Software Engineering

Software Engineering

Principles and Practice

Hans van Vliet
Vrije Universiteit, Amsterdam, The Netherlands

JOHN WILEY & SONS
Chichester · New York · Brisbane · Toronto · Singapore

Copyright © 1993 by John Wiley & Sons Ltd,
Baffins Lane, Chichester,
West Sussex PO19 1UD, England

Reprinted 1994, 1995
Reprinted May 1996
Reprinted July 1997

Other Wiley Editorial Offices

John Wiley & Sons, Inc., 605 Third Avenue,
New York, NY 10158-0012, USA

Jacaranda Wiley Ltd, G.P.O. Box 859, Brisbane,
Queensland 4001, Australia

John Wiley & Sons (Canada) Ltd, 22 Worcester Road,
Rexdale, Ontario M9W 1L1, Canada

John Wiley & Sons (SEA) Pte Ltd, 37 Jalan Pemimpin #05-04,
Block B, Union Industrial Building, Singapore 2057

Library of Congress Cataloging-in-Publication Data

Vliet, J. C. van.
   Software engineering : principles and practice / J.C. van Vliet.
     p.   cm.
   Includes bibliographical references (p.   ) and index.
   ISBN 0 471 93611 1
   1. Software engineering. 2. Computer software—Development.
I. Title.
QA76.5.V563   1993
005.1—dc20
                                  92-46773
                                    CIP

British Library Cataloguing in Publication Data

A catalogue record for this book is available from the British Library

ISBN 0 471 93611 1

Typeset in 10/12pt Palatino from author's disks by Text Processing Department,
John Wiley & Sons Ltd, Chichester
Printed and bound in Great Britain by Bookcraft (Bath) Ltd

To
Marjan, Jasper and Marieke

Contents

Preface

Several years ago, my wife and I discussed whether or not we should move. We were getting restless after having lived in the same house for a long time. For lack of space, my study had been changed into a child's bedroom. I definitely needed a room of my own in order to finish this book. My wife thought her kitchen too small.

The opportunity to buy a building lot in a new development plan arose. We gathered information, went to look for an architect, subscribed to the plan. Still, we were not sure whether we really wanted to leave our house. It was situated very nicely in a dead-end street, with a garden facing south and a playground in front. When asked, our children told us they did not want to move to a new neighbourhood.

So, we asked an architect about the possibility of rebuilding our house. He produced a blueprint in which the altered house had a larger kitchen and four extra rooms. We were sold immediately. We told ourselves that this rebuilding would be cheaper as well, though the architect could not give us a reliable cost estimate yet.

After giving the rebuilding plan some more thought, we decided this was the way to go. My brother, who is employed in the building industry, warned us of the mess it would create. We thought we could handle it. We started the regular procedure to get all permissions, which takes at least half a year in The Netherlands—and costs money (this was not accounted for).

In August, a year later, we were finally ready to start. The rebuilding was estimated to take 60 working days at most. Unfortunately, the contract did not mention any fine should this period be exceeded. We agreed on a fixed price. Certain things, such as the new electrical wiring, a new central heating unit, and the cost of plumbing were not included. We hardly knew what those 'extras' would cost in the end. We did estimate them on the back of an envelope, and felt confident.

On September 15, the first pile was driven. Counting on good weather throughout the fall, this should have meant that all would be finished by Christmas. The building contractor, however, had other urgent obligations, and progress was rather slow in the beginning. About one week's work was done during the first month.

In October, part of the roof had to be removed. We could interrupt work until next spring—the safe way; or continue—rather tricky in a country as wet as ours. We prayed for some dry weeks and decided to go on. The contractor started to demolish part of our house. While doing so, some surprises showed up and an even larger part of the house had to be demolished. We were real lucky—it only rained for two days while our roof was open. Our bedrooms became rather wet, and the kitchen was flooded. Sometime in November, the new roof was up and we could sleep quietly again.

By the end of November, we were getting nervous. There was still a lot of work to be done but several times, the workmen did not show up. In the meantime, we had made arrangements for our new kitchen to be installed the week before Christmas. Before this, a door had to be cut in an existing brick wall. The old central heating unit was placed right behind that wall and had to be removed first. The new central heating unit, unfortunately, was not available yet (fall is the peak season for central heating units).

Work continued as far as possible. A new wall was erected, after which we could enter our (old) kitchen only from the outside. For a while even, we lived with no kitchen at all. To make a long story short, the contractor made it, but only barely. The new kitchen was installed. Upstairs, however, much work remained. The project was finally finished by the end of January, only six weeks late.

During the rebuilding, life had been rather provisional. My computer was stored away in the attic. The children had virtually no space to play indoors. Dust was everywhere. These circumstances can be dealt with for a while, but we became frantic towards the end. Though the work seemed to be finished by the end of January, a lot still remained to be done: rooms had to be painted and decorated, and all that had been packed needed to be unpacked again. It took several more months before life took its normal course again.

Several months later, some of the new wooden planks on the back façade started to crack. They had expanded during the summer heat; either the tongue was too wide or the groove too narrow. This, and various other minor problems were, eventually, rectified.

On the financial side: various tiny expenses not accounted for added up to a pretty sum. I am still not sure whether we chose the cheapest option, but I am absolutely sure that knocking down a house and rebuilding it while you still try to live in it, is a nightmare. In that sense, my brother was more than right.

This story is fairly typical of a software development project. Software too is often delivered late, does not meet its specifications and is, moreover, faulty. Software projects also tend to underestimate the impact of non-technical factors.

The growing awareness of this in the late 1960s gave rise to the expression 'the software crisis'. Though we have made quite some progress since the term 'software engineering' was first coined back in 1968, the software crisis is still rampant.

The field of software engineering aims to find answers to the many problems that software development projects are likely to meet when constructing large software systems. Such systems are complex because of their sheer size, because they are developed in a team setting involving people from different disciplines, because they will be regularly modified to meet changing requirements, both during development and after installment.

Software engineering is still a young field compared to other engineering disciplines. All disciplines have their problems, particularly when projects reach beyond the engineers' expertise. It seems as if software development projects stretch their engineers' expertise all of the time.

The subject is rapidly moving and there are more questions than answers. In this book I have tried to collect the main principles and practices that have evolved in the thirty-odd years the field has existed.

I have not limited myself to a discussion of well-established practices. Rather, I decided to also pay attention to promising methods and techniques which have not yet outgrown the research environment, or hardly so: software reusability, quantitative assessment of software quality, and formal specifications, to name but a few. What is theory today, may become practice tomorrow.

It is compelling both to people actively involved in software development and maintenance—programmers, analysts, project managers—and to students of computer science and software engineering, to be abreast of the problems incurred by large-scale software development, and the solutions proposed.

I firmly believe that none of the solutions proposed are silver bullets. CASE, object-oriented software development, software reuse, formal specifications: they each contribute their mite. The fundamental problems will, however, remain. Software systems are extremely complex artifacts. Their successful realization requires experience and talent from their designers. If applied in a thoughtful, conscious manner, the methods and techniques discussed in this book may help you to become a professional software engineer too.

HOW THE BOOK IS ORGANIZED

Software development projects often involve several people for a prolonged period of time. Large projects may even range over several years and involve hundreds of people. Such projects must carefully be planned and controlled. The main aspects that deserve the continuous attention of project managers are introduced in Chapter 2, and further dealt with in chapters 3–7: progress, information, people, quality, cost and schedule.

To be able to assess progress during software development, one opts for a phased approach with a number of well-defined milestone events. The linear ordering of activities which underlies the most popular software development model, the waterfall model, renders it an impossible idealization of reality though. It assumes software development proceeds in an orderly, sequential manner. Real projects proceed in far less rational ways. The waterfall model of software development is not feasible, much like Escher's Waterfall, reproduced on the front cover, is unfeasible. Chapter 3 discusses various alternative models of the development process.

Many documents are produced during the lifetime of a project. Worse still, many changes to these documents must be accommodated. Careful procedures are needed to manage and control their consistency, a topic known as configuration management, which is dealt with in chapter 4.

Finding the right organizational framework and the right mix of skills for a development team is a difficult matter. Little well-founded theory is available for this. Yet, many stories of successful and less successful projects discern some of the intricacies of project team issues. Chapter 5 sketches the major issues involved.

Software quality is becoming an increasingly important topic. With the increasing penetration of automation in everyday life, more and more people are coming into contact with software systems, and the quality of those systems is becoming a major concern. Quality cannot be added as an afterthought. It has to be built in from the very beginning. Chapter 6 discusses the many dimensions of software quality.

Software development takes time, and money, and this is looked at in chapter 7. When commissioning a building project, you expect a reliable estimate of the cost and development time up front. Getting reliable cost and schedule estimates for software development projects is still largely a dream. Software development cost is notoriously difficult to estimate reliably at an early stage. Since progress is difficult to 'see'—just when is a piece of software 50% complete?—schedule slippages often go undetected for quite a while, and schedule overruns are the rule, rather than the exception.

The management part ends with chapter 8 in which I try to reconcile the various approaches sketched in chapters 3–7. A taxonomy of software development projects is given, together with recommended management practices for dealing with such projects. Chapter 8 also deals with some well-known techniques for project planning and control.

When designing a garden, you begin by formulating your requirements—how large should the grass area be, should you leave a corner to raise potatoes, where should the sand-bin be put, etc. After that, a design is drawn up which is carefully documented in a blueprint. Only then will the gardener cut the first sod. A similar approach is followed when developing software. In a number of phases— requirements analysis, design, implementation, testing—the software system will take shape. After the software is delivered to the client it must be maintained. Reiteration of phases occurs because changes have to be incorporated and errors must be corrected. The result is a highly cyclic process, the so-called software life cycle.

The various phases of the initial development cycle are the topics of chapters 9–13, and chapter 18 is devoted to software maintenance.

Chapters 14–17 deal with a number of additional important issues concerning large-scale software development.

The testing phase of a software development process is aimed at finding faults in the software. One may argue though that faults are not all that interesting. Failures, i.e. manifestations of faults, are what really count. Chapter 14 is concerned with assessing and improving software reliability: the probability that a given piece of software will not fail within a certain period of time.

Chapter 15 is concerned with tools. In the past years CASE (Computer Aided Software Engineering) has been touted as the ultimate answer to the problems faced by software developers. A large number of software tools are available nowadays, and the topic also receives considerable attention in the research community. Chapter 15 identifies and discusses major trends in the development of CASE tools.

Chapter 16 addresses another panacea that has become fashionable of late: software reusability. If we estimate the programmer population at three million people, and furthermore assume that each programmer writes 2000 lines of code per year, 6000 million lines of code are produced each year. There is bound to be a lot of redundancy in them. Reuse of software, or reuse of other artifacts that are produced in the course of a software development project, may lead to considerable productivity improvements and, consequently, cost savings.

Programs are written and read by humans. Software systems are used by humans. Cognitive issues are a major determinant of the effectiveness with which software engineers as well as users go about their work. Why is one program more understandable than another? Why is it useful to include comments in software? Why is system X more 'user-friendly' than system Y? Chapter 17 addresses cognitive aspects of software development and maintenance, and human factors issues relevant to the development of interactive systems.

LEARNING ABOUT SOFTWARE ENGINEERING

Most chapters of this book can be read and studied independently. For use in a classroom setting, the instructor has a large degree of freedom in choosing topics from this book, and the order in which to treat them. It is recommended that a first course in software engineering at least deals with the topics discussed in chapters 1–3, 9, 10, 12 and 13 (treated in this order). Additional material can be chosen at will from the other chapters, and/or be used as material for a secondary course.

A recurring problem in teaching software engineering is when and how to address project management issues. Computer science students often have difficulty in appreciating the importance of issues such as team organization and cost estimation. Software professionals know from the trenches that these non-technical issues are at least as important as the technical ones. For students of computer science or software engineering, it is more expedient to discuss management issues near the end of the course, possibly after they have been involved in some sort of practical work. However, a short treatment of the issues raised in Chapters 2 and 3 should be given near the beginning of the course.

Much of what is said in this book sounds obvious. In fact it is. As one speaker at a software engineering education conference said: 'You cannot teach it, you can only preach it.' So this book is one long sermon on how to practice software development. Just as you cannot become a good hand at carpentry from reading a textbook on the subject, you cannot become a serious software engineer by merely reading and absorbing the material contained in this book. You need to practice it as well.

Doing practical work in a university setting is not easy. The many risks that real-life software development projects run cannot be realistically mimicked in a term project. Yet certain recurring problems in software development can be successfully dealt with in a university setting. For example, small student teams may be asked to design, implement and test a nontrivial system, after which other teams get to maintain those systems. My own experience with this type of project has been very favorable [van Vliet89].

In addition to this, the exercises given at the end of each chapter provide further points to ponder. The exercises tend not to simply ask the reader to repeat the material from the text. Rather, they require him or her to seriously reflect on major issues and/or study additional sources to deepen his or her understanding.*

An *Instructor's Guide* is available to bona fide lecturers who adopt the book for course use. It contains solutions to selected problems and suggestions for software projects to supplement a software engineering course. The Guide is available on Internet. For access details, contact your Wiley representative or ask for details from gbjwslu1@ibmmail.com.

ACKNOWLEDGEMENTS

The present text is really a third edition. The first two editions appeared in Dutch only. I have used this material many times in courses, both for university students and software professionals. These people have, either consciously or unconsciously, helped to shape the text as it stands. I have received many useful suggestions from Anton Eliëns, Thomas Green, Wiebren de Jonge, Gerrit van der Veer and Roel Wieringa.

Many people from John Wiley & Sons contributed to this book. Special thanks are due to Gaynor Redvers-Mutton, for her editorial support and indefatigable optimism.

---

* Rather than writing 'him or her' all the time, I will use male pronouns throughout this text for brevity.

The drawings that go with the chapter headings were made by Tobias Baanders and Marieke Frohn. They accrue from artwork of Jan Snoeck that adorns the Centre of Mathematics and Computer Science in Amsterdam. The litho on the front cover is called 'Waterfall' (M.C. Escher, 1961). It is appropriate in name and message alike.

Finally I thank Marjan, Jasper and Marieke for their patience and support. The schedule overrun of this project has been worse than that of many a software development project. I may now comfortably turn my attention to tidying up our garden, which has been a wasteland since the house rebuilding project was finished.

Hans van Vliet
Amsterdam, July 1992

1
Introduction

Computer science is still a young field. The first computers were built in the mid 1940s, since when the field has developed tremendously.

Applications from the early years of computerization can be characterized somewhat as follows: the programs were in general quite small, certainly when compared to those that are currently being constructed. They were written by one person. They were written and used by experts in the application area concerned. The problems to be solved were mostly of a technical nature, and the emphasis was on expressing known algorithms efficiently in some programming language. Input typically consisted of numerical data, read from such media as punched tape or punched cards. The output, also numeric, was printed on paper. Programs were run off-line. If the program contained errors, one studied an octal or hexadecimal dump of memory. Sometimes, the execution of the program would be followed by binary reading machine registers at the console.

Present day applications are rather different in many respects. Present day programs are often very large and are being developed by teams that collaborate over periods spanning several years. The programmers are not the future users of the system they develop, and they have no expert knowledge of the application area in question. The problems that are being tackled increasingly concern everyday life: automatic bank tellers, airline reservation via a terminal connected to some host machine, salary administration, etc. Putting man on the moon was not conceivable without computers.

We may get an impression of the scale of current software development projects from the following examples:

- the Dutch KLM airline reservation system contains two million lines of (assembler) code;

- the UNIX operating system comprises over 3700 000 lines of source code (System V release 4.0, including Xnews and the X11 window system);

- the NASA Space Shuttle software counts 40 million lines of object code (this is 30 times as much as the software for the Saturn V project from the 1960s) [Boehm81];

- The IBM OS360 operating system took 5000 man years of development effort [Brooks75].

And this is by no means the end; neither with respect to the degree to which computerization penetrates other disciplines—it is a real possibility that by the year 2000, cows will be milked by a robot—nor with respect to size—one need only think of the US SDI (StarWars) efforts.

Programming techniques have lagged behind the developments in software both in size and complexity. To many people, programming is still an *art*, and has never become a *craft*. An additional problem is that many programmers have not been formally educated in the field. They have learned by doing. On the organizational side, solutions to problems are often attempted by adding more and more programmers to the project, the so-called 'million-monkey' approach.

As a result, software is often delivered too late, programs do not behave as the user expects, programs are rarely adaptable to changed circumstances, and many errors are detected only after the software has been delivered to the customer. This is commonly referred to as the 'software crisis'.

This type of problem became really manifest in the 1960s. Under the auspices of NATO, two conferences were devoted to the topic in 1968 [Naur68] and 1969, [Buxton69]. Here, the term 'software engineering' was coined in a somewhat provocative sense. Shouldn't it be possible to build software in the way one builds bridges and houses, starting from a theoretical basis and using sound and proven design and construction techniques, as in other engineering fields?

Software serves some organizational purpose. The reasons for embarking on a software development project vary. Sometimes, a solution to a problem is not feasible without the aid of computers, such as weather forecasting, or automated banktelling. Sometimes, software can be used as a vehicle for new technologies, such as typesetting, the production of chips, or manned spacetrips. In yet other cases software may increase user service (as in library automation), or simply save money (as in automated stock control).

In many cases though, the expected economic gain will be a major driving force. It may, however, not always be easy to prove that automation saves money (just think of office automation) because apart from direct cost savings, the economic gain may also manifest itself in such things as a more flexible production or a faster or better user service.

In [Boehm81], the total expenditure on software in the US was estimated to be $40 billion in 1980. This is approximately 2% of the GNP. In 1985, the total expenditure had risen to $70 billion in the US and $140 billion worldwide [Boehm87a].

So the *cost* of software is of crucial importance. This concerns not only the cost of developing the software, but also the cost of keeping the software operational once it has been delivered to the customer. In the course of time, hardware costs have decreased dramatically. Hardware costs now typically comprise less than 20% of total expenditure (figure 1.1). The remaining 80% comprise all non-hardware costs: the cost of programmers, analysts, management, user training, secretarial help, etc. Note that the curve depicted in figure 1.1 need not have the same dramatic shape in every organization [Cragon82, Frank83].

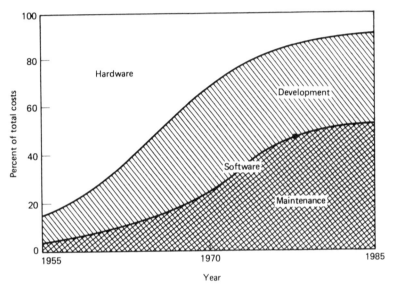

Figure 1.1:   Relative distribution of hardware/software costs. (*Source: B.W. Boehm, Software Engineering,* IEEE Transactions on Computers, © *1976 IEEE.*)

If automation saves money, this usually means a loss of jobs. In many cases, automation also entails a rise in the labor force in other jobs, with more interesting tasks, but the net effect still often is negative. We cannot and should not close our eyes to these effects of automation on society.

An aspect closely linked with cost is *productivity*. The quest for data processing personnel increases by 12% per year, while the population of people working in data processing and the productivity of those people each grow by approximately 4% per year [Boehm87a]. The net effect is a growing gap between demand and supply. The result is both a backlog with respect to the maintenance of existing software and a slowing down in the development of new applications. Eventually, the combined effect hereof will have repercussions as regards the competetive edge of an organization.

The problems of cost and productivity are large, and deserve our serious attention. However, this is not the complete story. Society is increasingly dependent on software. The quality of the systems we develop is increasingly determining the quality of our existence. Consider as an example the following message from a Dutch newspaper on June 6, 1980, under the heading 'Americans saw the Russians coming':

> For a short period last Tuesday the United States brought their atomic bombers and nuclear missiles to an increased state of alarm when, because of a computer error, a false alarm indicated that the Soviet Union had started a missile attack.

Efforts to repair the error were apparently in vain, for on June 9, 1980, the same newspaper reported:

> For the second time within a few days, a deranged computer reported that the Soviet Union had started a nuclear attack against the United States. Last Saturday, the DoD affirmed the false message, which resulted in the engines of the planes of the strategic air force being started.

It is not always the world that is in danger. On a smaller scale, errors in software may also have very unfortunate consequences, such as transaction errors in bank traffic; reminders to finally pay that bill of $0.00; a system for stock control that issues orders too late and thus lays off complete divisions of a factory.

The latter example indicates that errors in software systems may have serious financial consequences for the organization using it. An example of such a financial loss is the following. A large US airline company lost $50M because of an error in their seat reservation system. The system erroneously reported that cheap seats were sold out, while in fact there were plenty available. The problem was detected only after quarterly results lagged considerably behind those of both their own previous periods and those of their competitors. Errors in automated systems may even have fatal effects. One computer science weekly magazine contained the following message in April 1983:

> The court in Düsseldorf has discharged a woman (54), who was on trial for murdering her daughter. An erroneous message from a computerized system made the insurance company inform her that she was seriously ill. She was said to suffer from an incurable form of syphilis. Moreover, she was said to have infected both her children. In panic, she strangled her 15 year old daughter and tried to kill her 13 year old son and herself. The boy escaped, and with some help he enlisted, prevented the woman from dying of an overdose. The judge blamed the computer error and considered the woman not responsible for her actions.

With increasing applications of computers, the number of potential risks also increases. Baber compares the state of the art in the software engineering field with that in the fictitious land of Ret Up Moc where, around 2500 BC, great progress was being made at a few distinguished institutes in the area of designing buildings [Baber82]. The demand for engineers that were educated in this new way of designing buildings grew fast. The few experts at the engineering schools were snatched away by industry. Older practicing engineers had to be re-educated. Somebody therefore developed three-week crash courses and a designer kit that contained, amongst others, a designer's handbook, ruler, and sample forms and designs.

With these aids, many managed to draw up plans for new buildings. However, most designers did not really understand the underlying theory and 30% of the buildings collapsed before delivery. To tackle the danger to the workmen, elaborate test plans were developed. At certain critical moments during the construction process, everyone had to leave the workfloor and large amounts of sand and rubble were dumped in and on the building under construction. If the building did not collapse under this, the rubble was removed and construction could continue. Upon delivery, a similar final test was performed. The owner received a contract in which the builder disclaimed in advance any responsibility for possible defects.

Besides this very instructive parable, Baber's book contains many anecdotes about computer projects that failed or nearly failed. The bimonthly *ACM Software Engineering Notes* contains a column 'Risks to the public in computer systems', which contains reports on larger and smaller catastrophies caused by automation. Parnas' essays on the SDI program also point to the dangers of large-scale hazardous software development [Parnas85].

This all marks the enormous importance of the field of software engineering. Better methods and techniques for software development may result in large financial savings, in more effective methods of software development, in systems that better fit user needs, in more reliable software systems and thus a more reliable environment in which those systems function. Quality and productivity are the two most central themes in the field of software engineering.

1.1 WHAT IS SOFTWARE ENGINEERING?

In various texts on this topic, one encounters a definition of the term software engineering. An early definition was given at the first NATO conference [Naur68]:

> Software engineering is the establishment and use of sound engineering principles in order to obtain economically software that is reliable and works efficiently on real machines.

The definition given in the *IEEE Standard Glossary of Software Engineering Terminology* [IEEE83b] is as follows:

> Software engineering is the systematic approach to the development, operation, maintenance, and retirement of software.

These and other definitions of the term software engineering use rather different words. However, the essential characteristics of the field are always, explicitly or implicitly, present:

1. *Software engineering concerns the construction of large programs.*
   [DeRemer76] makes a distinction between **programming-in-the-large** and **programming-in-the-small**. The borderline between large and small obviously is not sharp; a program of 100 lines is small, a program of 50 000 lines of code certainly is not. Programming-in-the-small generally refers to programs written by one person in a relatively short period of time. Programming-in-the-large then refers to multi-person jobs that span, say, more than half a year. The traditional programming techniques and tools are primarily aimed at supporting programming-in-the-small. This not only holds for programming languages, but also for the tools (like flowcharts) and methods (like structured programming). These cannot be directly transferred to the development of large programs.

   In fact, the term program—in the sense of a self-contained piece of software that can be invoked by a user or some other system component—is not adequate here. Present-day software development projects result in systems containing a large number of (interrelated) programs.

2. *The central theme is mastering complexity.*
   In general the problems are such that they cannot be surveyed in their entirety. One is forced to split the problem into parts such that each individual part can be grasped, while the communication between the parts remains simple. The total complexity does not decrease in this way, but it does become manageable. In a stereo there are such components as an amplifier, receiver and tuner, and communication via a thin wire. In software, we strive for a similar separation of concerns. In a program for library automation, components such as user interaction, search processes and data storage could for instance be distinguished, with clearly given facilities for data exchange between those components. Note that the complexity of many a piece of software is not so much caused by the intrinsic complexity of the problem (as in the case of compiler optimization algorithms or numerical algorithms to solve partial differential equations), but rather by the vast number of details that must be dealt with.

3. *Regular cooperation between people is an integral part of programming-in-the-large.*
   Since the problems are large, many people have to work concurrently at solving those problems. There must be clear arrangements for the distribution of work, methods of communication, responsibilities, and so on. Arrangements alone are not sufficient, though; one also has to stick to those arrangements. In order to enforce them, standards or procedures may be employed. Those procedures and standards can often be supported by tools. Discipline is one of the keys to the successful completion of a software development project.

4. *Software evolves.*
   Most software models part of reality, such as processing requests in a library, or tracking money transfers in a bank. This reality evolves. If software is not to become obsolete fairly quickly, it has to evolve together with the reality

that is being modeled. This means that costs are incurred after delivery of the software system, and that we have to bear this evolution in mind during development.

5. *The efficiency with which software is developed is of crucial importance.*
   Total cost and development time of software projects is high. This also holds for the maintenance of software. The quest for new applications surpasses the workforce resource. The gap between supply and demand is growing. Important themes within the field of software engineering concern better and more efficient methods and tools for the development and maintenance of software.

6. *The software has to effectively support its users.*
   Software is developed in order to support users at work. The functionality offered should fit users' tasks. Users that are not satisfied with the system will try to circumvent it, or at best voice new requirements immediately. It is not sufficient to build the system in the right way, we also have to build the right system. Effective user support means that we must carefully study users at work in order to determine the proper functional requirements, and that we have to address usability and other quality aspects as well, such as reliability, responsiveness, user-friendliness. It also means that software development entails more than delivering software. User manuals and training material may have to be written, and attention must be given to developing the environment in which the new system is going to be installed. For example, a new automated library system will affect working procedures within the library.

The above list shows that software engineering has many facets. Software engineering certainly is *not* the same as programming, although programming is an important ingredient of software engineering. Mathematical aspects play a role since we are concerned with the correctness of software. Sound engineering practices are needed to get useful products. Psychological aspects play a role in the communication between human and machine, or between humans. Finally, the development process needs to be controlled, which is a management issue.

The term 'software engineering' hints at possible resemblances between the construction of programs and the construction of houses or bridges. These kinds of resemblances do exist. In both cases we work from a set of desired functions, using scientific and engineering techniques in a creative way. Techniques that have been applied successfully in the construction of physical artifacts, are also helpful when applied to the construction of software systems: development of the product in a number of phases, a careful planning of these phases, continuous audit of the whole process, construction from a clear and complete design, etc. For a more elaborate discussion of the differences and similarities between software engineering and a mature engineering discipline, viz. bridge design, see [Spector86].

Even though bridge design is a mature discipline, bridges do collapse once in a while too. According to Spector, most problems in bridge design occur when designers extrapolate beyond their models and expertise. A famous example is the Tacoma Narrows Bridge failure in 1940. The designers of that bridge extrapolated beyond their experience to create more flexible stiffening girders for suspension bridges. They did not think about aerodynamics and the bridge response to wind. As a result, that bridge collapsed shortly after it was finished. This type of extrapolation seems to be the rule rather than the exception in software development. We regularly embark on software development projects that go far beyond our expertise.

There are additional reasons for considering the construction of software as something quite different from the construction of physical products [Wegner79]. The cost of constructing software is incurred during development and not during production. Copying software is almost free. Software is logical in nature rather than physical. Physical products wear out in time and therefore have to be maintained. Software does not wear out. The need to maintain software is caused by errors detected late or by changing requirements of the user. Software reliability is determined by the manifestation of errors already present, not by physical factors such as wear and tear. We may even argue that software wears out *because* it is being maintained.

Two characteristics that make software development projects extra difficult to manage are visibility and continuity. It is much more difficult 'to see' progress in software construction than it is to notice progress in building a bridge. One often hears the phrase that a program 'is almost finished'. One equally often underestimates the time needed to finish up the last bits and pieces.

This '90% complete' syndrome is very pervasive in software development. Not knowing how to measure real progress, we often use a surrogate measure, the rate of expenditure of resources. For example, a project that has a budget of 100 person-days is perceived as being 50% complete after 50 person-days are expended. Because of the imprecise measurement of progress and the customary underestimation of total effort, problems accumulate as time elapses [Abdel-Hamid88].

Physical systems are often continuous in the sense that small changes in the specification lead to small changes in the product. This is not true with software. Small changes in the specification of software may lead to considerable changes in the software itself. In a similar way, small errors in software may have considerable effects. The Mariner space rocket to Venus for example got lost because of a typing error in a FORTRAN program.

We may likewise draw a comparison between software engineering and computer science. Computer science emerged as a separate discipline in the 1960s. It split from mathematics and has been heavily influenced by mathematics. Topics studied in computer science, such as algorithm complexity, formal languages, and the semantics of programming languages, have a strong mathematical flavor. PhD theses in computer science invariably contain theorems with accompanying proofs.

As the field of software engineering is emerging from computer science, we have a similar inclination to focus on clean, formalizable aspects of software development in both teaching and research. We tend to assume that requirements can be fully stated before the project starts, concentrate on systems built from scratch, and ignore the reality of trading of quality aspects against the available budget. Not to mention the trenches of software maintenance. According to [Gibbs91], much of what the academic (computer science) community does in universities can be viewed, like mathematics, as naive paper exercises that ignore reality.

Software engineering and computer science do have a considerable overlap. The practice of software engineering however also has to deal with such matters as the management of huge development projects, human factors (regarding both the development team and the prospective users of the system) and cost estimation and control. Software engineers must *engineer* software. In their effort to set up an elaborate educational program in software engineering, the Software Engineering Institute (SEI) pays ample attention to these issues. This and other initiatives are aimed at making software engineering less of an aspiration and more of a profession [Gibbs89].

Software engineering has many things in common both with other fields of engineering and with computer science. It also has a face of its own in many ways.

1.2 PHASES IN THE DEVELOPMENT OF SOFTWARE

When building a house, the builder does not start with piling up bricks. Rather, the requirements and possibilities of the client are analyzed first, taking into account such factors as family structure, hobbies, finances and the like. The architect takes these factors into consideration when designing a house. Only after the design has been agreed upon, is the actual construction started.

It is expedient to act in the same way when constructing software. First, the problem to be solved is analyzed and the requirements are described in a very precise way. Then a design is made based on these requirements. Finally, the construction process, i.e. the actual programming of the solution, is started. There are a distinguishable number of phases in the development of software. The phases as discussed in this book are depicted in figure 1.2.

The so-called **process model** depicted in figure 1.2 is rather simple. In reality, things will usually be more complex. For instance, the design phase is often split into a global design phase and a detailed design phase, and often various test phases are distinguished. The basic components, however, remain as given in figure 1.2. These phases have to be passed through in each project. Depending on the kind of project and the working environment, a more detailed scheme may be needed.

In figure 1.2, the phases have been depicted sequentially. For a given project these activities are not necessarily separated as strictly as indicated here. They

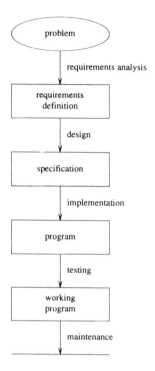

Figure 1.2:   A simple view of software development

may partly overlap. They usually will. It is, for instance quite possible to start implementation of one part of the system while some of the other parts have not been fully designed yet. As we will see in section 1.3, there is no strict linear progression from requirements analysis to design, from design to implementation, etc. Backtracking to earlier phases occurs, because of errors discovered or changing requirements.

Below, a short description is given of each of the basic components from figure 1.2. Various alternative process models will be discussed in chapter 3. These alternative models result from justifiable criticism to the simple-minded model depicted in figure 1.2. The sole aim of our simple model is to provide an adequate structuring of topics to be addressed. The maintenance phase is further discussed in section 1.3. All components of our process model will be treated much more elaborately in later chapters.

Requirements analysis. The goal of the requirements analysis phase is to get a complete description of the problem to be solved and the requirements posed by and to the environment in which the system is going to function. Requirements posed by the environment could include hardware and supporting software, or the number of prospective users of the system to be developed. Alternatively, the requirements analysis may lead to certain requirements imposed on hardware yet to be acquired or to the organization in which the system is to function. A description of the problem to be solved includes such things as:

— the functions of the software to be developed;

— possible future extensions to the system;

— the amount, and kind, of documentation required;

— response time and other performance requirements of the system.

Part of the requirements analysis is a **feasibility study**. The purpose of the feasibility study is to assess whether there is a solution to the problem which is both economically and technically feasible.

The more careful we are during the requirements analysis phase, the larger is the chance that the ultimate system will meet expectations. To this end, the various people involved have to collaborate intensively. This concerns among others the customer, prospective users, designers and programmers. These people often have widely different backgrounds, which does not ease communication.

The document in which the result of this activity is laid down, is termed **requirements specification**.

Design. During the design phase, a model of the whole system is developed which, when encoded in some programming language, solves the problem for the user. To this end the problem is decomposed into manageable pieces—**modules**; the functions of these modules as well as the **interfaces** between them are specified in a very precise way. The design phase is crucial. Requirements analysis and design are sometimes seen as an annoying introduction to programming, which is often seen as the real work. This attitude has a very negative influence on the quality of the resulting software.

During the design phase we try to separate the *what* from the *how*. We concentrate on the problem and should not let ourselves be distracted by implementation concerns. Modern specification methods adhere to this principle. They offer possibilities to formulate the operations of a module mathematically, by means of expressing their domain, range, and effect. These specification methods do not yield algorithms.

The result of the design phase, the **(technical) specification**, serves as a starting point for the implementation phase. If the specification is formal in nature, it can also be used to derive correctness proofs.

Implementation. During the implementation phase, we concentrate on the individual modules. Our starting point is the module's specification. It is often necessary to introduce an extra 'design' phase, the step from module specification to executable code often being too large. In such cases, we may take advantage of some high-level programming-language like notation, such as a **pseudocode**. (A pseudocode is a kind of programming language. Its syntax and semantics are in general less strict than those of Pascal, so that algorithms can be formulated at a higher, more abstract, level.)

It is important to note that the first goal of a programmer should be the development of a well-documented, reliable, easy to read, flexible, correct, program. The goal is *not* to produce a very efficient program full of tricks. We will come back to the many dimensions of software quality in chapter 6.

During the design phase, a global structure has been imposed through the introduction of modules and their interfaces. Certainly in the more classic programming languages, much of this structure tends to get lost in the transition from design to code. More recent programming languages such as Modula-2 and Ada*, offer possibilities to retain this structure in the final code through the module concept that has been built into the language.

The result of the implementation phase is an executable program.

Testing. Actually, it is wrong to say that testing is a phase following implementation. This suggests that you need not bother about testing until implementation is finished. This is not true. It is even fair to say that this is one of the biggest mistakes you can make.

Already during requirements analysis, attention has to be paid to testing. During the subsequent phases, testing is continued and refined. The earlier errors are detected, the cheaper their correction.

Testing at phase boundaries comes in two flavors. We have to test that the transition from phase i to phase $i + 1$ is correct (this is known as **verification**). We also have to check that we are still on the right track as regards fulfilling user requirements (**validation**). The result of adding verification and validation activities to the linear model of Figure 1.2 yields the so-called **waterfall-model** of software development (see also chapter 3).

In general, measuring efficiency and then tuning and optimizing the software in the light of these measurements are also considered part of the test phase.

Maintenance. After delivery of the software, there are often errors that have still gone undetected. Obviously, these errors must be repaired. In addition, the actual use of the system can lead to requests for changes and enhancements. All these types of changes are denoted by the rather unfortunate term maintenance. Maintenance thus concerns all activities needed to keep the system operational after it has been delivered to the user.

An activity spanning all phases is **project management**. Like other projects, software development projects must be managed properly in order to ensure that the product asked for is delivered on time and within budget. Visibility and continuity characteristics of software development, as well as the fact that for many software development projects undertaken there is insufficient prior experience to draw from, seriously impede project control. The many examples

---
* Ada is a registered trademark of the US Government (Ada Joint Program Office).

of software development projects that fail to meet their schedule provide ample evidence of the fact that we have by no means satisfactorily dealt with this issue yet. Chapters 2–8 deal with major aspects of software project management, such as project planning, team organization, quality issues, cost and schedule estimation.

An important activity not identified separately is **documentation**. A number of key ingredients of the documentation of a software project will be elaborated upon in the chapters to follow. Key components of the documentation of a system include the project plan, quality plan, requirements specification, design documentation and test plan. Certainly for larger projects, a considerable amount of effort will have to be spent on properly documenting those projects. Also, one will have to start documenting the various aspects of the system early on in the project. In practice, documentation is often seen as a balancing item. Since many projects are pressed for time, the documentation tends to get the worst of it. However, it is important to realize that software which is not sufficiently documented is bound to incur high costs later on. Since the program will undergo changes after delivery, because of errors that went undetected or changing user requirements, the documentation is of crucial importance during maintenance.

A particular noteworthy element of documentation is the user documentation. Software development should be task-oriented in the sense that the software to be delivered should support users in their task environment. Likewise, the user documentation should be task-oriented too. User manuals should not just describe the features of a system, they should help people getting things done [Rettig91]. We cannot simply rely on the structure of the interface to organize the user documentation. A programming language reference manual is not an appropriate source for learning how to program either.

In figure 1.3, the relative effort of the various activities up to delivery of the system is depicted. This figure is based on data from [Zelkowitz78]. From this and other such data a very clear trend emerges, the so-called 40–20–40 rule: only 20% of the effort is spent on actually programming (coding) the system, while the preceeding phases (requirements analysis and design) and testing each consume about 40% of the total effort.

Depending on specific boundary conditions, properties of the system to be constructed, and the like, variations to this rule can be found. For the majority of projects, however, this rule of thumb is quite workable.

This does not imply that the 40–20–40 rule is the one to be strived for. Errors made during requirements analysis are the ones that are most costly to repair (see also the chapter on testing). It is far better to put more energy into the requirements analysis phase, than try to remove errors during the time-consuming test phase or, worse still, during maintenance. According to [Boehm87b], successful projects nowadays follow a 60–15–25 distribution: 60% requirements analysis and design, 15% implementation and 25% testing.

Figure 1.3 does not show the extent of the maintenance effort. When we consider the total cost of a software system over its lifetime, it turns out that on average maintenance alone consumes 50–75% of these costs [Boehm76, Lientz80];

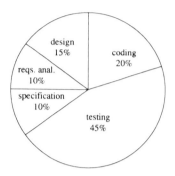

Figure 1.3: Relative effort for the various activities

see also figure 1.1. Thus, maintenance alone consumes more than the various development phases taken together.

1.3 MAINTENANCE OR EVOLUTION

The only thing we maintain is user satisfaction.
[Lehman80]

Once software has been delivered, it usually still contains errors which, upon discovery, must be repaired. Note that this type of maintenance is not caused by wearing. Rather, it concerns repair of hidden defects. This type of repair is comparable to that encountered after a newly built house is first occupied.

The story becomes quite different if we start talking about changes or enhancements to the system. Repainting our office or repairing a leak in the roof of our house is called maintenance. Adding a wing to our office is seldom called maintenance.

This is more than a trifle game with words. Over the total lifetime of a software system, more money is spent on maintaining that system than on initial development. If all these expenses merely concerned the repair of errors made during one of the development phases, our business would be doing very badly indeed. Fortunately, this is not the case.

Lientz distinguishes four kinds of maintenance activities [Lientz80]:

— **corrective** maintenance—the repair of actual errors;

— **adaptive** maintenance—adapting the software to changes in the environment, such as new hardware or the next release of an operating or database system;

— **perfective** maintenance—adapting the software to new or changed user requirements, such as extra functions to be provided by the system. Perfective maintenance also includes work to increase the system's performance or to enhance its user interface;

— **preventive** maintenance—increasing the system's future maintainability. Updating documentation, adding comments, or improving the modular structure of a system are examples of preventive maintenance activities.

Only the first category may rightfullly be termed maintenance. This category, however, accounts only for about a quarter of the total maintenance effort [Lientz80]. Approximately another quarter of the maintenance effort concerns adapting software to environmental changes, while half of the maintenance cost is spent on changes to accommodate changing user requirements, i.e. enhancements to the system (see figure 1.4).

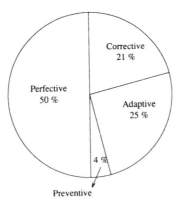

Figure 1.4: Distribution of maintenance activities

Changes in both the system's environment and user requirements are inevitable. Software models part of reality, and reality changes, whether we like it or not. So the software has to change too. It *has* to evolve. A large percentage of what we are used to calling maintenance is actually evolution. Maintenance because of new user requirements occurs in both high and low quality systems. A successful system calls for new, unforeseen functionality, because of its use by many satisfied users. A less successful system has to be adapted in order to satisfy its customers.

The result is that the software development process becomes cyclic, hence the phrase **software life cycle**. Backtracking to previous phases, alluded to above, does not only occur during maintenance. During other phases, we will from time to time iterate earlier phases as well. During design, it may be discovered that the requirements specification is not complete or contains conflicting requirements. During testing, errors introduced in the implementation or design phase may crop up. In these and similar cases an iteration of earlier phases is needed. We will come back to this cyclic nature of the software development process in chapter 3, when we discuss various alternative models of the software development process.

1.4 STATE OF THE ART

A lot of progress has been made over the past 20 years. For each of the major phases, numerous techniques and tools have been developed. A number of these have found widespread use. In their assessment of design and coding practices for example, DeMarco and Lister found that a number of widely acclaimed techniques (such as the use of small units, strong module binding and structured programming) are indeed applied in practice, and pay off [DeMarco89]. The short sketch of the field in the preceeding section has (and the more elaborate discussion in the following chapters will) also show that a lot of research is still needed to solve the software crisis.

Research in software engineering has been strongly stimulated in recent years. Some of the larger national and international efforts include (see also [Belady85]):

— The STARS program (Software Technology for Adaptable and Reliable Systems) [STARS83], [van Vliet85], [Lieblein86]. The US Department of Defense (DoD) has initiated the development of the programming language Ada (see also the later chapter on programming languages). As a follow-up, the STARS-program aims at the development of an integrated set of tools to support the software development process. Government support for this program is approximately US$50M per year.

— The Leonardo project [Myers85], [Frenkel85]. The Leonardo project has been initiated by the Micro-electronics Computer Corporation (MCC), in which a number of big computer companies cooperate. The aim of the Leonardo project is to get more, graphics-like, tool support during the early, exploratory phases of software development. About 60 people were involved in this project.

— SPC [Doe86]. The Software Productivity Consortium is an initiative of a number of US aerospace companies. The emphasis is on the development of tools to increase productivity and quality. Key topics are: software reuse, prototyping, and expert systems for software development.

— ESPRIT: European Strategic Programme in Information Technology [Kuntzmann-Combelles89]. ESPRIT is being sponsored by the EC. The research is divided into five areas, one of which is 'software technology'. In each ESPRIT project, industry and academic institutes from more than one member country cooperate. For the period 1984–89, about 1400 man-years of research in the area of software technology were funded. Projects from Phase 1 include: portable programming environments, formal specifications, an information system to support all activities that occur during the software life cycle, an expert sytem for managing the production and maintenance of software. Key results of the first phase are presented in [Software89b]. The second phase of ESPRIT builds on the experience gained in Phase 1 and includes some large projects in the area of software engineering.

— Alvey [Alvey85]. Alvey is the British version of ESPRIT. Within the software engineering part of the Alvey program, the emphasis is on formal specification, and an integrated programming environment with intelligent support from a knowledge base.

A striking denominator in the various research programs is the formation of centers in which software engineering expertise is being bundled. The Software Engineering Institute (SEI), for instance, has been established as part of the STARS program [Joyce86], [Barbacci85]. The main mission of the SEI is to speed up the transition of knowledge in the field of software engineering. Within the SEI Education Program a large number of curriculum modules are developed, each of which addresses a coherent body of knowledge relevant to the field of software engineering [Gibbs89].

It takes some time before technology developed in research laboratories gets applied in a routine way. This holds for physical products such as the transistor, but also for methods, techniques, and tools in the area of software technology. The first version of the UNIX operating system goes right back to 1971. Only recently, interest in UNIX spread widely. In the early 1960s, studies of the cost of software were first made. In the 1980s there was a growing interest in quantitative models for estimating software costs (see also the later chapter on cost estimation). Dijkstra's article on programming as a human activity appeared in 1965. In the late 1970s the first introductory textbooks on structured programming were published. The term software engineering was introduced in 1968. In the 1980s large national and international programs were initiated to foster the transition of this new technology. The above list can be extended with many other examples [Redwine85].

This maturation process in general takes at least 10 to 15 years. The primary goal of the SEI is to shorten this period. One way of trying to achieve this is to set up a showroom. Advanced products that may support software development are installed and tried out within the SEI. Also, an active exchange of researchers and representatives from industry is strived for. In this way, a bridge is built between theory and practice. Similar centers have been established in, for instance, England (the Software Tools Centre) and The Netherlands (the Software Engineering Research Centre). Technology transfer has become a major concern in software engineering [Raghavan89].

The other way round, there is a growing feeling that research should be more concerned with the practices and problems out in the field. According to a report from the US Science and Technology Board, the interaction between researchers and practitioners should be fostered, and academic exploration of large software systems in situ should be legitimized [CACM90].

In a seminal article entitled 'No silver bullet: essence and accidents of software engineering', Brooks discusses a number of potentially fruitful approaches to dramatically increase software productivity [Brooks87]. He distinguishes two types of reasons which hamper software construction: essential and accidental difficulties. Essential difficulties have to do with the essence of software, such as the high complexity of present-day systems. Accidental difficulties are just there because we have not adequately dealt with them yet. For example, hardware which is too slow or has insufficient memory constitutes an accidental difficulty. Accidental difficulties can be dealt with. Unfortunately, most of these have been dealt with already. What keeps us at work is the essence of software.

As a consequence, there is no single new technique which will bring us an order of magnitude improvement in software productivity. Quite a large number of developments are under way, though, each of which contributes its mite. According to Brooks, these developments will together lead to a significant productivity improvement. He comments on a number of these widely acclaimed developments.

Brooks advocates object-oriented program construction. Encapsulation and inheritance each remove an accidental difficulty. But the essence remains, so we should not expect miracles from these techniques. He does not expect spectacular improvements from artificial intelligence, graphical programming techniques and program verification either. Programming environments and other tools may yet make some useful contributions, but a lot of work has to be gone through in order to get a marginal return of investment. He expects by far the highest result from rapid prototyping, incremental development, the identification and development of great designers, and exploitation of the mass market to avoid constructing what can be bought.

While technology improvements do offer considerable potential, they are not enough. In many organizations, the software process is sufficiently confused and incoherent that non-technological factors impede the effective application of technology [Humphrey89a]. Thus, managerial, organizational, psychological and other non-technological issues deserve our attention as well.

There is no silver bullet. But we need not be afraid of the werewolf either. By a careful study of the many innovations and an investigation of their true merits, a lot of improvements in both quality and productivity can be achieved. The remainder of this text is devoted to a critical assessment of these technological and non-technological developments.

To close this chapter is a list of the important periodicals that contain material which is relevant to the field of software engineering:

— *Transactions on Software Engineering* (IEEE), a monthly periodical in which research results are reported;

— *Software* (IEEE), a bimonthly journal which is somewhat more general in scope;

— *Software Engineering Notes*, a bimonthly newsletter from the ACM Special Interest Group on Software Engineering;

— *Proceedings of the International Conference on Software Engineering* (ACM/IEEE), proceedings of the most important international conference in the field, organized every year;

— *Proceedings of the Conference on Software Maintenance* (IEEE), organized bi-yearly;

— *Software Maintenance: Research and Practice* (Wiley), quarterly journal devoted to topics in software maintenance;

— *Transactions on Software Engineering and Methodology* (ACM), a quarterly journal which reports research results.

1.5 SUMMARY

Software engineering is concerned with the problems that have to do with the construction of *large* programs. When developing such programs, a phased approach is followed. First, the problem is analyzed, and then the system is designed, implemented and tested. This practice has a lot in common with the engineering of physical products. Hence the term software engineering. Software engineering, however, also differs from the engineering of physical products in some essential ways.

Software models part of the real world surrounding us, like banking or the reservation of airline seats. This world around us changes over time. So the corresponding software has to change too. It has to evolve together with the changing reality. Much of what we call software maintenance, actually is concerned with ensuring that the software keeps pace with the real world being modeled.

We thus get a process model in which we iterate over earlier phases from time to time. We speak about the software life cycle.

The most important problems that we try to tackle in the field of software engineering are the quality of the software being delivered and the productivity of the people working in the field. On both a national and international scale, interest in this field is growing. Large research efforts are being undertaken, and the topic is slowly penetrating university curricula.

In most computer science curricula, software engineering does not have a very prominent place. In most cases, a one or two-semester course is offered in which some kind of practical project work is included. A number of full MSc programs in software engineering exist. [Gibbs91] speculates that there will be more than 100 such degree programs by the year 2000.

EXERCISES

1. Do you think the linear model of software development is appropriate at all? You may wish to reconsider this issue after having read the remainder of this text.

2. Discuss the major differences between software engineering and some other engineering discipline, such as bridge design or house building. Would you consider state-of-the-art software engineering as a true engineering discipline?

3. Quality and productivity are major issues in software engineering. It is often advocated that automated tools (CASE-tools) will dramatically improve both quality and productivity. Study a commercial CASE-tool and assess the extent to which it improves the software development process and its outcome.

4. Medical doctors have their Hippocratic oath. Could a similar ethical commitment by software engineers be instrumental in increasing the quality of software systems?

5. Suppose you are involved in an office automation project in the printing industry. The system to be developed is meant to support the work of journal editors. The management objective for this project is to save labor cost; the editors' objective is to increase the quality of their work. Discuss possible ramifications of these opposing objectives on the project. You may come back to this question after having read Chapter 9 and/or [Hirschheim89].

6. Study both the technical and user documentation of a system at your disposal. Are you satisfied with them? Discuss their possible shortcomings and give remedies to improve their quality.

7. Take a piece of software you wrote more than a year ago. Is it documented adequately? Does it have a user manual? Is the design rationale reflected in the technical documentation? Can you build an understanding of the system from its documentation that is sufficient for making non-trivial changes to it? Repeat these questions for a system written by one of your colleagues.

8. Try to gather quantitative data from your organization that reveals how much effort is spent on various kinds of maintenance activities. Are these data available at all? If so, is the pattern like that sketched in section 1.3? If not, can you explain the differences?

2
Software
Management

Many software development projects get into trouble, eventually. Software is delivered too late, budgets are overrun, customers are dissatisfied. Often, the underlying problems are of a technical nature. Equally often, however, the problems can be traced back to the organization and/or management of the project.

Some characteristic reasons people give when software is delivered too late, are exemplified by the following [Thayer81]:

— the programmers did not tell the truth about the actual status of their code;

— management grossly underestimated the time needed to complete the project;

— management did not allow sufficient time to carefully plan the project;

— the real status of the project was never made clear;

— the programmers' productivity turned out to be considerably lower than expected;

— the customer did not know what he wanted.

Apparently, it is not easy to complete successfully a software development project. This book mainly deals with technical aspects of software development: design, specification, implementation and testing of software systems. As we learn to control these aspects better, we will also learn to better satisfy our customers' demands. The organizational and managerial aspects of software development projects are at least as important as the technical aspects, though.

Before we embark on a discussion of these organizational and managerial aspects, let us first pay some attention to the boundaries of a software development project as they are drawn in this book.

A software development project is usually not started in complete isolation. There are other projects within the organization that this particular project needs to be tuned to, priorities between projects have to be decided upon, etc. The term **information planning** is often used to refer to this meta-project planning process.

Information planning results in a set of boundary conditions for each concrete project, much like a destination plan sets boundary conditions for building projects. Establishing a company-wide information plan is a problem on its own, and will not be addressed here. (We will, however, pay ample attention to some issues which will in general surpass the boundaries of individual software development projects, such as configuration control and quality assurance.)

Also in a more technical sense, software in general is not developed in isolation. In most cases, software is not written from scratch. It must interface with existing software, extend existing software, use existing subroutine libraries, and so on.

In some sense, the notion 'software development project' is a misnomer. We do not just develop software, we develop systems. Broadly speaking, a system transforms inputs into outputs. Software is an important ingredient of the systems we develop, but it is by no means the only ingredient. The technical and user documentation, the hardware, the procedures that govern the use of the system, and even the people using the software, may be considered as part of that same system.

Consider for example a system for library automation. The system will contain various software components, such as a data base component to store information on books and customers, and an interaction component to process user requests. Next to the development of these components, attention should be paid to matters like:

- techniques to electronically identify books, such as a barcode-like identification scheme;

- the selection and acquisition of special hardware both for scanning those identifications and for producing identifications for new books;

- setting up a scheme to provide all books with the new identification code;

- instruction of library employees to handle the new type of equipment (training material and courses, operating procedures, and the like);

- production of user-friendly documentation for the library customers.

Whenever the notion 'software development project' is used in the following, it should be understood in this wider sense. This is graphically illustrated in figure 2.1.

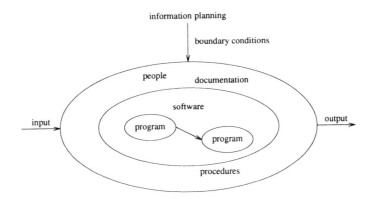

Figure 2.1:   The systems view of a software development project

Thus, our systems encompass a number of components. In a narrow sense, the software component itself may also consist of a number of interacting components. These latter components correspond to programs as we know them from introductory computer science textbooks. In general, a software development project results in a set of programs which collectively provide us with the desired functionality.

Given a project's boundary conditions, a concrete software development project may get started. Planning the project is the very first step to be undertaken, then. Part of this planning process is to identify the project characteristics and their impact on the development process. The result of the planning phase is laid down in a document, the **project plan**, which aims to provide a clear picture of the project to both the customers and the development team. The contents of the project plan are discussed in section 2.1.

During the subsequent execution of the project, a number of entities have to be managed. In section 2.2, we identify five major entities that need control during the execution of a software development project: time, information, organization, quality, and money. Each of these is further elaborated upon in a separate chapter.

2.1 PLANNING A SOFTWARE DEVELOPMENT PROJECT

Before we embark on a software development project, it has to be carefully planned. This entails, amongst others, an assessment of project properties that may impact the development process. A number of properties, however, will not be sufficiently well understood until the analysis phase has ended. Like many other aspects of a software development project, planning is not a one-shot activity. Rather, it is highly dynamic in nature. The project's plan can be laid down in a document that serves as a script during the execution of the project.

Cooper lists 13 important constituents of the project plan [Cooper84]:

1. **Introduction** In the introduction to the project plan, the background and history of the project are given, together with its aims, the names of the persons responsible, and a summary of the project.

2. **User's involvement** The prospective users will from time to time be involved in the project. The project plan has to state which information, services, resources and facilities are to be provided by the user and when these are to be provided.

3. **Risks** Potential risks have to be identified as early as possible. There will always be risks: hardware may not be delivered on time, qualified personnel not available when required, critical information lacking when it is needed, and so on. It is rather naive to suppose that a software development project runs smoothly. Even in well-established fields like construction there is always something that goes wrong. One should diagnose the risks of a software project early on, and provide measures to deal with them.
   As the uncertainties of the project become larger, so will the risks.

4. **Standards, guidelines, procedures** Software projects are big projects. Usually, a lot of people are involved. A strong working discipline is therefore needed, in which each person involved follows the standards, guidelines and procedures agreed upon. Besides being stated on paper, many of these can be supported or enforced by tools. Of extreme importance are clear agreements about documentation: when is documentation to be delivered, how is the quality of the documentation to be assessed, how does one ensure that the documentation is kept up to date?
   To a large extent, these standards and procedures will be described in separate documents, such as the Configuration Control Plan or the Quality Assurance Plan.

5. **Organization of the project** Under this heading, both the relation with other projects and the organization of the project itself are dealt with. Within the project team, various roles can be identified: project manager, tester, programmer, analyst, etc. One has to clearly delineate these roles and identify the responsibilities of each of them. If there are gaps in the knowledge required to fulfil any of these roles, the training and education needed to fill these gaps have to be identified. Different forms of team organization are discussed in chapter 5.

6. **Project phases** In chapter 1, we introduced a simple life cycle model in order to discuss the various activities to be dealt with in a software development project. There exist many variations of this process model, some of which are discussed in chapter 3. For each project, one has to decide upon the exact process model to be followed: which activities are being undertaken, which milestones can be identified, how do we ascertain whether those

milestones are reached, and which are the critical paths. The project must be broken down into manageable pieces that can be allocated to different team members. One also has to estimate, per phase and for the whole project, total cost and time. The topic of cost and time estimation will be dealt with extensively in chapter 7.

Different types of projects have different characteristics, and so call for different process models.

7. **Requirements analysis and design** Under this heading, the methods and techniques to be used during requirements analysis and design, are given. One should also indicate the resources and tools needed to support these methods and techniques.

8. **Implementation** In a similar way, the resources and tools needed to support implementation, are identified. Typically, the way version and configuration control for software components is dealt with, is described here too. A large proportion of the technical documentation will be produced during this phase. One thus has to state how this documentation will be taken care of.

9. **Testing** Here, the necessary test environment and test equipment is described. During testing, considerable pressure will normally be put on the test equipment. Therefore, this activity has to be planned carefully. After unit testing, the various components are integrated in some order. The order in which components are integrated and tested has to be stated explicitly. Also, the procedures to be followed during acceptance testing, i.e. the testing under user supervision, have to be given. Testing will be discussed in one of the later chapters.

10. **Resources** During the execution of the project, many resources are needed. The hardware, cpu-cycles and tools needed to support the project are listed under this entry.

11. **Quality assurance** Which organization and procedures will be used to assure that the software being developed meets the quality requirements stated? The many aspects of a Quality Assurance Plan may also be dealt with in a separate document. The topic of quality assurance is discussed in chapter 6.

12. **Changes**. It has been stated before that changes are inevitable. One has to ensure that these changes are being dealt with in an orderly way. One thus needs clear procedures on how proposed changes will be handled. Each such proposed change has to be registered and reviewed. When a change request has been approved, its impact (cost) has to be estimated. Finally, the change has to be incorporated into the project in execution. Changes that are entered via the back door lead to badly structured code, insufficient documentation and cost and time overruns. Since changes lead to different versions of both documentation and code, the procedures to be followed in dealing with such changes are often handled in the context of a Configuration Management Plan.

13. **Delivery** Finally, the procedures to be followed in carrying over the system to the customer must be given.

The project plan is aimed at providing a clear picture of the project to both the customers and the project team. If the objectives are not clear, they will never be achieved.

Despite careful planning, surprises will still crop up during execution of the project. However, careful planning early on leads to less surprises and makes one less vulnerable to these surprises. The project plan addresses a number of questions which anticipate possible future events. It gives orderly procedures for dealing with those events, so that justifiable decisions can be reached.

2.2 CONTROLLING A SOFTWARE DEVELOPMENT PROJECT

After a project plan has been drawn up and approved, the actual execution of the project may start. During that execution, control has to be exerted along the following dimensions:

— time,

— information,

— organization,

— quality, and

— money.

Progress of a software development project (the **time** aspect) is hard to measure. Before the proposed system has been finished, there is only a (large) pile of paper. Utterances such as '90% of the code has been written' should be taken with a pinch of salt. A much too rosy picture of the actual state of affairs is usually given. The phased approach introduced in chapter 1 as well as the many variants to this model that exist, aim at providing the manager with an instrument to measure and control progress. Some of these variants will be discussed in chapter 3.

The time needed to build a system is obviously related to the size of the system, and thus to the total manpower required. Larger systems simply require more time to develop, although we may try to shorten development time by allocating more personnel. Part of the control problem for software development projects is to trade off time against people. Shortening development time does not come for free, though. If more people are involved, more time will be needed for coordination and communication. After a certain point, adding more people will actually lengthen the development time. Part of the time control problem is phrased in Brooks' Law: 'Adding people to a late project only makes it later'. We will come back to this issue in the chapter on cost estimation.

The **information** that has to be managed above all concerns the documentation. Besides technical and user documentation, this also entails documentation on the project itself. Documentation concerning the project includes such things as: the current state of affairs, changes that have been agreed upon, decisions that have been made. This type of documentation can best be handled in the context of configuration management.

All members of the development team must know what their role in the team is, and understand what is expected of them. It is very important that these expectations are clear to all people involved. Unspoken and unclear expectations lead to situations in which individual team members set their own goals, either consciously or unconsciously. These **organizational** aspects deserve the continuous attention of the project manager. Secondly, the organization of a team and the coordination of the people involved will, at least partly, depend upon characteristics of the project and its environment. This dependence has to be recognized and taken into account when setting up a project team.

The **quality** aspect is gaining in importance. Customers are no longer satisfied with the purely technical solutions offered by computer specialists. They want systems that fit their real needs.

Quite a few quality requirements can be stated concerning software and its development. These quality requirements often conflict with one another. During the execution of a project we will have to assess whether or not the quality requirements are being met. This quality assessment has to occur on a regular basis, so that timely actions can be undertaken. Quality is not an add-on feature, it has to be built in.

Controlling expenses (the **money** aspect) largely means controlling labor costs. Though the cost of hardware and tools cannot be discarded, these can usually be estimated quite precisely early on in the project. Moreover, these are usually much less of an issue than personnel costs.

Estimating the cost of software thus means that we must estimate the manpower required to build the software. The manpower needed is very much dependent on the size of the software, for instance measured as the amount of code to be delivered. Many other factors, though, influence this cost or, alternatively, the productivity with which the software can be produced. A well-balanced team with experienced people will have a much higher productivity than a newly formed team with inexperienced people. Extreme quality constraints, such as an ultra-high reliability or a very fast response time, may also severely slow down productivity.

A number of models have been proposed that try to quantify the effect of those different cost drivers on the manpower required (see chapter 7).

Software development is a very labor-intensive process. One of our hopes is that better tools and the increased use of those tools will lead to a significant increase in productivity and, consequently, a significant decrease in the cost involved in developing software. A second way, at least in principle, to increase productivity dramatically, is reuse of existing software. Both these topics will be discussed in chapters to follow. As these trends continue, software development starts to become a capital intensive activity, rather than a labor intensive one [Wegner84].

Continuous assessment of the project with respect to these control aspects is of the utmost importance and will from time to time lead to adjustments: adjustments as regards time, cost, organization, information, or quality, or some combination thereof. Project management is a very dynamic activity.

In order to be able to adequately control a project, we need quantitative data which needs to be collected while the project is being executed. For instance, data on errors discovered during unit testing may help us in estimating further test effort needed. Data on time and effort spent up to a specific point will guide us in re-estimating schedule and cost. To measure is to know.

These data are also valuable in a post-mortem evaluation of the project. In a post-mortem evaluation we assess the present project in order to improve our performance on projects yet to come: what have we done wrong, what have we learned, what needs to be done differently on the next project?

Unfortunately, in practice very little hard data is ever gathered, let alone retained for later use. Most software development organizations have little insight in what they are doing. They tend to operate in a somewhat chaotic way, especially when facing a crisis. By identifying key factors that affect the controllability of the software development process, we may find ways to improve on it. This topic is further treated in chapter 8, when we discuss the process maturity framework introduced by Humphrey [Humphrey89a].

2.3 SUMMARY AND FURTHER READING

This chapter provides an introduction to the topic of software management.

Before we embark on a software development project, it has to be carefully planned. This planning process results in a document, the project plan, which provides a clear picture of the project to both the customers and the project team. Once the project plan has been drawn up and the project has started, its execution must be controlled. We identified five entities that require our continuous attention for project control:

1. Time: How do we assess progress towards the project's goals? Usually, some phased approach is followed which aims to provide management with a means to measure and control progress;

2. Information: How do we handle the vast number of documents that are produced in the course of a project? In particular, maintaining the integrity of the set of documents and handling all change requests require careful procedures;

3. Organization: How do we organize the project team and coordinate the activities of team members;

4. Quality: How do we define and assess quality requirements for both the development process and the resulting product;

5. Money: How do we estimate the cost of a project. These costs are to a large extent determined by the size of the software.

Each of these controlling aspects is further elaborated upon in a separate chapter (chapters 3–7). The various dimensions of project control will then be reconciled in chapter 8.

EXERCISES

1. Consider a software development project you have been involved in. Did the project have a project plan? Did the project plan address the issues listed in section 2.1? If some of these issues were not addressed, do you think it would have helped the project if they had been?

2. Do you think quantitative project data are important? In what way can they contribute to project planning?

3. Consider once again a software development project you have been involved in. To what extent were any environmental issues such as user training and working procedures adequately dealt with in the project?

4. A program written for personal use imposes rather less stringent requirements than a product that is also to be used by other people. According to [Brooks75], the latter may require three times as much effort. Discuss possible reasons for this considerable increase in cost.

3

The Software Life Cycle Revisited

In chapter 1, we introduced a simple model of the software life cycle. We distinguished several consecutive phases: requirements analysis, design, implementation, testing, maintenance. It was stated that, in practice, one often uses more sophisticated process models. In this chapter we continue this discussion. We will introduce various alternative models to structure the software development process.

Software development projects are often very large projects. A number of people work on such a project for a long time and therefore the whole process needs to be controlled: progress needs to be monitored, people and resources need to be allocated at the right point in time, etc. Earlier on, it was pointed out that progress of a software development project is particularly difficult to measure.

In order to control progress we employ a phased development in which a number of clearly identifiable milestones are established between start and finish of the project. We use a similar mechanism when constructing a house: foundations are laid, first floor is reached, house is weatherproofed, and so on. Often, the payment of installments is coupled to reaching those milestones.

In general, the milestones identified in a software development project correspond to points in time at which certain documents become available:

— after requirements analysis there is a requirements specification;

— after the design phase there is a (technical) specification of the system;

— after implementation there is a set of programs;

— after testing has been completed there is a test report.

Traditional models for the phased development of software are to a large extent 'document driven'. The pile of paper that is being produced in the course of the project guides the development process. This way of viewing the development process does not in general fit reality sufficiently well. In real projects, explicit feedback to earlier phases occurs after errors have been detected, prototyping techniques are applied, and software evolution entails rather more than is phrased in the term 'maintenance'. In the next section we discuss the waterfall model, a well-known variation of the process model introduced in chapter 1. In sections 3.2–5 we will discuss several other models that try to capture some or all of the drawbacks of the document-driven approach mentioned above.

Of these, the evolutionary-type models take into account that much of what is called maintenance is really evolution. It would then seem natural to explicitly bear this anticipated evolution in mind from the very start. This is usually not the case. Most often, the initial development of a software system is strictly separated from the subsequent maintenance phase. The major goal of a software development project then boils down to delivering a first version of the system to the user. Such may result in excessive maintenance costs to make the system fit the real user needs as yet. In section 3.6 it is argued that, in order to be able to properly assess costs and benefits, total life cycle cost rather than just development cost should be our primary focus. Going even one step further, we may argue that management should concentrate on product families rather than individual products, thereby granting an incentive both to the building of reusable parts and the reuse of (parts of) existing products when developing new ones.

From all the possible life cycle models we have to choose a particular one for any given project. This involves defining the individual steps and phases, their possible interaction, their deliverables, etc. By using an explicit modeling language, which may be supported by tools, management is provided with a handle to improve its control of software development. This type of process modeling is discussed in section 3.7.

3.1. THE WATERFALL MODEL

The waterfall model essentially is a slight variation of the model introduced in chapter 1. The waterfall model is generally attributed to Royce [Royce70] and became well known through Boehm [Boehm76]. However, a clearly phased approach to the development of software, including iteration and feedback, can already be found in earlier publications [Benington56], [Hosier61].

The waterfall model particularly expresses the interaction between subsequent phases. Testing software is not an activity which strictly follows the implementation phase. In **each** phase of the software development process, we have to compare the results obtained against that which is required. In all phases, quality has to be assessed and controlled.

This has been expressed in figure 3.1. V & V stands for Verification and Validation. Verification means: does the system meet its requirements (are we building the system right). Verification thus tries to assess the correctness of the transition to a next phase. Validation means: does the system meet the user's requirements (are we building the right system).

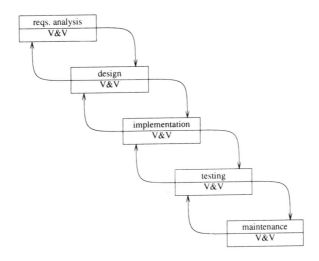

Figure 3.1: The waterfall model

Both in the model introduced in chapter 1 and in the waterfall model, considerable emphasis is placed on a careful analysis before the system is actually built. We want to prevent putting much energy into constructing a system which later turns out not to satisfy the user's requirements.

We therefore try to identify and tie down the user's requirements as early as possible. These requirements are documented in the requirements specification. On the basis of this document we may verify in subsequent phases whether or not these requirements are being met. Since it is difficult in practice, if not impossible, to completely specify the user's requirements, a regular test against the prospective user is desirable as well. These tests are termed validation. Through these validation steps we may prevent the appearance of a strong divergence between the system under development and possibly incompletely specified user requirements.

According to [Agresti86], a main reason for this type of approach is the fact that, in the past, insufficient tools were available to synthesize software. Design, implementation and testing of software are labor-intensive and time-consuming tasks. With the increasing availability of tools, for example to prototype software or execute specifications, considerable savings on these tasks come within reach. The development of software may then follow a more exploratory road. Eligible solutions can be tried out and, if needed, rejected.

McCracken and Jackson compare the waterfall model with a shop where the customer is obliged to give orders upon entering [McCracken81]. There is no possibility to look around, compare prices, change one's mind, or decide upon a different menu for today's dinner. Some things can be ordered by mail, but not all.

The waterfall model of software development is unrealistic, much like Escher's waterfall is.

[Zelkowitz88] provides insightful quantitative evidence that the classical document-driven model has many shortcomings. In many a software development project, the strict sequencing of phases advocated by the waterfall model is not actually obeyed. Figure 3.2 shows the average breakdown of activities across life cycle phases for a number of projects. In this figure, the label 'coding' refers to a phase which encompasses both implementation and unit testing.

Activity	Phase			
	Design	Coding	Integration testing	Acceptance testing
Integration testing	4.7	43.4	26.1	25.8
Coding	6.9	70.3	15.9	6.9
Design	49.2	34.1	10.3	6.4

Figure 3.2:   Breakdown of activities across life cycle phases, after [Zelkowitz88]

So, for example, only 50% of the design effort was found to occur during the actual design phase, while one-third of the design effort occurs during the coding period. Even worse, over 16% of the design effort takes place after the system is 'supposed' to be finished.

[Guindon88] also observed that software design behavior of individual designers is better characterized as an **oppportunistic process**. Designers move back and forth across levels of abstraction ranging from application domain issues to coding issues. Milestone dates seem to be somewhat arbitrary, and a significant part of the activities crosses phase boundaries.

3.2 PROTOTYPING

It became clear in the preceding section that it is often difficult to get and maintain a sufficiently accurate perception of the requirements of the prospective user. This is not surprising, though. It is in general not sufficient to take the *existing* situation as the one and only starting point for setting up software requirements. An important reason for embarking on a software development project is that one is not pleased with the present situation. What *is* wanted instead of the present situation often is not easy to determine. This holds even more in cases where we are concerned with a new application and the customer does not know the full possibilities of automation. In such cases, the development of one or more prototypes may help.

Analogies with the development of other products are appealing here. When developing a new car or chip one will also build one or more prototypes. These prototypes are tested intensively before a real production line is set up. For the development of the push-button telephone, about 2000 prototypes were tested, with variations in form, size and positioning of the buttons, size and weight of the mouthpiece, etc.

It is possible to follow a similar road with software development. In this context a prototype can be described as 'a working model of (possibly parts of) a software system, which emphasizes certain aspects' [Vonk87]. There is, however, one big difference between the development of software and the development of physical products such as cars, chips or telephones: in developing physical products, the highest costs are generally incurred during production, when multiple copies of the product are being produced. In software development, making multiple copies of the product is almost free. If we were to follow the hardware approach to prototyping in software development, and produce a prototype with the same functionality as the final product, we would in fact develop an operational system, with correspondingly high costs. It does not then seem plausible to start all over again and develop the 'real' system in a different way.

Using the definition given above and with the aim of developing a software prototype relatively cheaply, it is important that certain aspects are emphasized. This can be achieved through, for example:

— the use of very high-level languages, in which an executable version can be created quickly. This executable but probably rather inefficient version can be used to test the usability of the proposed system;

— the development of a system with less functionality, in particular as regards quality attributes such as speed, robustness, and the like.

One of the main difficulties for users is to express their requirements precisely. It then becomes natural to try to clarify these through prototyping. This can be achieved by developing the user interface fast. The prospective user may then work with a system that contains the interaction component but not, or to a much lesser extent, the software that actually processes the user's input. In this way, the user may get a good impression of what the future system will provide him with, **before** large investments are made to actually realize the system. Prototyping thus becomes a tool for requirements analysis. This is illustrated graphically in figure 3.3.

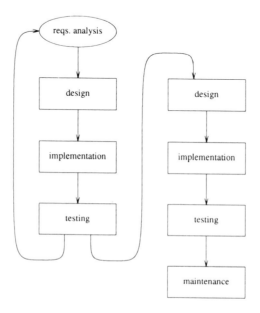

Figure 3.3:   Prototyping as a tool for requirements analysis

In this figure, the various phases are gone through in two different ways. The left-hand side of the figure is concerned with the prototyping stages. The iteration corresponds to the user-validation process, whereby new or changed requirements trigger the next cycle. The right-hand side concerns the actual production of the operational system. The difference between the two branches is that, by using different techniques and tools, the left-hand side can be traversed much more quickly and against much lower costs.

In figure 3.3, the prototyping phases and the later production phases have been clearly separated. This is appropriate, since we will use different techniques during the actual production phase, put much more emphasis on documentation, and so on. It is not necessary to make this distinction, though. The prototype then evolves to the final product. The user starts by formulating the raw requirements, on the basis of which a first version of the system is produced. The user starts to work with this system, which leads to new, or changed, requirements. The next version is then developed. After a number of such iterations, the user is satisfied and the last version developed is the product to be delivered.

This is very similar to the exploratory style of software development often used in AI-applications. In AI-programming, however, the goal often is not to produce a software product, but rather to explore some theory. In both cases though, the technique is aimed at *accommodating* design uncertainty rather than fighting it [Trenouth91].

We may thus employ two different definitions to the notion of prototyping. ([Floyd84], distinguishes a third approach, in which prototyping is used as a vehicle to experiment with different solutions proposed, before large investments are made to fully realize one of those solutions.) The first approach, the use of prototyping as a tool for requirements analysis, is very valuable. To make it an effective approach to the development of software, though, proper tools are needed. According to [Vonk87], most of the currently available fourth-generation tools are particularly well suited to prototype:

— data-oriented applications,

— with considerable emphasis on the user interface, and

— which show a high degree of user interaction.

The second approach, prototyping as an evolutionary development method, holds certain risks. If we are concerned with a short development time, certain necessary activities will receive less attention. The chances are that documentation is sacrificed for speed. The robustness of the system will often be less than is customary with a more traditional approach. Since with this evolutionary development method, maintenance will still be needed at some later stage, such quality defects may give a great deal of trouble later on. Incorporating quality after the system has been built is only possible against a very high price.

The points raised above are confirmed by one of the few experiments with prototyping which have been published [Boehm84a]. In this experiment, different groups of people developed one and the same system. Three groups took a traditional approach, in which a requirements specification was written after careful analysis. This requirements specification was then taken as the starting point for the subsequent development of the system. Four groups used a prototyping approach, in which the system was developed in a number of iterations with feedback to the prospective users.

The main conclusions of this experiment were:

— the prototyping approach took 40% less time and resulted in 45% less code;

— the traditional approach resulted in a more robust product, which was expected to be easier to maintain.

[Alavi84] reports on a similar experiment, in which prototyping (as an evolutionary development method) and the traditional approach to software development were applied to the development of an information system. In general, the users were more positive about the systems that were developed using the prototyping approach. This positive attitude concerned both the development process and the resulting product. The users felt more involved in the development process and had fewer conflicts with the designers. The designers themselves had some trouble with the frequent changes in user requirements that occured in the prototyping approach. They also had difficulties in trying to control the development process.

Finally, [Alavi91] reports on an experiment involving both prototyping and a more traditional data modeling step. Designers using the preliminary data modeling step required fewer iterations and delivered more efficient systems than designers using only prototyping. In this hybrid approach, data modeling was used to obtain robust and efficient data structures, while the prototyping steps addressed uncertainties in the requirements specification.

Alavi gives the following recommendations for the use of prototyping techniques:

— users and designers must be well aware of the prototyping approach and its pitfalls. Designers in particular may get frustrated by frequent changes in user requirements;

— prototyping is a relatively new approach and needs a positive attitude from those involved in order to get positive results;

— prototyping is particularly useful in those situations where user requirements are unclear or ambiguous. Prototyping seems a good way to clarify those requirements;

— prototyping too needs to be planned and controlled. We must impose limits on the number of iterations. We must establish explicit procedures for documenting and testing prototypes. The positive aspects of the traditional approach, which make the process manageable and controllable, should also be applied in this case.

Further research into the various ways in which prototyping techniques can be applied to the development of software is certainly needed in order to gain more insight into the boundary conditions to be imposed on the use of this technique.

3.3. INCREMENTAL DEVELOPMENT

In the preceding section, we discussed one way of using prototypes for which the final system is the last of a series of prototypes. Under careful management control in order to ensure convergence, the next version is planned to accommodate new or changed user requirements. There is yet another way to work towards the final system in a number of iterations.

We then proceed incrementally. The functionality of the system is produced and delivered to the customer in small increments. Starting from the existing situation we proceed towards the desired situation in a number of (small) steps. In each of these steps, the phased approach that we know from the waterfall model, is employed.

Developing software this way avoids the 'Big Bang' effect, i.e. for a long time nothing happens and then, suddenly, there is a completely new situation. Instead of building software, the software grows [Brooks87]. With this incremental approach, the user is closely involved in planning the next step. Redirecting the project becomes easier to realize, since we may anticipate changed circumstances faster.

Incremental development can also be used to fight the 'overfunctionality' syndrome. Since users find it difficult to formulate their real needs, they tend to demand too much. Lacking the necessary knowledge of the malleability of software and its development process, they may be inclined to think that anything can be realized. As a consequence, essential features appear next to bells and whistles in the list of requirements. Analysts are not able to distinguish one from the other, nor are they able to accurately estimate the effort required to implement individual features. Chances then are that much effort is spent on realizing features that are not really needed. As a result, many of today's systems offer a rich functionality, yet at the same time are ill-suited for the task at hand. For one thing, these systems are difficult to use simply because of the complexity incurred by their rich functionality.

This observation is confirmed by the prototyping example discussed above and several other studies [Fischer86]. With the incremental approach, attention is first focused on the essential features. Additional functionality is included only if and when it is needed. Systems thus developed tend to be leaner and yet provide sufficient support to their users.

Incremental development is strongly propagated in [Gilb88]. It is doubtful whether the time increments advocated by Gilb, up to a maximum of a few weeks, is always reasonable. But the advantages of incremental development are considerable even with different time increments. Surprises that are lurking with the traditional approach and that pose considerable difficulties on the management side of software development projects can be greatly diminished when software is being developed and delivered incrementally.

3.4 INTERMEZZO: MAINTENANCE OR EVOLUTION

Old payroll programs never die;
they just get fat around the middle.
Robert Granholm (*Datamation*, 1971)

In chapter 1, it was pointed out that a considerable maintenance effort is inevitable. Each maintenance task, whether it concerns repairing an error or adapting a system to new user requirements, in principle entails all aspects of the initial development cycle. During maintenance, we also have to analyze the problem and conceive a design which is subsequently implemented and tested.

The first big difference is that these changes are being made to an existing product. However, during initial development we often do not start from scratch either. If an existing organization decides to automate its order administration, such a system might also have to interface with already existing systems for, say, stock administration and bookkeeping. Thus, maintenance activities differ in degrees from initial development, rather than fundamentally. This relative difference is even more apparent when the system is being prototyped or developed incrementally.

The second main difference, time pressure, has a much larger impact. Time pressure is most strongly felt when repairing errors, for then it is quite possible that certain parts of the organization have to shut down because the software is not operational. In such cases, we have to work against time to identify and repair the errors. Often one patches the code and skips a thorough analysis and design step. It is the structure of the system that tends to suffer from such patches. The system's entropy increases, which hampers later maintenance activities. Worse still, the system's documentation may fail to get updated. Software and the corresponding documentation then grow apart, which will again hamper future maintenance activities. A more elaborate discussion of maintenance issues is given in chapter 18.

Lehman and Belady [Lehman85] have extensively studied the dynamics of software systems that need to be maintained and grow in size. Based on those quantitative studies, they formulated the following laws of software evolution (to be explained below):

1. **Law of continuing change** A system that is being used undergoes continuous change, until it is judged more cost-effective to restructure the system or replace it by a completely new version.

2. **Law of increasing complexity** A program that is changed, becomes less and less structured (the entropy increases) and thus becomes more complex. One has to invest extra effort in order to avoid increasing complexity.

3. **Law of program evolution** The growth rate of global system attributes may seem locally stochastic, but is in fact self-regulating with statistically determinable trends.

4. **Law of invariant work rate** The global progress in software development projects is statistically invariant.

5. **Law of incremental growth limit** A system develops a characteristic growth increment. When this increment is exceeded, problems concerning quality and usage will result.

In an early publication, Lehman compares the growth of software systems with that of cities and bureaucracies [Lehman74]. He makes a distinction between progressive and anti-regressive activities in software development. Lehman considers this model also applicable to socio-economic systems. In a city, for instance, progressive activities contribute to an increase in the living standard or quality of life. Anti-regressive activities, such as garbage collection, serve to maintain the status quo. If insufficient attention is being paid to those anti-regressive activities, decline will set in. Anti-regressive activities often are not interesting, politically speaking. It is an investment in the future, which had better be left to others. (The same phenomenon can be observed in the growth of the chemical industry and the resulting pollution problems.)

According to Lehman, the same kinds of activities occur within a software development project. Generating new code and changing existing code are progressive activities. These are interesting, challenging and rewarding activities. They provide the user with new and/or better functionality. Making documentation, improving the structure of the code, and taking care to maintain good communication between the people involved are anti-regressive activities. Neglecting these activities may not be harmful in the short term, but it certainly will be in the long term. For each system, we have to look for a proper balance between both kinds of activities.

The working of the third law (the law of program evolution) can be illustrated by means of figure 3.4 which depicts the growth pattern of system attributes over time. System attributes may refer to the length measured in lines of code, the number of modules, the number of user-callable functions, etc. The time axis may denote the release number, the number of months the system is operational, or the like. (The actual data studied by [Lehman74] concern the relation between the number of modules and the release number of the OS360 operating system.)

The relation depicted in figure 3.4 is almost linear. The ripples in the figure are very regular as well. Periods of more than linear growth alternate with periods of less than linear growth. Lehman explains the more than linear growth by pointing at the pressure from users to get more functionality as fast as possible. The developers/maintainers tend to bend under this pressure. As a consequence, one uses tricks and shortcuts in the code, documentation lags behind, errors are introduced and the system is insufficiently tested. After a while, more attention will be needed for anti-regressive activities: code needing to be restructured and documentation brought up to date, before further growth is possible. The two kinds of activities stabilize over time.

The fourth law (the law of invariant work rate) seems rather surprising at first sight. Lehman and Belady found that such things as allocated manpower and other resources do not correlate at all to the speed with which systems grow or change [Lehman78]. Apparently, large systems are in some sort of saturated state. One person more can be kept at work, but in the long run has no perceived impact on the evolution of the system.

More than average growth in some version of a system was in Lehman and Belady's observations almost always followed by a less than average growth in

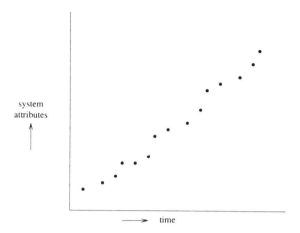

Figure 3.4:   Growth of system attributes over time

the next version (as expressed in the fifth law—law of incremental growth limit). In one of the systems they investigated, a substantially higher growth inevitably led to problems: lower reliability, higher costs, etc. Here too, a self-regulating feedback was observed.

From the preceding discussion, it follows that we have to be alert during maintenance. We have to preserve quality at each and every step. We may try to partly preclude the dangers sketched above by explicitly engaging ourselves in the various development phases during maintenance. The cyclic process followed during initial development then occurs during maintenance too. As with prototyping, the time needed to go through the complete cycle will in general be much shorter than during initial development. This way of looking at maintenance closely resembles the evolutionary view of software development. Realizing the first version of a software system is only the first step. True enough, this first step is more costly than most steps to follow, but it is not fundamentally different. In chapter 1 we noticed that such an approach may also have positive effects on the social and organizational environment in which software development takes place.

The waterfall model gives us a *static* view of the system to be developed. Reality is different. In developing software, and in particular during maintenance, we are concerned with an evolving system. As remarked before: software is not built, it grows.

3.5 THE SPIRAL MODEL

In the preceding sections we noticed that it is helpful to view software development as a cyclic process. In each cycle, the phases requirements analysis, design, implementation and testing are gone through. Some of those cycles serve to get a firmer grasp of user requirements (prototyping), other cycles serve to adapt an already existing operational system (maintenance).

If we look somewhat more closely at the main cycle of a software development effort, we notice that phases are not always executed strictly sequentially. It may be that the whole cycle is first traversed in order to build part of the system and, once this part is finished, the same cycle is gone through for other parts of that system. With the incremental approach, such is the intention from the beginning.

During the development of a software system, a number of problems have to be solved. In solving a problem, the most difficult parts are often tackled first, or the parts that have the highest risks—risks with respect to a successful completion of the project.

Following this line of thought, Boehm suggests a spiral model of the software development process, in which each convolution of the spiral gives rise to the following activities [Boehm86, 88a]:

— identifying the subproblem which has the highest risk associated with it;

— finding a solution for that problem;

The various process models discussed before can be coupled with Boehm's spiral model in a natural way (see figure 3.5):

— If obtaining the proper set of user requirements is seen as the area with highest risk, follow the spiral a few times around to solve this subproblem (= prototyping).

— If starting from a precise requirements specification, the main question is to obtain a robust and well-documented system, follow the spiral once, using the traditional process model with its phases and corresponding milestones as intermediate steps.

— Incrementally developing software boils down to tracking the spiral a number of times, once for each increment.

— During maintenance, the errors reported and/or changing requirements are triggers to track the spiral.

Viewed this way, the spiral model subsumes the other process models discussed so far.

3.6 TOWARDS A SOFTWARE FACTORY

Most software development organizations exhibit a fairly strict separation between initial development and subsequent maintenance of a product. A

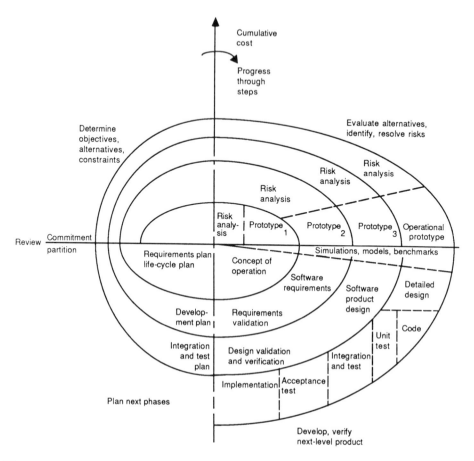

Figure 3.5:   The spiral model (*Source: B.W. Boehm A spiral model of software development and enhancement*, IEEE Computer **21**, 5 (1988) © 1988 IEEE.)

software development project ends as soon as the product is delivered to the clients. The subsequent evolution of the product is left to the maintenance department. As a consequence, the major goal of the development team is to get the product accepted.

In its worst form, quality, documentation, and even functionality may get sacrificed in order to deliver at least something to the user. Many necessary activities get deferred to the maintenance phase. But even in a more optimistic scenario, there is no real incentive for the development team to produce a system that can easily be maintained and adapted to changing requirements. That is simply not what they are being paid for.

To turn this bandwagon, assessment of a software product and its development should not be limited to the initial development phases. It should instead extend over its total life cycle. We should be concerned with *product* management rather than project management. Product management assesses the user-based quality aspects ('fitness-for-use'), costs and benefits of a product from its inception to its retention. In particular, the effort required to produce the initial system is not the only criterion that counts.

Going even one step further, we may consider managing the development of a family of (similar) products. When similar products are developed, we may hope to reuse elements from earlier products during the development of new products. Such is not the habit in software development though. In many an organization there is no incentive to reuse elements (code, design, or any other artifact) from another system since, again, that is not what we are being paid for. Similarly, there is no incentive to produce reusable elements, since the present project is all that counts.

As an alternative, we may conceive of the notion of a software factory.* The assets of a software factory are made up by the combined knowledge of its workers and its set of semi-products. When a new product is required, it is (mostly) built out of existing semi-products. The goal of the software factory is to optimize its ability to deliver products. It does so by increasing the combined knowledge of its workers and its set of semi-products [Curtis89a].

Applied to the development of software products, the software factory paradigm emphasizes the development of reusable elements. To make this a conceivable notion, we need to extend management responsibility to cover a family of products rather than an individual product.

Building reusable elements requires extra effort which is not paid back until those elements are indeed reused. It not only requires different cost estimating procedures and development paradigms, but also a different attitude amongst developers. One way to do so is to reward people both for producing reusable elements and for reusing elements produced by someone else [Prieto-Diaz91a].

A more elaborate discussion of software reusability is given in chapter 16. At the technical level, the shift from individual projects to product families is supported by the paradigm of object-oriented software development; see also chapters 10 and 12.

3.7 PROCESS MODELING

[Osterweil87] launched the idea to describe software development processes as programs. These **process programs** are written in a **process programming language**. Like other programming languages, process programming languages have a rigorously defined syntax and semantics. Process programs thus are descriptive representations of the development process. We may next envisage tools that process these programs and thus provide support for process management.

---

* The notion of a software factory is used here to emphasize one factory-like concept: reusability across products [McIlroy68]. The label is also often associated with Japanese efforts to improve software development productivity through standardization, division of labor, mechanization and automation, and the production of interchangeable (i.e. reusable) parts [Cusumano89].

As a simple example, consider the Pascal-like description of a test process in figure 3.6, adapted from [Osterweil87]. It describes the iterative execution of a number of test cases. The inputs and expected outputs are contained in an array `tests`. The test process is aborted as soon as some test does not produce the required output.

```
function all-tests-ok (executable, tests): boolean;
begin all-tests-ok:= true;
  for case:= 1 to number-of-testcases do
    derive(executable, tests[case].input, result);
    if not result-OK(result, tests[case].req-output)
      then all-tests-ok:= false; exit
    endif
  enddo
end all-tests-ok;
```

Figure 3.6:   A process program for testing

The above description of the test process is very deterministic. It can be completely automated, and executed without human intervention. Many aspects of the software development process, however, are heuristic in nature and do not lend themselves to this type of algorithmic description. Also, the aspects that tend to be described are those that are already well-understood [Lehman87], [Curtis87].

Most process models concentrate on activities that initiate and terminate a specific product, such as a requirements specification or test plan. Curtis identifies three mistakes that can be made if process models only focus on stages of transforming artifacts [Curtis89a]:

1. The progression of stages through which the artifact evolves gets confused with the organization of the processes through which people actually develop software. This argument was used earlier when we criticized the waterfall model. It is supported by the studies of Zelkowitz and Guindon reported in section 3.1. Parnas uses similar arguments when he criticizes the view that the software design process is a rational one [Parnas86].

2. Processes that do not directly transform artifacts tend to be ignored. Examples hereof include learning of the application domain, handling of fluctuating and conflicting requirements, and communication and coordination breakdowns [Curtis88].

3. The process is treated as discrete rather than continuous in time (i.e. each project invokes a separate process). This view inhibits the transfer of knowledge between projects, as was discussed in the previous section.

Yet, process programming does receive a lot of attention in the research literature. It is indicative of the need for more formal approaches to the description of the software process. The current trend in process modeling research is aimed at providing developers with computer guidance and assistance, rather than trying to fully automate the process. Such precise descriptions provide a basis for a range of support functions, ranging from the enactment of design steps to agenda management.

3.8 SUMMARY AND FURTHER READING

In this chapter we have paid ample attention to the software life cycle again. There are quite a few arguments against the strict sequential ordering of phases as discussed in chapter 1. The traditional approach is, to a large extent, document driven. On the way from start to finish, a number of milestones are identified. Reaching those milestones is determined by the availability of certain documents. These documents then play a key role in controlling the development process.

Several other development techniques, such as prototyping [Budde84], [Computer89], incremental development [Gilb88], software evolution [Lehman85], as well as daily practice, hardly fit this model. A more differentiated view of the software development process is needed. An interesting integrating model is being offered by Boehm's spiral model.

In most organizations, a fairly strict separation is found between software development and software maintenance. In section 3.6 we argued that software management should be concerned with the complete life cycle of a product. Going even one step further, we may put an incentive on the development of reusable elements by extending the scope of management responsibility to cover a range of products.

Finally, we introduced the notion of process modeling, which is aimed at describing the software development process in a precise and unambiguous way. Such descriptions are not intended to fully replace human activities, but rather to support them. The current state of process modeling is well reflected in the literature [Process89, 90].

EXERCISES

1. Suppose you are involved in a large project concerning the development of a patient planning system for a hospital. You may opt for one of two strategies. The first strategy is to start with a thorough analysis of user requirements, after which the system is built according to these requirements. The second strategy starts with a less complete requirements analysis phase, after which a pilot version is developed. This pilot version is installed in one or a few small departments. Further development of the system is guided by the experience gained in working with the pilot version. Discuss pros and cons of both strategies. Which strategy do you favor?

2. Discuss the relative merits of prototyping as a means to elicit the 'true' user requirements and prototyping as an evolutionary development method.

3. In what ways will the notion of a software factory impact the structure of the software development process?

4. Software maintenance increases system entropy. Discuss possible ways to counteract this effect.

5. One of the reasons for using 'document-driven' approaches in software development projects is that the documents produced provide some measure of project progress. Do you think this measure is adequate? Can you think of better ways to measure progress?

4
Configuration Management

Careful procedures are needed to manage the vast number of elements (source code modules, documentation, change requests, etc.) that are being created and updated over the lifetime of large software systems. This is called **configuration management**.

In the course of a software development project, quite a few documents are produced. These documents are also changed from time to time. Errors have to be corrected, change requests have to be taken care of, etc. Thus, at each point in time during a project, different versions of one and the same document may exist in parallel.

Often too, a software system itself is not monolithic. Rather, software systems exist in different versions and/or configurations. Different versions come about when changes are implemented after the system has been delivered to the customer. From time to time, the customer is then confronted with a new release. Different versions or components of a system may also exist during development. For instance, if a change request has been approved of, one programmer may be implementing that change by rewriting one or more components. Another programmer, however, may still be using the previous version of those same components.

Different configurations also come about if a set of components may be assembled into a system in more than one way. Take, for example, the system called ACK, the Amsterdam Compiler Kit [Tanenbaum83]. ACK consists of a set of programs to develop compilers for ALGOL-like languages. Important components of ACK are:

— front ends for languages such as Pascal, C, or Modula-2. A front end for language X will translate programs in that language into the universal intermediate code EM;

— different EM-optimizers;

— back ends, which translate EM-code to assembler-code for a variety of real machines.

A compiler is then obtained by selecting a front end for a specific language, a back end for a specific machine and, optionally, one or more optimizers. By now, more than 100 compilers have been produced using the ACK-system. Each of these compilers is a configuration, a certain combination of elements from the ACK-system.

The key tasks of configuration management are discussed in section 4.1. The procedures describing how to go about configuration management are laid down in a Configuration Management Plan. The contents of this document is discussed in section 4.2. Configuration management is often supported by tools. The discussion of those tools is largely postponed until chapter 15.

4.1 CONFIGURATION MANAGEMENT'S TASKS AND RESPONSIBILITIES

Configuration management is concerned with the management of all artifacts produced in the course of a software development project. Though configuration management also plays a role during the operational phase of a system, when different combinations of components can be assembled into one system and new releases of a system are generated, the discussion below centers around the role of configuration management during system development.

We will for the moment assume that, at any point in time, there is one official version of the complete set of documents related to the project. This is called the **baseline**. A baseline is 'a specification or product that has been formally reviewed and agreed upon, that thereafter serves as the basis for further development, and that can be changed only through formal change control procedures' [IEEE83b]. Thus, the baseline is the shared project data base, containing all approved items. The baseline may or may not be stored in a real data base and supported by tools to assist in retrieving and updating its elements. The items contained in the baseline are the **configuration items**. A configuration item is 'a collection of hardware or software elements treated as a unit for the purpose of configuration management' [IEEE83b]. Possible configuration items are:

— source code modules,

— object code modules,

— requirements specification,

— design documentation,

— test plan,

— test cases,

— test results, and

— user manual.

At some point in time, the baseline will contain a requirements specification. As time goes on, elements will be added: design documents, code modules, test reports, etc. A major task of configuration management is to maintain the integrity of this set of artifacts.

Such is especially important if changes are to be incorporated. Suppose that, during testing, a major flaw in some module is discovered. We then have to retrace our steps, and correct not only that code module, but also the corresponding design documents, and possibly even the requirements specification. Such may interact with work being done by other people still using the old version. Worse still, someone else may wish to make changes to the very same module at the same time. Configuration management takes care of controlling the release and change of these items throughout the software life cycle.

The way to go about this is to have one shared library or data base that contains all approved items, the so-called baseline. Adding an item to this data base, or changing an item, is subject to a formal approval scheme. For larger projects, such is the responsibility of a separate body, the Configuration (or Change) Control Board (CCB). The CCB ensures that any change to the baseline is properly authorized and executed. The CCB is staffed with people from the various parties involved in the project, such as development, test, and quality assurance.

Any proposed change to the baseline is called a change request. A change request may concern an error found in some code module, a discrepancy found between a design document and its implementation, an enhancement caused by changed user requirements, etc. A change request is handled as follows:

- The proposed change is submitted to the CCB. To be able to assess the proposed change, the CCB needs information as to how the change affects both the product and the development process. This includes information about the estimated amount of new or changed code, additional test requirements, the relation to other changes, potential costs, complexity of the change, the severity of the defect (if it concerns one), resources needed, etc. Usually, a special change request form is provided to specify the information needed by the CCB.

- The CCB assesses the change request. The change request may be approved, rejected, or deferred if further information is required. If the request is approved, it eventually results in a work order which has to be scheduled.

- The CCB will make sure that all configuration items affected will eventually be updated accordingly. Configuration management thus also provides a means to establish the status of all items, and thereby of the whole project.

We have to take care that the above formal scheme does not unnecessarily curtail the day-to-day working of the people involved in the project. New items should not be added to the baseline until they have been thoroughly reviewed and tested. Items from the shared data base may be used freely by the participants. If an item has to be changed, the person responsible for implementing the change gets a copy of that item. That item is then temporarily locked, so that others are not allowed to simultaneously update the same item. The person implementing the change is free to tinker with the copy. After the change has been thoroughly tested, it is submitted back to the CCB. Once the CCB has approved it, the revised item is included in the data base, the change itself is documented with the item, and the item is unlocked again. A sequence of documented changes thus provides a revision history of that item.

When an item is changed, the old version is kept as well. The old version still has to be used by others until they have adapted to the change. Also, we may wish to go back to the old version if another change is requested. We thus have different versions of one and the same item, and must be able to distinguish them. Such can be done through some numbering scheme, where each new version gets identified by the next higher number. We then get, for a component X, versions X.0, X.1, X.2, and so on.

In a more sophisticated environment, we may even create different branches of revisions. Figure 4.1 gives an example of such a forked development. In the example, module X.2.1 is, say, the result of fixing a bug in module X.2. Module X.3 may concern an enhancement to X.2. It should be noted that merging those parallel development paths again can be difficult. Also, the numbering schemes soon tend to become incomprehensible.

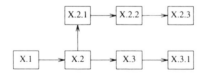

Figure 4.1:   Parallel development paths

At the level of source code elements, configuration management is generally supported by powerful tools. These tools take care of locking and unlocking elements, provide for automatic numbering of revisions, and by default provide users with the latest version of an item. Rather than keeping a copy of each version, such tools only keep track of what has changed from the previous version (the so-called **deltas**). If an item is changed, such tools prompt the user and ask him to document the change. In this way, the history of an item is recorded.

These tools also offer help in assembling an executable version of the system. One then writes a 'program' in which the various components of the required system are identified, together with their mutual dependencies. The system in question is then generated by executing this 'program': the components are retrieved automatically from the data base containing the source code modules, and all modules are subsequently translated and linked together into an executable system. If the system is smart enough, only those modules that have been changed are translated anew.

One example of such a tool is Make [Feldman78]. Such tools are a crucial element in environments where large software systems are being realized. Tools for configuration and version management will be discussed more extensively in chapter 15.

4.2 CONFIGURATION MANAGEMENT PLAN

The procedures for configuration management are laid down in a document, the Configuration Management Plan. As for the contents of this plan, we will follow the corresponding IEEE Standard [IEEE83a]. In this document, methods are described to identify configuration items, to control change requests, and to document the implementation of those change requests. A sample table of contents of the Configuration Management Plan is given in figure 4.2. The main constituents of this plan are:

Management section This section describes how the project is being organized. Particular attention is paid to responsibilities which directly affect configuration management: how are change requests being handled, how are development phases closed, how is the status of the system maintained, how are interfaces between components identified? Also, the relationship with other functional organizations, such as software development and quality assurance, is delineated. This section also contains a description of the procedures that are being followed for configuration management: naming conventions for components and versions, acceptance procedures, processing of change requests, and the like. A separate authority, the CCB, is usually established with the responsibility to evaluate and approve or disapprove proposed changes.

Activities This section describes how a configuration will be identified and controlled, and how its status will be accounted and reported. A configuration is identified by a baseline: a description of the constituents of that configuration. Such a configuration has to be formally approved of by the parties involved. One possible baseline could be a description of the functions to be delivered to the user, together with the associated acceptance criteria. This is called the **functional baseline**. Another baseline could define the version of the software to be delivered to the user (including the product identification, installation instructions and the like). This is called the **product baseline**.

To be able to control a software development project, clear and precise procedures are needed with respect to the processing of change requests. The authority, responsibility, and membership of the CCB have to be stated. Since software components are usually incorporated in a library, procedures for controlling this library have to be established as well.

In order to be able to control a software development project, data have to be collected and processed. Information that is normally required includes: the present status of components, versions and change requests, as well as reports of approved changes and their implementation.

Tools and techniques This section describes which tools and techniques are being applied for configuration and version management. Examples of possible tools are: data base management systems for storing documentation and software, or tools to generate an executable version from a description of its constituents (like Make, see chapter 15).

---

1. *Introduction*
    a. Purpose
    b. Scope
    c. Definitions and acronyms
    d. References

2. *Management*
    a. Organization
    b. Configuration management responsibilities
    c. Interface control
    d. Implementation of the Software Configuration Management Plan
    e. Applicable policies, directives and procedures

3. *Configuration management activities*
    a. Configuration identification
    b. Configuration control
    c. Configuration status accounting
    d. Audits and reviews

4. *Tools, techniques and methodologies*

5. *Supplier control*

6. *Records collection and retention*

Figure 4.2:   Sample structure of a Configuration Management Plan (*Source:* IEEE Standard for Software Configuration Management Plans, *IEEE Std 828-1983. Reproduced by permission of IEEE.*)

At some point, configuration items have to be approved. In the case of a requirement specification, this could entail a careful review or audit of that document. For source code modules, some strict testing scheme is likely to be specified. Though the Configuration Management Plan should identify the level of quality assurance required for each configuration item, the actual description of how this is tested had better be left to another document, the Quality Assurance Plan.

4.3 SUMMARY AND FURTHER READING

Configuration management is concerned with the management of all artifacts produced in the course of a software development project. It entails the following major activities:

— Configuration items must be identified and defined. A configuration item is a collection of elements that is treated as one unit for the purpose of configuration management. Examples of possible configuration items are: the requirements specification, a software module, a test report, the user documentation.

— The release and change of these items throughout the software life cycle must be controlled. This means that orderly procedures must be established as to whom is authorized to change or release configuration items.

— The status of configuration items and change requests must be recorded and reported. For example, the status of a change request could be: proposed, approved, rejected, or incorporated.

For larger projects, a Configuration Control Board is usually established. The CCB is responsible for evaluating all change requests and maintaining the integrity of the complete set of documents that relate to a project. Its tasks and the further procedures for configuration management are laid down in a separate document, the Configuration Management Plan.

A readable introduction to the topic of configuration management is given in [Babich86]. A complete reference source is [Bersoff80]. Further references on technical aspects of configuration management are given in a later chapter, when tools for configuration and version control are discussed.

EXERCISES

1. Discuss possible differences and similarities between configuration management during development and maintenance.

2. Configuration management at the implementation level is often supported by tools. Can you think of ways in which such tools can support the control of other artifacts (design documents, test reports, etc.) as well?

3. Device a configuration management scheme for both a small project (say, less than one person year) and a large project (say, more than ten person years). Give a rationale for the possible differences between those schemes.

4. To what extent could configuration management tools support the gathering of quantitative project data? To what extent could such tools support project control?

5
People Management and Team Organization

In most organizations that develop software, programmers, analysts and other professionals work together in a team. An adequate team structure will depend on many factors, such as the number of people involved, their experience and involvement in the project, the kind of project, individual differences and style. These factors also influence the way projects are to be managed. In this chapter, we will discuss various aspects of people management, as well as some of the more common team organizations for software development projects.

The work to be done within the framework of a project, be it a software development project, building a house, or the design of a new car, involves a number of tasks. A critical part of management responsibility is to coordinate the tasks of all participants.

This coordination can be carried out in a number of ways. There are both external and internal powers that influence the coordination mechanism. Internal powers originate from characteristics of the project. External powers originate from the project's organizational environment. If these powers ask for conflicting coordination mechanisms, conflicts between the project and the environment are lurking around the corner.

Consider as an example a highly innovative software development project, to be carried out within a government agency. The characteristics of the project may ask for a flexible, informal type of coordination mechanism, where the commitment of specialized individuals, rather than a strict adherence to formal procedures, is a critical success factor. On the other hand, the environment may be geared towards a bureaucracy with centralized control, which tries to impose formal procedures onto project management. These two mechanisms do not work harmoniously. As a consequence, management may get crushed between those opposing forces.

Section 5.1 further elaborates the various internal and external factors that affect the way projects are managed, and emphasizes the need to pay ample attention to the human element in project management.

Software development involves teamwork. The members of the team have to coordinate their work, communicate their decisions, etc. For a small project, the team will consist of up to a few individuals. As the size of the project increases, so will the team. Large teams are difficult to manage, though. Coordinating the work of a large team is difficult. Communication between team members tends to increase exponentially with the size of the team (see also chapter 7). Therefore, large teams are usually split into subteams such that most of the coordination and communication can be confined to within the subteams.

Section 5.2 discusses several ways to organize a software development team. Of these, the hierarchical and matrix type organization can be found in other types of business too, while the chief programmer team is rather specific to software development.

5.1 PEOPLE MANAGEMENT

A team is made up of individuals. Each of these individuals has his or her own personal goals. It is the task of project management to cast a team out of these individuals, whereby the individual goals are reconciled into one goal for the project as a whole.

Though the individual goals of people may differ, it is important to identify project goals at an early stage, and unambiguously communicate these to the project members. Project members ought to know what is being expected of them. If there is any uncertainty in this respect, team members will determine their own goals: one programmer may decide that efficiency has highest priority, another may choose efficient use of memory, while yet a third one will decide that writing a lot of code is what counts. Such widely diverging goals may lead to severe problems [Metzger87].

Once project goals are established and the project is under way, performance of project members with respect to the project goals is to be monitored and assessed. This can be difficult, since much of what is being done is invisible and progress is hard to measure.

Ideally, we would like to have an indication of the functionality delivered, and define productivity as the amount of functionality delivered per unit of time. Productivity is mostly defined as the number of lines of code delivered per man month. Anyone will agree that this measure is not optimal, but nothing better has been found [Boehm87a]. One of the big dangers of using this measure is that people tend to produce as much code as possible. This has a very detrimental effect. The most important cost driver in software development projects is the amount of code to be delivered (see also the chapter on cost estimation). Writing less code is cheaper, therefore, and reuse of existing code is one way to save time and money. It should therefore be strongly advocated. The present use of the amount of code delivered per man month as a productivity indicator offers no incentive for software reuse.

Another aspect of people assessment occurs in group processes like peer reviews, inspections and walkthroughs. These techniques are used during verification and validation activities, in order to discover errors or assess the quality of the code or documentation. In order to make these processes effective it is necessary to clearly separate the documents to be assessed from the authors of those documents. Weinberg used the term, egoless programming, in this context [Weinberg71]. An assessment of something produced by some person should not imply an assessment of that person.

Team management entails a great many aspects, not the least important of which concern the care for the human element. This chapter touches upon only a few aspects thereof. [Brooks75] or [Metzger87] give many insightful observations regarding the human element of software project management.

In the remainder of this section we will confine ourselves to two rather general taxonomies for coordination mechanisms and management styles.

5.1.1 Coordination mechanisms

[Mintzberg83] distinguishes between five different typical organizational configurations. These configurations reflect typical, ideal environments. Each of these configurations is associated with a specific coordination mechanism, a preferred mechanism to coordinate the tasks to be carried out within that configuration type. Mintzberg's configurations and associated coordination mechanisms are as follows:

1. **Simple structure** In a simple structure there may be one or a few managers, and there is a core of people who do the work. The corresponding coordination mechanism is called *direct supervision*. This configuration is often found in new, relatively small organizations. There is little specialization, training and formalization. Coordination lies with separate people, who are responsible for the work of others.

2. **Machine bureaucracy** When the content of the work is completely specified, it becomes possible to execute and assess tasks on the basis of precise instructions. Mass production and assembly lines are typical examples of this configuration type. There is little training, and much specialization and formalization. The coordination is achieved through *standardization of work processes*.

3. **Divisionalized form** This type of configuration is one where each division (project) is granted considerable autonomy as to how the stated goals are to be reached. The operating details are left to the division itself. Coordination is achieved through *standardization of work outputs*. Control is executed by regularly measuring the performance of the division. This coordination mechanism is possible only when the end result is specified precisely.

4. **Professional bureaucracy** If it is not possible to specify either the end result or the work contents, coordination can be achieved through *standardization of worker skills*. In a professional bureaucracy, skilled professionals are given considerable freedom as to how they carry out their job. Hospitals are typical examples of this type of configuration.

5. **Adhocracy** In projects that are big and/or innovative in nature, work is divided amongst many specialists. We may not be able to tell exactly what each specialist should do, or how they should carry out the tasks allocated to them. The project's success depends on the ability of the group as a whole to reach a non-specified goal in a non-specified way. Coordination is achieved through *mutual adjustment*.

The coordination mechanisms distinguished by Mintzberg correspond to typical organizational configurations, like a hospital, or an assembly line factory. In his view, different organizations call for different coordination mechanisms. Organizations are not all alike. Following this line of thought, factors external to a software development project are likely to exert an influence on the coordination mechanisms for that project.

Note that most real organizations do not fit one single configuration type. Different parts of one organization may well be organized differently. Also, Mintzberg's configurations represent abstract ideals. In reality, organizations may tend towards one of these configurations, but carry aspects of others as well.

5.1.2 Management styles

Reddin's theory of management styles emphasizes internal factors. His basic management styles can be related to Mintzberg's classification of coordination mechanisms, though. Reddin distinguishes between two dimensions in managing people [Reddin70]:

— **Relation directedness** This concerns the attention for the individual and his relations to other individuals within the organization.

— **Task directedness** This concerns the attention for the results to be achieved and the way in which these results must be achieved.

Both relation and task directedness may be high or low. This leads to four basic combinations, as depicted in figure 5.1. Obviously, these combinations correspond to extreme orientations. For both dimensions, there is a whole spectrum of possibilities.

		task directedness	
		low	high
relation directedness	low	separation style	committment style
	high	relation style	integration style

Figure 5.1:   The four basic management styles of Reddin

The style that is most appropriate for a given situation depends on the type of work to be done:

Separation style This management style is usually most effective for routine type of work. Efficiency is the central theme. Management acts like a bureaucrat and applies rules and procedures. This style closely corresponds to Mintzberg's coordination through standardization of work processes.

Relation style This style is usually most effective in situations where people have to be motivated, coordinated and trained. The tasks to be performed are bound to individuals. The work is not of a routine character, but innovative and specialized. This style best fits Mintzberg's mutual adjustment coordination mechanism.

Commitment style This is most effective if work is done under pressure. For this style to be effective, the manager has to know how to achieve goals without arousing resentment. This style best fits Mintzberg's professional bureaucracy.

Integration style This fits situations where the result is uncertain. The work is explorative in nature and the various tasks are highly interdependent. It is the manager's task to stimulate and motivate. Again, Mintzberg's coordination through mutual adjustment fits this situation well.

Each of the coordination mechanisms/management styles identified may be used within software development projects. It is only reasonable to expect that projects with widely different characteristics ask for different mechanisms. For an experienced team, asked to develop a well-specified application in a familiar domain, coordination may be achieved through standardization of work processes. For a complex and innovative application, this mechanism is not likely to work, though.

In chapter 8, we will identify various types of software development projects, and indicate which type of coordination mechanism/management style best fits those projects. It should be noted that the coordination mechanisms suggested in chapter 8 stem from internal factors, i.e. characteristics of the project on hand. As noted before, the project's environment will also exert influence on its organization.

5.2 TEAM ORGANIZATION

Within a team, different roles can be distinguished. There are managers, testers, designers, programmers, and so on. Depending on the size of the project, more than one role can be combined in one person, or different people may play the same role. The responsibilities and tasks of each of these roles have to be precisely defined in the project plan.

People cooperate within a team in order to achieve an optimal result. Yet it is advisable to strictly separate certain roles. It is expedient to compose a test team that is independent of the development team. Similarly, quality assurance should in principle be conducted by people not directly involved in the development process.

Large teams are difficult to manage and are therefore often split up into subteams. By clearly defining the tasks and responsibilities of the various subteams, communication between team members can be largely confined to communication between members of the same subteam. Quantifying the cost of interpersonal communication yields insights into effects of team size on productivity and helps to structure large development teams effectively. Some simple formulas for doing so are derived in chapter 7.

In the following subsections we discuss several organizational forms for software development teams.

5.2.1 Hierarchical organization

In an environment which is completely dedicated to the production of software, we often encounter hierarchical team structures. Depending on the size of the organization and/or project, different levels of management can be distinghuished.

Figure 5.2 gives an example of a possible hierarchical organization. The rectangles denote the various sub-teams in which the actual work is being done. Circled nodes denote managers. In this example, two levels of management can be distinguished. At the lower level, different teams are responsible for different parts of the project. The managers at this level have a primary responsibility

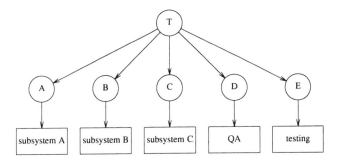

Figure 5.2: A hierarchical team organization

in coordinating the work within their respective teams. At the higher level, the work of the different teams is coordinated.

This type of hierarchical organization often reflects the global structure of the system to be developed. If the system has three major subsystems, there may be three teams, one for each subsystem, as indicated in figure 5.2. As indicated in this figure, there may also be functional units associated with specific project-wide responsibilities, such as quality assurance and testing.

It is not possible to uniquely associate the hierarchical organization with one of the specific coordination mechanisms introduced above. For each unit identified, each of the coordination mechanisms mentioned earlier is possible. Also, one need not necessarily apply the same mechanism in each node of the hierarchy. Having different coordination mechanisms within one and the same project is not without problems, though.

Based on an analysis of the characteristics of various subsystems, the respective managers may wish to choose a management style and coordination mechanism that best fits those characteristics. If one or more of the subsystems is highly innovative in nature, their management may opt for a mutual adjustment type of coordination. The higher levels within the hierarchy will usually tend towards a coordination mechanism based on some form of standardization, by imposing rules and procedures as in a machine bureaucracy, or measuring output as in a divisionalized configuration. In such cases, internal and external powers may well clash at one or more of the intermediate levels.

Another critical point in any hierarchical organization is the distance between top and bottom of the hierarchical pyramid. The 'real' work is generally done at the lower levels of this pyramid. The people at these lower levels generally possess the real knowledge of the application. The higher one rises in the hierarchy, the less specific this knowledge becomes (this is the main reason why management at these higher levels tends towards coordination through standardization). Yet, most decisions are taken at a fairly high level. In many cases, signals from the lower level somehow get subsumed at one of the intermediate levels.

If information seeps through the various levels in the hierarchy, it tends to become more and more rose-colored. The following scenario is not entirely fictitious:

— bottom: we have severe troubles in implementing module X;

— level 1: there are some problems with module X;

— level 2: progress is steady, I do not foresee any real problems;

— top: everything proceeds according to our plan.

These kinds of distortions are difficult to circumvent altogether. They are, however, reinforced by the fact that the organizational line along which progress is reported is also the line along which the performance of team members is being measured and evaluated. Everyone is favored by a positive evaluation and is thus inclined to color the reports accordingly. If data on a project's progress is being collected and processed by people not directly involved in the assessment of team members, you have a much higher chance that the information collected is of sufficient reliability.

An equally problematic aspect of hierarchical organizations lies in the fact that one is judged, both socially and financially, according to the *level* at which one stands within the organization. It is thus natural to aspire to higher and higher levels within the hierarchy. It is, however, not at all clear that such is desirable. The Peter Principle says: in a hierarchical organization each employee in general rises until reaching a level at which he is incompetent. A good programmer need not be a good manager. Good programming requires certain skills. To be a good manager, different skills are needed. In the long run, it seems wiser to maintain people at a level at which they perform well, and reward them accordingly.

5.2.2 Matrix organization

In an environment where software is a mere byproduct, we often encounter some sort of matrix organization. People from different departments are then allocated to a software development project, possibly part-time. In this type of organization it is sometimes difficult to control progress. An employee has to satisfy several bosses and may have the tendency to play off one boss against another.

We may also use a matrix organization in an environment completely dedicated to software development [Daly80]. The basic unit, then, is a small, specialized group. There may be more than one unit with the same specialization. Possible specializations are, for instance, graphics programming, data bases, user interfaces, quality control. The units are organized according to their specialty. Projects, on the other hand, may involve units with different specialties. Individuals are thus organized along two axes, one representing the various specialist groups and one representing the projects they are assigned to. This type of matrix organization is depicted in figure 5.3.

	real-time programming	graphics	databases	QA	testing
project C	X			X	X
project B	X		X	X	X
project A		X	X	X	X

Figure 5.3: A matrix organization

In such a situation, the project manager is responsible for the successful completion of the project. The manager in charge of one or more units with the same specialty has a longer-term mission, such as maintaining or enlarging the knowledge and expertise of the members of his team. Phrased in terms of Reddin's basic management dimensions, the project manager is likely to emphasize task directedness, while the unit manager will emphasize relation directedness. Such an organization can be very effective, provided there is sufficient mutual trust and the willingness to cooperate and pursue the project's goals.

5.2.3 Chief programmer team

A team organization known as the chief programmer team was proposed by Harlan Mills around 1970 and described in [Baker72]. The kernel of such a team consists of three people. The chief programmer is team leader. He takes care of the design and implements key parts of the system. The chief programmer is assisted by an assistant. If needed, the assistant stands in for the chief programmer. Thirdly, a librarian takes care of the administration and documentation. Besides these three people, an additional (small) number of experts may be added to the chief programmer team.

In this type of organization, fairly high demands are made upon the chief programmer. The chief programmer has to be very competent in the technical area, but he also has to have sufficient management capabilities. Put in other words: will there be enough chief programmers? Also, questions of competence may arise. The chief programmer plays a very central role. He takes all the decisions. The other team members may well challenge some of his qualities.

The early notion of a chief programmer team seems somewhat elitist. It resembles a surgeon team in its emphasis on highly specialized tasks and charismatic leadership. The benefits of a team consisting of a small group of peers over huge development teams struggling to produce ever larger software systems may be regained in a modified form of the chief programmer team though [Macro87].

In this modified form, peer group aspects prevail. The development team then consists of a small group of people collectively responsible for the task at hand. In particular, jobs are not structured around life cycle stages. There are no analysts, designers, or programmers, though the role of tester may be assigned to a specific person. Different levels of expertise may occur within the group. The most experienced persons act as chief programmer and deputy chief programmer, respectively. At the other end of the scale, one or two trainees can be assimilated and get the necessary on-the-job training. A trainee may well act as the team's librarian.

5.2.4 General principles for organizing a team

No matter how we try to organize a team, the key point is that it ought to be a *team*. From many tests regarding productivity in software development projects, it turns out again and again that factors concerning team capabilities have far greater influence than anything else. Factors such as morale, group norms and management style play more important roles than such things as the use of high-level languages, product complexity, and the like (see, for instance, [Lawrence81]).

Some general principles for team organization are given in [Koontz72]. In particular, these general principles also apply to the organization of software development projects:

Use fewer, and better, people Highest productivity is achieved by a relatively small group of people. This holds for novelists, football players and bricklayers. There is no reason to believe that it does not equally apply to programmers and other people working in the software field. Also, large groups require more communication, which has a negative effect on productivity and leads to more errors.

Try to fit tasks to the capabilities and motivation of the people available In other words: do take care that Peter's Principle does not apply in your situation. In many organizations, excellent programmers can be promoted only into managerial positions. It is far better to also offer career possibilities in the more technical areas of software development and maintenance.

In the long run, an organization is better off if it helps people to get the most out of themselves So you should not pursue either of the following:

— The reverse Peter Principle: people rise within an organization to a level at which they become indispensible. For instance, a programmer may become the only expert in a certain system. He will then not get a chance to work on anything else. It is not unlikely that this person, for want of another more interesting and challenging task, will leave your organization. At that point, you are in real trouble.

— The Paul Principle: people rise in an organization to a level at which their expertise becomes obsolete within five years. Given the speed with which new developments enter the marketplace in software engineering, and computer science in general, it is very important that people get the opportunity to grow and stay abreast of new developments.

It is wise to select people such that a well balanced and harmonious team results This in general means that it is not sufficient to have a few top-experts only. In a football team too, one needs water-carriers. Selecting the proper mix of people is a complicated task. There are various good texts available that specifically address this question (for example, [Weinberg71], [Metzger87]).

Someone who does not fit the team, should be removed If it turns out that a team does not function as a coherent unit, we are often inclined to wait a little while, see how things develop, and hope for better times to come. In the long run, this is detrimental.

5.3 SUMMARY AND FURTHER READING

Software is written by humans. Their productivity is partly determined by such factors as the programming language used, machine speed, and available tools. The organizational environment in which one is operating is equally important, though. A still very relevant source of information on allied psychological factors is [Weinberg71]. [Brooks75] and [Metzger87] also contain a number of valuable observations. Good team management distinguishes itself from bad team management above all by the degree to which attention is paid to these human factors. The human element in software project management is discussed in section 5.1, together with well-known taxonomies of coordination mechanisms and management styles.

There are different ways to organize software developers in a team. Hierarchical and matrix-type organizations are not specific to software development, while the chief programmer team originated in the software field. These organizational forms and some of their caveats are discussed in section 5.2.

EXERCISES

1. Consider a software development project you have been involved in. Which style of coordination mechanism and/or management style best fits this project? Do you consider management to have been adequate, or does the discussion in section 5.1 point at possible improvements?

2. From a management point of view, discuss possible pros and cons of having a true wizard on your development team.

3. Write an essay on the role of people issues in software development. To do so, you may consult some of the books that focus on people issues in software development, such as F.P. Brooks, *The Mythical Man-month*; P.W. Metzger, *Managing Programming People*; G.M. Weinberg, *The Psychology of Computer Programming*; or T. DeMarco and T. Lister, *Peopleware*.

4. Discuss pros and cons of an organization in which the primary departmentalization is vertical (i.e. along specialty such as data bases, human–computer interfaces, or graphics programming) as opposed to one in which the primary departmentalization is horizontal (design vs implementation vs testing).

5. Discuss pros and cons of letting people rotate between projects from different application domains as opposed to letting them become true experts in one particular application domain.

6

On Managing
Software Quality

In their landmark book *In Search for Excellence*, Peters and Waterman identify a number of key factors that set the very successful companies of the world apart from the less successful ones. One of those key factors is the commitment to quality of the very successful companies. Apparently, quality pays off.

Long-term profitability is not the only reason why attention to quality is important in software development. Because of the sheer complexity of software products and the often frequent changes that have to be incorporated during the development of software, continuous attention to, and assessment of, the quality of the product under development is needed if we ever want to realize satisfactory products. This need is aggravated by the increasing penetration of software technology into everyday life. Low-quality products will leave customers dissatisfied, will make users neglect the systems that are supposed to support their work, and may even cost lives.

One frightening example of what may happen if software contains bugs, has become known as 'Malfunction 54' [Joyce87]. A computerized radiation machine was blamed in incidents that caused the death of two people and serious injuries to others. The deadly mystery was eventually traced back to a software bug, named 'Malfunction 54' after the message displayed at the console.

The machine in question offered two types of radiation therapy, X-ray and electron. In X-ray mode, a high-intensity electron beam strikes a tungsten target, which absorbs much of the intensity and produces X-rays. In electron mode, the metal target is retracted from the beam path and the intensity is lowered by a factor of 100.

It turned out that, when the above-mentioned message appeared, the machine had mixed up the two modes. The target was retracted, as it should for electron mode, but the beam intensity was left high. The machine thus generated 25 000 rads in less than a second, a dose more than 100 times higher than the average treatment.

Commitment to quality in software development not only pays off, it is a sheer necessity.

The Council of the EC has issued a directive concerning product liability. The intention of the directive is stated in article 1: 'The producer shall be liable for damage caused by a defect in his product.' Thus, any product supplier is responsible for the quality of the product delivered. If, because of some defect, an individual suffers bodily harm or a financial loss, that individual may hold the supplier responsible under the directive. The supplier may not exonerate his responsibilities in any way.

In various European countries, a discussion is still going on as to whether software is to be considered a good as opposed to a service (the directive concerns goods, not services). (For a discussion of this Directive, see [Stuurman88].) Which way the coin will fall, stricter regulations as regards the quality of software products will certainly be established. And rightly so.

The commitment to quality products demands careful procedures. This has been widely recognized, and ISO, the International Standards Organization, has established several standards that pertain to the management of quality. The one most applicable to our field, the development and maintenance of software, is ISO 9001. This standard will be discussed in section 6.3.

ISO 9001 states general requirements for a quality system. This will have to be augmented by more specific procedures, procedures specifically aimed at quality assurance and control for software development. The IEEE Standard for Quality Assurance Plans is meant to provide such procedures. It is discussed in section 6.4.

Before we embark on a discussion of those standards, we will first elaborate on the notion of software quality itself. In the next section, we will discuss one possible taxonomy of quality attributes. This taxonomy is based on [McCall77]. It is a taxonomy widely used in practice. It is by no means the final word as regards software quality, but it is a good reference point to start from. This discussion also allows us to reflect on some pending problems as regards possibilities to measure quality in quantitative terms.

'Software quality' is a rather elusive notion. Different people will have different perspectives on the quality of a software system. A system tester may view quality as 'compliance to requirements', whereas a user may view it as 'fitness for use'. Both viewpoints are valid, but they need not coincide. As a matter of fact, they probably won't. Part of the confusion about what the quality of a system entails and how it should be assessed, is caused by mixing up these different perspectives. Section 6.2 elaborates on the different perspectives on quality.

Software quality assurance procedures provide the means to review and audit the software development process and its products. Quality assurance by itself does not guarantee quality products. Quality assurance merely sees to it that work is done the way it is supposed to be done.

It has to be augmented by quality actions within the software development organization itself, aimed at finding opportunities to improve the development process. These improvements require an understanding of the development process, an understanding that can be obtained only through carefully collecting and interpreting data that pertain to quality aspects of the process and its products. Some hints on how to start such a quality program are given in section 6.5.

6.1 A TAXONOMY OF QUALITY ATTRIBUTES

Some of the first elaborate studies on the notion of 'software quality' appeared in the late 1970s [McCall77], [Boehm78]. In these studies, a number of aspects of software systems are investigated which somehow relate to the notion of software quality. In the ensuing years, a large number of people have tried to tackle this very same problem. Many taxonomies of quality factors have been published. The fundamental problems have not been solved satisfactorily, though. The various factors that relate to software quality are hard to define. It is even harder to measure them quantitatively. On the other hand, real quality can often be identified surprisingly easily.

Quality can be defined as 'the totality of features and characteristics of a product or service that bears on its ability to satisfy given needs' [IEEE83b]. Applied to software, then, quality should be measured primarily against the degree to which user requirements are being met: correctness, reliability, usability, and the like. Software lasts a long time and is adapted from time to time in order to accommodate changed circumstances. It is important to the user that this is possible within reasonable costs. The customer is therefore also interested in quality factors which relate to the structure of the system rather than its use: maintainability, testability, portability, etc.

We will largely base our discussion of quality attributes on McCall's taxonomy [McCall77]. McCall distinguishes between two levels of quality attributes. Higher-level quality attributes are termed quality factors in his scheme. These quality factors can not be measured directly though. He therefore introduced a second level of quality attributes, termed quality criteria. Quality criteria can be measured, either subjectively or objectively. By combining the ratings for the individual quality criteria that affect a given quality factor, we obtain a measure for the extent to which that quality factor is being satisfied.

We may distinguish between internal and external (quality) attributes [Fenton91]. Internal attributes of a product, process, or resource, can be measured purely in terms of the product, process, or resource itself. Modularity, size, defects encountered, and cost are typical examples of internal attributes. External attributes of a product, process, or resource are those which can be measured only with respect to how the product, process or resource relates to its environment. Maintainability and usability are examples of external attributes. The high-level quality factors of McCall are external attributes. External attributes can be measured only *indirectly*, since they involve the measurement of other attributes. Users and managers tend to be interested in those external quality attributes.

For example, we cannot directly measure the reliability of a software system. We may however directly measure the number of defects encountered so far. This direct measure can be used to obtain insight into the reliability of the system. Such involves a theory of how the number of defects encountered relates to reliability. For reliability, such can be ascertained on good grounds. For most other aspects of quality though, the relation between the attributes that can be measured directly and the external attributes we are interested in is less obvious, to say the least.

Table 6.1 lists the quality factors and their definitions, as they are used by McCall et al. These quality factors can be broadly categorized into three classes. The first class contains those factors that pertain to the use of the software after it has become operational. The second class pertains to the maintainability of the system. The third class contains factors that reflect the ease with which a transition to a new environment can be made. These three categories are depicted in figure 6.1.

Table 6.2 lists the (lower-level) quality criteria and their definitions. Finally, table 6.3 indicates the relation between quality factors and quality criteria. Thus, column 1 of this table indicates that the factor Correctness is considered to be a function of the criteria Traceability, Consistency and Completeness. The definitions of the various terms as they are given in tables 6.1 and 6.2. should be borne in mind while interpreting table 6.3.

Product operation:
Correctness	Does it do what I want?
Reliability	Does it do it accurately all of the time?
Efficiency	Will it run on my hardware as well as it can?
Integrity	Is it secure?
Usability	Can I run it?

Product revision:
Maintainability	Can I fix it?
Testability	Can I test it?
Flexibility	Can I change it?

Product transition:
Portability	Will I be able to use it on another machine?
Reusability	Will I be able to reuse some of the software?
Interoperability	Will I be able to interface it with another system?

Figure 6.1:   Three categories of software quality factors (*Source: J.A. McCall, P.K. Richards & G.F. Walters*, Factors in Software Quality, *RADC-TR-77-369, US Department of Commerce, 1977.*)

Table 6.1: Quality factors

Correctness: The extent to which a program satisfies its specifications and fulfills the user's mission objectives.

Reliability: The extent to which a program can be expected to perform its intended function with required precision.[1]

Efficiency: The amount of computing resources and code required by a program to perform a function.

Integrity: Extent to which access to software or data by unauthorized persons can be controlled.

Usability: Effort required to learn, operate, prepare input, and interpret output of a program.[2]

Maintainability: Effort required to locate and fix an error in an operational program.[3]

Testability: Effort required to test a program to ensure that it performs its intended function.

Flexibility: Effort required to modify an operational program.

Portability: Effort required to transfer a program from one hardware and/or software environment to another.

Reusability: Extent to which a program (or parts thereof) can be reused in other applications.

Interoperability: Effort required to couple one system with another.

(*Source: J.A. McCall, P.K. Richards & G.F. Walters*, Factors in Software Quality, *RADC-TR-77-369, US Department of Commerce, 1977.*)

[1]This is a rather narrow definition of software reliability. A more complete definition is contained in the IEEE Glossary of Software Engineering Terminology [IEEE83b]: 'The probability that software will not cause the failure of a system for a specified time under specified conditions. The probability is a function of the inputs to and use of the system as well as a function of the existence of faults in the software. The inputs to the system determine whether existing faults, if any, are encountered.'

[2]Note that some factors seem to be defined in terms of attributes of some process. This is reflected in phrases like 'Effort required to learn . . .'. What is actually meant here is 'Properties that determine the effort required to learn . . .', i.e. the factor is meant to concern product attributes. Such is also reflected in the further decomposition into quality criteria, where Usability is decomposed into attributes that do concern the software itself rather than the process in which it is used.

[3]Again, this definition is rather narrow. It addresses only corrective maintenance activities (see also chapters 1 and 18).

Table 6.3 does not tell us yet what the exact relation is between quality factors and quality criteria. One possibility is to look for linear equations of the form

$$F_a = m_1 c_1 + m_2 c_2 + \ldots + m_n c_n$$

Here, F_a denotes the degree to which factor a is being met. m_i is a constant denoting the relative importance of criterion i, and c_i is the degree to which criterion i is being met. The constants m_i are to be determined by trial and error. This formula is one example of how to combine direct measurements into

Table 6.2:   Quality criteria

Access audit: The ease with which software and data can be checked for compliance with standards or other requirements.

Access control: The provisions for control and protection of the software and data.

Accuracy: The precision of computations and output.

Communication commonality: The degree to which standard protocols and interfaces are used.

Completeness: The degree to which a full implementation of the required functionality has been achieved.

Communicativeness: The ease with which inputs and outputs can be assimilated.

Conciseness: The compactness of the source code, in terms of lines of code.

Consistency: The use of uniform design and implementation techniques and notations throughout a project.

Data commonality: The use of standard data representations.

Error tolerance: The degree to which continuity of operation is ensured under adverse conditions.

Execution efficiency: The run-time efficiency of the software.

Expandability: The degree to which storage requirements or software functions can be expanded.

Generality: The breadth of the potential application of software components.

Hardware independence: The degree to which the software is dependent on the underlying hardware.

Instrumentation: The degree to which the software provides for measurements of its use or identification of errors.

Modularity: The provision of highly independent modules.

Operability: The ease of operation of the software.

Self-documentation: The provision of in-line documentation that explains the implementation of components.

Simplicity: The ease with which the software can be understood (this usually implies the avoidance of practices which increase the complexity of the software).

Software system independence: The degree to which the software is independent of its software environment — non-standard language constructs, operating system, libraries, data base management system, and the like.

Storage efficiency: The run-time storage requirements of the software.

Traceability: The ability to link software components to requirements.

Training: The ease with which new users can be made to use the system.

(*Source: J.A. McCall, P.K. Richards & G.F. Walters*, Factors in Software Quality, *RADC-TR-77-369, US Department of Commerce, 1977.*)

Table 6.3:   Relation between quality factors and quality criteria

	Correctness	Reliability	Efficiency	Integrity	Usability	Maintainability	Testability	Flexibility	Portability	Reusability	Interoperability
Access audit				x							
Access control				x							
Accuracy		x									
Communication commonality											x
Completeness	x										
Communicativeness					x						
Conciseness						x					
Consistency	x	x				x					
Data commonality											x
Error tolerance		x									
Execution efficiency			x								
Expandability								x			
Generality								x		x	
Hardware independence									x	x	
Instrumentation							x				
Modularity						x	x	x	x	x	x
Operability					x						
Self-documentation						x	x	x	x	x	
Simplicity		x				x	x				
Software system independence									x	x	
Storage efficiency			x								
Traceability	x										
Training					x						

(*Source: J.A. McCall, P.K. Richards & G.F. Walters*, Factors in Software Quality, *RADC-TR-77-369, US Department of Commerce, 1977.*)

an indirect measurement. There is as yet no accepted means to determine this relation more precisely.

Formulas such as the one given above presuppose that it is possible to measure quality quantitatively. Such is not all that easy, though. For lack of sound quality indicators, we often fall back onto the use of procedures and/or standards. These procedures and standards are our 'best guesses' [Kitchenham87]. We suspect that following certain procedures or adhering to certain standards yields a higher-quality product. In retrospect, the degree to which these procedures and standards are being followed, can be checked and used as quality indicators.

Following [Kaposi87], we will make a distinction between quality criteria which are based on objectively measurable properties and criteria which are based on subjective scores. Most of the quality criteria mentioned above can really only be assessed subjectively.

A subjective assessment of some criterion can be obtained by giving a rating on a scale from, say, 0 (extremely bad) to 10 (extremely good). Such a subjective metric is difficult to use, though. Different people assessing the same criterion are likely to give different ratings. This renders a proper quality assessment almost impossible.

We may do somewhat better by further decomposing a criterion into objectively measurable properties of the system. For example, rather than directly assessing consistency, we may take into consideration a number of properties that ascribe to consistency, such as the use of standard design representations, calling sequence conventions, error handling conventions, naming conventions, and so on. For each of these, procedures can be established, and we may simply count the percentage of modules that violate these rules. In the next step, we may combine the numbers thus obtained back into one number again. We must realize, however, that this indirect measure is still subjective. Though the properties we measure are objective, their combination into one criterion is still subject to a subjective interpretation. Yet, this approach is the one to be preferred, since different people will now assess a given system identically.

Another example of the indirect introduction of subjectivity occurs when we try to capture the notion of complexity (this criterion is not contained in McCall's taxonomy). McCabe defined the notion of complexity in terms of the number of elementary decisions in a program (see also chapter 10)[McCabe76]. Though this number is clearly an objective measure, its interpretation as a complexity metric is still subjective.

Subjectivity may thus enter the picture in two different ways: either directly because we can only measure the corresponding criterion subjectively, or indirectly via an interpretation of properties that can be measured objectively.

There are very few quality factors or criteria for which sufficiently sound numerical measures exist. The best, and in our view the only, example is software reliability, when software reliability is defined as we did in footnote 1 to table 6.1. Using solid statistical theory, we may predict the occurrence of future failures (i.e. reliability) based on data about past failures. (We will come back to this topic in the chapter on software reliability.)

McCall's taxonomy of quality factors and quality criteria may rightfully be criticized. For some factors, such as reliability for instance, better definitions can be given.

Similarly, one may dispute the list of quality criteria given in table 6.2. The most notable case in point is complexity. We all know that complex programs are hard to understand, error-prone, and difficult to adapt. We all know that it is a good programming practice to strive for clear, easy to understand, simple program structures. Thus, complexity bears on quality.

Complexity can be defined as 'the degree of complication of a system or system component, determined by such factors as the number and intricacy of interfaces, the number and intricacy of conditional branches, the degree of nesting, the types of data structures, and other system characteristics' [IEEE83b]. Various authors have added complexity to their taxonomy of quality criteria. Arthur did so, for instance; in his scheme, the criterion Complexity influences Flexibility, Reliability and Testability [Arthur85].

Complexity metrics are mostly used at the source code level, where they are used to assess the complexity of individual program components, such as modules and procedures. Some of the well-known complexity metrics are dealt with in the chapter on design.

Other, more fundamental, criticisms to schemes like the one discussed above, are [Kitchenham87]:

— The quality factors are not independent, but overlap. Some factors will impact one another in a positive sense, while others will do so negatively. An example from the first category is reliability versus correctness. Efficiency, on the other hand, will in general have a negative impact on most other quality factors. This means that we will have to make trade-offs between quality factors. If high requirements are decided upon for one factor, we may have to give in on others. Important trade-offs between quality factors are given in figure 6.2. A + in this figure indicates that factors reinforce one another; a — indicates conflicting goals.

— There is little relation between the quality factors identified and life cycle activities. Most quality factors can be assessed only after the fact. What we should do is to cross-reference quality factors to software engineering techniques [Gilb88]. For instance, though there are techniques and tools in existence to achieve reliable software, we cannot at present measure *progress* towards achieving reliable software.

In order to be able to control software quality, we have to know what it is. From the above discussion it follows that such can not be done in a satisfactory way as yet. We may, however, make a start. Within a given organization, quality factors and quality criteria may be defined. We may define the various criteria and describe the measurable properties and subjective scores they are based on. We may also indicate how these criteria contribute, in our view, to the various quality factors.

As the next step, we may determine to what extent the different quality factors must be fulfilled for a given project. In this way, the notion of software quality is precisely defined. We may then also determine whether or not the quality objectives are being met.

As Lord Kelvin said a century ago: 'When you can measure what you are speaking about, and express it in numbers, you know something about it; but when you cannot measure it, when you cannot express it in numbers, your knowledge is of a meagre and unsatisfactory kind; it may be the beginning of knowledge, but you have scarcely in your thoughts advanced to the stage of science.' [Kelvin]

Quality requirements that can not be quantified can not be controlled either.

	Correctness	Reliability	Efficiency	Integrity	Usability	Maintainability	Testability	Flexibility	Portability	Reusability	Interoperability
Correctness											
Reliability	+										
Efficiency											
Integrity			−								
Usability	+	+	−	+							
Maintainability	+	+	−		+						
Testability	+	+	−		+	+					
Flexibility	+	+	−	−	+	+	+				
Portability			−			+	+				
Reusability			−	−	−	+	+	+	+		
Interoperability			−	−					+		

Figure 6.2:   Trade-offs between quality factors

6.2 DIFFERENT PERSPECTIVES ON QUALITY

Users will judge the quality of a software system by the degree in which it helps them in accomplishing tasks and by the sheer joy they have in using it. The manager of those users is likely to judge the quality of the same system by its benefits. These benefits can be expressed in mere cost savings, or a better and faster service to clients.

During testing, the prevailing quality dimensions will be the number of defects found and removed, or the reliability measured, or the conformance to specifications. To the maintenance programmer, quality will be related to the system's complexity, its technical documentation, and the like.

These different viewpoints are all valid. They are also difficult to reconcile, though. Garvin distinguishes five definitions of software quality [Garvin84]:

1. Transcendent definition

2. User-based definition

3. Product-based definition

4. Manufacturing-based definition

5. Value-based definition.

Transcendent quality concerns innate excellence. It is the type of quality assessment we usually apply to novels. We may consider *Zen, Or the Art of*

Motorcycle Maintenance an excellent book, we may try to give words to our admiration, but these words are usually inadequate. Yet, the versed reader has gradually developed a good feeling for this type of quality. Likewise, the software engineering expert may have developed a good feeling for the transcendent qualities of software systems.

The user-based definition of quality concerns 'fitness for use' and relates to the degree in which a system addresses the user's needs. It is a subjective notion. Since different users may have different needs, they may assess a system's quality rather differently. The accidental user of a simple word processing package may be quite happy with its functionality and possibilities. A computer scientist may likewise be rather disappointed. The converse opinion may befall 'troff'.

In the product-based definition, quality relates to attributes of the software. Differences in quality are caused by differences in the values of those attributes. Most of the research into software quality concerns this type of quality. It also underlies the taxonomy of quality attributes discussed above.

The manufacturing-based definition concerns conformance to specifications. It is the type of quality definition used during system testing, whereas the user-based definition is prevalent during acceptance testing.

Finally, the value-based definition deals with costs and profits. It concerns balancing time and cost on the one hand, and profit on the other hand.

Software developers tend to concentrate on the product-based and manufacturing-based definitions of quality. The resulting quality requirements can be expressed in quantifiable terms, such as the number of defects found per module, or the number of decisions per module. The quality attributes discussed in the previous section fall into these categories. Such quality requirements however cannot directly be mapped onto the, rather subjective, quality viewpoints of the users, such as 'fitness for use'. Nevertheless, users and software developers will have to come to an agreement on the quality requirements to be met.

One way to try to bridge this gap is to define a common language between users and software developers in which quality requirements can be expressed. An example hereof is given in [Gilb88], where all quality attributes are quantified in user terms. Figure 6.3 gives one example of how a quality attribute can be expressed in user terms, and yet provides sufficient means to software developers to determine whether or not the requirement is met.

[Floyd88] also discusses the relation between quality as experienced by users and developers. Developers tend to have a mechanistic, product-oriented view on quality, whereby quality is associated with features of the product. In this view, quality is defined by looking from the program to the user (user friendliness, acceptability, etc.). To assess the quality of systems used in organizations, we have to adopt a process-oriented view on quality as well, where quality is defined by looking from the user to the program. This leads to notions like 'adequacy' and 'relevance'. In her view, both perspectives must be used when defining and assessing quality.

Attribute: friendliness

Scale: days on the job for employees to learn tasks supplied by the new system

Test: 90% successful completion of assigned tasks in employee test for the system, within twice the average time of an experienced user

Worst: 1 to 7 days

Plan: less than 1 day (to passing of test)

Best: less than 2 hours

Figure 6.3: Example of a quality attribute definition that can be used by both users and developers

6.3 THE QUALITY SYSTEM

ISO, the international organization for standardization, has issued several quality system standards [ISO87]. ISO 9000 gives guidelines for the selection and use of the series of standards on quality systems. ISO 9001–9003 discuss three different models for quality systems. The one most suited to software development is ISO 9001, 'Quality systems—Model for quality assurance in design/development, production, installation and servicing'.* ISO 9004 contains guidelines for the individual elements of the various standards.

Below, we will highlight the main constituents of ISO 9001. It should be emphasized that the requirements specified in this standard are complementary, and not alternative, to the technical requirements of the product.

ISO 9001 describes its scope as: 'This International Standard specifies quality system requirements for use when a contract between two parties requires the demonstration of a supplier's capability to design and supply products. The requirements specified in this International Standard are aimed primarily at preventing nonconformity at all stages from design to servicing.' The field of application is defined as:

contractual situations when: (a) the contract specifically requires design effort and the product requirements are stated principally in performance terms or they need to be established; (b) confidence in product conformance can be attained by adequate demonstration of certain supplier's capabilities in design, development, production, installation and servicing.

Thus, clause (a) indicates that the model still applies if the requirements are not completely specified in advance. This is very useful for software development, since requirements are usually not stable. Clause (b) specifies that we must be reasonably sure in advance that the supplier possesses sufficient capabilities to reach the goals set forth.

---

* ISO 9002 describes a model that applies only to production and installation; ISO 9003 describes a model applicable to final inspection and test.

---

1. Management responsibility
2. Quality system
3. Contract review
4. Design control
5. Document control
6. Purchasing
7. Purchaser supplied control
8. Product identification and traceability
9. Process control
10. Inspection and testing
11. Inspection, measuring and test equipment
12. Inspection and test status
13. Control of nonconforming product
14. Corrective action
15. Handling, storage, packaging and delivery
16. Quality records
17. Internal quality audits
18. Training
19. Servicing
20. Statistical techniques

Figure 6.4:   Ingredients of ISO 9001

The topics to be addressed in a quality system along the lines of ISO 9001 are listed in figure 6.4. Appendix C further elaborates upon these ingredients. As can be inferred from figure 6.4, a large number of issues need to be addressed in a quality system. Though ISO 9001 is not specifically aimed at software products (one might even claim that the standard suggests application to quality control for physical products) it is entirely possible to apply this standard to software quality control as well. Since software development projects have some rather peculiar characteristics (frequent changes in requirements during the development process, the rather invisible nature of the product during its development), there is a need for quality assurance procedures which are tailored towards software development. This is the topic of the next section.

6.4 SOFTWARE QUALITY ASSURANCE

The purpose of Software Quality Assurance (SQA) is to make sure that work gets done the way it is supposed to be done. More specifically, the goals of SQA [Humphrey89a] are:

- to improve software quality by appropriately monitoring the software and its development process;

- to ensure full compliance with the established standards and procedures for the software and the development process;

- to ensure that any inadequacies in the product, the process, or the standards are brought to management's attention so these inadequacies can be fixed.

Note that the SQA people themselves are not responsible for producing quality products. Their job is to review and audit.

There are potential conflicts of interest between the SQA organization and the development organization. The development organization may be facing deadlines and may want to ship a product, while the SQA people have revealed serious quality problems and wish to defer shipment. In such cases, the opinion of the SQA organization should prevail. For SQA to be effective, certain prerequisites must be fulfilled:

- It is essential that top management commitment is secured, so that suggestions made by the SQA organization can be enforced. If such is not the case, SQA soon becomes a costly padding and a mere nuisance to the development organization.

- The SQA organization should be independent from the development organization. Its reporting line should also be independent.

- The SQA organization should be staffed with technically competent and judicious people. They need to cooperate with the development organization. If the two organizations operate as adversaries, SQA won't be effective. We must realize that, in the long run, the aims of the SQA organization and the development organization are the same: the production of high-quality products.

The review and audit activities and the standards and procedures that must be followed are described in the Software Quality Assurance Plan.

IEEE Standard 730 offers a framework for the contents of a Quality Assurance Plan for software development [IEEE84a]. Figure 6.5 lists the entries of such a document. Appendix D contains a fuller description of its various constituents.

IEEE Standard 983 [IEEE86a] is a useful complement to standard 730. IEEE Standard 983 offers further guidelines as to the contents of a quality assurance plan, the implementation of a quality assurance plan, and its evaluation and modification.

The Software Quality Assurance Plan describes how the quality of the software is to be assessed. As noted before, some quality factors, such as reliability, can be determined objectively. Most factors at present can be determined only subjectively. Most often then, we will try to assess the quality by reading documents, by inspections, by walkthroughs and by peer reviews. In a number of cases, we may profitably employ tools during quality assurance. In particular, tools for static and dynamic analysis of program code can be used.

The actual techniques to be applied here will be discussed in the chapter on testing.

1. Purpose
2. References
3. Management
4. Documentation
5. Standards
6. Reviews and audits
7. Software configuration management
8. Problem reporting and corrective action
9. Tools, techniques and methodologies
10. Code control
11. Media control
12. Supplier control
13. Records collection, maintenance, and retention

Figure 6.5:   Main ingredients of IEEE Std 730

6.5 GETTING STARTED

In the preceding sections we discussed various ways to review the quality of a software product and the associated development process. The development organization itself should also actively pursue the production of quality products, by setting quality goals, assessing its own performance and taking actions to improve the development process.

Such requires an understanding of possible inadequacies in the development process, and possible causes thereof. Such an understanding is to be obtained through the collection of data on both the process and the resulting products, and a proper interpretation of those numbers. It is rather easy to collect massive amounts of data and apply various kinds of curve-fitting techniques to them. In order to be able to properly interpret the trends observed, they should be backed by sound hypotheses though.

An, admittedly ridiculous, example is given in figure 6.6. The numbers in this table indicate that black cows produce more milk than white cows. A rather naive interpretation is that productivity can be improved significantly by repainting all white cows.

Colour	Average production
White	10
Black	40

Figure 6.6:   Hypothetical relationship between the colour of cows and the average milk production

Though the example itself is ridiculous, its counterpart in software engineering is not all that far-fetched. Many studies, for example, have tried to determine a relation between numbers indicating the complexity of software components and the quality of those components. Quite a few of those studies found a positive correlation between such complexity figures and, say, the number of defects found during testing. A straightforward interpretation of those findings then is to impose some upperbound on the complexity allowed for each component. However, there may be good reasons for certain components for having a high complexity. For instance, [Redmond90] studied complexity metrics of a large number of modules from the MINIX operating system. Some of these, such as a module that handles 17 ANSI standard escape character sequences from the keyboard, were considered justifiably overcomplex. Experts judged a further decomposition of these modules not justified. Putting a mere upperbound on the allowed value of certain complexity metrics is too simple an approach.

An organization has to discover its opportunities for process improvements. The preferred way to do so is to follow a stepwise, evolutionary approach in which the following steps can be identified:

1. Formulate hypotheses

2. Carefully select appropriate metrics

3. Collect data

4. Interpret those data

5. Initiate actions for improvement

6. Iterate, whereby the effect of the actions is validated, and further hypotheses are formulated.

By doing so, the quest for quality will permeate your organization. You will subsequently reap the benefits.

One example of this approach is discussed in [van Genuchten91]. He describes an empirical study of reasons for delay in software development. The study covered six development projects from one department. Attention was focused on the collection of data relating to time and effort, viz. differences between plan and reality. A one-page data collection form was used for this purpose (see figure 6.7).

	Planned	Actual	Difference	Reason
Effort	—	—	—	—
Starting date	—	—	—	—
Ending date	—	—	—	—
Duration	—	—	—	—

Figure 6.7:   Time sheet for each activity

Some thirty reasons for delay were identified. These were classified into six categories after a discussion with the project leaders, and finalized after a pilot study. The reasons for delay were found to be specific to the environment.

A total of 160 activities were studied from mid 1988 to mid 1989. About 50% of the activities overran their plan by more than 10%. Comparison of planned and actual figures showed that the relative differences increased towards the end of the projects. It was found that one prime reason for the difference between plan and reality was 'more time spent on other work than planned'. The results were interpreted during a meeting with the project leaders and the department manager. The discussion confirmed and quantified some existing impressions. For some, the discussion provided new information. It showed that maintenance actions constantly interrupted development work. The meeting included a discussion on possible actions for improvement. It was decided to schedule maintenance as far as possible in 'maintenance weeks' and include those in quarterly plans. Another analysis study was started to gain further insights into maintenance activities. This study provides a number of useful insights, some of which reinforce statements made earlier:

- The 'closed loop' principle. The closed loop principle states that information systems should be designed such that those who provide input to the system are also main users of its output. Application of this principle results in feedback to the supplier of data. Thus, the data supplier is forced to provide accurate input. Second, it prevents users from asking more than they need. In the above example, the data was both collected and analyzed by the project leaders. The outcome was reported back to those same project leaders and used as a starting point for further actions.

- 'Local for local' data collection. Data collected may vary considerably between departments. Data is best used to gain insight in the performance of the department where the data is collected. Use in another department makes little sense.

- Focus on continuous improvement. The data collection effort was aimed at locating perceived deficiencies in the software development process. It revealed causes for these deficiencies and provided an opportunity for improvement. The question is not one of 'who is right and who is wrong', but rather 'how can we prevent this from happening again in future projects'.

- The study did not involve massive data collection. Simple data sheets were used, together with unambiguous definitions of the meaning of the various metrics. The approach is incremental, whereby the study gives an opportunity for small improvements, and shows the way for the next study.

6.6 SUMMARY AND FURTHER READING

In this chapter, we paid ample attention to the notion of quality. Software quality does not come for free. It has to be actively pursued. The use of a well-defined model of the software development process and good analysis, design and implementation techniques are a first prerequisite. However, quality must also be controlled and managed. To be able to do so, it has to be defined rigorously. Such is not without problems, as we have seen in sections 6.1 and 6.2. There exist numerous taxonomies of quality attributes. For each of these attributes, we need a precise definition, together with a metric that can be used to state quality goals, and to check that these quality goals are indeed being satisfied. Most quality attributes relate to aspects that are primarily of interest to the software developers. These engineer-oriented quality views are difficult to reconcile with the user-oriented 'fitness for use' aspects.

For most quality attributes, the relation between what is actually measured (module structure, defects encountered, etc.) and the attribute we are interested in is insufficiently supported by a sound hypothesis. For example, though programs with a large number of decisions are often complex, counterexamples exist which show that the number of decisions (essentially McCabe's cyclomatic complexity) is not a good measure for program complexity. We will further deal with the issue of software metrics and the associated problems in chapter 10. [Fenton91] contains a good discussion of these problems. [JSS90a], [JSS90b], [Software90b] are special journal issues on metrics. Many of the articles in these issues discuss the application of metrics in quality programs.

Major standards for quality systems have been defined by ISO and the IEEE. These standards give detailed guidelines as regards the management of quality. The importance of careful software quality assurance procedures is increasingly being recognized. For an extensive discussion of such procedures, see for instance [Vincent88].

Quality assurance by itself does not guarantee quality products. It has to be supplemented by a quality program within the development organization. Section 6.5 advocates an evolutionary approach to establishing such a quality program. A similar approach is discussed in [Grady87a]. Such an approach allows us to gradually build up expertise in the use of quantitative data to find opportunities for process improvements.

EXERCISES

1. Consider a software development project you have been involved in. How was quality handled in this project? Were quality requirements defined at an early stage? Were these requirements defined such that they could be tested at a later stage?

2. Define measurable properties of a software product that make up the quality criteria Modularity and Operability. Do these properties constitute an objective measure of these criteria? If not, in what ways is subjectivity introduced?

3. The quality factor Reusability influences several other quality factors, as indicated in figure 6.2. Can you think of arguments that explain these influences, both positive and negative?

4. Why should the SQA organization be independent of the development organization?

5. Give a possible staffing for an SQA group, both for a small development organization (less than 25 people) and a large development organization (more than 100 people).

6. Draw up a Quality Assurance Plan for a project you have been involved in.

7. Why should project members get feedback on the use of quality data they submit to the Quality Assurance Group?

8. One quality requirement often stated is that the system should be 'user-friendly'. Discuss possible differences between the developer's point of view and the user's point of view in defining this notion. Think of alternative ways to define system usability in measurable terms.

7
Cost
Estimation

When commissioning house construction, newly decorating the bathroom, or laying-out a garden, we expect a precise statement of the costs incurred by such an operation before that operation is started. A gardener is capable of giving a rough indication of the cost on the basis of, say, the area of land, the desired size of the terrace or grass area, whether or not a pond is desired, and similar information. Next, this statement can be made more precise in a further dialogue, before the first bit of earth is turned. If you expect a similar accuracy as regards the cost estimate for a software development project, you are in for a surprise.

Estimating the cost of a software development project is a rather unexplored field, in which one all too often relies on mere guesstimates. There are exceptions to this procedure, fortunately. There now exist a number of algorithmic models that allow us to estimate total cost and development time of a software development project, based on estimates for a limited number of relevant cost drivers. Some of the important algorithmic cost estimation models will be discussed in section 7.3.

In most cost estimation models, a simple relation between cost and effort is assumed. The effort may be measured in man-months, for instance, and each man-month is taken to incur a fixed amount, say, of $5000. The total estimated cost is then obtained by simply multiplying the estimated number of man-months by this constant factor. In this chapter, we will freely use the terms cost and effort as if they are synonymous.

The notion of total cost is usually taken to indicate the cost of the initial software development effort, i.e. the cost of the phases requirements specification, design, implementation and testing. Thus, maintenance costs are not taken into account. Unless explicitly stated otherwise, this notion of cost will also be used by us. In the same vein, development time will be taken to mean: the time between the start of the requirements specification and the point in time when the software is delivered to the customer. Lastly, the notion of cost as it is used here, does not include possible hardware costs either. It concerns only personnel costs involved in software development.

Research in the area of cost estimation is far from crystallized. Different models use different measures* and cost drivers, so that mutual comparisons are very difficult. Suppose some model uses an equation of the form:

$$E = 2.7 \, KLOC^{1.05}$$

This equation shows a certain relation between effort needed (E) and the size of the product ($KLOC$ = Kilo Lines Of Code = Lines Of Code/1000). The effort measure could be the number of man-months needed. Several questions come to mind immediately. What is a line of code, for instance? Do we count machine code, or the source code in some high-level language? Do we count comment lines, or blank lines that increase readability, as well, or don't we? Do we take into account holidays, sick-leave, and the like, in our notion of man-month, or does it concern a net measure? Different interpretations of these notions may lead to widely different results. Unfortunately, different models do use different definitions of these notions. Sometimes, it is not even known which definitions were used in the derivation of the model.

To determine the equations of an algorithmic cost estimation model, we may follow several approaches. Firstly, we may base our equations on the results of experiments. In such an experiment, we in general vary one parameter, while the other parameters are kept constant. In this way, we may try to determine the influence of the parameter that is being varied. As a typical example, we may consider the question of whether or not comments help to build up our understanding of a program. Under careful control of the circumstances, we may pose a number of questions about one and the same program text to two groups of programmers. The first group gets program text without comments, the second group gets the same program text, with comments. We may check our hypothesis using the results of the two groups. The, probably realistic, assumption in this experiment is that a better and faster understanding of the program text has a positive effect on the maintainability of that program.

This type of laboratory experiment is often performed at universities, where students play the role of programmers. It is not self-evident that the results thus obtained will also hold in industrial settings. In practice, there may be a rather complicated interaction between different relevant factors. Also, the subjects need not be representative. Finally, the generalization from the laboratory experiments that are (of necessity) limited in size, to the big software development projects that professionals get confronted with is not possible. The general opinion is

---

* In the literature, the term 'metric' is often used. Strictly speaking, a metric is a system of measures.

that results thus obtained have limited validity, and certainly need further testing. These remarks also apply if we want to generalize from the results of psychological experiments relating to software development, like the ones discussed in chapter 17.

A second way to arrive at algorithmic cost estimation models is based on an analysis of real project data, in combination with some theoretical underpinning. An organization may collect data about a number of software systems that have been developed. These data may concern the time spent on the various phases that are being distinguished, the qualification of the personnel involved, the points in time at which errors occurred, both during testing and after installation, the complexity, reliability and other relevant project factors, the size of the resulting code, etc. Based on a sound hypothesis of the relations between the various entities involved and a (statistical) analysis of these data we may derive equations that numerically characterize these relations. An example of such a relation is the one given above, which relates E to $KLOC$. The usability and reliability of such equations is obviously very much dependent upon the reliability of the data on which they are based. Also, the hypothesis that underlies the form of the equation must be sound.

The findings obtained in this way reflect an average, a best possible approximation based on available data. We therefore have to be very careful in applying the results obtained. If the software to be developed in the course of a new project cannot be compared with earlier products because of the degree of innovation involved, one is in for a big surprise. For example, estimating the cost of the Space Shuttle project cannot be done through a simple extrapolation from earlier projects.

We may hope, however, that the average software development project has a higher predictability as regards effort needed and the corresponding cost.

The way in which we obtain quantitative relations implies further constraints as regards the use of these models. The model used is based on an analysis of data from earlier projects. Application of the model to new projects is possible only insofar as those new projects resemble old projects, i.e. the projects on whose data the model is based. If we have collected data on projects of a certain kind and within a particular organization, a model based on these data cannot be used without further ado for different projects in a possibly different organization. A model based on data about administrative projects in a government environment has little predictive value for the development of realtime software in the aerospace industry. This is one of the reasons why the models of, for example, [Walston77] and [Boehm81] (see section 7.3 for more detailed discussions of these models) yield such different results for one and the same problem description.

The lesson to be learned is that blind application of the formulae from existing models will not solve your cost estimation problem. Each model needs tuning to the environment in which it is going to be used. This implies the need to continuously collect your own project data, and the application of statistical techniques to calibrate model parameters.

Other reasons for the discrepancies between different existing models are:

— Most models give a relation between man-months needed and size (in lines of code). As remarked before, widely different definitions of these notions are being used.

— The notion 'effort' does not always mean the same thing. Sometimes, one only counts the activities starting from the design, i.e. after the requirements specification has been fixed. Sometimes also, one does include maintenance effort.

Despite these discrepancies, the various cost estimation models do have a number of characteristics in common. These common characteristics reflect important factors that bear on development cost and effort. The increased understanding of software costs allows us to identify strategies for improving software productivity, the most important of which are [Boehm87a, 88b]:

• Writing less code. System size is one of the main determinants of effort and cost. By techniques that try to reduce size, such as software reuse and the use of high-level languages, significant savings can be obtained.

• Getting the best from people. Individual and team capabilities have a large impact on productivity. The best people are usually a bargain. Better incentives, better work environments, training programs and the like provide further productivity improvement opportunities.

• Avoiding rework. Studies have shown that a considerable effort is spent redoing earlier work. By applying process models like prototyping or evolutionary development, and the use of modern programming practices like information hiding, considerable savings can be obtained.

• Developing and using integrated project support environments. Tools can help us eliminate steps or make steps more efficient.

One often makes a distinction between **programming-in-the-small** and **programming-in-the-large** [DeRemer76]. Programming-in-the-small refers to small projects in which one single programmer exerts himself in a concentrated effort during a limited period of time. On the other hand, programming-in-the-large refers to projects in which a team of programmers is involved for a considerable period of time. Obviously, these are two extreme orientations, with many possible intermediate forms.

A number of studies have been done in which the main focus was to estimate the effort needed for a limited programming task. Some of the first experiments in this area were done by Halstead. Halstead developed a rather elaborate model that has become known as *software science* [Halstead77]. This model will be discussed more extensively in chapter 10. At the core of this model lies the observation that counting lines of code can be problematic, even if we have a very accurate definition of 'line of code'. Some lines are just more complicated than others. According to Halstead, it is better to start from the number of syntactic units, as they are recognized by a compiler. Halstead makes a distinction between *operators* and *operands*. Operators denote some action. Examples of operators are the standard operators (+, −, *, etc.), but also the semicolon that denotes composition of instructions, and constructs like **if-then-else** and **while-do**. Operands denote data: variables and constants. Counting the number of operators and operands in a program would then yield a better size measure than simply counting the number of lines.

The four basic entities in Halstead's model are, for a given program:

n_1 = the number of unique (i.e. different) operators
n_2 = the number of unique (i.e. different) operands
N_1 = the total number of occurrences of operators
N_2 = the total number of occurrences of operands

For the length of a program, Halstead gives the following equation:

$$N = N_1 + N_2$$

In this way, we obtain a refinement of the simple lines of code measure *LOC*. Both *LOC* and N (and also McCabe's complexity metric [McCabe76], also discussed in chapter 10) turn out to correlate well with programming effort [Curtis79]. It is therefore interesting to look for possibilities to estimate entities like *LOC* or N at an early stage. The value of N is highly dependent on the values of n_1 and n_2. Not surprisingly, the value for n_1 is rather constant for many programs in a given high-level language. This constant depends on the language chosen. For, given a particular programming language, the maximum number of operators that can be used in any program, is fixed: these are all listed in the syntax of the language. Most non-trivial programs will use a large percentage of these operators at least once. A further hypothesis could be that n_2 is mainly determined by the number of variables (*VARS*) that occur in the program. Based on these assumptions, the following empirical relation was found by [Wang84]:

$$LOC = 102 + 5.31 * VARS$$

Each program would thus contain about 100 lines of code, plus an additional five lines for each variable occurring in that program. First experiments indicate that reasonably accurate estimates of the size and effort required can indeed be obtained in this way. According to Wang, an estimated value of *VARS* can be obtained relatively early if a top-down design method is used in combination with a strongly-typed language like Pascal, so that such a model offers a good starting point for an early cost estimate.

Generalization of these results to really big programs is not straightforward. In large programs, factors like the complexity of the interfaces between components and the necessary communication between the people involved play a role which cannot be neglected. In [Conte86], a distinction is made between models for the micro and macro levels. At the macro level, the relations found will in general be more complicated. In the next sections, we will further discuss various models for estimating software cost at the macro level. In particular, we will discuss and compare some of the well-known algorithmic models in section 7.3.

Given an estimate of the size of a project, we will next be interested in the development time needed. With a naive view, we may conjecture that a project with an estimated effort of 100 man-months can be done in one year with a team of 8.5 people, but equally well in one month with a team of 100 people. This view is too naive. A project of a certain size corresponds to a certain nominal physical time period. If we try to shorten this nominal development time too much, we get into the 'impossible region', and the chance of failure will sharply increase. This phenomenon will be further discussed in section 7.4.

7.1 HOW NOT TO ESTIMATE COST

Cost estimates are often coloured in a political way, i.e. arguments other than the purely technical may (partly) determine the outcome. Typical lines of reasoning that reflect those non-technical arguments are:

- We were given 12 months to do the job, so it will take 12 months. This might be seen as a variation of Parkinson's Law: work fills the time available.

- We know that our competitor put in a bid of $1M, so we need to schedule a bid of $0.9M. This is sometimes referred to as 'price to win'.

- We want to show our product at the trade show next year, so the software needs to be written and tested within the next nine months, though we realize that such is rather tight. This could be termed the budget method of cost estimation.

- Actually, the present project needs one year, but I can't sell this to my boss. We know that ten months is acceptable, so we will settle for ten months.

Politically coloured estimates can have disastrous effects, as has been shown all too often during the short history of our field. Political arguments almost always play a role if estimates are being given by people directly involved in the project to be executed, such as the project manager, or someone reporting to the project manager. Very soon, then, estimates will influence, or get influenced by, the future assessment of those persons.

Many of the models to be discussed in the following sections are based on data about past projects. The arguments stated above may also influence this data collection process. A seemingly objective model may thus turn out to be useless, since the data on which the model is based are unreliable. A careful data collection procedure is therefore needed. In large organizations, one may set up a separate unit whose only task is to gather data and deliver accountable cost estimates. This unit has to treat the data supplied in a proprietary way.

Besides the reliability of the available data and the uncertainty of what exactly has been measured, one of the main problems is the sheer *lack* of quantitative data about past projects. There simply is not enough data available. Though the importance of such a data base is now being widely recognized we still do not routinely collect data on current projects. It seems as if we cannot spare the time to collect data; we have to write software. [DeMarco82] makes a comparison with the medieval barber who also acted as a physician. He could have made the same objection: 'We cannot afford the time to take our patient's temperature, since we have to cut his hair.'

For lack of hard data, the cost of a software development project is often estimated through a comparison with earlier projects. If the estimator is very experienced, reasonable cost estimates may result. However, the learning effect of earlier experiences may lead to estimates that are too pessimistic in this case. We may expect that experience gained with a certain type of application will lead to a higher productivity for subsequent projects. Similar applications thus give rise to lower costs.

[McClure68] describes a situation in which a team was asked to develop a FORTRAN compiler for three different machines. The effort needed (in man-months) for these three projects is given in figure 7.1.

Compiler	Number of man-months needed
1	72
2	36
3	14

Figure 7.1:   Learning effect in writing a FORTRAN compiler

On the other hand, peculiar circumstances and particular characteristics of a specific project tend to get insufficient attention if cost is estimated through comparison with earlier projects. For example, a simple change of scale (automation of a local library with 25 000 volumes as opposed to a university library with over 1 000 000 volumes), slightly harsher performance requirements, a compressed schedule (which incurs a larger team and thus increases overheads because of communication) may have a significant impact on the effort required in terms of man-months.

Careless application of the comparison method of cost estimation leads to estimates like: the cost of this project is equal to the cost of the previous project.

We may also involve more than one expert in the estimation process. In doing so, each expert gives an estimate based on his own experience and expertise. Factors that are hard to quantify, such as personality characteristics and peculiar project characteristics, may thus be taken into account. Here too, the quality of the estimate cannot exceed the quality of the experts.

If a group of people has to come up with a collective verdict, we will often find that some group members have a far higher impact on the outcome than others. Some members will not press their opinion or become impressed by the volubility of their companions. Such may well have a negative impact on the end result. In order to anticipate this undesirable effect, we may employ the Delphi-method if more than one expert is consulted. In the Delphi-method, each expert delivers his opinion on paper. A moderator collects the estimates thus obtained and redistributes them among the experts. In this process, the names of the experts and their estimates are decoupled. Each of the experts then delivers a new estimate, based on the information received from the moderator. This process is continued until a consensus is reached.

Another method that aims to get a more reliable estimate is to have the expert produce more than one estimate. We all have the tendency to conceive an optimistic estimate as being realistic. (Have you ever heard of a software system that got delivered ahead of time?) To obviate this tendency, Putnam suggests a technique in which the expert is asked for three estimates: an optimistic estimate a, a realistic estimate m, and a pessimistic estimate b. Using a beta-distribution, the expected effort then is $E = (a + 4m + b)/6$ [Putnam79]. Though this estimate will probably be better than the one simply based on the average of a and b, it seems justified to warn against too much optimism. Software has the tendency to grow, and projects have the tendency to far exceed the estimated effort.

A more elaborate discussion of the methods mentioned above can be found in [Boehm81], together with a discussion of their pros and cons.

7.2 EARLY ALGORITHMIC MODELS

The message from the preceding section is clear. To be able to get really reliable estimates, we need to extensively record historical data. These historical data can be used to produce estimates for new projects. In doing so, we will predict the expected cost on account of *measurable* properties of the project at hand. Like the cost of laying out a garden might be a weighed combination of a number of relevant attributes (size of the garden, size of the grass area, yes/no for a pond), so we would like to estimate the cost of a software development project. In this section, we will discuss some early efforts to get at algorithmic models to estimate software cost.

[Nelson66] gives a linear model for estimating the effort needed for a software development project. Linear models have the form

$$E = a_0 + \sum_{i=1}^{n} a_i x_i$$

Here, the a_i, $i = 0, \ldots, n$ are constants, and x_i, $i = 1, \ldots, n$ denote factors that impact the effort needed, i.e. cost. A large number of factors may influence productivity, and hence the effort required. By carefully analyzing data on past projects, and different combinations of factors, we may try to get a model with a small number of factors only. Nelson, for instance, suggests a model that takes into account 14 factors:

$$E = -33.63 + 9.15x_1 + 10.73x_2 + 0.51x_3 + 0.46x_4 + 0.40x_5 + 7.28x_6$$
$$- 21.45x_7 + 13.5x_8 + 12.35x_9 + 58.82x_{10} + 30.61x_{11} + 29.55x_{12}$$
$$+ 0.54x_{13} - 25.20x_{14}$$

In this equation, E denotes the estimate of the number of man-months needed. The meaning of the factors x_i and their possible values are given in figure 7.2.

Factor	Description	Possible values
x_1	Instability requirements specification	0–2
x_2	Instability design	0–3
x_3	Percentage of math instructions	percentage
x_4	Percentage of I/O instructions	percentage
x_5	Number of subprograms	number
x_6	Use of high-level language	0(yes)/1(no)
x_7	Business application	0(yes)/1(no)
x_8	Stand-alone program	0(yes)/1(no)
x_9	First program on this machine	1(yes)/0(no)
x_{10}	Concurrent development of hardware	1(yes)/0(no)
x_{11}	Use of random-access device	1(yes)/0(no)
x_{12}	Different host and target machine	1(yes)/0(no)
x_{13}	Number of trips	number
x_{14}	Development by defense organization	0(yes)/1(no)

Figure 7.2:   Factors from the model of [Nelson66]

Several observations can be made about this model. In developing software for defense applications, in which the software will often be embedded in target machines that differ from the host machine (an example might be flight-control software for missiles), factors like x_{12} and x_{14} will undoubtedly have a significant impact on cost. Such will probably not be the case in a completely different environment. This shows again that the data base with project data that underlies the model will have a significant impact on the factors that break the surface. Less likely in this model is the penalty for using an assembly language rather than some high-level language (x_6): about 7 man-months, regardless of the size of the project. Similarly, the negative constant a_0 and the two other factors that count negative strike as somewhat unlikely.

From a strict measurement theory point of view, Nelson's formula is not meaningful [Fenton91]. The scale type of factor x_1, for example, is ordinal, which means that only a linear ordering is imposed on possible values of x_1. Thus, larger values of x_1 mean a higher instability of the requirements specification.

The scale type of x_1 does not allow expressions like 'requirements specification A is twice as instable as requirements specification B'. If different measures are combined into a new measure, the scale type of the combined measure is the 'weakest' of the scale types of its constituents. In the case of Nelson's formula, the scale type of E would be ordinal too. We may then interpret different values of E as indicating that certain projects require more effort than others. The intention though is to interpret E as a ratio scale, i.e. actual effort in man-months. Strictly speaking, this is not allowed. The same objection can be raised against many other models discussed in this chapter.

In general, linear models don't work all that well. Though there is a large number of factors that impact productivity, it is very unlikely that they do so independently and linearly.

It is well to draw your attention at this point to the would-be accuracy of this type of formula. In Nelson's formula, the various constants are given with a precision of two decimals. Simply applying this formula would yield a point-estimate like, say, the cost of this project is 97.32 man-months. We have to watch for the pitfall phrased by the slogan: there are three kinds of lies: ordinary lies, big lies, and statistics. Nelson's formula is the result of a statistical analysis of real project data and has to be interpreted as such. This means that an estimate A obtained using this formula should be interpreted as: the probability that this project costs B man-months, where $(1 - \alpha)A \leq B \leq (1 + \alpha)A$, is greater than or equal to β, with suitable values for α and β (such as, for example, $\alpha = 0.2$ and $\beta = 0.9$). If the average height of men is 7 ft, this means that there is a fairly high chance that a randomly selected man has a height which is between 6 and 8 ft. The probability that he is exactly 7 ft high is very small. There also is a probability that his height is less than 6 feet or more than 8 ft.

Cost estimates obtained through this kind of model thus yield cost intervals and a certain non-zero probability remains that the real cost will lie outside this interval. The usability of those estimates then is strongly determined by the size of the interval and the probability that the real cost will indeed fall within that interval. Especially for large-scale development efforts, it is good practice to use the upper value of the cost interval rather than the point estimate that results from simply applying the formula [Myers89]. These remarks also hold for the algorithmic models to be discussed in section 7.3.

One way in which an expert could arrive at a cost estimate, is through a bottom-up process. For each module, a separate cost estimate can be obtained and the total cost is then taken to be the sum of the module costs, with some correction applied because of the integration of all the modules.

Wolverton describes a model in which a simple cost matrix is used as a starting point to determine module costs. In this matrix, a limited number of different types of modules is distinguished, together with a number of complexity levels [Wolverton74]. Figure 7.3 contains such a (hypothetical) cost matrix. The matrix elements reflect the cost (in dollars) per line of code.

Given a cost matrix C, a module of type i, complexity j and size S_k, will incur an estimated module cost $M_k = S_k * C_{ij}$.

This type of model also has its problems. Besides the difficulty of assessing module integration costs, the user has to subjectively assess the complexity class of each module, which yields a fair dose of uncertainty altogether. Other factors which may reasonably be expected to impact productivity as well, such as programming experience and hardware characteristics, are not taken into account. Extending the cost matrix in order to accommodate these factors only increases the subjectivity of the method.

Module type	Low		Complexity ⟷		High
	1	2	3	4	5
1. Data management	11	13	15	18	22
2. Memory management	25	26	27	29	32
3. Algorithm	6	8	14	27	51
4. User interface	13	16	19	23	29
5. Control	20	25	30	35	40

Figure 7.3:   A hypothetical cost matrix

7.3 LATER ALGORITHMIC MODELS

In the introduction to this chapter, we noticed that programming effort is strongly correlated with program size. There exist various (non-linear) models which express this correlation. A general form is

$$E = (a + bKLOC^c) \, f(x_1, \ldots, x_n)$$

Here, *KLOC* again denotes the size of the software (lines of code/1000), while *E* denotes the effort in man-months. *a*, *b* and *c* are constants, and $f(x_1, \ldots, x_n)$ is a correction which depends on the values of the entities $x_1, \ldots, x_n$. In general, the base formula

$$E = a + bKLOC^c$$

is obtained through a regression analysis of available project data. Thus, the primary cost driver is software size, measured in lines of code. This nominal cost estimate is next tuned by correcting it for a number of factors that influence productivity (so-called cost drivers). For instance, if one of the factors used is 'experience of the programming team', this could incur a correction to the nominal cost estimate of 1.50, 1.20, 1.00, 0.80 and 0.60 for a very low, low, average, high and very high level of expertise, respectively.

Figure 7.4 contains some of the well-known base formulas for the relation between software size and effort. For reasons mentioned before, it is difficult to compare these models. It is interesting to note, though, that the value of c fluctuates around the value 1 in most models.

Origin	Base formula	See section
Halstead	$E = 0.7\ KLOC^{1.50}$	10.2.4
Walston–Felix	$E = 5.2\ KLOC^{0.91}$	7.3.1
Boehm	$E = 2.4\ KLOC^{1.05}$	7.3.2

Figure 7.4: Some base formulas for the relation between size and effort

This phenomenon is well known from the theory of economics. In a so-called economy of scale, one assumes that it is cheaper to produce large quantities of the same product. The fixed costs are then distributed over a larger number of units, which decreases the cost per unit. We thus realize an increasing return on investment. In the opposite case, we find a diseconomy of scale: after a certain point the production of additional units incurs extra costs.

In the case of software, the lines of code are the product. If we assume that producing a lot of code will cost less per line of code, formulae like those of Walston–Felix ($c < 1$) result [Watson77]. Such may occur, for example, because the cost of expensive tools like program generators, programming environments and test tools can be distributed over a larger number of lines of code. Alternatively, we may reason that large software projects will be more expensive, relatively speaking. There will be a larger overhead because of the increased need for communication and management control, because of the problems and interfaces getting more complex, and so on. Thus, each additional line of code requires more effort. In such cases, we obtain formulas like those of Boehm and Halstead ($c > 1$).

There is no really convincing argument for either type of relation, though the latter ($c > 1$) may seem more plausible. Certainly for large projects, the effort required does seem to increase more than linearly with size.

[Banker89] suggests that there may be some, organization-specific, value A such that projects of size less than A exhibit an economy of scale, whereas projects of size greater than A exhibit a diseconomy of scale. This 'most productive scale size' A can then be used as an additional factor when tailoring projects.

It is clear that the value of the exponent c strongly influences the computed value E, certainly for large values of $KLOC$. Figure 7.5 gives the values for E, as they are computed for the earlier-mentioned models and some values for $KLOC$. The reader will notice large differences between the models. For small programs, Halstead's model yields the lowest cost estimates. For projects in the order of one million lines of code, this same model yields a cost estimate which is an order of magnitude higher than that of Walston–Felix. [Mohanty81] compares 13 different

KLOC	$E = 0.7\ KLOC^{1.50}$	$E = 2.4\ KLOC^{1.05}$	$E = 5.2\ KLOC^{0.91}$
1	0.7	2.4	5.2
10	22.1	26.9	42.3
50	247.5	145.9	182.8
100	700.0	302.1	343.6
1000	22135.9	3390.1	2792.6

Figure 7.5: *E* versus *KLOC* for various base models

quantitative cost estimation models. For one fictitious project, the estimated cost ranges from \$362 500 to \$2 776 667. Other studies show similar results [Thibodeau81], [Kemerer87].

From these observations, we should not immediately conclude that these models are thus useless. It is much more likely that there are big differences in the characteristics between the sets of projects that the various models are based on. Recall that the actual numbers used in those models result from an analysis of real project data. If these data reflect widely different project types and/or development environments, so will the models. We cannot simply copy those formulas. Each environment has its own specific characteristics and tuning the model parameters to the specific environment (a process called calibration) is necessary.

The most important problem with this type of model is to get a *reliable* estimate of the software size early on. How should we estimate the number of pages in a novel not yet written? Even if we know the number of characters, the number of locations and the time interval in which the story takes place, it is illusive to expect a realistic size estimate up front. The further advanced we are with the project, the more accurate our size estimate will get. If the design is more or less finished, we may (possibly) form a reasonable impression of the size of the resulting software. Only if the system has been delivered, do we know the exact number.

The customer, however, needs a reliable cost estimate early on. In such a case, lines of code is a measure which is too inexact to act as a base for a cost estimate. We therefore have to look for an alternative. In sections 7.3.4 and 7.3.5 we will discuss two models based on quantities which are known at an earlier stage.

7.3.1 The model of Walston and Felix

The base equation of Walston and Felix's model [Walston77] is

$$E = 5.2KLOC^{0.91}$$

Some 60 projects from IBM were used in the derivation of this model. These projects widely differed in size and the software was written in a variety of

Variable	Average productivity response group			|high-low| (PC)
Complexity user interface	< normal 500	normal 295	> normal 124	376
User participation during requirements specification	none 491	some 267	much 205	286
User originated changes in design	few 297	—	many 196	101
User-experience with application area	none 318	some 340	much 206	112
Qualification, experience of personnel	low 132	average 257	high 410	278
Percentage programmers participating in design	< 25% 153	25–50% 242	> 50% 391	238
Previous experience with operational computer	minimal 146	average 270	extensive 312	166
Previous experience with programming languages	minimal 122	average 225	extensive 385	263
Previous experience with application of similar or greater size and complexity	minimal 146	average 221	extensive 410	264
Ratio of average team size to duration (people/month)	< 0.5 305	0.5–0.9 310	> 0.9 171	134

Figure 7.6: Some productivity intervals (*Source: C.E. Walston and C.P. Felix, A method for programming measurement and estimation,* © IBM Systems Journal, *1977.*)

programming languages. It therefore comes as no surprise that the model, applied to a subset of these 60 projects, yields unsatisfactory results [Conte86].

In an effort to explain these wide-ranging results, Walston and Felix identified 29 variables that clearly influenced productivity. For each of these variables, three levels were distinguished: high, average and low. For a number of projects (51) Walston and Felix determined the level of each of these 29 variables, together with the productivity obtained (in terms of lines of code per man-month) in those projects. These results are given in figure 7.6 for some of the most important variables. Thus, the average productivity turned out to be 500 lines of code per man-month for projects with a user interface of low complexity. With a user interface of average or high complexity, the productivity is 295 and 124 lines of code per man-month, respectively. The last column contains the productivity change *PC*, the absolute value of the difference between the high and low scores.

According to Walston and Felix, a productivity index I can now be determined for a new project, as follows:

$$I = \sum_{i=1}^{29} W_i X_i$$

The weights W_i are defined by

$$W_i = 0.5 \log(PC_i)$$

Here, PC_i is the productivity change of factor i. For the first factor from figure 7.6 (complexity of the user interface), the following holds: $PC_1 = 376$, so $W_1 = 1.29$. The variables X_i can take on values $+1$, 0 and -1, where the corresponding factor scores as low, average or high (and thus results in a high, average or low productivity, respectively). The productivity index obtained can be translated into an expected productivity (lines of code produced per man-month). Details of the latter are not given in [Walston77].

The number of factors considered in this model is rather high (29 factors out of 51 projects). Also it is not clear to what extent the various factors influence each other. Finally, the number of alternatives per factor is only three, and does not seem to offer enough choice in practical situations.

Nevertheless, the approach taken by Walston and Felix and their list of cost drivers have played a very important role in directing later research in this area.

7.3.2 COCOMO

COCOMO (COnstructive COst MOdel) is one of the algorithmic cost estimation models best documented [Boehm81]. In its simplest form, called Basic COCOMO, the formula that relates effort to software size, reads

$$E = bKLOC^c$$

Here, b and c are constants that depend on the kind of project that is being executed. Boehm distinguishes three classes of projects:

Organic In projects of the organic type, a relatively small team develops software in a known environment. The people involved generally have a lot of experience with similar projects in their organization. They are thus able to contribute at an early stage, since there is no initial overhead. Projects of this type will seldom be very large projects.

Embedded Projects of the embedded type involve systems where the environment poses severe constraints. The product will be embedded in an environment which is very inflexible. An example of this type of project might be air traffic control, or some embedded weapon system.

Semidetached This is an intermediate form. The team may show a mixture of experienced and inexperienced people, the project may be fairly large, though not excessively large, etc.

For the various classes, the parameters of Basic COCOMO take on the following values:

organic: $b = 2.4, c = 1.05$

semidetached: $b = 3.0, c = 1.12$

embedded: $b = 3.6, c = 1.20$

Figure 7.7 gives the estimated effort for projects of each of those three modes, for different values of *KLOC* (though an 'organic' project of one million lines is not very realistic). Amongst others, we may read from this figure that the constant *c* soon starts to have a major impact on the estimate obtained.

		Effort in man-months	
KLOC	Organic $(E = 2.4 \, KLOC^{1.05})$	Semidetached $(E = 3.0 \, KLOC^{1.12})$	Embedded $(E = 3.6 \, KLOC^{1.20})$
1	2.4	3.0	3.6
10	26.9	39.6	57.1
50	145.9	239.4	392.9
100	302.1	521.3	904.2
1000	3390.0	6872.0	14333.0

Figure 7.7:   Size versus effort in Basic COCOMO

Basic COCOMO yields a simple, and hence a crude, cost estimate based on a simple classification of projects into three classes. In his book *Software Engineering Economics*, Boehm also discusses two other, more complicated, models, termed Intermediate COCOMO and Detailed COCOMO, respectively [Boehm81]. Both these models take into account 15 cost drivers—attributes that affect productivity, and hence costs. These cost drivers and the associated effort multipliers for Intermediate COCOMO are listed in figure 7.8.

All these cost drivers yield a multiplicative correction factor to the nominal estimate of the effort. (Both these models also use values for *b* which slightly differ from that of Basic COCOMO.) Suppose we found a nominal effort estimate of 40 man-months for a certain project. If the complexity of the resulting software is low, then the model tells us to correct this estimate by a factor of 0.85. A better estimate then would be 34 man-months. On the other hand, if the complexity is high, we get an estimate of $1.15 \times 40 = 46$ man-months.

In fact, Basic COCOMO is based on nominal values for each of the cost drivers.

Cost drivers	Rating					
	Very low	Low	Nominal	High	Very high	Extra high
Product attributes						
Reliability required	0.75	0.88	1.00	1.15	1.40	
Data base size		0.94	1.00	1.08	1.16	
Product complexity	0.70	0.85	1.00	1.15	1.30	1.65
Computer attributes						
Execution time constraints			1.00	1.11	1.30	1.66
Main storage constraints			1.00	1.06	1.21	1.56
Virtual machine volatility		0.87	1.00	1.15	1.30	
Computer turnaround time		0.87	1.00	1.07	1.15	
Personnel attributes						
Analyst capability	1.46	1.19	1.00	0.86	0.71	
Applications experience	1.29	1.13	1.00	0.91	0.82	
Programmer capability	1.42	1.17	1.00	0.86	0.70	
Virtual machine experience	1.21	1.10	1.00	0.90		
Prog. language experience	1.14	1.07	1.00	0.95		
Project attributes						
Use of modern prog. techniques	1.24	1.10	1.00	0.91	0.82	
Use of software tools	1.24	1.10	1.00	0.91	0.83	
Required development schedule	1.23	1.08	1.00	1.04	1.10	

Figure 7.8: Cost drivers and associated effort multipliers in Intermediate COCOMO (*Source: B.W. Boehm*, Software Engineering Economics, *table 8-2/page 118*, © *1981, Reprinted by permission of Prentice-Hall, Inc., Englewood Cliffs, NJ)*

On top of this set of cost drivers, the detailed model adds a further level of refinement. First of all, this model is phase-sensitive, the idea being that not all cost drivers influence each phase of the development cycle in the same way. So, rather than having one table with effort multipliers as in Intermediate COCOMO, Detailed COCOMO uses a set of such tables. These tables show, for each cost driver, a separate effort multiplier for each major development phase. Furthermore, Detailed COCOMO uses a hierarchy for the product to be developed, in which some cost drivers have an impact on the estimate at the module level, while others have an impact at the (sub)system level.

The COCOMO formulae are based on a combination of expert judgment, an analysis of available project data, other models, etc. The basic model does not yield very accurate results for the projects on which the model has been based. The intermediate version yields good results and, if one extra cost driver (volatility of the requirements specification) is added, it even yields very good results [Conte86]. Further validation of the COCOMO models using other project data is not straightforward, since the necessary information to determine the ratings of the various cost drivers is in general not available. So we are left with the possibility of only testing the basic model. Here, we obtain fairly large discrepancies between the effort estimated and the actual effort needed [Conte86], [Kitchenham84, 85].

A major advantage of COCOMO is that we know all its details.

7.3.3 The model of Putnam/Norden

Norden studied the distribution of manpower over time in a number of software development projects in the 1960s. He found that this distribution often had a very characteristic shape [Norden70]. This characteristic shape is well approximated by a Rayleigh distribution. Based upon this finding, Putnam developed a cost estimation model in which the manpower required (*MR*) at time t is given by

$$MR(t) = 2Kate^{-at^2}$$

a is a speed-up factor which determines the initial slope of the curve, while K denotes the total manpower required, including the maintenance phase [Putnam78]. K equals the volume of the area delineated by the Rayleigh curve. This Rayleigh curve is depicted in figure 7.9.

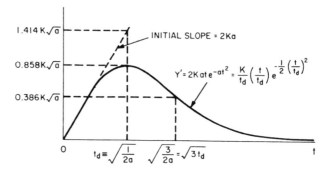

Figure 7.9:   The Rayleigh-curve for software schedules *(Source: M.L. Shooman,* Tutorial on software cost models, *IEEE Catalog nr TH0067-9 (1979), © 1979 IEEE.)*

The shape of this curve can be explained theoretically as follows [Parr80]. Suppose a project consists of a number of problems for which a solution must be found. Let $W(t)$ be the fraction of problems for which a solution has been found at time t. Let $p(t)$ be the problem-solving capacity at time t. Progress at time t then is proportional to the product of the available problem-solving capacity and the fraction of problems yet unsolved. If the total amount of work to be done is set to 1, this yields:

$$\frac{\mathrm{d}W}{\mathrm{d}t} = p(t)(1 - W(t))$$

After integration, we get

$$W(t) = 1 - \exp\left(-\int^t p(\alpha)d\alpha\right)$$

If we next assume that the problem-solving capacity is well approximated by an equation of the form $p(t) = at$, i.e. the problem-solving capacity shows a linear increase over time, the progress is given by a Rayleigh distribution:

$$\frac{dW}{dt} = ate^{-(at^2)/2}$$

Integration of the equation for $MR(t)$ that was given earlier yields the cumulative effort I:

$$I(t) = K(1 - e^{-at^2})$$

In particular, we get $I(\infty) = K$. If we denote the point in time at which the Rayleigh-curve assumes its maximum value by T, then $a = 1/(2T^2)$. This point T will be close to the point in time at which the software is being delivered to the customer. The volume of the area delineated by the Rayleigh curve between points 0 and T then is a good approximation of the initial development effort. For this, we get

$$E = I(T) = 0.3945K$$

This result is remarkably close to the often-used rule of thumb: 40% of the total effort is spent on the actual development, while 60% is spent on maintenance.

The above equations, together with many others, have been incorporated in SLIM, a commercial product [Putnam80]. Different studies [Conte86], [DeMarco82] indicate that Putnam's model is well suited to estimate the cost of very large software development projects (projects that involve more than 15 man-years). The model seems to be less suitable for small projects.

A serious objection against Putnam's model, in our opinion, concerns the relation it assumes between effort and development time if the schedule is compressed relative to the nominal schedule estimate: $E = c/T^4$. Compressing a project's schedule in this model entails an extraordinary large penalty (see also section 7.4).

A variant to Putnam's model is discussed in [Parr80]. This variant is based on the observation that for many a project the people involved will have a certain amount of applicable past experience. In such cases it seems realistic to assume a progress curve which does not start at the origin. This variant has been depicted in figure 7.10. It seems to be a useful alternative for small projects [Parr80].

7.3.4 DeMarco's model

Models like COCOMO are based on an early estimate of the amount of code to be delivered. Such an estimate is difficult, if not impossible, to obtain at an early

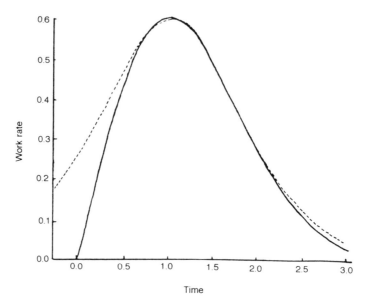

Figure 7.10:   Parr-curve (dotted) versus Rayleigh-curve *(Source: F.N. Parr, An alternative to the Rayleigh curve model for software development effort, IEEE Transactions on Software Engineering SE-6, 3 (1980), © 1980 IEEE.)*

stage. DeMarco proposed a model that would allow us to estimate cost at the requirements specification stage of software development [DeMarco82].

DeMarco uses dataflow diagrams to model a system. These dataflow diagrams depict the various data transformations. Together, they provide a network of functions to be performed. We may distinguish different levels in this network, levels that differ in the degree of abstraction with which we view the system being modeled.

DeMarco's cost estimation model is based on the number of functional primitives (*FP*) in the human–computer interface of the system. Functional primitives are those primitives that occur at the lowest level of the network depicted by the dataflow diagrams. Obviously, some primitives are 'bigger' and/or more complex than others, so that we need some correction in order to arrive at a more uniform metric.

With respect to size, such a correction can be achieved as follows: At the component level, the function network depicts the system as a sequence of interrelated primitive operations. Each of these operations involves some input and output elements. DeMarco estimates the relative size of a transformation (its information content) through a function of the number of elements *TC* involved in that transformation. Analogous to [Halstead77], this results in

$$\text{Size}(FP) = k \times TC_{FP} \times \log_2(TC_{FP})$$

for some constant *k*.

The complexity is next taken care of by applying some multiplicative corrective factor. To this end, each primitive function is classified using a taxonomy of function classes. Some of the classes from DeMarco's taxonomy are, with the multiplicative factors as in [DeMarco82] given between parentheses:

— functions that compose or decompose data (0.6)

— functions that update information (0.5)

— functions that analyze data and take subsequent actions (1.0)

— funtions that evaluate input from the human-computer interface (0.8)

— functions that check for internal consistency (1.0)

— functions for text manipulation (1.0)

— functions that synchronize the interaction with the user (1.5)

— functions that generate output (1.0)

— functions that do simple calculations (0.7)

— functions that do complex calculations (2.0)

So, rather than using the raw functional primitive metric *FP*, DeMarco uses an adjusted value *FP'* which involves a correction to accommodate differences in both size and complexity:

$$FP' = \sum_i \alpha_i \times TC_i \times \log_2 TC_i$$

Here, i goes through the set of functional primitives, while α_i denotes the correction factor associated with the class to which the ith primitive belongs.

Finally, we are left to decide on a relation between *FP'* and effort needed (*E*), such as, for example

$$E = aFP'^b$$

where a and b are again determined using data from past projects. DeMarco has not further elaborated this line of thought. He does point at the necessity to gather project data yourself and derive an organization-specific model from your own set of data.

The structure of this cost estimation model looks like that of some of the models we discussed before. The basic unit, however, is a functional primitive, rather than a line of code. This is attractive, since we may hope to be able to identify and count functional primitives at a relatively early stage. Such is not true if we stick to lines of code.

As of yet, we do not know of practical applications of this model. Its usefulness therefore remains unclear.

7.3.5 Function Point Analysis

Like DeMarco's model, function point analysis (FPA) is a method to estimate costs in which the problems associated with determining the expected amount of code are circumvented. FPA has been developed by Albrecht [Albrecht79, 83]. FPA is based on counting the number of different data structures that are being used. In the FPA method, it is assumed that this number of different data structures is a good size indicator. FPA is particularly suitable for projects aimed at realizing business applications. For, in these applications the structure of the data plays a very dominant role. The method is less suited for projects in which the structure of the data plays a less prominent role, and the emphasis is on algorithms (such as compilers and most real-time software).

The following five entities play a central role in the model as described in [Albrecht83]:

1. Number of input types (I). The input types refer only to user input that internally lead to changes in data structures. It does not concern user input which is solely meant to control the program's execution. Each input type that has a different format, or is treated differently, is counted. So, though the records of a master file and those of a mutation file may have the same format, they are still counted separately.

2. Number of output types (O). For the output types, the same counting scheme is used.

3. Number of inquiry types (E). Inquiry types concern input that controls the execution of the program and does not change internal data structures. Examples of inquiry types are: menu selection, and input meant to query certain data.

4. Number of logical internal files (L). This concerns internal data generated by the system, and used and maintained by the system, such as, for example, an index file.

5. Number of interfaces (F). This concerns data that is output to another application, or is shared with some other application.

By trial and error, weights have been associated with each of these entities. The number of (unadjusted) function points UFP then is a weighed sum of these five entities:

$$UFP = 4I + 5O + 4E + 10L + 7F$$

With FPA too, a further refinement is possible, by applying corrections to reflect differences in complexity of the data types. In that case, the constants used in the above formula depend on the estimated complexity of the data type in question. Figure 7.11 gives the counting rules when three levels of

Type	Simple	Complexity level Average	Complex
Input (*I*)	3	4	6
Output (*O*)	4	5	7
Inquiry (*E*)	3	4	6
Logical internal (*L*)	7	10	15
Interfaces (*F*)	5	7	10

Figure 7.11:   Counting rules for (unadjusted) function points

complexity are distinguished. So, rather than having each input type count as four function points, we may count three, four or six functions points for input types having, say, less than four fields, four to eight fields, or more than eight fields, respectively.

Like in other cost estimation models, the unadjusted function point measure is adjusted by taking into account a number of application characteristics that influence development effort. Figure 7.12 contains the 14 characteristics used in the FPA model. The degree of influence of each of these characteristics is valued on a six-point scale, ranging from zero (no influence, not present) to five (strong influence). The total degree of influence *DI* is the sum of the scores for all characteristics. This number is then converted to a technical complexity factor (*TCF*) using the formula

$$TCF = 0.65 + 0.01DI$$

The (adjusted) function point measure *FP* is now obtained through

$$FP = UFP \times TCF$$

Data communications
Distributed functions
Performance
Heavily used configuration
Transaction rate
On-line data entry
End-user efficiency
On-line update
Complex processing
Re-usability
Installation ease
Operational ease
Multiple sites
Facilitate change

Figure 7.12:   Application characteristics in FPA

Finally, there is a direct mapping from (adjusted) function points to lines of code. For instance, in [Albrecht79] one function point corresponds to 65 lines of PL/I, or to 100 lines of COBOL, on the average.

From the description given by Albrecht it is not simple to decide exactly when two data types should be counted as separate. Also, the difference between, for example, input types, inquiry types, and interfaces remains somewhat vague. Experiments show that analysts have difficulties in counting function points in a uniform way, even when provided with extensive guidance as to what the various classes entail.

Further problems with FPA have to do with its use of ordinal scales and the way complexity is handled [Symons88]. FPA distinguishes three levels of component complexity only. A component with 100 elements thus gets at most twice the number of function points as a component with one element. In a sense, complexity is counted twice: both through the complexity level of the component and through one of the application characteristics. Yet it is felt that highly complex systems are not adequately dealt with, since FPA is predominantly concerned with counting externally visible inputs and outputs.

In applying the FPA cost estimation method, it still remains necessary to calibrate the various entities to your own environment. This holds the more for the corrections that reflect different application characteristics, and the transition from function points to lines of code. You will also have to clearly delineate the different data types. Our conjecture is that the only way to satisfactorily do so is to refrain from manual counting, and provide a tool which does the counting for you.

7.3.6 Variations on a theme

The cost estimation models discussed above generally start out with some primary size estimate (such as *KLOC* or *UFP*) and next adjust this primary estimate by taking into account both technical complexity factors (such as performance requirements) and environmental factors (such as team capability). The primary size estimate and technical complexity factors together are meant to measure the 'intrinsic' size of the development task at hand [Symons88].

The underlying hypothesis then is that the primary size estimate is a proper first approximation of the intrinsic task size. For most cost estimation models this hypothesis has not really been validated. Moreover, such an hypothesis may become invalid as circumstances change.

To illustrate this point we will sketch two variations, on COCOMO and FPA, respectively.

The COCOMO model allows us to handle reuse in the following way. The three main development phases of design, coding and integration are estimated to take 40%, 30% and 30% of the average effort, respectively. Reuse can be catered for by separately considering the fractions of the system that require redesign

(*DM*), recoding (*CM*) and re-integration (*IM*). An adjustment factor *A* is then given by the formula

$$A = 0.4DM + 0.3CM + 0.3IM$$

An adjusted value *AKLOC*, given by

$$AKLOC = A \times KLOC / 100$$

is next used in the COCOMO formulas, instead of the unadjusted value *KLOC*. In this way a lower cost estimate is obtained if part of the system is reused.

By treating reuse this way it is assumed that developing reusable components does not require any extra effort. You may simply reap the benefits when part of a system can be reused from an earlier effort. This assumption does not seem to be very realistic. Reuse does not come for free (see also chapter 16).

In [Balda90], a variation of COCOMO is proposed which does take into account the fact that developing reusable parts requires additional effort. Its base formula is

$$E = \alpha KLOC_1^{\beta} + \alpha \gamma KLOC_2^{\beta}$$

α and β are constants, equal to those used in COCOMO. $KLOC_1$ is the amount of code uniquely developed in this project. $KLOC_2$ is the amount of code developed within this project, and intended for future reuse. γ is a 'penalty' factor reflecting the extra effort to develop reusable code. Balda assumes that γ takes on values between (approximately) 1.8 and 3.5. The actual value is organization-specific, and is affected by the reuse techniques used, the reuse attitude, and the like.

Our second variation concerns an FPA-type size measure. Function points as used in FPA are intended to be a user-oriented measure of system function. The user functions measured are the inputs, outputs, inquiries, etc. We may conjecture that these user-functions are technology-dependent, and that FPA primarily reflects the batch-oriented world of the 1970s.

Present-day administrative systems are perhaps better characterized by their number of menus or screens. This line of thought is pursued in a case study described in [Verner89]. Verner distinguishes four component types: relations (files in the relational context), menus, screens and reports. For each of these, a regression equation is derived for the estimated length (in either *LOC* or *FP*, whose ratio is assumed to be constant). For example, the length of a menu component is estimated at

$$LOC = 25.25 + 3.35 \times \text{number of choices}$$

For a given system, estimates for all system components can thus be made, and an FPA-like adjustment factor is next applied to the sum of these estimates.

We may conceive of many more variations, and indeed several such variations are reported upon in the literature. They reflect our growing understanding of factors that determine software cost and effort.

7.4 DISTRIBUTION OF MANPOWER OVER TIME

Having obtained an estimate of the total number of man-months needed for a given project, we are still left with the question as to how many calendar months it will take. For a project estimated at 20 man-months, the kind of schedules you might think of, include:

— 20 people work on the project for 1 month;

— 4 people work on the project for 5 months;

— 1 person works on the project for 20 months.

These are not actually realistic schedules. We noticed earlier that the manpower needed is not evenly distributed over the time period of the project. From the shape of the Rayleigh curve we find that we need a slowly increasing manpower during the development stages of the project. Cost estimation models generally provide us with an estimate of the development time (schedule) T as well. Contrary to the effort equations, the various models show a remarkable consistency if it comes to estimating the development time, as is shown in figure 7.13.

Walston–Felix	$T = 2.5 \, E^{0.35}$
COCOMO (organic)	$T = 2.5 \, E^{0.38}$
Putnam	$T = 2.4 \, E^{1/3}$

Figure 7.13:   Relation between development time and effort

The values T thus computed represent nominal development times. It is worthwhile to study possibilities to shorten these nominal schedules. Obviously, shortening the development time induces an increase in the number of people involved in the project.

In terms of the Rayleigh curve model, shortening the development time amounts to an increase of the value a, the speed-up factor which determines the initial slope of the curve. The peak of the Rayleigh curve then shifts to the left and at the same time it shifts up. We thus get a faster increase of manpower required at the start of the project and a higher maximum workforce.

Such a shift does not go unpunished. Different studies showed that individual productivity decreases as team size grows. According to [Brooks75], there are two major causes for this phenomenon:

1. If the team gets larger, this induces an increased communication overhead, since more time will be needed for consultation with other team members, tuning of tasks, and the like.

2. If manpower is added to a team during the execution of a project, the total team productivity decreases at first. New team members are not productive right from the start. At the same time, they do require time from the other team members during their learning process. Taken together, this causes a decrease in total productivity.

Combination of these two observations leads to the phenomenon that has become known as Brooks' Law: Adding manpower to a late project only makes it later.

By analyzing a large base of project data, Conte et al. [Conte86] found the following relation between average productivity L (measured in lines of code per man-month) and average team size P:

$$L = 777\ P^{-0.5}$$

Put in other words: individual productivity decreases exponentially with team size.

A theoretical underpinning hereof can be given on account of Brooks' observation regarding the number of communication links between the people involved in a project. This number is determined by the size and structure of the team. If, in a team of size P, each member has to coordinate his activities with those of all other members, the number of communication links will be $P\ (P - 1)/2$. If each member needs to communicate with one other member only, this number will be $P - 1$. Less communication than that seems unreasonable, since we then essentially get confronted with independent teams. (Phrased in other words: If we draw team members as nodes of a graph, and communication links as edges, we expect the graph to be connected.)

The number of communication links thus varies from roughly P to roughly $P^2/2$. In a true hierarchical organization, this leads to P^α communication paths, with $1 < \alpha < 2$.

For an individual team member, the number of communication links varies from 1 to $P - 1$. If the maximum individual productivity is L and each communication link results in a productivity loss l, the average productivity will be

$$L_\gamma = L - l(P - 1)^\gamma$$

where γ, with $0 < \gamma \leq 1$, is a measure for the number of communication links [Conte86]. (We assume that there is at least one person who communicates with more than one other person, so $\gamma > 0$.) For a team of size P, this leads to a total productivity

$$L_{tot} = P \times L_\gamma = P(L - l(P - 1)^\gamma)$$

For a given set of values for L, l and γ, this is a function which, for increasing values of P, goes from 0 to some maximum and then decreases again. There thus is a certain optimum team size P_{opt} that leads to a maximum team productivity. The team productivity for different values of the team size P is given in figure 7.14. Here, we assume that individual productivity is 500 LOC/man-month ($L = 500$), and the productivity loss is 10% per communication link ($l = 50$). With full interaction between team members ($\gamma = 1$) this results in an optimum team size of 5.5 persons.

Teamsize	Individual productivity	Total productivity
1	500	500
2	450	900
3	400	1200
4	350	1400
5	300	1500
5.5	275	1512
6	250	1500
7	200	1400
8	150	1200

Figure 7.14:   Impact of team size on productivity

Everything takes its time. We cannot shorten a software development project indefinitely by exchanging time against people. Boehm sets the limit at 75% of the nominal development time, on empirical grounds. A system that has to be delivered too fast, gets into the 'impossible region'. The chances for success become almost nil if the schedule is pressed too far. See also figure 7.15.

In any case, a shorter development time will induce higher costs. We may use the following rule of thumb: compressing the development time by X% results in a cost increase of X% relative to the nominal cost estimate [Boehm84d].

7.5 SUMMARY AND FURTHER READING

The discussion about which cost estimation model is best has not finished yet. The various models discussed yield widely different results. [Rubin85], for instance, gives estimates for one and the same (hypothetical) project, using different cost estimation models. Some of his results are given in figure 7.16 (ESTIMACS is a model based on function points, see [Rubin83]). The results given in figure 7.16 are symptomatic of many studies in this area; see, for instance, also [Thibodeau81], [Kemerer87]. Major reasons for these discrepancies have been hinted at in this chapter. Both differences in definitions of the

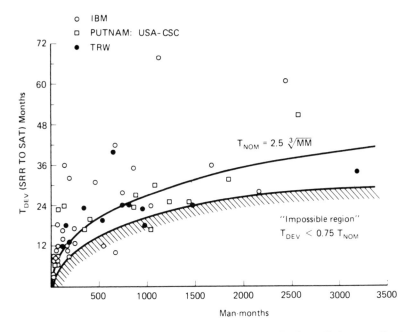

Figure 7.15: The impossible region (*Source: B.W. Boehm,* Software Engineering Economics, *fig. 27-8/page 471,* © *1981, Reprinted by permission of Prentice-Hall, Inc., Englewoods Cliffs, NJ*)

	Putnam	COCOMO	ESTIMACS
Effort	200 man-months	363 man-months	17 100 hours
Schedule	17 months	23 months	16 months
Peak teamsize	17	22	15

Figure 7.16:   Different estimates for one project

entities involved, and differences in environmental characteristics add to the phenomenon observed.

One of the main problems of this field is the lack of data. By now, this is realized by many organizations. In the STARS project (a large research project initiated by the US Department of Defense) the development of usable metrics and the associated need for collecting data has been marked one of the key themes [Van Vliet85]. The process of how to make an existing organization aware of the importance of data collection and the development of metrics is further discussed in [Grady87a].

In remains to be seen whether we will ever get at one, general, cost estimation model. The number of parameters that impact productivity simply seems to be too large. Yet, each organization may develop a model which is well suited for projects to be undertaken within that organization. An organization may, and should, by itself build a data base with data on its own projects. Starting with a model like COCOMO, the different parameters, i.e. applicable cost drivers and values for the associated effort multipliers, may then be determined. In the course of time, the model will get tuned better to the organizational environment, resulting in better and better estimates. [Bailey81] gives a procedure for doing so.

Though we strongly advocate the use of algorithmic cost estimation models, a word of caution should be made. Present-day models of this kind are not all that good yet. At best, they yield estimates which are at most 25% off, 75% of the time, *for projects used to derive the model.*

Even when a much better performance is realized, some problems remain when using the type of cost estimation model obtained in this way:

(a) Even though a model like COCOMO looks objective, quite some subjectivity is being introduced through the need to assign values to the various levels of a number of cost drivers. Based on an analysis of historical project data, [Jones86] lists 20 factors which certainly influence productivity, and another 25 for which such is probable. COCOMO's 15 cost drivers already allow for a variation of 1:800. A much smaller number of relevant cost drivers would reduce a model's vulnerability to the subjective assessment of project characteristics.

(b) The models are based on data from *old* projects and reflect the technology of those projects. In some cases, the project data are even fairly old. The impact of more recent developments, such as prototyping, the use of fourth-generation languages, and object-oriented programming, as well as changes in the kind of applications, such as a shift from batch-oriented systems to highly interactive, direct-manipulation type systems, cannot be taken into account, since we do not have sufficient data on projects which used those techniques.

(c) Almost all models take into account attributes that impact the initial development of software. Attributes which specifically relate to maintenance activities are seldom taken into account (an exception is [Boehm83b]). Also, factors like the amount of documentation required, the number of business trips (in case development is not localized at one spot) are often lacking. Yet, these factors may have a significant impact on the effort needed [Jones86].

A problem of a rather different nature is the following: In the introduction to this chapter we compared software cost estimation with cost estimation for laying out a garden. When laying out a garden, we often follow a rather different line of thought, namely: given a budget of, say, $10 000, what possibilities are there? What happens if we trade off a pond against something else?

Something similar is also possible with software. Given a budget of $100 000 for library automation, what possibilities are there? Which user interface can we expect, what will the transaction speed be, how reliable will the system be? To be able to answer this type of question, we need to be able to analyze the sensitivity of an estimate to varying values of relevant attributes. Given the still pending uncertainty about which attributes are relevant to start with, this trade-off problem is still largely unsolved.

While executing a task, people have to make a number of decisions. These decisions are strongly influenced by requirements set or proposed. The cost estimate is one such requirement which will have an impact on the end result. We may imagine a hypothetical case in which model A estimates the cost at 300 man-months. Now suppose the project actually takes 400 man-months. If model B would have estimated the project at 450 man-months, is model B better than model A? It is quite possible that, starting from the estimate given by model B, the eventual cost would have been 600 man-months. The project's behavior is also influenced by the cost estimate. Choices being made during the execution of a project are influenced by cost estimates derived earlier on [Abdel-Hamid86].

Finally, estimating the cost of a software development project is a highly dynamic activity. Not only may we switch from one model to another during the course of a project, estimates will also be adjusted on the basis of experiences gained. Switching to another model during the execution of a project is possible, since we may expect to get more reliable data while the project is making progress. We may, for instance, imagine the use of a cascade of cost estimation models, such as ESTIMACS–DeMarco–COCOMO.

We cannot, and should not, rely on a one-shot statistical cost estimate. Controlling a software development project implies a regular check of progress, a regular check of estimates made, re-establishing priorities and weighing stakes, as the project is going on [Gilb86].

EXERCISES

1. Discuss the major differences between COCOMO and FPA.

2. How may early cost estimates influence the way in which a project gets executed?

3. Suppose you are managing a project which is getting behind schedule. Possible actions include: renegotiating the time schedule, adding people to the project, and renegotiating quality requirements. In which ways can these actions shorten the time schedule? Can you think of other ways to finish the project on time?

4. Suppose you have a LOC-based cost estimation model available whose parameters are based on projects from your own organization that used COBOL as the implementation language. Can you use this model to estimate the cost of a project whose implementation language is Pascal? What if the model is based on projects that used C?

5. Can you give an intuitive rationale for the values of the COCOMO cost drivers (figure 7.8) that relate to project attributes?

6. Suppose you are involved in a project which is estimated to take 100 man-months. How would you estimate the nominal calendar time required for this project? Suppose the project is to be finished within six calendar months. Do you think such a schedule compression is feasible?

7. Why should software cost models be recalibrated from time to time?

8. How would you calibrate the COCOMO model as published in [Boehm81] to fit software development in your organization?

8

Project Planning and Control

Software development projects differ widely in nature. These differences are reflected in the different ways in which the projects are organized and managed. For some projects, the budget is fixed and the goal of the project is to maximize the quality of the end product. For others, quality constraints are fixed in advance, and the goal is to produce effectively a system that meets those quality constraints. If the developing organization has considerable experience with the application domain and the requirements are fixed and stable, a tightly structured approach may yield a satisfactory solution. In applications with fuzzy requirements and little previous experience of the development team, a much more exploratory approach may be desirable.

It is important to identify those project characteristics early on, because they will influence the way a project is organized, planned and controlled. In section 8.1, we will discuss project control from a systems point of view. This allows us to identify major dimensions along which software development projects differ. These dimensions lead to a taxonomy of software development projects, which will be discussed in section 8.2. For each of the project categories distinguished, we will indicate how best to control the various entities identified in previous chapters. This type of assessment is to be done at the project planning stage.

Software development projects consist of a number of interrelated tasks. Some of these will have to be handled sequentially (a module cannot be tested until it has been implemented), while others may be handled in parallel (different modules can be implemented concurrently). The dependencies between tasks can be depicted in a network from which a project schedule can be derived.

These and similar tools for the micro-level planning and control of software development projects are discussed in section 8.3.

In section 8.4 we turn our attention to a rather different topic, viz. aspects of the software development process that impact controllability. In many a software development organization, management can exert little control over the development organization. Humphrey identifies five process maturity levels, together with the necessary actions to get from one level to the next [Humphrey88, 89a]. These process maturity levels and their characteristics are the topic of section 8.4.

8.1 A SYSTEMS' VIEW OF PROJECT CONTROL

In the preceding chapters, we discussed several entities that need to be controlled. During the execution of a software development project, each of these entities needs to be monitored and assessed. From time to time, adjustments will have to be made. To be able to do so, we must know which entities can be varied, how they can be varied, and what the effect of adjustments is.

To this end, we will consider project control from a systems' point of view. The system we have in mind is slightly different from the one depicted in figure 2.1, though. We now consider the software development project itself as a system. Project control may then be described in terms of:

— the system to be controlled, i.e. the software development project;

— the entity that controls the system, i.e. the project manager, his organization and the decision rules he uses;

— information which is used to guide the decision process. This information may come from two different sources. It may either come from the system being controlled (such as a notice of technical problems with a certain component), or it may have a source outside the system (such as a request to shorten development time).

The variables that play a role in controlling a system may be categorized into three classes: irregular variables, goal variables, and control variables.

Irregular variables are those variables that are input to the system being controlled. Irregular variables cannot be varied by the entity that controls the system. Their value is determined by the system's environment. Examples of possible irregular variables are: computer experience of the user, or the project staffing level.

An important precondition for effective control is knowledge of the project's goals. In developing software, various conflicting goals can be distinguished. One possible goal is to *minimize development time*. Since time is often pressing, this goal is not unusual. Another goal might be to *maximize efficiency*, i.e. development should be done as cheaply as possible. Optimal use of resources (mostly manpower) is then needed. Yet a third possible goal is to *maximize quality*. Each of these goals is possible, but they can be achieved only if it is known which goals are being pursued. These goals collectively make up the set of goal variables.

Finally, the decision process is guided by the set of control variables. Control variables are entities which can be manipulated by the project manager in order to achieve the goals set forth. Examples of possible control variables are: tools to be used, project organization, efficiency of the resulting software.

It is not possible to make a rigid separation between the various sets of variables. It depends on the situation at hand whether a particular variable should be taken as an irregular variable, goal variable, or control variable. If the requirements are stable and fixed, one may for instance try to control the project by employing adequate personnel and using a proper set of tools. For another project, manpower might be fixed and one may wish to control a project by extending the delivery date, relaxing quality constraints, etc.

However, in order to be able to control a project, the different sets of variables must be known. It must be known where control is, and is not, possible. This is only one prerequisite, though. In systems theory, the following conditions for effective control of a system are used:

— the controlling entity must know the goals of the system;

— the controlling entity must have sufficient control variety;

— the controlling entity must have information on the state, input and output of the system;

— the controlling entity must have a conceptual control model. It must know how and to what extent the different variables depend on and influence each other.

When all these conditions are met, control can be rational, in which case there is no uncertainty, since the controlling entity is completely informed about every relevant aspect. The control problem can then be structured and formalized. Daily practice of software development is different, though. There is insufficient room for control, or the effect of control actions is not known. Control then becomes much more intuitive or primitive. It gets based on intuition, experience, and rules of thumb. The process maturity framework to be discussed in section 8.4 offers further opportunities to improve the controllability of software development projects.

The degree to which a software development project can be controlled increases as the control variety increases. This control variety is determined by the number of control variables and the degree to which they can be varied. As noticed before, the control variety is project dependent.

Controlling software development means that we must be able to measure both the project and the product. Measuring a project means that we must be able to assess progress. Measuring a product means that we must be able to determine the degree to which quality and functional requirements are being met.

Controlling software development projects implies that effective control actions are possible. Corrective actions may be required if progress is not sufficient, or the software does not comply with its requirements. Effective control means that we know what the effect of control actions is. If progress is insufficient and we decide to allocate extra manpower, we must know what the impact of this extra manpower is on the time schedule. If the quality of a certain component is less than required and we decide to allocate extra test time, we must know how much test time is required in order to achieve the desired quality.

In practice, controlling a software development project is not a rational process. The ideal systems theory situation is not met. There are a number of uncertainties which make managing such projects a challenging activity. Below, we will discuss a few ideal situations, based on the uncertainty of various relevant aspects.

8.2 A TAXONOMY OF SOFTWARE DEVELOPMENT PROJECTS

In the preceding section, we identified several conditions that need to be satisfied in order to be able to control projects rationally. Since these conditions are often not met, we will have to rely on a different control mechanism in most cases. The control mechanism best suited in any given situation obviously depends on relevant characteristics of the project at hand.

Based on an analysis of important characteristics of software development projects, important from the point of view of project control, we will distinguish several project situations, and indicate how projects can successfully be controlled in these situations. This discussion is based on [Heemstra89].

We will group project characteristics into three classes: product characteristics, process characteristics, and resource characteristics. From the point of view of project control, we are interested in the degree of *certainty* of those characteristics. For example, if we have clear and stable user requirements, product certainty is high. If part of the problem is to identify user requirements and/or these user requirements frequently change during the development project, product certainty is low.

In the first case, control can be quite rational, insofar as it depends on product characteristics. Since we know what the product is supposed to accomplish, we may check compliance with the requirements and execute corrective actions if needed. If product certainty is low, such is not feasible. We either do not know what we are aiming at, or the target is constantly moving. It is only reasonable to expect that control will be different in those cases.

For the present discussion, we are interested only in project characteristics that may differ between projects. Characteristics common to most or all of software development projects, such as the fact that it involves teamwork, will not lead to different control paradigms.

We will furthermore combine the characteristics from each of the three categories identified above, into one metric, the certainty of the corresponding category. This leaves us with three dimensions along which software development projects may differ:

Product certainty Product certainty is largely determined by two factors: the question whether or not user requirements are clearly specified, as regards both functionality and quality, and the volatility of those user requirements. Other product characteristics are felt to have a lesser impact on our understanding of what the end-product should accomplish.

Process certainty The degree of (development) process certainty is determined by such factors as: the possibilities to redirect the development process, the degree to which the process can be measured and the knowledge we have about the effect of control actions, the degree to which new, unknown tools are being used.

Resource certainty The major determinant here is the availability of the right, qualified personnel.

If we allow each of these certainty factors to take on two values (high and low, respectively), we get eight different control situations, although some of these are not very realistic. If we have little or no certainty about the software to be developed, we can hardly expect to be certain about the process to be followed and the resources needed to accomplish our goals. Similarly, if we do not know how to carry out the development process, we also do not know which resources are needed.

This leaves us with four archetypal situations, as depicted in figure 8.1. Below, we will discuss each of these control situations in turn. In doing so, we will pay attention to the following aspects of those control situations:

— the kind of control problem;

— the primary goals to be set in controlling the project;

— the coordination mechanism to be used;

— the development strategy, or process model, to be applied;

— the way and degree to which cost can be estimated.

1. **Realization problem** If the requirements are known and stable, it is known how the software is to be developed, there is sufficient control variety, the effect of control actions is known, and sufficient resources are available, we find ourselves in a rather ideal situation, a situation not often encountered in our field. The main emphasis will be on realization: how can we, given the requirements, achieve our goal in the most effective way. As for the development strategy, we may use some linear process model. Feedback to earlier phases, as in the waterfall model, is needed only for verification and validation activities.

	1	2	3	4
Product certainty	high	high	high	low
Process certainty	high	high	low	low
Resource certainty	high	low	low	low

Figure 8.1:   Four archetypal control situations

To coordinate activities in a project of this type, we may use direct supervision. Work output can be standardized, since the end result is known. Similarly, the work processes and worker skills can be fixed in advance. There will thus be little room for control variety as far as these variables are concerned.

Management can be done effectively through a separation style. The work to be done is fixed through rules and procedures. Management will allocate tasks and check the proper execution thereof.

As for cost estimation, we may successfully use one of the more formalized cost models, provided that the model has been calibrated for the current environment. A cost estimation thus obtained can be used to guard the project's progress. Cost estimation thus yields a target to be achieved.

2. **Allocation problem** This situation differs from the previous one in that there is uncertainty as regards the resources. The major problem then becomes one of the availability of personnel. Controlling a project of this kind tends to become one of controlling capacity. Questions such as: how do we get the project staffed, how do we achieve the desired end-product with limited means, become the crucial ones.

According to Mintzberg, one has to try to standardize the process as far as possible in this case. Such enlarges the interchangeability of personnel. Guidelines and procedures may be used to describe how the various tasks have to be carried out.

As regards the development strategy, we may again opt for the waterfall model. We may either contract out the work to be done, or try to acquire the right type and amount of qualified personnel.

As for cost estimation, we may again use some cost estimation model. Since there is uncertainty as regards resources, there is a need for sensitivity analyses in order to gain insight into such questions as: what will happen to the total cost/development time if we allocate three designers of level A rather than four designers of level B?

3. **Design problem** If the requirements are fixed and stable, but we do not know how to carry out the process, nor which resources to employ, the problem is one of design. Note that the adjective *design* refers to the design of the project, not the design of the software. We have to answer such questions as: which milestones are to be identified, which documents must be delivered and when, what personnel must be allocated, how will responsibilities be assigned?

In this situation, we have insufficient knowledge of the effect of allocating extra personnel, other tools, different methods and techniques. The main problem then becomes one of controlling the development process.

In Mintzberg's classification, this can best be pursued through standardization of work outputs. Since the output is fixed, control should be done through the process and the resources. The effect of such control actions is not sufficiently known, however.

In order to make a project of this kind manageable, one needs overcapacity. As far as the process is concerned, this necessitates margins in development time and budget. Keeping extra personnel is not feasible, in general.

In these situations, we will need frequently to measure progress towards the project's goals in order to allow for timely adjustments. Therefore, we may want to go from a linear development model to an incremental one. This preference will increase as the uncertainty increases.

Cost estimation will have to rely on data from past projects. We will usually not have enough data to use one of the more formalized cost estimation models. In this situation too, we will need sensitivity analyses. This need will be more pressing than in the previous situation, since the uncertainty is greater. The project manager will be interested in the sensitivity of cost estimates to certain cost drivers. He might be interested in such questions as: what will happen to the development schedule if two extra analysts are assigned to this project, or: what will the effect be on the total cost if we shorten the development time by x days? By viewing cost estimation in this way, the manager will gain insight in, and increase his feeling for, possible solution strategies.

4. **Exploration problem** If the product certainty, process certainty and resource certainty are all low, we get the most difficult control situation.

   Because of these uncertainties, the work will be explorative in nature. This situation does not fit a coordination mechanism based on standardization. In a situation as complex and uncertain as this one, coordination can best be achieved through mutual adjustment. The structure is one of adhocracy. Experts from various disciplines work together to achieve some as yet unspecified goal.

   A critical success factor in these cases is the commitment of all people involved. Work cannot be split up into neat tasks. Flexibility in work patterns and work contents is important. Adherence to a strict budget cannot be enforced upon the team from above. The team members must commit themselves to the project. Management has to place emphasis on their relations with the team members.

   Controlling a project of this kind is a difficult and challenging activity. To make a project of this kind manageable, our goal will be to maximize output, given the resources available to the project. This maximization may concern the quality of the product, or its functionality, or both.

Since requirements are not precisely known, some form of prototyping is appropriate as a process model. The larger the uncertainty, the more often we will have to check whether we are still on the right track. Thus, some development strategy involving many small steps is to be used. Cost estimation using some formalized model clearly is not feasible in these circumstances. The use of such models presupposes that we know enough of the project at hand to be able to compare it with previous projects. Such is not the case, though.

We may rely on expert judgments to achieve a rough cost estimate. Such a cost estimate, however, cannot and should not be used as a fixed anchor point as to when the project should be finished and how much it may cost. There simply are too many uncertainties involved. Rather, it provides us with some guidance as to the magnitude of the project. Based on this estimate, effort and time can be allocated for the project, for instance to produce a certain number of prototypes, a feasibility study, or a pilot implementation of part of the product. The hope is that in due time the uncertainties will diminish sufficiently, so that the project shifts to one of the other situations.

The four control situations discussed above are once more depicted in figure 8.2, together with a short characterization of the various control aspects discussed above.

By taking these aspects into account during the planning stage of a software development project, we are able to tailor the project's management to the situation at hand. In doing so, we will recognize that software development projects are not all alike. Neglecting those project-specific characteristics is likely to result in project failures, failures that have often been reported upon in the literature, but equally often remain unnoticed to the public at large.

8.3 TECHNIQUES FOR PROJECT PLANNING AND CONTROL

A project consists of a series of activities. We may graphically depict the project and its constituent activities by a **work breakdown structure** (wbs). The work breakdown structure reflects the decomposition of a project into subtasks down to a level needed for effective planning and control. Figure 8.3 contains a very simple example of a work breakdown structure for a software development project. The activities depicted at the leaves of the work breakdown structure correspond to unit tasks, while the higher-level nodes constitute composite tasks. We will assume that each activity has a well-defined beginning and end. This start or end of each activity is indicated by a milestone, a scheduled event for which some person is held accountable and that is used to measure and control progress. The end of an activity often is some deliverable, such as a design document, while the start of an activity is often triggered at the end of some other activity.

Activities usually consume resources, such as people or computer time, and always have a certain duration. Activities can not be executed in any order.

	1	2	3	4
Product certainty	high	high	high	low
Process certainty	high	high	low	low
Resource certainty	high	low	low	low
Problem type	Realization	Allocation	Design	Exploration
Primary goal in control	Optimize resource usage Efficiency and schedule	Acquisition, training of personnel	Control of the process	Maximize result Lower risks
Coordination, Management style	Standardization of product, process, and resources Hierarchy, separation style	Standardization of product and process	Standardization of process	Mutual adjustment Commitment Relation style
Development strategy	Waterfall	Waterfall	Incremental	Incremental Prototyping
Cost estimation	Models Guard progress	Models Sensitivity analysis	Database with project data Sensitivity analysis	Expert estimate Risk analysis Provide guidance

Figure 8.2: Four control situations (*Source: F.J. Heemstra*, How much does software cost, © *Kluwer Bedrijfswetenschappen, 1989.*)

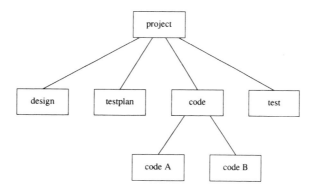

Figure 8.3: Simple work breakdown structure for a software development project

For example, we can not test a module before it is coded. This type of relation between tasks can be expressed as constraints. Usually, the constraints concern temporal relations between activities. Such constraints are also called precedence relations. Project planning involves the scheduling of all activities such that the constraints are satisfied and resource limits are not exceeded. Several techniques are available to support this scheduling task.

The activities from the simple wbs of a software development project, together with their duration and temporal constraints, are given in figure 8.4. Note that figure 8.4 contains more information on temporal relations than is given in the wbs. Though the left-to-right reading of the wbs suggests a certain time ordering, it does not give the precise precedence relations between activities.

Activity	Duration	Constraints
Design	10	—
Test plan	5	Design finished
Code A	10	Design finished
Code B	5	Design finished
Test	10	Code finished, Test plan finished

Figure 8.4: Activities, their duration and temporal constraints

The set of activities and their constraints can also be depicted in a network. For our example, this network is given in figure 8.5. The nodes in the network denote activities. This type of network is therefore known as an 'activity-on-node' network. Each node also carries a weight, the duration of the corresponding activity. An arrow from node A to node B indicates that activity A has to be finished before activity B can start.

These network diagrams are often termed **PERT charts**. PERT is an acronym for Program Evaluation and Review Technique. PERT charts were developed and first used successfully in the management of the Polaris missile program in the 1950s. While the original PERT technique was concerned solely with the time span of activities and their interrelations, subsequent developments have led to a variety of techniques that accommodate an increasing number of project factors.

From the PERT chart we can compute the earliest possible point in time at which the project can be completed. Let us assume that the network has a unique start node B and end node E. If there is more than one node with in-degree 0 (i.e. having no predecessors in the network), a new start node B is created with outgoing edges to all nodes having in-degree 0. This new node B gets a zero weight (duration). A similar procedure is followed to create the end node E if there is more than one node having out-degree 0.

We next label each node i in the network with an ordered pair of numbers (S_i, F_i). S_i and F_i denote the earliest possible time at which activity i can start and finish, respectively. The algorithm for doing so involves a breadth-first search of

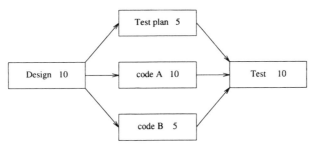

Figure 8.5:   Example of a PERT chart

the network (cf. [Boehm81]):

1. The start node B is labelled $(0, D_B)$, where D_B is the duration of activity B;

2. For all unlabelled nodes whose predecessors are all labelled nodes, the earliest possible starting time is the latest finishing time of all the predecessor nodes:

$$S_N = \max_{i \in P(n)} F_i$$

   where $P(N)$ is the set of predecessor nodes of N.
   The corresponding finishing time is $F_N = S_N + D_N$, where D_N is the duration of activity N.
   Node N is labelled as (S_N, F_N).

3. Repeat Step 2 until all nodes have been labelled.

   The earliest possible finishing time of the whole project now equals F_E, E being the end node of the network.
   We may subsequently compute the latest point in time at which activity L should finish: for each node N,

$$L_N = \min_{i \in Q(N)} S_i$$

where $Q(N)$ is the set of successor nodes of N.
   The results hereof can be graphically presented in a **Gantt chart** (these charts are named after their inventor). In a Gantt chart, the time span of each activity is depicted by the length of a segment drawn on an adjacent calendar. The Gantt chart of our software development example is given in figure 8.6. The grey areas show slack (or float) times of activities. It indicates that the corresponding activity may consume more than its estimated time, or start later than the earliest possible starting time, without affecting the total duration of the project. For each activity N, the corresponding segment in the Gantt chart starts at time S_N and ends at L_N.

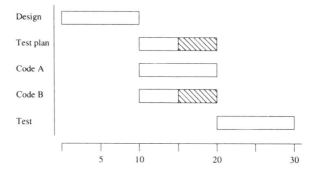

Figure 8.6:   Example of a Gantt chart

Activities without slack time are on a **critical path**. If activities on a critical path are delayed, the total project gets delayed as well. Note that there always is at least one sequence of activities that constitutes a critical path.

In an 'activity-on-node' network, the activities are depicted as nodes, while the arrows denote precedence relations between activities. Alternatively, we may depict a set of interrelated activities in an 'activity-on-arrow' network. In an activity-on-arrow network, the arrows denote activities, while the nodes represent the completion of milestone events. Figure 8.7 depicts the earlier example network as an activity-on-arrow network. The latter representation is intuitively appealing, especially if the length of an arrow reflects the duration of the corresponding activity. Note that this type of network may have to contain dummy activities which are not needed in the activity-on-node network. These dummy activities represent synchronization of interrelated activities. In our example, dummy activities (arrows) are needed to make sure that the activity *test* is not started until the activities *test plan*, *code A* and *code B* have all been completed.

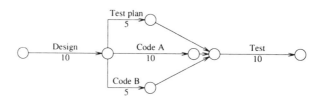

Figure 8.7:   An activity-on-arrow network

The PERT technique has evolved considerably since its inception 35 years ago. For example, next to constraints expressing that an activity B may start only after an activity A has ended, we may also specify that activity B may only start after activity A has started. We may also extend the technique such that it actually handles resource constraints. For instance, if we have only one programmer available, the Gantt chart of figure 8.6 would not work, since it assumes that coding of modules A and B is done in parallel. The PERT technique may even be extended further to allow for sensitivity analysis. By allowing so-called 'what-if' questions ('what if we allocate three designers rather than four', 'what if coding module A takes two months rather than one') we get a feeling for the sensitivity of a schedule to certain variations in resource levels, schedule overruns, and the like.

CPM—Critical Path Method—is, as the name already suggests, a technique very similar to PERT and developed at around the same time.

In our discussion, we presented Gantt charts as a graphical visualization of a schedule that results from network analysis. Actually, we may use Gantt charts as a scheduling mechanism of its own. We may simply list all activities and indicate their earliest starting time and latest ending time on the calendar. Gantt charts by themselves, however, do not carry information on dependencies between activities. This makes it hard to adjust schedules, for instance when a certain activity has slipped. As far as planning goes, we therefore prefer the use of Gantt charts as a means to visualize the result of network analysis.

Using the information contained in the Gantt chart and knowledge of personnel resources required for each activity, we may establish a personnel plan indicating how many people are required in each unit of time. Since people costs are a major part of project expenditures, this personnel plan provides a direct means to plan project expenditures.

When the project is under way, its control is based on monitoring the project's progress and expenditures. Time spent per activity per project member can be recorded on time cards. These time cards are the basis for determining cumulative effort and expenditure. These cumulative data can be compared with the planned levels of effort and expenditure. In order to properly judge whether the project is still on track, management needs progress information as well. The most common way to do so is via milestone reports: activities cannot be considered completed until a proper report has been produced and accepted.

The Gantt chart provides a very direct means to compare actual project status with the project schedule. Schedule slippage shows itself immediately. Slippage of activities on a critical path then necessitates prompt management action: renegotiation of the schedule, the project's deliverables, or both. Note that schedule slippage is a sneaky affair; projects get behind one day at a time. Note also that project schedules should at any point in time reflect the true project. An accepted change necessitates reconsideration of the schedule.

8.4 PROCESS MATURITY LEVELS

Consider the following course of events in a hypothetical software development project. Some organization is to develop a distributed library automation system. A centralized computer hosts both the software and the data base. A number of local libraries are connected to the central machine through telephone lines. The organization has some experience with library automation, albeit only with stand-alone systems.

In the course of the project, a number of problems manifest themselves. At first they seem to be disconnected and they do not alarm management yet. It turns out that the requirements analysis has not been all that thorough. Local requirements turn out to differ on some minor points. Though the first such deviations can be handled quite easily, keeping track of all change requests becomes a real problem after a while. When part of the system has been realized, the team starts to test the connections with the host machine. The telephone lines turn out not to be reliable enough, and special provisions are needed to prevent loss of data. Early back-of-the-envelope calculations as regards the speed of algorithms have been inadequate and some major algorithms will have to be redesigned.

The project gets into a crisis eventually. Management has no proper means to handle the situation. It tries to cut back on both functionality and quality in a somewhat haphazard way. In the end, some rather unsatisfactory system is delivered two months late. During the subsequent maintenance phase, a number of problems are solved, but the system never becomes a real success.

Though the above description is hypothetical, it is not all that unrealistic. Many an organization has insufficient control over its software development process. If a project gets into trouble, such is usually discovered quite late and the organization has no other means but to react in a somewhat chaotic way. More often than not, speed is confused with progress.

An important step in trying to address these problems is to realize that the software development process can indeed be controlled, measured, and improved. In order to gauge the process of improving the software development process, Humphrey developed a software maturity framework [Humphrey88, 89a]. He characterizes the process into one of five *maturity levels*, and gives improvement steps to get from one level to the next:

Initial At the initial process level, the organization operates without formalized procedures, project plans, or cost estimates. Tools are not adequately integrated. Many problems are overseen or forgotten, and maintenance poses real problems. Software development at this level can be characterized as being ad hoc. Performance can be improved by instituting basic project controls:

— a project management system to ensure control of commitments (through project plans and reviews);

— a quality assurance group to make sure that work gets done the way it is supposed to be done;

— a configuration management system to control change requests.

Repeatable The main difference between the initial process level and the repeatable process level is that the repeatable level provides control over the way plans and commitments are established. Through prior experience in doing similar work, the organization has achieved certain statistical control over costs, schedules, and change requests. The introduction of new tools, the development of a new type of product, and major organizational changes, however, represent major risks at this level. The main actions needed to advance to the next level are:

— the establishment of a software engineering process group, a small group of people whose sole task is to improve the software process;

— the establishment of a software development process architecture, a framework within which specific development processes are defined;

— the introduction of a family of software engineering methods and techniques, such as standards to be used, design and test methods, design and code inspection techniques.

Defined At the defined process level, the organization has achieved a foundation for continuous improvement and may start to examine the process and decide how to improve it. Major steps to advance to the next level are:

— the establishment of a set of process measurements, and a data base to manage and maintain the process data gathered;

— the establishment of a software quality plan, in which aggressive quality goals are set. Meeting those quality goals is assessed through quantitative measurements.

Managed At the managed process level, quantitative data is gathered and analysed on a routine basis. There is a large number of valuable measures, and collecting and maintaining all those data may become problematic. Attention is therefore focused on:

— supporting the automatic gathering of data;

— using those data to analyze and modify the development process in order to prevent problems.

Optimizing. At the final, optimizing, level, a stable base has been reached from which further improvements can be made. The step to the optimizing process level is a paradigm shift. Whereas attention at the other levels is focused on means to improve the product, emphasis at the optimizing level has shifted from the product to the process. The data gathered can now be used to improve the software development process itself.

Humphrey also investigated the state of software engineering practice with respect to the above framework [Humphrey89b]. Though this study concerned the DoD software community, there is little reason to expect that the situation will be much rosier in another environment. According to his findings, current software engineering practice is largely at the initial level. There were a few organizations operating at the repeatable level, and a few projects operating at the defined level. No organization or project operated at the managed or optimizing level.

Quite a few of the actions identified by Humphrey, especially those required to advance from the initial to the repeatable level, are extensively discussed elsewhere in this text.

8.5 SUMMARY AND FURTHER READING

In this chapter we looked at project control from a systems point of view, and gained insight into how different kinds of projects can be managed and controlled. We identified four archetypal situations, which demand different process models, coordination mechanisms and management styles.

In section 8.3, we focused on the planning and control of activities within a project. By depicting the set of activities and their temporal relations in a graph, techniques like PERT offer simple yet powerful means to schedule and control these activities (see for example [Boehm81]). More powerful models for doing so involve the use of AND/OR graphs or Petrinets [Liu89].

We finally sketched the software maturity framework as developed by Humphrey. This framework offers a means to assess the state of software engineering practice, as well as a number of steps to improve the software development process. Both the framework and the improvement steps are extensively discussed in [Humphrey89a].

EXERCISES

1. Classify a project you have been involved in with respect to product certainty, process certainty, and resource certainty. Which of the archetypal situations sketched in section 8.2 best fits this project? In what ways did actual project control differ from that suggested for the situation identified? Can you explain possible differences?

2. Consider the patient planning system mentioned in exercise 3.1. Suppose the project team consists of several analysts and two members from the hospital staff. The analysts have a lot of experience in the design of planning systems, though not for hospitals. As a manager of this team, which coordination mechanism and management style would you opt for?

3. Discuss pros and cons of a hierarchical as well as a matrix-like team organization for the patient planning project.

4. Consider a project you have been involved in. Identify the major irregular, control, and goal variables for this project. In what ways did the control variables influence project control?

5. Using Humphrey's classification, determine the maturity level that best fits your organization. Which steps would you propose to advance the organization to a higher maturity level? Are any actions actually pursued to get from the current level to a more mature one?

6. Suppose one of your team members is dissatisfied with his situation. He has been involved in similar projects for several years now. You have assigned him these jobs because he was performing so well. Discuss possible actions to prevent this employee from leaving the organization.

7. Suppose you are the manager of a project that is seriously getting behind schedule. Your team is having severe problems with testing a particular subsystem. Your client is pressing you to deliver the system on time. How would you handle this situation? How would you handle the situation if you were a member of the team and your manager was not paying serious attention to your signals?

9
Requirements Analysis

The requirements analysis phase is the first major step towards the solution of a data processing problem. During this phase, the user's requirements with respect to the future system are carefully identified and documented. These requirements concern both the actual functions to be provided and a number of additional requirements, such as those regarding performance, reliability, user documentation, user training, cost, and the like. During the requirements analysis phase we do not yet address the question as to *how* to achieve these user requirements in terms of system components and their interaction. Such is postponed until the design phase.

The result of the requirements analysis phase is documented in the **requirements specification**. This requirements specification reflects the mutual understanding of the analyst and the client of the problem to be solved. It is the basis for a contract, be it formal or informal, between the client of the system and the developing organization. Eventually, the system delivered will be assessed by testing its compliance with the requirements specification.

The requirements specification serves as a starting point for the next phase, the design phase. In the design phase the architecture of the system is devised in terms of system components and interfaces between those components. The design phase results in a specification as well: a precise description—preferably in some formal language—of the design architecture, its components, and its interfaces.

The notion 'specification' thus has several meanings. To prevent confusion, we will always use the prefix 'requirements' if it denotes the result of the analysis phase.

To make matters worse, the phase in which the user's requirements are being analyzed is also sometimes called specification. We feel this to be somewhat of a misnomer and will not use the term as such.

Requirements analysis and design generally cannot be strictly separated in time. In some cases, the requirements specification is very formal already and can be viewed as a high-level design specification of the system to be built. Often, a preliminary design will follow the requirements analysis. Based on the result of this design effort, the requirements specification may be changed and refined. This type of iteration also occurs when prototyping techniques are being used. Well-known techniques such as SADT and dataflow diagrams are used to structure and document both requirements specifications and designs.

It is only because of the ease of presentation that these phases are strictly separated and treated consecutively in this book.

During requirements analysis, a number of quite different matters are being addressed. Let us look at an example and consider the (hypothetical) case of a university's library automating its operation. We will start with the library containing a number of cabinets. These cabinets hold a huge number of cards, one per book. Each card contains the name(s) of the author(s), the book title, ISBN, publication year, and other useful data. The cards are ordered alphabetically by the name of the first author of each book.

This ordering system in fact presents major problems as it works well only if we know the first author's name. If we know only the title, or if we are interested in books on a certain topic, the author's catalogue is of little or no help.

By duplicating each card a number of times, and putting them in different catalogues—say, one ordered by author's names, one by title, one by topic, etc—this problem can be overcome. But, the process is error-prone and takes a lot of effort.

A software solution seems obvious. By storing the data of each book once in a data base, we may subsequently sort the entries in many different ways. Interactively searching this data base can be supported through appropriate tools. By placing a number of terminals in the library, service can be greatly enhanced.

During the requirements analysis phase, a number of user requirements will be raised. Some of those requirements will concern updating the data base, such as adding, deleting and changing records. Others will concern functions to be provided to ordinary users of the library, such as:

— Give a list of all books written by X.

— Give a list of all books whose title contains 'Y'.

— Give a list of all books on topic Z;

— Give a list of all books that arrived after date D.

It is expedient to try somehow to group user requirements into a few categories, ranging from 'essential requirements' to 'nice features'. As noted in chapter 3, users tend to have difficulties in articulating their real needs. Chances are, then, that much effort is spent on realizing features which later turn out to be mere bells and whistles. By using a layered scheme in both the formulation of user requirements and their subsequent realization, some of the problems that beset present-day software development projects can be circumvented. In our library system example, for instance, the requirement 'Give a list of all books that arrived after date D' could be classified as a nice feature. Service is not seriously degraded if this function is not provided, since we may temporarily place the accessions on a dedicated shelf.

It is also possible to try to predict a number of possible future requirements. These requirements will not be implemented in the present project. It is, however, sensible to pay attention to these matters at an early stage, so that they can be accommodated during the design of the system. Possible future requirements of our library system could include such things as:

— Storing information on books that have been ordered but have not been received.

— Storing information on books lent to users, such as their name and address, and the date on which the book is lent, which could then be used to generate a reminder notice for books not returned on time.

Besides these functions which directly relate to the software to be delivered, a number of other matters should be addressed during the requirements analysis phase. For our library example, at least the following points have to be addressed:

1. On which machine will the system be implemented, and which operating system will be used? If the data is to be stored in some DBMS, which (type of) DBMS is to be used? What type of terminal is to be used, and how many terminals will be supported?

2. Which classes of users can be distinguished? In our example, both library personnel and users will have to be served. What kind of knowledge do these users have? Will certain functions of the system be restricted to certain classes of users? Normal library users will probably not be allowed to update the data base or print the contents of the data base.

3. What is the size of the data base, and how is it expected to grow in the course of time? These factors influence both storage capacity needed and algorithms to be used. For a data base containing several thousands of books, some not very efficient searching algorithm might suffice. For the Library of Congress, the situation is quite different, though.

4. What response time should the system offer? A search request for a certain book will have to be answered fairly quickly. If the user has to wait too long for answers, he will become dissatisfied and search the shelves directly. Related questions concern the interaction between response time and the expected number of question sessions per unit of time.

5. How much will a system of this kind cost? In our library example, we should not only pay attention to the direct costs incurred by the software development effort. The cost of converting the information contained in the present file cabinets to a suitable data base format should not be neglected. These, less visible, indirect costs may well outweigh the direct cost of designing and implementing the new system.

This relatively simple example already shows that it is not sufficient to merely list the functional requirements of the new system. The system's envisioned environment and its interaction with that environment should be analyzed as well.

In our example, this concerns the library itself, to start with. The consequences of introducing a system like this one can be much greater than it seems at first sight. There may be changes in personnel functions, making some members of staff redundant. Checking whether membership fees have been paid might involve interfacing with the financial system, owned by another department.

In general, the setting up of an automated system may have more than just technical repercussions. Often, these other repercussions are not paid enough attention to. The lack of success of many software development projects can be traced back to a neglect of these non-technical aspects.

Before the actual design and implementation is started, the feasibility of a software development project should be assessed. Firstly, concerning the technical feasibility: can the hardware and software envisaged deliver the performance asked for; is the environment capable of timely delivery of the necessary data for the system? The latter could easily require more time than the design, implementation and testing of the new software.

[Elswijk87] contains a simple and yet insightful example of what may and may not be technically feasible. The example sketches an application in which two kinds of transactions may occur. Those transactions are characterized by their frequency, CPU-time needed and the number of physical I/O transports. The average I/O access time is also given. Using a statistical distribution describing the dynamics of these systems, one may then answer questions such as: 'how much capacity should the CPU have in order to achieve a response time of at most two seconds in $X\%$ of cases?' In this example, some given configuration satisfied the constraints for the case $X = 80$. A somewhat more stringent requirement ($X = 90$) required doubling the CPU-capacity. An even more severe requirement ($X = 95$) could not be satisfied at all by the range of machines available.

At first sight, the differences between these requirements seem marginal. They turn out to have a tremendous effect, though. An early and careful analysis of the technical feasibility may yield surprising answers to a number of important questions.There are many examples of projects in which lots of money was spent on software development efforts which turned out to be not practically feasible [Baber82].

Part of the feasibility study is an economic feasibility study. Do the gains outweigh the cost? The cost of a software development effort is largely determined by the time, in man-months, needed to develop the software. At the requirements analysis phase, only global attributes are known, so that a first cost estimation will be global in nature. As time goes by and the project progresses, the estimates will, hopefully, become more accurate. In chapter 7, we discussed the problems associated with estimating costs, and the various models that have been developed for this purpose.

The gains of a software development project are often difficult to express in dollars. For a stock control system, we may directly translate the benefits (less average stock and a higher availability of stock items) into money savings. The increased user service expected from our library automation project is, however, much more difficult to quantify.

In this chapter, we discuss the requirements analysis of an isolated software development project. Often, we will want to view a project within some wider organizational context. Requirements analysis and specification then follow a more general analysis of information requirements within a given organization. Such an environmental analysis results in boundary conditions and requirements for a range of software development projects.

In section 9.1, we give guidelines for the contents of a requirements specification document which describes the product to be delivered, not the process of how it is developed. Project requirements are described in another document, the project plan, discussed in chapter 2, which may be part of the contract between the client and developer. In this project plan, the cost, deliverables, and milestones of the project are discussed.

In general, the requirements analyst is not an expert in the domain being modeled. Through interaction with domain specialists, such as professional librarians, he has to build himself a sufficiently rich model of that domain. In section 9.2, we discuss various problems related to the fact that different disciplines are involved in the requirements analysis. This section also addresses the position of the analyst with respect to the universe of discourse (UoD) being modelled. In many cases, the analyst is not a mere outside observer of the UoD to be modelled, simply eliciting facts from domain specialists. He may have to take stands in power struggles or conflicting requirements, thereby actively participating in the construction of the UoD.

A number of techniques for documenting the requirements specification are discussed in section 9.3. Finally, some verification and validation techniques that can be applied at this early stage are sketched in section 9.4.

9.1 REQUIREMENTS SPECIFICATION

The end-product of the requirements analysis phase is a requirements specification. The requirements specification is an a posteriori reconstruction of the results of the analysis phase. Its purpose is to communicate these results to others. It serves as an anchor point against which subsequent steps can be justified.

The requirements specification is the starting point for the next phase: design. Consequently, a very precise, even mathematical description is preferable. On the other hand, the specification must also be understandable to the client. This often means: a readable document, using natural language and/or pictures. In practice, one will have to look for a compromise. Alternatively, the requirements specification may be presented in different, but consistent, forms to the different audiences involved. We will come back to this dilemma in section 9.2.

Besides readability and understandability, various other requirements for this document can be stated [IEEE84b]:

— A requirements specification should be *unambiguous*. We must be able to uniquely interpret requirements. Because of its very nature, this is difficult to realize in a natural language.

— A requirements specification should be *complete*. All significant matters relating to functionality, performance, constraints, and the like, should be documented. Both the responses to correct and the responses to incorrect input should be specified. Phrases like 'to be determined' are particularly insidious. Unfortunately, such is not always feasible. If certain requirements can be made specific only at a later stage, the requirements specification should at least document the ultimate point in time at which this should have happened.

— A requirements specification should be *verifiable*. This means that there must be a finite process to determine whether or not the requirements have been met. Phrases like 'the system should be user-friendly' are not verifiable. A requirement like 'for requests of type X, the system's response time is less than two seconds in 80% of cases, with a maximum machine load of Y', is verifiable.

— A requirements specification should be *consistent*. Conflicting requirements can be both logical and temporal. Using different terms for one and the same object may also lead to conficts.

— A requirements specification should be *modifiable*. Software models part of reality. Therefore it changes. The corresponding requirements specification has to evolve together with the reality being modelled. Thus, the document must be organized in such a way that changes can be accommodated readily (a loose-leaf form, for example kept in machine-readable form). Redundancy must be prevented as much as possible, for otherwise there is the danger that changes lead to inconsistencies.

— A requirements specification should be *traceable*. The origin of each and every requirement must be traceable. A clear and consistent numbering scheme makes it possible that other documents can uniquely refer to parts of the requirements specification.

— A requirements specification should be *useable* when the system is operational. Knowledge that is of importance when the requirements specification is being drafted and that is kept implicit, may lead to large problems during later maintenance of the software.

As a guideline for the contents of a requirements specification we will follow ANSI/IEEE Standard 830 [IEEE84b]. This standard does not give a rigid form for the requirements specification. The state-of-the-art simply has not advanced far enough yet. In our opinion, the precise ordering and contents of the elements of this document also is less essential. The important point is to choose a structure which adheres to the above constraints. In [IEEE84b], a global structure such as depicted in figure 9.1, is used. One of the possible refinements of the section on specific requirements is given in figure 9.2.

---

1. *Introduction*
    1.1. Purpose
    1.2. Scope
    1.3. Definitions, Acronyms and Abbreviations
    1.4. References
    1.5. Overview

2. *General Description*
    2.1. Product Perspective
    2.2. Product Functions
    2.3. User Characteristics
    2.4. General Constraints
    2.5. Assumptions and Dependencies

3. *Specific Requirements*

Figure 9.1:   Global structure of the requirements specification (*Source:* IEEE Guide to Software Requirements Specifications, *IEEE Std 830-1984. Reproduced by permission of IEEE.*)

A further clarification of the various components is given in Appendix E. As an example, figure 9.3 contains (part of) a possible requirements specification for the library example mentioned earlier, following the IEEE guidelines.

The IEEE framework for the requirements specification is especially appropriate in classic models for the software development process: the waterfall model and its variants. The framework is less useful when prototyping or incremental development techniques are used. A possible way out in the latter case is to add a section in which the hierarchy in user requirements is given.

3. Specific Requirements
  3.1. Functional Requirements
       3.1.1. Functional Requirement 1
              3.1.1.1. Introduction
              3.1.1.2. Inputs
              3.1.1.3. Processing
              3.1.1.4. Outputs
       3.1.2. Functional Requirement 2
       . . .
       3.1.n. Functional Requirement n
  3.2. External Interface Requirements
       3.2.1. User Interfaces
       3.2.2. Hardware Interfaces
       3.2.3. Software Interfaces
       3.2.4. Communications
              Interfaces
  3.3. Performance Requirements
  3.4. Design Constraints
       3.4.1. Standards Compliance
       3.4.2. Hardware Limitations
       . . .
  3.5. Attributes
       3.5.1. Security
       3.5.2. Maintainability
       . . .
  3.6. Other Requirements
       3.6.1. Data Base
       3.6.2. Operations
       3.6.3. Site Adaptation
       . . .

Figure 9.2: Prototype outline of the section on Specific Requirements (*Source: IEEE Guide to Software Requirements Specifications, IEEE Std 830-1984. Reproduced by permission of IEEE.*)

In that section we may start with a minimal set of requirements—the 'baseline'. Further requirements can be seen as extensions to this minimal—but working— system. Extensions anticipated also fit this model in a natural way.

When a prototyping technique is used to determine the user interface, the IEEE framework can be used to describe the outcome of that prototyping process.

The success of a product strongly depends upon the degree to which the desired system is properly described during the requirements analysis phase. Small slips in the requirements specification may necessitate large changes in the final software. Software is not continuous, as we noted earlier.

The importance of a solid requirements specification cannot be stressed often enough. Boehm states that in some cases 95% of the code of large systems had to be rewritten in order to adhere to the ultimate user requirements [Boehm74].

In our library example we could easily have overlooked the fact that in a number of cases the author's name as it appears on the cover of a book is not the 'canonical' author's name. This phenomenon occurs in particular with authors from countries that use non-Latin scripts. The transcription of the Russian name ЧЕХОВ reads 'Chekhov' in English and 'Tsjechow' in Dutch. In such cases librarians want to include the author's name twice: once the name is spelled as it appears on the book, and once the name is spelled as it is used in the various search processes. For, as an answer to questions like 'which books by Chekhov does our library possess', we would also like to be informed about the non-English titles.

Subtle mismatches between the analyst's notion of terms and concepts and their proper meaning within the domain being modelled can have profound effects. Such mismatches can most easily occur in domains we already 'know', such as a library. An illuminating discussion of potential problems in (formally) specifying requirements of a library system can be found in [Wing88]. Problems noted in [Wing88] include:

- A library employee may also be a user of the library, so the two sets of system users are not disjoint.

- There is a difference between a book (identified by its ISBN) and the (physical) copies of a book owned by the library. We have carefully made this distinction in the formal specification of a number of library functions in Appendix B.

- It is not sufficient to simply denote the status of a book by a boolean value present/not present (i.e. lent out). For instance, a book or, more properly, a copy of a book, may be lost, stolen, or in repair.

It depends on the experience of the people involved and their familiarity with the domain being modeled as to whether or not this type of omission is successfully circumvented and a good requirements specification gets produced. We will come back to this issue in the next section.

9.2 HUMANS AS INFORMATION SOURCES

In chapter 1, the first part of the software life cycle was depicted as it is reproduced in figure 9.4. The fact that the text 'requirements specification' is placed in a rectangle suggests, not unjustly, that it concerns something very concrete and explicit. The 'problem' is less well defined, less clear, even fuzzy in many cases. The primary goal of the requirements analysis phase is to elicit the contours and constituents of this fuzzy problem. This process is also known as **conceptual modeling**.

1. Introduction.

    1.1. *Purpose*. This document states the requirements of an automated library system for a medium-sized library of a research institute. The requirements stated serve as a basis for the acceptance procedure of this system. The document is also intended as a starting point for the design phase.

    1.2. *Scope*. The intended product automates the library functions described in DOC1. Its purpose is to provide a more effective service to the library users, in particular through the online search facilities offered. More details of the performance requirements are given in section 3.3 of this document. Once this system is installed, the incorporation of new titles will go from an average of 15 minutes down to an average of 5 minutes.

    1.3. *Definitions, Acronyms and Abbreviations*. Title catalogue: ..., PICA: ..., etc.

    1.4. *References*. DOC1: ..., DOC2: ..., etc.

    1.5. *Overview*. Section 2 of this document gives a general overview of the system. Section 3 gives more specific requirements for functions offered to (external) users and library personnel, respectively.

2. General Description.

    2.1. *Product Perspective*. The already installed data base system X will be used to store the various catalogues as well as the user administration. There are no interfaces to other systems. The system will be realized on the Y-configuration. System Y has a maximum capacity of 32 terminals of type Z. The maximum external storage capacity for the catalogues of the system is 1500 Mbyte.

    2.2. *Product Functions*. The system provides three types of functions:

        — Functions by which library users may search the catalogues of books and journal articles. A list of these functions is given in DOC1. A more detailed description is given in sections 3.1.2 and 3.1.3.

        — Functions by which library personnel may update the administration of borrowed titles; see section 3.1.4.

        — Functions by which library personnel may update the system's catalogues; see section 3.1.5.

    The user of the system selects one of the functions offered through the main menu (section 3.1.1).

    2.3. *User Characteristics*. The library users are incidental users of the system and have little knowledge of automated systems of this kind. The system therefore has to be self-instructing. Specific requirements are formulated in sections 3.2.1 and 3.3. The library personnel will be trained in the use of the system; see section 3.2.1.

    2.4. *General Constraints*. Library users may search only the catalogues of books and journal articles; they are not allowed to update a catalogue or the user administration. A password will be needed for these functions. Each library employee will be given his own password; see also section 3.5.2.

    2.5. *Assumptions and Dependencies*. ...

3. Specific Requirements.

    3.1. *Functional Requirements*.

        3.1.1. *Functional Requirement 1: Select Feature*.

            3.1.1.1. *Introduction*. The main menu appears after the system is started. The user next selects one of the options from the main menu. Subsequent actions are described in sections 3.1.2–3.1.5. If the option selected is constrained to library employees (Borrow Title or Modify Catalogue), the system asks for a password before a switch to the feature selected is made.

            At any point in time, the user has an option to return to the main menu.

            3.1.1.2. *Inputs*. ...

            3.1.1.3. *Processing*. ...

            3.1.1.4. *Outputs*. ...

        3.1.2. *Functional Requirement 2: Search Book Catalogue*.

Figure 9.3:   Partly worked-out requirements specification for the library example

3.1.2.1. *Introduction*. Given (part of) a book title or author name, the user may search the book catalogue for titles that match the user input given. The user is offered a screen with two fill-in-the-blank areas (one for the title and one for the author), one of which is to be filled in.

3.1.2.2. *Inputs*. The input may contain both upper and lower case letters. Special symbols allowed are listed in DOC1. Any other glyphs entered are discarded and are not shown on the screen. The input is considered complete when the processing command is issued.

3.1.2.3. *Processing*. All lower case letters are turned into upper case letters. The string thus obtained is used when querying the data base. A data base entry matches the title string given if the transformed input is a substring of the title-field of the entry. The same holds for the author-field if (part of) an author name is input.

3.1.2.4. *Outputs*. A list of titles that match the input is displayed. Up to four titles are shown on the screen. The user may traverse the list of titles found using the screen scrolling commands provided. A special warning is issued if no title matches the input given.

3.1.3. *Functional Requirement 3: Search Article Catalogue*.

. . .

3.1.4. *Functional Requirement 4: Borrow Title*.

. . .

3.1.5. *Functional Requirement 5: Modify Catalogue*.

. . .

3.2. *External Interface Requirements*.

3.2.1. *User Interfaces*. The screen formats for the different features are specified in Appendix A. Appendix B lists the mapping of commands to function keys. The user can get online help at any point in time by giving the appropriate command. Appendix C contains a list of typical usage scenarios. These usage scenarios will be used as acceptance criteria: 80% of the users must be able to go through them within ten minutes. An instruction session for library personnel should take at most two hours.

3.2.2. *Hardware Interfaces*. The user interface is screen-oriented. The system uses up to ten function keys.

3.2.3. *Software Interfaces*. The interface with data base system X is described in DOC2.

3.2.4. *Communications Interfaces*. Not applicable.

3.3. *Performance Requirements*. The system will initially support ten terminals. Its maximum capacity is 32 terminals. The present data base holds 25 000 book titles and 500 journal subscriptions. The storage capacity needed for these data is 300 Mbyte. On average 1000 books and 2000 journal issues enter the library per year. The average journal issue has six articles. This requires a storage capacity of 15 Mbyte per year.

The system must be able to serve 20 users simultaneously. With this maximum load and a data base size of 450 Mbyte, user queries as listed in sections 3.1.2 and 3.1.3 must be answered within five seconds in 80% of the cases.

3.4. *Design Constraints*.

3.4.1. *Standards Compliance*. Title descriptions must be stored in PICA-format. This format is described in DOC3.

3.4.2. *Hardware Limitations*. See section 2.1.

3.5. *Attributes*.

3.5.1. *Availability*. During normal office hours (9 am–5 pm) the system must be available 95% of the time. A backup of the system is made every day at 5 pm.

3.5.2. *Security*. The functions described in sections 3.1.4 and 3.1.5 are restricted to library employees and protected by passwords. Each library employee is issued a personal password. . . .

3.5.3. *Maintainability*. . . .

3.6. *Other requirements*. . . .

Figure 9.3:   cont'd

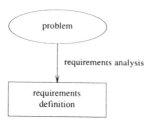

Figure 9.4:   The first part of the software life cycle

During requirements analysis we are modeling part of reality. The part of reality we are interested in is referred to as the **universe of discourse** (UoD). Example UoDs are a library system, a factory automation system, an assembly line, an elevator system.

The model constructed during the analysis phase is an **explicit conceptual model** of the UoD [Wieringa91]. The adjective 'explicit' denotes that the model must be communicatable to the relevant people (such as analysts and clients). To this end it should contain all relevant information from the UoD. One of the persistent problems of requirements analysis or, for that matter, analysis in general, is to account for all of the relevant influences and leave out irrelevant details.

People involved in a UoD have an **implicit conceptual model** of that UoD. An implicit conceptual model consists of the background knowledge shared by people in the UoD. The fact that this knowledge is shared gives rise to 'of course' statements by people from within the UoD, because this knowledge is taken for granted. ('Of course, a copy of a book is not the same as a book.') Part of the implicit conceptual model is not verbalized. It contains tacit knowledge, knowledge that is skillfully applied and functions in the background. Finally, an implicit conceptual model contains habits, customs, prejudices and possibly even inconsistencies.

During conceptual modeling, an implicit conceptual model has to be turned into an explicit one. In doing so, the analyst is confronted with two types of problems: analysis problems and negotiation problems. Analysis problems arise from the fact that part of the implicit conceptual model is not verbalized, that the implicit conceptual model evolves with time, that the client and analyst talk a different language, and that the implicit conceptual model cannot be completely codified. Negotiation problems arise because people in the UoD may counteract the analysis process, because the implicit conceptual models of people in the UoD may differ, or because of opposing interests of people involved (such as library personnel versus their managers). Both types of problems are discussed below.

The problem arises from the user, a human. This person must be able to describe the problem in both a correct and complete way. It must be communicated to a person who in general has a rather different background.

The analyst often lacks a sufficiently profound knowledge of the application domain in which the problem originated. He has to learn the language of the application domain and become acquainted with its terminology, concepts and procedures. Especially in large projects, the application knowledge tends to be thinly spread amongst the specialists involved, which easily leads to integration and coordination problems [Curtis88].

In our earlier example, it is the librarian who has to express his wishes. It is possible that the inclusion of two author names ('Tsjechow' and 'Chekhov') is seen as an obvious detail which need not be brought forward explicitly. The analyst at the other side of the table may still get the impression that he has a complete picture of the system. This type of omission may have severe consequences.

A number of years back a large automated air defense system was being developed in the US. During one of the final tests of this system, an alarm signal was issued. One of the computers detected an unknown missile. It turned out to be the moon. This possibility had not yet been thought of.

Eliciting correct and complete information is a crucial prerequisite for success. This turns out to be rather problematic in practice. Plainly asking the prospective user what is wanted does not generally work. More often than not we get a rather incomplete and inaccurate picture of the situation. According to Davis, important reasons for this are the human limitations for processing and selecting information, and problem solving [Davis82]. These limited human capabilities are yet aggravated by such factors as:

— the complexity and variation in requirements that can be imposed upon software;

— the differences in background between the client/user and the software specialist.

In research on human information processing one often uses a model in which human memory consists of two components: a short-term memory in which information is being processed, and a long-term memory in which the permanent knowledge is stored. Short-term memory has a limited capacity: it is often said that it has about seven slots [Miller56]. Long-term memory on the other hand has a very large capacity (more discussion on human memory will be given in chapter 17, in the context of other relevant psychological questions regarding software development).

So, information is processed in a relatively small part of human memory. Long-term memory is thus accessed in an indirect way. In addition, humans also employ external memories when information is being processed: a blackboard, a piece of paper, etc.

If a person being interviewed during requirements analysis uses only his short-term memory, the limitations thereof may have an impact on the results. This may easily occur if no use is being made of external memories. Things can be forgotten, simply because our short-term memory has limited capacity.

Humans are also inclined to be prejudiced when information is being selected and used. We are in particular inclined to let recent events prevail. In making up a requirements specification, this leads to requirements bearing on the present situation, presently available information, recent events, etc.

Humans are not very capable of rational thinking. They will simplify things and use a model which does not really fit reality. Other limitations that influence our model of reality are determined by such factors as education, prejudice, practice, etc. This same kind of simplification occurs when software requirements are drawn up. And the result will be limited by the same factors.

We cannot always expect the user to be able to precisely state his requirements at an early stage. The reason for studying the opportunities of automation is often because of a certain dissatisfaction with the present situation. One is not satisfied with the present situation and has the impression that automation will help. Whether this is true or not—many data processing problems are organizational problems—simply automating the present situation is not always the solution. Something different is wanted, though it is not clear what. Only when insight into the possibilities of automation is gained, will real requirements show themselves. This is one of the reasons for the sheer size of the maintenance problem. About half of the maintenance effort regards adapting software to (new) requirements of the user.

Through a careful analysis, we may hope to build a sound perspective of user requirements and anticipate future changes. However, no matter how much time is spent in a dialogue with the prospective users, future changes remain hard to foresee. In this respect, specifying requirements has much in common with weather-forecasting: there is a limit as to how far the future can be predicted.

For the requirements analysis phase to be successful we need methods and techniques that try to bypass the difficulties sketched above. The degree to which powerful techniques are required, depends on the experience of the people involved in the requirements analysis phase (both users and analysts) and the expertise of the analyst with the application domain. [Davis82] mentions four strategies that can be used in order to get the necessary information for the requirements specification:

1. **Asking** We may simply ask the users what they expect from the system. A presupposition then is that the user is able to bypass his own limitations and prejudices. Asking may take the form of an interview, brainstorming, or questionnaire.

2. **Derivation from from an existing system** Starting from an existing system, for instance a similar system in some other organization or a description in a text book, we may formulate the requirements of the new system. Obviously, we have to be careful and take the peculiar circumstances of the present situation into account.

3. **Synthesis of environmental characteristics** Software will be used in a certain environment. In order for the software to function successfully in that

environment, it has to follow the existing patterns of that environment. We may thus try to formulate requirements on the basis of that environment. This kind of technique is known by such names as process analysis, normative analysis, decision analysis.

4. **Prototyping** Given the fact that it is difficult, if not impossible, to build the right system from the start, we may decide to use prototypes. Starting from a first set of requirements, a prototype of the system is constructed. This prototype is used for experiments, which lead to new requirements and more insight into the possible uses of the system. In one or more ensuing steps, a more definite set of requirements is developed. As an alternative to the actual construction of prototypes, we may develop scenarios of possible system usage and corresponding system responses to gain an understanding of the requirements [Holbrook90].

Asking is the least certain strategy, while prototyping is the least uncertain. Besides the experience of both users and analysts, the uncertainty of the process is also influenced by the stability of the environment, the complexity of the product to be developed and the familiarity with the problem area in question. We may try to estimate the impact of those factors on the vulnerability of the resulting requirements specification, and then decide on a certain primary method for requirements analysis based on this estimate.

For a well-understood problem, with very experienced analysts, interviewing the prospective users may suffice. However, if it concerns an advanced and ill-understood problem from within a rapidly changing environment and the analysts have little or no experience in the domain in question, it seems wise to first construct one or more prototypes.

We should be very careful in our assessment of which technique to choose. It is all too common to be too optimistic about our ability to properly assess software requirements.

As an example, consider the following anecdote from a Dutch newspaper. A firm in the business of farm automation had developed a system in which chips were put in cows' ears. Subsequently, each individual cow could be tracked: food and water supply was regulated and adjusted, the amount and quality of the milk automatically recorded and analyzed, etc. Quite naturally, this same technique was next successfully applied to pigs. Thereafter, it was tried on goats. A million-dollar, fully automated goat farm was built. But alas, things did not work out that well for goats. Contrary to cows and pigs, goats eat everything, including their companions' chips.

Most requirements analysis methods, and software development methods in general, are Taylorian in nature. Around the turn of this century Taylor introduced the notion of 'scientific management', in which tasks are recursively decomposed into simpler tasks and each task has 'one best way' to accomplish it. By careful observations and experiments this one best way can be found and next formalized into procedures and rules. Scientific management has been successfully applied in many a factory operation. The equivalent in requirements analysis is to interview domain experts and observe users at work in order to obtain the 'real' user requirements. After this, the experts go to work and implement these requirements. During the latter process there is no further need to interact with the user community. This view of software development is a functional, and rational, one. Its underlying assumption is that there is one objective truth, which merely needs to be discovered during the analysis process [Denning91].

Though this view has its merits in drawing up requirements in purely *technical* realms, many UoDs of interest involve people as well–people whose model of the world is incomplete, subjective, irrational, and may conflict with the world view of others. In such cases, the analyst is not a passive outside observer of the UoD. Rather, he actively participates in the *shaping* of the UoD.

It is increasingly being recognized that the Taylorian, functional, approach is not the only, and need not be the most appropriate, approach to the requirements analysis process. Analysts share a set of assumptions about the nature of the subject of study. Such a set of assumptions is commonly called a 'paradigm'. It typically consists of assumptions about knowledge and how to acquire it, and about the physical and social world [Hirschheim89]. As noted above, analysts have to both inquire and intervene into the social world during the process of requirements analysis. It is thus natural to distinguish between two types of related assumptions: those associated with the way in which analysts acquire knowledge (epistemological assumptions) and those that relate to their view of the social and technical world (ontological assumptions).

In [Burrell79] the assumptions about knowledge result in a subjectivist–objectivist dimension, while the assumptions about the world result in an order-conflict dimension. The objectivist position 'is to apply models and methods derived from the natural sciences to the study of human affairs'. In the subjectivist position, 'the principal concern is with an understanding of the way in which the individual creates, modifies and interprets the world in which he or she finds himself (or herself)'. In the order-conflict dimension, the order view emphasizes order, stability, integration, consensus. On the other hand, the conflict view stresses change, conflict, disintegration.

In [Hirschheim89] these two dimensions and their associated extreme positions are used to yield four paradigms for requirements analysis and, more generally, information systems development:

Functionalism (objective–order). In the functionalist paradigm, the developer is the system expert who searches for measurable cause–effect relationships. An empirical organizational reality is believed to exist, independent of the observer. Systems are developed to support rational organizational operation. Their effectiveness and efficiency can be tested objectively, by tests similar to those used in other engineering disciplines.

Social-relativism (subjective–order). In this paradigm, the analyst operates as a facilitator. Reality is not something immutable 'out there', but is constructed in the human mind. The analyst is a change agent. He seeks to facilitate the learning of all people involved.

Radical-structuralism (objective–conflict). In the radical paradigm the key assumption is that system development intervenes in the conflict between social classes for power, prestige, resources. Systems are developed to support the interests of the owners, at the expense of the interests of labor. In order to redress the power balance, the analyst should act as a labor partisan. System requirements should evolve from a cooperation between labor and the analyst. This approach is thought to lead to systems that enhance craftmanship and working conditions.

Neohumanism (subjective–conflict). The central theme in this paradigm is emancipation. Systems are developed to remove distorting influences and other barriers to rational discourse. The system developer acts as a social therapist in an attempt to draw together, in an open discussion, a diverse group of individuals, including customers, labor, and various levels of management.

Admittedly, these paradigms reflect extreme orientations. In practice, some mixture of assumptions will usually guide the requirements analysis process. Yet it is fair to say that the majority of system development techniques stresses the functionalist view.

In the subjectivist–objectivist dimension, it is important to realize that a good deal of subjectivism may be involved in the shaping of the UoD. If we have to develop a system to, say, control a copying machine, we may safely take a functional stand. We may expect such a machine to operate purely rationally. In the analysis process, we list the functions of the machine, its internal signals, conditions, and the like, in order to get a satisfactory picture of the system to be developed. Once these requirements are identified, they can be frozen and some waterfall-like process model can be employed to realize the system.

If, however, our task is to develop a system to support people in doing their job, such as some office automation system, a purely functional view of the world may easily lead to ill-conceived systems. In such cases, user participation in the shaping of the UoD is of paramount importance. Through an open dialogue with the people concerned, we may encourage the prospective users to influence the system to be developed. Part of the analyst's job in this case is to reconcile the views of the participants in the analysis process. Continuous feedback during the actual construction phases with possibilities for redirection may further enhance the chance of success. It is the future users who are going to work with the system. It is of no avail to confront them with a system that does not satisfy their needs.

A dissatisfied user will try to neglect the system or, at best, express additional requirements immediately. The net result is that the envisaged gain in efficiency and/or effectivity is not reaped.

If the conceptual models of the participants differ, we may either look for a compromise, or opt for one of the views expressed. It is impossible to give general guidelines on how to handle such cases. Looking for a compromise can be a tedious affair, and may lead to a system that no one is really happy with. Opting for one particular view of the world will make one party happy, but may result in others completely neglecting the system developed. Worse yet, they may decide to develop a competing system.

9.3 TOOLS FOR DOCUMENTING THE REQUIREMENTS

The document that is produced during requirements analysis—the requirements specification—serves two groups of people. For the customer, the requirements specification is a clear and precise description of the functionality that the system has to offer. For the designer, it is the starting point for the design. It is not easy to serve both groups with one and the same document.

The customer is in general best served by a document which speaks his language, the language that is used within the application domain. In the example used before, this would induce the use of terms like 'title description' and 'catalogue'.

The designer on the other hand, is best served with a language in which concepts from his world are being used. In terms of the library example, he may prefer concepts like records (an instance of which might be termed 'title description') or files. In one sense the difference just boils down to a difference in language. However, this difference is of fundamental importance with respect to the later use of the system's description.

If the system is described in the user's language, the requirements specification is mostly phrased in some natural language. If we try to somewhat formalize this description, we may end up with a system in which certain forms have to be filled in, or certain drawing techniques have to be applied.

If, on the other hand, the expert language of the software engineer plays a central role, we often use some formal language. A requirements specification phrased in such a formal language may be checked using formal techniques, for instance with regard to consistency and completeness.

In [Abbott81] an outspoken prevalence for the user's expert language shows itself. We may then use existing concepts from the environment in which the system is going to be used. Admittedly, these concepts are not sharply defined, but in general there are no misconceptions between the experts in the application domain as regards the meaning of those concepts. A description in terms of those concepts can thus still be very *precise*. Since the first goal of the requirements specification is to get a *complete* description of the problem to be solved, the user's expert language is, according to Abbott, the best language for the requirements specification.

However, there are certain drawbacks attached to the use of natural language. [Meyer85] gives an example which illustrates very well what may go wrong when natural language is used in a requirements specification. Meyer lists seven 'sins' which may befall the analyst when using natural language:

1. **Noise** The presence of text elements that do not contain information relevant to the problem. Variants hereof are redundancy and regret. Redundancy occurs when things are repeated. Since natural language is very flexible, related matters can easily be phrased in completely different ways. When this happens the cohesion between matters gets blurred. Regret occurs when statements are reversed or shaded. In the library example, for instance, we could have used the phrase 'a list of all books written by author D' several times and only then realize that this list may be empty, necessitating some special reaction from the system.

2. **Silence** Silence occurs when aspects that are of importance for a proper solution of the problem, are not mentioned. An example of this occurred in the example given earlier: the fact that two author's names were needed was not stated explicitly.

3. **Overspecification** This occurs when elements of a requirements specification correspond to aspects of a possible solution, rather than to aspects of the problem. As an example, we could have specified that books be kept sorted by the first author's name. Overspecification limits the solution space for the designer.

4. **Contradictions** If the description of one and the same aspect is given more than once, in different words, contradictions may occur. This risk is especially threatening when one tries to be too literary. A requirements specification is not meant to be a novel.

5. **Ambiguity** Natural language allows for more than one meaning for one and the same phrase. Ambiguity can easily occur when terms are used that belong to the jargon of one or both parties. A 'book' may both denote a physical object and a more abstract entity of which several instantiations (copies) may exist.

6. **Forward references** References to aspects of the problem that are defined only later on in the text. This especially occurs in large documents that lack a clear structure. Natural language in itself does not enforce a clear structure.

7. **Wishful thinking** A description of aspects of the system such that a realistic solution will be hard to find.

A possible alternative given by Meyer is to first describe and analyze the problem using some formal notation and then translate it back into natural language. The natural language description thus obtained will in general represent a more precise notion of the problem. And it is readable to the user.

During requirements analysis, we may, as in other phases of the software life cycle, use all kinds of drawing techniques to depict the logical structure of the system. Most of these techniques are not very suitable for this task. They mostly originated as documentation techniques for software. (We will return to this topic in chapter 11.) An elaborate graphical technique, especially meant to be used during requirements analysis, is provided by SADT (Structured Analysis and

Design Technique) [Ross77a,b]. We will briefly cover SADT in the next subsection.

Following our discussion of SADT, we will pay some attention to PSL/PSA (Problem Statement Language/Problem Statement Analyzer) [Teichroew77]. PSL is a somewhat formalized language for requirements specification. PSA is a system that analyzes PSL-'programs'.

Finally, section 9.3.3 touches upon a few issues that impact requirements analysis in the wider context of software development, supported by an (integrated) collection of tools.

9.3.1 SADT

SA (Structured Analysis) is a graphical language developed by D.T. Ross in the 1970s [Ross77a,b]. SADT (Structured Analysis and Design Technique) is based on SA. SADT has been developed by Ross and his colleagues from SofTech. SADT also is a trademark of SofTech. SADT is both a graphics notation and an approach to system description. It includes guidelines on how to interview people, conduct reviews, and the like. The discussion below concentrates on the graphical aspects of SA(DT). A very elaborate discussion of SADT is provided in [Marca88].

SA contains about 40 basic components, some of which are depicted in figure 9.5. Each of these basic components has a very specific semantics. We may now describe a system using a combination of natural language and the drawing techniques from SA.

This way of graphically depicting a system is very much like a blueprint as it is used for buildings or radios. There is a clear philosophy behind SA. It is not a free-hand sketching technique. During requirements analysis, a clear description must be made of the actions to be performed by the system. This description is called the **functional architecture**. Based on this functional architecture, a **system architecture** is built during the subsequent design phase. This system architecture implements the functions of the functional architecture.

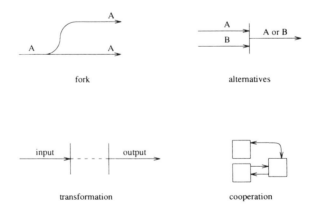

Figure 9.5: Some components of SA

The functional architecture is both hierarchical and modular. This is depicted schematically in figure 9.6. At the highest level, the global architecture of the system is sketched. Each of the components is further detailed at the second level. The component at the second level may in turn be further broken down, etc. In this way, a top-down hierarchical decomposition results.

A system may be described in SADT from different viewpoints. This is similar to the way in which one uses different drawings in house construction: one for the electrical wiring, another for the water supply, etc.

The most important viewpoints from which a system is described in SADT are activities and things, or, in our jargon, activities and data. These viewpoints are duals, in that they represent the same system (or system component), but viewed from a different perspective. Below, we will concentrate on the activity viewpoint, which is the one most often used.

Let us return to our library example. A customer who wants to borrow a book, addresses himself to one of the employees, who in turn satisfies the request. This has been depicted in figure 9.7 in the notation of SA. The activity—handling the user's request—is placed within the box. The input to this activity, the customer's request, is depicted by the arrow that enters the box from the left. The output is depicted by an arrow that exits the box at the right. The arrow that enters the box from above denotes things that constrain the activity. In this case, a catalogue constrains how the request is handled: a book can be borrowed only if it is available. Finally, the arrow entering the box from below denotes the mechanism by which the activity is handled. It represents, at least in part, *how* activities are realized. The mechanism arrow usually describes some physical aspects of an activity, such as storage places, people, or devices.

SADT diagrams are constraint diagrams. They describe both the input and output of an activity, and possible constraints that apply to the transformation. The arrows in the diagram depict the interfaces between activities and, especially at the higher levels, between the system and its environment.

In figures 9.8a–d, a small part of the library automation project is worked out in more detail, again using the SADT-notation. Figure 9.8a depicts a top-level view of the system, a slightly modified version of figure 9.7. The customer enters a request at the terminal. Handling this request is constrained by the library's catalogue and by passwords. The latter are used to distinguish between library personnel and clients; clients are not allowed to update the data base. Decomposition of this top-level view results in the diagram in figure 9.8b. Handling a user request involves two steps. First, the user selects an option, and next the action corresponding to that selection is executed. Finally, figures 9.8c and 9.8d give further refinements of two such actions, the searching of a catalogue and the modification of the data base.

9.3.2 PSL/PSA

PSL/PSA is part of the ISDOS-project, started in 1968 by D. Teichroew at the University of Michigan [Teichroew77]. ISDOS stands for Information System

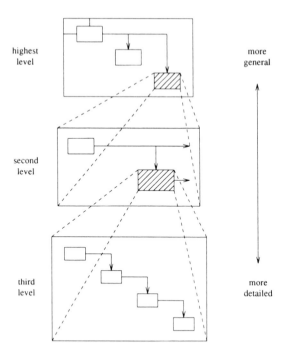

Figure 9.6:   Hierarchical decomposition in SADT

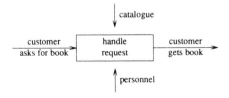

Figure 9.7:   An activity

Design and Optimization System. The two most important parts of ISDOS are:

— The Problem Statement Language (PSL). PSL is a language to describe information systems;

— The Problem Statement Analyzer (PSA). PSA is able to analyze a problem description written in PSL.

The user may express his problem in PSL at a fairly high level. In this description he concentrates on *which* actions have to be performed, and not on

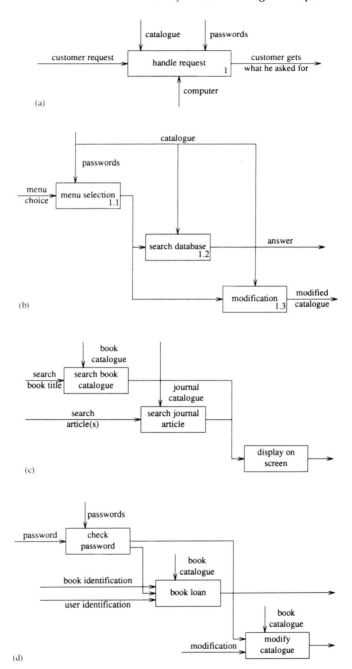

Figure 9.8: Library automation, (a) level 0, (b) level 1, (c) level 2, refinement of element 1.2, (d) level 2, refinement of element 1.3

how this will be realized. One should note that PSL is not a general-purpose programming language. The language does have enough structure though to allow PSA to analyze programs written in PSL. Figure 9.9 contains a typical fragment of PSL-code. Again, this concerns part of the library automation example used before.

PSL is kind of a relational language. There are objects (entities from the world being modelled, processes, data) and relations between those objects (is-a-part-of, consists-of, etc). Properties of the system to be constructed are expressed in PSL by specifying the appropriate relations between objects. This is a kind of free association. In this way the user may try to incorporate as much information as possible in a form which can be analyzed syntactically.

For example, figure 9.9 states that, when being executed, the process called main-menu may call processes request-password, search-for-booktitles, etc. The process main-menu gets interrupted when the condition F6-pressed becomes true. Besides processes, PSL knows 16 other object types (like INPUT, OUTPUT, GROUP, SET). [Dietz84] mentions 66 different relation types. This richness of expression allows the analyst to model a large number of aspects of the system. On the other hand, this richness may also be a burden. When will the future system be described in sufficient detail?

A description in PSL is next incorporated into a data base using PSA. After this has been done, it becomes possible to query that data base. These queries may for example yield:

— a list of modifications;

— reports in different formats, such as a list of all objects in the data base, together with their type and the date they were last changed, or a list of all properties and relations of a given object;

— summary reports, such as a report which depicts the system's hierarchy;

— analysis reports, in which for instance gaps in the information flow and unused objects are given.

The power of PSL largely results from the facilities offered by PSA: a central information repository, analysis of the information stored, and possibilities for report generation. There exist nowadays many tools that offer this type of support for the requirements analysis phase. These are called analyst workbenches. They will be discussed in chapter 15.

9.3.3 Ada-based analysis methods

Ada, the programming language that was developed on behalf of the US Department of Defense, will be embedded in an environment which offers support for all phases of the software life cycle (see chapter 12 for more

```
DEFINE PROCESS main-menu;
    DESCRIPTION: this process shows a menu to the user and, based
        on the user's choice, guides the further dialogue;
    RESPONSIBLE-PROBLEM-DEFINER IS: 'van Vliet';
    GENERATES: error-message, request-password, search-screen;
    RECEIVES: user's-choice;
    UTILIZES: request-password, search-book-titles,
        search-articles, book-loan, modify-book-catalogue;
    INTERRUPTED WHEN: F6-pressed BECOMES TRUE;
    CHANGES: F6-pressed;
    SECURITY IS: 'public';
    DERIVES: error-message, request-password, search-screen;
    HAPPENS: 300 TIMES-PER day;
    . . .
DEFINE PROCESS request-password;
    DESCRIPTION: request and check password;
    RESPONSIBLE-PROBLEM-DEFINER IS: 'van Vliet';
    GENERATES: error-message;
    RECEIVES: password;
    INTERRUPTED WHEN: F6-pressed BECOMES TRUE;
    CHANGES: F6-pressed;
    SECURITY IS: 'library only';
    DERIVES: error-message;
    HAPPENS: 10 TIMES-PER day;
    TRIGGERED BY: main-menu;
    TRIGGERED WHEN: personnel-choice BECOMES TRUE;
    . . .
DEFINE PROCESS search-book-titles;
    DESCRIPTION: given (part of) a title or an author's name, the
        user searches for books matching the pattern given;
    RESPONSIBLE-PROBLEM-DEFINER IS: 'van Vliet';
    GENERATES: error-message, list-of-books, no-match-present;
    RECEIVES: title-or-author;
    SUBPARTS ARE: search-data base, show-titles, show-no-titles;
    SECURITY IS: 'public';
    HAPPENS: 100 TIMES-PER day;
    TRIGGERED BY: main-menu;
    TERMINATION-CAUSES: main-menu;
    UTILIZES: search-data base, show-titles, show-no-titles;
    . . .
DEFINE OUTPUT list-of-books;
    DESCRIPTION: list of books that match a given title or author
        name;
    GENERATED BY: search-book-title;
    . . .
    DEFINE GROUP book-title;
    DESCRIPTION: PICA-format for book-titles;
    ATTRIBUTES ARE: type 'character';
    CONSISTS OF: title, author, isbn, . . .;
    . . .
DEFINE CONDITION F6-pressed;
    BECOMING TRUE CAUSES: main-menu;
    . . .
    DEFINE CONDITION personnel-choice;
    IS A FUNCTION OF: customer-choice;
    BECOMING TRUE TRIGGERS: request-password;
    . . .
```

Figure 9.9:   A typical PSL-fragment

information on Ada). In particular, such an environment will support the requirements analysis phase. [AdaMeth83] gives an overview of the requirements for any method supporting software development in Ada. These requirements are:

1. The method has to support all phases of the software life cycle. It should ease the transition between the different phases of a project. Thus, it should be easy to link program components during the implementation phase with the corresponding modules created at design time.

2. The method has to support the communication between the various parties involved. This concerns communication between designers and users, communication amongst designers, communication between designers and their managers, and so on. For this type of technical communication one will in general use some type of formal notation, such as data flow diagrams or algebraic specifications. The method should give specific guidelines for this.

3. The method has to support requirements analysis. The method should support effective problem-solving techniques. An important aspect of this concerns the possibility to model the future system. Techniques for problem-solving are employed when the system is decomposed and when the model is created. A formal model can be analyzed using tools.

4. Different approaches to the design and development of software systems must be supported. The method should not prescribe that a pure top-down or bottom-up approach be followed. Each combination of top-down and bottom-up should be allowed.

5. The method should support the construction of correctness proofs. The method should emphasize error detection at the earliest possible moment. Test and validation techniques should be integrated into the method.

6. The method should offer organizational support. It must allow effective communication between all people involved. It must be possible to deliver clearly delineated intermediate products, so that the project's progress can be measured. The method should incorporate techniques for cost estimation, project planning and other managerial duties.

7. The method should support the evolution of software systems. For this, effective documentation is required. The use of flexible and well-structured design and implementation techniques also contributes to a product that can easily be adapted.

8. Where possible, the method should be supported by tools. Such a collection of tools constitutes a **programming support environment**. The requirements of this type of environment are given in the STONEMAN report. The topic of CASE—Computer Aided Software Engineering—in its different flavors will be dealt with in chapter 15.

9. The Ada-method must be able to support different configurations of the system. These configurations may differ both in their hardware and in their software components.

10. The method must be learnable. To promote knowledge transfer, training material must be available, such as user documentation, exercises, examples.

11. The method must be open-ended. It should be possible to add and integrate new techniques and tools.

These requirements sound rather general. One may paraphrase them as 'an Ada-method should be a good method'.

[Porcella83] compares a number of methods in order to assess their suitability as Ada-methods. This comparison is based on answers to a questionnaire given by the designers of those methods. None of those methods came out as superior. One may view the requirements listed in [AdaMeth83] as the union of the positive characteristics of a number of existing methods, as they appear in [Porcella83].

A possible direction for specific support of the requirements analysis phase by an Ada-method is sketched in [Crew82]. The method proposed there is called ARM (Ada Requirements Methodology). In ARM, the requirements analysis consists of four phases, which preferably are executed in the order given:

1. Determining functional requirements, using data flow diagrams (see also chapter 10) and data models.

2. Determining non-functional requirements, such as response time, reliability, adaptability.

3. Developing concurrency requirements.

4. Collecting all requirements in a requirements specification.

The functional decomposition in phase 1 of ARM is very similar to the method underlying SADT. The result is partly documented in pictures and partly in a mixture of plain English and Ada-constructs. If the language Ada itself is used as a means of communication during the subsequent design phase, one may profitably use the result of the requirements analysis.

9.4 VERIFICATION AND VALIDATION

In chapter 1, we argued that a careful study of the correctness of the decisions made at each stage is a critical success factor. This means that we should already start verifying and validating the decisions laid down in the requirements specification during requirements analysis.

The verification and validation techniques to be applied during requirements analysis depend on the way in which requirements are documented. The least we can, and should, do, is to conduct a careful inspection or review to assess whether all aspects of the system have indeed been described. This involves an evaluation of the requirements for correctness, completeness, consistency, accuracy, readability, and testability. In a similar vein, the interfaces of the anticipated system with its environment (hardware, other software, people) is evaluated. A good way to assess requirements is to construct possible scenarios for future use together with prospective users.

Assessing the testability of requirements requires special attention. Requirements such as 'the system should be flexible', 'the system should be user-friendly', or 'response times should be fast', can never be tested and should not therefore appear in the requirements specification either. Other phraseology can be used such as 'for activities of type A the system should have a maximum response time of one second in 80% of the cases, while a maximum response time of three seconds is allowed in the remaining 20% of the cases' (see also section 9.1).

Besides testing the requirements specification itself, we also generate at this stage the test plan to be used during system and/or acceptance testing. A test plan is a document prescribing the scope, approach, resources and schedule of the testing activities. It identifies the items and features to be tested, the testing tasks to be performed, and the personnel responsible for these tasks [IEEE86b]. We may at this point develop such a plan for the system testing stage, i.e. the stage at which the developing organization tests the complete system against its requirements. Acceptance testing is similar, but is performed under supervision of the user organization. Acceptance testing is meant to determine whether or not to accept the system.

If a clear framework is available for documenting the requirements specification, such as is available in systems like PSL/PSA, we may often actually test the requirements specification itself, using the tools that come with such systems. We may then, for instance, test whether the requirements are complete and consistent.

A more elaborate treatment of the various verification and validation techniques will be given in chapter 13.

9.5 SUMMARY AND FURTHER READING

During requirements analysis we try to get a complete and clear description of the problem to be solved and the constraints that must be satisfied by any solution to that problem. During this phase, we do not only consider the functions to be delivered, but we also pay attention to requirements imposed by the environment. The result of this process is documented in a requirements specification. A good framework for the contents of the requirements specification is given in [IEEE84b]. It should be kept in mind that this document contains an a posteriori reconstruction of an as yet ill-understood iterative process.

During requirements analysis we are modeling part of reality. The part of reality we are interested in is referred to as the universe of discourse (UoD). The modeling process is termed conceptual modeling [Wieringa91].

People involved in a UoD have an implicit conceptual model of that UoD. During conceptual modeling, an implicit model has to be turned into an explicit one. The explicit conceptual model is used to communicate with other people, such as clients and designers, and to assess the validity of the system under development during all subsequent phases. During the modeling process, the analyst is confronted with two types of problems: analysis problems and negotiation problems. Analysis problems have to do with getting the requirements right. Negotiation problems arise because different people involved may have different views on the UoD to be modelled, opposing interests, and the like.

The techniques that are being applied during requirements analysis have not been developed very far yet. A number of them are aimed at overcoming our limitations as humans in conveying information. An overview of this type of problem is given in [Davis82].

Humans apply certain techniques when solving problems. These techniques have their limitations. Humans are limited in their capabilities to solve problems. Yet the problems to be solved are often complex. It is therefore useful to know these human abilities and limitations, so that we may bear them in mind during the analysis phase. Well-known sources on problem solving are [Newell72] and [Polya68].

The techniques alluded to above are largely Taylorian in nature. They fit a functional view of software development, in which the requirements analysis phase serves to elicit the 'real' user requirements. It is increasingly being recognized that the Taylorian approach need not be the most appropriate approach to requirements analysis. Many UoDs of interest involve people whose world model is incomplete, irrational, or in conflict with the world view of others. In such cases, the analyst is not a passive outside observer of the UoD, but he actively participates in shaping the UoD. He will get involved in negotiation problems. He will have to choose the view of some party involved, or assist in obtaining some compromise. [Hirschheim89] gives a very illuminating discussion of major paradigmatic issues involved in our approach to requirements analysis.

The following description techniques are often used for the requirements specification:

— natural language,

— pictures, and

— formal language.

An advantage of using natural language is that the specification is very readable and understandable to the user and other non-professionals involved. Pictures may be put to advantage in bringing across the functional architecture of the system. A well-known example from this category is SADT [Ross77a,b]. A formal language allows us to use tools in analyzing the requirements. Because of its precision, it is a good starting point for the design phase. PSL/PSA is a well-known and successful example [Winters79]. We may also argue that both formal and informal notations be used, since they augment and complement each other. For each of the parties involved, a notation should be chosen that is appropriate to the task at hand [Fraser91].

Developments regarding an Ada-based method to support requirements analysis were discussed in section 9.3.3. Ongoing research in this area is aimed at supporting the full software life cycle by means of an integrated toolset (see also chapter 15). The same holds for the other description techniques discussed in section 9.3. Insofar as this type of system supports requirements analysis, it can usually be traced back to one of the techniques discussed here. Examples are SREM [Alford77], which builds on PSL/PSA and is specifically directed towards real-time systems, and SAMM [Stephens78], which is strongly influenced by SADT and is somewhat more formal and richer in notation. Yet another form of structured analysis uses data flow diagrams. Like SADT, it concentrates on the description of the input–output behavior of system components. Data flow oriented techniques are further discussed in chapter 10.

It is very difficult to make a comparative evaluation of requirements analysis techniques and environments that support them. Tentative efforts have been undertaken by [Prentice81], [Porcella83], [Celko83], [Davis88a, b] and [Tse91].

EXERCISES

1. Draw up a requirements specification for a system whose development you have been involved with, following IEEE 830. Discuss the major differences between the original specification and the one you wrote.

2. What are major differences in the external environment of an office automation system and that of an embedded system, like an elevator control system. What impact will these differences have on the way the requirements specification problem is tackled?

3. Discuss pros and cons of the following descriptive means for a requirements specification: full natural language, constrained natural language, a pictorial language like SADT, and a formal language like VDM (see chapter 11).

4. Which of the above descriptive means would you favor for describing the requirements of an office automation system? And which one for an elevator control system?

5. Take the requirements specification document from a project you have been involved in, and assess it with respect to the requirements for such a document as listed in section 9.1 (unambiguity, completeness, etc.).

6. How would you test the requirements stated in the document from the previous exercise? Are the requirements testable to start with?

7. How would you go about in determining the requirements for a hypertext-like browsing system for a technical library. Both users and staff of the library have experience with keyword-based retrieval systems only.

8. As an analyst involved in the development of this hypertext browsing system, discuss possible stands in the subjectivist–objectivist and order-conflict dimensions. What are arguments for and against these stands?

9. Write a requirements specification for a hypertext browsing system.

10. Study the following specification for a simple line formatter:
    The program's input is a stream of characters whose end is signalled with a special end-of-text character, ET. There is exactly one ET character in each input stream. Characters are classified as:

    - break characters—BL (blank) and NL (new line);

    - nonbreak characters—all others except ET;

    - the end-of-text indicator—ET;

    A *word* is a non-empty sequence of nonbreak characters. A *break* is a sequence of one or more break characters. Thus, the input can be viewed as a sequence of words separated by breaks, with possible leading and trailing breaks, and ending with ET.
    The program's output should be the same sequence of words as in the input, with the exception that an oversize word (i.e. a word containing more than MAXPOS characters, where MAXPOS is a positive integer) should cause an error exit from the program (i.e. a variable, Alarm, should have the value TRUE). Up to the point of an error, the program's output should have the following properties:

    1. A new line should start only between words and at the beginning of the output text, if any.

    2. A break in the input is reduced to a single break character in the output.

    3. As many words as possible should be placed on each line (i.e. between successive NL characters).

    4. No line may contain more than MAXPOS characters (words and BLs).

    Identify as many trouble spots as you can in this specification.
    Compare your findings with those in [Meyer85].

11. What are the major uses of a requirements specification. In what ways do these different uses impact the style and contents of a requirements document?

10
Software Design

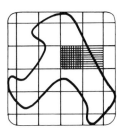

The starting point for the design phase is a clear, accurate description of the requirements of the prospective user. This description is part of the requirements specification which is the result of the requirements analysis phase. Besides a functional description of the system at the user level, the requirements specification may also discuss other requirements, for instance those concerning hardware and software needed, standards to be adhered to, or training needs.

A good design is the key to a successful product. A well-designed system is easy to implement, is understandable and reliable, and allows for smooth evolution. Badly designed systems may work at first, but they are hard to maintain, difficult to test, and unreliable. The design phase is a most crucial step in the software development process.

During software development, we should adhere to a planned approach. If we want to travel from point A to point B, we will (probably) consult a map first. According to some criterion, we will then plan our travel scheme. The time-loss caused by the planning activity is bound to outweigh the misery that occurs if we do not plan our trip at all but just take the first turn left, hoping that this will bring us somewhat closer to our destination.

In designing a garden we will also follow some plan. We will not start by planting a few bulbs in one corner, an apple tree in another, and a poplar next to the front door.

The above examples sound ridiculous. They are. Yet, many a software development project is undertaken in this way. Somewhat exaggerated, we may call it the 'programmer's approach' to software development. Far too much software still is being developed without a clear design phase. The reasons for this 'code first, design later' attitude are many:

- We do not want to, or are not allowed to, 'waste our time' on design activities.

- We have to, or want to, quickly show something to our customer.

- We are judged by the amount of code written per man-month.

- We are, or expect to be, pressed for time.

Such an approach grossly underestimates the complexity of software and its development. Just as with the furnishing of a house or the undertaking of a long trip, it is paramount to put in a well thought-out plan, resulting in a blueprint, which is then followed during actual construction. The outcome of this process (the blueprint) will be termed the **design** or, if the emphasis is on its notation, the (**technical**) **specification**. The process of making this blueprint is also called design. To a large extent, the quality of the design determines the quality of the resulting product. Errors made during the design phase often go undetected until the system is operational. At that time, they can be repaired only against very high costs.

Design is a problem-solving activity, and as such very much a matter of trial and error. In the presentation of a mathemathical proof, subsequent steps dovetail well into each other and everything drops into place at the end. The actual discovery of the proof was probably quite different. The same holds for the design of software. We should not confuse the outcome of the design process with the process itself. The outcome of the design process is a 'rational reconstruction' of that process. (Note that we made precisely the same remark with respect to the outcome of the requirements analysis process.)

The design process can hardly be separated from either the preceeding requirements analysis phase or the subsequent documentation of the design in a specification. These activities will in practice overlap and influence each other. At the more global (architectural) stages of system design the designer will interact with the user to assess fitness-for-use aspects of the design. This may lead to adaptations in the requirements specification. The more detailed stages of design often cannot be separated from the specification method used.

During design we may opt for a Taylorian, functionality centered, view and consider the design problem as a purely technical issue. Alternatively, we may realize that design involves user issues as well and therefore needs some form of user involvement. The role of the user during design need not be restricted to that of a guinea pig in shaping the actual user interface. It may also involve much deeper issues.

Rather than approaching system design from the point of view that human weaknesses need to be compensated for, we may take a different stand and consider computerized systems as a means to support human strengths. Likewise, systems need not reflect the interests of system owners only. In a democratic world, systems can be designed such that they contribute to the values of all those involved. This less technocratic attitude leads to extensive user involvement during all stages of system development.

Whereas traditional system development has a *production* view in which the technical aspects get optimized, the 'Scandinavian school' pays equal attention to the human system as well, and holds the view that technology must be compatible with organizational and social needs. [Floyd89] contains a discussion of this alternative approach to system development. The various possible modes of interaction between the designer/analyst on the one hand and the user on the other hand are also discussed in section 9.2. In this chapter, we concentrate on the technical issues of software design.

During the design phase, the system is decomposed into parts that each have a lower complexity than the system as a whole, while the parts together solve the user's problem. Since the complexity of the individual components should be surveyable, it is important that the interaction between components not be too complicated.

The design problem can now be formulated as follows: how to determine this decomposition. There really is no universal method for this. The design process is a creative one, and the quality and expertise of the designers is a critical determinant for its success. Yet, during the course of the years, a number of ideas and guidelines have emerged which may serve us in designing software.

In the next section, an elaborate example will be given. This example illustrates the single most important principle of software design: **information hiding**. The example shows how to apply **abstraction** in software design. Abstraction means that we concentrate on the essential issues and ignore, abstract from, details that are irrelevant at this stage. Considering the complexity of the problems we are to solve, applying some sort of abstraction is a sheer necessity. It is simply impossible to take in all details at once.

Section 10.2 discusses desirable design features that bear on maintainability and reusability. Five issues are identified that have a strong impact on the quality of a design: abstraction, modularity, information hiding, complexity, and system structure. Assessment of a design with respect to these issues allows us to get an impression of design quality, albeit not a very quantitative one yet.

A vast number of design methods exist, many of which are strongly tied to a certain notation. These methods give strategies and heuristics to guide the design process. Most methods use a graphical notation to depict the design. Though the details of those methods and notations differ widely, it is possible to provide broad characterizations in a few classes. The essential characteristics of those classes are elaborated upon in section 10.3.

In section 10.4 we discuss the various notations that may support the design process. This discussion is fairly brief, since a number of important notations are extensively dealt with in section 10.3, and chapters 9 (requirements analysis) and 11 (specification).

During the design process too, quite a lot of documentation will be generated. This documentation serves various users, such as the project manager, designers, testers, and programmers. Section 10.5 discusses IEEE Standard 1016. This standard contains useful guidelines for describing software designs. The standard identifies a number of roles and indicates, for each role, the type of design documentation needed.

Finally, section 10.6 discusses some verification and validation techniques that may fruitfully be applied at the design stage.

10.1 AN EXAMPLE: PRODUCING A KWIC-INDEX

If we are looking for a book on software engineering, we may consult the title catalogue of our library. If we are lucky, this book would be found under 'S'. A book entitled 'Introduction to software engineering' would be harder to find, since it might be categorized under 'I'. This problem can be solved by referencing each title a number of times, once for each word in the title. Doing so by hand is a cumbersome process and error-prone. Automation of this process seems an obvious choice.

A program for doing so is part of many software packages used by libraries. The input consists of a number of lines, corresponding to the titles we want to include in our catalogue. From each line, we generate n 'shifts', where n is the number of words in that line. If w_i is the i-th word from a line, then the first shift equals $w_1, ..., w_n$ (i.e. the original line). The second shift equals $w_2, ..., w_n, w_1$; the third shift is $w_3, ..., w_n, w_1, w_2$; and so on. A title

Software engineering should be a compulsory topic.

thus results in the following shifts:[*]

Software engineering should be a compulsory topic.
engineering should be a compulsory topic. Software
should be a compulsory topic. Software engineering
be a compulsory topic. Software engineering should
a compulsory topic. Software engineering should be
compulsory topic. Software engineering should be a
topic. Software engineering should be a compulsory

These shifts are then, together with those of other lines, sorted in the standard lexicographic order. The output is a KWIC-index. KWIC stands for Key Word In Context. It is easy to search for titles in a KWIC-index once you know part of the title.

When designing software to solve a problem like this one, we try to identify a number of components (modules) that each solve part of the problem and, taken

---

[*] In practice, one will only generate shifts that start with a relevant word. Shifts starting with words such as 'a', 'be', 'the' or 'some' are not all that interesting. We will not deal with this and other complications here.

together, solve the whole problem. Such a decomposition is sometimes called modularization. In this section we discuss two possible modularizations for this problem. The example is taken from a seminal paper by Parnas [Parnas72b].*

Except for very large data collections, this example is fairly easy to solve. A solution in Pascal results in a program that counts less than 400 lines. Real problems that crop up in practice and underpin the need for a proper modularization, will not be encountered. The purpose of the following exposition is to contrast two different modularizations of this problem and highlight the differences. The first modularization is typical for a large fraction of software designs commonly found. It is strongly geared towards an ordering of the various actions to be performed with respect to time. Information hiding is the central theme of the second modularization. We will further elaborate upon this notion later on in this chapter.

10.1.1 First modularization

A closer inspection of the problem formulation shows that the following tasks must be accomplished:

1. reading and storing the input;

2. determining all shifts;

3. sorting the shifts;

4. output of the sorted shifts.

These tasks are allocated to different modules which will then be called, in the appropriate order, from a control module.

As a next step, we have to decide on the internal representation of the data. The module that determines all shifts must know how the input is stored by the preceeding input module. These agreements on the internal representation of data are thus part of the design.

Following this line of thought we may distinguish the following modules in our first modularization.

Module 1: Input This module reads the input. The input is stored in memory such that the lines are available for further processing by subsequent modules. The input will be stored in a table. Each table entry holds up to ten characters. An otherwise not used character, termed `EndOfLine`, denotes the end of a line. We will use a second table to indicate the start address of each input line. These tables will be called `Store` and `StartOfLine`, respectively.

---

*   Source: D.L. Parnas, On the criteria to be used in decomposing systems into modules, *Comm. of the ACM* **15**, 12 (1972), ACM, New York. Reproduced by permission of the Association for Computing Machinery, Inc.

Module 2: Shift The shift module is called after all input lines have been read and stored. It builds a table called `Shifts` which contains, for each shift, the index in `Store` of the first character of that shift, and the index of the corresponding line in `StartOfLine`.

Module 3: Sorting This module employs the tables produced by modules 1 and 2. It produces a new table, `Sort`. `Sort` has the same structure as `Shifts`. The ordering of the entries in `Sort` is such that the corresponding shifts are in lexicographic order. Thus, `Sort` is a permutation of `Shifts`.

Module 4: Output The output module uses the tables from modules 1 and 3 to produce a neat output of the sorted shifts.

Module 5: Control The control module does little more than calling the other modules in the appropriate order. It may also take care of error messages, memory organization and other bookkeeping duties.

The control and data flow between the modules of this decomposition are depicted in figure 10.1. The control flow is indicated by solid arrows, the data flow by dashed arrows. A dashed arrow from A to B means that module B uses data from module A. Double arrows denote the input and output of the program.

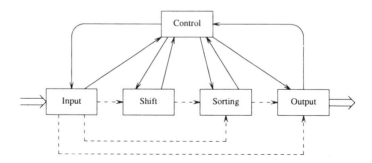

Figure 10.1:   First modularization of the KWIC-index program

A precise description of the interfaces between modules and the precise structure of the various tables has yet to be added to the description given above. However, even though incomplete, still a lot can be said about the decomposition. It is the kind of decomposition often used in practice. The system is decomposed into modules with well-defined interfaces. Each module has a well-defined task. The modules are limited in size. Each module is simple enough to be understood with relative ease.

Probably, quite a few programmers will arrive at such a modularization.

Appendix A, figure A.1, contains a solution in Pascal along these lines. Pascal does not offer modules as a language feature, so the text given has to be reshuffled a bit in order to get a correct Pascal program. The reshuffling merely boils down to moving the main program to the end of the text. The various type and variable declarations have been incorporated in the control module. This is necessary, since each of the other modules makes use of these variables. They are global variables.

10.1.2 Second modularization

In the first modularization we observed that various modules need knowledge about the precise storage of data. As a consequence, decisions about data representations have to be made at an early stage. When the module Shift is being implemented, for instance, we must know how the data is stored by the input module. Decisions about data representations are in fact a mutual property of the modules that use those data.

We may also try to make such decisions locally rather than globally. In that case the user does not get direct access to the data structures, but is offered a procedural interface. The data can be accessed only through appropriate procedure calls.

This means that we only have to get an agreement on this procedural interface at the design stage. We must know which procedures to call, which parameters to provide and which results to expect. The way in which the procedures obtain those results is of no concern to the caller. The implementer of a module can make those decisions locally. These decisions do not interfere with internals of other modules.

A first obvious candidate to apply this technique to is the module that takes care of the input's storage. Viewed abstractly, the input can be seen as a set of lines. The order in which these lines are stored is not relevant for the application. However, we do need a way to obtain information about lines stored. In order to get a simple mapping between lines stored and the subsequent retrieval of information about those lines, we stipulate that input lines are numbered from 1 onwards. This rank number will later be used to retrieve information. Furthermore, each line consists of an ordered number of words and each word consists of an ordered number of characters. In both cases the numbering starts at 1. We thus get the following.

Module 1: Store This module contains the following set of routines, callable by users of the module:

— InitStore, to initialize the module. This routine should be called before any of the other routines;

— PutCharacter(r, w, c, d), a routine to actually store characters. Character d is stored at position c of word w of line r;

— CloseStore, a routine to finish local administration. It is called after all input lines have been stored through successive calls of PutCharacter.

After `CloseStore` has been called, the user may retrieve the data stored through the following routines:

— `Lines`: delivers the number of lines stored;

— `Words(r)`: delivers the number of words in line `r`;

— `Characters(r, w)`: delivers the number of characters in word `w` of line `r`;

— `Character(r, w, c)`: delivers the character at position `c` of word `w` of line `r`.

In the above description of the module `Store`, we assume a sequential input of data, especially in `PutCharacter`. An implementation that accepts input in any order is conceivable, though not very realistic. This closely links up with the operation of the second module:

Module 2: Input The input module starts by initializing the module `Store` (through a call of `InitStore`). Next, the lines to be processed are read and stored through a series of calls of `PutCharacter`. Finally, `CloseStore` is called to close the administration kept by module 1.

As a next step, the shifts have to be determined. In the first modularization, we decided on a particular way of doing so: some table which contains the start address of each shift. This is a design decision. We could also have taken a different decision, e.g. to explicitly construct the textual representation of each shift. The latter may be more advantageous if the input is not voluminous and the shifts are to be used a number of times.

Again, a more abstract view may help. Rather than making any assumptions about the exact representation of shifts, we may limit ourselves to agreements about the information that is needed and the way this information can be obtained. This again amounts to an agreement about a procedural interface. This interface shows a striking resemblance to that of module `Store`.

Module 3: Shift This module offers the following routines:

— `InitShift`: a routine to initialize the module;

— `ShiftLines`: a routine that yields the total number of shifts;

— `ShiftWords(l)`: a routine that yields the number of words in shift `l`;

— `ShiftCharacters(l, w)`: a routine that yields the number of characters in word `w` of shift `l`;

— `ShiftCharacter(l, w, c)`: a routine that yields the `c`-th character of word `w` of shift `l`.

Whereas we spoke about lines in module `Store`, this module speaks about shifts. We still have to relate shifts to lines, though. This can be done as follows:

1. if $i < j$, the shifts of line i precede those of line j;

2. for each line, the first shift will be the original line, the second one will be the line shifted one word to the left, etc.

In this way we have ensured that, by calling ShiftCharacter with increasing values of 1 (counting from 1), all shifts will be obtained exactly once. The routine ShiftToLine uses the above ordering to determine the line number of a given shift 1.

The last important step concerns sorting. Here again, we may hide decisions pertaining to representations and algorithms by choosing a different interface to the user of the sorting module:

Module 4: Sorting The sorting module offers two functions to its users. The first one, InitSort, serves as an initialization routine. The second one, Ith, serves as an index. Ith(i) delivers the rank number of the shift that is i-th in the lexicographic ordering of all shifts. This rank number is to be used as a parameter to calls of routines from module Shift to obtain the textual representation of that shift.

Finally, we need an output and control module. These are very similar in function to those from the first decomposition.

Figure 10.2. shows the architecture of the second decomposition. Solid arrows indicate control flow. A dashed arrow A → B denotes that module A uses (calls) functions from module B.

Figure A.2 (see appendix A) gives a realization of the second decomposition in Pascal. Remarks made earlier with respect to modularization 1 hold here as well. Note however that the type and variable declarations are now included in the various modules that use them. This is reasonable, since they are not used outside their respective modules. All information needed is communicated through procedure calls.

10.1.3 Comparison of the modularizations

Both schemes will work. The first scheme is fairly conventional. The second scheme is in some sense more surprising. The data representations and their access are very similar in both modularizations. The difference lies in the modularization itself.

The difference becomes apparent if we compare both modularizations with respect to the following aspects:

— adaptability,

— degree to which modules can be implemented independently, and

— comprehensibility.

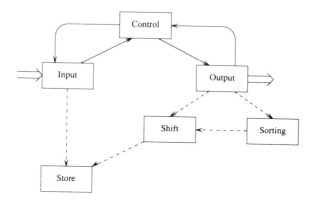

Figure 10.2: Modularization 2 of the KWIC-index program

Adaptability When conceiving a solution to the KWIC-index problem, a number of disputable decisions are taken. Some of these may be subject to change. Examples are:

1. The input format.

2. The decision to store all input in main memory. If the input is very large, such may be impractical.

3. The decision to store the input in units of ten characters. If there are few lines only, it may not be worth the effort. Some other format is conceivable as well.

4. The decision to use a table from which shifts can be deduced, rather than storing the shifts themselves. With a small input and/or a large memory, it may be more advantageous to actually construct the shifts once.

5. The decision to sort the shifts all at once, rather than using some partial sorting algorithm, or even searching for each element when it is needed. In a number of cases it may be worthwhile to divide the sorting time over the time needed to produce the complete index on paper.

The difference between the two modularizations with respect to adaptability becomes clear if we consider the impact of those changes. The first change remains restricted to one module in both decompositions. The second change necessitates adaptations in *each* module in the first decomposition. The same holds for the third change also because knowledge about internal representations is shared by all modules. In the second decomposition, this knowledge is kept by the module Store only. It is completely hidden to the other modules. The necessary changes thus remain restricted to that one module.

The fourth change necessitates adaptations in modules Shift, Sort and Output in the first decomposition. We need only adapt module Shift in the second decomposition. In the implementation of the second decomposition that is given in Appendix A, a simple computation is performed in the initializing routine `InitShift`, while the other routines search for the information needed. We could as well construct all shifts in this initializing routine which would lead to proportional simplifications in the other routines from this module.

The fifth change also affects more than one module in the first decomposition (`Sort` and `Output`). The sort module in decomposition 2 has been designed such that it is not visible to the user when the actual sorting takes place. To illustrate this, appendix A also contains an alternative implementation of the sorting module (figure A.3). In this alternative implementation, sorting takes place within the routine `Ith`. This implementation may replace the original version without any change to the other modules.

Independent development In the first decomposition the interfaces between the various modules consist of fairly complex descriptions of formats and tables. These correspond to design decisions that are essential to the final structure of the system. Documenting the organization thereof is a part of the development of those modules which cannot be neglected during design. In a sense, these decisions are a common property of those modules. They are visible to, and used by, the implementers of those modules.

The interfaces in the second decomposition are much more abstract. They consist of function names and information about the number and type of their parameters. Such decisions are fairly easy to make, and the independent development of modules can easily be started.

We may illustrate this by mentally depicting the implementation of the KWIC-index program by two people. In order to do so, we split the program into two parts of approximately the same size. As far as modularization 1 is concerned, all types and variables defined in the control module must be known to both developers. In modularization 2, these types and variables are declared locally, so the developers have only to agree on the way functions are to be called.

Comprehensibility In order to fully comprehend the sorting module of the first modularization, you also have to know something of the input and shift module. Certain aspects of the table organization derive their meaning from specific choices made in other modules. As a consequence, the system can be comprehended only as a whole. This does not hold for the second modularization.

What *criteria* were the design decisions based on? In the first decomposition, emphasis is on the time ordering of actions: module 1 is executed first, module 2 is executed next, etc. It is as if a rough diagram of the control flow has been made, and the modularization follows directly from that control flow diagram.

In the second decomposition, the *data* are the focal point. We have tried to make a decomposition that will allow decisions about implementations of data to remain hidden inside a module. As a consequence, these representations remain hidden to other components of the system. This is called **information hiding**

[Parnas72b]. The data structures and the functions that operate on those data structures are incorporated in one module. Recent programming languages like Ada [Ada83] and Modula-2 [Wirth85] also offer language features to support this way of programming. See also chapter 12. In chapter 11 we will discuss the formal specification of this type of software component (abstract data types).

10.2 DESIGN CONSIDERATIONS

Up till now we have used the notion of 'module' in a rather intuitive way. It is not easy to give an accurate definition of that notion. It appears from our example problem that a module in general does not denote some random piece of software. We tend to apply certain criteria in order to decompose a system into modules.

At the programming language level, a module usually refers to an identifiable unit with respect to compilation. We will use a similar definition of the term 'module' with respect to design: a module is an identifiable unit in the design. In the decomposition from section 10.1.1 these units tended to be procedures. The modules from section 10.1.2 usually contain more than one procedure. The latter will often be the case.

There are, in principle, many ways to decompose a system into modules. Obviously, not every decomposition is equally desirable. In this section we are interested in desirable features of a decomposition. These features can in some sense be used as a measure for the quality of the design. Designs that have those features are considered superior to those that do not have them.

The design features we are most interested in are those that facilitate maintenance and reuse: simplicity, a clear separation of concepts into different modules, and restricted visibility (i.e. locality) of information.* Systems that have those properties are easier to maintain since we may concentrate our attention on those parts that are directly affected by a change. These properties also bear on reusability, because the resulting modules tend to have a well-defined functionality that fits concepts from the application domain. Such modules are likely candidates for inclusion in other systems that address problems from the same domain.

In the following subsections we discuss five interrelated issues that have a strong impact on the above features:

- abstraction,
- modularity,
- information hiding,
- complexity, and
- system structure.

---

* Obviously, an even more important feature of a design is that the corresponding system should perform the required tasks in the specified way. To this end the design should be validated against the requirements.

10.2.1 Abstraction

We applied abstraction in both decompositions discussed above. Abstraction means that we concentrate on the essential features and ignore, *abstract from*, details that are not relevant at the level we are currently working. The sorting module from either modularization is a case in point. From the outside we cannot (and need not be able to) discern how exactly the sorting process takes place. We need only know that the output is indeed sorted. At a later stage, when the details of the sorting module are decided upon, then we can rack our brains about the most suitable sorting algorithm.

The complexity of most software problems makes applying abstraction a sheer necessity. In the ensuing discussion, we distinguish two types of abstraction: *procedural abstraction* and *data abstraction*.

The notion of procedural abstraction is fairly traditional. A programming language offers if-constructs, loop-constructs, assignment statements, and the like. The transition from a problem to be solved to these primitive language constructs is a large one in many cases. To this end a problem is first decomposed into subproblems, each of which is handled in turn. These subproblems correspond to major tasks to be accomplished. They can be recognized by their description in which some verb plays a central role (for example: *read* the input, *sort* all shifts, *process* the next user request, *compute* the net salary). If needed, subproblems are further decomposed into even simpler subproblems. Eventually we get at subproblems for which a standard solution is available. This type of (top-down) decomposition is clearly recognizable in the modularization discussed in section 10.1.1.

The result of this type of stepwise decomposition is a hierarchical structure. The top node of the structure denotes the problem to be solved. The next level shows its first decomposition into subproblems. The leaves denote primitive problems. This is schematically depicted in figure 10.3.

The procedure concept offers us a notation for the subproblems that result from this decomposition process. The application of this concept is known as procedural abstraction. With procedural abstraction the name of a procedure (in section 10.1.1: Input, Shift, etc.) is used to denote the corresponding sequence of actions. When that name is used in a program, we need not bother ourselves about the exact way in which its effect is realized. The important thing is that, after the call, certain prestated requirements are fulfilled (such as the appropriate filling of some tables in the case described in section 10.1.1).

This way of going about the process closely matches the way in which humans are inclined to solve problems. Humans too are inclined to the stepwise handling of problems. Procedural abstraction thus offers an important means to tackling software problems.

When designing software, we are inclined to decompose the problem so that the result has a strong time orientation. A problem is decomposed into subproblems that follow each other in time and this is clearly shown in the decomposition of section 10.1.1. In its simplest form, this approach results in

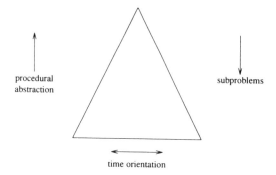

Figure 10.3: The idea of procedural abstraction

input–process–output schemes: a program first has to read and store its data, next some process computes the required output from these data, and the result finally is output. As we noticed, application of this technique may result in programs that are difficult to adapt and hard to comprehend. Applying data abstraction results in a decomposition which shows this affliction to a far lesser degree.

Procedural abstraction is aimed at finding a hierarchy in the program's control structure: which steps have to be executed, and in which order. Data abstraction is aimed at finding a hierarchy in the program's data. Programming languages offer primitive data structures for integers, reals, truth values, characters and possibly a few more. Using these building blocks we may construct more complicated data structures, such as stacks and binary trees. Such structures are of general use in application software. They occur at a fairly low level in the hierarchy of data structures. Application-oriented objects, such as 'paragraph' in text processing software or 'shift' in our example, are found at yet higher levels of the data structure hierarchy. This is schematically depicted in figure 10.4.

For the data, too, we wish to abstract from details that are not relevant at a certain level. In fact, we already do so when using the primitive data structures offered by our programming language. In using these, we abstract from details such as the internal representation of numbers and the way in which the addition of two numbers is realized. At the programming language level we may view the integers as a set of objects $(0, 1, -1, 2, -2, \ldots)$ and a set of operations on these objects $(+, -, *, /, \ldots)$. These two sets together determine the data type `integer`. To be able to employ this datatype we need only name the set of objects and specify its operations.

We may proceed along the same lines for the data structures not directly supported by the programming language. A data type `binary-tree` is characterized by a set of objects (all conceivable binary trees) and a set of operations on those objects. When using binary trees, their representation and the implementation of the corresponding operations need not concern us. We need to ascertain only the intended effect of the operations.

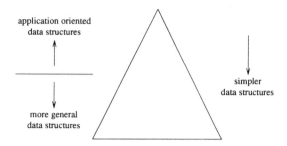

Figure 10.4:   The idea of data abstraction

This technique was applied in section 10.1.2. Within the module `Store` we have lines. How `lines` are represented is not known to the user of that module. The user has only a number of operations on lines (`Lines`, `Words`, and the like) at his disposal.

Applying data abstraction during design is sometimes called **object-oriented design**, since the type of object and the associated operations are encapsulated in one module. The buzzword 'object-oriented', however, also has a subtly different meaning. We will further elaborate upon this notion in section 10.3.4 and chapter 12.

Both with procedural abstraction and data abstraction the *what* (the specification) is separated from the *how* (the implementation). In chapter 11 we will elaborate upon the what when discussing different specification techniques. In chapter 12 we elaborate upon the how, when we discuss the module concept as it appears in various programming languages.

Recent languages such as Ada and Modula-2 offer a language construct (called **package** and **module**, respectively) that allows us to maintain a syntactic separation between the implementation and specification of data types. Note that it is also possible, though somewhat cumbersome, to apply data abstraction during design, when the ultimate language does not offer the concept. The example in section 10.1.2 is a case in point.

We noticed before that procedural abstraction fits in nicely with the way humans tend to tackle problems. To most people, data abstraction is a bit more complicated.

When searching for a solution to a software problem we will find that the solution needs certain data structures. At some point we will also have to choose a representation for these data structures. Rather than making those decisions at an early stage and impose the result on all other components (as was the case in the first decomposition of our example), you are better off if you create a separate subproblem and make only the procedural, implementation-independent, interfaces public (as was done in the second decomposition). Data abstraction thus is a prime example of information hiding.

The development of these abstraction techniques went hand in hand with other developments, particularly those in the realm of programming languages. Way back, procedures were introduced to avoid repetition of instruction sequences. Only at a later stage did we view the name of a procedure as an abstraction of the corresponding instruction sequence. Only then did the notion of procedural abstraction get its present connotation. In a similar vein, developments in the field of formal data type specifications and language notions for modules (starting with the **class** concept of SIMULA 67) strongly contributed to our present notion of data abstraction [Shaw84].

As a final note we remark that we may identify yet a third type of abstraction, **control abstraction**. In control abstraction we abstract from the precise order in which a sequence of events is to be handled. Though control abstraction is often implicit when procedural abstraction is used, it is sometimes convenient to be able to explicitly model this type of nondeterminacy, for instance when specifying concurrent systems. This topic falls outside the scope of this book; see [Shatz89].

10.2.2 Modularity

During design the system is decomposed into a number of modules and the relations between those modules are indicated. In a second design of the same system, different modules may show up and there may be different relations between the modules. We may now try to compare those designs by considering both a typology for the individual modules and the type of connections between them. This leads us to two structural design criteria: *cohesion* and *coupling*.

Cohesion may be viewed as the glue that keeps the module together. It is a measure for the mutual affinity of the components of a module. In general we will wish to make the cohesion as strong as possible. [Yourdon75] identifies the following seven levels of cohesion of increasing strength:

1. **Coincidental cohesion** With coincidental cohesion components have been grouped into modules in a haphazard way. There is no significant relation between the components.

2. **Logical cohesion** With logical cohesion, the components realize tasks that are logically related. One example is a module that contains all input routines. These routines do not call one another and they do not pass information to each other. Their function is just very similar.

3. **Temporal cohesion** A typical example of this type of cohesion is some initialization module. The various components hereof are independent, but are activated at about the same point in time.

4. **Procedural cohesion** A module exhibits procedural cohesion if it consists of a number of components that have to be executed in some given order. For instance, a module may have to first read some datum, then search a table, and finally print a result.

5. **Communicational cohesion** This type of cohesion occurs if the components of a module operate on the same (external) data. For instance, a module may read some data from a disk, perform certain computations on those data, and print the result.

6. **Sequential cohesion** Sequential cohesion occurs if the module consists of a sequence of components where the output of one component serves as input to the next component.

7. **Functional cohesion** In a module exhibiting functional cohesion all components contribute to the one single function of that module. Such a module often transforms a single input datum in a single output datum. The well-known mathematical subroutines are a typical example hereof. Less trivial examples are modules like 'execute the next edit-command' and 'translate the program given'.

In their classic paper on structured design, Stevens et al provide some simple heuristics that may be of help in establishing the degree of cohesion of a module [Stevens74]. They suggest to write down a sentence that describes the function (purpose) of the module and next examine that sentence. Properties to look for include the following:

- If the sentence is compound, has a connective like a comma or the word 'and', or contains more than one verb, then that module is probably performing more than one function. It is likely to have sequential or communicational cohesion.

- If the sentence contains words that relate to time, such as 'first', 'next', 'after', 'then', then the module probably has sequential or temporal cohesion.

- If the sentence contains words like 'initialize', the module probably has temporal cohesion.

The levels of cohesion identified above reflect the cohesion between the *functions* that a module provides. Abstract data types cannot be easily accommodated within this scheme. Macro and Buxton therefore propose to add an extra level, **data cohesion**, to identify modules that encapsulate an abstract data type [Macro87]. Data cohesion is even stronger than functional cohesion.

It goes without saying that it is not always an easy task to obtain the strongest possible cohesion between the components of a module. Though functional cohesion may be attainable at the top levels, and data cohesion at the bottom levels, we will often have to settle for less at the intermediate levels of the module hierarchy. The trade-offs to be made here are what makes design such a difficult, and yet challenging, activity.

The second structural criterion is **coupling**. Coupling is a measure for the strength of the intermodule connections. A high degree of coupling indicates a strong dependence between modules. A high degree of coupling between modules means that we can only fully comprehend this set of modules as a whole.

High coupling easily results in ripple effects when a module has to be changed, because such a change is likely to incur changes in the dependent modules as well. Loosely coupled modules on the other hand are relatively independent and are easier to comprehend and adapt. Loose coupling therefore is a desirable feature of a design (and its subsequent realization). From highest to lowest, the following types of coupling can be identified:

Content coupling With content coupling, one module directly affects the working of another module. Content coupling occurs when a module changes another module's data, or when control is passed from one module to the middle of another (as in a jump). This type of coupling can, and should, always be circumvented.

Common coupling With common coupling, two modules have shared data. The name originates from the use of COMMON blocks in FORTRAN. Its equivalent in block-structured languages is the use of global variables.

Control coupling. With control coupling, one module directs the execution of another module by passing the necessary control information. This is usually accomplished by means of flags that are set by one module and reacted upon by the dependent module.

Stamp coupling Stamp coupling occurs when complete data structures are passed from one module to another. With stamp coupling, the precise format of these data structures is a common property of those modules.

Data coupling With data coupling, only simple data is passed between modules, as is the case when abstract data types are used.

Coupling and cohesion are dual characteristics. If the various modules exhibit strong internal cohesion, the intermodule coupling tends to be minimal, and vice versa.

Simple interfaces—weak coupling between modules and strong cohesion between the module's components—are of crucial importance for a variety of reasons:

— Communication between programmers becomes simpler. When different people are working on one and the same system, it helps if decisions can be made locally and do not interfere with the working of other modules.

— Correctness proofs become easier to derive.

— It is less likely that changes will propagate to other modules, which reduces maintenance costs.

— The reusability of modules is increased. The less assumptions are made about a component's environment, the greater the chance of fitting another environment.

— The comprehensibility of modules is increased. Humans have limited memory capacity for information processing. Simple module interfaces allow for an understanding of a component independent of the context in which it is used.

— Empirical studies show that interfaces exhibiting weak coupling and strong cohesion are less error prone than those that do not have these properties (see for example [Selby91]).

10.2.3 Information hiding

The concept of information hiding originates from the seminal paper of Parnas that was discussed in section 10.1. The principle of information hiding is that each module has a secret which it hides to other modules. Its use as a guiding principle in design is aptly illustrated in the KWIC-index example. In the second modularization, for example, module `Store` hides how lines are stored, and module `Sort` hides how and when shifts are sorted.

Design involves a sequence of decisions, such as how to represent certain information, or in which order to accomplish tasks. For each such decision we should ask ourselves which other parts of the system need to know about the decision, and how to hide it to parts that need not.

Information hiding is closely related to the notions of abstraction, cohesion, and coupling. If a module hides some design decision, the user of that module may abstract from, ignore, the outcome of that decision. Since the outcome is hidden, it cannot possibly interfere with the use of that module. If a module hides some secret, that secret does not permeate the module's boundary, thereby decreasing the coupling between that module and its environment. Finally, information hiding increases cohesion, since the module's secret is what binds the module's constituents together.

It depends on the programming language used whether the separation of concerns obtained during the design stage will be identifiable in the ultimate code. To some extent, this is of secondary concern. The design decomposition will in any case be reflected implicitly in the code and should be explicitly recorded in the technical documentation. As such it is of great importance for the later evolution of the system. A confirmation of the impact of such techniques as information hiding on the maintainability of software can be found in [Boehm83b].

10.2.4 Complexity

In a very general sense, the complexity of a problem refers to the amount of resources required for its solution. In the present context complexity refers to the effort needed to construct or change a piece of software. This is very different from the complexity of the computation performed (with respect to time or memory needed).

The latter is a well-established field in which many results have been obtained; see for example [Garey79]. Such is much less true for the type of complexity we are interested in. Software complexity in this sense still is a rather elusive notion.

Serious efforts have been made to measure software complexity in quantitative terms. The resulting metrics are intended to be used as anchor points for the decomposition of a system, to assess the quality of a design or program, to guide re-engineering efforts, etc. We then measure certain attributes of a software system, such as its length, the number of if-statements, or the information flow between modules, and try to relate the numbers thus obtained to the system's complexity. The type of software attributes considered can broadly be categorized into two classes [Fenton91]:

- **intra-modular attributes**: attributes of individual modules, and

- **inter-modular attributes**: attributes of a system viewed as a collection of modules with dependencies.

In this subsection we are dealing with intra-modular attributes. Inter-modular attributes are discussed in the next subsection. With respect to individual modules, Basili distinguishes two classes of complexity metrics [Basili80]:

1. **Size-based** complexity metrics. The size of a piece of software, such as the number of lines of code, is fairly easy to measure. It also gives a fair indication of the effort needed to develop that piece of software (see also chapter 7). As a consequence, it could also be used as a complexity metric.

2. **Structure-based** complexity metrics. The structure of a piece of software is a good indicator of its design quality, because a program that has a complicated control structure or uses complicated data structures is likely to be difficult to comprehend and maintain, and thus be more complex.

The easiest way to measure software size is to count the number of lines of code. We may next impose limits on the number of lines of code per module. In [Weinberg71] for instance the ideal size of a module is said to be 30 lines of code. In a variant hereof, limits are imposed on the number of components per module. Some people claim that a module should contain at most seven components as is prescribed for SADT, for instance. This number seven can be traced back to research in psychology. [Miller56] suggests that human memory is hierarchically organized with a short-term memory of about seven slots, while there is a more permanent memory of almost unlimited capacity. If there are more than seven pieces of information, these cannot all be stored in short-term memory and information gets lost. This type of psychological factor is further discussed in chapter 17.

There are serious objections to the direct use of the number of lines of code as a complexity metric. Some programmers write more verbose programs than others. We should at least normalize the counting to counteract these effects and be able to compare different pieces of software. This can be achieved by using a prettyprinter, a piece of software that reproduces programs in a given language in a uniform way.

A second objection is that this technique makes it hard to compare programs written in different languages. If the same problem is solved in different languages, the results may differ considerably in length. For example, APL is more compact than COBOL.

Finally, some lines are more complex than others. An assignment like

```
a:= b
```

looks simpler than a loop

```
while p↑.next <> nil do p:= p↑.next,
```

though they each occupy one line.

Halstead's method, also known as 'software science', uses a refinement of counting lines of code [Halstead77], [Fitzsimmons78]. This refinement is meant to overcome the problems associated with metrics based on a direct count of lines of code.

Halstead's method uses the number of operators and operands in a piece of software. The set of operators includes the arithmetic and Boolean operators, as well as separators (such as a semicolon between adjacent instructions) and (pairs of) reserved words. The set of operands contains the variables and constants used. Halstead then defines four basic entities:

1. n_1 is the number of unique (i.e. different) operators in the program;

2. n_2 is the number of unique (i.e. different) operands in the program;

3. N_1 is the total number of occurrences of operators;

4. N_2 is the total number of occurrences of operands;

Figure 10.5 contains a simple sorting program. Tables 10.1 and 10.2 list the operators and operands of this program together with their frequency. Note that there is no generally agreed upon definition of what exactly an operator or operand is. So the numbers given have no absolute meaning. This is part of the critique of this theory.

Using the primitive entities defined above Halstead defines a number of derived entities, such as:

— Size of the vocabulary: $n = n_1 + n_2$.

— Program length: $N = N_1 + N_2$.

```
1        procedure sort(var x: array; n: integer);
2        var i, j, save: integer;
3        begin
4           for i:= 2 to n do
5              for j:= 1 to i do
6                 if x[i] < x[j] then
7                    begin save:= x[i];
8                          x[i]:= x[j];
9                          x[j]:= save
10                   end
11       end;
```

Figure 10.5:   A simple sorting routine

Table 10.1:   Counting the number of operators

Operator	Number of occurrences
procedure	1
sort()	1
var	2
:	3
array	1
;	6
integer	2
,	2
begin ... end	2
for ... do	2
if ... then	1
:=	5
<	1
[]	6
$n_1 = 14$	$N_1 = 35$

— Program volume: $V = N \log_2 n$.
  This is just the minimal number of bits needed to store N elements from a set of cardinality n.

— Program level: $L = V^*/V$. Here V^* is the most compact representation of the algorithm in question. For the example in figure 10.5 this is *sort(x, n);* , so $n = N = 5$, and $V^* = 5 \log_2 5$. From the formula it follows that L is at most 1. Halstead postulates that the program level increases if the number of different operands increases, while it decreases if the number of different operators and/or the total number of operands increases. As an approximation of L he therefore suggests: $\hat{L} = (2/n_1)(n_2/N_2)$.

Table 10.2:   Counting the number of operands

Operand	Number of occurrences
x	7
n	2
i	6
j	5
save	3
2	1
1	1
$n_2 = 7$	$N_2 = 25$

— Programming effort: $E = V/L$.
The effort needed increases with volume and decreases as the program level increases. E represents the number of mental discriminations (decisions) to be taken while implementing the problem solution.

— Estimated programming time in seconds: $\hat{T} = E/18$.
The constant 18 is determined empirically. Halstead explains this number by referring to [Stroud67] where the speed with which human memory processes sensory input is discussed. This is said to go at 5–20 units per second. In Halstead's theory, the number 18 is chosen. This number is also referred to as Stroud's number.

The above entities can be determined only after the program has been written. It is also possible to get an estimate of a number of these entities. When doing so, the values for n_1 and n_2 are assumed to be known. Such could be the case, for instance, after the detailed design step. Halstead then estimates program length as:

$$\hat{N} = n_1 \log_2 n_1 + n_2 \log_2 n_2$$

An explanation for this formula can be given as follows. There are $n_1 2^{n1} * n_2 2^{n2}$ ways to combine the n given symbols such that operators and operands alternate. Next to the program we are looking for, this also results in a lot of rubbish. The program itself is organized, and organization generally attends with a logarithmic reduction in the number of possibilities. Doing so yields the above formula for $\hat{N}$.

Table 10.3 lists the values for a number of entities from Halstead's theory for the example program in figure 10.5.

A number of empirical studies have addressed the predictive value of Halstead's formulas. These studies often give positive evidence of the validity of the theory; see, for example, [Curtis79], [Elshoff76].

Table 10.3:   Values of 'software science' entities for the example program in figure 10.5

Entity	Value
Size vocabulary	21
Program length	60
Estimated program length	73
Program volume	264
Level of abstraction	0.044
Estimated level of abstraction	0.040
Programming effort	6000
Estimated programming time	333 s

The theory has also been heavily criticized. The underpinning of Halstead's formulas does not convince some people. [Coulter83] argues that results from cognitive psychology like Stroud's number are ill-used which weakens the theoretical foundation of the theory. [Hamer82] heavily criticizes the theory as well: Halstead concentrates on the coding phase and assumes that programmers are 100% devoted to a programming task for an uninterrupted period of time. Practice is likely to be quite different. [Moranda78] criticizes the statistical tests that are used to measure the relation between theory and reality. It is also noted that different people may use quite different definitions of the notions of operator and operand, which may lead to widely different outcomes for the values of entities [Shen83].

Yet, Halstead's work has been very influential. It was the first major body of work to point out the potential of software metrics for software development.

If we try to derive a complexity metric from the structure of a piece of software, we may focus on the control structure, the data structures, or a combination of these [Basili80].

If we base the complexity metric on the use of data structures, we may for instance do so by considering the number of instructions between successive references to one and the same object. If this number is large, information about these variables must be retained for a long period of time when we try to comprehend that program text. Following this line of thought, complexity can be related to the average number of variables for which information must be kept by the reader (see also chapter 17).

The best-known complexity metric from the class of structure-based complexity metrics is McCabe's *cyclomatic complexity* [McCabe76]. McCabe bases his complexity metric on a (directed) graph depicting the control flow of the program. He assumes that the graph of a single procedure or single main program has a unique start and end node, while each node is reachable from the start node and the end node can be reached from each node. In that case, the graph is connected. If the program consists of a main program and one or more procedures, then the control graph has a number of connected components, one for the main program and one for each of its procedures.

The cyclomatic complexity CV now equals the number of linear independent paths in this control graph. Its formula reads

$$CV = e - n + 2p,$$

where e, n and p denote the number of edges, nodes, and connected components in the control graph, respectively.

Figure 10.6 shows the control flow graph of the example program from figure 10.5. The numbers inside the nodes correspond to the line numbers from figure 10.5. The edges have been labelled with letters. The cyclomatic complexity of this graph is $15 - 11 + 2 = 6$. A set of linear independent paths for this graph is:

a–b–c–l–o
d–k
e–j
f–g–h–i
m
n

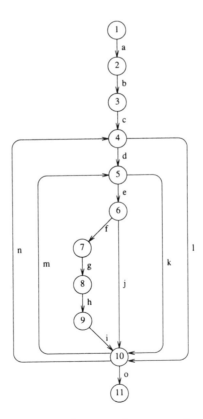

Figure 10.6:   Control flow graph of the example program from figure 10.5

Each possible execution-time path through this graph can be obtained through a linear combination of these linear independent paths.

McCabe suggests imposing an upper limit of ten for the cyclomatic complexity of a program component. McCabe's complexity metric is also applied to testing. One criterion used during testing is to get a good coverage of the possible paths through the program. Applying McCabe's cyclomatic complexity leads to a structured testing strategy involving the execution of all linearly independent paths (see also chapter 13).

As with Halstead's theory, we may try to establish a relation between cyclomatic complexity and required programming time. Woodfield, for example, established a (linear) relation with programming effort, based on data from a number of projects [Woodfield81a]:

$$T = \alpha CV + \beta$$

Here, α and β are constants whose values are obtained through regression analysis.

Complexity metrics like those of Halstead, McCabe and many others, all measure attributes which are in some sense related to the size of the task to be accomplished, be it the time in man-months, the number of lines of code, or something else. As such they may serve various purposes: determining the optimal size of a module, estimating the number of errors in a module, or estimating the cost of a piece of software.

All known complexity metrics suffer from some serious shortcomings, though [Harrison82]:

- They are not very context sensitive. For example, any program with five if-statements has the same cyclomatic complexity. Yet we may expect that different organizations of those if-statements (consecutive versus deeply nested, say) have their effect on the perceived complexity of those programs. In terms of measurement theory, this means that cyclometic complexity does not fulfill the 'representation condition' [Fenton91]. The representation condition says that the empirical relations should be preserved in the numerical relation system. If we empirically observe that program A is more complex than program B, then any complexity metric F should be such that $F_A > F_B$.

- They measure few facets only. Halstead's method does not take into account the control flow complexity, for instance.

We may formulate these shortcomings as follows: present complexity metrics do tell us something about the complexity of a program (i.e. a higher value is likely to induce a higher complexity), but the reverse certainly is not true. Complexity is made up of many specific attributes. According to [Fenton91] it is unlikely that there will be a 'general' complexity metric.

We should thus be very careful in the use of these complexity metrics. Since they seem to measure along different dimensions of what is perceived as complexity, the use of multiple metrics is likely to yield better insights. But even then the results must be interpreted with care. [Redmond90] for instance evaluated various complexity metrics for a few systems, including the MINIX operating system [Tanenbaum87]. Of the 277 modules, 34 have a cyclomatic complexity greater than ten. The highest value (58) was observed for a module that handles a number of ASCII escape character sequences from the keyboard. This module, and most others with a large cyclomatic complexity, were considered 'justifiably complex'. An attempt to reduce the complexity by splitting those modules would increase the difficulty of understanding them while artificially reducing its complexity value.

Finally, we may note that various validations of both software science and cyclomatic complexity indicate that they are not substantially better indicators of coding effort, maintainability, or reliability than the length of a program (number of lines of code) [Basili83], [Li87], [Shepperd88], [Wake88]. The latter is much easier to determine, though.

10.2.5 System structure

We may depict the outcome of the design process, a set of modules and their mutual dependencies, in a graph. The nodes of this graph correspond to modules, and the edges denote relations between modules. We may think of many types of intermodule relations, such as:

— module A contains module B;

— module A follows module B;

— module A delivers data to module B;

— module A uses module B.

The type of dependencies we are interested in are those that determine the complexity of the relations between modules. The amount of knowledge that modules have of each other should be kept minimal. To be able to assess this, it is important to know, for each module, which other modules it *uses*, since that tells us which knowledge of each other they (potentially) use. In a proper design the information flow between modules is restricted to flow that comes about through procedure calls. The graph depicting the uses-relation is therefore often termed **call graph**.

The call graph may have different shapes. In its most general form it is a directed graph (figure 10.7a).* If the graph is acyclic, i.e. it does not contain a

---

* We assume that the graph is connected, i.e. that there is a path between each pair of nodes if we ignore the direction of the arrows that link nodes. This assumption is reasonable, since otherwise the graph can be split into two or more disjoint graphs between which there is no information flow. These disjoint graphs then correspond to independent programs.

path of the form M_1, M_2, ..., M_n, M_1, the uses-relation forms a hierarchy. We may then decompose the graph in a number of distinct layers such that a module at one layer uses only modules from lower layers (figure 10.7b). Going one step further, we get at a scheme like the one in figure 10.7c, where modules from level i only use modules from level $i + 1$. Finally, if each module is used by one other module only, the graph reduces to a tree (figure 10.7d).

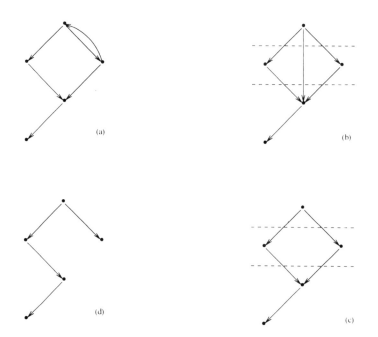

Figure 10.7:   Different module hierarchies. (a) directed graph, (b) directed acyclic graph, (c) layered graph, (d) tree

There are various aspects of the call graph that can be measured [Fenton91]. Directly measurable attributes that relate to the 'shape' of the call graph include:

- its *size*, measured in terms of the number of nodes, the number of edges, or the sum of these;
- its *depth*, the length of the longest path from the root to some leaf node (in an acyclic directed graph);
- its *width*, the maximum number of nodes at some level (in an acyclic directed graph).

We do not know of studies that try to quantitatively relate those measures to other complexity-related aspects such as debugging time, maintainability, etc. They may be used, though, as one of the parameters in a qualitative assessment of a design.

It is often stated that a good design should have a tree-like call graph. It is therefore worthwhile to consider the **tree impurity** of a call graph, i.e. the extent to which the graph deviates from a pure tree. Suppose we start with a connected (undirected) graph (like the ones in figures 10.7b–d if we ignore the direction of the arrows). If the graph is not a tree, it has at least one cycle, i.e. a path from some node A via one or more other nodes back to A again. We may then remove one of the edges from this cycle, and the result will still be a connected graph. We may continue removing edges from cycles until the result is a tree. We did so in the transition from figure 10.7b to 10.7c to 10.7d. The final result is called the graph's **spanning tree**. The number of edges removed in this process is an indication of the graph's tree impurity.

In order to obtain a proper measure of tree impurity we proceed as follows. The complete graph K_n is the graph with n nodes and the maximum number of edges. This maximum number of edges is $n(n - 1)/2$. A tree with n nodes has $(n - 1)$ edges. Given a connected graph G with n nodes and e edges, we define its tree impurity $m(G)$ as the number of extra edges divided by the maximum number of extra edges:

$$m(G) = 2(e - n + 1)/(n - 1)(n - 2)$$

This measure of tree impurity fits our intuitive notion of that concept. The value of $m(G)$ lies between 0 and 1. It is 0 if G is a tree, and 1 if it is a complete graph. If we add an edge to G, the value of $m(G)$ increases. Moreover, the 'penalty' of extra edges is proportional to the size of the spanning tree [Fenton91].

From the example given in section 10.1 we see that the uses-structure is closely allied to the different levels of abstraction. The modules in decomposition 1 are at the same level and we may observe a fairly complex interaction between them. Each module from decomposition 2 only uses modules from the same level, or 'lower' levels. These lower levels are 'closer' to the executable machine. Here, the structure is hierarchical.

In retrospect, we observe that the system is decomposed into subcomponents in modularization 1 such that each subcomponent ranges over all levels of abstraction. In modularization 2 we may distinguish several layers of abstraction. Decisions that bring us closer to the executable machine lead to modules from a lower layer. This philosophy has considerably contributed to the simplicity of the relations between modules.

It is not always easy, or even meaningful, to strive for a neat hierarchical decomposition. We will often have to settle for a compromise. It may for instance be appropriate to decompose a system into a number of clusters, each of which contains a number of modules. The clusters may then be organized hierarchically, while the modules within a given cluster show a more complicated interaction pattern. Also, tree-like call graphs do not allow for reuse (if a module is reused within the same program, its node in the call graph has at least two ancestors).

The call graph allows us to assess the structure of a design. In deriving the measures above, each edge in the call graph is treated alike. Yet, the complexity of the information flow that is represented by the edges is likely to vary. As noted in the earlier discussion on coupling, we would like the intermodule connections to be 'thin'. Therefore, we would like a measure which does not merely count the edges, but which also considers the amount of information that flows through them.

The best-known attempt to measure the total level of information flow between the modules of a system is due to Henri and Kafura [Henri81]. Their measures were able to identify change-prone UNIX procedures and evaluate potential design changes. Shepperd extensively studied the information flow measure and proposed several refinements, thus obtaining a 'purer' metric [Shepperd90]. Using Shepperd's definitions, the information flow measure is based on the following notions of local and global data flow:

- A **local flow** from module A to module B exists if
  (a) A invokes B and passes it a parameter, or
  (b) B invokes A and A returns a value.

- A **global flow** from module A to module B exists if A updates some global data structure and B retrieves from that structure.

Using these notions of local and global data flow, Shepperd defines the 'complexity' of a module M as

$$complexity(M) = (fan\text{-}in(M) * fan\text{-}out(M))^2$$

where

- fan-in(M) is the number of (local and global) flows whose sink is M, and
- fan-out(M) is the number of (local and global) flows whose source is M.

A weak point of the information flow metric is that all flows have equal weight. For instance, the fan-in and fan-out module `Shift` in modularization 1 of the KWIC-index example is 2 (`Shift` reads the variables `Store` and `NumberOfLines`, while it updates variables `Shifts` and `ShiftIndex`). The corresponding module from the second modularization has a fan-in of 7 and a fan-out of 5 (if unique data items are counted once only). Yet, the information flow both to and from the latter looks simpler. It concerns only simple integers and characters.

In a more qualitative sense, the information flow metric may indicate spots in the design that deserve our attention. If some module has a high fan-in, this may indicate that the module has little cohesion. Also, if we consider the information flow per layer, an excessive increase from one layer to the next might indicate a missing level of abstraction [Yin78].

Though much work remains to be done, a judicious use of available design metrics already is a valuable tool in the design and quality assurance of software systems.

10.3 DESIGN METHODS

Having discussed the properties of a good system decomposition, we now come to a question which is at least as important: how do you get a good decomposition to start with?

There exists a vast number of design methods, a sample of which is given in table 10.4. These design methods generally consist of a set of guidelines, heuristics, and procedures on how to go about designing a system. Next to that, they offer a notation to express the result of the design process. Together these provide a *systematic* means for organizing and structuring the design process and its products.

For some, such as FSM or Petrinets, emphasis is on the notation, while the guidelines as to how to go about during design are not very well developed. Methods like JSD on the other hand offer extensive prescriptive guidelines as well. Most notations are graphical and somewhat informal, but OBJ and Meta IV use a very formal mathematical language. Some methods concentrate on the design stage proper, while others are part of a wider methodology covering other life cycle phases as well. Examples of the latter are SSADM and JSD. Finally, some methods offer features that make them especially useful for the design of certain types of applications, such as SA/WM (real time systems) or Petrinets (concurrent systems).

In the following subsections we discuss four design methods often used:

- Functional decomposition. Functional decomposition is a rather general approach to system design. It is not tied to any specific method listed in table 10.4. To depict the resulting design, many different notations can be used, ranging from flowcharts or pseudocode to algebraic specifications.

- Data flow design, as exemplified by SA/SD.

- Design based on data structures, as is done in JSP, LCP and JSD.

- Object-oriented design. Whereas the first three methods concentrate on identifying the functions of the system, object-oriented design focuses on the data that the system is to operate on. This method has become very popular of late.

A fifth design method, the constructive use of pre- and postconditions in the derivation and specification of software, is addressed in the chapter on specifications.

Table 10.4: A sample of design methods

Name	Description
Decision tables	Matrix representation of complex decision logic at the detailed design level.
Draco	Framework to design domain-specific representation languages and transformations between those languages; see also chapter 16.
E–R	Entity–Relationship Model. Family of graphical techniques for expressing data-relationships [Chen76].
Flowcharts	Simple diagram technique to show control flow at the detailed design level. Exists in many flavors, see [Tripp88] for an overview.
FSM	Finite State Machine: way to describe a system as a set of states and possible transitions between those states; the resulting diagrams are called state transition diagrams.
JSD	Jackson System Development; see section 10.3.3. Successor to, and more elaborate than, JSP; has an object-oriented flavor.
JSP	Jackson Structured Programming. Data structure oriented method; see section 10.3.3.
KEE	Knowledge representation system. Though primarily intended for the development of expert systems, its representational features are also of potential interest for the development of other types of software [Wall86].
LCP	Logical Construction of Programs, also known as the Warnier–Orr method; data structure oriented, similar to JSP.
Meta IV	Model oriented specification language of VDM; highly mathematical [Björner82]; see appendix B.
NoteCards	Example hypertext system. Hypertext systems make it possible to create and navigate through a complex organization of unstructured pieces of text [Conklin87].
OBJ	Algebraic specification method; highly mathematical [Goguen86b].
OOD	Object oriented design; exists in many flavors, see section 10.3.4.
PDL	Program Design Language; example of a constrained natural language ('structured English') to describe designs at various levels of abstraction. Offers the control constructs generally found in programming languages. See [Caine75] for an example, and [Pintelas89] for an overview.
Petrinets	Graphical design representation, well-suited for concurrent systems. A system is described as a set of states and possible transitions between those states. States are associated with tokens and transitions are described by firing rules. In this way, concurrent activities can be synchronized [Peterson81].
PSL/PSA	Program Statement Language/Program Statement Analyzer. Semi-formal language to describe and analyze a large number of system aspects; see section 9.3.2.

Table 10.4: cont'd

Name	Description
SA/SD	Structured Analysis/Structured Design. Data flow design technique; see also section 10.3.2.
SA/WM	Ward–Mellor extension to Structured Analysis so that real-time aspects can be described [Ward85].
SADT	Structured Analysis and Design Technique. Graphical language emphasizing hierarchical relations; see also section 9.3.1.
SARA	System ARchitects Apprentice. Design environment to support the development of concurrent systems; supported by a number of tools [Estrin86].
SREM	Builds on PSL/PSA, intended for real-time applications [Alford77].
SSADM	Structured Systems Analysis and Design Method. A highly prescriptive method for performing the analysis and design stages; UK standard [Downs88].
Statecharts	Finite state transition diagrams, with extensions to allow for the expression of concurrency [Harel88].

10.3.1 Functional decomposition

Both decompositions discussed in section 10.1 are functional in nature. In a functional decomposition the intended function is decomposed into a number of subfunctions that each solve part of the problem. These subfunctions themselves may be further decomposed in yet more primitive functions, and so on. Functional decomposition is a design philosophy rather than a design method. It denotes an overall approach to problem decomposition which underlies many a design method.

With functional decomposition we apply **divide-and-conquer** tactics. These tactics are analogous to, but not the same as, the technique of **stepwise refinement** as it is applied in programming-in-the-small [Wirth71].

Using stepwise refinement, the refinements tend to be context-dependent. As an example, consider the following pseudo-code algorithm to insert an element into a sorted list:

```
procedure insert(a, n, x);
begin insert x at the end of the list;
    k:= n + 1;
    while element_k is not at its proper place
    do swap element_k and element_{k-1};
        k:= k-1
    enddo;
end insert;
```

The refinement of a pseudo-code instruction like `element_k is not at its proper place` is done within the context of exactly the above routine, using knowledge of other parts of this routine. In the decomposition of a large system, it is precisely this type of dependency that we try to avoid. The previous section addressed this issue at great length.

During requirements analysis the base machine has been decided upon. This base machine need not be a 'real' machine. It can also be a programming language or some other set of primitives that constitutes the bottom layer of the design. During this phase too, the functions to be provided to the user have been fixed. These are the two ends of a rope. During the design phase we try to get from one end of this rope to the other. If we start from the user function end and take successively more detailed design decisions, the process is called top-down design. The reverse is called bottom-up design.

Top-down design Starting from the main user functions, the top, we work down by decomposition of functions into subfunctions. Assuming we do not make any mistakes on the way down, we can be sure to construct the system specified.

With top-down design, each step is characterized by the design decisions it embodies. To be able to apply a pure top-down technique, the system has to be fully described. This is hardly ever the case.

Bottom-up design Using bottom-up design, we start from a set of base functions available. From there we proceed towards the requirements specification through abstraction. This technique is potentially more flexible, especially since the lower layers of the design could be independent of the application and thus have wider applicability. This is especially important if the requirements have not been formulated very precisely yet, or if a family of systems has to be developed.

A real danger of the bottom-up technique is that we miss the target.

In its pure form, neither the top-down nor the bottom-up technique is likely to be used all that often. Both techniques are feasible only if the design process is a pure and rational one. And this is an idealization of reality. There are many reasons why the design process cannot be rational. Some of these have to do with the intangibles of design processes per se, some originate from accidents that happen to befall many a software project. Parnas lists the following such reasons, amongst others [Parnas86]:

— Mostly, users do not know exactly what they want and they are not able to tell all they know.

— Even if the requirements are fully known, a lot of additional information is needed. This information is discovered only when the project is under way.

— Almost all projects are subject to change. Changes influence earlier decisions.

— People make errors.

— During design, people use the knowledge they already have, experiences from earlier projects, and the like.

— In many projects we do not start from scratch, but we build from existing software.

Design exhibits a 'yo-yo' character. Something is being devised, tried, rejected again, new ideas crop up, etc. Designers frequently go about in rather opportunistic ways. They frequently switch from high-level application domain issues to coding and detailed design matters, and use a variety of means to gather insight into the problem to be solved [Guindon88], [Rosson88]. At most, we may present the result of the design process as if it came about through a rational process [Parnas86].

A general problem with any form of functional decomposition is that it is not immediately clear along which dimension the system is decomposed, as is shown in the example given in section 10.1. If we decompose along the time-axis, modules like the ones from modularization 1 result. In Yourdon's classification, the resulting cohesion type is temporal [Yourdon75]. If we decompose with respect to the grouping of data we obtain the type of data cohesion exhibited in modularization 2.

Parnas offers the following useful guidelines for a sound functional decomposition [Parnas78]:

1. Try to identify subsystems. Start with a *minimal* subset and next define minimal extensions to this subset.

     The idea behind this guideline is that it is extremely difficult, if not impossible, to get a complete picture of the system during requirements analysis. People ask too much, or they ask the wrong things. Starting from a minimal subsystem, we may add functionality incrementally, using the experience gained with the actual use of the system. The idea is very similar to that of incremental development, as discussed in chapter 3.

2. Apply the information-hiding principle.

3. Try to define extensions to the base machine step by step. This holds for both the minimal machine and its extensions. Such incremental extensions lead to the concept of a **virtual machine**. Each layer in the system hierarchy can be viewed as a machine. The primitive operations of this machine are implemented by the lower layers of the hierarchy. This machine view of the module hierarchy adds a further dimension to the system structuring guidelines offered in section 10.2.5.

4. Apply the uses-relation and try to place the dependencies thus obtained in a hierarchical structure.

Obviously, the above guidelines are strongly interrelated. It has been said before that a strictly hierarchical tree structure of system components is often not

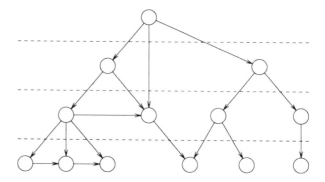

Figure 10.8: A layered system structure

feasible. A compromise that often is feasible is a layered system structure as depicted in figure 10.8.

The arrows between the various nodes in the graph indicate the uses-relation. Various levels can be distinguished in the structure depicted. Components at a given level only use components from the same, or lower, levels. The layers distinguished in this picture are not the same as those induced by the acyclicity of the graph (as discussed in section 10.2.5) but are rather the result of viewing a distinct set of modules as an abstract, virtual machine. Deciding on how to group modules into layers in this way involves considering the semantics of those modules. Lower levels in this hierarchy bring us closer to the 'real' machine on which the system is going to be executed. Higher levels are more application-oriented. The choice for the number of levels in such an architecture is a, problem-dependent, design decision.

10.3.2 Data flow design

The data flow design technique originated with Yourdon and Constantine [Yourdon75] and is also known as **composite design** or **structured design**. In its simplest form it is but a functional decomposition with respect to the flow of data. A component (module) is a black box which transforms some input stream into some output stream. There are various graphical conventions for depicting those data flow diagrams. We will use the notation from [Gane79].

Four types of data entities are distinguished in data flow diagrams:

External entities: the source or destination of a transaction. These entities are located outside the domain considered in the data flow diagram. External entities are indicated as squares.

Processes, inside which the transformation of data takes place. Processes are denoted by squares with rounded angles.

Data flows between processes, external entities and data stores. A data flow is indicated by an arrow. Data flows are paths along which data structures travel.

Data stores in between two processes. This is indicated by two parallel lines with the name of the data store in between. Data stores are places where data structures are stored until needed.

At the highest level we draw a **context diagram** in which the environment (the collection of external entities) of the system is indicated. This is done for the KWIC-index example in figure 10.9. This diagram must be supplemented by a description of the structure of both the input and output.

Figure 10.9:   Context diagram for the KWIC-index program

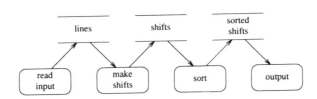

Figure 10.10:   Data flow diagram for the KWIC-index program

This top-level diagram is next further decomposed. For our example, this could lead to the data flow diagram of figure 10.10. In the lower level diagrams, the external entities are usually omitted. For more complicated applications, various diagrams could be drawn, one for each subsystem identified. These subsystems in turn are further decomposed into diagrams at yet lower levels. We thus get a hierarchy of diagrams.

These diagrams constitute part of the **context model**. As well as these diagrams, the context model also contains natural language descriptions of each of the processes and the structure of each data store in a **data dictionary**.

This data dictionary contains the documentation of all components from the set of data flow diagrams. The smallest unit of information in the analysis is called a **data item**. Data items are combined into **data structures**. For data items, the data dictionary contains at least its name and type. For data structures it is indicated how these are built out of their components. Deciding on *how* to structure the data involves techniques from the realm of data base design, such as normalization; see for instance [Date86]. The data structures are next used to document the elements of the data flow diagrams:

- For processes, the incoming and outgoing data flows are specified. A short description of the transformation realized is given, as well as a more detailed description of the logic of that transformation. For the latter, a variety of techniques is available, including structured English and decision tables.

- For data flows, a specification of its structure is given, together with an indication of its source and sink, and possibly an indication of its volume.

- For data stores, a specification of its structure is given, together with a list of data flows leading to and from the store.

The context model is a logical model of the system. In a subsequent step a **structured design** is derived from the data flow diagrams. The structured design is expressed in a hierarchical set of **structure charts**. There are no strict rules for this step. Text books on the data flow technique do give guidelines, and sometimes even well-defined strategies, for how to get from a context model to a hierarchical model for the implementation [Gane79], [DeMarco79]. These guidelines are strongly inspired by the various notions discussed in section 10.2, most notably cohesion and coupling.

The major heuristic involves the choice for the top level structure chart. Many data processing systems are essentially transform centered. Input is read and possibly edited, a major transformation is done, and the result is output. One way to decide upon the central transformation is to trace the input through the data flow diagram until it can no longer be considered input. The same is done, in the other direction, for the output. From this we may directly derive the global hierarchy of the system, as is depicted in figure 10.11.

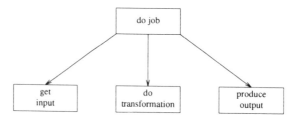

Figure 10.11: Global system hierarchy

For our example, it is not a priori clear which bubble(s) from the data flow diagram represent the central transformation. There are three feasible solutions:

1. Shift is the central transformation, and the sorting process is considered part of the output process;

2. Sort is the central transformation, and producing the shifts is considered part of the input process;

3. Shift and Sort together constitute the central process.

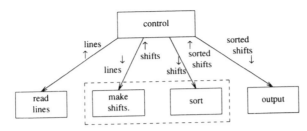

Figure 10.12: Structure chart for the KWIC-index program

In the structure chart given in figure 10.12, we have opted for the latter solution. The single arrows in this picture denote control flow, while the data flow is indicated by the symbol →.

Because of the tranformation orientation of the structure chart, the relations between modules in the graph have a producer–consumer character. One module produces a stream of data which is then consumed by another module. The control flow is one whereby modules call subordinate modules so as to realize the required transformation. There is a potentially complex stream of information between modules, corresponding to the data flow that is passed between producer and consumer. The guidelines used in the transformation from data flow diagrams to structure charts aim to reduce the complexity of the interaction between modules, though.

In the above discussion, we viewed data flow design as a two-step process. First, a logical design is derived in the form of a set of data flow diagrams. Next, this logical design is transformed into a program structure represented as a set of structure charts.

Sometimes, an explicit distinction is made between these two steps. The two steps are then referred to as *Structured Analysis* and *Structured Design*, respectively. Structured analysis can be viewed as a proper requirements analysis method insofar it addresses the modeling of some Universe of Discourse. It should be noted though that, as data flow diagrams get refined, the analyst performs an implicit functional decomposition of the system as well. At the same time, the diagram refinements result in corresponding data refinements. The analysis process thus has design aspects as well.

Structured Design, being a strategy to map the information flow contained in data flow diagrams into program structure, is a genuine component of the design phase.

10.3.3 Design based on data structures

The best-known technique for design based on data structures originates with Jackson [Jackson75]. The technique is known as JSP—Jackson Structured

Programming. Essentials of JSP have been carried over to JSD—Jackson System Development [Jackson83]. We will discuss both methods in turn.

The basic idea of JSP is that a good program reflects the structure of both the input and the output in all its facets. Given a correct model of these data structures, we may straightforwardly derive the corresponding program from the model.

Jackson distinguishes elementary and compound components. Elementary components are not further decomposed. There are three types of compound components: sequence, iteration and selection. Compound components are represented by diagrams (also called **Jackson diagrams** or **structure diagrams**) and/or some sort of pseudocode (called **structure text** or **schematic logic**). The base forms of both are given in figure 10.13.

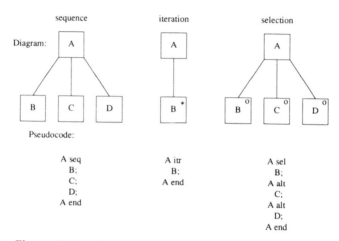

Figure 10.13:   Compound components in Jackson's notation

In Jackson's notation the global structure of the input and output of the KWIC-index program are as given in figure 10.14. These structure diagrams should be read as: 'the input consists of zero or more lines' and 'the output consists of zero or more lines'.

For each of these diagrammatic notations for the structure of data or, for that matter, the corresponding pseudocode, notations in most modern programming languages are available (loops, if-statements and sequential composition). The essence of Jackson's technique is that the structure diagrams of the input and output can be merged, thus yielding the global structure of the program. This is rather simply demonstrated for the diagrams in figure 10.14 and the resulting program has the following structure:

```
until EOF loop
    read line;
    process line;
    write line
endloop.
```

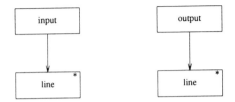

Figure 10.14:   Global structure of the data in Jackson's diagram notation

Obviously, this does not work for our problem. The cause is something called a **structure clash**: the input and output data structures do not really match. The reasons are twofold. First, the repetition at the input side is not the same as the repetition at the output side. One input line in general results in a number of output lines. Secondly, the shifts have to be sorted before being output. As a consequence, we have to restructure the system, for instance as depicted in figure 10.15.

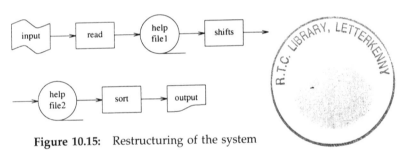

Figure 10.15:   Restructuring of the system

A clear disadvantage of the structure thus obtained is that there are now two intermediate files. Closer inspection shows that we do not really need the first of those. This is immediately clear if we depict the first part of the structure as done in figure 10.16.

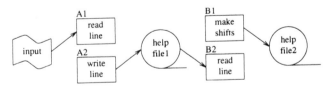

Figure 10.16:   A different view of the system

Here, we may *invert* component A1 and code it such that it may serve as a replacement of component B2. Alternatively, we may invert B1 and substitute the result for component A2. In either case, the FIFO (first in, first out)-type intermediate file in between the two components is removed by making one of the components a subordinate of the other. The second structure clash cannot be circumvented.

This example shows the fundamental issues involved in the use of JSP:

- modeling input and output using structure diagrams,

- merging these to create the program structure, meanwhile

- resolving possible structure clashes, and finally

- optimizing the result through program inversion.

The hierarchy in the structure diagrams denotes a relation of the type 'consists of' between components of the data structures. The same type of relation occurs in the resulting modular structure of the system.

If we choose a linear notation for the structure diagrams, the result falls into the class of 'regular expressions' [Hopcroft79]. Thus, the expressive power of these diagrams is that of a finite automaton. Some of the structure clashes crop up if the problem cannot be solved by a finite automaton.

For a fuller exposition of JSP, the reader is referred to [Jackson75] or [King88]. JSP is very similar to a method developed by J.-D. Warnier in France at about the same time [Warnier74]. The latter is known as LCP (Logical Construction of Programs) or the Warnier–Orr method, after Ken Orr who was instrumental in the translation of Warnier's work.

Both in the functional decomposition and in the data flow design methods, the problem structure is mapped onto a functional structure. This functional structure is next mapped onto a program structure. In contrast, JSP maps the problem structure onto a data structure, and the program structure is derived from this data structure. JSP is not much concerned with the question as to how the mapping from problem structure to data structure is to be obtained.

JSD—Jackson System Development—tries to fill this gap. The key concepts of JSD are discussed below. For a fuller exposition of this method, see [Jackson83], [Cameron89] or [Sutcliffe88]. The graphical notations used are those of [Sutcliffe88].

JSD distinguishes three stages in the software development process:

1. A **modeling stage** in which a description is made of the real world problem through the identification of entities and actions.

2. A **network stage** in which the system is modeled as a network of communicating concurrent processes.

3. An **implementation stage** in which the network of processes is transformed into a sequential design.

The first step in JSD is to model the part of reality we are interested in, the UoD. JSD models the UoD as a set of entities, objects in the real world that participate in a time-ordered sequence of actions. For each entity a process is created which models the life cycle of that entity. Actions are events that happen to an entity. For instance, in a library the life cycle of an entity Book could be as depicted in figure 10.17. The life cycle of a book starts when it is acquired. After that it may be borrowed and returned any number of times. The life cycle ends when the book is either archived or disposed of. The life cycle is depicted using **process structure diagrams** (PSDs). PSDs are hierarchical diagrams that resemble the structure diagrams of JSP, with its primitives to denote concatenation (ordering in time), repetition and selection. PSDs have a pseudocode equivalent called **structure text** which looks like the schematic logic of JSP.

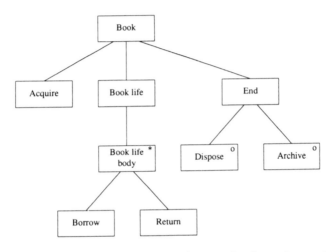

Figure 10.17: Process structure diagram for the entity Book

Process structure diagrams are finite state diagrams. In traditional finite state diagrams, the bubbles (nodes) represent possible states of the entity being modelled while the arrows denote possible transitions between states. The opposite is true for PSDs. In a PSD, nodes denote state transitions and arrows denote states.

In the same way, an entity Member can be described as is done in figure 10.18: members enter the library system, after which they may borrow and return books until they cease to be a member.

The modeling stage is concerned with identifying entities and the events (actions) that happen to them. These actions collectively constitute the life cycle of an entity. As with other design methods, there is no simple recipe to determine the set of entities and actions. The approach generally taken has a linguistic stance. From notes, documentation, interviews and the like, we may draw up a preliminary list of actions and entities. One heuristic used is to look for real-world objects that the system is to interact with. Since a library is all about books, an

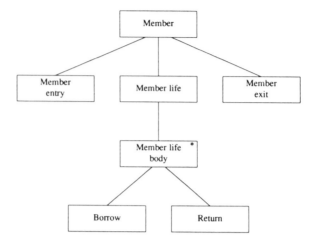

Figure 10.18:   Process structure diagram for the entity `Member`

entity `Book` immediately suggests itself. From statements like 'members borrow books' we may infer that an event `Borrow` occurs in the life cycle of both books and members. Once such a preliminary list is made up, further reflection should lead to a precisely demarcated life cycle of the entities identified.

Entities are made up of actions. These actions are atomic, i.e. they cannot be further decomposed into subactions. Actions respond to events in the real-world. The action `Acquire` that is part of the life cycle of the entity `Book` is triggered when a real-world event, the actual acquisition of a book, takes place. In the process structure diagram, actions show up as leaf nodes.

Events are communicated to the system through data messages, called **attributes**. In a procedural sense these attributes constitute the parameters of the action. For the action `Acquire` we may have such attributes as `ISBN`, `date-of-acquisition`, `title` and `authors`.

Entities have attributes as well: local variables that keep information from the past and collectively determine its state. The entity `Book` for example may retain some or all of the information that was provided upon acquisition (`ISBN`, `title`, etc.). Next to that, entities have two special attributes. First, the *identifier attribute* uniquely identifies the entity. Second, each entity has an attribute which indicates its status. This attribute can be viewed as a pointer to some leaf node of the process structure diagram.

Each entity can be viewed as a separate, long-running, process. In the library example, each book and each member has its own life cycle. The processes though are not completely independent. They communicate and synchronize by sending messages. During the network stage the system is modelled as a network of interconnected processes. This network is depicted in a **system specification diagram** (SSD).

The major type of interprocess communication is shown in figure 10.19. Recall that the actions `Borrow` and `Return` occur in the life cycle of both `Book`

Figure 10.19:   Datastream between processes Member and Book

and `Member` (see figures 10.17 and 10.18). Such common actions create a link between these entities. As a consequence, the life cycles of these entities will be synchronized with respect to these events.

A member may borrow and return books. Doing so produces a **datastream** BR, which is read by the process `Book` on a FIFO basis. There may be multiple instances of both the `Member` and `Book` process type. This many-to-many relation is indicated by the double bar on either side of the bubble. If there is no double bar, or it shows up on one side only, there is a 1–1 or 1–n (n–1) relation, respectively, between the entities.

The final stage of JSD is the implementation stage. In the implementation stage the concurrent model that is the result of the network stage is transformed into an executable system. One of the key concepts for this stage is **program inversion**: the communication between processes is replaced by a procedure call, so that one process becomes a subordinate to another process. This is very similar to the notion of program inversion as present in JSP.

10.3.4 Object oriented design (and analysis)

My guess is that object-oriented programming will be in the 1980s what structured programming was in the 1970s. Everyone will be in favor of it. Every manufacturer will promote his products as supporting it. Every manager will pay lip service to it. Every programmer will practice it (differently). And no one will know just what it is.
T. Rentsch, Object-oriented programming, *SIGPLAN Notices* **17**, 9 (1982) 51–57.

My cat is object-oriented.
R. King, **in** W. Kim & F. Lochovsky (Eds), *Object Oriented Concepts, Databases and Applications*, Addison-Wesley (1989) pp 23–30.

Every now and then some people claim to have found the ultimate solution to the software crisis. In the 1970s, structured programming was widely claimed to provide a definite answer to our problems. For a while, everything had to be structured: structured methods, structured design, structured testing, etc. Though many of these developments have considerably advanced the field of software engineering, our problems have not disappeared yet.

Something similar is presently happening with the adjective object-oriented. Today, objects are 'the right stuff'. We have object-oriented languages, object-oriented data bases, object-oriented design methods, etc. But, as has been argued convincingly in [Brooks87], there is no silver bullet. Software development will simply remain a difficult and painstaking process. At the same time we must admit that the object-oriented viewpoint does have a number of advantages over other approaches. These advantages make it into an approach worthwhile considering.

The concept of object orientation has its roots in the development of programming languages, most notably Simula 67 and Smalltalk. These language issues of object orientation will be dealt with in chapter 12. With respect to design (and requirements analysis), object orientation is best viewed by highlighting the differences with more traditional design methods such as functional decomposition and data flow design. As noted in our discussion on JSD, these traditional techniques focus on identifying the *functions* that the system is to perform. In contrast, object-oriented methods focus on identifying and interrelating the *objects* that play a role in the system.

The world around us is full of objects, animate and inanimate, concrete and abstract: trees and tables, cars and legal cases. Objects are characterized by a set of attributes (properties). A table has legs, a table top, size, color, etc. At the programming language level, objects that have the same set of attributes are said to belong to the same *class*. Individual objects of a class are called *instances* of that class. So we may have a class `Table`, with instances `MyTable` and `YourTable`. These instances have the same attributes, with possibly different values. They must be different for at least one attribute value, for otherwise they cannot be distinguished.

Collectively, the set of attributes of an object constitutes its state. In the object-oriented approach, however, an object not only encapsulates its *state*, but also its *behavior*, i.e. the way in which it acts upon other objects and is acted upon by other objects. The behavior of an object is described in terms of *services* provided by that object. These services are realized by *sending messages*, from the object that requests the service to the object that is acted upon.

The major behavioral aspect of an object concerns state changes. The state of an object instance is not static, but changes over time: the object instance is created, updated, and eventually destroyed. Also, certain information may be requested from an object. This information may concern the state of the object instance, but it may also involve a computation of some sort.

For example, a customer of a library may have attributes like `Name`, `Address`, and `BooksOnLoan`. It must be possible to create an instance of the object type `Customer`. When doing so, suitable values for its attributes must be provided. Once the instance has been created, state changes are possible: books are loaned and returned, the customer changes address, etc. Finally, the instance is destroyed when the customer ceases to be a member. Information requested may concern such things as a list of books on loan, or the number of books on loan. The former is part of the state that describes a particular customer and can be directly retrieved from that state. `NumberOfBooksOnLoan` is a service that requires a computation of some sort, for example the counting of the number of elements in `BooksOnLoan`.

In the discussion below, we will generally not be concerned with individual objects. Our goal at this stage is to identify and relate the object types (i.e. classes). Following [Coad90], we will simply use the term object to denote an object type.

We may then define an object as follows [Coad90]: 'An Object is an encapsulation and an abstraction: an encapsulation of Attributes and exclusive Services on those Attributes; an abstraction of the problem space, representing one or more occurrences of something in the problem space.'

One of our major concerns during object-oriented analysis and design is to identify this set of objects, together with their attributes (state) and services (behavior).

Relations between objects can be expressed in a classification structure. If we have objects Table and Chair, we may also define a more general object Furniture. Table and Chair are said to be *specializations* of Furniture, while Furniture is a *generalization* of Table and Chair. These relations are also known as 'is-a' relations. The is-a relation is a well-known concept from entity–relationship modeling [Chen76].

The generalization/specialization relations can be expressed in a hierarchical structure like the one in figure 10.20. In its most general form the classification structure is a directed acyclic graph. Many classification structures can be depicted as a tree though, in which case each object is a direct descendant of exactly one other object.

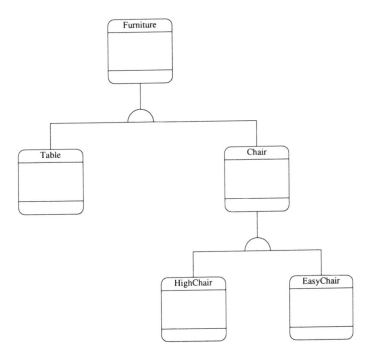

Figure 10.20: Object hierarchy

Different objects may share some of their attributes. Both tables and chairs have a height, for instance. Rather than defining the full set of attributes for each object, we may define common attributes at a higher level in the object hierarchy, and let descendants *inherit* those attributes. We may therefore define the attribute `Height` at the level of `Furniture` rather than at the level of each of its descendants. Obviously, this is just a dual way of looking at the object hierarchy. The fact that `Chair` and `Table` are both descendants of `Furniture` already suggests that they share certain properties, properties that are common to the various types of furniture. The fact that they are different descendants of `Furniture` also suggests that they each have unique properties as well.

We may alternatively view the object hierarchy as a *type hierarchy*. `Chair` and `Table` are *subtypes* of `Furniture`, just like `Cardinal` is a subtype of `Integer`. In this view, an object is a restriction of the object(s) of which it is a specialization. Each chair is a piece of furniture, but the reverse is not generally true.

By explicitly relating objects in the object hierarchy, a much tighter semantic binding between related objects is realized than is possible in more traditional design approaches. In a functional decomposition of our library automation problem for example, there is virtually no way to make the similarities between books and journals explicit in the design. In an object oriented design, objects `Book` and `Journal` can be made descendants of a more general object `Publication`, and attributes like `Publisher` can be inherited from this more general type of object.

The above discussion identified the key concepts that play a role in the object-oriented approach to analysis and design: objects, attributes and services, classification, and inheritance. It follows quite naturally from the above that the object-oriented approach to systems analysis and design involves three major steps:

1. identify the objects;

2. determine their attributes and services;

3. determine the object hierarchy.

Obviously, these steps are highly interrelated and some form of iteration will be needed before the final design is obtained. The guidelines for finding objects and their attributes and services are mostly linguistic in nature, much like the ones discussed in the previous section on JSD. Indeed, the modeling stage of JSD is object-oriented too. The guidelines presented below are based on [Coad90]. Their general flavor is similar to that found in other object-oriented approaches, such as those presented in [Booch91] and [Wirfs-Brock90].

A major guiding principle for identifying objects is to look for important concepts from the application domain. Objects to be found in a library include `Books`, `FileCabinets`, `Customers`, etc. In an office environment, we may have `Folders`, `Letters`, `Clerks`, etc. These domain-specific entities are our prime candidates for objects. They may be real-world objects like books, roles played like the customer of a library, organizational units like a department, locations like an office, or devices like a printer. Potential objects can also be found by considering existing classification or assembly (whole-parts) structures. From interviews, documentation and the like, a first inventory of objects can be made.

We next identify the attributes of objects. Attributes describe an instance of an object. Collectively, the attributes constitute the state of the object. Attributes are identified by considering the characteristics that distinguish individual instances, yet are common properties of the instances of an object type. We thereby look for atomic attributes rather than composite ones. For our library customer, we would for example obtain attributes `Name` and `Address` rather than a composite attribute `NameAndAddress`. At this stage, we also try to prevent redundancies in the set of attributes. So rather than having attributes `BooksOnLoan` and `NumberOfBooksOnLoan`, we settle for the former only, since the latter can be computed from that attribute.

The major services provided by an object are those that relate to the object's life cycle: an object instance is created, updated zero or more times, and finally it gets destroyed. Finite state diagrams depicting the possible states of an object and the transitions between those states are a good help in modeling this life cycle. We discussed a variant hereof, PSDs in the previous section.

A second type of service concerns those that provide information about the state of an object. These services may or may not involve some type of computation. Note that it is always possible to optimize the actual implementation by keeping redundant information in the state as it is maintained by the object. For example, we may decide to include the number of books on loan in the state as implemented, rather than computing it when required. This need not concern us at this stage though. Whether services are actually implemented by computational means or by a simple lookup procedure is invisible to the object that requests the information.

Note also that, over time, the set of attributes of and services provided by an object tends to evolve, while the object hierarchy remains relatively stable. If our library decides to offer an extra service to its customers, say borrowing records, we may simply adapt the set of attributes and extend the set of services for the object `Customer`.

Part of the classification of objects may result from the pre-existing real-world classifications that the system is to deal with. Further classification of objects into an object hierarchy involves a search for relations between objects. To start with, we may consider an object as a generalization of other possible objects. For instance, the object `Book` may be viewed as a generalization of objects `Novel`, `Poetry` and `ReferenceBook`. Whether these specializations are meaningful depends on the problem at hand. If the system does not need to distinguish between novels and poetry, we should not define separate objects for them either. The distinction between novels and poetry on the one hand and reference books on the other is sensible, though, if novels and poetry can be borrowed, but reference books cannot.

In a similar way, we may consider similarities between objects, thus viewing them as specializations of a more general object. If our library system calls for objects `Book` and `Journal` that have a number of attributes in common, we may introduce a new object `Publication` as a generalization of these objects. The common attributes are lifted to the object `Publication`; `Book` and `Journal` then inherit these attributes. Note that generalizations should still reflect meaningful real-world entities. There is no point in introducing a generalization of `Book` and `FileCabinet` simply because they have a common attribute `Location`.

The object `Publication` introduced above is an *abstract object*. It is an object for which there are no instances. The library contains only instances of objects that are a specialization of `Publication`, such as `Book` and `Journal`. Its function in the object hierarchy is to relate these other objects, and to provide an interface description to its users. The attributes and services defined at the level of `Publication` together constitute the common interface for all its descendants.

The generalization/specialization hierarchy also makes it possible to lift services to higher levels of the hierarchy. Doing so often gives rise to so-called **virtual functions**. Virtual functions are services of an object for which a (default) implementation is provided which can be redefined by specializations of that object. The notion of virtual functions greatly enhances reusability, since a variant of some object can now be obtained by constructing a specialization of that object in which some services are redefined.

Decisions as to which objects and attributes to include in a design, and how to relate them in the object hierarchy, are highly intertwined. For instance, objects should have more than one attribute. If an object has one attribute only, it is generally better to include it as an attribute in other objects. Also, the instances of an object should have common attributes. If some attributes are meaningful only for a subset of all instances, then we really have a classification structure. If some books can be borrowed, but others cannot, such is an indication of a classification structure where the object `Book` has specializations, such as `Novel` and `ReferenceBook`.

Object-oriented design can be classified as a **middle-out** design method. The set of objects identified during the first modeling stages constitutes the middle level of the system. In order to implement these domain-specific entities, lower-level objects are used. These lower-level objects can often be taken from a library. For the various object-oriented programming languages, quite extensive class libraries already exist. We may envisage a future in which collections of domain-specific classes will become available as well in the form of 'domain libraries'. The higher levels of the design constitute the application-dependent interaction of the domain-specific entities.

There are a number of potential advantages of the object-oriented approach over the more traditional, function oriented, approaches to design:

- The object-oriented approach is more natural. It fits the way we view the world around us. The concepts that show up in the design have a direct counterpart in the UoD being modeled, thus providing a direct link between the design and the world being modeled. This makes it easier for the client to comprehend the design and discuss it with the analyst.

- The object-oriented approach focuses on structuring the problem rather than any particular solution to it. This point is closely related to the previous one. In designs based on the functional paradigm the modules tend to correspond to parts of a solution to the problem. It may then not be easy to relate these modules to the original problem. The result of an object-oriented analysis and design is a hierarchy of objects with their associated attributes which still resembles the structure of the problem space.

- The object-oriented approach provides for a smoother transition from requirements analysis to design to code. Such is clearly demonstrated in our discussion of the object oriented approach, where it is difficult to strictly separate UoD modeling aspects from design aspects. The object hierarchy that results from this process can be directly mapped onto the class hierarchy of the implementation (provided the implementation language is object-oriented too). The attributes of objects become encapsulated by services provided by the objects in the implementation. They are implemented by so-called messages (see also chapter 12).

- The object-oriented approach leads to more flexible systems, systems that are easier to adapt and change. Because the real-world objects have a direct counterpart in the implementation, it becomes easy to link change requests to the corresponding program modules. Through the inheritance mechanism, changes can often be realized by adding another specialized object rather than through tinkering with the code. For example, if we wish to extend our system dealing with furniture with another type of chair, say wheelchair, we do so by defining a new object `WheelChair`, together with its own set of attributes, as another specialization of `Chair`.

- The object-oriented approach promotes reuse by focusing on the identification of real-world objects from the application domain. In contrast, more traditional approaches focus on identifying functions. In an evolving world, the objects tend to be stable, while the functions tend to change. For instance, in an office environment the functions performed are likely to change with time, but there will always be letters, folders, and the like. Thus, an object-oriented design is less susceptible to changes in the world being modeled.

- The inheritance mechanism adds to reusability as well. New objects can be created as specializations of existing objects, inheriting attributes from the existing objects. At the implementation level, this kind of reuse is accomplished through code sharing. The increasing availability of class libraries contributes to this type of code reuse.

- Objects in an object-oriented design encapsulate abstract data types. As such, an object-oriented design potentialy has all the right properties (information hiding, abstraction, high cohesion, low coupling, etc.).

The object-oriented approach, however, does not by definition result in a good design. It is a bit too naive to expect that the identification of domain-specific entities is all there is to a good design. The following issues must be kept in mind:

- There are other objects besides the ones induced by domain concepts. Objects that have to do with system issues such as memory management or error recovery do not naturally evolve from the modeling of the UoD. Likewise, 'hypothetical' objects that capture implicit knowledge from the application domain may be difficult to identify.

- The separation of concerns that results from the encapsulation of both state and behavior into one component need not be the one that is most desirable. For example, for many an object it might be necessary to be able to present some image of that object to the user. In a straightforward application of the object-oriented method such would result in each object defining its own ways for doing so. This, however, is against good practices of system design, where we generally try to isolate the user interface from the computational parts. A clearly identifiable user interface component adds to consistency and flexibility.

- With objects too, we have to consider the uses-relation. An object uses another object if it requests a service from that other object. It does so by sending a message. The bottom-up construction of a collection of objects may result in a rather loosely coupled set, in which objects freely send messages to other objects. With a wink at the term spaghetticode to denote overly complex control patterns in programs, this is known as the *ravioli* problem. If objects have a complicated usage pattern, it is difficult to view one object without having to consider many others as well.

Next to problems that have to do with the design process as such, there is the question as to how to integrate object-oriented methods, tools and languages with those that already exist. We often tend to reinvent the wheel and do not build on previous results. Designers of object-oriented systems have often failed to incorporate features that have long proven to be useful. For example, present-day object-oriented data bases generally do not offer features like authorization and protection (let alone speed) at the level non-object-oriented data bases do. Object-oriented languages are similarly not equipped with the type of tool support (version control, debugging, etc.) known from other environments. Finally, object-oriented design methods are still based on immature guidelines and notations, compared to the more traditional design methods.

10.3.5 How to select a design method

It is not easy to compare the many design methods that exist. They all have their pros and cons. None of them gives us a straightforward recipe as to how to proceed from a list of requirements to a successfully implemented system. We always need some sort of magic in order to get a specific decomposition. The expertise and quality of the people involved do have a major impact on the end result of the design process [Boehm81].

[Greeno80] claims that all types of problem solving are based on experience. Simon estimates that an expert has over 50 000 chunks of domain-specific knowledge at his disposal [Simon80]. When solving a problem, we try to map the problem at hand onto the knowledge available. The larger this knowledge is, and the more accessible it is, the more successful this process will be.

The prescriptiveness of the design methods differs considerably. The various variants of functional decomposition as well as the object-oriented design methods heavily rely on heuristic knowledge of the designers. Jackson's techniques seem to suffer less from this need. Especially if structure clashes do not occur, JSP provides a well-defined framework for how to go about a design. The prescriptive nature of JSP possibly explains to some extent its success, especially in the realm of administrative data processing. JSD offers similar advantages. Its strict view of describing data structures as a list of events may lead to problems, though, if the data structures do not fit this model.

JSP has a static view of the data. More importantly, it does not tell us *how* to organize the data. As such, this technique seems most suited for problems where the structure of the data has been fixed beforehand. JSD and object-oriented methods offer better support as regards the structuring of data. Though these methods give useful heuristics for the identification of objects, obtaining a well-balanced set of objects is still very much dependent on the skills of the designer.

The data flow technique has a more dynamic view of the data streams that are the base of the system to be constructed. We may often view the bubbles from a data flow diagram as clerks that perform certain transformations on incoming data to produce data for other clerks. The technique seems well suited for circumstances where an existing manual system is to be replaced by a computerized one. A real danger, though, is that the existing system is just copied, while additional requirements get overlooked.

If we take into account that a substantial part of the cost of software is spent in *maintaining* that software, it is clear that factors such as flexibility, comprehensibility and modularity should play a crucial role when selecting a specific design technique. The ideas and guidelines of Parnas are particularly relevant in this respect. The object-oriented philosophy incorporates these ideas, and is well matched to current developments in programming languages, which allow for a smoother transition between the different development phases.

The above arguments relate to characteristics of the problem to be solved. There are several other factors that may impact the choice for a particular design technique:

- Familiarity with the problem domain. If the designers are well acquainted with the type of problem to be solved, a top-down technique or a technique based on data structures, may be very effective. If the design is experimental, one will go about it in a more cautious way, and a bottom-up design technique then seems more appropriate.

- Designer's experience. Designers that have a lot of experience with a given method will in general be more successful in applying that method. They are aware of the constraints and limitations of that method and will be able to successfully bypass the resulting potential problems.

- Available tools. If tools are available to support a given design method, it is only natural to make use of them. In general, this also implies that the organization has chosen for that design method.

- Overall development philosophy. Many design methods are embedded in a wider philosophy which also addresses other aspects of system development, ranging from ways to conduct interviews or reviews to full-scale models of the software life cycle. The organized and disciplined overall approach endorsed by such a development philosophy is an extra incentive for using the design method that goes with it.

10.4 NOTATIONS THAT SUPPORT THE DESIGN PROCESS

It is often said that a picture is worth a thousand words. In all sorts of designs, be it houses, radios or other electronic appliances, extensive use is being made of various drawing techniques. In many cases, the resulting drawings are the major outcome of the design process. It seems obvious to do the same when designing software.

There are a number of reasons why this is not as simple as it may at first appear:

- Software is far more subject to change. Incorporating those changes in the design takes a lot of effort and, if things have not been automated, reality and its pictorial counterpart will soon diverge.

- One of the major issues in software design is the hierarchical decomposition of the system. This seems to play a lesser role in other types of design, possibly because most radios and houses have a less complex structure than the average 5000-line program. Many drawing techniques do not impose very strict rules for this hierarchical decomposition.

- The outcome of the design is the major source of information for the programmer. The programmer is best served by a very precise description. Existing drawing techniques tend to be fairly simple and the pictures thus obtained have to be extensively decorated through natural language annotations. The text added often allows for multiple interpretations.

Yet, pictures may be a powerful tool in the design of software. This holds in particular for the global stages of design. In those stages there tends to be frequent interaction with the user. The user is often more at ease with pictures than with some formal description. Examples of this type of drawing technique are SADT (see also chapter 9) and data flow diagrams (see section 10.3.2).

In the more detailed stages of design, flowcharts or variants thereof such as Nassi–Shneiderman charts [Nassi73] or structured flowcharts [Dewhurst79] are often used. These techniques emphasize control-flow relations between components through a spatial arrangement of these components. They are not very useful as documentation of the design. They tend to be voluminous, they use natural language (which is inherently ambiguous) and offer little or no means to indicate the structure of data. This topic is discussed in greater depth in chapter 11.

We may envisage pictures to be generated automatically from a formal description. If such is done, these pictures at least have a sound semantics. As of now, quite a number of tools are available for applying this kind of drawing technique. Many of the shortcomings of these techniques are overcome by such tools.

Various types of symbology can be used to describe a design. Narrative text and formal languages represent extreme orientations along this dimension. Examples of formal languages include PSL/PSA (see chapter 9) and VDM (see chapter 11). A major advantage of formal languages is that they allow for formal checks. Narrative text tends to be wieldy and ambiguous.

The low-level design is often documented in a constrained language, or pseudocode. A pseudocode generally supports the control structures as offered by most high-level languages, such as **if-then-else** constructs, **while** and/or **repeat** constructs and block structures like **begin-end**. They often provide for a number of useful data structures such as stacks, sequences, lists and sets, together with their usual operations. Apart from that there are hardly any strict rules imposed as regards syntax or semantics and you may freely add new names and notations. PDL is one example of such a pseudocode [Linger79]. [Pintelas89] provides an overview of this type of software design language.

Software design languages based on an existing high-level programming language like Ada allow for a smooth transition from (detailed) design to code. The advantage of a special-purpose pseudocode language remains largely limited to the freedom offered as regards syntax and semantics. This seems marginal and need not be a real benefit. The use of low-level pseudocode hardly offers extra advantages over a high-level programming language. This shows the more from experiments that have demonstrated that the use of pseudocode hardly surpasses the level of a language like Pascal. One tends to repeat the story in pseudocode [Zelkowitz84].

There is little evidence that one design notation is consistently better than another. An interesting experiment comparing different notations for the detailed design stage is described in [Curtis89b]. The notations were compared along two dimensions: spatial arrangement and symbology. Spatial arrangement concerns the visualization of control flow on the page. The symbology dimension includes narrative text, constrained language and ideograms. The authors conclude that for most tasks the contrained language is best suited. The spatial arrangement appeared to be important only when control flow information plays an essential role in the task at hand.

10.5 DESIGN DOCUMENTATION

During requirements analysis a requirements specification is developed. That document serves a number of purposes. It specifies the users' requirements and as such it often has legal meaning. It is also the starting point for the design and thus serves another class of users.

The same fate befalls the design documentation. The description of the design serves different users as well, users that have different needs. A proper organization of the design documentation is therefore very important.

IEEE Standard 1016 discusses guidelines for the description of a design [IEEE87]. This standard mainly addresses the kind of information needed and its organization. For the actual description of its constituent parts any of the notations discussed in section 10.4 can be used.

[Barnard86] distinguishes between seven user roles for the design documentation:

1. The **project manager** needs information to plan, control and manage the project. He must be able to identify each system component and understand its purpose and function. He also needs information to make cost estimates and define work packages.

2. The **configuration manager** needs information to be able to assemble the various components into one system and to be able to control changes.

3. The **designer** needs information about the function and use of each component, and its interfaces to other components.

4. The **programmer** must know about algorithms to be used, data structures and the kind of interaction with other components.

5. The **unit tester** must have detailed information about components, such as algorithms used, required initialization and data needed.

6. The **integration tester** must know about relations between components and the function and use of the components involved.

7. The **maintenance programmer** must have an overview of the relations between components. He must know how the user requirements are realized by the various components. When changes are to be realized he assumes the role of the designer.

In IEEE Standard 1016, the project documentation is described as an information model. The entities in this model are the components identified during the design stage. We used the term 'modules' for these entities. Each of these modules has a number of relevant attributes, such as its name, function, and dependencies. We may now construct a matrix in which it is indicated which attributes are needed for which user roles. This matrix is depicted in table 10.5.

Table 10.5:   User roles and attributes

Attributes	User roles						
	1	2	3	4	5	6	7
Identification	X	X	X	X	X	X	X
Type	X	X				X	X
Purpose	X	X					X
Function	X		X			X	
Subordinates	X						
Dependencies		X				X	X
Interface			X	X	X	X	
Resources	X	X				X	X
Processing				X	X		
Data				X	X		

(*Source: H.J. Barnard et al., A recommended practice for describing software designs: IEEE Standards Project 1016*, IEEE Transactions on Software Engineering SE-12, 2, *Copyright* © *1986, IEEE.*)

IEEE Standard 1016 distinguishes ten attributes. These attributes are minimally required in each project. The documentation about the design *process* is strongly related to the above design documentation. The design process documentation includes information pertaining to, among others, the design status, alternatives that have been rejected, and revisions that have been made. It is part of configuration control as discussed in chapter 4. The attributes from IEEE Standard 1016 are:

1. **Identification**: the component's name, for reference purposes. This name must be unique.

2. **Type**: the kind of component, such as subsystem, procedure, module, file.

3. **Purpose**: what is the specific purpose of the component. This entry will refer back to the requirements specification.

4. **Function**: what does the component accomplish. For a number of components, this information will already occur in the requirements specification.

5. **Subordinates**: which components the present entity is composed of. It identifies a static is-composed-of relation between entities.

6. **Dependencies**: a description of the relationships with other components. It concerns the uses-relation from section 10.2.5 and includes more detailed

information on the nature of the interaction (including common data structures, order of execution, parameter interfaces, and the like).

7. **Interface**: a description of the interaction with other components. This concerns both the method of interaction (how to invoke an entity, how communication is achieved through parameters) and rules for the actual interaction (encompassing things like data formats, constraints on values and the meaning of values).

8. **Resources**: the resources needed. Resources are entities external to the design, such as memory, printers, or a statistical library. This includes a discussion of how to solve possible race or deadlock situations.

9. **Processing**: a description of algorithms used, way of initialization and handling of exceptions. It is a refinement of the function attribute.

10. **Data**: a description of the representation, use, format and meaning of internal data.

Table 10.5 shows that different users have different needs as regards design documentation. A sound organization of this documentation is needed so that each user may quickly find the information he is looking for.

Incorporation of all attributes in one and the same document is not self-evident. Each user will then get at least twice the amount of information needed to play his role. Nor is it obvious to provide separate documentation for each user role. For in that case quite a few items will occur three or four times. This is difficult to handle and complicates the maintenance of the documentation.

In IEEE 1016 the attributes have been grouped into four clusters. The decomposition is made such that most users need information from only one cluster, while these clusters contain a minimum amount of superfluous information for that user. This decomposition is given in table 10.6. It is interesting to note that each cluster has its own view on the design. Each such view gives a complete description, thereby concentrating on certain aspects of the design.

The **decomposition description** describes the decomposition of the system into modules. Using this description we may follow the hierarchical decomposition and as such describe the various abstraction levels.

The description of the **dependencies** gives the coupling between modules. It also sums up the resources needed. We may then derive how parameter passing is achieved and which common data are used. This information is helpful when planning changes to the system and when isolating errors or problems in resource usage.

The **interface description** tells us how functions are to be used. This information constitutes a contract between different designers and between designers and programmers. Precise agreements hereabout are especially needed in multi-person projects.

The **detail description** gives internal details of each module. Programmers need these details. This information is also useful when composing module tests.

Table 10.6: Different views on the design

Design view	Description	Attributes	User roles
Decomposition	Decomposition of the system into modules	Identification, type, purpose, function, subcomponents	Project manager
Dependencies	Description of the relations between modules and between resources	Identification, type, purpose, dependencies, resources	Configuration manager, maintenance programmer, integration tester
Interface	Everything a designer or tester should know in order to use modules	Identification, function, interfaces	Designer, integration tester
Detail	Description of internal details of modules	Identification, computation, data	Module tester, programmer

(*Source: H.J. Barnard et al., A recommended practice for describing software designs: IEEE Standards Project 1016*, IEEE Transactions on Software Engineering SE-12, 2, *Copyright* © *1986, IEEE.*)

10.6 VERIFICATION AND VALIDATION

Errors made at an early stage are difficult to repair and can be repaired only against high costs if discovered at a late stage of development. It is therefore incumbent to pay extensive attention to testing and validation issues during the design stage.

The way in which the outcome of the design process can be subject to testing strongly depends upon the way in which the design is recorded. If some formal specification technique is used, the resulting specification can be tested formally. It may also be possible to do static tests, such as checks for consistency. Formal specifications may sometimes be executed, which offers additional ways to test the system. Such prototypes are especially suited to test the user interface. Users often have little idea of the possibilities to be expected, and a specification-based prototype offers good opportunities to mutually atune users' requirements and designers' ideas.

Often, the design is stated in less formal ways, limiting the possibilities for testing to forms of reading and critiqueing text, such as inspections and walkthroughs. Yet, such design reviews provide an extremely powerful means for assessing designs.

During the design process the system is decomposed into a number of modules. We may develop test cases based on this process. These test cases may be used when functionally testing the system at a later stage.

A more comprehensive discussion of the various test techniques is given in chapter 13.

10.7 SUMMARY AND FURTHER READING

Just like designing a house, designing software is an activity which demands creativity next to a fair dose of craftmanship. The quality of the designer is of paramount importance in this process. Mediocre designers will not deliver excellent designs.

The essence of the design process is that the system is decomposed into parts that each have less complexity than the whole. Some form of abstraction is always used in this process. We have identified several guiding principles for the decomposition of a system into modules. These principles result in desirable properties for the outcome of the design process, a set of modules with mutual dependencies:

- Modules should be internally cohesive, i.e. the constituents of a module should 'belong together'. By identifying different levels of *cohesion*, a qualitative notion of module cohesion is obtained.

- The interfaces between modules should be as 'thin' as possible. Again, various levels of module *coupling* have been identified, allowing for an assessment of mutual dependencies between modules.

- Modules should hide secrets. *Information hiding* is a powerful design principle, whereby each module is characterized by a secret which it hides from its environment. Abstract data types are a prime example of the application of this principle.

- The structure of the system, depicted as a graph whose nodes and edges denote modules and dependencies between modules, respectively, should have a simple and regular shape. The most constrained form of this graph is a tree. In a less constrained form the graph is acyclic, in which case the set of modules can be split into a number of distinct layers of abstraction.

Abstraction is central to all of these features. In a properly designed system we should be able to concentrate on the relevant issues and ignore the irrelevant ones. Such is an essential prerequisite to comprehend a system, to successfully implement parts of it without having to consider design decisions made elsewhere, and to implement changes locally, thus allowing for a smooth evolution of the system.

The above features are highly interrelated and reinforce one another. Information hiding results in modules with high cohesion and low coupling.

Cohesion and coupling are dual characteristics. A clear separation of concerns results in a neat design structure.

We have discussed several measures to quantify properties of a design. The most extensive research in this area concerns complexity metrics. These complexity metrics concern both attributes of individual modules (called intra-modular attributes) and attributes of a set of modules (called inter-module attributes). A very complete source on complexity metrics is [Zuse90] which discusses just about every complexity metric ever proposed. Several journals have devoted special issues on the application of metrics in the software development process [JSS90a, b], [Software90b]. This is a sure sign of the growing importance of quantitative approaches to assess both the process and its products (see also chapter 6).

A word of caution is needed, though. Software complexity is a very illusive notion, which cannot be captured in a few simple numbers. Different complexity metrics measure along different dimensions of what is perceived as complexity. Also, large values for any such metric do not necessarily imply a bad design. There may be good reasons to incorporate certain complex matters into one component.

[Fenton91] presents a rigorous approach to the topic of software metrics. He explains the essentials of measurement theory, and illustrates these using a number of proposed metrics (including those for complexity, quality assessment, and cost estimation).

A judicious and knowledgeable use of multiple design metrics is a powerful tool in the hands of the craftsman. Thoughtless application though is bound not to help you any further.

There exist a great many design methods. They consist of a number of guidelines, heuristics and procedures on how to go about designing a system, and notations to express the result of that process. Design methods differ considerably in their prescriptiveness, formality of notation, scope of application, and extent of incorporation in a more general development paradigm. Several tentative efforts have been made to compare design methods along different dimensions. A fairly extensive such comparison is described in [Webster88]. Dimensions considered by Webster include the application range, formality, expressiveness and tool support.

We discussed four design methods in this chapter:

- functional decomposition,
- data flow design,
- data structure design, and
- object-oriented design.

Of these, the former three are in widespread use. The object oriented approach to system development has become very popular of late. It has a number of advantages, but still suffers from certain shortcomings as well. Its design guidelines and notation have not matured yet. Tool support and integration of object-oriented techniques with more traditional ones needs to be improved.

An overview of a number of design methods is given in [Peters81] and [Yau86]. [Bergland81] and [Freeman83a] are compilations of seminal articles on software design. There are many text books that extensively discuss a particular design method. A number of these are mentioned in section 10.3.

Finally, the design itself must also be documented. IEEE Standard 1016 may serve as a guideline for this documentation. It lists a number of attributes for each component of the design. These attributes may be clustered into four groups, each of which represents a certain view on the design.

Unfortunately, the design documentation typically describes the design *result* only, but not the process that led to that particular result. Yet, information about choices made, alternatives rejected, and deliberations on the design decisions is a valuable additional source of information when a design is to be implemented, assessed, or changed [Potts88].

EXERCISES

1. Make an object-oriented design of the KWIC-index example. Discuss any major differences with the decompositions given in section 10.1.

2. Assess the design obtained in exercise 1 with respect to: abstraction, modularity, information hiding, complexity, and system structure.

3. Assess the coupling and cohesion level of the modules in both decompositions derived in section 10.1.

4. Determine the cyclomatic complexity of the program text in figure A-3 of appendix A.

5. Draw the call graphs for the two decompositions from section 10.1, and determine their tree impurity. Do the numbers obtained agree with our intuitive idea about the 'quality' of the decompositions?

6. Compute Henri and Kafura's information flow metric for the two decompositions from section 10.1. Do these numbers agree with our intuitive understanding?

7. What are the differences between object-oriented design and the simple application of the information hiding principle?

8. Why would object-oriented design be more 'natural' than, say, data flow design? Assess the naturalness of the design obtained in exercise 1 above as opposed to the decompositions from section 10.1.

9. Write the design documentation for a project you have been involved in, following IEEE 1016.

10. Discuss the pros and cons of:
    — functional decomposition,
    — data flow design,

— design based on data structures, and
— object-oriented design
for the design of:
— a compiler,
— a patient monitoring system, and
— a stock control system.

11. Discuss the possible merits of those design techniques with respect to reusability.

12. Augment IEEE Standard 1016 such that it also describes the design rationale. Which user roles are in need of this type of information?

13. Is cyclomatic complexity a good indicator of system complexity?

14. According to [Fenton91], any tree impurity metric m should have the following properties:

   1. $m(G) = 0$ if and only if G is a tree;
   2. $m(G_1) > m(G_2)$ if G_1 differs from G_2 only by the insertion of an extra arc;
   3. For $i = 1, 2$ let A_i denote the number of arcs in G_i and N_i the number of nodes in G_i. Then if $N_1 > N_2$ and $A_1 - N_1 + 1 = A_2 - N_2 + 1$, then $m(G_1) < m(G_2)$.
   4. For all graphs G, $m(G) \leq m(K_N) = 1$ where N = number of nodes of G and K_N is the (undirected) complete graph of N nodes.

   Give an intuitive rationale for these properties. Show that the tree impurity metric discussed in section 10.2.5 has these properties.

11
Formal Specification

When decomposing a system into modules, we employ two important kinds of abstractions: procedural abstraction and data abstraction. Procedural abstraction has been with us for a long time: a sequence of instructions is grouped into a (parameterized) procedure. In data abstraction a module is built out of some data type and the operations on that data type.

In this chapter we deal with specification techniques for these types of software components. A specification is here taken to mean: a very precise description of the possible effects of a software component. Sometimes this is called a functional specification. Other types of specifications may concern, for example, performance requirements or reliability requirements. In a functional specification we deal with the question of *what* the component has to establish. We do not deal with *how* this is to be realized.

The emphasis will be on *formal* methods, like **input–output specifications** for components resulting from procedural abstraction, and **algebraic specifications** for components resulting from data abstraction.

These are both examples of **local specifications** [Horning82]. In local specifications we deal with the behavior of individual, fairly small, software components, such as procedures and modules. In contrast, **system specifications** deal with requirements imposed on the system's behavior with respect to the user. We use the term requirements specification for this latter type of specifications. As an intermediate form, structural specifications emphasize the building of a system out of individual modules.

Obviously, writing specifications cannot be totally decoupled from the design process. During the design process, specifications are written, refined, tuned. As such, they are important to the designer as well. Thus, there is a whole spectrum, ranging from system specifications (requirements specifications) to the (formal) specifications that provide a starting point for the implementation of individual components.

Given this wide spectrum, it comes as no surprise that specifications may serve a number of different goals (cf. [Horning82]):

- Specifications may serve to clarify things. If we try to write precise specifications, we are almost inevitably forced to answer a great number of questions. The answers to these questions need not always be given in the specification itself. Sometimes, they continue to serve as a parameter to the specification. It does, however, prevent things being overlooked.

- A well-documented specification may serve as a contract. Somewhat less formally, a specification plays a role in the communication between parties involved.

- Specifications may serve as an aid during the design process. They constitute an essential element of the documentation of the design process. As such, design decisions, design alternatives, and the like, may be documented.

- Specifications may serve as a starting point for the actual implementation. During implementation we decide how the components specified will be realized.

  It is often written that the specification tells us *what* should be done, not *how* it should be done, which also is the tack taken in this book. It is really an oversimplification, because the borderline between what and how cannot be sharply drawn. Some people speak about programs as 'specifications'. Also, systems exist in which the kind of specification we are discussing, may even be executed. These are so-called executable specifications.

  It is probably better to view a specification as a (not necessarily executable) 'program' at a more abstract level. In a specification, we abstract from certain details that become concrete at lower levels. This is not fundamentally different from what happens when we program in a specific language. There, for instance, we abstract from the precise representation of data in memory. The difference is merely a difference in the level of abstraction.

- Specifications may serve as a starting point for verification and validation. Formal specifications can be subjected to all kinds of tests. In this way, errors may get detected and corrected early on.

- Specifications may serve as a starting point for maintenance activities. In particular, specifications should not be discarded once the system has become operational. Specifications should evolve together with the system specified.

Each of the above uses is feasible only if the specifications are very precise. To that end, we had best use formal techniques. Formal descriptions are less amenable to ambiguity than informal descriptions. Moreover, ambiguities in a formal description can be detected through a formal analysis of that description. Such an analysis may be supported by tools. In that way, for instance, the consistency of a specification can be guaranteed.

Formal specifications may also be used as a starting point for correctness proofs. Certain properties of the specification itself can be proved. We may also try to prove the correctness of the final program with respect to its specification. We may do so automatically. As a third possibility, we may systematically try to derive the program from its specification. If each step in this derivation is correct, the program will evidently also be correct with respect to the original specification. And again, this derivation can be supported by automated tools. We will come back to this stepwise software development strategy in section 11.2.

Obviously, we cannot formally specify each and every aspect of a system. This, however, should not preclude us from formally specifying as much as possible. Formal specifications force us to be very precise about matters, and thereby help to prevent ambiguities, misunderstandings and unclarity.

According to [Liskov75], the first requirement of a specification technique is that it be formal. Additional requirements of a specification technique are:

- It must be possible to construct specifications with reasonable effort. This also means that the (abstract) object to be specified must still be recognizable in the specification. The 'cognitive distance' between the specification and the object specified should be surveyable.

- With some training, it must be possible to read and 'understand' specifications. Understanding a specification means that we must be able to determine what is being specified.

  Obviously, these first two requirements are relative. The ease of construction and our understanding of the specification ought to be viewed in relation to the complexity of the concept that is being specified.

- A specification must be minimal. A specification should describe all interesting aspects, and nothing more. For example, in specifying some function we indicate what effect the function has to achieve, but we usually do not specify how this effect is to be achieved. At the level of the specification, the precise implementation is an irrelevant detail.

- Each specification technique allows us to specify some class of concepts in a natural way. Concepts outside this class can only be specified in a more complex way and involve a lot of effort. Obviously, we would like to use specification techniques that can be applied to a wide range of applications.

- We would like a specification to be continuous. A specification is continuous if a small change in the concept to be specified incurs a small change in the specification as well.

In the sections to follow, we will assess to what extent the various formal specification techniques meet the above requirements.

We start off in section 11.1 with a short discussion of some well-known informal specification techniques and their shortcomings.

Sections 11.2–4 are devoted to formal specification techniques. Formal specification techniques can be broadly characterized as either **model oriented** or **property oriented**. Model-oriented techniques provide a direct means to describe the system's behavior. The system is specified in terms of mathematical structures like sets, sequences, tuples and maps. In contrast, the property-oriented techniques use indirect means to specify the system's behavior, by stating the properties (constraints) that the system is to satisfy.

The property-oriented techniques can be further broken down in two categories, which are referred to as the **axiomatic** and **algebraic** specification techniques. The axiomatic technique has its origin in the early work on program verification. It uses (first-order predicate) logic in pre- and postconditions to specify operations. In the algebraic technique, data types are viewed as algebras, and axioms are used to state properties of the data type's operations.

Section 11.2 discusses the use of pre- and postconditions. Pre- and postconditions may serve a variety of purposes. They they can be used to prove the correctness of programs, to specify the intended behavior of the program, and to (manually or automatically) guide the derivation of a program that satisfies the conditions.

Section 11.3 and 11.4 discuss the model-oriented and algebraic specification techniques, in particular their role in the specification of abstract data types. Further examples to illustrate these specification techniques are given in appendix B.

Finally, section 11.5 sketches some characteristics of AFFIRM, an example system to specify and verify algebraic specifications.

11.1 INFORMAL SPECIFICATION TECHNIQUES

We often emphasize that specifications ought to be formal. In practice, they often are not. As with a requirements specification, specifications for subsystems, modules, and the like, are mostly expressed informally, using natural language or pictures with an unspecified structure, or some combination.

It seems as if this type of specification is even more dangerous than an informal requirements specification. A requirements specification is used by people having different backgrounds. They know this and may anticipate the possibility of misunderstanding each other. Local specifications, on the other hand, are used by programmers and analysts, people with the same background, using the same jargon. When using natural language, subtle differences in interpretation may arise. These differences might easily go unnoticed and lead to errors that are hard to detect. The seven sins of the analyst, discussed in chapter 9, strongly apply here as well. Parnas gives the following, non-fictitious, examples [Parnas77]:

- 'The first parameter should be the address of the new PSW.' The author may have meant the absolute (physical) address, while the reader thought of it as the virtual address in the namespace of the calling routine.
- 'The value returned by the routine is the top of the stack.' Does this refer to the address of the top element, or does it concern its value?
- 'The date to be printed is the one three months after the input date.' What should be printed if the input date is November 30?

You may claim that these examples are not very honest, since these specifications are not sufficiently precise and complete. Indeed, they are neither precise nor complete. They are realistic, though. When using natural language, there are so many opportunities for the kind of subtle ambiguities given above, that we strongly advise not using it when specifying software components.

These objections against the use of natural language as a descriptional tool may be partly circumvented if we restrict ourselves to a very constrained version of it—various forms of pseudocode being an example. A disadvantage of pseudocode is that it often strongly resembles some specific programming language. This increases the probability that implementation details creep into the specification.

The use of flowcharts (figure 11.1), Nassi–Shneiderman diagrams (figure 11.2), or similar drawing techniques, hardly provide us with a better alternative.* Some reasons for this are:

— The structure depicted by the drawings is a *control* structure. In this structure we may put components of widely different complexity or widely different levels of abstraction next to each other. This difference need not be obvious from the picture. A possible hierarchical structure is difficult to detect. Worse still, these drawing techniques hardly ever offer possibilities to depict the data structure organization.

— The resulting diagrams tend to be large. Even for individual routines, we often need more than one page which can mean that we have to leaf through many pages, thus losing an overview. Realizing this type of diagram takes a lot of time and there is a tendency not to update them as the software evolves. They thus become worthless as a means of documentation. This objection is obviously less paramount if the picture is automatically generated from some other, usually formal, description.

— In these diagrams, we use natural language as well. The objections raised before as regards the use of natural language in specifications, hold equally well for pictures.

We may summarize this by saying that the various well-known drawing techniques fall short as a specification technique. You would be advised not use them as such.

---

* Note that figures 11.1 and 11.2 do not correspond to the same program.

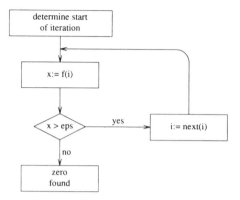

Figure 11.1:   A flowchart

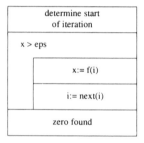

Figure 11.2:   A Nassi–Shneiderman diagram

11.2 SPECIFICATION BY PRE- AND POSTCONDITIONS

If we want to formally prove that some program performs a given function, we will start by searching for assertions that have to hold before and after execution of that program, respectively. Next, we prove that the program transforms one assertion—the precondition—into the other—the postcondition. Founders of this method for proving program correctness are Floyd [Floyd67] and Hoare [Hoare69]. The usual notation in this technique is:

    {P} S {Q}

Here, S denotes some program while P and Q denote the pre- and postcondition, respectively. This expression should be read as follows: if the execution of S is started in a state where P holds, then Q will hold afterwards, provided that S terminates. For a simple summation program, this might look as follows:

```
{sum = 0}
for i:= 1 to n do sum:= sum + a[i]
```
$$\{ \text{sum} = \sum_{j=1}^{n} a[j] \}$$

Finding a correctness proof of a program after the program has been written, often is a tedious affair. To prove the correctness of the above program, we have to find an assertion which is an invariant of the loop construct. For the summation example, this invariant is

$$\text{sum} = \sum_{j=1}^{i} a[j]$$

Unfortunately, there is no algorithm for finding these invariants.

For a larger program, the proof has to be split into a number of smaller steps. We then put an assertion between each pair of subsequent instructions and prove each transition separately. Again, these intermediate assertions may be hard to find.

Proving termination is usually done by induction. For instance, to prove the termination of a loop, we may look for a function f which is monotonically decreasing and has some lowerbound, say 0. For the above example, f could be the function $n - i$.

As an alternative to this tedious process, we may let the proof go hand in hand with the construction of the program. At each step in the derivation, the set of pre- and postconditions obtained so far is viewed as a specification of the program to be constructed. In the above example, the two assertions may be viewed as a specification of a certain summation program. An example of the stepwise manual derivation of a program from its specification is given in the next subsection.

Software development is then seen as a series of correctness-preserving transformations. The high-level initial specification is refined and transformed a number of times until an executable version is obtained. This approach to software development is known as the **transformational approach** [Balzer83]. We may also conceive of tools that support the stepwise derivation of executable code from high-level specifications. Starting from a high-level formal specification, such a tool assists in finding successively more detailed specifications. Languages that allow expression of the whole spectrum of such specifications are called **wide-spectrum languages** [Bauer89].

Even if the actual construction of the program does not follow this procedure, pre- and postconditions are still a valuable means to specify software components. The pre- and postconditions give the constraints that the implementation has to satisfy. This axiomatic specification technique is often used to specify the properties of the operations of an abstract data type. As an example, figure 11.3 gives the pre- and postcondition of an operation to search for some element x in a list A. These pre- and postconditions give a formal characterization of the relation between the input and output of this procedure. For that reason, they are also known as input–output specifications. They constitute a precise

```
proc Search (A, n, x) int:
    pre n ≥ 0
    post (result = 0 ∧ ∀i ∈ 1, .. , n: A[i] ≠ x) ∨
        (result = i ∧ 1 ≤ i ≤ n ∧ A[i] = x ∧
            ∀ ∈ 1, .. , i-1: A[i] ≠ x)
```

Figure 11.3:   Input–output specification of a search operation

description of what a user may expect when the operation is invoked. They also constitute a precise description of the implementor's task.

11.2.1 An example: the derivation of a line-justifier program

To illustrate the use of pre- and postconditions in the derivation of programs we will show part of the construction of a simple program to justify lines in a text formatter.* The complete example can be found in [Gries76] or as chapter 20 of [Gries 81].

The line justifier program inserts extra spaces between the words of a line, so that all the lines balance in length. We want the number of spaces between different pairs of words to differ by at most one. So the extra spaces are to be divided evenly amongst the open spaces between words. Finally, the justifier uses an alternating technique for insertion. When necessary, more spaces are added toward the left and right of the line, depending on the line number being even or odd, respectively. For example, the text

```
This program is meant to add
extra spaces until all
lines have equal length
```

will be transformed into

```
This program is meant to add
extra     spaces    until    all
lines    have    equal    length
```

if the total line length is 30.

The procedure that will do the job may be described as follows:

```
proc justify (n, z, s: integer; var b: array [ ] of integer);
    {line number z contains n words, starting at column b[1], ..., b[n].
    There is exactly one space between two consecutive words.
    s equals the number of spaces to be added.
    The routine determines new column numbers b[1 .. n] such that the lines
    will be justified. If s is not a multiple of n - 1, the remaining spaces will
    alternatingly be added left and right.}
```

*   Source: D. Gries, An illustration of current ideas on the derivation of correctness proofs and correctness programs, *IEEE Transactions on Software Engineering* SE-2, 4 (1976). Copyright © 1976, IEEE.

For a proper specification, we need formal pre- and postconditions. If the initial value of b[i] is denoted by B_i, then the precondition can be stated as follows:

$$s \geq 0 \text{ and } b[i] = B_i, \text{ for } 1 \leq i \leq n \tag{1}$$

An input line then has the form

$$W_1 \, [1] \, W_2 \, [1] \ldots [1] \, W_n[s]$$

W_i, $1 \leq i \leq n$, denotes the *i*th word. An expression between square brackets denotes some number of spaces. From this, we see that b[1] = 1, b[2] = b[1] + length(W_1) + 1. In general, for $j > 1$, b[j] = b[j-1] + length(W_{j-1}) + 1.

After a call of the routine justify we may characterize the output line as follows:

$$W_1[p + 1]W_2[p + 1]\ldots[p + 1]W_t[q + 1]\ldots[q + 1]W_n \tag{2}$$

with the following constraints as regards the values of p, q and t:

$$\begin{aligned}
&1 \leq t \leq n, \\
&p \geq 0, q \geq 0, \\
&p * (t - 1) + q * (n - t) = s, \\
&\text{even}(z) \text{ and } p = q + 1 \text{ or uneven}(z) \text{ and } q = p + 1
\end{aligned} \tag{3}$$

These formulas represent the following facts:

— W_t is one of the words $W_1, \ldots, W_n$.

— We cannot add a negative number of spaces.

— The total number of spaces added equals s.

— The extra spaces are divided evenly among the $(n - 1)$ interword gaps. If s is not an exact multiple of $(n - 1)$, the remaining s **mod** $(n - 1)$ spaces are alternatingly added to the left and right.

The goal of the routine justify is to change the array b such that the resulting line looks as indicated by (2). Starting from precondition (1) and having defined p, q and t as in (3), we may derive the following postcondition:

$$\begin{aligned}
&b[1] = B_i + p * (i - 1), \text{ for } 1 \leq i \leq t, \\
&b[i] = B_i + p * (t - 1) + q * (i - t), \text{ for } i < t \leq n
\end{aligned} \tag{4}$$

A first approximation for the algorithm sought then is:

{(1)}
Compute *p*, *q* and *t* satisfying (3)
{(1) and (3)};
Compute new values b[1 .. t] satisfying (4);
{(3) and (b[i] = $B_i + p * (i - 1)$ for $1 \leq i \leq t$)
  and (b[i] = B_i for $i < t \leq n$)}
Compute new values b[t + 1 .. n] satisfying (4);
{(3) and (4)}

In the next step, the algorithm may further be refined. We will start by computing the values of *p*, *q* and *t* from (3). If we assume *z* to be uneven, then $q = p + 1$. This yields the equality

$$p * (t - 1) + (p + 1)(n - t) = s$$

From this, it follows that

$$p * (n - 1) + n - t = s$$

A solution then is:

$$p = s \text{ } \textbf{div} \text{ } (n - 1)$$
$$q = p + 1$$
$$t = n + p * (n - 1) - s$$

This solution is only valid if $n > 1$. In fact, we have found a new constraint while constructing a solution. The constraint does not come as a surprise: we can satisfy only the requirements if the number of words on a line exceeds 1.

The computation is completely analogous for the case where the line number *z* is even.

If the values of *p*, *q* and *t* are known, we may compute new values for b[1 .. n] satisfying (4). We start with b[1 .. t]. An obvious solution is:

```
for k:= 2 to t do
  b[k]:= b[k] + (k - 1) * p;
```

We may, however, use a different, more efficient formulation. Successive computations of $(k - 1) * p$ yield values that differ by *p*. We will successively obtain the values *p*, 2*p*, 3*p*, ... The multiplication may thus be changed into an addition. This yields

```
incr:= 0;
for k:= 2 to t do
begin incr:= incr + p; b[k]:= b[k] + incr end;
```

The computation of b[t+1] .. b[n] is analogous. The final version of our routine then looks as depicted in figure 11.4.

```
proc justify (n, z, s: integer; var b: array [] of integer);
var p, q, t, k, incr: integer;
begin
   {the two loop constructs use the following invariants P1
         and P2:
   P1: 1 ≤ k ≤ t, incr = p * (k-1),
        b[i] = Bᵢ + p * (i-1) for 1 ≤ i ≤ k,
        b[i] = Bᵢ for k < i ≤ n.
   P2: t ≤ k ≤ n, incr = p * (t-1) + q * (k-t),
        b[i] = Bᵢ + p * (i-1) for 1 ≤ i ≤ t,
        b[i] = Bᵢ + p * (t-1) + q * (i-t) for t < i ≤ k,
        b[i] = Bᵢ for k < i ≤ n.}
   if n > 1 then
   begin {determine p, q and t such that (3) holds}
     if odd(z)
     then
         begin p:= s div (n-1); q:= p+1;
              t:= n + p * (n-1) - s
         end
     else
         begin q:= s div (n-1); p:= q+1;
              t:= s - q * (n-1) + 1
         end;

     {determine new values for b[1..t].
           The invariant is (3) and (P1)}
     incr:= 0;
     for k:= 2 to t do
     begin incr:= incr + p; b[k]:= b[k] + incr end;

     {determine new values for b[t+1..n].
           The invariant is (3) and (P2)}
     for k:= t+1 to n do
     begin incr:= incr + q; b[k]:= b[k] + incr end
   end
end justify;
```

Figure 11.4:   The final version of the justification routine

11.3 MODEL-ORIENTED SPECIFICATIONS

The specification techniques to be discussed in this section and the next one both serve to formally specify the behavior of software components, in particular abstract data types. An abstract data type consists of a set of values together with a set of operations that can be applied to these values.

In mathematics we may, for example, think of the positive integers with operations NULL (initialization), SUCC (successor function), +, *, ... In computer science we may think of examples such as:

— a stack, with operations `Create`, `Top`, `Pop` and `Push`;

— a binary tree, with operations `Create`, `Insert`, `Isin`;

— a hierarchical table, with operations `Create`, `IncrLevel`, `DecrLevel`, `Add`, `Isin`, `Retrieve`.

The set of values that concerns us here is the set of all stacks whose elements are of some given type, the set of all binary trees whose elements are of some given type, and the set of all hierarchical tables whose elements are of some given type, respectively.

The specification of an abstract data type is an implementation-independent description of all relevant properties of that data type. This specification concerns both the syntax of the operations (how it is written) and their semantics (what it means). Only at the implementation phase will we decide on a certain representation of the values of the data type. After that, the operations are implemented using the representation chosen.

The two main specification techniques for abstract data types are model-oriented specifications and algebraic specifications. Figures 11.5 and 11.6 give an example of both. The main difference between the two techniques concerns the way in which the semantics of the operations is given. In an algebraic specification, the semantics is given through relations between the operations. These relations are also called axioms, or rewrite rules. For example, the line `Pop(Push(s, i))` = s in figure 11.5 denotes the well-known fact that popping the last element pushed onto a stack yields the old stack again. We will return to these issues in the next section.

```
type Intstack;
operators
    Create:                      -> Intstack
    Push: Intstack x Int         -> Intstack
    Pop: Intstack                -> Intstack
    Top: Intstack                -> Int
    Isempty: Intstack            -> Boolean
axioms
    Isempty(Create) = true
    Isempty(Push(s, i)) = false
    Pop(Create) = Create
    Pop(Push(s, i)) = s
    Top(Create) = 0
    Top(Push(s, i)) = i
end Intstack;
```

Figure 11.5: Algebraic specification of a stack

In model-oriented specifications, some abstract object is chosen to represent the data type to be specified. The semantics of the various operations is then given by specifying the effect of those operations on the abstract object. In figure 11.6, the abstract object is a sequence, denoted as $< \ .. \ x_i \ .. \ >$. We further use a number of operations on sequences, such as $\sim$ (concatenation) and `length`.

```
let stack = < .. xᵢ .. > where xᵢ is int;
invariant 0 ≤ length(stack);
initially stack = nullseq;
function
   push(s: stack, x: int)
       pre 0 ≤ length(s)
       post s = s' ~ x,
   pop(s: stack)
       pre 0 < length(s)
       post s = leader(s'),
   top(s: stack) returns x: int
       pre 0 < length(s)
       post x = last(s'),
   isempty(s: stack) returns b: boolean
       post b = (s = nullseq)
```

Figure 11.6:   Model-oriented specification of a stack

Figure 11.6 uses the notation of Alphard. In Alphard, the postfix accent denotes the value of a variable prior to the call of a routine. Alphard is a programming language that will be discussed in chapter 12.

Parnas already proposed a model-oriented specification technique back in 1972 [Parnas72a]. Its notation resembles that of a programming language and provides a precise description of possible effects of routines. The notation mimics Parnas' ideas about information hiding and modularization, as discussed in the previous chapter. Parnas' ideas have had a strong influence on the model-oriented specification language SPECIAL.

The acronym SPECIAL stands for SPECIfication and Assertion Language. It is part of HDM (Hierarchical Development Method), a large system that supports software development. HDM has been developed at SRI, the Stanford Research Institute [Robinson77, 79]. The system is particularly meant to support the development of systems with severe safety requirements. For example, the system has been successfully applied in the construction of a flight control system [Wensley78]. SPECIAL denotes a first step in the direction of mechanically verifiable specifications.

Since that time a number of other model-oriented specification techniques have been developed. The most well known of these are Z and VDM.

There are many similarities between Z and VDM. Both use mathematical structures like sets, sequences and functions to model a system, and the notation of predicate logic to describe operations. One striking feature of Z is the way in which its building blocks, called **schemas**, are laid out. A simple Z-schema to obtain the address of a person from a (name, address) mapping is given in figure 11.7. The top line contains the name of the operation. Next, some variables are declared. Both `entry` and `entry'` are partial functions with domain `Name` and range `Address`. Following Z conventions, a postfix accent denotes the value of the state after the operation. A name ending in ? denotes an input to the operation, and a name ending in ! denotes an output. The bottom part of the schema contains both the pre- and postconditions of the operation.

The VDM version of this specification is given in figure 11.8. This example assumes a global state variable `entry`, a mapping from names to addresses. Since `entry` is a read-only variable, which is indicated by the prefix **rd**, the postcondition need not specify that its value has not changed. By default, the reference to n in the precondition denotes its value prior to the routine call, while the reference to `addr` in the postcondition denotes its value upon completion of the operation.

For a detailed discussion of Z, see [Spivey88]. VDM is dealt with in more detail in appendix B.

```
 ____ Lookup _____
 entry, entry' : Name ↦ Address
 name? : Name
 addr! : Address
|_____
 name? ∈ dom (entry) ∧
 addr! = entry (name?) ∧ entry' = entry
```

Figure 11.7:   An example Z schema

```
LookUp (n: Name) addr: Address
     ext rd entry
pre n ∈ dom entry
post addr = entry (n)
```

Figure 11.8:   An example VDM specification

In the next subsection we look at a variety of model-oriented specifications. From the examples given there it shows that it is very important to have a suitable base of abstract objects that can be used in subsequent specifications.

11.3.1 Some potential problems

Figure 11.9 contains yet another model-oriented specification of a stack. The abstract object chosen to model the data type is a triple $< S, V, T >$. In this example, the order of the elements on the stack is kept in the linear relation T. This relation stores pairs $< x, y >$, in which x comes right on top of y. Such is only unique if all elements are different. Since this need not be the case for stacks, we do not directly store the user-supplied integers in T. Instead, we use 'nodes' that are being constructed within the module. V is the mapping from nodes to integers.

In both the specifications of figures 11.6 and 11.9 we use structures and relations that are assumed to be known already. In the Alphard-specification, use is made of a sequence, an empty sequence, the length of a sequence, and so on. In

```
type intstack
logical structure
   objects node
   attributes value: node to int
   relationships ontopof: node to node
   state <S: collection of node, V: collection of value,
         T: ontopof>
   invariant assertions
     ontopof is linear
operations
   syntax
     create:                  -> intstack
     push: intstack * int     -> intstack
     pop: intstack            -> intstack ∪ {error}
     isempty: intstack        -> int ∪ {error}
   semantics
     x, y, z: node; val: int; s: intstack;
     create = s with [S:= ∅ ; V:= ∅ ; T:= ∅]
     push(s, val) = s with
        [S:= S ∪ {x}, V:= V ∪ {<x, val>},
        T:= if s = create then ∅
            else T ∪ {<x, topnode(s)>}]
        where (x ∉ S)
     pop(s) = if S = ∅ then error else s with
        [S:= S - {x}, V:= V - {<x, V(x)>},
              T:= T - {<x, y> | <x, y> ∈ T}]
        where x = topnode(s)
     topnode(s) = if s = create then error else x
        where x ∈ S and (¬ ∃ y ∈ S) (<y, x> ∈ T)
     top(s) = val where val = V(topnode(s))
     isempty(s) = if S = ∅ then true else false
```

Figure 11.9: Abstract model specification of a stack (*Source: B.G. Claybrook, M.P. Wyckoff, Module: an encapsulation mechanism for specifying and implementing abstract data types*, Proceedings of the ACM'80 Conference, *Reproduced by permission of the Association for Computing Machinery, Inc.*)

the example taken from [Claybrook80], we use sets together with the familiar operations on sets, as well as a linear relation ontopof. In both cases, the new type is being defined in terms of types already known, types which are, in a sense, more primitive. To start with, the system contains a fixed set of primitive types. In specifying new types, we may use this fixed set of primitive types as well as types specified earlier on. When specifying new types, use is made of the constructors (such as the set- and sequence-constructor) provided by the system.

The above examples do indicate a certain weakness in the model-oriented specification technique. If the type to be specified 'fits' the type constructors provided, then the specification looks fairly natural (as in figure 11.6). However, if the new type has some property which cannot easily be expressed in the abstract model, then the specification will soon become rather complex (as in figure 11.9).

In the specification in figure 11.9, the complexity is due to the fact that the *order* of the elements is crucial for a stack. This property is inherent in the notion of a sequence as we know it and it is also inherent in the corresponding Alphard-notion. But sequencing is not incorporated in the notion of a set so it has to be taken care of explicitly. Moreover, a stack may contain several elements having the same value. This is not true for a set either, so that special precautions have to be made in order to cater for duplicate elements as well.

A similar illustration of this phenomenon is found in the following example, taken from [Van Amstel89]. This text contains a number of model-oriented specifications. Two of those concern queues. In a normal queue, elements are added at one end of the queue and removed from the other end. This can be neatly specified using the notion of a sequence, as shown in figure 11.10.

```
structure queue(type item);
procedure CreateQ(var q: queue(item));
   pre true
   post q = ()
procedure PutQ(var q: queue(item); i: item);
   pre q = x
   post q = x ~ (i)
procedure GetQ(var q: queue(item); var i: item);
   pre q = (c) ~ x
   post q = x and i = c
```

Figure 11.10:   Abstract model specification of a queue

In this example, () denotes the empty queue, and x ~ (i) denotes the concatenation of the (possibly empty) queue x and an element i. The pre- and postconditions of the various routines speak for themselves.

In a second example, priority queues are specified. The elements in a priority queue are placed in descending order of priority. Removing the first element thus means removing the element with highest priority. Adding an element in a priority queue does not necessarily take place at the end of the queue. Rather, it is inserted such that the invariant—the elements being in descending order—remains satisfied.

This cannot easily be specified in terms of ordinary sequences. [Van Amstel89] therefore uses sets as the abstract object when specifying priority queues. In this case also, we have to be careful. All elements of a set are different, which need not be the case for priority queues. If, for the sake of simplicity, we assume that all elements are different, the resulting specification may look as shown in figure 11.11.

The only special point to make about this specification is the function min. min(x, f) simply delivers some element from the set x for which f is minimal.

So model-oriented specifications of two very similar data types may look rather different. This clearly is a disadvantage of the technique. The drawback holds the more, since we may be inclined to take the kind of objects used in the specification as a starting point when implementing the data type.

```
structure priorityqueue(type item);
procedure CreatePQ(var q: priorityqueue(item));
    pre true
    post q = ∅
procedure PutPQ(var q: priorityqueue(item); i: item);
    pre q = x and i ∉ x
    post q = x ∪ {i}
procedure GetPQ(var q: priorityqueue(item); var i: item);
    pre q = x
    post q = x \ {c} and c = min(x, priority) and i = c
```

Figure 11.11:   Abstract model specification of a priority queue

11.4 ALGEBRAIC SPECIFICATIONS

Algebraic specifications constitute another very formal approach to the specification of abstract data types. The technique looks fairly simple if we restrict ourselves to small examples such as the specification of a stack or binary tree. Dangers lurk around the corner, however. A full treatment of this fairly mathematical topic is far beyond the scope of this book. If you are sufficiently well versed in mathematics, you may consult [Goguen78a], for example. Without going too deep into the mathematics involved, we will try to put across the essentials of the technique. We will largely do so by discussing a number of simple examples.

Let us start by looking at an algebraic specification for the natural numbers:

```
type  Nat
operators
   0:                   -> Nat
   Suc: Nat             -> Nat
   Add: Nat × Nat       -> Nat
axioms
   Add(i, 0) = i
   Add(i, Suc(j)) = Suc(Add(i, j))
```

Here, i and j stand for arbitrary elements from the set Nat, i.e. they are universally quantified over the set of natural numbers.

The first function, 0, yields some natural number, i.e. some start element from the set Nat. We will denote this element by the same glyph, 0. The two other functions, Suc and Add, are obviously meant to denote the successor and plus function, respectively.

You can easily see that, by choosing

```
Suc(i) = i + 1
```

and

```
Add(i, j) = i + j
```

we indeed obtain the well-known natural numbers 0, 1, 2, 3, ...

The axioms give us the well-known relations in that case:

```
i + 0 = i
```

and

```
i + (j + 1) = (i + j) + 1
```

However, this is not the only possible choice. If we take the trivial set containing just one element, 0, and furthermore choose

```
Suc(0) = 0
```

and

```
Add(0, 0) = 0
```

then the axioms are satisfied as well. So there is more than one 'solution'. An important question which arises when using algebraic specifications is: given such a specification, how do we determine whether it really specifies the data type we had in mind to start with?

An algebraic specification, such as the one given above for natural numbers, comprises two parts:

- a **syntactic** part, in which the names of the data types involved (also called **sorts**) are listed together with the names of the operators and their domains. This part is also called the **signature**;

- a **semantic** part, in which we list the properties that the actual implementation of the data type should have. This is done by giving a set of **axioms**, or rewrite rules. In general, the semantic part is allowed to contain conditional equations. We will encounter examples of this in the following.

The syntactic part can be viewed as a context-free grammar for the terms that can be constructed using those symbols. Examples of such terms are:

```
Suc(Suc(Add(Suc(0), Suc(0)))))
```

and

```
Add(Suc(0), Suc(Suc(0)))
```

Viewed in this way, the axioms from the semantic part can be considered as *rewrite rules* for these terms. As an example, the last term can be rewritten, using the second axiom, as:

```
Suc(Add(Suc(0), Suc(0)))
```

Applying the second axiom once more yields

```
Suc(Suc(Add(Suc(0), 0)))
```

Next, applying the first axiom yields

```
Suc(Suc(Suc(0)))
```

So, an algebraic specification is a completely *formal* system, in which the only thing we can do is manipulate sequences of symbols.

In the end, we are interested in very down-to-earth things, such as natural numbers, stacks with elements of type integers, bags of marbles, and so on. In mathematics, these are called algebras (in general **heterogeneous algebras** [Birkhoff70]). Algebras are very concrete. They consist of a set of objects and clearly defined functions from objects to objects. An algebraic specification in general characterizes a *collection* of algebras.

So, besides the algebraic specification, we need a mechanism to couple the specification to one of the algebras it characterizes. We need to attach a *semantics* to the specification. This semantics is of a rather different type than the one expressed by the axioms of the specification. By means of this second type of semantics, we make a choice from the class of algebras possible.

11.4.1 Initial and final semantics

There are two semantics that are often used in conjunction with algebraic specifications: **initial semantics** and **final semantics**. Informally speaking, initial semantics yields the algebra with the largest number of elements, while final semantics yields the algebra with the least number of elements. Obviously, the algebras have to obey the axioms in both cases.

In our example `Nat`, the initial semantics results in the algebra of natural numbers, the one intended from the start. The final semantics, however, results in the trivial algebra mentioned before. In many cases, the initial semantics yields the algebra sought for. We will come across an example where this is not the case, though.

We saw earlier that an algebraic specification defines terms which can be rewritten into other terms using the axioms from the specification. In this way, we obtain a number of equivalence classes. Each equivalence class contains all terms which can be transformed into one another using the rewrite rules, in a finite number of steps.

Obviously, all terms from one and the same equivalence class should denote the same real object. In the initial semantics, this is all that is required. In the initial semantics, two terms correspond to one and the same object *if and only if we can prove them to be equivalent using the axioms given.*

On the other hand, in the final semantics two terms denote the same object, *unless we can prove them to be not equal, using the axioms given.* The mechanism we use, in which conditional equations are allowed, does not allow us to give a formal definition of final semantics. It would also be beyond the scope of the present discussion. The interested reader is referred to [Kamin80] or [Bergstra83].

The initial and final semantics are not the only two possibilities to assign a meaning to an algebraic specification. They represent two extreme possibilities. There is a large spectrum of algebras in between both.

We will try to further clarify the distinction between initial and final semantics through the following example. The datatype Set, with parameter Item, corresponds to sets of elements of type Item. It could be algebraically specified as in figure 11.12.

```
type Set[Item]
   operators
      Create:                -> Set
      Isempty: Set           -> Boolean
      Insert: Set × Item     -> Set
      Isin: Set × Item       -> Boolean
   axioms
      Isempty(Create) = true
      Isempty(Insert(s, i)) = false
      Isin(Create, i) = false
      Isin(Insert(s, i), j) =
         if Eq(i, j) then true else Isin(s, j)
```

Figure 11.12:   Algebraic specification of a data type 'set'

In this specification we assume the presence of an equality operator Eq for objects of type Item. Sets as specified here may contain multiple copies of one and the same element. So it really is a bag. In the initial semantics for this specification, the order in which the elements are inserted into the bag, is 'remembered'. If i and j denote different elements of type Item, we cannot prove from the above axioms that

```
Insert(Insert(s, i), j) = Insert(Insert(s, j), i)
```

In the initial semantics, therefore, these objects are different. The final semantics would not register this. If we wish to specify a 'real' set using initial semantics, the above commutativity rule should be added, together with an axiom to prevent multiple copies in the set:

```
Insert(Insert(s, i), i) = Insert(s, i)
```

We may summarize this as follows: in the initial semantics the order in which an object is built up, is remembered, unless the axioms specifically tell us not to do so. In the final semantics this order is forgotten, unless we provide for extra features to prevent this, such as some counter. In this sense, the final semantics is most 'economic', while the initial semantics is most 'conservative'.

11.4.2 Some difficulties

We would like an algebraic specification of a data type to be *consistent* and *complete* with respect to the semantics used. All necessary axioms should be there and they should not contradict one another.

Even for simple examples it is not always easy to show the consistency and completeness. In general, both problems are undecidable.

This observation may give you the impression that algebraic specifications merely offer a nice mathematical framework and have no practical merit whatsoever. This is not true. Practical specifications are mostly of a kind for which interesting results can be obtained using computer-supported tools.

There are some serious problems, though, which make practical use of algebraic specifications not a simple affair. We will discuss three such problems:

- hidden functions,
- error treatment, and
- readability.

Suppose we want to write an algebraic specification of the natural numbers, with operations 0, Suc (the successor function as introduced earlier) and $Square(x)$, yielding the square of x.

One can prove that the proper axioms for this can be given only if at least one extra function is introduced [Bergstra82]. If, for example, we add the operator Add, introduced earlier, the axioms for $Square$ may be phrased as folllows:

```
Square(0) = 0
Square(Suc(x)) = Suc(Add(Square(x), Add(x, x)))
```

Here, Add is a so-called **hidden function**. The operator Add is not needed for the application itself, but is merely introduced to allow us to define the proper axioms for the other operations. If we want to algebraically specify some data type, there is always the possibility that the axioms cannot be expressed directly, but that we first need to invent some new operators. These new operators, with their own axioms, only serve the purpose of making the specification complete. As with the invariants used in program correctness proofs, there is no algorithm for finding those hidden functions.

A second problem occurs when we try to specify errors. To illustrate this, let us consider the specification of a queue. In a first approximation it might look as depicted in figure 11.13.

```
type Queue [Item]
operators
   Create:                      -> Queue
   Append: Queue x Item         -> Queue
   Remove: Queue                -> Queue
   First: Queue                 -> Item
   Isempty: Queue               -> Boolean
axioms
   Isempty(Create) = true
   Isempty(Append(q, i)) = false
   First(Append(q, i)) = if Isempty(q) then i else First(q)
   Remove(Append(q, i)) = if Isempty(q) then q
                             else Append(Remove(q), i)
```

Figure 11.13: Algebraic specification of a data type 'Queue'

In this type of queue, the elements (of type `Item`) are appended at the back end using `Append`. Elements are removed from the other end using `Remove`. `First` yields the first element. The above specification is not complete, since `First(Create)` and `Remove(Create)` have not been defined yet. As a first try, we may add undefined elements to the sets involved and specify

```
First(Create) = undefined item
Remove(Create) = undefined queue
```

This, however, results in the introduction of meaningless terms such as

```
Append(Create, First(Create))
```

If this term is denoted by q, we get, amongst others

```
Isempty(q) = false
```

It seems better to have errors propagated, so:

```
Append(undefined queue, i) = undefined queue
Append(q, undefined item)  = undefined queue
Isempty(undefined queue)   = undefined boolean
```

etc. This has disastrous effects, though, since it introduces inconsistencies into the specification. By completely rewriting the axioms of `Queue` and `Item`, this can be remedied but this is not the way to go. It is highly desirable to separate the 'normal' axioms from those that deal with any erroneous cases.

Guttag proposed a better way to deal with errors in algebraic specifications [Guttag80]. He adds a section **restrictions** to the specification. For the above specification of a queue, it could read as follows:

```
restrictions
   pre (Remove(q)) = ¬ Isempty(q)
   pre (First(q)) = ¬ Isempty(q)
```

These preconditions constrain the applicability of the axioms. Guttag also allows error specifications. If the latter occur, the corresponding call fails. The difference between preconditions and error specifications is that the user has to make sure that the preconditions are satisfied in the former case, while the implementor is responsible for a correct treatment in the latter case.

A very similar mechanism is used in Larch [Guttag85, 86]. Larch combines axiomatic and algebraic specifications in a two-tiered specification. The axiomatic part describes state-dependent information by giving pre- and postconditions for the operations. The algebraic part specifies state-independent properties through its axioms. Exceptional conditions are then 'caught' in the preconditions of the axiomatic component and need not be handled in the algebraic component.

[Goguen78b] extends the range of the functions with error values and adds specific axioms which result in these error values.

Both techniques require a lot of work on the user's part, and neither is very robust. In inauspicious cases also, the length of the specification will sharply increase.

Finally, there is a quite practical problem to cope with: the readability of algebraic specifications. One of the reasons why the, admittedly simple, specifications in this section are still quite understandable, is the fact that we have chosen simple examples and mnemonic names. All of you know what we mean by the operator Square. All of you can understand its axioms. Probably, you could have come up with them yourself. If the names used do not ring a bell, it becomes much more difficult to grasp the meaning of an algebraic specification. As an example, you may try to deduce the data type specified in figure 11.14.

```
type x
operators
    e:          x                   -> x
    t:          x X y               -> x
    c:                              -> x
    l:          x                   -> y
    s:          x                   -> z
axioms
    e(t(a, b)) = if s(a) then a else t(e(a), b)
    s(t(a, b)) = false
    l(t(a, b)) = if s(a) then b else l(a)
    s(c) = true
    e(c) = c
    l(c) = 0
```

Figure 11.14:   A somewhat obscure algebraic specification

If the examples become more complex, and certainly when they are generated by some system, it will become hard to understand what they mean.

This problem is not so different from what we experience in ordinary programming. Small programs with well-chosen variable names don't give us any problems. Large programs tend to become incomprehensible.

11.4.3 How to construct an algebraic specification

In the previous sections, we already came across some simple algebraic specifications. You probably had no difficulty in reading and understanding the axioms. The situation becomes different if you are being asked to come up with a set of axioms for a given data type all by yourself. In this section, we will present some guidelines as to how to get at these axioms.

Suppose we have the following signature for a data type `Intstack`:

```
type Intstack;
operators
   Create:                 -> Intstack
   Push: Intstack X Int    -> Intstack
   Pop: Intstack           -> Intstack
   Top: Intstack           -> Int
   Size: Intstack          -> Int
   Isempty: Intstack       -> Boolean
```

These operators all have their obvious meaning. For instance, `Size` yields the number of elements in the stack. We may categorize the operators into four classes [Liskov86]:

1. **Basic constructors** The set of basic constructors allows us to generate each possible element of the data type being defined. In our case, the routines `Create` and `Push` are the basic constructors. For, all possible values of type `Intstack` can be expressed in terms of those two operators.

2. **Extra constructors** This set constitutes the remaining operators that yield a value of the data type being specified. In our case, `Pop` is the only extra constructor.

3. **Basic observers** Let S be the set of operators whose range is not the data type being specified. The set of basic observers $S1$ is a subset of S such that each operator from $S-S1$ can be expressed in terms of operators from $S1$. In our case, `Top` and `Size` are the basic observers, since `Isempty(s)` is equivalent to `Size(s) = 0`.

4. **Extra observers**: All that remains, i.e. $S-S1$. In our case, `Isempty`.

In order to satisfy certain desirable properties, an algebraic specification should be *sufficiently complete* [Liskov86]. This means that there is a set of operators F which suffices to generate all possible values of the data type that is being specified. For an algebraic specification of a data type X to be sufficiently complete, we have to prove the following two facts:

1. Each closed term with range X which contains an operator not in F, can be rewritten such that we obtain a term which only contains operators from F. This rewriting is to be done using the axioms of the specification. This

generating set *F* is exactly the set of basic constructors introduced before. For the `Intstack` example this means that we should be able to rewrite a closed term containing `Pop` to some term which contains only `Create` and `Push`.

2. Each closed term with a range other than *X* can be rewritten to a term which does not contain an operator with range *X*. A term which has as its range a data type other than *X*, has an observer as its outermost operator. For the `Intstack` example, therefore, this requirement means that each term starting with any of `Top`, `Size` or `Isempty` can be rewritten so that the resulting term does not contain either `Create`, `Push` or `Pop`.

One procedure that leads to an algebraic specification which is sufficiently complete, is given below. In explaining its various steps, we refer back to the `Intstack` example. The procedure runs as follows:

1. Determine a set of basic constructors: `Create` and `Push`.

2. For each extra constructor, add as many axioms as there are basic constructors. A closed term `Pop(s)` is either of the form

    ```
    Pop(Create)
    ```

    or

    ```
    Pop(Push(s, i))
    ```

    For both cases, we need an axiom. (If we have an extra constructor whose domain contains the data type specified more than once, the situation becomes somewhat more complex. In principle, each combination of basic constructors in the domain has to be considered in that case. Appendix B contains some examples hereof, such as the `Merge` operator for `Slists`.)

3. For each basic observer, we also have to give as many axioms as there are basic constructors, one for each possible head of one of the parameters of the data type to be specified. In our case, this leads to the following left-hand sides of the axioms:

    ```
    Top(Create)
    Top(Push(s, i))
    Size(Create)
    Size(Push(s, i))
    ```

4. For each extra observer, we need an axiom which relates this observer to the basic observers. In the `Intstack` example, we thus have a left-hand side

    ```
    Isempty(s)
    ```

5. The right-hand sides of these axioms have to be such that the earlier-mentioned proofs can be given. These proofs are usually done by induction on the length of the term in question. A complete set of axioms for the `Intstack` example could read as follows:

```
Pop(Create) = Create
Pop(Push(s, i)) = s
Top(Create) = 0
Top(Push(s, i)) = i
Isempty(s) = (Size(s) = 0)
Size(Create) = 0
Size(Push(s, i)) = 1 + Size(s)
```

Only the last axiom might need some clarification. By induction on the length of the argument of Size, i.e. the number of occurences of Push and Create, it is easy to prove that it is possible to rewrite any term starting with Size into one which no longer contains any of the basic constructors.

The specifications given in the previous subsections all satisfied the requirements for being sufficiently complete. If a set of axioms is sufficiently complete, this does not necessarily mean that it also completely specifies the data type we are interested in. For instance, the above procedure does not yield a commutativity rule for sets as given in section 11.4.1.

In Appendix B, the guidelines for producing sufficiently complete algebraic specifications will be applied to a couple of other examples.

11.4.4 Large specifications

A large specification that has no structure imposed on it, is unreadable, just like a large, unstructured, program is unreadable. In chapter 10 we introduced the module concept in order to impose structure on a design. In chapter 12 we will discuss various programming languages which offer the module concept as a means to structure software. In order to retain an overview of large specifications, one also looks for similar constructs. In a notation which supports the modular construction of algebraic specifications, the signature of a data type Set could start as follows:

```
type Set [Item];
    imports true, false from Boolean, Eq from Item;
    exports Create, Isempty, Insert, Isin;
```

Such a notation resembles that of modules in programming languages like Modula-2 and Ada. If an import clause states that module A imports module B, then this could be taken to mean that the signature and axioms of B are added to those of A. The export clause indicates which part of the signature is exported. Operations not exported remain hidden to the users of the module. If a specification has parameters, different instantiations of the specification are obtained by substituting suitable actual values for these parameters.

Research in this area is far from finished. The technical problems involved are similar to those of module constructs in programming languages. However, they are much harder to tackle, because of the strict formal framework in which they occur. Examples of formalisms for structured algebraic specifications are ASF [Bergstra89] and Larch [Guttag85, 86].

11.5 AFFIRM

AFFIRM is an interactive system to specify and verify abstract data types and programs (in Pascal style) that use those data types. The system was developed in the 1970s at the Information Sciences Institute of the University of Southern California.

In the discussion here, we will confine ourselves to those parts of the system that are used to specify and verify abstract data types. The techniques applied obviously are not unique to AFFIRM. They can also be found in other systems that support the construction of algebraic specifications, such as LP, the Larch Prover [Garland89, 90].

AFFIRM is an interactive system. Finding a proof strategy is left to the user: the user guides the system. In each step, the proof structure is adapted by the user. Next, this structure is simplified by the system, using knowledge embedded within the system. Part of this knowledge takes the form of axioms and theorems about abstract data types that have been proven before.

The axioms of an algebraic specification were sometimes called rewrite rules in the previous section. AFFIRM uses this view in an essential way. When searching for a proof, new rules are obtained from old rules through substitution. The axioms, or rewrite rules, tell us which substitutions are valid.

The specification in AFFIRM of a sequence of integers might look as given in figure 11.15. Except for some syntactic sugar and the final two axioms, this specification is the same as the one given in figure 11.13. The final two axioms concern the treatment of errors. As in most systems for algebraic specifications, the solution adopted is not very elegant.

The axioms from the specification are used as rewrite rules when searching for some proof. Suppose some axiom is of the form $L = R$, where both L and R may contain (universally quantified) variables, such as q and i in figure 11.15. If, by some suitable substitution of the variables in L, an expression T can be obtained which occurs in some proof, then T may be replaced by the expression T' which is obtained by applying the same substitution in R. In this context, we speak about a term rewriting system (TRS). See [Klop80] or [Huet80] for more theoretical background.

In AFFIRM, these rewrite rules are applied until no further reduction is possible. An essential requirement for this method to work is that the set of rewrite rules does not allow infinite sequences of rewrites. Only then is the rewrite process guaranteed to stop. (A commutativity axiom as used in the previous section violates this requirement.)

```
type Queue;
declare q: Queue;
declare i: Integer;
interface First(q): Integer;
interface Isempty(q): Boolean;
interfaces Empty, Append(q, i), Remove(q): Queue;
axioms
   Isempty(Empty) = true,
   Isempty(Append(q, i)) = false,
   First(Append(q, i)) = if Isempty(q) then i else First(q),
   Remove(Append(q, i)) =
      if Isempty(q) then q else Append(Remove(q), i),
   First(Empty) = 0,
   Remove(Empty) = Empty;
end Queue;
```

Figure 11.15:   Specification of sequence of integers in AFFIRM ([Musser80])

A second important requirement is that the order in which rewrite rules are applied, does not matter. In such a case, it does not matter which axiom is applied first, or which subexpression is first chosen to be replaced by another subexpression.

If a set of axioms satisfies both requirements (finite *and* unique termination) then it is called **convergent**. If the set of axioms of an algebraic specification has this property, one of the nice corrolaries is that each equality can be proved or disproved by simply rewriting both sides until none of the axioms apply any more. Both sides are then in normal form, and equality is proved if both sides are identical.

Finite termination is, in general, undecidable. AFFIRM imposes some further restrictions, which make finite termination decidable [Musser80]. Once finite termination is ensured, then there is an algorithm to decide about unique termination, and thus about convergence.

AFFIRM has been successfully applied in a number of small to medium examples. Since the user is responsible for the proof strategy, and since there do not exist general decision procedures for some important aspects (such as convergence), one needs a certain familiarity with the system and the underlying techniques to achieve successful results.

This is still a very active research area, and future systems will certainly offer more and better opportunities to manipulate algebraic specifications.

11.6 SUMMARY AND FURTHER READING

In this chapter we discussed a number of specification techniques. We argued that informal specification techniques may lead to all kinds of problems and had better not be used. Fortunately, formal aproaches to software specification provide a good alternative.

Formal specification methods are beginning to mature. It used to be the case that formal approaches were dispatched by their detractors using arguments like [Hall90]:

- formal methods are difficult;

- only highly critical systems benefit from their use;

- formal methods involve complex mathematics;

- formal methods increase the cost of development;

- formal methods are incomprehensible to clients;

- nobody uses formal methods for real projects.

The increased use of formal specification methods is shown in special journal issues [Software90d], [TrSE90]. The papers in these journals reflect state-of-the-art applications of formal approaches in real projects. It shows from these examples that the primary purpose in using formal approaches often is not to prove the correctness of the system. Rather, the process of building a formal specification helps to get insight into the universe being modeled. It helps to unveil ambiguities and inconsistencies. It helps to get better specifications and, as a consequence, better systems.

We distinguished model-oriented and property-oriented specification techniques. Model-oriented techniques provide a direct means to specify the system's behavior. In model-oriented techniques, the system is specified in terms of mathematical structures like sets and sequences. Property-oriented techniques provide an indirect means, and state the properties (constraints) that the system is to satisfy. Often, a mixture of several techniques is used.

The use of pre- and postconditions is an example of a property-oriented technique. It is widely used to specify procedural abstractions. This type of input–output specification can also be used as a starting point for constructively deriving software from a statement of its pre- and postconditions. Well-known texts on this topic are [Dijkstra76] and [Gries81].

The most well-known model-oriented specification formalisms are VDM and Z. There are many similarities between these formalisms. Both use mathematical structures like sets, sequences and functions to model a system, and the notation of predicate logic to describe operations. There are good textbooks for both methods: [Spivey88] for Z, and [Jones90a] for VDM. Case studies in using these methods for a variety of problems are collected in [Haies87] and [Jones90b], respectively.

Algebraic specifications are the major type of property-oriented methods. The idea to algebraically specify data types and their operations emerged in the 1970s [Zilles74], [Guttag75], [Goguen75]. A good overview of this material can be found in [Berztiss83]. [Liskov75] also provides an introduction to this topic. The more mathematically oriented reader should look to [Goguen78a] or [Ehrig85]. [Guttag82] elaborates on the problem of practical applications of algebraic specifications.*

AFFIRM [Gerhart80] is one of the successful systems based on algebraic specifications. Amongst others, it has been used to specify and verify communication protocols [Sunshine82].

EXERCISES

1. The following signature of a data type `List` is given:

```
Create:                                              -> List
Add:          List x Course * Points * Score   -> List
PartyTime:    List                                   -> Boolean
GradePoints:  List                                   -> Integer
```

The data type `List` is used to store data about student scores. `Create` is used to create an empty list. `Add` adds a new entry to the list. Such an entry consists of the course name, the grade points for that course (a cardinal number), and the student's score (a cardinal number between 0 and 100). If an entry is added whose course name equals that of an entry already in the list, then the new entry replaces the old one, provided the score of the new entry is larger than that of the old one. Only entries whose scores exceeds 50 are incorporated in the list. `GradePoints` yields the sum of the grade points of all entries in the list. `PartyTime` yields true if and only if the total number of grade points exceeds 126.

Give the axioms for the data type `List`, using initial semantics. You are free to use any operations needed for the auxiliary types `Course`, `Points`, `Score`, `Integer` and `Boolean`. You may also use if-then-else constructs in the right-hand sides of axioms. Axioms for hidden functions of the data type `List` must be given though.

2. Would the axioms for the data type `List` from exercise 1 be any different if final semantics were used instead of initial semantics?

3. The following signature is given for a data type `String`:

```
Create:                                  -> String
Append:     String x Char                -> String
Delete:     String x Integer             -> String
Substring:  String x String              -> Boolean
```

`Create` creates an empty string. `Append` adds a character at the end of a string. The second parameter of `Delete` denotes the position of the character that is to be deleted. The character positions are numbered from 1 onwards. `Delete` is a void operation if the position given is out of bounds. Finally, `Substring($s_1$, $s_2$)` yields true if and only if s_2 is a substring of s_1.

Give the axioms for the data type `String`, using initial semantics.

---

* For the reader who has not solved the puzzle in figure 11.14: the specification concerns a queue. Substitute `Remove` for e, `Append` for t, `Create` for c, `First` for l and `IsEmpty` for s. The types x, y and z stand for `Queue`, `Integer` and `Boolean`, respectively. a and b are variables of type `Queue` and `Integer`, respectively.

4. Prove the following equality, using the axioms derived in exercise 3:

```
Substring(Append(Append(Append(Append(Create, a), a), b), a),
    Append(Append(Create, a), a)) = true
```

5. Give a model-oriented specification for the string operations of exercise 3, assuming the sequence type and its usual operations are predefined.

6. Try to do the same if only the set type and associated operations are predefined.

7. Consider a sequence of numbers $A = (a_1, ..., a_n)$. A subsequence of length $n - 1$ is obtained by deleting l (not necessarily adjacent) elements from A. A subsequence is called an *upsequence* if its values are in non-decreasing order.

   State pre- and postconditions for a program to calculate the length of the longest subsequence of a given sequence A, and constructively develop the program from these pre- and postconditions. (After having done so, you may wish to study section 20.2 of [Gries81].)

8. The Knuth–Morris–Pratt (KMP) algorithm searches a string for the (first) occurrence of some other string. It has a running time proportional to the length of the string to be searched. (Unfortunately, this is of little help since the dumbest string searching algorithm has the same running time in practice. Actual string searching algorithms in application programs like text editors are more complicated.) For a given string S and substring p to be looked for, KMP is as follows:

```
j:= k:= 1;
while k <= n do
    while j > 0 and S[k] # p[j] do j:= F[j] end;
    if j = m
        then return "substring found at position k-m"
        else k:= k+1; j:= j+1
    end
end;
return "substring not found"
```

In this algorithm, m and n are positive integers denoting the length of p and S, respectively. F is an auxiliary array of length m. Prior to the execution of the above algorithm, F is determined as follows:

```
j:= 1; i:= 0; F[1]:= 0;
while j < m do
    while i > 0 and p[j] # p[i] do i:= F[i] end;
    i:= i + 1; j:= j + 1;
    if p[j] = p[i]
        then F[j]:= F[i]
        else F[j]:= i
    end
end;
```

State pre- and postconditions for the KMP-algorithm and next prove its correctness. (Hint: F[j] is the largest index i < j such that p[1 .. i-1] = p[j - (i-1) .. j-1] and p[i] # p[j].)

Also prove that the running time of the KMP-algorithm is $O(n + m)$. (See also [Smit82].)

9. Add an operation `ChangeAddr` to the VDM-specification in figure B.5 (appendix B) that updates the address-field of a client, given the identification number of that client.

10. In the VDM-specification of the library system given in appendix B, a copy of a book is either borrowed by some client or it is available from the library. Change the specification such that a copy of a book may also be temporarily unavailable (it could for instance be in repair).

11. Write an essay on the virtues of formal specifications as opposed to natural language specifications.

12
Programming
Languages

The question 'How does one write good programs in X?' is very similar to the question 'How does one write good English prose?' There are two kinds of answers: 'Know what you want to say,' and 'Practice. Imitate good writing.' Both kinds of advice appear to be as appropriate for X as they are for English—and as hard to follow.
Paraphrase of [Stroustrup91], p10

Eventually, a program or a set of programs must be written. In principle, the programmer can choose from among thousands of programming languages. In practice, the choice, if any, will most likely be limited to just a few languages. In this chapter we address a number of important characteristics of some of the better-known programming languages.

It is not our intention to teach you how to program (in a structured way). We assume you already know how to do so. Neither is it our intention to present an elaborate assessment of different programming languages and their concepts. You should consult other sources for that, such as [Sethi89] or [Watt90]. However, as a programmer you do need a fairly thorough understanding of the main concepts of programming languages in order to be able to make a reasoned choice as to which language suits your applications best.

In practice you will not always have a decisive voice as regards this choice. In many an environment the implementation language is fixed from the very beginning. Perhaps company policy dictates that all software be written in language X. Possibly also, the application is to be part of a larger system, for which a decision has already been made.

One reason for spending some time in discussing programming language concepts in a text like this is that there is a distinctive mutual relation between developments in the area of software engineering and developments in the area of programming languages. Such is paramount in, for instance, the development of the module concept in programming languages parallel to the development of notions such as abstract data types, information hiding, (algebraic) specifications in software engineering.

Differences in programming languages in general far surpass the precise syntax of individual program constructs. A language such as FORTRAN does not allow for recursive procedures. Therefore, you will not be immediately inclined to develop a recursive algorithm if it is known that the algorithm will eventually be encoded in FORTRAN. Both FORTRAN and ALGOL 60 are not particularly suited for character manipulations, which will have its bearing on the structure of a certain class of programs written in those languages. Writing a set of routines for numerical calculations in COBOL is not simple.

These and similar examples show that the choice of a particular programming language may well have far-reaching repercussions. Our way of thinking is, at least partly, controlled by the language concepts at our disposal.

Also, most programs are more often read than executed. Programming style issues are therefore important. In a number of cases these style issues are related to programming language features. We will address these issues in chapter 17 when discussing cognitive aspects of program design and comprehension.

Thousands of programming languages have been designed and implemented [Sammet69]. Most of these are used by one person, the designer of the language, or serve some specific application area. Examples from the latter category include: LISP and Prolog for Artificial Intelligence applications, SNOBOL4 for text manipulation, CHILL for applications in telecommunications.

In the next section we will present a, by no means exhaustive, discussion of programming language features and their consequences. The discussion is constrained to features from **imperative languages**. In imperative languages, programs are built out of individual instructions. Data is contained in *variables* that are accessible by these instructions. In contrast, **functional languages** do not contain variables. In functional languages, complicated functions are built up recursively, starting from some set of basic functions. In functional languages, communication is achieved through parameter passing. LISP [McCarthy65] and FP [Backus78] are typical examples of functional languages. Besides variables (originally names of memory cells), imperative languages also have an assignment instruction (to put a value in some memory location) and a repeat instruction, both of which are lacking in functional languages.

The module concept will be discussed more extensively, because of its role in capturing the structure-in-the-large of a program. This structure is the main result of the design phase. In particular, the embedding of the module concept in Modula-2 and Ada will be discussed.

Finally, we include a section on object-oriented programming. Sometimes, object-oriented programming is taken to be synonymous with the use of modules to implement abstract data types [Booch85]. Enrichment of the classical module concept from Modula-2 and Ada with notions such as inheritance, however, gives new perspectives to software design and construction. This development goes back to languages such as Simula-67 [Birtwistle73] and Smalltalk [Goldberg83]. The language C++, an object-oriented extension of the UNIX systems implementation language C, gains increasing popularity.

12.1 LANGUAGE CONSTRUCTS

The availability of suitable language constructs may influence the reliability and maintainability of software. Selecting a particular solution for some given problem can be strongly influenced by the implementation language, as argued above. If a language supports the module concept, it becomes possible to decompose the software into largely independent chunks that can be developed independently. Characteristic errors that are made because of the absence of certain language constructs are, for example, type inconsistencies caused by the absence of declarations.

Knowledge of the effects of the presence or absence of certain language constructs may therefore have an impact on our choice of a particular language. Obviously, this choice is not only determined by language characteristics. Other factors that play a role in this process, include:

• arguments that surpass an individual project, such as some global company policy;

• the quality, availability, or speed of available implementations for some programming language;

• the availability of tools to support software development in some programming language, such as syntax-directed editors, programming environments, language sensitive debuggers, or a version management system (these topics are discussed extensively in chapter 15).

Finally, the presence of 'good' language constructs by itself does not guarantee good software. High-quality software can also be written in languages that are generally considered to be inferior. In order to get high-quality software, you need to proceed in a very disciplined way. The availability of certain language constructs most certainly helps you in obeying that discipline, though.

12.1.1 Declarations

Declarations are used to indicate which names are allowed to be used in a program. If the types of the names are specified as well, the correct use of these names in expressions can be checked. In this way the compiler may reject a program in which, say, a character is added to a number. This process is known as **type-checking**.

Names often have a certain scope. For instance, inclusion of a declaration within some procedure then means that use of the name being declared is only valid within the scope of that procedure.

In many programming languages, semantically different operators are denoted by one and the same symbol (a phenomenon known as **operator overloading**). The symbol +, for instance, is used to indicate the addition of both integers and real numbers. If types are specified in declarations, the language compiler may determine which operator is meant in each case. For some expression a+b, the compiler is thus able to bind the + at compile time to some routine implementing the addition.

In languages like Pascal, the programmer cannot define new infix operators. User-defined operations then have to be moulded as procedures or functions. An add-operation for vectors may then look like

```
function add(a, b: vector): vector; ...
```

In Ada, such an operator may be called + as well. It may also be used as an infix operator. In Ada, though, the compiler still determines the operator definition for each operator application, be it an infix operator or a procedure or function call. In a 'real' object-oriented language, binding an application of an operator to its definition is done at runtime and then operator binding becomes dynamic rather than static.

Some languages do not require explicit declarations. In both FORTRAN and BASIC, the first occurrence of a name is considered an implicit declaration of that name. If a name starts with one of the letters I through N, it is taken to denote an integral number. In all other cases, a real number is assumed. If the programmer wants something else, such as a variable COUNT denoting an integer, or a variable A denoting some array, an explicit declaration at the start of the corresponding program unit is required.

An often recurring side-effect of (implicit) declarations in FORTRAN is that the variable in question is initialized to 0 which can have surprising effects. I once spent a considerable amount of time porting some FORTRAN program from one machine to another. One of the major problems was that the compiler on the original machine initialized all variables to 0 while the other one did not. (This was around 1970, when all those wonderful tools such as cross referencers were unheard of.)

If you are forced to explicitly declare all variables, such errors are immediately reported by the compiler.

Explicit declaration of names, together with an indication of their type and (implicitly, through the position of the declaration) their scope, has a positive impact on the readability, understandability, reliability and maintainability of software.

12.1.2 Types

The possibility of declaring new types is closely allied to the possibility of declaring names. Once new types have been introduced, you may declare objects of that type. Operations on those objects are allowed only if they have been defined for that class of objects.

The notion of **type checking** was first used in ALGOL 60. Over the course of years this notion has been refined quite a bit. In programming languages like Pascal type checking also applies to user-defined types. Suppose a Pascal program contains the following declarations:

```
type color = (red, yellow, green);
var TrafficLight: color;
```

Through the first declaration a new type, color, is introduced. Objects of this type, such as TrafficLight, may take on only the values red, yellow and green.

In fact, this type denotes a discrete set of values. Along the same lines, we may declare

```
type age = 0 .. 114;
type letter = 'a' .. 'z';
```

These are so-called subtype declarations, by which subsets of known types (integers and characters, respectively) are being declared. Objects of those new types may take only values within the bounds given in the declaration.

Unfortunately, as much as we would like it, this is impossible to check during compilation. Subtypes simply inherit the operations that have been defined for the parent type. For example, objects of type age are added using the standard operator + for integers. Hopefully, the Pascal-compiler will generate code for a runtime bounds check.

In many languages, or rather implementations of those languages, this type checking is handled somewhat pragmatically. We are all used to adding numbers without paying much attention to the precise type of those numbers. Not only do we add integers to integers, but we also add integers to real numbers. The type checking algorithm must be able to handle these mixed-type expressions. This means that there are often implicit conversions, i.e. conversions that are invisible to the programmer, such as from integer to real to complex, or character to string, or from color to integer. Combined with the possibility to define new operations, such as offered in Ada, this may lead to obscure situations.

Implicit conversions do not occur in Ada if we use so-called *derived* types, as in

```
type age is new integer range 0 .. 114;
```

Derived types are brand new types which merely inherit the operations from the parent type. Thus, an object declared of the above type `age` cannot be added to an integer.

12.1.3 Structured types

Many programming languages offer the possibility to declare **arrays**. Arrays are sequential collections of objects of the same type. Each element is identified by an index, its position in the set.

In this way, sets of objects of different type cannot comfortably be represented. For instance, if we wish to characterize a person by name and telephone number, it is expedient to be able to use a type with two elements, viz. a string and an integer. This can be achieved in languages like Pascal through a record declaration:

```
type person =
   record
      name: array [1 .. 20] of char;
      phonenumber: integer
   end;
```

Each element of this record has a name, and reference to this element is made through its name. If A is an object of type person, then A's name is obtained by writing A.name, and A.phonenumber identifies the appropriate telephone number.

Obviously, type checking is also extended to structured types. Besides, structured types offer us a powerful abstraction mechanism. By introducing type names for user-defined types, we can program in terms of person, color, and the like, without bothering about precise representations for these types. Together with the ability to incorporate such type declarations together with operations on objects of that type in one logical program unit, the module, we obtain so-called abstract data types.

In other kinds of structured types, objects may take on values from a fixed set of predefined types. For instance, after the ALGOL 68 declaration

```
mode human =union (man, woman)
```

variables of type **human** may take on values of either type **man** or **woman** which may vary dynamically, and type consistency is guaranteed. Something similar is possible in Pascal through the variant-part of a record-declaration:

```
type list =
   record
      element: array [1 .. 10] of char;
      case end: boolean of
         true: (last: 1 .. 10);
         false: (next: ↑ list);
   end;
```

Variables of type `list` can be used to store character strings of arbitrary length. An object of type `list` consists of an array element that contains up to ten characters, a boolean marker `end` (the **discriminator**) which indicates whether the end of the list has been reached and, depending on the value of this marker, a pointer to the next part of the list or an index which denotes the position of the last character in the list.

In most implementations of Pascal, type checking is not waterproof. If the variant part of an object of type `list` contains a pointer, we may also read it as if it is an integer. In this way we may directly access memory from a Pascal program or, worse, overwrite the program itself.

The reason for this is that the above-mentioned discriminant is considered a separate entity in Pascal, which can be manipulated in its own right. Ada is safe in this respect. If we want to change the value of the discriminant in an Ada program, we are forced to assign a new value to the *whole* record object. Conversely, the variant part of an Ada record object can be accessed only through its discriminant.

In an Ada record type declaration we may assign initial values to its fields, including the discriminant of a variant part. Alternatively, initial values may be included in the declaration of an object of that type. If the latter is not done, the type of the variant part is determined by the initial value of the discriminant as given in the record type declaration. But this can be changed by assigning a new value to the complete object. If the record type declaration does not give an initial value for the discriminant, you are forced to do so when an object of that type is declared. In the latter case, however, this binding is definite. It is not then possible to assign a new value to the discriminant, not even through an assignment to the complete object.

12.1.4 Pointers

Sometimes, programming languages allow you to manipulate objects in an indirect way, through pointers. We already did so in the list example above. The ↑ notation was used for that purpose. Pointers are particularly handy to define recursive, dynamic structures, such as lists or binary trees. A binary tree of integers can easily be defined in Pascal through the following declaration:

```
type tree =
   record
      elem: integer;
      left, right: ↑ tree
   end;
```

Here, an object of type `tree` is a structure with three components: a number `elem`, and pointers `left` and `right` to objects of type `tree`.

In Ada, declaration of the above recursive data structure takes three steps, and the order of those steps is important. First, the record type is declared incompletely. Next, the type of the pointers, the so-called *access-type*, is declared. Finally, the full record type is given. (The order of those steps makes it easy for the compiler to determine whether some identifier denotes a type.) The full declaration then looks as follows:

```
type tree;
type treeptr is access tree;
type tree is
    record
      elem: integer;
      left, right: treeptr;
    end record;
```

Given a pointer variable `root`, assigning a new value to the left subtree is written in Pascal as

```
root↑.left:= value
```

The symbol ↑ is thus to be read as 'follow pointer'. Ada does not have this symbol. In Ada, following the pointer is implicit in the symbol '.', so we just write

```
root.left:= value
```

If an Ada pointer p points to some scalar object, we are forced to write

```
p.all:= value
```

if a new value is to be assigned to the scalar object. The selector `all` is defined for each pointer variable and stands for 'the complete object referred to'. You have to realize that

```
root1:= root2
```

and

```
root1.all:= root2.all
```

yield different results. In the first case, `root1` and `root2` both point to the same object after execution of the assignment. In the second case, `rcot1` and `root2` point to different objects with the same value.

Though pointers provide us with an elegant means to build powerful data structures, they are also dangerous. If more than one pointer variable points to any given object, such is called **aliasing**. Assignment of a new value to this object through one of these variables then implicitly changes the value referenced through the other variables. Note that aliasing may also occur in procedure calls (see section 12.1.11).

The use of pointers to define recursive data structures also entails the need to dynamically allocate and deallocate storage. For instance, in the above example of trees, you will from time to time want to add elements to the tree, which necessitates allocation of fresh storage space. Similarly, when elements are deleted from the tree, the storage occupied by those elements can be used by the runtime system again. As a result, storage occupation will look like Swiss cheese after a while. The runtime system then has to determine which parts of memory are still in use, and which parts are available if memory requests are to be handled.

This process is called 'garbage collection'. It has been known since the first LISP implementations. For a language like Pascal, the problem is more complicated since the units being allocated and deallocated may vary in size. In many a Pascal implementation, the storage released is not available for reuse.

Memory allocation and deallocation in Pascal is explicit through standard procedures `new` and `dispose`. The dispose instruction has to be handled with care. If multiple pointers to the same object exist and memory is deallocated through one of these, the other pointers point nowhere. They are called **dangling references**.

12.1.5 Initialization

Some programming languages allow you to initialize variables at their declaration point. Implementations of other languages (such as FORTRAN) may do so automatically. Both mechanisms are somewhat unsatisfactory. Rather, we would like to force the programmer to specify an initial value for every object declared.

As an alternative, the language definition could specify that each non-initialized variable takes on a special value 'not-initialized'. Subsequently, use of such variables in an expression may be prohibited. For a number of cases, the compiler could check for initialization of variables. For the remaining cases a runtime check, similar to that for, say, overflow, would be needed.

12.1.6 Constants

Many an object in a program is not variable at all. It would be nice to be able to declare such objects as constants. The type checking algorithm may check that these objects are not being assigned to inadvertently. For instance, a Pascal program may contain a declaration like

```
const pi = 3.1415926589;
```

and subsequently use the identifier `pi` wherever an object of type `real` is allowed. In Pascal, constant declarations precede type declarations. As a consequence, constants of user-defined types cannot be declared. So the following declaration sequence is illegal:

```
type color = (red, yellow, green);
const safe = color(green);
```

Languages like Modula-2 and Ada do not enforce a strict ordering of declarations. In those languages, the above sequence is therefore legal.

It is convenient to be able to declare program parameters, such as the maximum length of an input line, as constants. Such constants recur frequently. Without declaring them once at the start of the program, it becomes a tedious and error-prone process to change them later on. Finally, constants can be given mnemonic names, which increases readability.

12.1.7 Loops

Many programming languages have a loop construct of the form

```
for i = l step t to u do
```

In ALGOL 60 it was possible to manipulate both the count i and the parameters l, t and u within the body of the loop, though obviously not rendering the loop construct particularly comprehensible. A much more reliable loop construct is obtained if the values of l, t and u are computed once upon entry of the loop, and the value of the controlling variable i cannot be changed in the loop-body.

The above for-loop is a special case, well suited to traverse arrays and the like. In general, programming languages also offer **while** loops and/or **repeat** loops. They have the following form:

```
while condition do statements
repeat statements until condition
```

In both cases, the programmer has more control about when to end the loop. Both the **while** construct and the **repeat** construct have their pros and cons. There will always be cases where either construct is less suited. Both constructs do not allow us to put the termination condition somewhere in the middle of the statement sequence. Yet, such will often be the natural way to go about.

Suppose you want to read and process a sequence of numbers. The length of the input is not known in advance. For that reason, the input is terminated by some special number. A natural description of this algorithm is:

```
repeat read element;
   if end of input then exit loop;
   process element
end loop
```

In most programming languages, there is no neat way to code the above algorithm. We are forced to either exit the loop with a jump or introduce an extra variable which is tested both in the condition guarding the loop and in some instruction following the loop.

In most cases, this phenomenon can be formulated as follows: it is not possible to exit the loop with some value. Once you have exited a loop, you no longer know under which conditions you did so. Zahn proposed an interesting construct to handle such cases [Zahn74].

Suppose we want to find the first occurrence of an element X in a sequential table A. If X is found, we increase a counter in table B. If X does not occur in A, we add a new entry and initialize the corresponding counter in B to 1. In Zahn's notation, a first version of this algorithm might look as follows:

```
until found or not found do
    search table
then case
    found: increase counter
    not found: create new entry
```

After refining this algorithm we obtain:

```
until found or not found do
    repeat for i:= 1 to n
        if A[i] = X then
            index:= i; found
        not found
then case
    found: B[index] +:= 1
    not found: n +:= 1; A[n]:= X; B[n]:= 1
```

Note that the above **until-then-case** construct is one single language construct. It is *not* a repeat instruction followed by a select instruction. Obviously, what it really amounts to is a tied-up multiple-exit loop.

A somewhat similar construct is available in Ada. An Ada loop can be left through an instruction

```
exit when condition
```

Execution of this construction causes program execution to be continued at the first instruction following the innermost loop which contains the exit instruction. Modula-2 offers a similar construct.

The Ada exit instruction may also have the form

```
exit idf when condition
```

In the latter case, a jump occurs to the instruction following the enveloping loop labeled idf. However, in both cases and in contrast to Zahn's construct, it is not known upon exit of the loop under what condition the loop was ended.

12.1.8 Select instructions

Select instructions allow us to make a choice out of several alternatives. The standard form is

```
if condition then statement else statement
```

The else-part is often optional. If select statements are nested, omitting the else-part may easily lead to ambiguities. In a select statement like

```
if A then if B then E1 else E2
```

it is not clear whether the else-part belongs to the inner or outer construct. This is known as the 'dangling else problem'. Sometimes the language definition prescribes which alternative prevails. The problem is also solved by explicitly ending the select statement with **fi** or **endif**. The latter solution is more robust and results in fewer errors.

The condition generally is a boolean expression yielding true or false. In order to be able to choose from more than two alternatives, languages like Pascal provide for a case statement. Case statements allow us to select on scalar values such as integers, characters and values from user-defined types like color, defined above.

For an integer selection, the case statement in Pascal has the form

```
case integer expression of
   S₁: action₁;
   S₂: action₂;
   ...
   Sₙ: actionₙ
end;
```

The labels S_i have to be disjoint subsets of the integers. If the integer expression evaluates to some value e, the alternative whose S_i contains e is selected. The corresponding action$_i$ is then executed, after which the case statement is ended. If none of the S_i contains e, none of the alternatives are selected and execution of the case statement amounts to a void action which is not particularly robust, since programmer errors may easily go undetected.

In Ada, a simple solution to this problem has been adopted. If the case-expression is of type T, then the list of alternatives should contain entries for each possible value of type T. There is obviously a way to indicate 'all other cases'.

For instance, given

```
type day is (su, mo, tu, we, th, fr, sa);
```

and a variable today of type day, an Ada case statement might look as follows:

```
case today is
   when mo => bad day;
   when tu .. fr => workday;
   when others => weekend;
end case.
```

12.1.9 Gotos

Since 1968, a vast amount of papers have been written on this controversial topic. Even now, the discussion seems not yet finished; see [CACM87], for example. We won't try to add new arguments. The general consensus is that gotos tend to clutter a program, thus making it more difficult to comprehend or assess its correctness. Therefore, gotos are better circumvented.

On the other hand, there are circumstances where it is just plain awkward to write down a clear and crisp algorithm without gotos. An example would be the case in algorithms where one might want to stop in the middle of an algorithm, because the answer has already been found. In a number of cases, constructs like the one proposed by Zahn or the `exit` construct of Ada, may fruitfully be applied.

12.1.10 Exceptions

Exceptional cases may occur in many circumstances. In most programming languages, there will be exceptions that just cannot be handled by the user (e.g. overflow, array out of bounds, etc). Even if they can be checked by the user, there is often no natural way to solve the problems that caused the exception to occur.

Suppose we are developing some subroutine library which contains routines for numerical computations. It would be convenient to be able to notify the user of some exceptional condition and leave it up to him to handle the exception. Suppose one of the routines computes a matrix inverse. Such an inverse matrix does not always exist. If the routines were written in Ada, we could write

raise singular

in the matrix inverse routine when it is found out that the matrix has no inverse, i.e. is singular. singular then is one of the possible exceptions of the package containing this routine. The user may now indicate what to do in case a matrix is singular in the program unit using this package:

when singular => statements

At the spot where the exception is being handled, it is no longer possible to determine the cause of the exception. For instance, there could be multiple calls of the matrix inverse routine in this program unit. There is no way to tell which one caused the exception to be raised. As a consequence, it is not always easy to find the proper remedy.

The effect of exceptions can also be realized through (indirect) jump instructions if labels can be passed as routine parameters. The above exception construct, however, seems to be safer and easier to comprehend.

12.1.11 Parameter passing

Most programming languages have the procedure concept. Upon declaration of a procedure, *formal* parameters are used. When calling a procedure, *actual* parameters are provided. There are various mechanisms for (dynamically) binding actual parameters to formal parameters. The main ones are:

Call-by-name Using the call-by-name mechanism, the actual parameter is substituted wherever the corresponding formal parameter occurs in the procedure body. If the formal parameter is encountered more than once when the procedure body is executed, then the actual parameter is also evaluated more than once. These different evaluations need not always yield the same result. For instance, a procedure to sum a sequence of real numbers may be written in ALGOL 60 as follows:

```
real procedure sum (x, i, l, u); value l, u;
integer i, l, u; real x;
begin real s; s:= 0;
   for i:= l step 1 until u do s:= s + x;
   sum:= s
end;
```

Both i and x are call-by-name parameters. This procedure may now be called as follows:

```
sum(a[i], i, 1, n);
sum(f(i, j), i, 0, 10);
```

In the first call, a number of different elements of some array a is summed. In the second call a number of different function values is summed. This powerful use of the call-by-name mechanism has become known as Jensen's device.

Assignment of a new value to a formal parameter has a global effect: the new value is assigned to the corresponding actual parameter, which then has to be a variable. Here too, the parameter need not always evaluate to the same variable. For example, different evaluations of a[i] may well yield different array elements.

Call-by-reference When using call-by-reference parameter substitution, the actual parameter is evaluated once and the resulting reference is substituted for each occurrence of the corresponding formal parameter.

The above summation procedure thus would not yield the desired answer in this case. The first call would yield n * a[α], where the value of i is α upon calling the procedure. Here too, assigning a new value to a formal parameter has a global effect. Multiple assignments to the same formal parameter now affect the same variable.

Call-by-value-result (also called **copy-restore**) Using this mechanism, the value of the actual parameter is assigned to a fresh local variable upon entry of the procedure. This local variable is substituted for each free occurrence of the corresponding formal parameter. Upon exit of the procedure, the value of the local variable is assigned to the formal parameter again.

Schematically, a procedure of the form

```
procedure f(x); real x;
block;
```

results in

```
begin real x';
    x':= a;
    block';
    a:= x'
end
```

upon execution of a call f(a). Here, x' is a new variable, one which does not occur freely within block, while block' is obtained from block by substituting x' for each free occurrence* of x in block.

Call-by-value The call-by-value mechanism behaves like the call-by-value-result mechanism, except for the assignment a:= x' at the exit point. Thus, assignment to a formal parameter has no global effect in this case.

In Pascal and Modula-2, both the call-by-reference mechanism and the call-by-value mechanism are used. In a declaration

```
procedure f(i: integer; var x: real);
```

the formal parameter i is evaluated according to the call-by-value mechanism, while x is evaluated according to the call-by-reference mechanism.

The language definition of FORTRAN does not specify which mechanism to use. Most implementations use the call-by-reference mechanism. Some, however, use the call-by-value-restore mechanism.

---

* The adjective 'free' ensures that only those occurrences of x are affected in which x denotes the formal parameter x. If x is being redeclared in some inner block, occurrences of x within this inner block are bound to the newly declared name, *not* to the formal parameter. Thus, the latter occurrences are not being substituted either.

Ada uses a variant of the call-by-value-restore mechanism. By specifying such at the declaration of the formal parameter it is indicated whether the initial assignment (x' := a in the above schema), the final assignment (a := x'), or both are to be done. These three possibilities are indicated by prefixing the formal parameter with **in**, **out**, or **in out**, respectively. A special proviso holds for **in** parameters: these may not be assigned a new value in the procedure body. Thus, **in** parameters are treated as real constants within the procedure body.

However, the Ada definition explicitly allows implementations to use the call-by-reference mechanism for complicated objects, such as arrays or records.

The difference between call-by-reference and call-by-value-result is rather subtle. If some variable is used as an actual parameter in a procedure call and that same variable is also accessible along a different path (for instance, through some other parameter or through direct use as a global variable), the two mechanisms may yield different results. This is yet another form of aliasing.

Let us look at an example:

```
a: integer;
procedure g(in out n);
begin
   . . .
   n:= 3;
   write(standard input, a);
   . . .
end;
. . .
a:= 4; g(a);
```

If the call-by-reference mechanism is used, the number 3 will be printed. If the call-by-value-restore mechanism is used, the number 4 will be printed instead.

If variables are accessible along one path only (and, in the case of Ada, exceptions do not occur), the result will be the same for both substitution mechanisms.

Obviously, it is to be considered a weak point if the precise effect of executing some construct depends on specific implementation details. Porting software from one implementation to another may then become notoriously difficult. In the case of Ada, on the other hand, we cannot always afford the call-by-value-result mechanism, especially not in real-time applications. For, in the call-by-value-result mechanism it is not a priori known how much time execution of a procedure will take. 'Big' actual parameters take more copy time than 'small' ones. Such dependencies between the size of objects and procedure start-up time do not occur with the call-by-reference mechanism.

12.1.12 Separate compilation

Parts of a system can usually be compiled separately. The allowable grouping of program components into compilation units depends on the programming language and/or its environment. For languages supporting the module concept, individual modules tend to be the unit of compilation. In FORTRAN environments, individual routines are treated as compilation units. In C environments we may freely group components into compilation units.

If information is passed between compilation units, this information can be used to check the compatibility of components. This is called *separate compilation*. If such information is not passed on, the units are compiled *independently*.

In FORTRAN, program components are compiled independently, so the compiler does not know where and how such components will be used. Only at a very late stage will components be glued together into an executable system. This may have strange effects, as shown in the following example:

```
SUBROUTINE THREE(I)
I = 3
RETURN
END
...
CALL THREE(5)
K = 5
WRITE(6, 100) K
```

Quite opposed to expectations, the above program fragment will result in the number 3 being printed. The subroutine THREE expects some variable as its actual parameter. In the call, however, a constant is given as actual parameter. Next, a different value will be stored at the constant's address.

With separate compilation the parts of a system are not completely independent. For instance, information on the type and number of parameters of procedure calls will be passed between module compilations. This scheme allows for full type checking amongst separately compiled system components.

The information needed is usually gathered in a component of its own, such as a definition module in Modula 2, or a header file in C. A consequence of these dependencies between components is that they have to be compiled in a certain order. For the Modula-2 case, this issue is dealt with in section 12.2.4.

Though separate compilation is a powerful concept, its possibilities depend on features of the programming language (and its implementation). Many environments offer a mechanism that prevents unnecessary recompilation of components. In its simplest form, components and their object-code counterparts are time-stamped. If a component has not been changed since it was last compiled, that component and its dependent components need not be recompiled. We will further elaborate on this issue in chapter 15.

12.1.13 Further implementation concerns

In the above discussion of the various language constructs we have already noticed that the precise effect of a program fragment need not always follow from the language definition. Language definitions leave certain things undefined or allow for several options. As a consequence we often need knowledge of the implementation used in order to be able to decide on a program's semantics.

In particular, differences between implementations of one and the same language show up manifestly where it concerns communication between the program and the outside world: input/output, file management, character codes, storage allocation, and the like. At these points also, problems often crop up when a program is to be ported to another machine or implementation.

```
Main program:
    PROCEDURE DIVISION.
    PARA.
        DISPLAY "MAIN PROGRAM" ERASE.
        CALL "MODA".
        CALL "MODB".
        CALL "MODA".
    EXITPARA.
        STOP RUN.

MODA:
    WORKING STORAGE SECTION.
    01 DATA-A PIC X VALUE "1".
    PROCEDURE DIVISION.
    PARA.
        DISPLAY DATA-A.
        MOVE "2" TO DATA-A.
    EXITPARA.
        EXIT PROGRAM.

MODB:
    PROCEDURE DIVISION.
    PARA.
        DISPLAY "MODULE B".
    EXITPARA.
        EXIT PROGRAM.
```

Figure 12.1:   An ambiguous COBOL program (*Source: R.L. Baber*, Software Reflected, *North-Holland Publishing Company (1982), Amsterdam.*)

A rather salient example of implementation-dependent program semantics is the following. Consider the COBOL program given in figure 12.1. Which output would you expect? It is fairly easy to see that there are two possible answers. The output will be either

```
"MAIN PROGRAM" "1" "MODULE B" "1"
```

or

```
"MAIN PROGRAM" "1" "MODULE B" "2"
```

Surprisingly, though, some COBOL implementations may yield *both* outcomes. The explanation goes as follows. Large programs do not fit in a computer's memory in their entirety. The user may then try to isolate some largely independent program components (these components are called **overlays**) and assign them to the same memory segment. During execution of the program, parts that do not reside in memory will have to be (re)loaded from time to time. The precise decomposition into overlays is usually indicated through some sequence of operating system commands.

If, in the above example, MODA and MODB are assigned to the same memory segment, the code of MODA has to be reloaded when the second call is to be executed. DATA-A is then seen as a local variable which is re-initialized to 1. As a consequence, the second output of that variable will yield 1 too. If MODA and MODB are not assigned to the same segment, the value of DATA-A is still available at the second call. We then get output 2.

12.2 MODULES

During the design phase we try to decompose the system into logical units, modules. In this section we discuss the extent to which this decomposition and a description of the interfaces between components can be expressed in existing programming languages. An important point is to what extent programming languages offer possibilities to *syntactically enforce* a properly structured decomposition. Well-structured programs can be written in *any* language. In practice, some help turns out to be indispensible.

A general principle of structured programming is that names of objects are introduced near the place where they are used, while they are accessible only in those parts where they are needed. Many languages, though not COBOL, work to this principle and offer some means to limit the scope of names. If some name is declared, it holds for only part of the program (the scope) and the object in question is accessible only from within its scope.

Some languages, including FORTRAN, know only one scoping level. Usually, names are then local to the program piece, such as a subroutine, that is being compiled independently. The main program is considered some sort of subroutine as well, so its variables are not global to the other subroutines. In fact, the set of variables is just partitioned. There is no name hierarchy. (The COMMON block feature however offers a means to share memory and can be used to simulate global variables.)

Languages with a block structure like ALGOL 60, Pascal, Modula-2 and Ada offer multiple levels at which local names can be introduced. Storage for these local names is requested upon entry of the block containing the declarations. Upon exit of the block, the storage is released again. During execution, the set of names constitutes a stack. Pushing and popping of names occurs at block entry and exit, respectively. If there are multiple occurrences of the same name, the most local one (i.e. the one nearest to the top of the stack) is chosen during execution.

For a proper understanding of the following discussion it is important to distinguish between the *existence* of names and their *visibility*. The essence of the module concept is that certain information remains hidden. But it works two ways. In a modular decomposition we wish to limit both the export of names *from* a module and the import of names *into* a module. In both cases, we wish certain information to exist, while at the same time this information is invisible. Most languages with a block structure do not offer this possibility. Each object that exists is visible. Each object that is not visible, does not exist either.*

We may also formulate this as follows: upon entry of a block, all information from surrounding blocks is imported. A block does not export any information.

The ways in which the existence of names and their visibility have been decoupled in various programming languages that offer a module concept, are the topic of the subsections to follow. We will not delve into syntactic details or implementation aspects, though.

Often, a module coincides with a separately compiled component. When this happens there will be restrictions on the *order* in which components are to be compiled. We will shortly discuss the consequences in the case of Modula-2 and Ada.

It is not easy to realize modules in classic languages that lack a block structure (assembler, FORTRAN, COBOL). They usually offer only the possibility to declare subroutines. Some separation of concerns can be obtained through separate compilation. This, however, does not offer the safety required.

Languages that do have a block structure (ALGOL 60, Pascal, PL/I) offer more opportunities to create local data. But the one-way traffic of information across block boundaries (everything goes in, nothing goes out) is often a hindrance.

12.2.1 SIMULA 67

The first step in the right direction was taken in the language SIMULA 67 [Birtwistle73].

The original goal of SIMULA 67 was to create an extension of ALGOL 60 in order to ease the writing of simulation software. The first SIMULA compilers merely translated SIMULA programs to ALGOL 60 programs, after which the ALGOL 60 compiler took over.

If we want to simulate procedures in a post office we may define several *processes*, for both customers and clerks. These processes have little to do with each other. They all have their own local data. Once in a while we might wish to stop one process temporarily and continue with another. The data (status) of the halted process obviously has to be retained because that process will be restarted sometime in the future.

---

* Except for the somewhat artificial shielding of names through redeclaration of the same name in an inner scope.

To express the above in an elegant way, a programming language should offer the possibility to make information temporarily inaccessible so as to prevent processes to interact in an uncontrolled way.

SIMULA's **class** feature allows us to do so. A class strongly resembles a normal procedure. It has a heading and body. The body contains local declarations and instructions. However,

- A class behaves as a type as well, i.e. we may declare various instances of a class.

- After such a declaration the local names of the class can be accessed using the familiar dot notation (like in Pascal: `A.name`, where `A` is an instance of some class).

- The execution of a class, which is started upon creation of an instance of that class, can be halted (through the instruction `DETACH`) and restarted later on (through the instruction `RESUME`). This will often occur in the form of 'co-routines', whereby execution jumps back and forth between two or more routines under control of the program itself.

Through the SIMULA class, we have introduced a kind of an *antiblock*: in essence local names are accessible from outside the class.

In 1976 it was proposed to limit the export of names from a class [Palme76]. The list of names to be hidden should be given at the start of the class, prefixed by the words **hidden protected**. With this extra feature it becomes possible to really hide information. The distinction between the existence of an object and its visibility becomes a fact.

As in other block-structured languages, everything visible from within a class can still be used inside that class. So the import of names is not restricted.

SIMULA offers limited means to parameterize classes. Values of known types can be used as parameters, types themselves cannot. So it is possible to define a class that can handle stacks of different maximum lengths. It is impossible to instantiate stacks containing integers and stacks containing real numbers from one and the same class.

The definition of a class `stack` in SIMULA might look like figure 12.2. In a similar way, the class `item` is defined. Next, stacks and items are declared as follows:

```
ref (stack) books;
ref (item) book;
```

A new instantiation of a stack is obtained through, say,

```
books:-new stack(100);
```

which creates a stack of maximum depth 100. It is empty initially. We may next push an element onto the stack through

```
books.push(book);
```

Other examples of languages with a module concept are Alphard [Shaw77], CLU [Liskov77, 86], Euclid [Lampson77], Modula-2 [Wirth85] and Ada [Ada83]. Interesting aspects of some of these languages are discussed in the subsections to follow.

```
class stack(stacksize);
    integer stacksize;
    hidden protected store, index;
    begin
        ref (item) array store [1 : stacksize];
        integer index;

        procedure push(x); ref (item) x;
            if index < stacksize
                then begin index:= index + 1;
                    store[index]:- x
                end;

        procedure pop;
            if index ≠ 0
            then index:= index - 1;

        ref (item) procedure top;
            if index ≠ 0
            then top:- store[index]
            else top:- none;

        boolean procedure isempty;
            isempty:= index = 0;

        comment initialization;
        index:= 0
    end stack;
```

Figure 12.2:   Outline of a stack module in SIMULA 67

12.2.2 Alphard

Alphard is interesting in that it offers us the possibility to separate the correctness proof of a module (called **form**) from the use of that module. In this way, correctness proofs can be modularized as well. A possible Alphard stack module is given in figure 12.3. The following aspects of this module are worth noting:

- The module may have types, i.e. forms, as parameters. The operations applicable to objects of those types must be given with the parameters. In the

```
form stack (item: form <←>, stacksize: integer) =
specification
    requires stacksize > 0;
    let stack = < ... xᵢ... > where xᵢ is item;
    invariant 0 ≤ length(stack) ≤ stacksize;
    initially stack = nullseq;

function
    push(s: stack, x: item)
        pre 0 ≤ length(s) < stacksize
        post s = s' ~ x,
    pop(s: stack)
        pre 0 < length(s) ≤ stacksize
        post s = leader(s'),
    top(s: stack) returns x: item
        pre 0 < length(s) ≤ stacksize
        post x = last(s'),
    isempty(s: stack) returns b: boolean
        post b = (s = nullseq);

representation
    unique v: vector (item, 1, stacksize), stackpointer: integer
        init stackpointer ← 0;
    rep (v, stackpointer) = seq (v, 1, stackpointer);
    invariant 0 ≤ stackpointer ≤ stacksize;
    states
        empty when stackpointer = 0,
        normal when 0 < stackpointer < stacksize,
        full when stackpointer = stacksize,
        error otherwise;

implementation
    body push out (s.stackpointer = s.stackpointer' + 1 ∧
        s.v = ∝ (s.v', s.stackpointer, x)) =
        empty, normal:: (s.stackpointer ← s.stackpointer + 1;
            s.v[s.stackpointer] ← x);
        full:: overflow;
        error:: failure;
    body pop out (s.stackpointer ← s.stackpointer - 1) =
        normal, full:: s.stackpointer ← s.stackpointer - 1;
        empty:: underflow;
        error:: failure;
    body top out (x = s.v[s.stackpointer]) =
        normal, full:: x ← s.v[s.stackpointer];
        empty:: underflow;
        error:: failure;
    body isempty out (b = (s.stackpointer = 0)) =
        normal, full:: b ← false;
        empty:: b ← true;
        error:: failure;
    ...
endform;
```

Figure 12.3:   A stack module in Alphard (*Source: R. Kimm et al,* Einfuhrung in software engineering *(1979). Reproduced by permission of Walter de Gruyter & Co, Berlin.*)

example of figure 12.3, the only operation needed is the assignment, denoted by ←. So the stack module parameter takes the form

```
item:form <←>
```

- The module consists of three parts: **specification**, **representation** and **implementation**. Simple mathematical means are used in the specification part to indicate properties that must hold at the abstract level. For instance, $< \ldots x_i \ldots >$ denotes a sequence. It is further specified that the stack is initially empty (`nullseq`). The pre- and postconditions of all routines are given in the specification part. A condition like

```
post s = s' ~ x
```

should be read as: after execution of this routine s is equal to the concatenation (~) of the old value of s (denoted by s') and x. This type of specification is known as an abstract model specification. In abstract model specifications, new types (such as stacks) are specified in terms of types already known (such as sequences, which are built into the Alphard language). Abstract model specifications have been discussed in chapter 11.

- The representation of the abstract data type in terms of language primitives is given in the representation part.

- Finally, the implementation part contains the bodies of the various routines.

It is now possible to separate a correctness proof of a program using the stack module into two parts:

1. Locally, the correctness of the representation and implementation with respect to the specification is proven. To do so, a number of steps are required. This number depends on the number of routines; see also [Shaw77].
2. At the place where the module is used we need only to prove that the requirements of the module are being fulfilled. These requirements are given in the specification part. In our stack module example, there is but one simple requirement:

```
requires stacksize > 0;
```

12.2.3 CLU

Modules are often used to implement data types whose implementation details are to be hidden from the user. The user may inspect or change values of that data type only through the operations provided. For compound types such as sets or binary trees the internal structure also remains hidden. As a consequence, it is not easy to apply an operation to *all* elements of that compound type. We are then inclined to define, say, procedures `first`, `next` and `last`, and next iterate over a value in the following way:

```
x:= first;
while not last do begin process(x); x:= next end;
process(last);
```

CLU provides an elegant solution to this problem [Liskov77, 86]. Besides procedural and data abstraction, CLU distinguishes yet a third form: iterator abstraction. CLU allows us to define one or more loop constructs within a module defining a compound type (CLU modules are called **cluster** for a change). These constructs may be exported, just like variables, procedures, etc. Outside the module, the syntax of these constructs is the same as that of ordinary loop constructs. In the next example, an iterator elements is defined.

```
set = cluster is create, insert, elements, ...
   rep = array[int]

   create = proc () returns (cvt)
      return (rep$new())
      end create
   insert = proc (s: set, i: int)
      if ~ member(s, i) then rep$addh(down(s), i) end
      end insert
   elements = iter (s: cvt) yields (int)
       i: int:= rep$low(s)
      while true do
          yield (s[i])
            except when bounds: return end
          i:= i + 1
          end
      end elements

   ...
end set
```

Figure 12.4: A CLU module implementing sets

Figure 12.4 sketches what a module implementing sets of integers might look like. Objects in CLU, like the set in this example, are seen as abstract objects outside the module. Inside the module we will often want to use the concrete representation. CLU provides two special operators to switch from concrete representation to abstract object and vice versa, called **up** and **down**, respectively. These operations may be used only within a cluster, and only for the data type being defined by that cluster. Quite often, we will want to execute a **down** operation upon entry of a routine and an **up** operation on exit. As a shortcut for this combination, the reserved word **cvt** (convert) is introduced. It may only be used in routine headings.

In the above example, sets are represented by arrays and this is indicated in the line **rep** = array[int]. Inside the cluster we may from now on use the token rep to stand for the data type being defined. In CLU, arrays are also defined by some cluster. So, functions on arrays follow the same notation as functions on user-defined types, though the language provides shortcuts to make certain expressions resemble the more familiar array-notation. For example, array[int]$store(a, i, 5) may be abbreviated to a[i]:= 5. The $ symbol is the equivalent of the period in languages like Pascal or Ada. In the routine insert, **rep** has been used as an abbreviation of array[int] in the call **rep**$addh(**down**(s), i). CLU arrays are dynamic. The routine addh makes the array grow one element and assigns a value to that new element.

Finally, we come to the iterator elements. Initially, the local variable i is set to the lower bound of the array s. The elements s[i] are next returned one after the other. The exception bounds occurs when i exceeds the upper bound of the array. In that case the iterator is ended. Use of the iterator outside the cluster takes the form of an ordinary loop construct. The example given at the start of this section may now be written as

```
for i: int in set$elements(s) do
   process(i)
end
```

12.2.4 Modula-2

Modula-2 is the successor of Pascal. Both languages were designed by Niklaus Wirth. We will base our discussion on version 3.

The main extension of Modula-2 with respect to Pascal is the addition of the module concept. Other features of Modula-2 include various low-level constructs to ease the writing of systems programs, a co-routine mechanism, and correction of some of the less pleasant properties of Pascal. For instance, the order of type, constant, variable declarations and the like is free in Modula-2, whereas Pascal prescribes some strict ordering of these.

Modula-2 has two kinds of modules: local modules and global modules. Local modules are textually included within a procedure or some other module. A global module comes in two parts: a definition part and an implementation part. Both these parts are compilation units. They are compiled separately from each other and the rest of the program. The definition part contains information that is relevant to the user of the module. The implementation part contains the implementation details. The main program itself is a module also. It is an implementation module that has no definition part. Below, we discuss only global modules.

Figure 12.5 gives the outline of a stack module in Modula-2. The definition module contains names of procedures, constants, types, etc., that are accessible to the user of that module. Export of these names is implicit. The fact that these names are included in the definition module implies their export.

```
definition module stacks;
   from defs import item;
   type stackptr;
   procedure create(var s: stackptr);
   procedure push(s: stackptr; x: item);
   procedure pop(s: stackptr): item;
   ...
end stacks.

implementation module stacks;
   from defs import stacksize, item;
   from Storage import ALLOCATE;
   type stackptr = pointer to stack;
      stack = record
         index: cardinal;
         store: array [1 .. stacksize] of item
      end;

   procedure create(var s: stackptr);
   begin
      ALLOCATE(s, SIZE(stack));
      s↑.index:= 0
   end create;

   procedure push(s: stackptr; x: item);
   begin
      if s↑.index = stacksize
      then ...
      else s↑.index:= s↑.index + 1;
         s↑.store[s↑.index]:= x
      end push;

   ...
end stacks.
```

Figure 12.5:   Outline of a stack module in Modula-2

A main program that uses the module stacks may now look as follows:

```
module main;
   import stacks;
   var st1, st2: stacks.stackptr;

begin
   stacks.create(st1);
   stacks.create(st2);

   stacks.push(st1, 1);
   stacks.push(st2, 2);

   ...
end main.
```

Both definition and implementation modules may import names. The names to be imported are to be listed in an import clause which is of the form

```
import A, ...
```

or

```
from A import name₁, name₂, ...
```

Using the first form, all names from A's definition module are imported. The familiar dot notation is used to refer to them, as in A.name. In the second form, only those names that are listed are imported. Also, when referring to them, the dot notation is not used and we may simply write name₁, name₂, ...

The export of types merits some further discussion. The definition module in figure 12.5 contains just the type name, while further details are given in the implementation module. This type of export is called non-transparant, or opaque. The details of the type remain hidden from the user. Alternatively, we may also include the full type definition in the definition module (so-called transparant export). But then the user also has access to these details. With opaque export we are forced to implement the type as a pointer type. (This obligation can be explained as follows. We may use the module stacks without any knowledge of the implementation module. In that case the compiler must be able to generate code for a call of, say, push. Generating code for such a call implies allocation of storage for the parameters of the procedure. Therefore, the size of these parameters must be known. Values of a pointer type have constant size, hence there is no problem in doing so.)

In the stack example we have not yet specified the type of the stack elements. Yet, all our stacks will have the same element type. The compiler will statically bind the module stacks and the module defs which contains a definition of type item.

We may decide on the order in which some set of Modula-2 modules must be compiled in the following way: the set of modules making up some program can be viewed as a directed graph. One of its nodes corresponds to the main program. Outgoing edges from this node lead to nodes $A_1, \ldots, A_n$. These nodes correspond to modules that are (directly) used by the main program, i.e. the main program contains import clauses in which these modules are named. In order for the compiler to be able to do the necessary type checking, it must have access to the type information of imported objects. Thus, the definition parts of modules A_i must have been compiled first. Therefore, we had better speak of a dependency between the main program and the definition modules DA_i. Each of these definition modules may itself also contain import clauses. So the graph contains outgoing edges from DA_i to $DA_{i1}, \ldots, DA_{im}$. This process may go on for a while. The end nodes correspond to definition modules that do not contain any import clause.

The implementation part of a module A may also contain import clauses. This happens if modules used by A are not visible at the definition level. We may thus, starting from some implementation module IA, build a graph indicating the (definition) modules that are used, directly or indirectly, by IA.

Finally, each definition module is bound to the corresponding implementation module. We may view the implementation module as a 'user' of the corresponding definition module as the implementation module must fulfill the requirements stated in the definition module, such as the right spelling of names, and the number and type of procedure parameters.

The graph thus obtained is connected: we cannot split the nodes of the graph into two disjoint sets such that there is no edge connecting some node from one set with some node from the other set. If this were the case, the main program (a node in either set) would bear no direct or indirect relation with a number of definition and/or implementation modules. The connectivity of the graph also follows from the construction sketched above.

The graph is not allowed to contain cycles. In other words: there should not be a path that goes from some node A, through zero or more other nodes, back to A again. In that case, module A would use itself, directly or indirectly, through some chain of import clauses. It is not possible to determine a compilation order for such a chain of modules.

From this directed, connected, acyclic graph of module dependencies a compilation order can be obtained through topological sorting (see, e.g. Stubbs87]). Suppose we denote an edge from node A to B as B < A. In that case, module A uses module B, so B has to be compiled before A. Topologically sorting the graph using this relation < results in a sequence of modules $x_1, \ldots, x_n$, such that $\forall\, i, j: x_i < x_j => i < j$. Compilation in the order $x_1, \ldots, x_n$ is then allowed. Note that in general this order is not unique, i.e. the sequence is only partially ordered.

To illustrate this algorithm, consider the following program outline:

```
module main;
    import B, C;
definition module B;
    import A;
definition module C;
    import A, D;
implementation module B;
    import D;
implementation module C;
    import E;
```

The definition modules of A, D and E do not contain import clauses. The graph of module dependencies for this program is given in figure 12.6. In this figure, subscripts def and impl denote the definition and implementation part of a module, respectively.

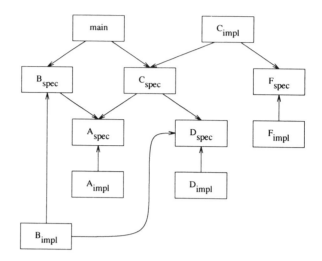

Figure 12.6: Module dependencies in a Modula-2 program

One possible compilation order for this program is given by the following sequence:

A_{def}, D_{def}, E_{def}, B_{def}, C_{def}, A_{impl}, D_{impl}, E_{impl}, B_{impl}, C_{impl}, main

Another possible order is given by

A_{def}, D_{def}, E_{def}, A_{impl}, D_{impl}, E_{impl}, B_{def}, C_{def}, B_{impl}, C_{impl}, main

12.2.5 Ada

Around 1974 the first efforts were started on the design of a new programming language for the US DoD. The language was to be suitable for all DoD applications.

A first list of requirements was published in a 1975 report that became known as STRAWMAN. After various iterations (WOODENMAN, TINMAN, IRONMAN), the final requirements were laid down in the STEELMAN-report (1978). After publication of the IRONMAN-report in 1977, an open invitation was issued to solicit contracts to develop the new language. After a first selection, four groups were selected and asked to design a language.

The four languages developed became known as RED, GREEN, YELLOW and BLUE. After a thorough selection process, the 'green' language was chosen, developed by a French team (CII-Honeywell) led by Jean Ichbiah.

The language was called Ada, after Ada Augusta Byron, Countess of Lovelace, daughter of the poet Lord Byron. She was Charles Babbage's secretary. Amongst others, Charles Babbage designed the analytical engine (1834), a precursor to our present-day computers. It is said that Ada Byron wrote a 'program' to compute Bernouilli numbers on the analytical engine. Hence she is called the first programmer.

The first publicly available Ada report appeared in 1979 [SIGPLAN79]. Various revisions followed. The ANSI-standard appeared in 1983 [Ada83].

Ada is strongly influenced by Pascal. The main goals behind Ada are the following (cf. STEELMAN):

- The language must be suited for the development of **embedded computer systems**. Those are systems where the computer is but a small part of the overall system, e.g. large weapon systems. These computers are often geared towards a very specific task. They are not equipped with the kind of supporting software that comes with general-purpose computers. Embedded computers are not well-suited to *develop* software.

  This leads to a so-called *host–target* approach. The software that has to run on the target computer is developed on a host machine, which has a number of consequences: for instance, with respect to services to be provided by the programming environment.

- The language must be suited for the design, implementation and maintenance of *large* systems, that change over time and yet have a long lifetime.

- The language must be machine-independent.

- It must be possible to create a usable programming environment (APSE— Ada Programming Support Environment) for the language. APSEs are further discussed in chapter 15.

The major extensions of Ada with respect to Pascal are:

1. The introduction of the `package` concept as a means to achieve data abstraction (information hiding).

2. The notion of a `task` to express parallel processes.

3. The possibility to independently compile a module specification (heading) and the corresponding module implementation (body).

4. Facilities for exception handling, whereby exceptional cases can be handled on a level different from the one where these exceptions occur.

In our discussion we will concentrate on the first point mentioned. An Ada package offers great potential to describe abstract data types. Even if the encapsulated piece of software does not encapsulate an abstract data type in the strict sense, packages provide a useful means to group logically related routines and limit the export and import of objects.

A package comes in two parts, the *package specification* and *package body*. They may be separately compiled. The specification part contains the information needed by the outside world. Roughly, this boils down to names of types and procedure headings. Implementation details are hidden in the package body.

```
generic
   size: positive;
   type elem is private;
package stack is
   procedure push(e: in elem);
   function pop return elem;
   overflow, underflow: exception;
end stack;

package body stack is
   s: array (1 .. size) of elem;
   index: integer range 0 .. size:= 0;

   procedure push(e: in elem) is
   begin
      if index = size then raise overflow; end if;
      index:= index + 1; s(index):= e;
   end push;

   function pop return elem is
   begin
      if index = 0 then raise underflow; end if;
      index:= index - 1; return s(index + 1);
   end pop;
   ...
end stack;
```

Figure 12.7:   Outline of a stack module in Ada

An Ada package may have types as parameters. In that case it is called a
generic package. Upon instantiation, some concrete type has to be given as an
actual parameter. The example below will illustrate the use of generic packages.

There are two rather different ways to define packages. They differ in the exact
location where objects of the encapsulated type are declared. One does so in the
program part using the package, the other declares them in the package body.
Except for some implementation details (and possible philosophical arguments)
both ways are to a large extent interchangeable.

Figure 12.7 contains one possible formulation of a generic stack package. Both
the maximum size of the stack and the type of the stack elements are parameters
to the package. Instances of this generic package can be obtained and used along
the following lines:

```
declare
   package stackint is new stack(200, integer);
   package stackbool is new stack(100, boolean);
   use stackint, stackbool;
begin
   ...
   push(n);
   b:= pop;
   ...
end;
```

The **use** clause of Ada has a function similar to the Pascal **with** clause. It allows us to use the names exported by some module X without the prefix 'X.'. If, in the above program fragment, n is an integer and b a boolean variable, then the compiler can recognize that the call of push necessarily refers to stackint, while pop refers to stackbool. In case the compiler is not able to uniquely determine the package that some routine belongs to, for instance because we are using two stacks of integers, we are obliged to use the dot notation.

Ada also has a **with** clause. Its purpose is similar to that of the import clause of Modula-2. Just like in Modula-2, export in Ada is implicit. Names given in the specification part of a module are available to the user of that module.

An alternative generic formulation of a generic package for stacks runs as follows (the package body is omitted):

```
generic
    type elem is private;
package stacks is
    type stack(size: positive) is limited private;
    procedure push(s: in out stack; e: in elem);
    function pop(s: in out stack) return elem;
    overflow, underflow: exception;
private
    type stack(size: positive) is
      record
        s: array (1 .. size) of elem;
        index: integer range 0 .. integer'last:= 0
      end record;
end;
```

To be able to use the above package, an instantiation of it must be created, just as in the previous example. Next, stacks with the desired type of elements can be declared:

```
declare
    package stackint is new stacks(integer);
    use stackint;
    s: stackint(100);
begin
    ...
    push(s, 20);
    ...
end.
```

The latter version closely resembles the stack module as given for Modula-2 in the previous section. For the Modula-2 version we noted the restriction that the actual stack type had to be a pointer type. This restriction does not hold in Ada. However, in order to make it possible for the compiler to generate code for a call like push(s, n) in a module using stacks, the full declaration of the stack type has to be included in the specification part. The postfix **(is) private** in the type definition of the specification part prevents details of the definition to be exported. If the postfix **(is) private** is used, a program using this module may use only the operations : =, = and ≠ next to the operations explicitly exported by the module. The postfix **limited** excludes the assignment and (in)equality operators as well. We may then use only the operations exported by the module.

Modules in Ada can be parameterized with types. Such modules are called generic. Upon translation of a generic package the actual parameter type provided in some instantiation is yet unknown. The question then is: which operations are allowed on objects of that type within the package being defined? For example, suppose we define a generic package and within this package we wish to add values of a type given as parameter using an operator '+'. We must then be sure that such an operator is available for each type used in an instantiation of the package. The operations expected to be available for such a type are given in the parameter part of a generic package. The construct

```
generic
    type elem is private;
```

indicates that within the package only the operations : =, = and ≠ are allowed on objects of type elem. Here too, the postfix **limited private** excludes these operations as well. If we wish to apply other operations, these extra operations must be included in the parameter part, as in

```
generic
    type elem is private;
    with function "*" (u, v: elem) return elem;
```

In this case, a binary operation '*' can be applied to objects of type elem. The compiler will check whether such an operator is available for each type used in an instantiation of this package.

The package specification and body may be compiled separately. Obviously, the specification has to be compiled first. When a system consists of a group of modules and various import clauses, the compilation order is determined by the visibility rules for objects. This is similar to the procedure as discussed for Modula-2 programs.

12.3 OBJECT-ORIENTED PROGRAMMING

Up until now, we have discussed the module concept as it is incorporated into various high-level programming languages. A major use of modules concerns the implementation of abstract data types. The specification part of such a module contains the names of types and procedures accessible to the user. The representation of these types together with other implementation details are contained in the implementation part of the module. Thus, the module provides for *data encapsulation*, or *data hiding*. It is a black box, the internals of which remain hidden to its users. Some people call this object-oriented programming [Booch85].

Others associate object-oriented programming primarily with the language Smalltalk, developed at Xerox PARC in the 1970s. The notion of object-oriented programming originated in that environment. Its roots can be traced back as far as SIMULA-67, though, where the class concept was introduced for the first time. SIMULA-67 classes encapsulate both operations and a state, and subclasses in SIMULA-67 inherit operations and state from their parent class.

In the early 1970s Alan Kay was involved in the development of a visionary hardware/software system called Dynabook at Xerox PARC. The hardware part eventually evolved into the Xerox Star. The software part became Smalltalk. The first version of Smalltalk was released in 1972. The present version is known as Smalltalk-80.* The language is described in [Goldberg83, 84]. Smalltalk-80 is more than a programming language. It comprises a rather elaborate language-oriented programming environment as well. Programming environments are the topic of chapter 15.

In a language like Pascal or Ada, a program contains a number of routines. Each of these routines manipulates certain data structures. If we wish to manipulate these data, we call the appropriate routine, passing the proper data as parameters.

This relation is reversed in the paradigm of object-oriented programming. In that paradigm, the world consists of objects. Each object is an instance of some *class*. Classes encapsulate common properties of a set of objects. An object contains data, its state, and knows a number of operations. These operations are contained in the definition of the object's class. Operations can inspect and/or change the state of an object. If we want to execute an operation, we send a *message* to an object. The operation is given as a parameter. In the terminology of object-oriented programming, an operation is called a *method*.

Up to this point, the difference between object-oriented programming and 'ordinary' programming in languages like Modula-2 or Ada seems philosophical at best. Instead of `sqrt(x)` we might write `x <- sqrt`, but the intention seems to be the same. Languages with the module concept also allow us to put similar objects together with operations on those objects in one component, the module.

A language that allows us to encapsulate abstract data types in modules is sometimes termed **object-based** [Wegner90]. The adjective object-oriented then is reserved for languages supporting **inheritance**. Inheritance is discussed below.

Now, quite a few object-oriented languages are available. [Saunders88] reviews 88 object-oriented languages, about half of which have been introduced since 1984. Many of these are hybrid languages in that they combine a traditional high-level language with some of the features that distinguish object-oriented languages from traditional high-level languages. Examples of the latter are C++ [Stroustrup91] and Objective-C [Cox86]. Both are extensions of C, well known in UNIX circles. C++ is discussed in section 12.3.1. Other object-oriented languages find their origins in AI and are often Lisp-based. In such languages, objects tend to be dynamic, in that operations on objects may be added dynamically. Some

---

* Smalltalk-80 is a trademark of ParcPlace Systems.

of the object-oriented languages originate from work on concurrent systems. In these, objects correspond to processes that can be executed concurrently.

In the following discussion, we will restrict ourselves to object-oriented languages having one thread of control, i.e. we do not discuss concurrent languages. Moreover, the objects are assumed to be passive, i.e. objects have a statically known set of operations associated with them. This excludes most of the Lisp-based object-oriented languages. A more elaborate assessment of the design space of object-oriented languages can be found in [Wegner87].

We discuss the main principles of object-oriented programming through the 'seven steps towards object-oriented happiness', as given in [Meyer88]. Meyer developed a 'pure' object-oriented language called Eiffel. Figure 12.8 gives the outline of some Eiffel classes. This example will be used to illustrate the various issues that set object-oriented languages apart from other languages. The line numbers obviously are not part of the program text; they are used as references in the text. The syntax used is that of Eiffel Version 3, which slightly deviates from that used in [Eiffel88]. For example, features are exported by default in Eiffel 3, so that we generally do not need an export-clause.

Step 1: Systems are modularized on the basis of their data structures.

Step 2: Objects should be described as implementations of abstract data types.

From a design point of view, these principles have been discussed extensively in chapter 10. If we modularize a system according to its data structures we obtain a system that scores well on the various design criteria identified. At the language level these steps are supported by languages offering the module concept.

A word of caution is needed as well. There are many aspects that influence a design, and a properly designed system may well contain modules that do not encapsulate some data structure.

Step 3: Unused objects should be deallocated by the underlying language system, without programmer intervention.

In a traditional block-structured language, local variables can easily be managed using a stack. Upon entering a new block, space for local variables is claimed on a stack. Upon leaving the block, the corresponding stack frame is released again. Things become somewhat more complicated if dynamic data structures are implemented using pointers. A language then forces you to explicitly allocate memory through calling a routine ALLOCATE. You also have to explicitly deallocate such space once it is no longer needed. Since allocation and deallocation of memory for dynamic objects need not follow a stack-like behavior, reusing such memory becomes a problem. A system function known as *garbage collection* takes care of collecting this unused space. However, quite a few implementations of languages supporting dynamic data structures do not support garbage collection.

```
1    class POLYGON
2    feature
3       vertices: LINKED_LIST[POINT];
4       translate (a, b: REAL) is
5             -- Move by a horizontally, b vertically
6          do
7             from vertices.start until vertices.offright
8             loop
9                vertices.value.translate (a, b);
10               vertices.forth
11            end
12         end; -- translate
13      rotate (center: POINT; angle: REAL) is
14            -- Rotate by angle around center
15         do ... end;
16      perimeter: REAL is
17            -- Length of the perimeter
18         local this, previous: POINT
19         do
20            from vertices.start; this:= vertices.value
21            until vertices.islast
22            loop
23               previous:= this;
24               vertices.forth;
25               this:= vertices.value;
26               Result:= Result + this.distance (previous)
27            end;
28            Result:= Result + this.distance (vertices.first)
29         end; -- perimeter
30   end -- class POLYGON
31   class RECTANGLE
32   inherit
33      POLYGON redefine perimeter
34   feature
35      side1, side2: REAL; -- The two side lengths
36      diagonal: REAL;
37      perimeter: REAL is
38            -- Redefinition of the POLYGON version
39         do
40            Result:= 2 * (side1 + side2)
41         end; --perimeter
42   end -- class RECTANGLE
```

Figure 12.8:   Outline of some Eiffel classes (*Source: B. Meyer*, Object-oriented Software Construction, *Prentice-Hall, 1988. Reproduced by permission of Prentice-Hall.*)

Explicit deallocation by the programmer can be somewhat tricky. The programmer may simply forget to do so. Worse still, memory that is still needed may be deallocated—an easy occurrence when two pointers point to the same object and memory is deallocated through one of these while the other pointer is still used (so-called *dangling references*).

In traditional languages, the main structure of a program is hierarchical. Thus, dynamic memory allocation is needed only for a small part of the variables. This is rather different in object-oriented programming, where the main structure of a program tends to be that of a loose collection of classes that implement abstract data types. Keeping track of which objects are still needed at any point in time then becomes rather tricky and leaving the job of memory management to the system a great relief.

Garbage collection has its price though. The overhead caused by automatic garbage collection may not be affordable. Worse still, we cannot predict when the garbage collection routine will be called. Intermediate forms, in which the user can indicate whether or not garbage collection is to be done automatically, offer an interesting alternative.

Step 4: Every non-simple type is a module, and every high-level module is a type.

Let us for the moment ignore the adjective 'non-simple'. Then a type is a module and a module is a type.

In Modula-2, the implementation part of a module implementing polygons could have the form expressed in figure 12.9. In here, the coupling of type polygon and routines that operate on polygons is *syntactic* in nature. Objects of type polygon do not carry their operations with them.

By identifying the notions of type and module, the binding between a type and the associated operations becomes a semantic one. Rather than having a routine perimeter which has a parameter of type polygon, objects of type polygon have an 'attribute' (or feature) perimeter. Modules then become first-class entities, that can be passed as parameter, or organized into structures.

In Modula-2, a call of the routine perimeter is written as perimeter(p), where p is an object of type polygon. In Eiffel this is written as p.perimeter. The close binding of an object and its operators has a somewhat peculiar effect for binary operators. An addition x:= x + y or x:= Plus(x, y) is written as x.Plus(y) in Eiffel. The message Plus(y) is sent to the object x. This type of asymmetry in expressions is typical for object-oriented languages. It is a consequence of the tight coupling of state data and operations on those data.

The adjective 'non-simple' has a dual purpose. It allows the user to employ familiar notations for simple objects (like a+b rather than a.plus(b)) and these simple objects can often be implemented more efficiently—a restriction that is pragmatic rather than fundamental.

Step 5: A class may be defined as an extension or restriction of another.

This is the notion of **inheritance**, which truly distinguishes object-oriented languages from mere object-based languages.

```
implementation module Polygon;
   type polygon = pointer to edge_list;
       edge_list = record
          edge: point;
          next_edge: polygon
       end;

       procedure perimeter (p: polygon): real;
       var s: real;
          this, next: polygon;
          p_this, p_next: point;
       begin
          if p = nil then return(0)
          else
             s:= 0;
             this:= p; p_this:= this↑.edge; next:= this↑.next;
             while next # nil do
                p_next:= next↑.edge;
                sum:= sum + distance(p_this, p_next);
                this:= next; p_this:= p_next;
                next:= this↑.next
             end;
             return(sum)
          end
       end perimeter;

   ...
end Polygon.
```

Figure 12.9: Outline of a module Polygon in Modula-2

In biology, we are used to depicting species in a tree structure. One of the nodes in this tree is labelled 'mammals'. Properties common to all mammals are associated with this node. At any descendent node hereof we list only additional properties, properties which are not common to all mammals. So the property 'lacteal glands' is associated with the node labelled 'mammals'. The property 'can fly' is not: bats fly, but most of the other subspecies of mammals cannot. If we want to know all the properties of bats, we take the union of the properties at the node labeled 'bats' and the properties at any ancestor node. Bats thus inherit properties from mammals, their parent node in the species tree.

The same idea can be used when we try to relate data types. As an example, consider the class POLYGON from figure 12.8. Polygons have features such as vertices, rotate and perimeter. Next, we may wish to define, say, RECTANGLE. Since rectangles are a special kind of polygon, the features defined for polygons also hold for rectangles. Polygons and rectangles share certain properties. It would be natural to be able to explicitly share these properties in an implementation of those data types, which is possible if the notion of inheritance is supported.

If you look at an implementation of related data types in, say, Modula-2, you will often notice a certain redundancy in the code. Some routines are likely to have identical code. In a language supporting inheritance, RECTANGLE may be defined as a *subclass* of POLYGON. RECTANGLE then inherits the features of POLYGON. Only additional features need be defined. For instance, an additional feature `diagonal` may be defined for rectangles.

If RECTANGLE is a subclass of POLYGON, POLYGON is a *superclass* of RECTANGLE. The notions subclass and superclass are sometimes termed *heir* and *parent*, respectively. The subclass relation obviously is transitive. If we define a class SQUARE as a subclass of RECTANGLE, SQUARE directly inherits properties from RECTANGLE, and indirectly also from POLYGON.

The notions subclass and superclass reflect a linguistic point of view. They allow us to build abstract data types on top of one another. They allow us to explicitly share code between such related data types. In that view, a subclass is best seen as an extension of its superclass. It has all the properties of its parent class, plus a few others.

When viewed as types, rectangles are a restricted form of polygons. A rectangle is a polygon, but the converse is not always true. In this view, a subclass is a restriction of its superclass.

Step 6: Program entities should be permitted to refer to objects of more than one class, and operations should be permitted to have different realizations in different classes.

If we build a Modula-2 program that makes use of polygons and rectangles, program entities like variables denote objects of either type. If P and R are of type POLYGON and RECTANGLE, respectively, Modula-2 assignments

```
P:= R
```

and

```
R:= P
```

are both illegal since the two types involved are incompatible. Once inheritance is supported and RECTANGLE is defined as a subclass of POLYGON, it is natural to allow for an assignment

```
P:= R
```

That is, an object of type POLYGON may be assigned an object of type RECTANGLE. Operations defined for polygons may be applied to P, whether it denotes a polygon or an object of one of its subclasses. The reverse need not be allowed, however (see below).

This concept is known as **polymorphism** (the ability to take more than one form). It is phrased in the first part of step 6.

One of the operations defined for polygons is perimeter. If a polygon is represented as a set of vertices, the implementation of perimeter amounts to adding the distances between adjacent vertices, as is done in lines 19–29 of figure 12.8. For rectangles there might be a much easier way to compute its perimeter. Thus, we would like to be able to redefine perimeter within RECTANGLE. The redefinition is indicated in line 33. The new definition of perimeter follows in line 37–41.

Once redefinitions are allowed, it is no longer possible to statically bind operator invocations with their definition. If P is defined to be of type POLYGON, we would like P.perimeter to denote the definition in either POLYGON or RECTANGLE, depending on the actual type of P. Since this may vary at runtime, so will the actual operation to be invoked.

This process is known as **dynamic binding**. In languages like Modula-2, the binding between a routine call and its definition is made statically, i.e. at compile time.

The flexible binding between operator invocations and their definition alluded to in this context is caused by the type inclusion property of related classes. Other kinds of such flexible, but not necessarily dynamic, bindings are:

- implicit type coercions, as in a+b where both a and b may be of type integer or real;

- operator overloading as is offered in Ada, where the compiler can identify a routine call P(x) on the basis of the type of x (which is known at compile time);

- generic modules such as offered by Ada, which allow us to parameterize modules with types.

There is a relation between the rules for dynamic binding and those for type checking.

In Smalltalk, entities may denote objects of any type. Thus, there is no static type checking. The classes in a Smalltalk-program constitute a tree, i.e. each class has exactly one parent class. If during execution of a program a message M with parameter B is sent to an object A, then the actual message identified is found as follows:

1. Let AA be the class of A (A is of type AA).

2. If AA contains a definition of a message M with a parameter of type BB, where BB is the type of B, then that message is selected. Otherwise

3. if AA is the root of the class hierarchy, the message cannot be identified and an error message is given. Otherwise

4. replace AA with the superclass of AA, and reiterate step 2.

In this process, the path from class AA to the root of the class hierarchy is searched for the first matching message definition.

The virtues of strong typing are well known. Strong typing leads to fewer programming errors and more reliable programs. In the object-oriented language Eiffel, the notions of strong typing and inheritance have been reconciled. Part of this reconciliation has been hinted at above. If P and R are declared to be of type POLYGON and RECTANGLE, respectively, then the assignment

```
P := R
```

is valid in Eiffel, but

```
R := P
```

is not. Whether P denotes a polygon or a rectangle, the compiler can still check whether P.X is valid. It is valid only if X is defined in POLYGON. The binding of P.X to some definition of X, however, still has to be postponed until runtime. If X is redefined in RECTANGLE and P happens to denote a rectangle, the redefined version must be selected.

The reverse is not true. A reference R.X cannot be checked for type conformancy. Though X could be defined for rectangles, it need not be for polygons.

As noted above, routines may be redefined in subclasses. There are circumstances in which you would like to *force* such a redefinition. Suppose we have a class FIGURE. Its instances denote figures. FIGURE has several subclasses, such as POLYGON, CIRCLE, and LINE. A routine Draw cannot effectively be defined in FIGURE. We really have to know which type of figure it concerns in order to be able to generate a picture of it. To that end, FIGURE may contain a definition of Draw which merely tells us that some implementation is to be found in each of its subclasses. Draw is called a **deferred routine**. A class containing a deferred routine is called a **deferred class**. (In other languages deferred classes are called **abstract classes**.)

By using deferred routines, the type checking rules can still be applied. If D is a figure, the compiler knows that D.Draw is a valid routine call. Note that objects cannot be of a type that corresponds to a deferred class. Though D.Draw is a valid routine call, an actual definition thereof exists only for subclasses of Figure. As such, deferred classes serve as a mere means to share attributes between related types.

Step 7: It should be possible to declare a class as heir to more than one class, and more than once to the same class.

The Smalltalk class hierarchy is a tree, i.e. each class is a direct descendant of exactly one other class. Thus, it directly inherits from one class only. This is called **single inheritance**. For some applications, this restriction forces you to organize classes in a somewhat unnatural way.

Suppose we want to write an application that allows us to draw graphs of certain mathematical functions. We may define one class MATH which encapsulates our mathematical objects. Another class GRAPHS contains our drawing primitives. With single inheritance, we are forced to define MATH as a superclass of GRAPHS, or vice versa. Both views are unnatural, though, since the two classes are not really related.

With so-called **multiple inheritance** we may define a class MATHGRAPHS as a subclass of both MATH and GRAPHS. Eiffel supports multiple inheritance.

Multiple inheritance may lead to naming conflicts. If A is an object of type MATHGRAPHS, a reference to a routine A.X may be ambiguous. X may be defined in both MATH (or one of its ancestors) and GRAPHS (or one of its ancestors). Rules are needed for solving such conflicts. The Eiffel rules resemble those for solving naming conflicts in Ada programs that have multiple imports.

Repeated inheritance occurs when a class is an ancestor of another class in more than one way and this often occurs in the context of multiple inheritance. If both MATH and GRAPHS inherit from some class BASICS, MATHGRAPHS inherits from BASICS in two ways.

Again, the general rule is that the proper definition is identified if it can be done unambiguously. If not, the programmer has to disambiguate things through renaming of routines.

The major distinguishing feature of object-oriented languages is inheritance. Inheritance offers excellent opportunities for reuse and extensibility. If we are in need of software which resembles existing software, we are not forced to tinker with the existing code. We may rather define one or more new classes which inherit most of the code from existing classes, and need only rewrite what is different. By defining collections of reusable classes, we may build up a base of reusable components. Examples of such class libraries are discussed in [Meyer90], [Booch90].

If we want to extend a system, the inheritance mechanism and the associated polymorphism and dynamic binding facilities ensure that the existing code remains valid.

Inheritance also holds some dangers. Object-oriented languages differ substantially in their inheritance rules. In its most simple form, subclasses simply extend the set of features of their parent class. This is also known as the 'is-a' relation. It is the type of class hierarchy that reflects a proper classification structure.

However, features may undergo almost any transformation in the mapping from class to subclass. For instance, we could have redefined perimeter within RECTANGLE into something semantically very different from its counterpart in POLYGON. Obviously, such is not to be recommended.

We favor a very disciplined use of the class hierarchy and the inheritance mechanism induced. As noted in our discussion of object-oriented analysis and design in chapter 10, the relation between classes in the class hierarchy should be a semantic one. Relating classes for the mere sake of code sharing is a very bad idea.

When redefining a feature, its effect must stay within the realm of the original definition. This can be stated more formally in terms of pre- and postconditions [Meyer88]. In redefining a feature, the precondition may be replaced only by a weaker one, while the postcondition may only be replaced by a stronger one.

This can also be interpreted in view of a 'contracting' metaphor. The features of class POLYGON with their pre- and postconditions constitute a contract. The contract says that the client is bound to the precondition and entitled to the postcondition. The converse is true for the implementer. Class POLYGON may in turn subcontract certain features to someone who can do it better or cheaper, as we did with the redefinition of perimeter in RECTANGLE. Obviously, the subcontractor should at least do the job requested.

If these guidelines are adhered to, object-oriented happiness may truly come about.

12.3.1 C++

C++ is designed to be a 'better C'. C is the prevalent programming language in UNIX circles. The name C++ signifies the evolutionary changes that led from C to C++. The name is inspired by the increment operator of C which is written as '++'. By far the larger part of C is retained as a subset of C++. So C++ is a hybrid object-oriented language. It offers the features that are typical of object-oriented languages, but it also allows you to write in the more traditional imperative style of programming. Features from C not supported by C++ are mostly minor ones dwarfed by the extensions offered by C++. Obviously, the major extension concerns the ability to define and interrelate classes.

The first version of C++ dates from 1985 and is described in [Stroustrup86]. A number of features have been added since then. These additions caused the language manual to more than double in size. The revised version of C++ is described in the second edition [Stroustrup91]. The current ANSI and ISO standardization efforts largely follow this second edition. From an object-oriented point of view, the most striking difference is that the second edition supports multiple inheritance, while the first version supported only single inheritance. We will base our discussion on the second edition.

An outline of a C++ class POLYGON along the lines of the example from figure 12.8 is given in figure 12.10. Reserved words of the language are written in boldface for legibility. The first part defines objects of type POLYGON to consist of a state vertices and operators translate, rotate and perimeter. The operators are called **member functions** in C++. They are accessed using the dot-notation, as in P.perimeter.

In this example we included vertices in the public part (the class interface), so that users may access it. Alternatively, we could have included the state in the private part of the class by starting the example as follows:

```
class POLYGON {
    lslist <point> vertices;
public:
```

```
class POLYGON {
public:
    Islist <point> vertices;
    void translate (real, real);
    void rotate (point, real);
    virtual real perimeter ();
};

real POLYGON:: perimeter ()
{
    real Res = 0;
    point this = vertices.first;
    while (vertices.islast == 0) do
        {
            point previous = this;
            this = vertices.forth;
            Res = Res + this.distance (previous);
        }
    Res = Res + this.distance (vertices.first);
    return Res;
}

class RECTANGLE: public POLYGON {
public:
    real side1, side2;
    real diagonal;
    real perimeter ()
};

real RECTANGLE:: perimeter ()
{
    return 2* (side1 + side2);
}
```

Figure 12.10: Outline of some C++ classes

and incorporate routines to access the state in the public part. The actual definition of the operations follows the class definition. The definition of an operation, like `perimeter`, includes the name of its class. The second part of the example contains the definition of RECTANGLE as a subclass of POLYGON. In C++ terminology, a subclass is called a **derived class**, and a superclass is called a **base class**.

The vertices of a polygon are represented by a list of points. Lists are supposed to be implemented in a generic class Islist, much like the LINKED_LIST[POINT] in the Eiffel example. Generic classes are termed **templates** in C++. Templates have been added in the second edition of C++.

C++ is a statically typed language. In the context of an expression or routine call, the compiler will identify a particular definition on the basis of the name of the operator or routine and the types of its parameters. The precise rules are fairly complicated because of the many conversions between types that are

312 Programming Languages

possible in C++. Suffice it to say that the identification algorithm has to come up with exactly one applicable definition.

In a true object-oriented language we would like to be able to have different definitions of operations in different subclasses. Since an object P of type POLYGON may actually be a RECTANGLE, we would like to invoke the proper definition based on the runtime type of P. This was referred to as dynamic binding in the previous section. Whereas dynamic binding is the default mechanism in Eiffel, such has to be explicitly indicated in C++. We do so by writing

```
virtual real perimeter ();
```

in the superclass definition. To ensure type compatibility at compile-time, the type of the operation is fixed by the superclass and cannot be overridden in a subclass.

If a definition of a virtual function can be given only at the subclass level (such as a print operation for arbitrary figures), it can be defined as a **pure virtual function** at the base class level. That base class then is an **abstract class**. We cannot create objects of such a type. (So abstract classes and pure virtual functions behave like deferred classes and deferred features, respectively, in Eiffel.)

As this discussion shows, many features offered by C++ are also offered by Eiffel. They are often called by different names though. More importantly, C++ is designed to enable the writing of efficient software. Some of the features that are typical for object-oriented languages induce a runtime overhead that may not be affordable in all circumstances. The notion of dynamic binding is a case in point. Rather than imposing the use of these features all of the time, C++ lets the user (programmer) decide when and where the full capabilities of the object-oriented style of programming are warranted.

C++ contains a wide range of additional features which cannot possibly be addressed in this short space. To fully appreciate the capabilities of the language the reader should consult [Stroustrup91].

12.4 SUMMARY AND FURTHER READING

Programming (still) is a central activity in the software construction process. Programming in some higher-level language generally leads to better results. In this chapter we discussed a number of features commonly found in such high-level languages. Many of these languages still require a strong discipline in order to achieve reliable products.

Many text books are available for each of the languages discussed. Good overviews can be found in [Sethi89], [Appleby91], [Friedman91], [Watt90], [Dershem90].

Conventional languages generally offer just the procedure concept as a unit of abstraction. This concept is not particularly useful for indicating the structure-in-the-large of software. To that end, a number of languages offer the module concept. A module allows us to group a number of related routines. A module has a well-defined interface with its environment. Often, modules can be compiled separately from the environment in which they are used. Modules offer a very natural means to implement abstract data types.

Traditional imperative languages lead to rather static programs. Through inheritance and related notions, object-oriented languages offer a means to obtain more flexible software, software that is easier to adapt to new circumstances. They offer promising ways to build reusable component libraries.

The object-oriented language Smalltalk-80 and its associated programming environment are discussed in [Goldberg83, 84]. [Kaehler86] is an introductory text book for Smalltalk-80. Hybrid object-oriented languages such as C++ and Objective-C are discussed in [Stroustrup91] and [Cox86], respectively.

Lately, object-oriented languages have drawn a lot of attention. Special conferences are devoted to the topic (see for example [OOPSLA89, 90, 91]). There is no concensus yet as to what 'object-oriented' exactly means. Different languages use slightly different definitions of concepts like 'object', 'class', 'type', with subtle but sometimes far-reaching consequences as regards the use of such languages. [Wegner89], [Korson90] and [Nierstrasz89] discuss object-oriented concepts and their different interpretations. [Saunders88] gives a survey of a large number of object-oriented languages. [Blaschek89] compares C++, Eiffel and Smalltalk.

EXERCISES

1. What problems and/or opportunities do you foresee if the KWIC-index example from chapter 10 were to be implemented in FORTRAN? What if the implementation language is Ada?

2. What are the advantages/disadvantages of a 'pure' object-oriented language such as Eiffel or Smalltalk over a hybrid language like C++?

3. Discuss differences between single and multiple inheritance in object-oriented languages. Assess both consequences for design and implementation concerns such as naming conflicts.

4. Under what circumstances do you consider gotos admissible, or possibly even preferable, to structured language constructs?

5. Assess the differences in the module constructs as provided by Ada and Modula-2. Which approach do you favor?

6. Assess the advantages of typed programming languages over untyped ones.

7. In what ways do language constructs like the module or class support the development of reusable building blocks?

8. What is your favorite language for the implementation of:

— a text-processing system,
— a numerical package,
— a system for salary administration,
— a window-management system.

Motivate your choice.

13
Testing

Suppose you are asked to answer the kind of questions posed in [Baber82]:

— Would you trust a completely automated nuclear power plant?

— Would you trust a completely automated pilot whose software is written by yourself? What if it is written by one of your colleagues?

— Would you dare to write an expert system to diagnose cancer? What if you are personally held liable in a case where a patient dies because of a malfunction of the software?

You will (probably) have difficulties answering all these questions in the affirmative. Why? The hardware of an aeroplane probably is as complex as the software for an automatic pilot. Yet, most of us board an aeroplane without any second thoughts.

As our society's dependence on automation ever increases, the quality of the systems we deliver increasingly determines the quality of our mere existence. We cannot hide from this responsibility. The role of automation in critical applications and the threats these applications pose should make us ponder. *ACM Software Engineering Notes* runs a column 'Risks to the public in computer systems' in which we are told of numerous (near) accidents caused by software failures. The recent discussion on software reliability provoked by SDI is a case in point [Parnas85], [Myers86], [Parnas87a].

Software engineering is still a very immature field. During software construction, many errors are still made. To locate and fix those errors through excessive testing is a laborious affair and mostly not all the errors are found. Good testing is at least as difficult as good design.

With the current state of the art we are not able to deliver fault-free software. Different studies indicate that 30–85 errors are made per 1000 lines of source code [Boehm81]. During testing, quite a few of those errors are found and subsequently fixed. Yet, some errors do remain undetected. [Myers86] gives examples of extensively tested software that still contains 0.5–3 errors per 1000 lines of code.

A fault in the seat reservation system of a major airline company incurred a loss of $50M in one quarter. The computerized system reported that cheap seats were sold out while this was in fact not the case. As a consequence, clients were referred to other companies. The problems were not discovered until quarterly results were found to considerably lag behind those of their competitors.

As yet, scant theory on testing has been developed. Fortunately, however, there do exist a number of test methods and test techniques that have proven to be effective in practice. A number of these will be discussed in this chapter.

Testing is often taken to mean: the execution of a program to see whether it produces the correct output for a given input, which boils down to testing the end-product, the software itself. As such, the testing activity often gets the worst of it. By the time the software has been written, we are often pressed for time, which does not benefit the thoroughness of the testing activity. According to [Boehm83a], postponing test activities for too long is one of the most severe mistakes that is currently made in software development projects.

This postponement makes testing a rather costly affair. Figure 13.1 shows the results of a study by Boehm about the cost of error correction [Boehm76], [Boehm81]. The cost of error correction is depicted relative to the phase in which the error is discovered. This picture shows that errors which are not discovered until after the software has become operational incur costs that are 10 to 90 times higher than those of errors which had been discovered during the design phase.

The development methods and techniques that are applied in the pre-implementation phases are least developed, relatively. It is therefore not surprising that most of the errors are made in those early phases. A study by Boehm shows that over 60% of the errors are introduced during the design phase, as opposed to 40% during implementation [Boehm75]. Worse still, most of the errors introduced at the design phase (two-thirds shaded in figure 13.2.) are not discovered until after the software has become operational.

It is therefore incumbent on us to plan carefully our testing activities as early as possible. We should also start the actual testing activities at an early stage. If we do not start testing until after the implementation stage, we are really far too late. The requirements specification, design, and design specification may also be tested. The rigor hereof depends on the form in which these documents are expressed. This has been hinted at in previous chapters. In section 13.2, we will again highlight the various verification and validation activities that may be applied at the different phases of the software life cycle. The planning and documentation of these activities is discussed in section 13.3.

Before we decide upon a certain approach to testing, we have to determine our test objectives. If the objective is to find as many errors as possible we

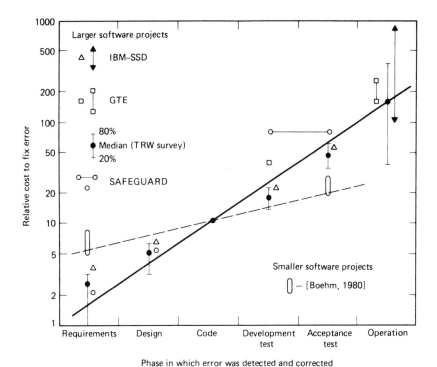

Figure 13.1: Relative cost of error correction (*Source: Barry B. Boehm*, Software Engineering Economics, *fig. 4.2/page 40,* © *1981, Reprinted by permission of Prentice Hall, Inc. Englewood Cliffs, NJ.*)

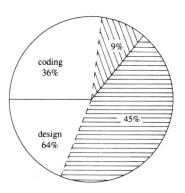

Figure 13.2: Distribution of errors

will opt for a strategy which is aimed at revealing errors. If the objective is to increase our confidence in the proper functioning of the software we may well opt for a completely different strategy. So the objective will have its impact on the test approach chosen, since the results have to be interpreted with respect to the objectives set forth. Different test objectives and the degree to which test approaches fit these objectives are the topic of section 13.1.

Testing software shows only the presence of errors, not their absence. As such, it yields a rather negative result: up to now, only n ($n \geq 0$) errors have been found. Only when the software is tested exhaustively, are we certain about its functioning correctly. In practice this seldom happens. A simple program like

```
for i from 1 to 100 do
   print (if a[i] = true then 1 else 0 endif);
```

has 2^{100} different outcomes. Even on a very fast machine—say a machine which executes 10 million print instructions per second—exhaustively testing this program would take 3×10^{14} year.

An alternative to this brute force approach to testing is to prove the correctness of the software. Proving the correctness of software very soon becomes a tiresome activity, however. It furthermore applies only in circumstances where software requirements are stated formally. Whether these formal requirements are themselves correct has to be decided upon in a different way.

We are thus forced to make a choice. It is of paramount importance to choose a sufficiently small, yet adequate set of test cases. For example, if our objective is to find errors, the set of test cases should be designed such that it leads to the discovery of as many errors as possible. Globally, we may distinguish two methods for the systematic derivation of test cases:

Black box testing, also called **functional analysis**. Using this method, test cases are being derived from the specification of the software, i.e. we do not consider implementation details.

White box testing, or **structural analysis**. This is a complementary method, in which we *do* consider the internal logical structure of the software. In this method we often use tools to keep track of the degree to which the system has been covered by the tests so far. This degree of coverage is used as a measure for the completeness of our test effort.

Different techniques for functional and structural analysis will be discussed in sections 13.5 and 13.6, respectively. These techniques involve the actual execution of a program. Manual techniques which do not involve program execution, such as code reading and inspections, are discussed in section 13.4. In section 13.7 we assess some empirical and theoretical studies that aim to put these different test techniques in perspective.

The above techniques are applied mainly at the module level. This level of testing is often done concurrently with the implementation phase. It is also called

unit testing. Besides the module level, we also have to test the integration of a set of modules into a system. Possibly also, the final system will be tested once more under direct supervision of the prospective user. In section 13.8 we will sketch these different test phases.

13.1 TEST OBJECTIVES

Up till now, we have not been very precise in our use of the notion of an 'error'. In order to appreciate the following discussion, it is important to make a careful distinction between the notions *error*, *fault* and *failure*. In [IEEE83b], an error is defined as a human activity that results in software containing a fault. A fault then is the manifestation of an error. If encountered, a fault may result in a failure.

So, what we observe during testing are failures. These failures are caused by faults, which are in turn the result of human errors. A failure may be caused by more than one fault, and a fault may cause different failures. Similarly, the relation between errors and faults need not be 1–1.

One possible aim of testing is to find faults in the software. Tests are then intended to expose failures. It is not easy to give a precise, unique, definition of the notion of failure. A programmer may take the system's specification as reference point. In this view, a failure occurs if the software does not meet the specifications. The user, however, may consider the software erroneous if it does not match expectations. 'Failure' thus is a relative notion. If software fails, it does so with respect to something else (a specification, user manual, etc.). While testing software, we must always be aware of what the software is being tested against.

In this respect a distinction is often made between 'verification' and 'validation'. [IEEE83b] defines verification as: the process to determine whether the product conforms to the requirements specified in the previous phase. Verification thus tries to answer the question: Have we built the system right?

The term 'validation' is defined in [IEEE83b] as: the process at the end of the software life cycle in which it is tested whether the software conforms to the requirements specification. This type of testing, however, may also be done at earlier stages. Validation then boils down to the question: Have we built the right system?

Even with this catch in mind, the situation is not all that clear-cut. Generally, a program is considered correct if it consistently produces the right output. We may, though, easily conceive of situations where the programmer's intention is not properly reflected in the program, but the errors made simply do not manifest themselves. For example, some entry in a case statement may be wrong, but this fault never shows up because it happens to be subsumed by a previous entry. Is this program correct, or should it rather be classified as a program with a 'latent' fault? Even if it is considered correct within the context at hand, chances are that we get into trouble if the program gets changed, or parts of it get reused in a different environment.

With the above definitions of error and fault, such programs must be considered faulty, even if we cannot devise test cases that reveal the faults. This still leaves open the question of how to define errors. Since we cannot but guess what the programmer's real intentions were, such can only be decided upon by an oracle.

Given the fact that exhaustive testing is infeasible, the test process can be thought of as depicted in figure 13.3. The box labelled P denotes the object (program, design document, etc.) to be tested. The test strategy involves the selection of a subset of the input domain. For each element of this subset, P is used to 'compute' the corresponding output. The expected output is determined by an oracle, something outside the test activity. Finally, the two answers are compared.

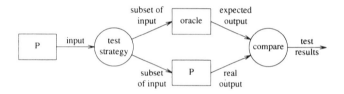

Figure 13.3: Global view of the test process

The most crucial step in this process is the selection of the subset of the input domain which will serve as the test set. This test set must be adequate with respect to the test objective. In section 13.1.1 we discuss the two main test objectives, fault detection and confidence building, and their impact on the test selection problem.

To test whether the objectives are reached, test cases are tried in order that faults manifest themselves. A quite different approach is to view testing as fault prevention. This leads us to another dimension of test objectives, which to a large extent parallels the evolution of testing strategies over the years. This evolution is discussed in section 13.1.2.

Finally, the picture so far considers each fault equally hazardous. In reality, there are different types of faults, and some faults are more harmful than others. All methods to be discussed in this chapter can easily be generalized to cover multiple classes of faults, each with its own acceptance criteria.

Some faults are even critical and we will have to exert ourselves in order to find those critical faults. Special techniques, such as fault tree analysis [Leveson86] have been developed to this end. Using fault tree analysis, we try to derive a contradiction by reasoning backwards from a given, undesirable, end situation. If such a contradiction can be derived, we have shown that that particular situation can never be reached. For a further discussion of safety issues, see [Abbott90] or [Leveson91].

13.1.1 Fault detection versus confidence building

Failures are needles in the haystack of the input domain.
[Hamlet90]

Suppose we wish to test some module P which sorts an array A[1..n] of
integers, and $1 \leq n \leq 1000$. Since exhaustive testing is infeasible, we are looking
for a strategy in which only a small number of tests are exercised. One possible
set of test cases is the following:

let n assume values 0, 1, 17 and 1000. For each of n = 17 and n = 1000, choose
three values for the array A:

— A consists of randomly selected integers;

— A is sorted in ascending order;

— A is sorted in descending order.

In following this type of constructive approach, the input domain is partitioned
in a finite, small number of subdomains. The underlying assumption is that
these subdomains are **equivalence classes**, i.e. from a testing point of view each
member from a given subdomain is as good as any other. For example, we have
tacitly assumed that one random array of length 17 is as good a test as any other
random array of length i with $1 < i < 1000$.

Suppose the actual sorting algorithm used is the one from figure 13.4. If the
tests use positive integers only, the output will be correct. The output will not
be correct if a test input happens to contain negative integers.

The test set using positive integers only does not reveal the fault because the
inputs in the subdomains are not really interchangeable (instead of comparing
the values of array entries, the algorithm compares their absolute values). Any
form of testing which partitions the input domain works perfectly if the right

```
procedure selection-sort (A, n);
integer i, j, small, temp;
begin
   for i:= 1 to n-1 do
      small:= i;
      for j:= i+1 to n do
         if abs(A[j]) < abs(A[small]) then small:= j endif
      enddo;
      temp:= A[i]; A[i]:= A[small]; A[small]:= temp
   enddo
end selection-sort;
```

Figure 13.4: Erroneous selection sort procedure

subdomains are chosen. In practice, however, we generally do not know where the needles are hidden, and the partition of the input domain is likely to be imperfect.

Both functional and structural testing schemes use a systematic means to determine subdomains. They often use peculiar inputs to test peculiar cases. Their intention is to provoke failure behavior. Their success hinges on the assumption that we can indeed identify subdomains with a high failure probability. Though this is a good strategy for fault detection, it does not necessarily inspire confidence.

The user of a system is interested in the probability of failure-free behavior. Following this line of thought, we are not so much interested in the faults themselves, but rather in their manifestations. A fault which frequently manifests itself will in general cause more damage than a fault which seldom shows up. This is precisely what we hinted at in the previous section when we discussed fault detection and confidence building as possible test objectives.

If failures are more important than faults, the goal pursued during the test phase may also change. We will then not pursue the discovery of as many faults as possible, but we will rather strive for a high reliability. Random testing does not work all that well if we want to find as many faults as possible—hence the development of functional and structural test techniques. When pursuing a high reliability, however, it is well possible to use random input.

In order to obtain confidence in the daily operation of a software system, we have to mimic that situation. Such requires the execution of a large number of test cases that represent typical usage scenarios. Random testing does at least as good a job in this respect as any form of testing based on partitioning the input domain [Duran84]. Further evidence hereof can be found in [Hamlet90].

This approach has been applied in the Cleanroom development method [Selby87, Mills87]. In the Cleanroom development method, the development of individual modules is done by programmers who are not allowed to actually execute their code. A programmer then must manually convince himself of the correctness of his modules, using techniques such as stepwise abstraction (see also section 13.4).

In the next step these modules are integrated and tested by someone else. The input for this process is generated according to a distribution which follows the expected operational use of the system. During this integration phase, one tries to reach a certain required reliability level [Currit86]. Experiences with this approach are very promising.

The quantitative assessment of failure probability brings us into the area of software reliability. Chapter 14 is fully devoted to this topic.

13.1.2 From fault detection to fault prevention

In the early days of computing, programs were written and then debugged to make sure that they ran properly. Testing and debugging were largely synonymous terms. Both referred to an activity near the end of the development process when the software had been written, but still needed to be 'checked out'.

Today's situation is rather different. Testing activities occur in every phase of the development process. They are carefully planned and documented. The execution of software to compare actual behavior with expected behavior is only one aspect out of many.

In [Gelperin88], four major testing models are identified. These roughly parallel the historical development of test practices. The models and their primary goals are given in figure 13.5.

Model	Primary goal
Phase models	
Demonstration	Make sure that the software satisfies its specification
Destruction	Detect implementation faults
Life cycle models	
Evaluation	Detect requirements, design and implementation faults
Prevention	Prevent requirements, design and implementation faults

Figure 13.5: Major testing models (*Source: D. Gelperin & B. Hetzel, The growth of software testing*, Communications of the ACM **31**, *6 (1988) 687–695. Reproduced by permission of the Association for Computing Machinery, Inc.*)

The primary goal of the demonstration model is to make sure that the program runs and solves the problem. The strategy is like that of a constructive mathematical proof. If the software passes all tests from the test set, it is claimed to satisfy the requirements. The strategy gives no guidelines as to how to obtain such a test set. A poorly chosen test set may mask poor software quality.

Most programmers will be familiar with the process of testing their own programs by carefully reading them or executing them with selected input data. If such is done very carefully, it can be beneficial. This method also holds some dangers, though. We may be inclined to consider this form of testing as a method to convince ourselves or someone else that the software does *not* contain errors. We will then, partly unconsciously, look for test cases which support this hypothesis. This type of demonstration-oriented approach to testing is not to be advocated.

Proper testing is a very destructive process. A program should be tested with the purpose of finding as many faults as possible. A test can only be considered successful if it leads to the discovery of at least one fault. (In a similar way, a visit to your physician is successful only if he finds a 'fault', and we will generally consider such a visit unsatisfactory if we are sent home with the message that nothing wrong could be found.)

In order to improve the chances of a high quality product, we should therefore reverse the strategy and start looking for test cases that *do* reveal faults. This may be termed a proof by contradiction. The test set is then judged by its ability to detect faults.

Since we do not know whether any residual faults are still left, it is difficult to decide when to stop testing for both these models. In the demonstration-oriented model, the criteria most often used to determine this point in time seem to be the following [Myers79]:

— stop if the test budget has run out;

— stop if all test cases have been executed without any failures occurring.

The first criterion is pointless, since it does not tell us anything about the quality of the test effort. If there is no money at all, this criterion is most easily satisfied. The second criterion is pointless as well, since it does not tell us anything about the quality of the test cases.

The destruction-oriented model usually entails some systematic (functional or structural) way of deriving test cases. We may then base our criterion on the test techniques used. An example of this might be: 'We stop testing if all test cases that result from the boundary value analysis and cause–effect graphs, yield an unsuccessful result.'

Both these models view testing as one phase in the software development process. As noted before, such is not a very good strategy. The life cycle testing models extend testing activities to earlier phases as well. In the evaluation-oriented model, the emphasis is on analysis and review techniques to detect faults in requirements and design documents. In the prevention model, emphasis is on the careful planning and design of test activities. For example, the early design of test cases may reveal that certain requirements cannot be tested and thus such an activity helps to prevent errors from being made in the first place.

We may observe a gradual shift of emphasis in test practice, from a demonstration-like approach to prevention-oriented methods. Though many organizations still concentrate their test effort late in the development life cycle, leading-edge organizations have shown that upstream testing activities can be most effective. Quantitative evidence hereof is provided in section 13.7.2.

13.2 VERIFICATION AND VALIDATION ACTIVITIES FOR THE VARIOUS PHASES OF THE SOFTWARE LIFE CYCLE

In the following subsections we will discuss the various verification and validation activities which can be performed during requirements analysis, design, implementation and maintenance, respectively. In doing so, we will also

Phase	Activities
Requirements analysis	determine test approach
	test requirements specification
	generate functional test data
Design	check consistency between design and requirements specification
	test the design
	generate structural and functional test data
Implementation	check consistency between design and implementation
	test implementation
	generate structural and functional test data
	execute tests
Maintenance	repeat the above tests in accordance with the degree of redevelopment

Figure 13.6: Activities in the various phases of the software life cycle (*Source: W.R. Adrion, M.A. Branstad & J.C. Cherniavski, Validation, verification, and testing of computer software,* ACM Computing Surveys **14**, 2 (1982), *Reproduced by permission of the Association for Computing Machinery, Inc.*)

indicate the techniques and tools that may be applied. These techniques and tools will be further discussed in subsequent sections. A summary is given in figure 13.6.

13.2.1 Requirements analysis

The verification and validation techniques applied during this phase are strongly dependent upon the way in which the requirements specification has been laid down. Something which should be done at the very least is to conduct a careful review or inspection in order to check whether all aspects of the system have been properly described. As we saw earlier, errors made at this stage are very costly to repair if they go unnoticed until late in the development process. Boehm gives four essential criteria for a requirements specification [Boehm84b]:

— completeness;

— consistency;

— feasibility;

— testability.

Testing a requirements specification should primarily be aimed at testing these criteria.

The aim of testing the completeness criterion then is to determine whether all components are present and described completely. A requirements specification is incomplete if it contains such phrases as 'to be determined' or if it contains references to undefined elements. We should also watch for the omission of functions or products, such as back-up or restart procedures and test tools to be delivered to the customer.

A requirements specification is consistent if its components do not contradict each other and the specification does not conflict with external specifications. We thus need both internal and external consistency. Moreover, each element in the requirements specification must be traceable. It must for instance be possible to decide whether a natural language interface is really needed.

According to Boehm, feasibility is more than feasibility with respect to functional and performance requirements. The benefits of a computerized system should outweigh the associated costs. This must be established at an early stage and necessitates timely attention to user requirements, maintainability, reliability, and so on. In some cases, the project's success is very sensitive to certain key factors, such as safety, speed, availability of certain type of personnel, in which case these risks must be analyzed at an early stage.

Lastly, a requirements specification must be testable. In the end, we must be able to decide whether or not a system fulfills its requirements. So requirements must be specific, unambiguous, and quantitative.

Many of these points are raised by [Poston87a]. According to Poston, the most likely errors in a requirements specification can be grouped into the following categories:

— missing information (functions, interfaces, performance, constraints, reliability, and so on);

— wrong information (not traceable, not testable, ambiguous, and so forth);

— extra information (bells and whistles).

Using a standard format for documenting the requirements specification, such as IEEE Standard 830, discussed in chapter 9, may help enormously in preventing these types of errors to occur in the first place.

Useful techniques for testing the degree to which criteria have been met, are mostly manual (reading documents, inspections, reviews). If a clear framework for documenting the requirements specification is available, as is offered by systems such as ISDOS (PSL-PSA) [Teichroew77] or SADT [Ross77a], we may often execute tests using the accompanying tools. Such tests may for instance concern the completeness or consistency of the requirements specification. Together with the prospective users of the system, scenarios for the expected use of the system can be devised. In this way, a set of functional tests is generated.

At this stage also, a general test strategy for subsequent phases must be formulated encompassing: the choice for particular test techniques; the formulation of evaluation criteria; the formulation of a test plan; test scheme; and test documentation requirements. Possibly also, a test team will already be formed at this stage. These planning activities are dealt with in section 13.3.

13.2.2 Design

The criteria mentioned in the previous subsection (completeness, consistency, feasibility and testability) are also essential for the design. The most likely errors in design, as listed in [Poston87b], also resemble the kind of errors one is inclined to make in a requirements specification: missing, wrong, and extraneous information. For the design, too, a precise standard for documenting the design is of great help in preventing these types of errors. IEEE Standard 1016, discussed in chapter 10, is one such standard.

During the design phase, we decompose the total system into subsystems, components and modules, starting from the requirements specification. We may then develop tests based on this decomposition process. Design is not a one-shot process. During the design process a number of successive refinements will be made, resulting in layers showing increasing detail. Following this design process, more detailed tests can be developed as the lower layers of the design are decided upon.

During the design phase, we may also test the design itself. This includes tracing elements from the requirements specification to the corresponding elements in the design description, and vice versa. The quality of the design as such is to be assessed as well. Well-known techniques for doing so are, amongst others, simulation, design walkthroughs, design inspections.

At the requirements analysis phase the possibilities to formally document the resulting specification are limited. Most requirements specifications make excessive use of natural language descriptions. For the design phase, there are ample opportunities to formally document the resulting specification. The more formally the design is specified, the more possibilities we have for applying verification techniques, as well as formal checks for consistency and completeness.

Support tools in this area are provided by systems like PDL [Caine75], LP, a debugging tool for the Larch family of specification languages [Garland90], and EPROS, an environment that supports the development of VDM specifications [Hekmatpour88].

13.2.3 Implementation

During the implementation phase, we do the 'real' testing. One of the most effective techniques to find errors in a program text is to carefully read that text, or have it read. This technique has been successfully applied for a long time past. Somewhat formalized variants are known as code-inspection and code-walkthrough. We may also apply the technique of stepwise abstraction. In stepwise abstraction, the function of the code is determined in a number of abstraction steps, starting from the code itself. The various manual test techniques will be discussed in section 13.4.

There are many tools to support the testing of code. We may distinguish between tools for static analysis and tools for dynamic analysis. Static analysis tools inspect the program code without executing it. It includes tests like: Have all variables been declared, and have all variables been given a value before they are used? Dynamic analysis tools are used in conjunction with the actual execution of the code, for example a tool which keeps track of which portions of the code have been covered by the tests so far. Examples of the latter are RXVP80 for FORTRAN and COBOL [Andrews83], and nvcc for C and C++ [Frakes91b].

Using formal verification techniques, we may try to prove the correctness of the code.

The above techniques are aimed at evaluating the quality of the source code as well as its compliance with design specifications and code documentation.

It is crucial to properly control the test information while testing the code. Tools may help us in doing so, for example test drivers, test stubs and test data generators. A test driver is a tool to generate the test environment of a component to be tested. A test stub does the opposite. It simulates the function of a component not yet available. In bottom-up testing we will in general make much use of test-drivers, while top-down testing implies the use of test stubs. The test strategy (top-down versus bottom-up) may be partly influenced by the design technique used.

Tools may also be profitable while executing the tests (test harnesses, test systems). Examples are TPL [Panzl78], PRUFSTAND [Sneed78], ASSET [Frankl88] or Mothra [DeMillo91]. A simple, and yet effective tool is one which compares test results with expected results. The eye is a very unreliable medium. Fairly soon, results look OK. One additional advantage of this type of tool support is that it helps to achieve a standard test format. This in turn helps for regression testing.

13.2.4 Maintenance

On average, more than 50% of total life-cycle costs is spent on maintenance. If we modify the software after a system has become operational (because an error is found late on, or because the system must be adapted to changed requirements), we will have to test the system anew. This is called regression testing. To have this proceed smoothly, the quality of the documentation and the possibilities for tool support, are crucial factors.

13.3 VERIFICATION AND VALIDATION PLANNING AND DOCUMENTATION

Like the other phases and activities of the software development process, the testing activities need to be carefully planned and documented. Since test activities start early on in the development life cycle and span all subsequent phases, timely attention to the planning of these activities is of paramount importance. A precise description of the various activities, responsibilities and procedures must be drawn up at an early stage.

The planning of test activities is described in a document called the software verification and validation plan. We will base our discussion of its contents on the corresponding IEEE Standard 1012 [IEEE86b]. Standard 1012 describes verification and validation activities for a waterfall-like life cycle in which the following phases are identified:

- Concept phase

- Requirements phase

- Design phase

- Implementation phase

- Test phase

- Installation and checkout phase

- Operation and maintenance phase

The first of these, the concept phase, is not discussed in the present text. Its aim is to describe and evaluate user needs. It produces documentation which contains, for example, a statement of user needs, results of feasibility studies, and policies relevant to the project. The verification and validation plan is also prepared during this phase. In our approach, these activities are included in the requirements analysis phase.

The sections to be included in the verification and validation plan are listed in figure 13.7. V&V stands for verification and validation. The structure of this plan resembles that of other standards discussed earlier. The plan starts with an overview and next gives detailed information on each and every aspect of the topic being covered. The various constituents of the Verification and Validation Plan are discussed in appendix F.

More detailed information on the many V&V tasks covered by this plan can be found in [IEEE86b]. Following the organization proposed in this standard, the bulk of the test documentation can be structured along the lines identified in figure 13.8. The Test Plan is a document describing the scope, approach, resources, and schedule of intended test activities. It can be viewed as a further refinement of the Verification and Validation Plan, and describes in detail the test items,

1. Purpose
2. Referenced documents
3. Definitions
4. Verification and validation overview
   4.1. Organization
   4.2. Master schedule
   4.3. Resources summary
   4.4. Responsibilities
   4.5. Tools, techniques and methodologies
5. Life-cycle verification and validation (V&V)
   5.1. Management of V&V
   5.2. Requirements phase V&V
   5.3. Design phase V&V
   5.4. Implementation phase V&V
   5.5. Test phase V&V
   5.6. Installation and checkout phase V&V
   5.7. Operation and maintenance phase V&V
6. Software verification and validation reporting
7. Verification and validation administrative procedures
   7.1. Anomaly reporting and resolution
   7.2. Task iteration policy
   7.3. Deviation policy
   7.4. Control procedures
   7.5. Standards, practices and conventions

Figure 13.7:   Sample contents of the verification and validation plan (*Source:* IEEE Standard for Software Verification and Validation Plans, *IEEE Std. 1016, 1986, Reproduced by permission of IEEE.*)

Test Plan
Test Design
Test Cases
Test Procedures
Test Reporting

Figure 13.8:   Main constituents of test documentation, after [IEEE83c]

features to be tested, testing tasks, who will do each task, and any risks that require contingency planning.

The Test Design documentation specifies, for each software feature or combination of such features, the details of the test approach and identifies the associated tests. The Test Case documentation specifies inputs, predicted outputs and execution conditions for each test item. The Test Procedure documentation specifies the sequence of actions for the execution of each test. Lastly, the Test Report documentation provides information on the results of testing tasks. It addresses the issues mentioned in section 6 of the Verification and Validation Plan.

A detailed description of the contents of these various documents is given in the IEEE Standard for Software Documentation [IEEE83c].

13.4 MANUAL TEST TECHNIQUES

A lot of research effort is spent on finding techniques and tools to support testing. Yet, a plethora of heuristic test techniques have been applied since the beginning of the programming era. These heuristic techniques, such as walkthroughs and inspections, often work quite well, although it is not always clear why.

Test techniques can be separated into **static** and **dynamic analysis** techniques. During dynamic analysis, the program is executed. With this form of testing the program is given some input, and the results of the execution are compared with the expected results. During static analysis, the software is generally not executed. Many static test techniques can also be applied to non-executable artifacts such as a design document or user manual. It should be noted, though, that the borderline between static and dynamic analysis is not very sharp.

A large part of the static analysis is nowadays done by the language compiler. For languages like Pascal and Ada, the compiler checks whether all variables have been declared, whether each function call has the proper number of actual parameters, and so on. These constraints are part of the language definition. We may also apply a more strict analysis of the program text, such as a check for initialization of variables, or a check on the use of non-standard, or error-prone, language constructs. In a number of cases, the call to a compiler is parametrized to indicate the checks one wants to be performed. Sometimes, separate tools are provided for these checks.

The techniques to be discussed in the following subsections had best be classified as static techniques. The techniques for functional and structural analysis, to be discussed in sections 13.5 and 13.6, are mostly dynamic in nature.

13.4.1 Reading

We all read, and reread, and reread, our program texts. It is the most traditional test technique we know of. It is also a very successful technique to find faults in a program text (or a specification, or a design).

In general, it is better to have someone else read your texts. The author of a text knows all too well what the program (or any other type of document) ought to convey. For this reason, the author may be inclined to overlook things, suffering from some sort of trade blindness.

A second reason why reading by the author himself might be less fruitful, is that it is difficult to adopt a destructive attitude towards one's own work. Yet such an attitude is needed for successful testing.

A somewhat institutionalized form of reading each other's programs is known as **peer review** [Myers79]. This is a technique for anonymously assessing programs as regards quality, readability, usability, and the like.

Each person partaking in a peer review is asked to hand in two programs: a 'best' program as well as one of lesser quality. These programs are then randomly distributed amongst the participants. Each participant gets four programs to assess: two 'best' programs and two programs of lesser quality. After all results have been collected, each participant gets the (anonymous) evaluations of their programs, as well as the statistics of the whole test.

The primary goal of this test is to give the programmer insight into his own capabilities. The practice of peer reviews shows that programmers are quite capable of assessing the quality of their peers' software.

A necessary precondition for successfully reading someone else's code is a businesslike attitude. Weinberg coined the term **egoless programming** for this [Weinberg71]. Many programmers view their code as something personal, like a diary. Denunciatory remarks ('how could you be so stupid as to forget that initialization') can disastrously impair the effectiveness of such assessments. The chances for such an 'asocial' attitude to occur seem to be somewhat smaller with the more formalized manual techniques.

13.4.2 Walkthroughs and inspections

Walkthroughs and inspections are both manual techniques that sprout from the traditional desk checking of program code. In both cases it concerns teamwork, whereby the product to be inspected is evaluated in a formal session, following precise procedures.

Inspections are sometimes called **Fagan inspections**, after their originator [Fagan76, 86]. In an inspection, the code to be assessed is gone through statement by statement. The members of the inspection team (mostly four) get the code, together with its specification and the associated documents, a few days before the session takes place.

Each member of the inspection team has a well-defined role. The *moderator* is responsible for the organization of inspection meetings. He chairs the meeting and ascertains that follow-up actions agreed upon during the meeting are indeed performed. The moderator must ensure that the meeting is conducted in a businesslike, constructive way, that the participants follow the right procedures and act as a team. The team usually has two *inspectors* or *readers*, knowledgeable peers that paraphrase the code. Finally, the *code author* largely is a silent observer. He knows the code to be inspected all too well and is easily inclined to express what he intended rather than what is actually written down. He may, though, be consulted by the inspectors.

During the formal session, the inspectors paraphrase the code, usually a few lines at a time. They express the meaning of the text at a higher level of abstraction than what is actually written down. This gives rise to questions and discussions which may lead to the discovery of faults. At the same time, the code is analyzed using a checklist of faults that often occur. Examples [Myers79] of possible entries in this checklist are:

— wrongful use of data: uninitialized variables, array index out of bounds, dangling pointers, etc.;

— faults in declarations, such as the use of undeclared variables, or the declaration of the same name in nested blocks;

— faults in computations; division by zero, overflow (possible in intermediate results too), wrong use of variables of different types in one and the same expression, faults caused by an erroneous conception of operator priorities, etc.;

— faults in relational expressions, such as using an incorrect operator ($>$ instead of $\geq$), or an erroneous conception of priorities of Boolean operators;

— faults in control flow, such as infinite loops, or a loop that gets executed $n+1$ or $n-1$ times rather than n;

— faults in interfaces, such as an incorrect number of parameters, parameters of the wrong type, or an inconsistent use of global variables.

The result of the session is a list of faults found. These faults are not corrected during the formal session itself. Such may easily lead to quick fixes and distract the team from its primary goal. After the meeting, the code author fixes all defects found and the revised code is verified once again. Depending on the amount of faults detected and/or their severity, this second inspection may be done by the moderator only or by the complete inspection team.

Since the goal of an inspection is to find as many faults as possible in order to increase the quality of the software to be developed, it is important to maintain a constructive attitude towards the programmer whose code is being assessed. The results of an inspection therefore are often marked confidential. These results should certainly *not* play a role in the formal assessment of the programmer in question.

In a walkthrough, the team is guided through the code using test data. These test data are mostly of a fairly simple kind. Otherwise, tracing the program logic soon becomes too complicated. The test data serves as a means to start a discussion, rather than as a serious test of the program. In each step of this process, the designer may be questioned regarding the rationale of the decisions. In many cases, a walkthrough boils down to some sort of manual simulation.

Both walkthroughs and inspections may profitably be applied at all stages of the software life cycle. The only precondition is that there is a clear, testable document. Both techniques not only serve to find faults. If properly applied, these techniques may help to promote team spirit and morale. At the technical level, the people involved may learn from each other, enrich their knowledge of algorithms, programming style, programming techniques, error prone constructions, and so on.

A potential danger of this type of review is that it remains too shallow. The people involved become overwhelmed with information, they may have insufficient knowledge of the problem domain, their responsibilities may not have been clearly delineated. As a result, the review process does not pay off sufficiently. Parnas describes a type of review process in which the people involved have to play a more active role [Parnas87b].

Parnas distinguishes between different types of specialized design reviews. Each of these reviews concentrates on certain desirable properties of the design. As a consequence, the responsibilities of the people involved are clear. Next, the reviewers get a list of questions they have to answer ('under which conditions may this function be called', 'what is the effect of this function on the behavior of other functions', and the like). In this way, the reviewers are forced to study carefully the design information received. Problems with the questionnaire and documentation can be posed to the designers, and the questionnaires filled in are discussed by the designers and reviewers. First results with these active design reviews are positive.

13.4.3 Correctness proofs

The most complete static analysis technique is the proof of correctness. In a proof of correctness we try to prove that a program meets its specification. In order to be able to do so, the specification must be expressed formally as well. We mostly do so by expressing the specification in terms of two assertions which hold before and after the program's execution, respectively. Next, we prove that the program transforms one assertion (the precondition) into the other (the postcondition). This is generally denoted as

$$\{P\} \ S \ \{Q\}$$

Here, S is the program, P is the precondition, and Q is the postcondition. Termination of the program is usually proved separately. The above notation should thus be read as: if P holds before the execution of S, and S terminates, then Q holds after the execution of S.

Formally verifying the correctness of a not too trivial program is a very complex affair. Some sort of tool support is helpful, therefore. Tools in this area are often based on heuristics, and proceed interactively (for example AFFIRM, discussed in chapter 11 [Gerhart80]).

Correctness proofs are most often applied to program code. However, if we do use a formal language at an earlier stage, we may also construct correctness proofs at this earlier stage. LP, the Larch Prover [Garland90] and Gypsy [Good79], [Cheheyl81], [Young89] are examples of systems which offer this facility.

Gypsy is both a specification language and a high-level programming language. Its notation resembles that of Pascal. A Gypsy program consists of a set of small units that are to be verified independently. Such a unit has an external specification (pre- and postconditions). It may also have internal specifications to indicate certain constraints on the implementation. In the correctness proof of a unit we may use only the external specification of other units, but not their internal specification.

In this way, the correctness proofs of units are independent, and the implementation of a unit is independent of its possible uses (insofar as the implementation does not violate the external specification). Gypsy offers extensive tool support for the construction of these proofs.

Correctness proofs are very formal and, for that reason, they are often difficult to construct for the average programmer. The value of formal correctness proofs is sometimes disputed [DeMillo79]. We may state that the thrust in software is more important than some formal correctness criterion. Also, we cannot formally prove every desirable property of software. Whether we built the right system can only be decided upon through testing (validation).

On the other hand, it seems justified to state that a thorough knowledge of this type of formal technique will result in better software.

Heated debates in the literature show that this issue has by no means been resolved yet [Fetzer88].

13.4.4 Stepwise abstraction

In the top-down development of software components we often employ stepwise refinement. At a certain level of abstraction the function to be executed will then be denoted by a description of that function. At the next level, this description is decomposed into more basic units.

Stepwise abstraction is just the opposite [Linger79]. Starting from the instructions of the source code, the function of the component is built up in a number of steps. The function thus derived should comply with the function as described in the design or requirements specification.

Below, we will illustrate this technique with a small example. Consider the search routine of figure 13.9. We know that the elements in array A are sorted when this routine is called, from the accompanying documentation, for instance.

We start the stepwise abstraction with the instructions at the innermost nesting level, the if-statement on lines 7–10. In these lines, x is being compared with A[mid]. Depending on the result of this comparison, either of high, low and found is given a new value. If we take into account the initializations on lines 4 and 6, the function of this if-statement can be summarized as

stop searching (found:= **true**) if x = A[mid], or
shorten the interval [low .. high] that might contain x, to an
  interval [low' .. high'], where high' - low' < high - low

```
1    procedure binsearch
2        (A: array [1..n] of integer; x: integer): integer;
3    var low, high, mid: integer; found: boolean;
4    begin low:= 1; high:= n; found:= false;
5        while (low ≤ high) and not found do
6            mid:= (low + high) div 2;
7            if x < A[mid] then high:= mid - 1 else
8            if x > A[mid] then low:= mid + 1 else
9                found:= true
10            endif
11        enddo;
12        if found then return mid else return 0 endif
13    end binsearch;
```

Figure 13.9:   A search routine

Alternatively, this may be described as a postcondition to the if-statement:

```
(found = true  and x = A[mid])  or
(found = false  and x ∉ A[1 .. low' - 1]  and
    x ∉  A[high' + 1 .. n]  and high' - low' < high - low)
```

Next, we consider the loop in lines 5–11, together with the initialization on line 4. As regards termination of the loop, we may observe the following. If $1 \leq n$ upon calling the routine, then low ≤ high at the first execution of lines 5–11. From this, it follows that low ≤ mid ≤ high. If the element searched for is found, the loop stops and the position of that element is returned. Otherwise, either high gets assigned a smaller value, or low gets assigned a higher value. Thus, the interval [low .. high] gets smaller. At some point in time, the interval will get length 1, i.e. low = high (assuming the element still is not found). Then, mid will be assigned that same value. If x still does not occur at position mid, either high will get the value low − 1, or low will get the value high + 1. In both cases, low > high, and the loop terminates. Together with the postcondition given earlier, it then follows that x does not occur in the array A. The function of the complete routine can then be described as:

```
result = 0 ⟼ x ∉ A[1 .. n]
1 ≤ result ≤ n ⟼ x = A[result]
```

So, stepwise abstraction is a bottom-up process to deduce the function of a piece of program text from that text.

13.5 TECHNIQUES FOR FUNCTIONAL TESTING

In functional analysis, also called **black-box testing**, test cases are derived from the specifications of the software. Implementation details thus are not taken into account.

The most obvious technique for functional testing is exhaustive testing. This is in general not feasible. A program that can be tested exhaustively could as well be replaced by a finite table that contains all the answers.

The crux therefore is to determine an adequate set of test cases. Unfortunately, there is no algorithm to do so. We will have to rely on a number of techniques and heuristics which work well in practice, but largely lack an underlying theory.

In each of the techniques discussed below, characteristics of the input domain are sought so as to find ways to determine a representative set of test cases. In practice, it is often better to use a combination of those techniques.

13.5.1 Equivalence partitioning

The main problem in determining a set of test cases is to partition the program domain into a (small) number of equivalence classes. We try to do so in such a way that testing a representative element from a class suffices for the whole class.

Determining these equivalence classes is a heuristic process. We may base our partitioning on the design description. In the design, the system has been decomposed into a number of components. Ideally, this has resulted in a hierarchical structure (a tree, or a directed acyclic graph), whereby the lower levels reflect more detail.

Each input condition that plays a role in one of these components results in two or more sets of values. These sets can be classified as either *valid* or *invalid* equivalence classes. A condition like

each book has a 6-digit number

results in three equivalence classes: one valid, and two invalid ones (corresponding to a number with more, or less, than six digits, respectively).

Given these equivalence classes, we may next construct test cases. In doing so, the test cases are chosen such that as many equivalence classes as possible are 'covered' by the test cases so far. We may stop when all equivalence classes have been covered.

The weak point in this procedure is the underlying assumption that the program behaves equivalently on all data from a given class. If this assumption is true, the partition is perfect and so is the test set. This assumption will in general not hold however (see also section 13.1.1).

13.5.2 Boundary value analysis

Boundary value analysis can be considered a variant of the equivalence class partition technique. It is based on the observation that software often fails at boundary values. Common extreme values are: 0, *nil*, lists with 0 or 1 element, etc.

Rather than testing some random element from each equivalence class, boundary value analysis concentrates on the extreme values from each class. In using this technique, we do not consider only the input side. The output is also partitioned into equivalence classes, and extreme values from each such class are tested as well.

13.5.3 Cause–effect graphs

One weakness of the above techniques is that they do not test combinations of input and/or output conditions. Since the number of equivalence classes is likely to grow fast with program size, it may not be feasible to test all possible combinations in practice. The technique which is based on cause–effect graphs is meant to find the interesting combinations.

Given the equivalence classes as determined by the earlier techniques for both input and output, we may connect input classes (cause) to output classes (effect). This yields a directed graph.

For this graph, we may set up a decision table in which causes act as conditions, and effects as actions. As a final step we may reduce this table using standard optimization techniques [Metzner77].

The nice part of this technique is that most of it can be supported through tools.

13.6 TECHNIQUES FOR STRUCTURAL TESTING

In structural testing techniques, we test the actual implementation. Structural testing techniques are most often applied when testing the final code. If we have available formal documents at an earlier stage, for example an algorithm in some pseudocode, structural testing techniques may also be applied to those.

Again, the crux is to achieve full coverage of the object to be tested. For this, we need a metric. Depending on the type of metric used, we speak about coverage-based testing or complexity-based testing.

13.6.1 Coverage-based testing

Coverage-based testing is often based on the number of instructions, branches or paths being visited during the execution of a program. It is helpful to base the discussion of coverage-based testing on the notion of a control graph. In this control graph, nodes denote actions, while the (directed) edges connect actions with subsequent actions (in time). A path is a sequence of nodes connected through edges. The graph may contain cycles, i.e. paths $p_1, ..., p_n$ such that $p_1 = p_n$. These cycles correspond to loops in the program (or gotos). A cycle is called simple if its inner nodes are distinct and do not include p_1 (or p_n for that matter).

During the execution of a program, we will follow a certain path through this graph. If some node has multiple outgoing edges, we choose one of those (which is also called a **branch**). In the ideal case, the tests collectively traverse all possible paths. This so-called **All-Paths coverage** is equivalent to exhaustively testing the program.

In general, this is not possible. A loop often results in an infinite number of possible paths. If we do not have loops, but only branch-instructions, the number of possible paths increases exponentially with the number of branching points. There may also be paths that are never executed (quite likely, the program contains a fault in that case). We therefore search for a metric which expresses the degree to which the test data approximates the ideal covering.

Many such metrics can be devised. The most obvious is the metric which counts the number of statements (nodes in the graph) executed. It is called the **All-Nodes coverage**, or **statement coverage**. This metric is rather weak because it is relatively simple to construct examples in which 100% statement coverage is achieved, while the program is nevertheless incorrect.

Consider as an example the program given in figure 13.10. It is easy to see that one single test, with n = 2, a[1] = 5, a[2] = 3, will result in each statement being executed at least once. So, this one test achieves a 100% statement coverage. However, if we change, for example, the test a[i] $\geq$ a[i - 1] in line 6 by a[i] = a[i - 1], we still obtain a 100% statement coverage with this test. Although this test also yields the correct answer, the mutilated program is incorrect.

We get a stronger metric if we require that at each branching node in the control graph, all possible branches are chosen at least once. This metric is known as **All-Edges coverage** or **branch coverage**. Here too, a 100% coverage is no guarantee for program correctness.

```
1    procedure bubble
2       (var a: array [1..n] of integer; n: integer);
3    var i, j, temp: integer;
4    begin
5       for i:= 2 to n do
6          if a[i] ≥ a[i-1] then goto next endif;
7          j:= i;
8       loop: if j ≤ 1 then goto next endif;
9          if a[j] ≥ a[j-1] then goto next endif;
10         temp:= a[j];
11         a[j]:= a[j-1];
12         a[j-1]:= temp;
13         j:= j-1;
14         goto loop;
15         next: skip;
16      enddo
17   end;
```

Figure 13.10:   A sort routine

[Chusho87] notes a disadvantage of the use of branch coverage. In branch coverage, certain segments (paths between two branching nodes) will be tested very often, simply because they occur in many possible execution paths. Chusho therefore distinguishes between essential and non-essential segments. A segment is considered non-essential if it is being executed *because* some other segment is executed. He next defines a metric based on coverage of the essential segments only. Such a technique may greatly reduce the number of tests to be done.

Since a stronger metric induces more tests, and thus higher costs, financial arguments tend to influence the choice of a metric.

Starting from the control graph of a program, we may also consider how variables are treated along the various paths. This is termed data flow analysis. With data flow analysis too, we may define metrics and use these metrics to guide testing.

In data flow analysis, we consider the definitions and uses of variables along execution paths. A variable gets *defined* in a certain statement if it gets assigned a (new) value because of the execution of that statement. After that, the new value will be used in subsequent statements. A definition in statement X is *alive* in statement Y if there exists a path from X to Y in which that variable does not get assigned a new value at some intermediate node. In the example in figure 13.10, for instance, the definition of j at line 7 is still alive at line 13 but not at line 14. A path such as the one from line 7 to 13 is called **definition-clear** (w.r.t. j). Algorithms to determine such facts are commonly used in compilers in order to allocate variables optimally to machine registers; see for example [Hecht77].

We distinguish between two types of uses of variables: **P-uses** and **C-uses**. P-uses are predicate uses, like those in the conditional part of an if-statement. All other uses are C-uses. Examples of the latter are uses in computations or I/O statements.

A possible test strategy is now to construct tests which traverse a definition-clear path between each definition of a variable to each (P- or C-) use of that definition and each successor of that use. (We have to include each successor of a use to force all branches following a P-use to be taken.) We are then sure that each possible use of a definition is being tested. This strategy is known as **All-Uses coverage** [Rapps85]. A slightly stronger condition requires that each definition-clear path is either cycle-free or a simple cycle. This is known as **All-DU-Paths coverage**. Several weaker data flow criteria can be defined as well:

- **All-Defs coverage** simply requires the test set to be such that each definition is used at least once.

- **All-C-Uses/Some-P-Uses coverage** requires definition-clear paths from each definition to each computational use. If a definition is used only in predicates, at least one definition-clear path to a predicate use must be exercised.

- **All-P-Uses/Some-C-Uses coverage** requires definition-clear paths from each definition to each predicate use. If a definition is used only in computations, at least one definition-clear path to a computational use must be exercised.

- **All-P-Uses coverage** requires definition-clear paths from each definition to each predicate use.

A question that may be raised now is whether, say, the All-Uses coverage metric is stronger or weaker than the All-Nodes or All-Edges coverage metrics mentioned earlier. We may define the notion 'stronger' as follows: metric X is stronger than metric Y if a 100% X-coverage implies a 100% Y-coverage for all programs P and all sets of test data T [Rapps82]. In this sense, All-Edges coverage is stronger than All-Nodes coverage. The All-Uses coverage, however, is not stronger than All-Nodes coverage. This is caused by the fact that programs may contain statements which refer only to constants. For the program

```
if a < b
    then print(0)
    else print(1)
```

the All-Uses coverage will always be 100%, while the test set need not result in each statement being executed. If we ignore references to constants, the All-Uses coverage is stronger than All-Nodes coverage. With the same exception, the All-Uses criterion is also stronger than the All-Edges criterion.

Quite a few other coverage metrics have been defined. There does not exist a simple linear scale along which the strength of those coverage metrics can be depicted. For the metrics introduced in this section, the subsumption hierarchy is depicted in figure 13.11. An arrow A → B indicates that A is stronger than (subsumes) B. A more elaborate discussion of the relation between a number of coverage criteria can be found in [Clarke89].

A problem with any of the path selection criteria is that none is able to deal with infeasible paths. Infeasible paths are paths which cannot be executed because of the semantics of the program. Infeasible paths result if parts of the program are unreachable, as in

```
if true
    then x:= 1
    else x:= 2
```

The else-branch never gets executed. Yet, most coverage metrics require this branch to be taken. Infeasible paths also result from loops. If a loop is of the form

```
for i from 1 to 10 do
    body
```

there will be no feasible paths that traverse the resulting cycle in the graph any other than ten times.

The theoretical upper bounds for the number of test cases needed to satisfy most of the coverage criteria are quadratic or exponential. Empirical studies, however, show that, in practice, these criteria are usually linear in the number of conditional statements [Weyuker90].

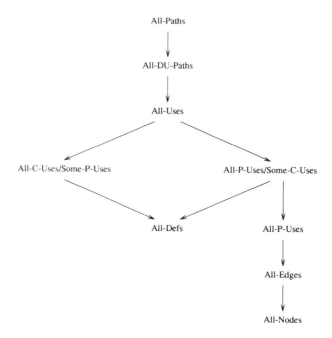

Figure 13.11:   Subsumption hierarchy for coverage metrics

13.6.2 Complexity-based testing

Different metrics have been designed to measure software complexity. Well-known examples are the cyclomatic complexity of McCabe, and Halstead's complexity metric. Both of these were discussed in chapter 10.

McCabe's metric [McCabe76] has also been applied to testing. McCabe suggests three complexity metrics: **cyclometic complexity**, **essential complexity**, and **actual complexity**. These are all based on a graphical representation of the system's flow of control. The cyclomatic and essential complexity are determined statically, while the actual complexity is determined dynamically.

The notion **basis set** is known from graph theory. A basis set is a maximal linearly independent set of paths through a graph. The cyclomatic complexity (*CV*) equals this number of linearly independent paths (see also section 10.3.3). Its formula is

$$CV(G) = V(G) + p$$

Here, $V(G)$ is the graph's cyclomatic number:

$$V(G) = e - n + \mathrm{p},$$

where

e = the number of edges in the graph

n = the number of nodes

p = the number of components (a component is a maximal subgraph that is connected, i.e. a maximal subgraph for which each pair of nodes is connected by some path)

As an example, consider the program text of figure 13.12. The corresponding control graph is given in figure 13.13. For this graph, e = 13, n = 11, and p = 1. So $V(G)$ = 3 and $CV(G)$ = 4.

```
1     procedure insert(a, b, n, x);
2     begin bool found:= false;
3       for i:= 1 to n do
4         if a[i] = x
5         then found:= true; goto leave endif
6       enddo;
7     leave:
8       if found
9       then b[i]:= b[i] + 1
10      else n:= n + 1; a[n]:= x; b[n]:= 1 endif
11    end insert;
```

Figure 13.12:   An insertion routine

The actual complexity AV equals the number of linearly independent paths being traversed during execution. So we have $AV \leq CV$. A possible test strategy is to construct tests such that all linearly independent paths are covered, i.e. $AV = CV$.

The essential complexity is an entropy measure, a measure of the program's unstructuredness. This complexity measure depends on the number of proper subgraphs that have exactly one entry point and one exit point, and contain more than one node. We are interested in a decomposition of the original graph in the minimum number of such subgraphs. There exists a simple algorithm by Hecht and Ullman for doing so [Hecht72]. The subgraphs as identified by Hecht and Ullman's algorithm have been indicated in figure 13.13 as well.

If we denote this minimal number of subgraphs by m, then the essential complexity $EV(G)$ is defined by:

$$EV(G) = CV(G) - m$$

m will always satisfy the inequality $m \leq CV(G) - 1$. So, $EV(G) \geq 1$. McCabe postulates that a program is well structured if $EV(G) = 1$. There obviously exist tools to compute these complexity metrics for a given program [Maitland80].

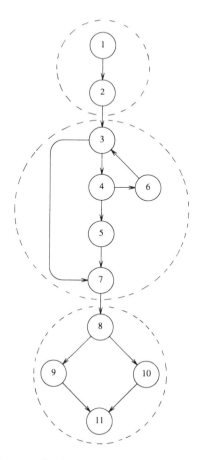

Figure 13.13:   Control flow graph of the insert routine from figure 13.12, with subgraphs identified

13.7 COMPARISON OF TEST TECHNIQUES

Most test techniques are heuristic in nature and lack a sound theoretical basis. Manual test techniques heavily rely on the qualities of the participants in the test process. But even the systematic approaches taken in functional and structural test techniques have a rather weak underpinning and are based on assumptions that are generally not true.

Experiments show that it is sometimes deceptively simple to make a system produce faults or even let it crash. [Miller90] describes one such experiment, in which they were able to crash or hang approximately 30% of the UNIX utilities on seven versions of the UNIX operating systems. The utilities tested included commonly used text editors and text formatters.

Similar results have been obtained in **mutation analysis** experiments. By applying some algorithm to a program text, we may generate a number of variants of that program. Each of those variants, or mutants, slightly differs from the original version. The faults thus created are termed **seeded faults**. This mutation technique can be used to estimate software reliability (see also chapter 14). As far as testing is concerned, this simple mutation technique may yield surprising results, as is shown by an experiment described in [Knight85]. The algorithms used to generate mutants were fairly simple. An example of such an algorithm is one in which the value v_1 in a loop of the form

```
for var:= v₁ to v₂ do
```

is changed into $v_1 + 1$ or $v_1 - 1$.

Seventeen programs developed by different programmers from one and the same specification were used in this experiment. These programs had all been thoroughly tested. Some of them had successfully stood one million tests. For each of those programs, 24 mutants were created using algorithms like the one given above, each mutant containing one seeded fault. The programs thus obtained were each tested 25 000 times. The results can be summarized as follows:

— some seeded faults were found quickly, some needed quite a few tests, and some remained undetected even after 25 000 tests. This pattern was found for each of the 17 programs;

— in some cases, the original program failed, while the modified program yielded the right result.

The Competent Programmer Hypothesis states that competent programmers write programs that are 'close' to being correct. So the program actually written may be incorrect, but it will differ from a correct version by relatively minor faults. This hypothesis is used in mutation-based test techniques, where mutants are generated using simple algorithms like the one given above. These mutants are then used in tests to reveal faults [Morell88]. Though it is difficult to prove or disprove this hypothesis, we may draw a more discouraging conclusion from experiments like the one discussed above: even simple faults can be very hard to detect and easily go unnoticed using test techniques in vogue today.

In past years, several attempts have been made to obtain more insights into the theoretical aspects of test techniques. An example hereof is the research that is aimed at relating different coverage metrics, as discussed in section 13.6.1. These metrics are used to systematically construct test cases. They also serve as test adequacy criteria, i.e. as rules used to determine whether or not testing can be terminated. An important issue then is to decide whether these test adequacy criteria are in fact adequate. Given the number of faults that remain undetected, the answer seems to be 'no'. In section 13.7.1 we investigate a number of fundamental properties of test adequacy criteria. This type of research is aimed at gaining a deeper insight into properties of different test techniques.

Several experiments have been done to compare different test techniques. From a number of projects also, real data are available on the fault-detection capabilities of test techniques used in those projects. In section 13.7.2 we discuss several of these findings which may provide some practical insight into the virtues of a number of test techniques.

13.7.1 Properties of test adequacy criteria

A major problem with any test technique is to decide when to stop testing. As noted, functional and structural test techniques provide only weak means for doing so. [Weyuker88] provides an interesting set of properties of test adequacy criteria. Although it is intuitively clear that any test adequacy criterion should satisfy all of the properties listed, it turns out that even some of the well-known test techniques such as All-Nodes coverage and All-Edges coverage fail to satisfy several of them.

The characteristics identified relate to program-based adequacy criteria, i.e. criteria that involve the program's structure. In particular, coverage-based test techniques fall into this category. The first four criteria, however, are fairly general and should apply to any test adequacy criterion. The following 11 properties are identified in [Weyuker88]*:

1. **Applicability property** For every program, there exists an adequate test set. Exhaustive testing obviously satisfies this criterion, but in general we will look for a reasonably sized test set. Both All-Nodes and All-Edges coverage criteria do not fulfill this property. If the program contains unexecutable code, there simply are no tests to cover those parts of the program.

2. **Non-exhaustive applicability property** This property says that, even if exhaustive testing may be required in some cases, a criterion should certainly not require exhaustive testing in all circumstances.

3. **Monotonicity property** This property states that once a program has been adequately tested, running some additional tests can do no harm. Obviously, the additional tests may reveal further faults, but this does not deem the original test set inadequate. It merely improves the quality of the test process.

4. **Inadequate empty set property** The empty test set is not an adequate test set for any program. A test adequacy criterion should measure how well the testing process has been conducted. If a program has not been tested at all, it certainly has not been adequately tested.

5. **Antiextensionality property** This property states that semantic equivalence is not sufficient to imply that the programs are to be tested in the same way. For instance, routines BubbleSort and QuickSort are likely to require different

---

* Reproduced by permission of the Association for Computing Machinery, Inc.

test sets. This property is specific for *program-based* adequacy criteria, which depend on the implementation rather than the function being implemented. In a *specification-based* approach such as functional testing, this property need not hold.

6. **General multiple change property** Whereas the previous property states that semantic 'closeness' is not sufficient to imply that two programs can be tested in the same way, this property states that syntactic closeness is not sufficient either. Programs are said to be syntactically close if they have the same structure and the same data flow characteristics. Such is the case for instance when some of the relational or arithmetic operators in those programs differ. Though the shape of such programs is the same, testing them on the same data may well cause different paths through the flow graph being executed.

7. **Antidecomposition property** This property states that if some component is adequately tested in some environment, this does not imply that it is adequately tested for some other environment. Put in other words: if some assembly of components is adequately tested, this does not imply that the individual components have been adequately tested as well. For example, a sorting routine may well be adequately tested in an environment where the size of the array is always less than ten. If we next move that routine to an environment which requires much larger arrays to be sorted, it must be tested anew in that environment.

8. **Anticomposition property** This property reflects just the opposite: even if components have been adequately tested in isolation, we still have to test their composition in order to ascertain that their interfaces and interactions work properly.

9. **Renaming property** If two programs differ only in inessential ways, as is the case when different variable names are used, then an adequate test set for one of these programs also suffices for the other.

10. **Complexity property** Intuitively speaking, more complex programs require more testing. This property reflects this intuition by stating that, for every program there exists other programs that require more testing.

11. **Statement coverage property** One central property of program-based adequacy criteria is that they should at least cause every executable statement of the program to be executed.

As noted, the All-Nodes and All-Edges coverage metrics fail to satisfy the applicability criterion. This is rather unsatisfactory, since it implies that we may not be able to decide whether testing has been adequate. If a 50% coverage has been obtained using either of these criteria, we do not know whether additional tests will help. It may be that the other 50% of the statements or branches is not executed by any input.

Both the All-Nodes and All-Edges criteria do not satisfy the antidecomposition and anticomposition criteria either. For example, if all statements of individual components are executed using some given test set, then this same test set is likely to satisfy that criterion on their composition. Further research along these lines is expected to deepen our insight into what test techniques may or may not accomplish.

13.7.2 Experimental results

When one vacuums a rug in one direction only, one is likely to pick up less dirt than if the vacuuming occurs in two directions.
[Cha88], p. 386.

The most common techniques for module testing have been discussed in the previous sections. The effectiveness of those techniques is discussed in [Basili87]. There, Basili and Selby describe an experiment in which both professional programmers and students participated. Three techniques were compared:

— stepwise abstraction;

— functional testing based on equivalence classes and boundary value analysis;

— structural testing with 100% statement coverage.

Basili and Selby compared the effectiveness of these techniques as regards detecting faults, the associated costs and the kinds of faults found. Some of the results of this experiment were:

1. The professional programmers detected more faults with stepwise abstraction. Also, they did so faster than with the other techniques. They discovered more faults with functional testing as compared with structural testing. The speed with which they did so did not differ.

2. In one group of students the various test techniques yielded the same results as regards the number of faults found. In a second group structural testing turned out to be inferior to both other techniques. The speed with which faults were detected did not differ.

3. The number of faults found, the speed of fault detection and total effort needed depended upon the kind of program being tested.

4. More interface faults were found with stepwise abstraction.

5. More faults in the control structure were found with functional testing.

Other experiments, such as those discussed in [Myers79] and [Girgis86], also indicate that there is no uniform 'best' test technique. Different test techniques tend to reveal different types of faults. The use of multiple test techniques certainly results in the discovery of *more* faults. It is difficult though to ascribe the discovery of faults to the use of a specific technique. It may well be that the mere fact that test techniques force us to pay systematic attention to the software is largely responsible for their success [Hamlet88].

Several studies have reported on the fault detection capabilities of (Fagan) inspections. [Myers88] reports that about 85% of the major errors in the Space Shuttle software were found during eariy inspections. [Ackerman89] reports that inspections were found to be superior to other manual techniques such as walkthroughs. Inspections were found to have the additional benefit of improving both quality and productivity.

Finally, there is ample empirical evidence that early attention to fault detection and removal really pays off. Boehm's data presented in the introduction to this chapter can be augmented by other results, such as those of [Collofello89]. His data stem from a large real-time software project, consisting of about 700 000 lines of code developed by over 400 people. Some of his findings are reproduced in figure 13.14. For example, of the 676 design faults that could have been caught, 365 were caught during the design review (=54%). The overall design review efficiency was not much different from code review efficiency, while the testing phase was somewhat less efficient. The latter is not all that surprising, since the design and code reviews are likely to have removed many of the faults that were easy to detect. These results again suggest that the use of multiple techniques is preferable to the use of a single technique.

	% of design faults found	% of coding faults found	Combined efficiency
Design review	54	–	54
Code review	33	84	64
Testing	38	38	38

Figure 13.14:   Fault-detection efficiency

The results become much more skewed if we take into account the cost effectiveness of the different test techniques. The cost effectiveness metric used is the ratio of 'costs saved by the process' to 'costs consumed by the process'. The costs saved by the process are the costs that would have been spent if the process had not been performed and faults would have to be corrected later. The cost effectiveness results found in this study are given in figure 13.15. These results indicate that, for every hour spent in design reviews and correcting design faults, more than eight hours of work are saved. The cost effectiveness of the testing phase itself is remarkably low. This is not really surprising, since much time is wasted during the actual testing phase in performing tests that do not reveal any faults. These findings once more confirm the statement that early testing really pays off.

Design review	Code review	Testing
8.44	1.38	0.17

Figure 13.15:   Cost-effectiveness results found in [Collofello89]

13.8 DIFFERENT TEST STAGES

During the design phase, the system to be built has been decomposed into modules. In the ideal case, these modules form some hierarchical structure. During testing, we will often let ourselves be led by this structure. We do not immediately start to test the system as a whole but start by testing the individual modules (called **module testing** or **unit testing**). Next, these modules are incrementally integrated into a system. Testing the composition of modules is called **integration testing**.

In so doing, we may essentially take two approaches. In the first approach, we start by testing the low-level modules which are then integrated and coupled with modules at the next higher level. The subsystem thus obtained is tested next. Then gradually we move towards the highest-level modules. This is known as bottom-up testing. The alternative approach is top-down testing. In top-down testing, the top-level modules are tested first, and are gradually integrated with lower-level modules.

In bottom-up testing, we often have to simulate the environment in which the module being tested is to be integrated. Such an environment is called a test driver. In top-down testing the opposite is true. We then have to simulate lower-level modules, through so-called test stubs.

Both methods have their advantages and disadvantages [Myers79]. For instance, in bottom-up testing it may be difficult to get a sound impression of the final system during the early stages of testing because whilst the top-level modules are not integrated, there is no system, there are only bits and pieces. This is not the case with top-down testing. On the other hand, writing the stubs can be rather laborious.

In practice, it is often useful to combine both methods. It is not necessarily the case that some given design or implementation technique drives us in selecting a particular test technique. If the testing is to partly parallel the implementation, ordering constraints induced by the order of implementation have to be obeyed, though.

Other forms of testing exist besides module testing and integration testing.

One possibility is to test the whole system against the user documentation and requirements specification after integration testing has finished. This is called the **system test**. A similar type of testing is often performed under supervision of the user organization, and is then called **acceptance testing**. During acceptance testing, emphasis is on testing the usability of the system, rather than compliance of the code against some specification. Acceptance testing is a major criterion upon which the decision to accept or reject a system is based. In order to ensure a proper delivery of all necessary artifacts of a software development project it is useful to let the future maintenance organization have a veto right in the acceptance testing process.

In case the system has to become operational in an environment different from the one it has been developed in, a separate **installation test** is usually performed.

The test techniques discussed in the previous sections are often applied during module and integration testing. When testing the system as a whole, the tests often use random input, albeit that the input is chosen such that it is representative of the system's operational use. Such tests can also be used to quantitatively assess the system's reliability. Software reliability is the topic of chapter 14.

The use of random input as test data has proven to be successful in the Cleanroom development method [Mills87]. [Duran84] also concludes that random testing can be very effective. In their experiments, they found that aselect testing resulted in a high degree of statement and branch coverage. Branches not executed often concerned the treatment of exceptional cases.

13.9 SUMMARY AND FURTHER READING

In this chapter we discussed a great number of test techniques. We emphasized the importance of early fault detection. It is important to pay attention to testing during the early stages of the software development process. Early testing activities are the ones that are most cost effective. Early testing activities provide opportunities to prevent errors from being made in the first place.

In practice the various manual test techniques seem to be used most often. They turn out to be at least as successful as the various structural and functional techniques. Next to the test techniques used, a major element in software fault detection and removal is the choice of people—some people are significantly better at finding and removing faults than others.

The interest in random testing as a technique for assessing the system's reliability during system testing is growing. Experiments with this type of test data selection have been promising.

Like any other life cycle activity, testing has to be carefully planned, controlled, and documented. Some of the IEEE Standards provide useful guidelines for doing so [IEEE83c, 86b].

There is as yet little theory on testing. Some attempts can be found in [Goodenough75], [Howden76, 85, 86], [Weyuker88], [Hamlet89] and [Clarke89].

Well-known textbooks on testing are [Myers79] and [Beizer90]. [Miller81] contains a compilation of well-known articles on the subject. Some review articles are [Adrion82], [Howden82a], [Dunlop82]. [Software89a] contains a series of articles on verification and validation.

EXERCISES

1. Read [DeMillo79], [Fetzer88], and the reactions to the latter article (cited in the reference section). Write a position paper on the role of correctness proofs in software development.

2. For a (medium-sized) system you have developed, write a Software Verification and Validation Plan (SVVP) following IEEE Standard 1012. Which of the issues addressed by this standard were not dealt with during the actual development? Could a more thorough SVVP have improved the development and testing process?

3. Consider the following routine (in Modula-2):

```
procedure SiftDown(var A: array of integer; k, n: integer);
var parent, child, Ak: integer;
begin
    parent:= k; child:= k + k;
    Ak:= A[k];
    loop
      if child > n then exit end;
      if child < n then
          if A[child] > A[child+1] then child:= child+1 end
      end;
      if Ak <= A[child]
          then exit
          else A[parent]:= A[child];
              parent:= child; child:= child + child
      end
    end;
    A[parent]:= Ak
end SiftDown;
```

(This operation performs the sift-down operation for heaps; if needed, you may consult any text on data structures to learn more about heaps.) The routine is tested using the following input:

```
n = 5, k = 2,
A[1] = 80, A[2] = 60, A[3] = 90, A[4] = 70, A[5] = 10.
```

Will the above test yield a 100% statement coverage? If not, provide one or more additional test cases such that a 100% statement coverage is obtained.

4. For the example routine from exercise 3, construct a test set that yields a 100% branch coverage.

5. Consider the following sort routine:

```
procedure selectsort(var r: array [1 .. n] of integer);
var j, k, small: integer;
begin
    if n > 1 then
        for k:= 1 to n - 1 do
            small:= k;
```

```
         for j:= k + 1 to n do
            if r[j] < r[small] then small:= j end
         end;
         swap(r[k], r[small])
      end
   end
end selectsort;
```

Determine the function (by means of pre- and postconditions) of this routine using stepwise abstraction.

6. Consider the following two program fragments:

Fragment 1:
```
found:= false; counter:= 1;
while (counter < n) and (not found)
do
   if table[counter] = element then found:= true end;
   counter:= counter + 1
end;
if found then writeln ("found") else writeln ("not found")
end;
```

Fragment 2:
```
found:= false; counter:= 1;
while (counter < n) and (not found)
do
   found:= table[counter] = element;
   counter:= counter + 1
end;
if found then writeln ("found") else writeln ("not found") end;
```

Can the same test set be used if we wish to achieve a 100% branch coverage for both fragments?

7. Construct an example showing that the antidecomposition and anticomposition axioms from section 13.7.1 do not hold for the All-Nodes and All-Edges testing criteria. Why are these axioms important?

8. With one or two fellow students or colleagues, do an inspection of a requirements or design document not produced by yourself. Is the documentation sufficient to do a proper inspection? Discuss the findings of the process with the author of the document. Repeat the process with a document of which you are the author.

9. Assess the strengths and weaknesses of:

   — functional/structural testing,
   — correctness proofs,
   — random testing, and
   — inspections

for fault finding and confidence building, respectively.

10. One way of testing high-level documents like a requirements specification is to devise and discuss possible usage scenarios with prospective users of the system to be developed. What additional merits can such a technique have over other types of reviews?

11. How do you personally feel about a Cleanroom-like approach to software development?

14
Software Reliability

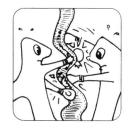

Creating reliable software is one of the central objectives of the field of software engineering. Unreliable software can be a nuisance to its users. Unreliable software may incur (large) financial losses to its users. It may even cause deaths. The column 'Risks to the public in computer systems' in the *ACM Software Engineering Notes* gives many examples of (near) accidents caused by faulty software.

In a narrow sense, we may consider reliability aspects of programming languages and programming language constructs. For instance, the use of goto's is often discouraged. Goto's result in complex and error prone software. The intended effect can often be obtained through alternative constructs, such as exceptions or an exit-statement. Another example is type-checking. Type-checking as it is done in languages like Pascal detects both clerical typing errors and more subtle mistakes. As a third example, automatic garbage collection frees the programmer from book-keeping tasks concerned with storage management. In this sense, reliability has been discussed extensively in chapter 12. See also [Gannon75].

A second aspect of reliability shows up when we consider the input domain of a software component. Most often, the legal input to a component is somehow constrained. We may expect the system to issue a proper error message or otherwise notify the caller of a component for those cases in which these constraints are not met.

The set of correct inputs to some software component is sometimes called its **standard domain**, while the set of incorrect inputs is referred to as the **exception domain** [Cristian82]. Some subset of the exception domain is caught by the software: the **expected exception domain**. The part not caught makes the component unreliable. Errors in this category may have quite unexpected effects.

For example, suppose we implement a module that manipulates stacks of a certain maximum length. This maximum length is given as a parameter to the routine `Create`. The routines `Pop`, `Push` and `Top` properly test for the stack being empty or full. These cases belong to the expected exception domain. However, the routine `Create` does not test whether its actual parameter has some positive value. The latter is an unexpected exception.

In an ideal situation, the domain of unexpected exceptions is empty. We have then taken precautions against all possible interface faults in routine invocations. Such can be obtained by assuming a precondition true for all routines of a program.

In any case, we must try to keep the domain of unexpected exceptions as small as possible. Prudence is the mother of wisdom. Even if we know that a component is only invoked from within a certain context, it is better to ensure the proper functioning of that component irrespective of this context. Such will increase the program's reliability. This technique is called **robust programming** [Cristian84] or **defensive programming**.

In general, we assume that our programs work perfectly. That is, if a sorting routine is being called, we expect the resulting file to be sorted; if a binary tree is built, we expect the resulting data structure to be a binary tree; if we write certain information to a disk, we expect the disk to contain that information and we expect to be able to retrieve that information at a later stage.

But what if this is not true? The sorting component may contain a fault, the system's memory allocation facilities may run havoc, disk tracks may become unreadable.

There are various techniques to detect and correct this type of hazard. When storing data we may add some redundant information and use this redundancy later to check the correctness of the data stored. Simple forms hereof are the addition of a parity bit or a checksum. In section 14.1, we will give a more elaborate example of the use of redundant information to increase the reliability of a piece of software.

For all kinds of physical products, reliability requirements are set. Cars, bridges, radios, etc., are not 100% reliable. They do function properly most of the time, though. By setting thresholds like 'the probability that component A will not fail within 5000 hours of operational use is greater than 0.999', and through extensive testing and a proper statistical analysis of the test data, the validity of such reliability claims can be assessed.

We may apply the same statistical notion of reliability to software, and try to answer such questions as: what is the probability that a given software system will not fail during the next hour of operational use? Answering such questions hinges on the use of a valid model of failure behavior for software, and the availability of data on past failures of the system. Some of these statistical software reliability models are discussed in section 14.2.

14.1 AN EXAMPLE: FAULT-TOLERANT DISKS

Information written to a disk does get lost once in a while. How then should we design and implement a system in which the probability that information gets lost irrevocably is less than some threshold α?

This example is taken from [Cristian85]. In the solution given there, the information is written to *two* disks. The redundancy thus obtained can be used when reading information from the disk: if one disk fails, we try the second one. The corresponding routines `safewrite` and `saferead` are given in figure 14.1.

The system under discussion is able to handle two types of adverse events:

— The contents of one or more blocks from a disk may become unreadable. The frequency with which this happens is supposed to be known from some hardware analysis procedure. As usual, an exponential distribution is assumed for the frequency with which such failures occur.

— The processor on which the system runs crashes. If this happens during a write operation, we assume that the block in question becomes unreadable. The content of the disk is not affected if the crash occurs somewhere else in the program. This process is also assumed to follow an exponential distribution, with known parameters.

By combining these two types of adverse events, something will go wrong with frequency *s*. If this occurs, we would like quickly to bring both disks in line again. This is achieved by regularly calling the routine `recover` from figure 14.1. `Recover` compares the information on both disks, and if necessary takes corrective action.

```
proc safewrite(a: address, b: block);
    begin write(disk1, a, b); write(disk2, a, b) end;

proc saferead(a: address, b: block);
    begin
        if ¬ read(disk1, a, b) then read(disk2, a, b)
    end;

proc recover;
var s1, s2: boolean; x, y: block; a: address;
    begin
        for a from 0 to max do
        begin s1:= read(disk1, a, x);
          s2:= read(disk2, a, y);
          if ¬ s1 then write(disk1, a, y);
          if (¬ s2) or (x ≠ y) then write(disk2, a, x)
        end
    end;
```

Figure 14.1: Read, write and recovery routines for fault-tolerant disks. (*Source: F. Cristian, A rigorous approach to fault-tolerant programming*, IEEE Transactions on Software Engineering, © *1985 IEEE.*)

The routine `recover` treats the two disks asymmetrically. For, if we are able to read a certain block from both disks and their contents differ, then the processor must have crashed between the two write actions of `safewrite`. In that case, the first disk was written last, so we still have to adjust the contents of the second disk accordingly.

It is the intention that `recover` is called with a frequency such that the probability of more than one failure in between two successive calls is less than the given threshold α. Note that the routine `recover` as given is also capable of handling multiple failures, provided they affect mutually disjoint sets of blocks.

Each of the disks can be in any of two states:

ok—each block is readable and has the right contents, and

ko—at least one block is unreadable or has incorrect contents.

We may view each disk as a random variable d_i ($i = 1, 2$). Each of these random variables is in one of the states {ok, ko}. The stochastic process (d_1, d_2) thus has four possible states.

Transitions $(x, \text{ok}) \to (x, \text{ko})$ or $(\text{ok}, y) \to (\text{ko}, y)$ occur if one or more blocks of the disk in question get the wrong contents. As noted before, the frequency hereof is assumed to be s.

Transitions in the opposite direction occur when `recover` is called. If the frequency of calling `recover` is $1/2\delta$, then the time between the occurrence of a fault and the start of the next corrective action is δ hours, on average. If the corrective action itself takes ρ hours on average, then the frequency of the transition $(\text{ko}, \text{ok}) \to (\text{ok}, \text{ok})$ or $(\text{ok}, \text{ko}) \to (\text{ok}, \text{ok})$ equals $r = 1/(\delta + \rho)$.

If the system inadvertently reaches the state (ko, ko), the routine `recover` will still work correctly if the faults concern different blocks. If not, we will have to fall back onto a different procedure, such as manual repair. Obviously, our goal is to prevent this situation occurring—which is why we built the model to start with. However, this situation cannot be ruled out altogether. If this latter procedure takes ω hours on the average, then the frequency of the transition $(\text{ko}, \text{ko}) \to (\text{ok}, \text{ok})$ equals $R = 1/(\delta + \omega)$.

The various possible states and transitions are depicted graphically in figure 14.2. It easily follows that the system in equilibrium satisfies the following equations:

$$2\, s\, p_{\text{ok, ok}} = r\, p_{\text{ok, ko}} + r\, p_{\text{ko, ok}} + R\, p_{\text{ko, ko}}$$
$$s\, p_{\text{ok, ko}} + r\, p_{\text{ok, ko}} = s\, p_{\text{ok, ok}}$$
$$s\, p_{\text{ko, ok}} + r\, p_{\text{ko, ok}} = s\, p_{\text{ok, ok}}$$
$$s\, p_{\text{ok, ko}} + s\, p_{\text{ko, ok}} = R\, p_{\text{ko, ko}}$$

We may safely assume the process to be symmetric—there is no a priori reason to think that one disk is better than the other—so:

$$p_{\text{ok, ko}} = p_{\text{ko, ok}}$$

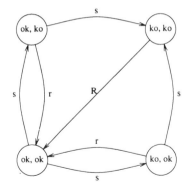

Figure 14.2:   Possible states and their transitions (*Source: F. Cristian. A rigorous approach to fault-tolerant programming*, IEEE Transactions on Software Engineering, © *1985 IEEE.*)

The various probabilities add up to 1, so:

$$p_{ok,ok} + p_{ok,ko} + p_{ko,\,ok} + p_{ko,\,ko} = 1$$

Finally, the probability that the system reaches state (ko, ko) is given through the threshold α:

$$p_{ko,\,ko} \leq \alpha$$

If values for α, ρ, ω and s are given, the value of r (i.e. the frequency with which `recover` has to be called) can be determined by solving the above set of equations [Cristian85].

In certain applications, such as data bases containing financial data, this type of analysis and the resulting algorithms are often applied. We term these systems **fault-tolerant**.

The routine `saferead` employs a fault tolerance technique that resembles **recovery blocks**. Another main technique that has evolved for software fault tolerance is **N-version programming**. Both these techniques are based on design diversity. Different versions of the software are developed independently and it is hoped that these versions are (at least partly) independent in their failure behavior. This is not necessarily true though. In one analysis of faults in N-version programming for example it was found that programmers do make identical errors [Brilliant90].

When using recovery blocks, versions are executed serially. An acceptance test is used to check their outcomes. An alternative version is executed only if the current version fails the acceptance test. In N-version programming, the different versions are executed in parallel, and the results are voted on. The reader is referred to [Abbott90] for an overview of different approaches to fault tolerance.

14.2 ESTIMATING SOFTWARE RELIABILITY

In much of this book the reader will find references to the fact that most software does not function perfectly. Faults are found in almost every run-of-the-mill software system: the software is not 100% reliable. In this section we concentrate on quantitative, statistical, notions of software reliability.

One benefit of such information is that it can be put to use in planning our maintenance effort. Another reason for collecting reliability information could be contractual obligations regarding a required reliability level. Software for telephone switching systems, for instance, requires such quantitative knowledge of the system's expected availability. We need to know what the probability is of wrong connections being due to faults in the software.

A second application of reliability data is found in testing. A major problem with testing is deciding when to stop. One possibility is to base this decision on reaching a certain reliability level. If the required reliability level is not reached, we need an estimate of the time it will take to reach that level.

In order to be able to answer this type of question, a number of **software reliability models** have been developed which strongly resemble the well-known hardware reliability models. These are statistical models where the starting point is a certain probability distribution for expected failures. The precise distribution is not known a priori. We must measure the points in time at which the first n failures occur and look for a probability distribution that fits those data. We can then make predictions using the probability distribution just obtained.

In this section we will concentrate on two models which are not too complicated and yet yield fairly good results: the *basic execution time model* and the *logarithmic Poisson execution time model*. Both models are extensively discussed, and compared with a number of other models, in [Musa87].

Text books on statistics often contain examples along the following lines: If we want to estimate the number of pikes in Lake Soft, we proceed as follows:

(a) catch a number of pikes, say N;

(b) mark them, and throw them back into the lake;

(c) a second time, catch a number of pikes, say M.

Supposing that M' out of the M pikes are found to be marked, the total number of pikes is then estimated as $M \times N/M'$.

A somewhat unsophisticated technique is to try to estimate the number of faults in a program in a similar way. The easiest way to do this is to artificially seed a number of faults in the program. When the program is tested, we will discover both seeded faults and new ones. The total number of faults is then estimated from the ratio of those two numbers.

We must be aware of the fact that a number of presuppositions underly this method—amongst others, the assumption that both real and seeded faults have the same distribution.

There are many ways of determining which faults to seed in the program. Probably the least satisfactory technique is to construct them by hand. It is unlikely that we will be able to construct very realistic faults in this way. Faults thought up by one person have a fair chance of having been thought up already by the person that wrote the software to start with.

An interesting alternative is to generate so-called **program mutants**. By applying some algorithm to a program text, we may generate a number of variants of that program. Each of those variants, or mutants, slightly differs from the original version. The faults thus created may be considered as the seeded faults (see also chapter 13).

Yet a third technique is to have the program independently tested by two groups. The faults found by the first group can then be considered seeded faults for the second group. In using this technique, though, we must realize that there is a chance that both groups will first detect (the same type of) simple faults. As a result, the picture might well get distorted.

A useful rule of thumb for this technique is the following: if we find many seeded faults and relatively few others, the result can be trusted. The opposite is not true. This phenomenon is more generally applicable: if, during testing of a certain component, many faults are found, it should not to be taken as a positive sign. Quite the contrary, it is an indication that the component probably is of low quality. As Myers observed: 'The probability of the existence of more errors in a section of a program is proportional to the number of errors already found in that section.' [Myers79]. The experimental findings reported in [Yu88] suggest the same phenomenon. Yu et al found a strong linear relationship between the number of defects discovered during early phases of development and the number of defects discovered later.

The goal of the various test techniques discussed in chapter 13 is to find as many faults as possible. The fault-seeding technique discussed above aims at estimating the number of faults. What we in fact observe are *manifestations* of faults, i.e. failures. The system fails if the output does not meet the specification. Faults in a program are static in nature, failures are dynamic. A program can fail only when it is executed. From the user's point of view, failures are much more important than faults. For example, a fault in a piece of software that is never, or hardly ever, used is in general less important than a fault which manifests itself frequently. Also, one and the same fault may show up in different ways, and a failure may be caused by more than one fault.

In the following discussion on reliability, we will not be concerned with the expected number of faults in a program. Rather, the emphasis will be on the expected number of failures. The notion of time plays an essential role. For the moment, we will define reliability as: the probability that the program will not fail during a certain period of time.

The notion of time deserves further attention. Ultimately, we are interested in statements regarding calendar time. For example, we might want to know the probability that a given system will not fail in a one-week time period, or we might be interested in the number of weeks of system testing still needed to reach a certain reliability level.

Both models discussed below use the notion of execution time. Execution time is the time spent by the machine actually executing the software. Reliability models based on execution time yield better results than those based on calendar time. At a later stage, we will return to possibilities to a posteriori translate execution time to calendar time. To emphasize this distinction, execution time will be denoted by τ and calendar time by t.

The failure behavior of a program depends on many factors: quality of the designers, complexity of the system, development techniques used, etc. Most of these cannot adequately be dealt with as variables in a reliability model and therefore are assumed to be fixed. Reliability, when discussed in this section, will therefore always concern one specific project.

Some factors impacting failure behavior can be dealt with, though. As noticed before, the models discussed are based on the notion of execution time. This is simple to measure if we run one application on a stand-alone computer. Translation between machines that differ in speed can be taken care of relatively easy. Even if the machine is used in multiprogramming mode, translation from the time measured to proper execution time may be possible. Such is the case, for instance, if time is relatively uniformly distributed over the applications being executed.

The input to a program is also variable. Since we estimate the model's parameters on the basis of failures observed, the predictions made will hold only insofar as future input resembles the input which led to the observed failure behavior. The future has to resemble the past. In order to get reliable predictions, the tests must be representative of the later operational use of the system. If we are able to allocate the possible inputs to different equivalence classes, simple readjustments are possible here too.

We may summarize this discussion by including the environment in the definition of our notion of software reliability. Reliability then is defined as: the probability that a system will not fail during a certain period of time in a certain environment.

Finally, software systems are not static entities. Software is often implemented and tested incrementally. Reliability of an evolving system is difficult to express. [Musa87] gives certain rules which allow us to accommodate such changes. In the ensuing discussion, however, we assume that our systems are stable over time.

We may characterize the failure behavior of software in different ways. For example, we may consider the expected time to the next failure, the expected time interval between successive failures, or the expected number of failures in a certain time interval. In all cases, we are concerned with stochastic variables, since we do not know exactly when the software will fail. There are at least two reasons for this uncertainty. Firstly, we do not know where the programmer made errors. Secondly, the relation between a certain input and the order in which the corresponding set of instructions is being executed is not usually known. We may therefore model subsequent failures as a stochastic process. Such a stochastic process is, amongst others, characterized by the form and probability distribution of the stochastic variables.

When the software fails, we try to locate and repair the fault that caused this failure. In particular, this situation arises during the test phase of the software life cycle. Since we assume a stable situation, the application of reliability models is particularly appropriate during system testing, when the individual modules have been integrated into one system. This system-test situation in particular will be discussed below.

In this situation, the failure behavior will not follow a constant pattern but will change over time, since faults detected are subsequently repaired. A stochastic process whose probability distribution changes over time is called *non-homogeneous*. The variation in time between successive failures can be described in terms of a function $\mu(\tau)$ which denotes the average number of failures until time τ. Alternatively, we may consider the failure intensity function $\lambda(\tau)$, the average number of failures per unit of time at time τ. $\lambda(\tau)$ then is the derivative of $\mu(\tau)$. If the reliability of a program increases through fault correction, the failure intensity will decrease.

The relation between $\lambda(\tau)$, $\mu(\tau)$ and τ is graphically depicted in figure 14.3. The models to be discussed below, the basic execution time model BM and the logarithmic Poisson execution time model LPM, differ in the form of the failure intensity function $\lambda(\tau)$.

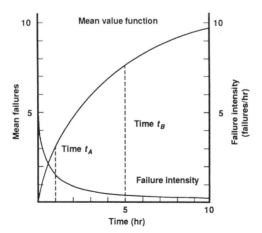

Figure 14.3:   Failure intensity $\lambda(\tau)$ and mean failures $\mu(\tau)$ as functions of τ (*Source: J.D. Musa, A. Iannino and K. Okumoto*, Software Reliability, *Copyright McGraw-Hill Book Company, 1987. Reproduced by permission of McGraw-Hill, Inc.*)

Both BM and LPM assume that failures occur according to a non-homogeneous Poisson process. Poisson processes are often used to describe the stochastic behavior of real-world events. Examples of Poisson processes are: the number of telephone calls expected in a given period of time, or the expected number of car accidents in a given period of time. In our case, the processes are non-homogeneous, since the failure intensity changes as a function of time, assuming a (partly) successful effort to repair the underlying errors.

In BM, the decrease in failure intensity, as a function of the number of failures observed, is constant. The contribution to the decrease in failure intensity thus is the same for each failure observed. In terms of the mean number of failures observed (μ), we obtain

$$\lambda(\mu) = \lambda_0 (1 - \mu/\nu_0)$$

Here, λ_0 denotes the initial failure intensity, i.e. the failure intensity at time 0. ν_0 denotes the number of failures observed if the program is executed for an infinite time period. Note that, since λ is the derivative of μ, and both are functions of τ, λ in fact only depends on τ. We will return to this later.

In LPM, the first failure contributes more to the decrease in failure intensity than any subsequent failures. More precisely, the failure intensity is exponential in the number of failures observed. We then get:

$$\lambda(\mu) = \lambda_0 \; e^{-\theta \mu}$$

In this model, θ denotes the decrease in failure intensity. For both models, the relation between λ and μ is depicted in figure 14.4. (Note that the two curves intersect in this picture. This need not necessarily be the case. It depends on the actual values of the model parameters.)

Both models have two parameters: λ_0 and ν_0 for BM, and λ_0 and θ for LPM. These parameters have yet to be determined, for instance from the observed failure behavior during a certain period of time.

We can explain the shape of these functions as follows: given a certain input, the program in question will execute a certain sequence of instructions. A completely different input may result in a completely different sequence of instructions to be executed. We may partition all possible inputs into a number of classes such that input from one and the same class results in the execution of the same sequence of instructions. Some example classes could be: a certain type of command in an operating system, a certain type of transaction in a data base system.

The user will select input from the various possible classes according to some probability distribution. We define the **operational profile** as the set of possible input classes together with the probabilities that input from those classes is selected.

The basic execution time model implies a uniform operational profile (see for instance [Downs85]). If all input classes are selected equally often, the various

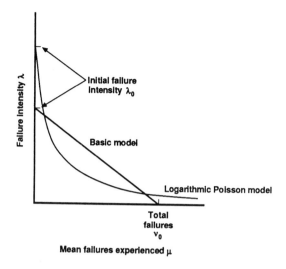

Figure 14.4:   Failure intensity λ as a function of μ (*Source: J.D. Musa, A. Iannino and K. Okumoto*, Software Reliability, *Copyright McGraw-Hill Book Company, 1987. Reproduced by permission of McGraw-Hill, Inc.*)

faults have an equal probability of manifesting themselves. Correction of any of those faults then contributes the same amount to the decrease in failure intensity.

With a strong non-uniform operational profile the failure intensity curve will have a convex shape, like in LPM. Some input classes will then be selected relatively often. As a consequence, certain faults will show up earlier and be corrected sooner. These corrections will have a larger impact on the decrease in failure intensity.

[Musa87] emphasizes that BM still models the situation fairly well in the case of a fairly non-uniform operational profile.

In both models, λ and μ are functions of τ (execution time). Furthermore, failure intensity λ is the derivative of mean failures μ. For BM, we may therefore write

$$\lambda(\mu) = \lambda_0 \left(1 - \mu/\nu_0\right)$$

as

$$\frac{\mathrm{d}\mu(\tau)}{\mathrm{d}\tau} = \lambda_0(1 - \mu(\tau)/\nu_0)$$

Solving this differential equation yields

$$\mu(\tau) = \nu_0(1 - \exp(-\lambda_0 \tau/\nu_0))$$

and

$$\lambda(\tau) = \lambda_0 \exp(-\lambda_0 \tau / \nu_0)$$

In a similar way, we obtain for LPM:

$$\mu(\tau) = \ln(\lambda_0 \theta \tau + 1)/\theta$$

and

$$\lambda(\tau) = (\lambda_0 \theta \tau + 1)/\lambda_0$$

For LPM, the expected number of failures in infinite time is infinite. Obviously, the number of failures observed during testing is finite.

Both models allow that fault correction is not perfect. In BM the effectiveness of fault correction is constant, though not necessarily 100%. This again shows up in the linearity of the failure intensity function. In LPM, the effectiveness of fault correction decreases with time. Possible reasons could be that it becomes increasingly more difficult to locate the faults, for example because the software becomes less structured, or the personnel less motivated.

If the software has become operational and faults are not being corrected any more, the failure intensity will remain constant. Both models then reduce to a homogeneous Poisson process with failure intensity λ as the parameter. The number of failures expected in a certain time period will then follow a Poisson-distribution. The probability of exactly n failures being observed in a time period of length τ is then given by

$$P_n(\tau) = (\lambda \tau)^n \times \exp(-\lambda \tau)/n!$$

The probability of 0 failures in a time frame of length t then is $P_0(\tau) = \exp(-\lambda \tau)$. This is precisely what we earlier denoted by the term software reliability.

Given a choice of one of the models BM or LPM, we are next faced with the question of how to estimate the model's parameters. We may do so by measuring the points in time at which the first N failures occur. This gives us points $T_1, \ldots, T_n$. These points can be translated into pairs $(\tau, \mu(\tau))$. We may then determine the model's parameters so that the resulting curve fits the set of measuring points. Techniques like Maximum Likelihood or least squares are suited for this. For more details, see [Musa87].

Once these parameters have been determined, predictions can be made. For example, suppose the measured data result in a present failure intensity λ_P and the required failure intensity is λ_F. If we denote the additional test time required to reach failure intensity λ_F by $\Delta \tau$, then we obtain for BM:

$$\Delta \tau = (\nu_0/\lambda_0) \ln(\lambda_P/\lambda_F)$$

And for LPM we get

$$\Delta\tau = (1/\theta)(1/\lambda_F - 1/\lambda_P)$$

Obviously, we may also start from the equations for μ. We then obtain estimates for the number of failures that have yet to be observed before the required failure intensity level is reached.

For BM, this extrapolation is graphically depicted in figure 14.5. Since estimating the model's parameters is a statistical process, we actually do not obtain one solution. Rather, we get reliability intervals. Such a reliability interval denotes the interval which will contain a parameter with a certain probability. For example, λ_0 may be in the interval [80,100] with probability 0.75. So the curve in figure 14.5 actually is a band. The smaller this band is, the more accurate the parameters have been estimated, for the same reliability of the interval. In general the estimates will be more accurate if they are based on more data.

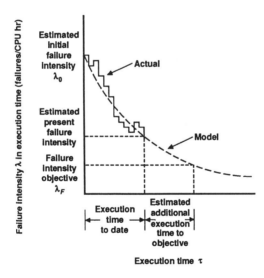

Figure 14.5: A conceptual view of the parameter-estimating process (*Source: J.D. Musa, A. Iannino and K. Okumoto,* Software Reliability, *Copyright McGraw-Hill Book company, 1987. Reproduced by permission of McGraw-Hill, Inc.*)

In the above discussion, we used the notion of execution time. That calendar time is a less useful notion on which to base our model can be seen as follows: suppose the points in time at which the first N failures occured were expressed in terms of calendar time. Suppose also that we try to correct a fault as soon as it manifests itself. If the manpower available for fault correction is limited, and this manpower is capable of solving a fixed number of problems per day, the failure intensity will be constant if it is based on calendar time. We then do not observe any progress.

Translation from execution time to calendar time is possible, though. [Musa87] mentions three aspects which are relevant for the progress of the testing process:

— the available manpower for detecting and identifying failures;

— the available manpower for identifying faults that led to the failures observed, and the correction of those faults;

— the available computer time.

The capacity of each of these entities is assumed constant. This is not unreasonable, since large fluctuations in available manpower do not seem to be very effective anyway [Brooks75]. Note also that the effect of changing values for these resources can be computed relatively easy.

Each of these resources may hinder the actual decrease in failure intensity. Based on an analysis of actual project data, [Musa87] postulates equations of the form

$$X_r = \theta_r \tau + \mu_r \, \mu(\tau)$$

In this formula, r denotes one of the above mentioned resources. X_r is the total need for this resource. θ_r and μ_r are constants denoting the use of resource r per hour of computer time and per failure observed, respectively. For example, identifying faults may induce six hours of work per failure observed. So, this relation is linear in both the execution time τ and the average number of failures observed.

Again, the values of these parameters can be computed using a least squares approximation. Rather peculiar in [Musa87] is that the value of θ for correcting faults is 0. This is somewhat against our intuition. One would think that failures occuring late are more complicated and require more time to correct but observations of real projects do not concur.

Differentiating the above equation gives insight to the change in the use of resources:

$$\frac{dX_r}{d\tau} = \theta_r + \mu_r \lambda(\tau)$$

Since $\lambda(\tau)$ decreases with time, the required effort per hour of execution time will also decrease and asymptotically approach θ_r. As far as the ratio between execution time and calendar time is concerned, we still have to divide the right-hand side of this expression by $P_r \rho_r$. Here P_r denotes the available capacity of resource r and ρ_r denotes the average use of that resource. We then get

$$\frac{dt}{d\tau} = (\theta_r + \mu_r \lambda(\tau))/P_r \rho_r$$

in which t denotes calendar time. We now have three relations between calendar time and execution time, one for each of the resources that may hinder progress. At each point in time, we have to take the maximum of those three.

In practice, it turns out that we may often distinguish between three different time intervals:

— in the first period the capacity of personnel available for failure correction will be the limiting factor: they are not able to correct faults fast enough;

— in the next period, the capacity of personnel identifying failures is limiting: they do not find the next fault fast enough;

— finally, computer time will be limiting: both for the identification and correction of faults, more personnel is available than is needed.

In [Musa87], quite a few other reliability models are discussed. The question then arises as to which model to choose. [Iannino84] gives the following evaluation criteria for choosing a particular model:

1. The degree to which future failure behavior can be predicted from previous failure behavior. Based on an analysis of a large amount of project data, [Musa87] concludes that in this respect the different models do not yield significant differences. [Abdel-Ghaly86] claims that there is no uniform best model. One would have to look for the model that gives the best prediction on a project-by-project basis.

2. The degree to which a model allows us to estimate relevant entities, such as present reliability, or the expected point in time at which a required level of reliability will be reached. Both models discussed in this section give good possibilities for doing so, because they are based on execution time rather than calendar time.

3. Each of the models makes certain assumptions. The question then arises as to whether these assumptions match our knowledge of the software construction field. A general evaluation hereof has not been done yet.

4. Applicability of the model. To what extent is the model applicable to software of different kinds and different sizes, different development environments, etc.? In practice, software evolves, software runs on different machines, and data are incomplete or inaccurate. Most models are applicable to different types of software and different development environments. As of now, procedures to handle software that strongly changes in size, have been developed only for the basic execution time model. These procedures are discussed in [Musa87].

5. Simplicity: it must be easy to collect the necessary data. The model's concepts must be easy, so that people lacking a serious mathematical background are able to understand the model and its underlying assumptions. Also it must be easy to construct tools that support the use of the model. Both models discussed above satisfy this criterion.

By far, most experiments have been done using BM. However, LPM seems to yield slightly better predictions. A possible strategy is to start by using BM, particularly when we do not have much data available and the software is still evolving. After the various components have been integrated and the system has become fairly stable, we may then shift to LPM.

14.3 SUMMARY AND FURTHER READING

This chapter focused on software reliability, a topic of increasing importance, not least because of the many accidents and near-accidents that are caused by software failures.

The reliability of software may be increased in various ways. First, we may study programming languages in order to identify error prone constructs. The reliability of software will be increased by using only safe constructs. Secondly, reliability may be increased through robust programming, in which program components as far as possible test for faulty input. Finally, by adding redundancy, we can use it to repair later, inadvertent events, which is called **fault-tolerant programming**. This is somewhat similar to techniques developed for fault tolerancy, in which multiple versions of a piece of software are developed and next used to tolerate faults in some of the versions.

The major part of this chapter has been devoted to a discussion of how to quantitatively estimate the reliability of a piece of software. Recently an increasing interest in this topic has been adopted by both researchers and practitioners. The currently available software reliability models are limited in their immediate practical value. Much research and experimentation is needed to further refine and validate these models.

Software reliability is more extensively discussed in [Myers76], [Anderson79], chapter 5 of [Shooman83], [TrSE85] and [TrSE86]. Recently, an excellent text book was published [Musa87].

EXERCISES

1. Discuss the possible contribution of
   — strongly-typed programming languages,
   — *goto*-less programming,
   — abstract data types,
   — object-oriented programming languages, and
   — procedures having precondition *true*
   to the construction of reliable software.

2. Discuss arguments for and against the use of N-version programming to increase software reliability.

3. Why is it important to consider the operational profile of a system while assessing its reliability?

4. With a colleague or fellow student, do a fault-seeding exercise. Try to include both 'deep' and 'shallow' faults. Did the exercise reveal any faults not known yet? Did the exercise increase your confidence in the software in question?

5. Can you think of reasons why reliability models based on execution time yield better results than those based on calendar time?

6. Discuss the following claim: 'Reliability assessment is more important than testing.' Can you think of reasons why both are needed?

7. Can software reliability be determined objectively?

8. Give an intuitive account of the role of pre- and postconditions in software development (consider the contract-theory proposed by Meyer—see chapter 12 and [Meyer88]).

15

Software
Tools

The demand for software grows faster than the increase in software development productivity and available manpower. [Musa85] estimates the demand to grow at 12% annually, and the increase in productivity and available manpower at 4% each. The result is an ever increasing shortage of personnel; we are less and less able to satisfy the quest for software. To turn the tide, we must look for techniques that result in significant productivity gains.

One of the most obvious routes to pursue is automation itself. We may use the computer as a tool in the production of software. In the past, all sorts of things were automated, save software development itself. Programmers knew better than that.

We have long been accustomed to employ the computer as a tool for the *implementation* of software. To this end, programmers have a vast array of tools at their disposal, such as compilers, linkers and loaders. Also during testing, tools like test drivers and test harnesses have been used for a long time. The development of tools to support earlier phases of the software life cycle is much more recent. One example of the latter is software to aid the drawing and validation of data flow diagrams.

The use of software tools may have a positive effect on both the productivity of the people involved and the quality of the product being developed. Tools may support checking conformance to standards. Tools may help to quantify the degree of testing. Tools may support progress tracking. And so on. Boehm estimates that even the use of very modest tools may result in cost savings of up to 10% [Boehm81]. The study reported on in [Norman89] also shows that, in the perception of software engineers, productivity is improved with the use of automated tools. We may hope that as better tools become available and, in particular, a better integration and mutual tuning of tools is achieved, significant productivity gains can be realized.

The application of tools in the software development process is referred to as **CASE—Computer Aided Software Engineering**. Save the traditional implementation and test tools, CASE has a very short history. The first tools to support design activities appeared in the early 1980s. Today, in the early 1990s, the number of CASE-tools is overwhelming.

As the amount of available tools proliferates, it becomes expedient to structure things. We would like to attune the various tools and incorporate them into a single system. Depending on the scope of the tool collection thus obtained, different names are used:

- A collection of tools is called an **analyst workbench** (AWB) if it supports the requirements specification/global design phase.

- A **programmer workbench** (PWB) contains tools that mainly support the implementation and test phases.

- A **management workbench** (MWB) contains tools to support management tasks.

- If the collection of tools is intended to support *all* phases of the software life cycle, the term **Integrated Project Support Environment** (IPSE) is used. Terms with roughly the same connotation are **Software Engineering Environment** (SEE) and **Software Development Environment** (SDE).

The above classification suggests a certain relation between a given model of the software life cycle and a corresponding tool collection. Ideally, this would indeed be the case. Starting from a given life cycle model, a set of techniques that fit the model would be decided upon, and then (an integrated collection of) tools that would support such techniques could be sought. In reality, however, this line of thought is not always followed, to say the least.

As noted in chapter 1, the classic waterfall model of software development is often disputed, one reason being that the number of available tools is rapidly increasing. These tools render other process models, such as prototyping and evolutionary development, viable alternatives. There is an interaction between trends in support environments and trends in process models.

It is yet too early to give a precise and unambiguous tool taxonomy. Developments in this area rapidly follow each other, as is apparent from the large body of literature on this topic. Research into (integrated) tool sets is very prominent in the various national and international software engineering research programs.

We will sketch the developments in this area following a taxonomy given in [Dart87]. Dart distinguishes four categories, based on trends that have a major impact on support environments:

1. Environments based on a *specific programming language* contain tools specifically suited for the support of software development in that language;

2. Environments based on the *structure* of programming languages contain tools aimed at manipulating program structures. These environments can be generated from a grammatical description of those program structures.

3. In *toolkits* we find tools that are generally not so well integrated. The support offered is independent of a specific programming language. A toolkit merely offers a set of useful building blocks. In particular, toolkits tend to contain tools that specifically support programming-in-the-large.

4. Finally, tools may be based on certain techniques used in specific phases of the software life cycle, while integrated tool sets aim at supporting the full spectrum of the software life cycle in a coordinated fashion.

These various approaches are addressed in sections 15.1 to 15.3. Section 15.1 discusses programming environments. In Dart's taxonomy, this encompasses both environments created manually around some given programming language, and environments generated from a grammatical description of the program structures being manipulated. In both cases, the support offered mostly concerns the individual programmer. Environments in which tools are not well integrated are discussed in section 15.2. UNIX is a prime example from this category.

As far as the scope of support offered is concerned, the environments discussed in these sections can be classified as programmer workbenches. Section 15.3 is mainly devoted to environments that support other phases of the software life cycle.

Tools may be classified in many different ways. Besides the classification used above we may, for instance, classify tools with respect to the type of systems whose development they support, their merit in relation to the size of the systems to be realized, or their merits as perceived by their users. These alternative classifications and some expectations with respect to future developments are discussed in section 15.4.

The discussion below is fairly global in nature. We will skim over details of individual tools. Our aim is to sketch discernible trends in this rapidly evolving area and to have a critical look at the possible role of tools in the software development process.

15.1 PROGRAMMING ENVIRONMENTS

In this section we will concentrate on those tools that specifically support programming tasks and associated activities such as testing, debugging and editing. In Dart's taxonomy given above, this concerns both environments based on a specific programming language and environments based on the structure of program objects.

Nowadays, most software is developed interactively; changes are made interactively and programs are tested and executed interactively. Much research in the area of programming environments is aimed at developing a collection of useful, user-friendly, effective tools for this type of activity.

Conventional operating systems are not well suited for these activities, for the following reasons:

- Most operating systems in use today have evolved out of earlier, non-interactive, operating systems: the man–machine interface often strikes as unnatural and impractical; the user dialog is rigid in form and sometimes, the 80-column punched card format is still evident.

- Most operating systems support a large variety of programming languages. Part of the facilities offered, such as the text editor and file system, are the same for all languages. As a consequence, these facilities are either too dumb, or too complicated for most tasks. For example, a text editor may well perform simple syntactic checks (more about this later on). The file system is usually very complex; peculiarities of all kinds of programming languages as well as different I/O devices come forward;

- When using an operating system to develop software, you have to master a number of different languages: the programming language itself, the editor's language, the system's command language, the debugger's language, etc. Each of these languages has its own syntax and semantics.

In short, many operating systems have become overly complex and the solution to this problem commonly comes in one of two forms:

— try to make a better operating system (the toolkit approach of UNIX could be classified as such);

— try to make the operating system 'invisible' by building a collection of tools on top of the operating system. This collection can be based on and built around a specific programming language. The principle then is that, to the software developer, the programming environment replaces the operating system.

15.1.1 Language-based environments

Environments that are built around a specific programming language exploit the fact that a program entails more than a mere sequence of characters. Programs have a clear structure. This structure can be used to make the editing process more effective, to handle debugging in a structured way, and the like. Knowledge of properties of the objects to be manipulated can be built *into* the tools and subsequently used by these tools.

In a language-based environment, the set of tools supports software development in one specific language. Well-known examples of language-based environments are Interlisp [Teitelman81] and the Smalltalk-80 environment [Goldberg84].

In such an environment, it is often not easily possible to make a clear separation between the language and its environment. The Smalltalk-environment is a case in point. Smalltalk-80 is an object-oriented programming language. The Smalltalk-environment is aimed at supporting a single user. This user creates object classes (modules) with the corresponding messages (procedures). The new object classes are added to the environment the user is working in. To start with, the environment already contains a number of useful classes. Working this way tends to be exploratory in nature. The user builds himself an evolving system. The state of the machine can be saved at the end of a working session and restored at the start of the next session. The user is thus provided with a persistent virtual memory which is not shared with other users.

One tool often available in such an environment is a browser. Browsers offer introspective capabilities to their users. They allow us to traverse and inspect the set of program objects in a systematic way. Such tools know about the *semantics* of the objects to be manipulated. As a consequence, they provide powerful support for tasks like program comprehension or debugging.

Language-based environments mostly run on workstations or PCs with good graphical capabilities. They support the individual programmer during the implementation and test phases. They offer little or no support for group activities such as configuration control and sharing information between group members. If the latter type of support is provided, such usually requires abandoning the exploratory programming paradigm offered by the environment.

Environments specifically aimed at supporting software development in Ada are also being developed. In this context, the acronym APSE stands for **Ada Program Support Environment**. It is important to realize that many Ada applications will have a real-time character and concern embedded systems. The tools to be incorporated in an APSE will have to be directed at this type of application. For example, in an APSE we may expect tools that allow us to test software on machine Y, though ultimately it will run on machine X.

The goals of an APSE are more far-reaching than those of most other language-based programming environments. Not only does an APSE have to support the implementation phase, but it also has to support the design phase, maintenance phase, documentation activities, and the like. As such, APSEs had better be classified as integrated support environments. Figure 15.1 gives the general idea of an APSE, as shown in the STONEMAN report. Four layers are distinguished in this picture:

0: Hardware, and underlying software as far as present.

1: Kernel Ada Program Support Environment (KAPSE). This level represents a machine-independent interface to port Ada software. The KAPSE contains functions to support the use of data bases and to execute Ada programs.

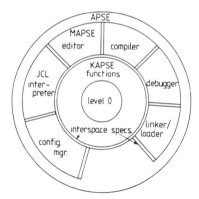

Figure 15.1:   Global structure of an APSE

2: Minimal Ada Program Support Environment (MAPSE). The MAPSE contains a minimal set of tools necessary and sufficient to develop and support Ada programs. Standard tools such as an editor, linker, loader, debugger, compiler, belong to the MAPSE. The MAPSE is written in Ada on top of a KAPSE.

3: Ada Program Support Environments (APSEs). APSEs are the result of extensions to the MAPSE on behalf of specific applications or development techniques. At this level, a certain diversity is expected to occur.

Early developments in the area of Ada environments are discussed in [Goos83], [McDermid84] and [Software85], for example. Two major efforts at developing an APSE resulted in systems having quite different interfaces at the KAPSE level. Because of these divergent approaches, attention was shifted to the development of a common interface for Ada environments. This resulted in the definition of CAIS—the Common APSE Interface Set [Munck88]; see also section 15.3.4.

15.1.2 Structure-oriented environments

In general, a standard editor can handle only text, i.e. unstructured sequences of characters. A special editor for language X could have built-in knowledge of that language. The Cornell Program Synthesizer [Teitelbaum81] is one example of such an editor. If the user of the Cornell Program Synthesizer wants to create an if-statement, he indicates so by typing a one- or two-character code. As a result, the following template appears:

```
IF (<condition>)
  THEN <statement>
  ELSE <statement>
```

The user is next asked to fill in the holes ('placeholders'). In this way, the user is supported in keying in a program text. Trivial mistakes, like the omission of parentheses around the condition, cannot be made.

Quite often, systems like the one described above offer additional support as well. For example, the system may easily take care of program indentation. Programs can also be analysed incrementally, so that the user is immediately informed about, say, an undeclared variable. In the Cornell Program Synthesizer, an incomplete program can even be executed. For example, if the ELSE-part of some if-statement is left open, the program could be executed up to that ELSE-part. Only if the ELSE-branch has to be executed does program execution stop. The system then brings you back into edit mode in order to enable you to fill in the missing code, and then execution of the program can be resumed. In systems such as this, where incremental software development is supported, users may sometimes guide program execution. They may for instance inspect the values of all variables after each instruction or procedure call and interactively assign them new values. Like in language-based environments, the tools in a structure-based environment know the semantics of the objects manipulated.

The above list can be extended with numerous other bells and whistles. The net result is an interactive system with a great many possibilities. Structure-oriented environments provide capabilities for the direct manipulation of program structures, multiple views of programs, incremental checking of static semantics, and program debugging [Pintelas91]. Obviously, having such a system available changes the working procedures of the programmer. The compile–load–execute cycle of program development is replaced by an incremental program construction paradigm.

The Cornell Program Synthesizer works for PL/CS, an educational subset of PL/I. Similar systems exist for other languages, such as Pascal (see, for instance, [Shapiro81], [Delisle84]). Again, these systems tend to support the individual programmer. Tasks that relate to team activities are generally not supported.

Many language-based systems have been developed from scratch. A more recent endeavor is the development of systems with which such environments can be generated. One example is the Synthesizer Generator [Reps84, 87] which evolved from the Cornell Program Synthesizer. With such systems, a programming environment is generated from a grammatical description of the structure of the language (including rules for prettyprinting program texts and static semantics). [Pintelas91] contains a comparative study of several such environments.

The Gandalf project [Habermann86], [JSS85] also makes use of a system to generate programming environments from a grammar. In the Gandalf project, the editor generator ALOE is used [Medina-Mora82]. Using this generator, environments have been created for Modula-2 and Ada, amongst others. The Gandalf prototype (GP) is an environment which supports version control and project management, in addition to the programming task of the individual.

The GP support for version control has two parts: a description of the components of a system with their mutual dependencies, and the possibility to automatically generate executable versions of the system. To that end, a grammar has been developed for a language in which we may express the tree structure of a collection of system components. Different realizations (versions) can be developed for each module, and each version may have multiple revisions. Programmer actions, such as modifying code, creating alternative implementations, creating executable versions and indicating dependencies between components, now amounts to writing a program that expresses these actions. While doing so, the programmer is supported by a syntax-directed editor generated from the grammar mentioned above.

On behalf of project control, each node in the tree structure of system components has attributes which describe the rights of its various classes of users. Also, a revision history is kept for each node, module and module version, in which a short description of each revision is kept. These functions are similar to those of other systems for configuration control, such as SCCS [Rochkind75]; see also section 15.3.2.

With this type of extension, the work of a multiperson development team can be supported. Because of the way in which the system is generated, the user interface for version and configuration management tasks is similar to that for the development of 'ordinary' programs. So the user need not learn yet another language.

15.2 TOOLKITS

The tools discussed in the previous section show a large cohesion because of their orientation towards one specific programming language. We may also envisage a situation in which programmers are supported by a rather loosely coupled collection of tools, each of which serves a specific, well-defined, task. The analogy with a carpenter is obvious. His toolkit contains hammers, screw drivers, a saw, and the like. These tools each serve a specific task. However, they are not 'integrated' in the way a drill with its attachments is.

The prime example of a toolkit environment is UNIX. UNIX may be viewed as a general programming environment, not aimed at one specific programming language. UNIX offers a number of very convenient, yet very simple, building blocks with which more complicated things can be realized [Kernighan81]:

- The file system is a tree. The leaves of this tree are the files, while inner nodes correspond to directories. A specific file can be addressed both absolute and relative to the current directory. The addressing is through a pathname, analogous to the selection of record fields in Pascal. Directories are files too, though the user cannot change their contents.

- Files have a very simple structure. A file is but a sequence of characters (bytes). So there are no physical or logical records, there is no distinction between random access files and sequential access files, and there are no file types.

An I/O device is a file, too, which, if it is opened, automatically activates a program which handles the traffic with that device. In this way, a user may write programs without knowing (or, indeed, without having to know) where the input comes from or where the output goes to.

- All system programs (and most user programs) assume that input comes from the user's terminal, while the output is again written to that terminal. The user can easily redirect both input and output. Through a call of the form

  ```
  prog <in >out
  ```

  input is read from file `in`, while output is written to file `out`. The program itself need not be changed.

- UNIX offers its users a very large set of small, useful, programs. To name but a few: `wc` counts the number of lines, words and characters in files, `lpr` prints files, `grep` does pattern matching.

- UNIX programs can easily be combined to form larger programs. If the output of one program is to serve as input to another program, both programs can be connected through a *pipe*, denoted by '|':

  ```
  ls | pr
  ```

  makes a list of all file names and subsequently prints that list. There is no need for an auxiliary file to store intermediate results.

In this way, users are led to try to reach their goals by gluing existing components together, rather than writing a program from scratch. To illustrate some of UNIX's possibilities: a UNIX guru could solve the KWIC-index problem from chapter 10 in the following way:

```
ptx -i /dev/null <input |
sed -e 's/.xx "" "\([^"]*\)" "\([^"]*\)".*$/\/2 \1' |
lpr
```

The above program may require some clarification:

— `ptx` generates a permuted index of the input. It is often used in conjunction with one of the available text processing programs. The parameter '-i' is used to indicate a file that contains words to be ignored in the permutation. The file `/dev/null` is a standard empty file. So in this case all words count in the permutation. For an input line

```
This is an example.
```

the above call to `ptx` would generate the following output:

```
.xx "" "This is " "an example." ""
.xx "" "This is an " "example." ""
.xx "" "This " "is an example." ""
.xx "" "" "This is an example." ""
```

Note that `ptx` already takes care of sorting. Sorting is done lexicographically on the third string of each line.

— `sed` is a stream editor. The above cryptic command makes sure that the second and third substring on each line are output in reverse order, while the rest of the line is deleted (the command assumes that the symbol '"' itself does not occur in the original input).

— Finally, `lpr` prints the resulting file.

Quite a few users of UNIX will not immediately think of the above solution. Another disadvantage of UNIX is that there is little consistency in interfaces and the choice of command names. For different programs, the '-k' option, say, may well mean something rather different. To stop a dialogue, you may try `kill`, `stop`, `quit`, `end`, `leave`, and a few others. If you get tired, CTRL–c is likely to work too.

The average UNIX user knows only a fairly limited subset of the available commands and tools [Fischer86]. Quite likely, a workable set of commands will be known and used after a while, and then the learning process stops. Inevitably, the facilities offered under UNIX are then far from optimally used.

In UNIX, the different tools have minimal knowledge of the objects they manipulate. Both input and output are a mere stream of characters. Systems like PCTE [Gallo87] build on UNIX and offer better possibilities to type objects. Various other development environments have been built on top of UNIX. They make use of the attractive features of UNIX, but try to overcome its disadvantages by imposing more structure; see also section 15.3.4.

Besides tools that support the individual programmer, UNIX also offers support for programming-in-the-large, through configuration management and system build facilities like SCCS and Make. These will be discussed in section 15.3.2.

15.3 METHOD-BASED ENVIRONMENTS

Finally, environments have been developed based on a specific model of (parts of) the software development process. Depending on the scope of the set of tools available, such an environment is called an analyst workbench (AWB), programmer workbench (PWB), management workbench (MWB) or Integrated

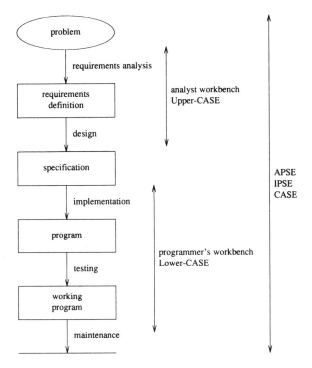

Figure 15.2: Scope of tool sets

Project Support Environment (IPSE). See also figure 15.2. The acronym CASE (Computer Aided Software Engineering) is often used to indicate any type of tool support in the software development process. The qualified terms Upper-CASE and Lower-CASE then refer to tool support during the analysis/design and implementation/test phases, respectively.

In the ideal case, the choice for a specific set of tools will be made as follows. First, a certain approach to the software development process is selected. Next, techniques are selected that support the various phases in that development process. As a last step, tools are selected that support those techniques. Possibly, some steps in the development process are not supported by well-defined techniques. Some techniques may not be supported by tools. Thus, a typical development environment will have a pyramidal shape as in figure 15.3.

In practice, we often find the reverse conical form: a hardly developed model of the development process, few well-defined techniques, and a lot of tools. In this way, the benefits of the tools will be limited at best. To paraphrase the situation: for many a CASE, there is a lot of Computer Aided, and precious little Software Engineering.

[Freeman87a] views software development itself as a system. Under control of certain rules this system transforms some input—the user's requirements—into

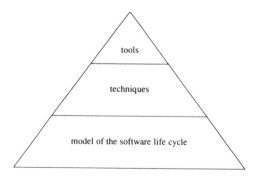

Figure 15.3:   Support in a typical development environment

some output—an automated system. Within this development system, a number of elements work together in a more or less harmonious way: Goals, Rules, Procedures, People, Tools and Information. To make optimal use of tools, they have to fit the other system elements.

The different tool sets as identified above are discussed in the subsections to follow.

15.3.1 Analyst workbenches

Analyst workbenches serve to support the activities in the early phases of software development: requirements analysis and (global) design. In these phases, analysis and design data is gathered. Often, a graphical image of the system is made, for instance in the form of data flow diagrams. From a practical point of view, important problems concern the drawing and redrawing of those diagrams and guarding the consistency and completeness of the data gathered. AWB tools specifically address these points.

The kernel of an AWB is a data base in which the information gathered is being stored. The structure of the data base can be rather free, or it can be derived from the technique(s) supported. Next, the AWB will contain tools to support the following types of activities:

- Drawing, changing and manipulation of pictures. This may vary from simple drawing programs that have no knowledge of the pictures' semantics, to programs that have an elaborate knowledge of the semantics of the drawing technique in question. As far as the latter is concerned, we may think of automatic generation of pointers to subpictures, the automatic reconfiguration of pictures to circumvent intersecting lines, and the like. If the drawing technique has been formalized sufficiently, the user support can be comparable to that offered by a syntax-directed editor for programming languages.

- Analysis of data produced, as regards consistency and completeness. The possibilities to do so are strongly dependent upon the degree to which the drawing technique itself imposes strict rules. There is a choice as to when this checking takes place. If the user is immediately notified as an error is being made, there is little chance that errors cascade. On the other hand, the freedom to 'play' during the exploratory development stages is also limited. If checking is done at a later stage, the user may continue on the wrong track for quite a while before detection, and it then becomes more difficult to identify the proper error messages.

- Generating reports and documentation. It is important to be able to adapt the precise form of reports and documentation to the requirements of the user. For instance, internal standards of some organization may enforce certain report formats. It should be possible to configure the tools to adhere to these standards.

Further tools of an AWB may support, amongst others, prototyping, the generation of user interfaces, or the generation of executable code. [Perrone87] compares the capabilities of four products for drawing and manipulating data flow diagrams (Visible Analyst Workbench, Teamwork/PCSA, Anatools and PowerTools). His conclusion is that the capabilities of these tools (as of 1987) are surprisingly large. He also remarks that we are at only the beginning of a long road.

[Oman90a] is a more recent source of information on a number of state-of-the-art CASE tools for analysis and design, one example being Software Through Pictures (STP). STP is an extendable and customizable environment that supports a number of well-known graphical notations, such as those of Gane/Sarson (data flow diagrams), Jackson (data structure design) and Booch (object-oriented design).

Given the number and variety of Upper-CASE tools on the market and the rapid progress in the capabilities of these tools, their selection process can be a bewildering task. Choosing an Upper-CASE tool requires a thorough analysis of the needs of the software development organization that is about to procure such a tool. [Zucconi89] and [Baram89] give useful guidelines for this selection and evaluation process.

15.3.2 Programmer workbenches

A Programmer workbench consists of a set of tools to support the implementation and test phases of software development. The term originated in the UNIX-world [Dolotta78]. The support offered by UNIX mainly concerns these types of activities. Many programming environments constructed around a certain programming language also support these phases in particular. In a PWB, we find tools to support, amongst others:

— editing and analysis of programs;

— debugging;

— generation of test data;

— simulation;

— test coverage determination.

The tools that support teamwork on large projects deserve our special attention. In a typical environment a group of programmers will be working on the same system. The system will have many components, developed, tested, and changed by different people. During the evolution of the system, different versions of components will result. Automatic support for the control of such a set of components, both technically and organizationally, is a sheer necessity.

One of the early systems for configuration control is the Source Code Control System (SCCS), originally developed for IBM OS, and best known from UNIX [Rochkind75]. SCCS enables the user to keep track of modifications in files (which may contain such diverse things as program code, documentation, or test sets). The system enables the user to generate any version of the system. New versions can be generated without old versions getting lost. Important aspects of SCCS [Bazelmans85] are:

— no separate copies of versions are being kept. Only the modifications (so-called deltas) to previous versions are being stored;

— access to files is protected–only authorized users can make changes;

— each file is identified by an author, version number, date and time of modification;

— the system asks the user for information on the reason for a change, which change is made, where, and by whom.

Figure 15.4 illustrates the main operations provided by SCCS. Within SCCS, all information is kept in so-called **s-files**. The operation create creates the s-file for the first time. If the original file is named prog, then the SCCS file is named s.prog. The operation get yields a read-only copy of the file requested. This read-only copy can be used for compiling, printing, and the like. It is *not* intended to be edited. The operation edit retrieves a copy to be edited. SCCS takes care of protection in the sense that only one person can be editing a file at one time. Finally, the delta operation stores the revised version of the file edited.

Versions of SCCS files get numbered, like in 1.1, 1.2, 1.3, 2.1, etc. The number to the left of the period is the major version number (release number). The number to the right of the period is the minor version number. The first version is numbered 1.1. By default, get and edit retrieve the latest version of a file, while delta results in an increase of the minor version number. If an older version is required or the major version number is to be increased, such is to be specified explicitly.

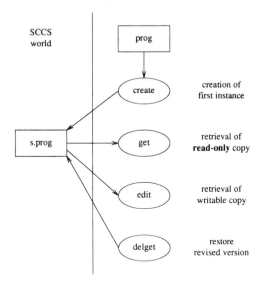

Figure 15.4: Main operations of SCCS (© 1986 *Sun Microsystems, Inc. Reproduced with permission.*)

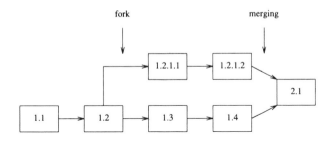

Figure 15.5: Forking and merging of development paths

The above scheme results in a linear sequence of versions. SCCS also provides possibilities to create branches (**forks**), as illustrated in figure 15.5. For example, starting from version 1.2 we may create versions 1.3, 1.4, etc. to represent normal development of a system component, and versions 1.2.1.1, 1.2.1.2, etc. to represent bug fixes in version 1.2. In SCCS, the merging of development paths must be done manually. RCS (the Revision Control System, a system very similar to SCCS) allows for automatic merging of branches, but this is by no means a foolproof operation and should be used with the utmost care.

When different versions of one and the same system are being maintained in this way, the need to automate the construction of new executable versions arises. Make [Feldman78] is one such tool. Make uses a description of the various components of a system and their mutual dependencies. When generating a new executable system, Make inspects the date and time of the latest changes to components and recompiles components only when needed (i.e. components that have been changed after the last compilation). A tool like Make not only saves machine time, but it also ensures that the most recent version of each component is used.

One of the most advanced tools for software configuration control is DSEE, the Domain Software Engineering Environment [Leblang84, 87]. Amongst others, the functions of SCCS and Make have been integrated in DSEE. DSEE has three basic concepts:

— a system model, in which the components of a system and their mutual dependencies are described: this is comparable to a description as used by Make;

— a 'configuration thread' which describes, for each component, which version to use;

— a set of object files that are the result of earlier compilations. Object files which have not been used for a long time are garbage collected by the system.

If a command is issued to assemble a system according to some system model, the configuration thread is used to determine which versions of which components are needed. Once this list of versions is known, it is determined which object files are already present, and which must be compiled anew.

Different users of DSEE may generate different versions of a system at the same time. All users make use of the same set of object files. In DSEE Version III [Leblang87], parallel use is made of the available processing capacity in a pool of computers connected through a network. These facilities together make DSEE a very efficient tool for configuration control.

Programming environments as discussed in section 15.1 support the individual developer. These environments are dominated by issues of software construction. The emphasis is on tools that support software construction: editors, debuggers, compilers, etc. Environments that offer configuration management and system build facilities like those offered by SCCS and Make can be classified as belonging to the *family model* of software development environments [Perry91]. In the family model, a great deal of freedom is left to the individual developers, while a number of rules are agreed upon to regulate critical interactions between developers.

It is argued in [Perry91] that this model is not appropriate anymore if projects get really big. Larger populations require more complicated rules and restrictions on individual freedom. Within my family, a few simple rules suffice (Jasper and Marieke take turns in washing dishes) while adjustments and local deviations are easily established (Jasper having a party today and asking Marieke to take over). Within a large company, policies have to be more strictly obeyed and cooperation between individuals is enforced. Likewise, environments to support the development of very large systems should enforce the proper cooperation between individual developers.

Current software development environments usually offer a family type of support. For example, Make assumes that files whose names end in .c, are C source files. Members of the development family follow this rule and may even have agreed upon further naming conventions. The development environment, however, has no means to enforce those rules. It is up to management to make sure that the rules are being followed.

15.3.3 Management workbenches

A Management workbench contains tools that assist the manager during planning and control of a software development project. Example tools in an MWB include:

Configuration control Besides the control of software components as discussed in the previous section, we may also think of the control of other project-specific information, like design and analysis data, or documentation. An essential aspect of this type of configuration control concerns the control of change requests. Changes are proposed, assessed, (dis)approved, given a priority and cost estimate, planned and executed. The corresponding procedures are described in a Configuration Management Plan, as discussed in chapter 4. The administration of those change requests may well be supported through a tool.

Work assignment Given a number of components, their mutual dependencies, and resources needed (both people and hardware), tools can be used to determine critical paths in the network of tasks, and work packages may be assigned accordingly.

Cost estimation Various quantitative cost estimation models have been developed. These models yield cost estimates, based on project characteristics. Tools have been developed that assist in gathering quantitative project data, calibrating cost estimation models based on these data, and making cost estimates for new projects.

Reliability For reliability models like the ones discussed in chapter 14, tools have been developed that give estimates of the present reliability, test time needed, and the like, based on project data.

15.3.4 Integrated project support environments

An Integrated Project Support Environment is meant to support all phases of the software life cycle. Thus, such an environment has to contain the various tools as discussed in the previous sections. Really mature environments in that sense do not yet exist. In [Porcella83], for example, 24 development methods are compared. For none of these methods did an environment exist that provided full support for all phases of the software life cycle. A number of prototype IPSEs has been described in the literature; see for example [Computer87], [SIGSOFT88, 90]. State-of-the-art developments in this area are exemplified by systems like Sigma, a major Japanese effort in this area [Akima89], ISTAR [Dowson87], and Pact, a large ESPRIT project [Thomas89b].

Environments that span the complete life cycle usually emphasize the support of either front-end activities (analysis/global design—Upper-CASE) or back-end activities (implementation/test—Lower-CASE). They then contain tools specifically geared at supporting tasks from the corresponding part of the life cycle, augmented by a more general support for the other phases (such as for editing, text processing, or a data base interface).

When developing an IPSE, we may strive for either a strong or a weak integration of its tools. A strong integration, as realized in the programming environments discussed in section 15.1, has both advantages (like better control capabilities) and disadvantages. One disadvantage is that such an IPSE tends to be less flexible. If the tools are not integrated, as in UNIX, there is more flexibility. On the other hand, a more stringent management control is then needed.

We may also look for intermediate forms. The Software Productivity System (SPS) is one such intermediate form, based on UNIX [Boehm84c]. SPS uses a central data base in which all project information is stored. The objects are stored in the UNIX file system, controlled by SCCS, and the relations between objects are represented using a relational data base system. Many of the tools of SPS originate from UNIX. Boehm classifies the SPS tools into three classes:

1. General tools, to generate menu interfaces, forms ('fill-in-the-blank') and the like.

2. Tools for office automation and project support, such as an electronic mail system, a tool catalogue, an agenda system, text processing facilities.

3. Tools for software development. Next to the facilities offered by UNIX this includes, amongst others, a set of tools to support SREM, a requirements analysis technique for real time systems, resembling PSL/PSA.

According to Boehm, the first experiences with SPS are encouraging. From a subjective estimate of its users, SPS increased productivity by about 40%.

Support environments are built on top of an (existing) operating system. Current operating systems do not offer a suitable platform to directly base an integrated environment on. For example, the UNIX file system does not allow us to type files or indicate relations between objects stored in different files. Moreover, environments based on existing operating systems are not portable.

A very active area of research within the field of (integrated) environments concerns the definition of an infrastructure for such environments. Portable, integrated tool sets are to be built on top of such an infrastructure and should not directly refer to the underlying operating system. An early effort in this area is represented by the basic interface level to be provided by KAPSE mentioned in section 15.1.1.

A major example of this research is the ESPRIT project that resulted in PCTE, the Portable Common Tool Environment [Thomas89a]. PCTE is a public tool interface intended to serve as a platform for environment builders. PCTE's objectives include (i) the definition of a 'complete' interface, sufficient for all of the needs of tool writers, (ii) support for tools written in a variety of languages, and (iii) a well-defined migration path for existing tools [Boudier88]. The latter has been achieved by ensuring that PCTE primitives are upwardly compatible with UNIX primitives in the X/OPEN standard.

The PCTE interface offers four general classes of services:

- Basic mechanisms for the execution, composition and communication of tools. This includes functions for starting up and stopping processes, functions that handle the I/O between a file system and a process, message-passing functions to handle data traffic between processes, and the like.

- Distribution mechanisms. PCTE is designed to be implemented on a distributed hardware platform which is made transparent by this set of features.

- User-interface facilities to enable uniform interfaces across tools.

- Object-management facilities. The Object Management System (OMS) provides functions to manipulate the various objects within the development environment.

The major novel aspect of PCTE is the OMS. The OMS generalizes the notion of a file system. The OMS lets you store information on objects and relations between objects in an entity-relationship style. Object types in OMS are organized into a hierarchy and object types inherit the attributes and links defined for their ancestor types.

The root of the hierarchy is Object. Predefined subtypes of Object include, amongst others, File and Pipe. Objects of type File have contents, an unstructured sequence of bytes as found in the file systems of most operating systems. An OMS object is further characterized by:

- a set of attributes that describe characteristics of the object;

- a set of links that associates the object with other objects.

For example, an element representing a module may have attributes like 'id' and 'status'. It may be linked to an element that constitutes the subsystem of which the module is a component, and to an element that represents the person responsible for the module. In this way we are able to create an explicit model of both the development environment and the application to be developed.

Several prototype implementations of PCTE have been developed and several environments have been built on top of PCTE. One such environment is Pact,

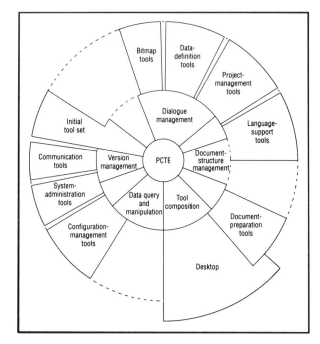

Figure 15.6:   An overview of the Pact environment's architecture (*Source: I. Thomas, PCTE interfaces: supporting tools in software-engineering environments*, IEEE Software **6**, *6 (1989)* © *1989 IEEE.*)

which is a separate large ESPRIT project [Thomas89b]. Figure 15.6 gives an overview of the Pact environment and illustrates the central role of PCTE. A number of improvements to PCTE will be incorporated in a successor, PCTE+ [Boudier88]. Similar efforts within the Ada community have led to the definition of CAIS—the Common APSE Interface Set [Munck88]. Both PCTE+ and CAIS are aimed at providing public tool interface definitions for the development of high-security applications.

15.4 QUO VADIS

We have discussed a number of developments as regards computer-aided software engineering. Whilst many tools have so far been developed not many are able to demonstrate significant productivity gains. It is like a garden, where all kinds of seeds are sprouting, but where it is not yet clear which ones will be weeds, and which ones will grow to beautiful flowers.

We previously classified tools by the degree to which they cover the various phases of the software life cycle. [Houghton87], [Penedo88a] and [Perry91] discuss various alternative tool classifications.

No development method is suited for all classes of problems. Likewise, there is no development environment for all problem classes. Specific properties of a given class of problems will impact the tools for that class of problems. An important property of embedded systems is that its software is often developed on some host machine which is different from the ultimate target machine. Specific tools will be required for the development of such systems, for instance tools that allow us to test the software on the host machine. An Ada environment will have to contain such tools.

For many business applications, the human–computer interaction plays a prominent role, while the requirements analysis of such systems tends to be problematic. A development environment for such systems had better contain tools that support those aspects (AWB, prototyping facilities, and facilities to generate screen layouts).

As a final example, when developing realtime software, it would be preferable to have tools that allow us to analyze system performance at an early stage.

A second possible classification of tools is based on the degree of support offered by the environment. One way to do so is to relate the set of tools to the size of the system to be developed. In practice, it shows that tool usage increases with problem size [Hecht82]. [Howden82b] gives a four-level classification of tool usage:

1. Minimal support for a medium-size project (two years development time, one manager, seven programmers). Use is made of a data base to store documents, a simple configuration control system, and simple test tools.

2. More advanced support for a medium-size project. Central in this environment is a structured data base, with objects such as design documentation, test plans, source code modules. Relations between objects in the data base, such as object A implements object B, or object A uses object B, are maintained. The various tools use these relations. The environment contains tools to support all phases of the software life cycle. There are also tools to support management tasks, for example to create CPM or PERT charts.

3. Support for a medium to large project. A large project has a 3–5 year development time, and involves 70 programmers and 5–7 managers. This environment contains all tools from class 2, with the additional requirement that the tools should be mutually compatible. As far as possible, they use the objects from the project data base.

4. Support for large projects. The environment contains the tools from class 2 to start with. All tools use the project data base. The environment contains facilities to archive documents, so that earlier versions can be recalled.

Finally, we may also relate the degree of support to the importance that users attach to the various tools. Within the framework of a study into tools for an Ada environment, a number of tools were classified by their users

[Houghton83]. These users rated tools for the implementation/test phase as definitely needed: configuration control, management of Ada libraries, type analysis, debugging, interface analysis, compilation, optimization, etc. Tools that were considered moderately important included: control of specifications and tests, cost estimation, work assignment, test coverage determination, regression testing. Tools considered useful included: complexity measurement, checking for completeness and consistency.

This user classification seems to be somewhat application-dependent. By the sheer nature of the class of problems to be solved in the average Ada environment, support is felt to be most strongly needed for the technical parts of the software development process. Users with a background in the development of business applications may well have other priorities.

Such is confirmed by the study reported in [Norman89]. This study addresses CASE productivity perceptions of management information systems professionals. From the study it appears that the data flow diagram and data dictionary functions of the CASE products contribute the most to the software engineer's productivity improvements over manual methods.

One of the essential requirements of a collection of tools concerns their flexibility. Not only do the systems developed with the help of these tools evolve, the tools themselves evolve as well. Our ideas and insights as regards desirable functions of tools change rapidly. Our ideas about process models evolve. Tools that support us in the construction of software should evolve as well. It is as yet an open question as to how this can be realized satisfactorily. Research into interfaces that may serve as a platform upon which IPSEs are built addresses this issue.

An essential property of future software engineering environments is that it provides an integrated collection of tools. This integration has two sides. On the one hand, a mutual tuning of individual tools is needed. Such may be achieved by letting all tools use the information from a central project data base/data dictionary. Secondly, the tools should have a uniform user interface. The earlier mentioned programming environments do reasonably well in this respect.

Finally, the environment of the future should offer support during all phases of the software life cycle. This brings us to the following list of important components:

- A central data base in which all system data is stored. Systems like the Object Management System of PCTE have been identified as the core of software development environments. They serve as a key mechanism for tool integration [Penedo88b].

- A uniform way to input, inspect, or change the requirements specification, design, source code, and any other documents produced along the way. The various stages of a system component must be interconnected, so that changes in one stage cannot be made without the corresponding changes in other stages.

- Elaborate tools for the static and dynamic analysis of the various development stages of system components.

- Tools for management support. It should be possible to track the stage of each system component, so that progress can be controlled, critical paths can be determined, and the like. It must also be possible to make new cost and schedule estimates based on the present state of the project.

- Tools to support system evolution. For instance, tools may track reasons for certain decisions, or consequences of changes proposed. Present environments are strongly aimed at supporting initial software development. They provide little or no support for the subsequent system evolution.

The rules that a program in some language must satisfy are very strict. Because of this formalization it becomes possible to develop syntax-directed editors for these languages. Besides syntax checking, these editors may also perform a number of semantic checks. It is already possible to generate this type of editor from a grammatical description of the structures to be manipulated. For other tasks as well, formalization offers opportunities to develop better tools [Goguen87]. A more effective support of configuration control is possible by specifying a syntax and semantics of possible actions [Habermann86]. Similar possibilities exist for tools that draw diagrams, as present in many AWBs [Moriconi85]. The advent of visual technology further improves the capabilities of support environments [Ambler89]. It opens possibilities for visual editing of diagrams, and allows for multiple views on the same internal structure, as is offered by Software Through Pictures for example [Wasserman87].

15.5 SUMMARY AND FURTHER READING

For many an organizational problem, automation seems to be the panacea. Likewise, the use of tools is often seen as panacea for our problems in software engineering. CASE as prosthesis. Tools, though, remain mere tools. Within the software development process, other factors play a role as well. If the tools do not fit the procedures used within your organization, they are likely to have a far from optimal effect. Also, tools cannot replace an ineffective development method, or ill-qualified personnel. Good people deliver good products, mediocre people deliver mediocre products, irrespective of the tools they use.

Present developments in the area of (integrated) collections of tools go very fast. For many a facet of the software development process, good tools are available. Integration and mutual tuning of tools, as well as their flexibility with respect to changing user needs and changing process models, are current research themes.

[Barstow84] contains a collection of well-known articles on programming environments. [Charette86] is a text book on software engineering which emphasizes tools. Some sources for recent developments include [Computer87], [Software87, 88, 90c], [SIGPLAN87], [SIGSOFT88, 90]. [Houghton85] and [Tahvanainen90] contain annotated bibliographies of articles on software engineering environments.

EXERCISES

1. Discuss strengths and weaknesses of:
   — programming environments,
   — toolkits, and
   — method-based support environments.

2. For the development environment you are currently working in, prepare a list of:
   — utilities you use on a regular basis;
   — utilities you use infrequently and/or vaguely know about.
   Next compare these lists with the manual(s) describing the environment. What percentage of the environment's functionality do you really need?

3. Select and evaluate some commercial Upper-CASE tool using the criteria given in [Zucconi89] and/or [Baram89].

4. Discuss the possible role of automatic support for configuration control in the management of artifacts other than source code modules.

5. One of the claims of CASE-tool providers is that CASE will dramatically improve productivity. At the same time though, customers seem to be disappointed with CASE and take a cautionairy stand. Can you think of reasons for this discrepancy?

6. Why is tool integration such an important issue?

16
Software Reusability*

Meanwhile Daedalus, tired of Crete and of his long absence from home, was filled with longing for his own country, but he was shut in by the sea. Then he said: 'The king may block my way by land or across the ocean, but the sky, surely, is open, and that is how we shall go. Minos may possess all the rest, but he does not possess the air.' With these words, he set his mind to sciences never explored before, and altered the laws of nature. He laid down a row of feathers, beginning with tiny ones, and gradually increasing their length, so that the edge seemed to slope upwards. In the same way, the pipe which shepherds used to play is built up from reeds, each slightly longer than the last. Then he fastened the feathers together in the middle with thread, and at the bottom with wax; when he had arranged them in this way, he bent them round into a gentle curve, to look like real birds' wings.
P. Ovidus Naso: Metamorphoses, VIII, 183–194.

Daedalus deserves a place in the mythology of software engineering. In King Minos' days, software did not exist and yet the problems and notions did which we still find in today's software engineering. One example is of the construction of complex systems. Daedalus certainly has a track record in that field. He successfully managed a project that can stand a comparison with today's software development projects: the construction of the Labyrinth at Knossos.

After a while, Daedalus wanted to leave Crete, as narrated above in Naso's words. King Minos, however, did not want to let him go. We know how the

---

* This chapter is partly based on the MSc Thesis of K. Sikkel, 'Can software last longer?', Department of Mathematics and Computer Science, Vrije Universiteit, Amsterdam, February 17, 1988.

story continues: Daedalus flies with his son Icarus from Crete. Despite his father's warnings, Icarus flies higher and higher. He gets too close to the sun and the wax on his wings melts. Icarus falls into the sea and drowns. Daedalus safely reaches the mainland of Italy.

Daedalus' construction is interesting from the point of view of reuse. The fact that it concerns hardware rather than software is not important here. What concerns us in the present framework, is the application of certain principles in the construction:

- **reuse of components**: Daedalus used real feathers;

- **reuse of design**: he imitated real wings;

- **glue to connect the various components together**: at that time, people used wax to glue things together. The quality of the glue has a great impact on the reliability of the end product.

Through a justified and determined application of these principles, a successful and ambitious project (Daedalus' flight to Italy) was realized. An effort to storm heaven with an insufficient technology turned into a disaster (Icarus' fall into the sea).

We make a small jump in history, to the end of the 1970s. The software crisis has been rampant for many years. The demand for new applications far surpasses the ability of the collective workforce in our field. This gap between demand and supply is still growing. Software reuse is one of the paths being explored in order to achieve a significant increase in software productivity.

Why code well-known computations over and over again? Cannot reliability and productivity be drastically increased by using existing high-quality software components?

It sounds too good to be true. But then, it isn't that simple. The use of existing software components requires standardization of naming and interfaces. The idea of gluing together components is not directly transferable to software.

Some people already term the idea an unfulfilled promise.

Is software reuse a myth, or can it really be achieved? In the following sections, we will give an overview of the developments, opportunities and expectations of software reusability. A tentative conclusion is that we should not expect miracles. By patiently developing a sound reuse technology, a lot of progress is possible, though. There is no philosopher's stone. There are a great number of different developments that may reinforce and supplement one another, though.

The modern view does not restrict the notion of software reuse to component reuse. Design information can be reused also, as can different other forms of knowledge gathered during software construction.

Closely coupled to software reuse is software flexibility. Software is continuously adapted to changed circumstances. In developing the next release of a system, we would like to reuse as much as possible from the present release. This is sometimes considered to be software reuse too. Flexibility aspects have been extensively discussed in previous chapters, notably chapters 6 and 10, albeit not explicitly in the context of reusability.

Various aspects of software reuse are discussed in sections 16.1 to 16.4. Section 16.1 addresses the reuse of intermediate products. Specific tools and techniques to support reuse are the topic of section 16.2. Section 16.3 addresses the perspectives of software reuse. In particular, a domain-oriented, evolutionary approach is advocated. Lastly, non-technical aspects of software reuse are addressed in section 16.4.

16.1 REUSE OF INTERMEDIATE PRODUCTS

This section follows a more or less chronological order. Libraries with ready-to-use pieces of code, such as those for numerical or statistical computations, have been with us for a long time and their use is widespread. This form of software reuse is not necessarily suited for other domains. In other domains we may be better off by reusing 'skeleton' components, components in which some details have not been filled in yet. In an environment in which the same type of software gets developed over and over again, these skeletons may be moulded in a reusable design. A similar technique is to reuse the architecture of a software system, as is found in the construction of compilers, for example.

By incorporating domain knowledge in supporting software, we arrive at the area of transformation systems, application generators and fourth generation languages.

The various reuse technologies to be discussed can be roughly subdivided into two categories [Biggerstaff89a]:

- composition-based technologies, and
- generation-based technologies.

In a **composition-based** technology, reuse is achieved by (partly) composing a new system out of existing components. The building blocks used are passive fragments that are copied from an existing base. In a **generation-based** technology, it is much more difficult to identify the components that are being reused. Rather, the knowledge reused is to be found in some program that generates some other program. In a generation-based technology, reusable patterns are an active element used to generate the target system [Seppänen87]. Prime examples of these two technologies are subroutine libraries and application generators, respectively. Most reuse systems, however, carry aspects of both approaches.

The various approaches to software reuse are discussed below. We conclude with a discussion of the Draco system, in which different techniques for software reuse have been combined.

16.1.1 Libraries of software components

No one in his right mind would think of writing a routine to compute a cosine. If it is not built into the language already, there is bound to be a library routine `cos`. By investigating the question why reuse of mathematical functions is so easy, we come across a number of stumbling blocks that hamper reuse of software components in other domains:

- **a well-developed field, with a standardized terminology**: 'cosine' means the same to all of us;

- **a small interface**: we need exactly one number to compute a cosine;

- **a standardized data format**: a real number may be represented in fixed point, floating point, or double precision, and that's about all.

Reuse of subroutines works best in an application domain that is well disclosed, one whose notions are clear and where the data to be used is in some standardized format.

The modern history of software reuse starts with McIlroy, who envisaged a bright future for a software component technology at the NATO Software Engineering Conference back in 1968. In his view, it should be possible to assemble larger components and systems out of a vast number of ready-to-use building blocks, much like hardware systems are assembled using standard components [McIlroy68].

It hasn't come to that, yet. In order for a large-scale reuse of software components to become feasible, we first have to solve the following problems:

- **Search** We have to search for the right component in a data base of available components which is possible only if we have proper methods available to describe components. If you don't know how to specify what you are looking for, there is little chance you will find it.

- **Understanding** To decide whether some component is usable, we need a precise and sufficiently complete understanding of what a component does.

- **Adaptation** The component selected may not exactly fit the problem at hand. Tinkering with the code is not satisfactory, and in any case only justified if it is thoroughly understood.

- **Composition** A system is wired out of many components. How do we glue components together? We will return to this topic in section 16.2.1.

Hardware components are usually classified in a multi-level hierarchy. Since the naming conventions in that field have been standardized, people are able to traverse the hierarchy. At the lowest level, alternative descriptions of components are given, such as a natural language description, logic schema, and timing information, which describe different aspects of the components.

Several efforts have been made to classify software components in a hierarchical fashion. One such effort is described in [Booch87]. In his taxonomy, a component is first described by the abstraction it embodies. Part of this taxonomy is depicted in Figure 16.1. Secondly, components are described by their time and space behavior.

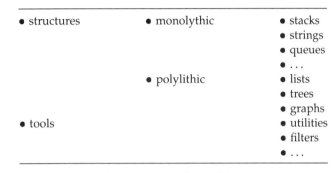

Figure 16.1:   Part of a taxonomy of reusable software components

As for the latter dimensions, Booch distinguishes between four categories:

1. **Concurrency**: objects may or may not preserve their semantics in the presence of multiple threads of control.

2. **Space**: objects may or may not be static in size.

3. **Garbage collection**: objects may or may not handle memory management themselves.

4. **Iterator**: the component may or may not provide operations to visit all parts of the objects embodied by the component.

Figure 16.2 depicts an alternative taxonomy of some well-known data structures. The structural relationships between elements of a compound data structure have been used to set up this taxonomy. For example, there is a 1–1 relationship between elements of a linear structure such as a list or queue. The taxonomies in figures 16.1 and 16.2 both seem to be reasonable. Each of them can be used effectively, provided the user knows how the hierarchy is organized.

This phenomenon holds for component hierarchies in general. If you don't know how the hierarchy is organized, there is little chance that you will be able to find the component you were looking for.

The examples contained in figures 16.1 and 16.2 are somewhat misleading, in that the components found at the leaf nodes of the hierarchy embody abstractions that are known all too well. In other domains, there will be less mutual understanding as regards primitive concepts and their naming. Therefore, setting up a usable taxonomy is likely to be much more difficult in other domains.

structures	0–0	sets
	1–1	stacks
		queues
		lists
		. . .
	1–n	trees
	n–m	graphs

Figure 16.2:   An alternative component hierarchy

A second observation that can be made about the reuse of components regards their granularity. The larger a component is, the larger the pay off will be once it is reused. On the other hand, larger components tend to become less reusable, since the reusability of a component decreases as its size grows. Such is caused by the fact that larger components tend to put larger constraints on their environment. This is analogous to Fisher's fundamental theorem of biology: the more an organism is adapted to some given environment, the less suited it is for some other environment.

Some of the most advanced work so far in the area of component classification has been done by Prieto-Diaz [Prieto-Diaz85, 87, 91a]. A component library based on his classification scheme helps in localizing potentially useful components. It also helps in estimating the effort needed to adapt a component once it is found.

Prieto-Diaz' classification scheme uses a number of different characteristics, or *facets*, to describe each component. For example, components in a UNIX environment could be classified according to the action they embody, the object they manipulate, the data structure used, and the system they are part of [Prieto-Diaz91a]. Classifying a component amounts to choosing an n-tuple which best fits that component.

Faceted classification has certain advantages over the enumerative classification as used in the examples of figures 16.1 and 16.2. Strictly enumerative schemes use a predefined hierarchy and force you to search for a node that best fits the component to be classified. Though cross-references to other nodes can be included, the resulting network soon becomes fairly complicated.

We will often not succeed in finding a component which exactly matches our requirements. But that does not imply that a usable component cannot be found. Prieto-Diaz' system offers the possibility to *expand* questions by also considering components that are 'close to' the one sought for, for any of the facets. Being 'close to' is determined through appropriate measures of the distance between notions that make up the facets.

Once a set of candidate components has been found, an evaluation system may order these components for their (presumed) suitability. Besides conceptual distance, properties like the length (lines of code), structure (number of modules, complexity) and documentation (a subjective assessment) play a role in the selection process.

A research project that builds on the work of Prieto-Diaz is described in [Burton87]. Burton et al. have developed a prototype Reusable Software Library. In their system, the description of each software component consists of a great number of attributes, such as the length of the component, its complexity, test results, errors reported, quality of the documentation, and readability. If there is a choice between different components, the reuser may interactively indicate the relevance of each of the attributes. A rank order is then obtained, based on the user's indications. By varying the values for different attributes, the reuser quickly gains insight into the relative value of the eligible components.

The approach of Prieto-Diaz has been successfully applied in reuse programs at both GTE Laboratories and Contel. Further experiences in building and using component libraries are described in [Tarumi88], [Maarek91] and [Matsumoto87]. These and other projects vary considerably with respect to their classification and retrieval schemes, and the amount of tool support provided by the environment. Classification schemes vary from a simple Key Word In Context approach to fully automated keyword retrieval from existing documentation, and may even involve elaborate knowledge of the application domain. With respect to retrieval, systems may employ an extensive thesaurus to relate similar terms, or offer browsing facilities to inspect 'similar' components. A survey of methods for representing reusable software components is given in [Frakes90].

Some of the actual experience suggests that practical, useful component libraries will not contain a huge number of components. For example, [Prieto-Diaz91a] reports that the asset collection of GTE went from 190 in 1988 to 128 in 1990. For that reason, the classification and retrieval of components often is not the main impediment for a successful reuse program. Rather, filling the library with the *right* components is the real issue. This aspect will be taken up again in section 16.3.

16.1.2 Templates

In the preceding section, we silently assumed library components to be ready-to-use pieces of code. The applicability of a component can be increased by leaving certain details unspecified. **Templates** or **skeletons** are 'unfinished' components. By *instantiating* them, i.e. by filling in the holes, a (re)usable component results.

An example of a possible template is a procedure implementing the quicksort algorithm. Details like the bounds of the array to be sorted, the type of the array elements and the relational operator used to compare array elements, are not important for the essence of the algorithm.

This very much boils down to separating the functionality and the data types used in the realization. Potential reusability is greatly enhanced if the library contains templates besides abstract data types. Volpano and Kieburtz have developed a prototype instantiator that can instantiate templates in Pascal and C to complete components [Volpano85]. A similar principle is embedded in Ada through the concept of a *generic package*.

As more and more details are being left open, a template can be applied more generally. However, there is a price to be paid. The cost of obtaining a complete application is likely to increase proportionally with the number of holes to be filled in.

Templates need not be constrained to just subroutines. It is realistic to think of a template which can be instantiated into a full program for a very specific application domain. Such templates are called application generators, which are the topic of section 16.1.6.

16.1.3 Design reuse

It seems plausible that design reuse pays off in an environment where the same type of program is developed over and over again. In many a business environment, applications are wrongfully considered to be unique. As a consequence, they are designed and coded from scratch each time the need for yet another application arises. Lanergan and Grasso state that there are but a few different basic operations in business Cobol programs, like sorting, updating and reporting [Lanergan84]. Based on an analysis of a vast number of existing programs at Raytheon Company, MA, they designed seven 'logic structures'. A logic structure is an unfinished Cobol program. Some data declarations are empty, i.e. have a 01-level only. Some paragraphs have no code yet.

After some experimentation it was decided that all new programs to be developed at Raytheon were to use one of these predefined logic structures. The biggest advantage of using logic structures, according to Lanergan and Grasso, shows up during maintenance. It seems as if all software is written by the same team. If a programmer adapts a program written by someone else, there are likely to be few surprises, since the structure and much of the code will already be familiar.

At Raytheon, one also uses a library of Cobol components besides the logical structures. Standard components are certain data types (file descriptors or record descriptors) and a great number of routines. After a start-up phase, the combination of standard designs and standard components resulted in a productivity increase of 50%.

Reuse is an integrated part of software production at the Toshiba Software Factory in Japan [Matsumoto84a, 84b, 87]. Toshiba mostly produces software for industrial process control. Most emphasis on reuse is in the design phase, though it rather differs from that at Raytheon.

At Toshiba, a piece of software starts off with a formal specification. This specification is composed of (largely) independent modules. The specification is transformed into executable code via two intermediate abstraction levels, the so-called functional and logic design. A library module then is composed of four parts: the specification, functional design, logic design and code of that module. Note the difference with Raytheon's approach. At Raytheon, design modules need not be linked to code modules.

Before a new module for some application is included in Toshiba's library, it is first rewritten into a more general form. At the same time, a 'presentation' of the module is prepared. This presentation consists of a specification and a description of those module properties that can be easily changed if the module is to be reused in a different context. According to Matsumoto, reuse of modules at higher levels of abstraction results in a much higher increase in the amount of code reused. About half of the code delivered by Toshiba is reused code.

16.1.4 Reuse of architecture

Reuse of architecture—i.e. the way in which the various parts of a system hang together—is rather different from reuse of software components, templates or designs. A library of software architectures is not all that useful. For each problem, we had better look for an architecture specifically tuned to that problem. An inappropriate architecture can never be the basis for a good system. The situation becomes rather different if a problem recurs over and over again in different variants. If a useful standard architecture exists for a particular type of problem, it can be applied in all future variants.

The prime area within computer science where a software architecture can be reused is in building compilers. Most compilers are built out of the same components: a lexical analyzer, parser, symbol table, code generator, and a few others. There exist certain well-defined types of parsers, such as LL(1) or LALR(1) parsers. There is a large body of theory about how compilers function, and this theory is known to the people building compilers. In this way, a generally accepted standard architecture for compilers has evolved. Obviously, it has never been proved that this is the only, or best, way to build compilers. But it constitutes a sound and well-known method to attack problems in a notoriously difficult domain.

Reuse of architecture is seldom found in other areas. (One interesting exception is in the area of software development environments, most of which employ a central information repository surrounded by a small number of layers containing tools that become more specific at the outer layers.) The main reason being that a similar body of shared, crystallized, knowledge just does not exist. We may, however, observe how certain types of standard architectures have developed in other engineering disciplines. [Spector86] for instance describes the procedures used in building motorway bridges from the software engineering point of view. [Standish84] notes that in each engineering discipline an enormous amount of work has to be done, and experience has to be gained, before such standardization takes place. [Freeman83b] states that we may start documenting existing architectures, so that others may take advantage from those experiences.

16.1.5 Transformation systems

We already mentioned the transformational nature of the software development process earlier on. A requirements specification describes the system to be realized in some notation, be it a natural language, a formal language, or a pictorial language. Through a number of intermediate stages this description is transformed into the final product, encoded in some programming language.

Two types of transformations recur in this process:

- **refinements**: by adding details and implementation decisions, the product's description is refined;

- **linguistic transformations**: during some steps, the product's description in one language is translated into an equivalent description in some other language.

Obviously, both types of transformation can be carried out manually; they often are. We may, however, also consider the possibility of having a computer assist us in realizing those transformations—precisely the aim of a transformation system.

The easiest starting point for doing so is provided by the class of linguistic transformations. A construct like

```
IfExists i in 1..N SuchThat A[i] = x
then ...
```

leaves no doubt as to its meaning. Unfortunately, this construct does not exist in most high-level programming languages that are in use today. So, at some point in time the IfExists-construct will have to be replaced by a semantically equivalent code sequence in some existing language.

The IfExists-construct is of a fairly low level. It is immediately obvious that the formalism is already fairly close to, say, Pascal. An important point is that it is indeed a *formalism*. Translations between formal languages are far easier to realize than a translation to or (especially) from a natural language. A design completely written in Dutch or English is hardly palatable to a transformation system. The use of transformation systems incurs a further formalization of higher-level product descriptions.

In a so-called **wide-spectrum language**, the solution to a problem can be expressed at different levels of abstraction. Correctness-preserving transformations from one level to the next are guided by transformation rules, while all intermediate results stay within the realm of the same, formal language. See [Bauer89] for an example of this approach.

An interesting question is whether we can formalize *all* levels, and build an intelligent compiler which translates a design into executable code without human intervention. This is indeed possible if we restrict ourselves to a very narrow application domain. In order to be able to *meaningfully* rewrite a design, a sufficient amount of application domain knowledge somehow has to be built into the system. Such systems are called **application generators**. Application generators are the topic of section 16.1.6.

A transformation system for a broad application domain will in general need human guidance in making refinements. For example, if some high-level description talks about *sets* of objects, such may be refined into a representation using binary trees, or one using hash tables, or yet another one. In general, the programmer will decide which data structure best fits the application, since the transformation system lacks the knowledge to do so properly.

The most difficult task for a user of a transformation system is to identify some well-defined, consistent, intermediate levels to be used in the transformation process. If we manage to decompose the transformation process into some conceptually well-separated steps, the transformations become much easier to realize. A nice example of this is given by Boyle and Muralidharan [Boyle84]. Their transformation system, originally written in Lisp, was translated into Fortran using that same transformation system. They did so in two steps: from Lisp to 'recursive Fortran', and next to Fortran77.

16.1.6 Application generators and fourth-generation languages

Application generators write programs. An application generator has a fair amount of application-domain knowledge. Usually, the application domain is quite narrow. In order to obtain a program one obviously needs a specification of that program. Once the specification is available, the program is generated automatically.

The principle being used is the same as that behind a generic package or template: the actual program to be generated is built into the application generator already. Instantiation of an actual program is done by filling in a number of details. The difference with a template is that the size of the code being delivered is much bigger with an application generator. Also, the details are generally provided at a higher level of abstraction, in terms of concepts and notions drawn from the application domain.

An application generator can be employed in each domain with a structure such that complicated operations within that domain can be largely automated. One example is the production of graphical summaries from a data base. So-called compiler-compilers are another typical example of application generators: given a grammar (i.e. the details) of some programming language, a parser for that language results.

Fourth-generation languages or **very high level languages** (VHLLs) are often mentioned in one and the same breath with application generators. Fourth-generation languages offer programming constructs at a much higher level than third-generation programming languages.

Expressions from a given application domain can be directly phrased in the corresponding fourth-generation language. Consequently, the fourth-generation language must have knowledge of that application domain. This generally means that fourth-generation languages are only suited for one specific, limited, domain.

There is no fundamental difference between fourth-generation languages and application generators. When one wants to stress the generative capabilities of a system, the term application generator is mostly applied. The term fourth-generation language highlights the high-level programming constructs being offered. For a number of systems, such as Focus and dBase II, both terms are used interchangeably [Horowitz85], [Boehm87a].

Application generators and fourth-generation languages potentially offer a number of cost savings, since implementation details need not be bothered with: less code to be written, software that is more comprehensible, fewer errors, software that is easier to maintain. In practice, this theory often does not come up to expectations. For one thing, the user may want something which is not offered by the system. In that case, a piece of handwritten Cobol is to be added to the software being generated automatically. By doing so, one of the main advantages of using fourth-generation languages, viz. easily comprehensible programs at a high level of abstraction, gets lost.

We may ask ourselves whether it is possible to embed a fourth-generation language within a general-purpose programming language. [Horowitz85] concludes that this is not without problems. If we want to activate a report generator from within some program, such can be done only by first allocating sufficient memory in which the report generator can write its answer. Such greatly reduces the ease of use of the report generator. He therefore suggests going the other way around: extend fourth-generation languages to general-purpose programming languages by adding conventional programming language constructs.

16.1.7 An integrated approach

Different types of reuse are combined in the Draco-system [Neighbors84], [Freeman87b]. Two starting points are essential to this system, developed at the University of California at Irvine:

- reuse of design information is more important than reuse of code, but optimal reuse can be obtained only by a combination of reuse strategies at different levels;
- for each application domain a special, domain-specific, language should be used, in which the notions, objects and functions from that domain can be described.

To construct similar systems, which is the goal of Draco, two types of activities are needed. As a first step, a new domain language is implemented in Draco, using Draco. Next, Draco is used as a transformation system for specifications written in that domain language. Thus, Draco had best be described as a transformation system generator.

Analyzing an application domain is particularly difficult. It can be done properly only by very experienced people. As Neighbors puts it: 'One sure way to make the Draco method fail is to have unexperienced people observe the work of the "old hands" to construct a domain. It is easy to construct a poor domain, and very hard to construct a good one.' [Neighbors84]

As a bottom domain, some ordinary high-level language must be present. New domains are built using existing domains. To each Draco domain, the following constituents belong:

A **parser** This parser maps the domain language onto some internal representation.

A **pretty printer** The pretty printer is the inverse of the parser: it translates the internal representation back into a specification in the domain language.

Rewrite rules Rewrite rules are used to simplify pieces of text written in the domain language.

Components Components are implemented in underlying domains. A component consists of one or more **refinements** which implement that component in various ways.

Procedures If there exist certain domain-specific algorithms, procedures for those algorithms are present in that domain.

Transforming a specification in an already implemented domain proceeds by executing the following steps in alternating fashion:

- **refinement**: elements from one domain are replaced by an implementation of those elements in another, lower-level, domain;

- **rewriting**: a specification (program) in one domain is being optimized by applying one of the rewrite rules.

It is important that optimizations be applied at the right level of abstraction. To give an example: the domain of algebraic manipulation contains a component EXP(A, B) for exponentiation. If we start with an expression EXP(A, 2), it is sensible to rewrite this expression to A * A. If this rewriting is not done at this level and the bottom domain, some ordinary programming language, does not know the standard exponentiation operator, then EXP(A, 2) would eventually be rewritten to some rather complicated piece of code. From that piece of code it is difficult, if not impossible, to deduce that multiplication would have sufficed in this case. If EXP(A, 2) is rewritten as A * A, that expression can be left as it is, or changed into something like SQR(A).

During the transformation of a specification to an equivalent program, Draco retains the **refinement history**. This refinement history is of importance when making changes to the program. Using a **refinement replay**, the desired change can be effected at the proper place.

The version discussed in [Freeman87b], Draco 1.2, is a working prototype. Considering the effort needed to extend the system with good domain languages, it will take a long time before we will have a production-quality system of this kind. The important contribution of Draco is that it constitutes the most advanced effort so far in which the reuse of components, design and application domain knowledge are combined.

16.2 REUSE TOOLS AND TECHNIQUES

In this section we consider a number of concepts, methods and techniques that may have a positive impact on software reuse. In doing so, we will reconsider the approaches discussed in the previous section, thus establishing a relation between the reusable software assets discussed in the previous section and the notions to be discussed here.

16.2.1 Module interconnection languages

The relation between different modules of a system can be formally expressed in a Module Interconnection Language (MIL) [Prieto-Diaz86]. MILs are an important tool when designing and maintaining large systems consisting of many different modules. A MIL-description is a formal description of the global structure of a software system. It can be used to verify the integrity of the system automatically. It can be used to check whether the various modules conform to the agreed interfaces.

Figure 16.3 contains a small fragment of MIL-code to illustrate the general flavor. The example concerns the structure of a one-pass compiler. The notation used is that of INTERCOL [Tichy79]. A description in INTERCOL consists of a sequence of module and system families followed by a set of compositions. The example in figure 16.3 contains one system family. A member of that family is a version of a system. Note that module family `scan` has multiple implementations, one for each language supported. The composition given at the end of the description selects a number of building blocks defined previously.

MILs originated as a consequence of the separation between programming-in-the-small and programming-in-the-large. The essential ideas behind the development of MILs are:

- **A separate language for system design** A MIL is not a programming language. Rather, it describes desirable properties of modules that are to become part of the system being considered.

- **Static type-checking between different modules** This automatically guarantees that different modules obey the interface. An interface can be changed only after the corresponding change has been realized in the design.

- **Design and binding of modules in one description** In the early days of programming-in-the-large the various modules of a system were assembled by hand. Using a MIL, it is done automatically.

```
system compile
   provide compile

   module compiler
      provide procedure compiler
      require scanner, parser, postfix_generator, symtbl_funct
   end compiler

   module scan
      provide package scanner is
         type token: ALPHA
         function nextchar_funct return: CHARACTER
         procedure backup_proc
      end scanner
      require symtbl_proc, errormsg_proc
      implementation SCAN02 .. PL/I
      implementation SCAN03 .. Pascal
   end scan

   ...

   module errormsg
      provide procedure errormsg_proc
      implementation ERRMSG
   end errormsg

   COMPOSITION
   compile_A = [compile, SCAN02, PARSE.NIP, SYMBL.PL/I,
         POSTFIXGEN.NIP, SYSLBL, VRFY, ERRORMSG]
end compile
```

Figure 16.3: Partial INTERCOL code for a single one-pass compiler (*Reprinted by permission of the publisher from Module interconnection languages, by R. Prieto-Diaz & J.M. Neighbors,* Journal of Systems and Software **6** *pp. 307–334. Copyright 1986 by Elsevier Science Publishing Co., Inc.*)

- **Version control** Keeping track of the different versions of (parts of) a system during development and maintenance requires a disciplined approach.

A number of different MILs have been developed. The basic concepts, however, are the same. These are:

- **resources**, everything that can have a name in a programming language (constant, type, variable, procedure) and can be made available by a module for use in another module;

- **modules** that make resources available, or use them;

- **systems**, groups of modules which together perform a well-defined task. To the outside world, a system can be viewed as one single module.

The coupling between modules can be modeled as a graph: the nodes of the graph denote modules while the (directed) edges denote the uses-relation.

Depending on the sophistication of the MIL, this graph can be a tree, an acyclic directed graph, or a directed graph without any restrictions.

Important ideas that underlie the concept of a MIL are abstract data types and information hiding. More recent notions that have had their impact on the world of MILs are version control and programming environments. According to Prieto-Diaz and Neighbors, the Gandalf system is the best example of an environment in which a MIL (INTERCOL, used in figure 16.3) has been integrated; see also chapter 15.

All MILs discussed in [Prieto-Diaz86] show the same limitations: they engage themselves only in the *syntax* of interfaces. Whether the resources passed on are meaningful or not cannot be assessed. Goguen tries to go one step further in his effort to supply a MIL with a limited knowledge of semantics [Goguen86a]. His system is called LIL (Library Interconnection Language). This language is an extension of Ada, but other languages can be similarly extended using the same principles. LIL consists of the following entities:

- **Packages**, comparable to those of Ada. An important addition is that these packages may have **axioms** associated with them. These axioms tell something about the operation of the package. Axioms can be formal (in first-order logic) or informal (such as natural language).

- **Theories** resemble packages, but do not contain any code. They indicate only that certain types and functions should be provided, and they give axioms that describe the behavior of those functions.

- **Views** show how a given theory is fulfilled.

An example may clarify this. Let SORT be a generic package for sorting a sequence. We have not yet specified the type of the elements in the sequence. The theory ORDEREDSET tells us what an ordering is, by means of the following axioms:

- E ≤ E (reflexivity)

- E1 ≤ E2 and E2 ≤ E3 -> E1 ≤ E3 (transitivity)

- E1 ≤ E2 and E2 ≤ E1 -> E1 = E2 (antisymmetry)

- E1 ≤ E2 or E2 ≤ E1 (complete ordering)

For example, the natural numbers with ordering '≥' satisfy these axioms. But there are many other orderings possible (such as: all even numbers are larger than all odd numbers, and both the even and odd numbers follow the natural ordering). If we wish to sort a sequence in descending order, we choose a **view** with the natural numbers as elements of ORDEREDSET and the relation ≥ as ordering.

The above construction is called *horizontal* composition by Goguen. The view describes an interface between two components at the same level of abstraction. One component looks for a theory, the other one satisfies the axioms, and the view tells us how they match. *Vertical* composition is also possible. In the SORT package it has not been defined yet how a sequence is to be implemented. Thus, SORT still has to be connected to a component at some lower level of abstraction that implements a sequence.

Axioms not expressed in a formal notation obviously cannot be verified automatically. Goguen therefore proposes a **truth management system**. This system should keep track of the probability that the axioms have been verified (such as: approved by a theorem prover; the programmer saw that it was OK; some tests have been executed successfully). If an error occurs, some critical path analysis could indicate the weakest link in the proof chain.

With respect to the previous section we may note that MILs fit in well with transformation systems (section 16.1.5) and other forms of reuse where design plays an essential role (sections 16.1.3, 16.1.7). When searching a module library for a suitable component, its semantics are much more important than the syntax of the interface. Goguen's work represents a first step in that direction. [Biggerstaff87] notes that *semantic binding* is one of the major issues in really getting reuse off the ground.

16.2.2 Object-oriented programming

Object-oriented programming was one of the buzzwords of the 1980s. What is the potential of object-oriented languages as regards software reuse? [Cox84] and [Meyer87] both argue that reuse is primarily a technical problem that can be solved by using the right, i.e. object-oriented, techniques. Many others also see managerial, organizational and psychological problems that hinder the fast promulgation of a large-scale reuse technology.

It goes without saying that module libraries become much more usable if they contain object-oriented modules. If the module looked for is not present, it is not necessary to adapt an almost fitting module by tinkering with the code—always a dangerous affair. Desirable features can be inherited from a suitable class already present in the library, and the extra bells and whistles can be added to a newly defined subclass.

Conversely, the inheritance and polymorphism features of object-oriented languages by themselves provide opportunities for constructing reusable parts. They promote the emergence of abstract classes that may serve as a starting point from which more specific components are derived.

A study conducted by Lewis et al. supports the claim that the object-oriented paradigm has a particular affinity to software reuse [Lewis91]. In their experiments the increase in software productivity due to reuse was greater for the object-oriented paradigm than for the procedural paradigm.

16.2.3 Programming environments

A programming environment is a set of facilities offered to a programmer or a team of programmers. As a minimum requirement, such an environment contains at least the following tools: a file system, editor and compiler. But a module library, for example, becomes meaningful only if the programming environment also contains tools to locate modules and glue modules together. Examples of programming environments that contain tools specifically geared towards reuse are discussed in [Browne90], [Devanbu91], [Wood88] and [Ramamoorthy88].

The programming environment is of limited use only if the reuse assets offered are just (passively) present. A more optimal use of the environment can be made if it has *knowledge* of the information that can be reused, and actively uses this knowledge. Not accidentally, the AI contribution to reuse will be discussed here. If the environment *knows* the intention of the programmer, if it knows how and where to find that information, we are far better off. An interesting project in this area is the 'Programmer's Apprentice' (PA).

The PA has been developed at the MIT Artificial Intelligence Laboratory [Waters82], [Rich83, 88]. As its name suggests, the PA acts as an apprentice to the programmer using it. The PA serves as an active agent in the development process rather than as a passive tool. The PA fills in the coding details, helps with the documentation, debugging and changing of programs, while the programmer does the real hard work. In order to be able to do its job properly, the PA must *understand* what is going on. There must be a body of shared knowledge between the programmer and the PA. A central focus in the PA-project is to develop a knowledge representation for programs and program fragments (**clichés**). This type of knowledge is codified and stored in **plans**. Plans constitute the representation underlying the whole system.

Plans describe an *algorithmic* structure. They abstract from syntactic constructs that characterize different programming languages. The programmer interacts with the PA in terms of such algorithmic structures. These plans fit in well with the way experienced programmers go about their work. [Soloway86a] argues that experienced programmers use similar plans, i.e. they employ standard stereotyped solutions to solve standard problems; see also chapter 17.

Let us give a small example to illustrate some of the key ideas from the PA project. Suppose we are going to write a function (in Lisp) to compute the square root of a number. If we start with

```
(DEFINE SQRT (NUM) ...)
```

we may instruct the PA to

```
implement SQRT as a successive approximation
```

The PA then retrieves the stepwise approximation plan from the plan library. This plan is instantiated to Lisp and included in the as of yet incomplete function:

```
    (DEFINE SQRT (NUM)
  (PROG (RESULT)
    (SETQ RESULT ..initialization..)
LP (COND (..test.. (RETURN RESULT)))
    (SETQ RESULT ..approximation..)
    (GO LP)))
```

During the interaction with the PA, we may use known algorithmic terms. The pieces not yet instantiated are given in between double periods. They can be called by their name. If we continue with

```
implement the test as an equality within epsilon
```

the line containing `..test..` will be changed into

```
LP (COND ((< (ABS (- ..arg.. ..arg..)) ..epsilon..)
    (RETURN RESULT)))
```

and so on.

For the interaction with the outside world, the PA contains the following components:

- the **coder** translates plans into program text;

- the **analyzer** abstracts program text into plans;

- the **drawer** depicts a plan as a diagram;

- the **plan editor** helps the programmer in changing a program by changing its plan.

So, besides its ability to write programs by using known plans, the PA can also do the reverse: building plans from a given program. In this way, programs that have been written without assistance from the PA can be adapted using the PA. The PA will first make a plan of the program given, and the programmer may tell the PA, at the algorithm level, which changes to accommodate.

The Programmer's Apprentice idea is very elegant. It is used as a starting point to explore opportunities to provide knowledgeable assistance at the design and requirements analysis stages through a Design Apprentice [Waters91] and Requirements Apprentice [Reubenstein91]. Both employ a cliché library, a repository of codified fragments of reusable knowledge. Through its very nature, a Programmer's Apprentice is best suited to an environment where explicit knowledge from a limited domain is available.

This resembles the application generators from section 16.1.6. Application generators also manage to achieve high productivity gains by limiting their domain of application. It is feasible that a new generation of application generators can be developed using an AI-approach like the one used in the Programmer's Apprentice. Such application generators could be more dynamic, more flexible, and easier to handle than their limited, rigid, predecessors.

Programming environments may in principle concern themselves with all types of reuse discussed in section 16.1. The practical value of a data base of reusable modules increases if the environment automatically checks the interface consistencies. A transformation system will always be embedded in some kind of programming environment. The added value of a programming environment over a set of loose tools is that the various constituents are integrated, which results in a potentially more directed and uniform support for reuse.

16.3 PERSPECTIVES OF SOFTWARE REUSE

Useful abstractions are discovered, not invented.
[Johnson88]

In any reuse technology, the building blocks being reused, whether in the form of subroutines, templates, tranformations, or problem solutions known to the designers, correspond to crystallized pieces of knowledge, pieces of knowledge that can be used in circumstances other than the one for which they were envisaged originally.

A central question in all reuse technologies discussed above is how to exploit some given set of reusable building blocks. This is most paramount in the various projects in the area of component libraries, where the main goal is to provide ways of retrieving a usable component for the task at hand.

Alternatively, we may look at software reusability from an entirely different angle: what building blocks do we need in order to be able to use them in different applications?

Reuse is not the same as reusability [Tracz88]. Reuse of software is profitable only if the software is indeed reusable. The second approach addresses the question of how to identify a useful, i.e. reusable, collection of components in an organized way.

Such a collection of reusable components is tied to a certain application domain. Examples are: a mathematical subroutine library, Lanergan's collection of 'logic structures', the primitives of a fourth-generation language. The latter two both aim at providing useful primitives for business-type applications.

When trying to identify a reusable set of components, the main question is to decide *which* components are needed. A reusable component is to be valued, not for the trivial reason that it offers relief from implementing the functionality yourself, but for offering a piece of the *right* domain knowledge, the very functionality you need, gained through much experience and an obsessive desire to find the right abstractions.

Components should reflect the primitive notions of the application domain. In order to be able to identify a proper set of primitives for a given domain, considerable experience with software development for that domain is needed [Neighbors84]. While this experience is being built up, the proper set of primitives will slowly evolve.

Actual implementation of those primitives is of secondary importance. A collection of primitives for a given domain defines an *interface* that can be used when developing different programs in that domain. The ideas, concepts and structures that play an important role in the application domain have to be present in the interface. Reuse of that interface is more important than reuse of its implementation. The interface structures the software. It offers a focal point in designing software for that application area.

In [Sikkel88], such a collection of primitives is called a Domain-Oriented Virtual Machine (DOVM).

A domain is a 'sphere or field of activity or influence'. A domain is defined by consensus, and its essence is the shared understanding of some community [Arango89]. It is characterized by a collection of common notions that show a certain coherence, while the same notions do not exist or do not show that coherence outside the domain. Domains can be taken more or less broadly. Example domains are, for instance:

- accounting software,

- accounting software for multinationals,

- accounting software for multinationals, developed by Soft Ltd.

All accounting software will incorporate such notions as 'ledger' and 'balance'. Accounting software for multinationals will have some notions in common, such as provisions for transborder cash flow, notions that do not exist in accounting systems for the grocery store or milkman. Representation of notions in software developed by Soft Ltd. will differ from those of other firms because of the use of different methodologies or conventions.

The essential point is that certain notions play an important role in the domain in question. Those notions also play a role in the software for that domain. If we want to attain reuse within a given domain, these domain-specific notions are important. These notions have certain *semantics* which are fixed within the domain, and are known to people working in that domain. These semantically primitive notions should be our main foci in trying to achieve reusability.

For most domains, it is not immediately clear which primitives are the right ones. It is very much a matter of trial and error. By and by, the proper set of primitives show themselves. As a domain develops, we may distinguish various stages:

- At the start, there is no clear set of notions yet and all software is written from scratch. Experience is slowly building up, while we learn from previous mistakes.

- At the second stage, similar problems are being recognized and solved in a similar way. The first semantic primitives will be recognized. By trial and error, we find out which primitives are useful, and which are not.

- At the third stage, the domain is ripe for reuse. A reasonable amount of software has been developed, the set of concepts has stabilized, there are standard solutions for standard problems.

- Finally, the domain has been fully explored. Software development for the domain can largely be automated. We do not program in the domain anymore. Instead, we use a standard interface formed by the semantic primitives of the domain.

Most reuse occurs at the last stage, though it is not recognized as such anymore. A long time ago, computers were programmed in assembly language. In high-level languages, we 'just write down what we want', and the compiler makes this into a 'real' program. This is generally not seen as reuse anymore. A similar phenomenon occurs in the transition of a third-generation language to a fourth-generation language.

From the reusability point of view, the above classification is one of a normal, natural, evolution of a domain. The various stages are categorized by reuse at qualitatively different levels:

- at the first stage, there is no reuse;

- at the second stage, reuse is ad hoc;

- at the third stage, reuse is structured – existing components are reused in an organized way when new software is being developed;

- at the fourth stage, reuse is institutionalized and automated – human effort is restricted to the upper levels of abstraction.

Within a given domain, an informal language is used. In this informal domain language, the same thing can be phrased in quite different ways, using concepts that are not sharply defined. Yet, informal language is understandable, because the concepts refer to a universe of discourse that both speaker and listener share.

Concepts in a formal language do not refer to experience or everyday knowledge. They merely have a meaning in some formal system. A virtual machine is such a formal system, and its language is a formal language.

To formalize a domain is to construct a formal (domain) language that mimics an existing informal language. We then have to choose from the different semantic primitives that exist informally. Sometimes also, it is convenient to add new primitives, primitives that fit neatly within the formalized domain.

As an example of the latter, consider the domain of computerized typesetting. Part of formatting a document concerns assembling words into lines and lines into paragraphs. The sequence of words making up a paragraph must be broken into lines such that the result is typographically pleasing.

Knuth describes this problem in terms of 'boxes', 'glue' and 'penalties' [Knuth81]. Words are contained in boxes, which have a certain width. White space between words is phrased in terms of glue, which may shrink or stretch. A nominal amount of white space between adjacent words is preferred, and a penalty of 0 is associated with this nominal spacing. Putting words closer together (shrinking the glue), or wider apart (stretching the glue), incurs a non-negative penalty. The more this glue is stretched or shrunk, the higher the penalty. The penalty associated with formatting a complete paragraph in some given way then is the sum of the penalties associated with the interword spacings within that formatted paragraph. The problem may now be rephrased as: break the paragraph into lines such that the total penalty is minimal. (Note that penalties may also be associated with other typographically less desirable properties, such as hyphenation.)

The notions 'box', 'glue' and 'penalty' give a neat formalization to certain aspects of typography. They also lead to an efficient solution for the above problem, using a dynamic programming technique.

In practice, formalizing is not a one-shot activity. Rather, it is an iterative process. The formalized version does not exactly describe the informal language. It fixes one possible interpretation. If we study its semantics, it may have some undesirable aspects. In due course, an acceptable compromise is reached between those who use the language (in higher domains) and those who implement it (in lower domains). Once the formal domain language is fixed, it also affects the informal domain language. People working within the domain start to use the primitives of the formal language.

It is now clear that it is in general not wise to go directly from stage one (no reuse) to stage three (structured reuse). Formalization has a solidifying effect on the semantic primitives of the domain. Our notion of these primitives changes, because we do not any longer consider them as coming from the intuitive universe of discourse, but as being based on the underlying formalism. A crucial question, namely whether we formalized the *right* semantic primitives, then becomes harder to answer.

Formalization has much in common with standardization. In this respect, it may be noted that some experts consider present standardization efforts regarding window systems premature.

Stage two (ad hoc reuse) is crucial. In this stage, we get insight into the application domain and discover *useful* semantic primitives. This experience, both in working with the primitives and in implementing them, is of vital importance for the formalization of the domain in the right way.

The notion of a virtual machine is not new. Parnas used it as a guideline for the design of software systems [Parnas78]. One of the rules for a good design is to build a hierarchy of virtual machines. Currently there is not much theory as to what constitutes a good virtual machine. Notions like coupling and cohesion are often used as design criteria [Yourdon75]. These criteria, however, concern the after-the-fact structure of design abstractions. What we need is a way to get the proper abstractions. The usefulness of a virtual machine and the reusability of its building blocks critically depends on the degree to which we manage to capture the primitive concepts of a domain.

The above discussion suggests an evolutionary approach to reuse. To start with, potentially reusable building blocks can be extracted from existing software products. While gaining experience with the reuse of these building blocks, better insight is obtained and better abstractions of concepts and mechanisms from the application domain are discovered. The library of reusable building blocks will thus evolve and stabilize over time.

This evolutionary process can be structured and guided through **domain analysis**, a process in which information used in developing software for a particular domain is identified, captured, structured, and organized for further reuse [Prieto-Diaz90]. Domain analysts and domain experts may use a variety of sources when modeling a domain, including expert knowledge, existing implementations and documentation. They extract and abstract the relevant information and encapsulate them in reusable building blocks.

16.4 NON-TECHNICAL ASPECTS OF SOFTWARE REUSE

The problem is not lack of technology but unwillingness to address the most important issues influencing software reuse: managerial, economic, legal, cultural, and social.
[Prieto-Diaz91b]

Myth #1: Software reuse is a technical problem.
[Tracz88]

Up until now, we have discussed only technical aspects of software reuse. Software engineering is not concerned only with technical aspects but with people and other environmental aspects as well.

By being embedded within a society, the field of software engineering will also be influenced by that society. Software reuse in the US is likely to be different from software reuse in Japan or Europe. Because of cultural differences and different economic structures, it is not *a priori* clear that, say, the Toshiba-approach can be copied by Europeans, with the same results.

Though our discussion so far has concerned the technical aspects of software reuse, it is not complete without a few words on non-technical issues. These non-technical issues are intimately intertwined with the more technical ones. Recently, various practitioners in the field of software reuse have argued that the technology needed for software reuse is available, but that the main problems inhibiting a prosperous reuse industry are non-technical in nature [Prieto-Diaz91b], [Tracz88, 90], [Barnes91].

Successful reuse programs share the following characteristics [Prieto-Diaz91b]:

- Unconditional and extensive management support. A reuse program requires changes in the way software is developed. Management commitment is essential for making such changes work. In particular, building a base of reusable assets requires an upfront investment which may not pay off until after some time.

- Establishment of an organizational support structure. The organization must provide the initiative for the reuse program, funding, and policies. A separate body is needed to assess potential candidates for inclusion in the reuse library. A librarian is needed to maintain the library.

- Incremental program implementation. A first catalog with potential reusable assets can be built at a relatively low cost. Positive experiences with such an initial library will raise awareness and provide the necessary incentives (and funding) to expand the library, devise a classification scheme, etc.

- Significant success, both financial and organizational. Raytheon for example reports a 50% increase in productivity over a period of several years.

- Compulsory, or highly incentivized. Programmers suffer from the 'not invented here' syndrome. By creating an environment that values both the creation of reusable software and the reuse of software, an atmosphere is established in which reuse may become a success.

- Domain analysis was conducted either consciously or unconsciously. Domain analysis is a process in which the concepts and mechanisms underlying some well-understood domain are identified and captured in reusable resources.

Some of the non-technical aspects are discussed in the subsections below.

16.4.1 The economics of software reuse.

Reuse is a long term investment
[Tracz90]

Reuse does not come for free. In a traditional development environment, products get tailored to the situation at hand. Similar situations are likely to require slightly different products or product components. For a software component to become reusable, it has to be generalized from the situation at hand, thoroughly documented and tested, incorporated in a library and classification scheme, and maintained as a separate entity. Such requires initial investments, investments which start to pay off only after a certain period of time.

Quite immediate returns on investment can be obtained if the reuse program starts small, with an initial library whose members are extracted from existing products. Expansion of the program can then be justified on the basis of positive early experiences. But even then, non-project specific funds must be allocated to the reuse program.

The economic consequences of software reuse go beyond cost savings in production and maintenance. The nature of the software development process itself changes. Software becomes a *capital* good. High initial costs are coupled with returns over a longer time period. The production of software thus becomes a *capital intensive* process [Wegner83, 84]. The production of non-reusable software, on the other hand, is a *labor intensive* process. Many man-months are spent, but the profits are reaped as soon as the project is finished.

Whereas labor-intensive software production tends to concentrate on the project at hand to be finished in time and within budget, capital-intensive software production takes into account long-term business concerns such as the collective workers' knowledge and the collection of reusable assets. The software factory paradigm discussed in section 3.6 fits this view of the software development organization.

16.4.2 Management and software reuse

Myth #9: Software reuse will just happen.
[Tracz88]

Getting software reuse off the ground cannot depend on spontaneity. Rather, software production ought to be organized so that reuse is promoted. In chapter 3 we noted that the traditional waterfall model tends to impede software reuse. In the waterfall model, emphasis is placed on measuring and controlling project progress. The product quality with respect to reusability is hard to measure. There is no real incentive to pursue reusability either, since the primary (and often the only) goal is to finish the current project within time and budget. There is no motivation to make the next project look good. Consequently, software reusability tends to get low priority.

If reuse is not a clear objective of our software development process, it is bound to remain accidental. Programmers then tinker with code they have written before, if and when they happen to notice similarities between successive problems. This unplanned approach to reuse is also known as **code scavenging** or **code salvaging**. According to [Tracz90], this is distinct from the process of reusing software that was *designed* to be reused.

Software reuse has to be incorporated in the software development process. Reusable assets have to be actively sought. The concepts and mechanisms underlying some domain have to be identified and captured in reusable resources (see also section 16.3). The focus of software management then shifts from the delivery of individual products to maintaining and nurturing a rich collection of reusable artifacts. Some of the successful reuse programs, such as those reported in [Prieto-Diaz91b], have followed this approach.

The library of reusable assets itself needs to be managed as well. An organizational infrastructure must be created which makes the library accessible (documentation, classification schemes), assesses candidates for inclusion in the library, maintains and updates the library, etc. A separate organizational role, the librarian, may be created for this purpose. Its tasks resemble that of a data base administrator.

One type of reuse only mentioned in passing, is *reuse of good people*. Expert designers are worth their weight in gold. Every average programmer is capable of writing a complicated, large program. In order to obtain a better, smaller, more elegant, radically new solution for that same problem, we need a person who has bright ideas from time to time.

A major problem in our field is that managers are rated higher than programmers or designers. If you are really good, you will sooner or later, but usually sooner, rise in the hierarchy and become part of the management. According to Brooks, there is only one way to counteract this phenomenon [Brooks87]. To ensure that these bright people remain system designers, we need a dual ranking scheme, one in which good designers have the same job prospects as good managers. Once again: the software process must be reconceived as one both of growing people and the base of reusable assets [Curtis89a].

16.4.3 Psychological aspects of software reuse

Reusing other people's code would prove that I don't care about my work. I would no more reuse code than Hemingway would reuse other authors' paragraphs.
[Cox90]

Software reuse means that programmers have to adapt, incorporate, or rejuvenate software written by other programmers. There are two important psychological aspects to this process:

- are programmers willing to do so?

- are they capable of doing so?

The first aspect is often mentioned as a major stumbling block to establishing a positive attitude towards software reuse. [Barnes91] phrases this image dilemma as follows: 'Anyone who has ever gone to an auto salvage yard to pick up a spare part for his old car "knows" what reuse is'.

Many authors suggest a both simple and effective solution to this problem: change the programming culture. The experiences at Raytheon and Toshiba suggest that it is indeed possible, given the right incentives and, more importantly, a management attitude which pays attention to longer-term goals, goals that go beyond those of the present project.

From research into the comprehensibility of software, such as reported in [Soloway84], it shows that programmers use certain standard schemes in standard situations. Experienced programmers tend to get confused when a known problem has been tackled using (to them) non-standard solutions. As a consequence, the reusability of components is likely to be increased if the components embody abstractions the programmers are familiar with. We will return to this phenomenon in chapter 17. Domain analysis addresses the same issues by trying to identify the notions that are shared by experts in a particular domain.

In the studies of Lanergan and Grasso, discussed in section 16.1.3, it appeared that one side-effect of the use of standard designs and standard components is the increased comprehensibility of the resulting software. Once all programmers got used to the Raytheon house style, it seemed as if all programs were written by one and the same team. Any team could understand and adapt a program written by some other team.

16.5 SUMMARY AND FURTHER READING

Software reusability is an objective, rather than a field. It emerged as an issue within software engineering, not because of its appeal as a scientific issue per se, but driven by the expected gain in software development productivity.

The first conference on software reuse was held in 1983 [ITT83]. Since then, the topic has received increased attention. A number of recent articles on the subject are collected in [TrSE84] and [Freeman87c]. The most comprehensive collection of such articles is to be found in [Biggerstaff89a].

In section 16.1, we discussed the main approaches to the reuse problem. The various reuse technologies discussed can be roughly subdivided into two categories [Biggerstaff89a]:

- composition-based technologies, and

- generation-based technologies.

A composition-based technology aims at incorporating existing components into software to be newly developed. In a generation-based technology, it is much more difficult to explicitly identify components that are being reused. Rather, the knowledge reused is to be found in some program that generates some other program. Prime examples of these two technologies are subroutine libraries and application generators, respectively. Most reuse systems, however, carry aspects of both approaches.

A central question in all reuse technologies discussed is how to exploit some set of reusable building blocks. As argued in section 16.3, an equally important, yet largely neglected, question is which building blocks are needed to start with. Answering the latter question requires a much deeper understanding of the software development process than we currently have. Successful reuse programs share a number of characteristics [Prieto-Diaz91b]:

- Unconditional and extensive management support.

- Establishing an organizational support structure.

- Incremental program implementation.

- Significant success, both financial and organizational.

- Compulsory, or highly incentivized.

- Domain analysis was conducted either consciously or unconsciously.

Reuse is not a magic word with which the productivity of the software development process can be substantially increased at one blow. But we do have a sufficient number of departure-points for further improvements to get a remunerative reuse technology off the ground. Foremost amongst these are the attention to non-technical issues involved in software reuse, and an evolutionary approach in conjunction with a conscientious effort to model limited application domains [Prieto-Diaz91b], [Tracz90], [Arango89], [Frakes91a].

EXERCISES

1. For a domain you are familiar with, identify a set of potentially reusable software components and devise a classification scheme for them. Consider both a hierarchical and a faceted classification scheme and assess their merits with respect to ease of classification and search, and extendability.

2. For the same domain, assess its maturity level and that of the components identified. Can you relate the maturity level of components to their perceived reusability?

3. Devise a managerial setting and a software development process model for a component-based software factory.

4. Assess one or more of the following domains and determine the extent and kind of reuse that has been achieved:
   — window management systems;
   — (2D-) computer graphics;
   — user-interface development systems;
   — office automation;
   — salary administraion;
   — hypertext systems.

5. For the domain(s) studied in the previous exercise, is there any relation between the reuse level achieved and (de facto or de jure) standardization within the domain? Can you discern any influence of standardization on reuse, or vice versa?

6. Discuss possible merits of knowledge-based approaches to software reusability.

7. To what extent do you consider a domain-independent library of reusable software components a realistic option?

8. From your own past in software development, make an inventory of:
   — components developed by yourself which you reused more than once, and
   — components developed by others and reused by you.

   To what extent does the Not-Invented-Here syndrome apply to your situation? Is reuse in your situation accidental or deliberate? Were the components designed for reuse, or was it rather a form of code scavenging?

9. Suppose you developed a routine to determine the inverse of a matrix. The routine is to be incorporated in a library of reusable components. Which aspects of this routine should be documented in order that others may determine the suitability of the routine for their application?

10. In developing abstract data types (ADTs) we try to strictly separate (and hide) implementation concerns from the users of those ADTs. To what extent could these implementation concerns be relevant to the reuser?

17

Software
Psychology

We still think too readily of programs as just being for compilation. We should think of them also as being for communication from ourselves to others, and as vehicles for expressing our own thoughts to ourselves.
[Green90]

Today, user needs are recognized to be important in designing interactive computer systems, but as recently as 1980, they received little emphasis.
[Grudin91]

Why would it be useful to include comments in a program? Why would it be better not to use goto's? Why would design technique X be any better than design technique Y? Why do users of one system get confused and irritated while users of a functionally similar system with a different user interface do not, and may even enjoy their work?

Almost all texts on programming and software engineering give you their own answers to such questions. Often, these answers are not well founded. The arguments mostly appeal to our intuition, common sense, and the reader's assumed experience.

However useful intuition and common sense may be, they are not enough. We need theories, supported by valid empirical evidence and carefully controlled experiments in order to get well-founded answers to such questions as raised above.

Tom Love once coined the term *software psychology* to indicate the 'marriage' between psychology and computer science. It is also the title of a book in which many of the results obtained in the 1970s have been collected [Shneiderman80].

Software psychology addresses human factors that relate to the construction and use of software, such as:

- the ease with which programmers handle certain language constructs;
- problems associated with learning to program;
- the error-proneness and robustness of language constructs;
- the types of errors programmers make;
- the ease of use of application software, such as word processors, by non-programmers;
- the role of on-line help facilities.

Little research of this kind had been done before 1970. Interest in the area grew considerably after publication of Weinberg's classic text *The Psychology of Computer Programming* [Weinberg71]. Weinberg's book contains an abundance of insightful anecdotes, many of which still apply today.

Unfortunately, many of the early results have little cogency. The early empirical research on how programmers go about their work has been heavily criticized (see, for example, [Sheil81]). The need for a sound methodological design of such experiments has been stressed repeatedly, for instance in [Curtis80]. The quality of the human factors experiments has strongly improved in recent years and some useful theory has been built up.

When doing experiments, attention has to be paid to the *ecological validity* of those experiments. Ecological validity (or *external validity*) refers to the issue of being able to generalize from laboratory situations to real-world situations. Ecological validity is a matter of concern both when we assess usability aspects of user interfaces [Thomas89c] and when we experimentally study programmer behavior [Moher82]. The factors that deserve our attention, are:

The subject population Differences between individuals may well color the results obtained. Many tests with programmers have used inexperienced programmers, such as university students, as subjects. Other experiments showed that the same results need not necessarily hold for expert programmers. Similar expert–novice differences may occur when we assess user-interfaces. Especially in the latter case, motivation differences may play a role as well. Real users often have a production-bias. For instance, real users do not read manuals. They have better things to do.

The system context In order to test a certain language construct one often uses some toy language. In a fully-fledged programming language, language features interact. User interfaces are often assessed in isolation, so that consistency across applications is not taken into account. It is not clear that results thus obtained can be directly transferred to our daily practice.

The problem size For practical purposes, most tests use small applications, and the problems posed are neat. Here too, direct generalizations to large applications and ill-defined problems are questionable, to say the least. This is known as the school-exam fallacy.

The work context In reality, people are often confronted with the interleaving of multiple tasks (while we are busy trying to find some bug, the phone rings).

Many experiments show a large variation in the results obtained. [Curtis81], for example, contains data about the time programmers need to find and repair ·errors in software. The best subject outperformed the worst by a factor of 23. [Boehm81] discusses the COCOMO cost estimation models (see also chapter 7). The cost drivers of COCOMO that relate to personnel factors, such as team and programmer capabilities, have by far the largest influence on the estimates derived.

This variation is usually ascribed to individual differences. For instance, in an experiment evaluating different documentation formats, it was found that individual differences accounted for between a third and one-half of the variation observed [Curtis89b]. [DeMarco85] shows that a considerable part of performance variation may possibly be explained from differences in organization and layout of the work place. Programmers with adequate secretarial support, opportunities to work uninterrupted for long periods of time, and sufficient floor space turn out to be significantly more productive than their colleagues that are worse off.

Large variations may also be caused by the different goals that subjects try to achieve. [Weinberg74] shows that if different goals are set forth, such as minimal use of memory, fast delivery, or readability of the output, the results may be widely diverging. In experiments we have to take care that the goals to be pursued have been described very precisely. In that respect, experiments do not differ from real projects.

Notwithstanding these somewhat negative notes, some positive results have emerged. This type of research has only just started, however. It is essential for the further development of our field to deepen our understanding of human factors that impact the development and use of software. The insights obtained should lead to a better understanding of the relevant cognitive skills, information processing capacities, and personality traits. Results that come out of this research should lead to better programming languages, better programming and design techniques, better productivity metrics, better user interfaces and better software management. All this adds to the quality of the software delivered.

Our point of departure in the discussion of human factors that relate to the construction and use of software is a model of human memory as an information processing system. A simple variant is discussed in section 17.1.

Next, section 17.2 discusses perceptual cues that aim to enhance program understanding, such as comments and program indentation. The results from some experiments will be explained using the memory model sketched in section 17.1.

The same line of reasoning will be followed in section 17.3, where we discuss a number of programming language features.

Psychological aspects that relate to group processes have been hinted at in chapter 5, where we addressed different ways to organize software development teams.

The issues raised in sections 17.2 and 17.3 all relate to the construction of software. How about the user? In the distant past, users hardly came into direct contact with the machine. Nowadays, many a piece of software works interactively. The number of non-programmers that make regular use of computers is rapidly increasing. This raises questions as to how this type of interaction has to be shaped in order to make it effective, learnable, usable.

These questions too are largely psychological in nature. To address them, we may fruitfully apply the model introduced in section 17.1. Some aspects of human–machine interaction will be addressed in section 17.4.

17.1 PROGRAMMING AS A HUMAN ACTIVITY

Programmers write programs. They express algorithms using the language constructs of some programming language. They must know the syntax and semantics of these language constructs. They must also know how to build meaningful programs out of the building blocks offered. The better you are able to use the programming language as a tool, the better you are able to perform these tasks.

Usually, mere coding is not the one and only task programmers are faced with. They must also be able to design software, to test it, document it, and maintain it. The latter requires programmers to understand software that is written by someone else. Many a piece of software is more often read than executed.

A descriptive model of the way programmers go about their work should cover all these activities. These activities may be described in terms of **cognitive structures** and **cognitive processes**. Cognitive structures denote the way in which knowledge is stored in human memory. Cognitive processes enter the picture when the knowledge is stored (i.e. during the learning process) and when it is used.

Research in the area of human information processing has resulted in a model as shown in figure 17.1.

Information from perception is entered in **short-term memory**. Short-term memory has a limited capacity. [Miller56] estimates its size at about seven units. We really do not know the precise size of our short-term memory. The important point to note here is that its capacity is very limited.

Entries in short-term memory need not correspond to elementary pieces of information. People join together bits of information into larger units. This process is called **chunking**, and the units of information are called **chunks**. For example, the sequence of digits '85884' could occupy five entries in short-term

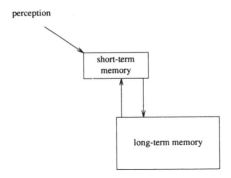

Figure 17.1:   Memory components for problem solving

memory. However, if it is recognized as being mom's telephone number, it is encoded as such and only occupies one entry. Entries in short-term memory can thus be viewed as labels denoting some unit of information, like a digit, mom's telephone number, or the routine *quicksort*.

When information is to be processed or operations have to be performed, short-term memory acts as a **working-memory**, much like the registers of a computer.

Finally, permanent knowledge is stored in our **long-term memory**.

Within the simple model sketched in figure 17.1, two important questions may be raised: what type of knowledge (**cognitive structures**) are available to the programmer from long-term memory, and what type of cognitive processes are used in constructing a solution in his working memory?

Expert programmers have stored a vast and complex amount of knowledge in their long-term memory. This partly concerns knowledge about general concepts, not directly connected to a specific programming language. It concerns both low-level concepts (what is an assignment to a variable) and high-level concepts (what is sorting). A yet higher level of knowledge is needed to develop solution methods, for example those for solving dynamic programming problems. We may thus distinguish different, hierarchical, levels. This type of knowledge is collectively referred to as **semantic knowledge**.

Long-term memory also contains **syntactic knowledge**, such as the format of a loop construct in Pascal. Syntactic knowledge is more arbitrary in kind and is therefore easily forgotten. It is actually easier to learn a new syntactic structure when the corresponding semantic structure is already known. As a consequence, learning a first programming language in general turns out to be more difficult than the learning of the next or subsequent languages. After a while you need only to master a new syntax. Obviously, this holds to a much lesser degree if the new language has a very different semantic structure (as in FORTRAN versus LISP).

Semantic knowledge has to be learnt. It has to be assimilated. Syntactic knowledge can be mastered through mere instruction. For that reason too, learning a first programming language is different from learning a second one.

Knowledge of semantics and knowledge of syntax are not closely integrated in human memory. For example, the knowledge of what an assignment is, is not intertwined with knowledge about the way it is written down in a particular programming language. Syntactic knowledge gets mixed up easily. We are inclined to confuse syntactic constructs from different programming languages.

The knowledge in our long-term memory may also be decomposed according to the domains they refer to. Besides knowledge of computer science and software engineering, an expert programmer also possesses knowledge about one or more application domains, such as financial accounting, oil exploration or chemical technology. When working on concrete problems, knowledge from different domains is used to derive a solution.

In order to complete our model, we also need to investigate the problem-solving processes associated with the programmer's task. [Polya68] distinguishes four steps in problem solving:

1. understanding the problem;

2. making a plan, discovery of a solution strategy;

3. executing the plan;

4. checking the results.

If a programmer is given some problem, we assume it enters short-term/working memory. When the problem is actually analyzed, general information from long-term memory is called in to aid. These are first steps towards a solution.

Many uncertainties still remain as far as the second step, devising a design, is concerned. Often, techniques like **stepwise refinement** [Wirth71] and **top-down design** are advocated. Using stepwise refinement, a solution is first formulated in quite general terms. Next, it is refined in one or more steps. In this refinement process, techniques like structured programming and modularization can be applied. Reality is probably more complicated. Design is not a pure top-down, rational, process.

Guindon argues that deviations from top-down design are a natural consequence of the ill-structuredness of problems during the early stages of design [Guindon90]. A top-down decomposition seems to be a special case for well-structured problems when the designer already knows the correct solution. Guindon found that designers rapidly shift between levels of abstraction. For example, if they recognize a partial solution to some part of the problem, they will immediately enter a detailed design stage to work out that solution. The other way round, the development of a solution may lead to the discovery of new or additional requirements, which then become the immediate focus of attention. The design process seems best characterized as *opportunistic*.

Because of the vast number of possible solutions, the software design process seems to be qualitatively different from the design process in other domains. [Kant84] discusses a problem-solving theory known from the works of Newell and Simon [Newell72]. A problem space is searched, starting from some initial state, until a desired end state is reached. Several experiments show that there are large differences as regards the effectiveness with which different people search the problem space, viz., solve problems. Amongst others, the structure of the problem description plays an important role.

[Carroll80a] describes an experiment in which a number of people designed a solution to two problems that had a very similar structure. One was to solve a spatial problem—placing people in an office. The other was to schedule a production process. Better results were obtained for the spatial problem. For the spatial problem, a spatial representation was self-evident, and most subjects used that representation. Apparently, people are not very good at exchanging information between isomorphic problems. Another experiment from Carroll showed that better results were obtained if subjects were given a more hierarchically structured problem description [Carroll80b].

[Soloway84, 86a] discusses an interesting theory of problem solving in the programming domain. This theory states that programmers solve such problems using **programming plans**, program fragments that correspond to stereotypic actions, and rules that describe programming conventions. For example, to compute the sum of a series of numbers, a programmer uses the 'running total loop plan'. In this plan, some counter is initialized to zero and incremented with the next value of a series in the body of a loop. Experts tend to recall program fragments that correspond to plan structures before they recall other elements of the program. This nicely maps onto the idea that knowledge is stored in meaningful units (chunks).

Programming plans are related to the concept of a **beacon**. Beacons were proposed in [Brooks83] as knowledge structures used in program comprehension. Beacons are key features that typically indicate the presence of a particular structure or operation. They seem to be very diagnostic of program meaning. For example, the kernel idea or central operation in a sorting program is a swap operation. If we are presented with a program that contains a swap operation, our immediate reaction would then be that it concerns some sorting program.

[Wiedenbeck91] describes experiments in which it was found that sorting programs containing a swap operation are indeed more often recognized as such than sorting programs in which the swap operation is disguised. Even worse, the presence of a false beacon was found to have a strong tendency to mislead programmers. Experienced programmers rely more heavily on the presence of beacons than do novices. This reflects their stronger association of a beacon with a particular program type because of their experience.

An expert programmer has at his disposal a much larger number of knowledge chunks than a novice programmer. This concerns both programming knowledge and knowledge about the application domain. Both during the search for a solution and during program comprehension, the programmer tries to link up with knowledge chunks already present. As a corollary, part of our education as programmer or software engineer should consist of acquiring a set of useful knowledge chunks.

Expert programmers rely on the proper use of programming clichés. They are easily misled by false beacons, i.e. the use of stereotypical program fragments in an unusual context. Likewise, **delocalized plans**, i.e. the physical location of conceptually related pieces of code in non-contiguous parts of a program, causes comprehension problems [Soloway88]. At the typographical level, inconsistent naming and indentation hinder program understanding.

Acquiring expertise entails more than assimilating an ever increasing number of units of information, though. New knowledge must also be integrated in a meaningful way with already acquired knowledge. In that way, a rich network is built up, a network in which information can be traced effectively.

We have already noted that programmers build an internal semantic structure of a solution in multiple levels. A component at one level is associated with a more detailed structure at the next level down. In the same way, the actual program code is retained hierarchically. Code is not stored in human memory on a line-by-line basis. Rather, it is grouped into meaningful chunks. This process of decomposition and retainment becomes easier as the program has a more logical structure. In that case, the association with knowledge already present becomes easier to accomplish.

Similarly, programmers try to comprehend a piece of software. The software is decomposed and encoded into chunks having a meaningful structure and some label denoting them. The chunks are subsequently stored in memory [Barfield86], [Vessey85].

Again, a clear difference between expert and novice programmers is noticeable. Expert programmers 'recognize' a sorting procedure, search process, etc. They recognize larger pieces without inspecting all of its details. They are triggered by the key idea embodied in the program (the beacon) and are less bothered by peripheral details. The other way round, details are being interpreted in the wider context in which they appear (see also figure 17.2). We might call this top-down perception.

A whole spectrum of perceptual cues, such as indentation, naming of variables, and syntactic notation, is called upon during this recognition process.

Programmers with little experience do not yet possess a richly forked network of knowledge chunks, while perceptual cues do not ring bells either. They will have more problems in comprehending software.

Really, this should not come as a surprise. Early research on chess players revealed that chess masters are much better at recalling positions than less experienced colleagues, provided these positions are realistic ones [DeGroot65, Chase73]. If the pieces are randomly scattered about the chess-board, the performance is the same for both groups. Experienced chess players are much better at grouping and encoding the pieces into meaningful chunks ('queen is threatened'), and remembering and reconstructing them as such.

The precise structure of the model of human memory is disputable. Some authors view short-term and working memory as different components. Sometimes working memory is considered to be (the active) part of long-term memory, sometimes the two are considered to be separate. [Card83] contains

THE CAT

Figure 17.2:   Effect of context on letter recognition

a more elaborate discussion of models of human memory for the purpose of information processing.

In reality, the situation certainly is more complex than has been sketched above. Before sensory information enters short-term memory, it is already 'pre-processed' in a peripheral part of our memory (known as 'perceptive memory' or 'primary memory'). This type of processing occurs before conscious attention is given to the stimuli. It is driven by both the environment and knowledge already present, and often involves some kind of contextual pattern matching. Figure 17.2 gives an example hereof. It illustrates how context influences the recognition of letters. Similar pattern matching processes occur, for example, when programmers use indentation patterns to comprehend program texts.

From all these models, though, a picture sprouts forth in which human memory consists of an active component with a very limited capacity and a background memory whose capacity is, for all practical purposes, unlimited. Information is grouped into meaningful units called chunks and stored in an associative way. The degree to which we are able to remember and recall information is to a large extent dependent on our experience in the knowledge domain concerned. Experiments suggest that breadth and depth of programming experience are more important (i.e. better predictors of programmer performance) than mere years of experience or years of education [Curtis79], [Boehm-Davis92].

17.2 TYPOGRAPHIC GUIDELINES

Almost all texts on programming contain guidelines aimed at increasing software comprehensibility. These guidelines concern such matters as: adding comment, giving meaningful names to variables, the use of indentation, the use of flowcharts.

We may ask ourselves if and under which circumstances application of those guidelines will indeed yield better results. What interests us here is the effect of such perceptual cues on software comprehension. While studying a program text, an internal semantic structure must be built that conforms to the program. We may expect that each of the above-mentioned aids will to some extent ease that process.

We will give an overview of experiments on issues related to programming practice, and draw some tentative conclusions as to the merits of obeying some well-known guidelines.

17.2.1 Comment

Experts do not fully agree on the amount and kind of comment to be incorporated in software. Each introductory text book on programming does tell you to document your programs through comments, although this can be dangerous as well. Often, comments are not updated if the program is changed. Out-of-date comments may easily lead you astray.

Results of a fairly old experiment suggest that misleading comments work counterproductively [Okimoto70]. From the same experiment, it appears that programs without comments are comprehended even faster than programs with comments, even if the comments are correct.

[Shneiderman80] discusses an experiment in which 62 students were asked to study a 26-line FORTRAN-program. One group (H) received the program with some high-level comments at the start of the program text. The comments described the function of the program. The second group (L) were given a text with a number of low-level comments, such as 'reserve 500 words of memory'. Both groups were asked to make some small changes to the program. They were also given a memory test, viz. the number of lines of code that could be reproduced. For both these tests, group H scored higher than group L.

[Sheppard79] describes an experiment in which 36 professional programmers were asked to modify some fairly small (39–56 lines of code) programs. He used three types of commentary: global comments, in-line comments, and no comments at all. The results did not differ significantly. Also in the experiment described in [Norcio83], no significant performance differences were measured between programs with comments and those without.

Finally, [Woodfield81b] investigated the relation between modularization and comments. The subjects in this experiment were for the most part expert programmers. Woodfield used four versions of a program of some 100 lines of code: a monolithic version consisting of one large module, two versions obtained through functional decomposition, and one version obtained through data abstraction. All versions with comments scored higher than those without. For the monolithic version, though, the difference was rather small. The version with abstract data types *and* comments showed by far the best performance.

Comments are not stored in the internal semantic structure being built, they just ease its construction, is what reported experiments tend to confirm. Novice programmers pay significantly more attention to comments than experienced programmers [Crosby90]. For fairly small programs expert programmers do not really need comments, particularly if its structure shows through other means already. For instance, [Sheppard79] used mnemonic names, which might have provided sufficient cues to build up the internal structure of the program. [Woodfield81b] used meaningless names. Here, the comments provided the only anchor. The combination of meaningless names and a monolithic piece of software might explain the difficulties programmers had in comprehending that version.

So, commentary eases the talking and thinking about a piece of software. This agrees with the practice often advocated. Functional comments are preferable to low-level comments. Comments should not echo the code, as in

```
x:= 0; /* x is set to zero */
```

Proper comments ease the construction of an internal semantic structure. In writing your comments, you should use problem domain terminology, in order to facilitate bridging the gap between the problem and program domain. Some instruction sequence should be explained through

```
Search for the student with the highest average score
```

rather than

```
Search for the largest value in the table.
```

17.2.2 Variable names

If you are confronted with a program in which variables are denoted by names like P, Q, and R, you may have some difficulties in establishing their meaning. Mnemonic names like account or bill, on the other hand, reflect some semantic role and may provide for a direct link as to what those variables stand for. We would thus assume that mnemonic names facilitate the comprehension process. However, it would be worthwhile to investigate the true merits.

One experiment showed surprising results [Newsted73]. Four programs were used in the test. One group of subjects used mnemonic versions of both a 'difficult' and an 'easy' program. Another group used non-mnemonic versions of these programs.

The mnemonic group scored higher on the difficult program than on the easy program. The non-mnemonic group showed equal scores on the difficult and easy program. For both programs, though, the non-mnemonic group scored *higher* than the mnemonic group. The results may be somewhat distorted, since the meaning of the variables was explained at the start of the program.

In a similar test without explanatory comments, the mnemonic group scored higher in all cases. The results are depicted in figure 17.3.

In yet another experiment, the value of mnemonic names for debugging was investigated. The results did not show significant differences between subjects that received a program with mnemonic names and those that received one with non-mnemonic names [Shneiderman80]. This is not really surprising, since the subjects were familiar with the algorithms used in the test.

Finally, [Sheppard79] tested the degree to which reproduction of a program is influenced by the use of meaningful names. No significant differences were found. Strikingly, though, the subjects invariably preferred meaningful names in the versions reproduced.

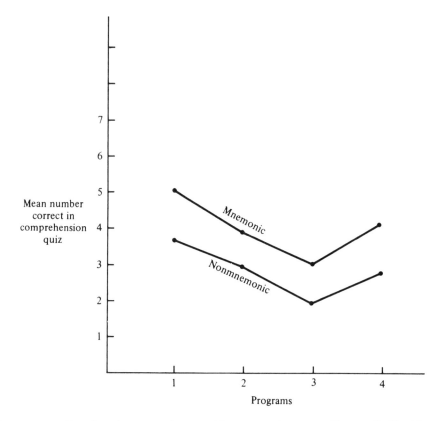

Figure 17.3:   Results of an experiment with mnemonic names (*Source: B. Shneiderman, Software Psychology (1980), Winthrop Publishers, Inc., Cambridge.*)

With respect to our model of human memory, the above results suggest that conversion from syntax to internal semantic structure is eased through the use of mnemonic names. If such help is not needed, for instance because one already knows the algorithm or a sufficient amount of comment has been added, then mnemonic names don't help either. Meaningless names seem to hinder the conversion.

17.2.3 Indentation

Programmers generally apply some form of indentation to increase the readability of their programs. If asked, they invariably prefer indentation. The style of indentation may differ considerably, though, even for programs written in the same programming language. Various experiments have assessed the merits of indentation.

In a test done by Shneiderman two groups of students were asked to find and repair some error in a program. Both groups received one program with indentation and one program without. No significant performance differences were found [Shneiderman75].

From these and similar experiments, a consistent pattern emerges: apparently, indentation is of no help. Quite likely, a wrongly indented program will be less easily understood.

It is hard to imagine, though, that indentation is of no help at all, because that would imply the superfluity of any form of visual help in program comprehension.

It is quite possible that many programmers have developed their own indentation style. They apply this style when reading programs and trying to build the corresponding internal structure. When confronted with a program in which a different indentation style has been used, the deviating visual form might not be of much help. It might even act counterproductively [Kesler84].

For a long time, indentation provided the only means to visualize program structure. With the advent of more powerful printing devices such as laser printers, other visual cues can be used. We may, for example, print variables in bold, use grey scales to highlight comments, or print procedure headings in a larger typeface [Baecker88].

Though these additional visual cues do seem to help, their support is restricted to highlighting the surface structure of software. A deeper analysis of program text is needed to isolate semantically meaningful chunks.

Experts seem to recognize well-known patterns in program texts. Soloway's plan theory and Brooks' notion of 'beacons' relate to this phenomenon. It would then be more useful to bring those semantically meaningful units to the foreground.

17.2.4 Flowcharts

Flowcharts have been popular for a long time. Is their widespread use warranted? There has always been quite some controversy about the use of flowcharts. Some people consider flowcharts a major tool for documenting software. Others criticize flowcharts because they allow programmers to violate the rules of structured programming. Brooks for instance considered flowcharts 'an obsolete nuisance' [Brooks75]. Experiments with flowcharts have yielded quite contradictory results as well.

Shneiderman discusses a series of five experiments to evaluate the merits of flowcharts for program comprehension, debugging and modification [Shneiderman77]. For each of the experiments the results were statistically insignificant. Shneiderman though used inexperienced students in his experiments and used very simple algorithms. His results have been criticized by a number of authors [Scanlan89], [Curtis89b].

A possible explanation of Shneiderman's results is that once the programming language is known, it is much easier to just read the code—especially if the programs are small. For one thing, the program code is usually much smaller in size than the corresponding flowcharts. At best, the program is repeated in the flowcharts.

Often, things that are viewed as a conceptual unit in the programming language, such as an if-statement, are further decomposed in the corresponding flowchart. When 'reading' the flowchart this structure has to be regenerated.

It seems fair to conclude that for programs whose structure can be derived easily through some other means, flowcharts are of little or no help. This is in line with the results in [Ramsey83]. For many programs the control logic is not complicated enough to warrant a graphical presentation to highlight its logic. A well-structured (restricted) natural language description seems at least as effective [Curtis89b].

In an experiment discussed in [Scanlan88] the subjects themselves turned out to have a clear preference for flowcharts above program code. The experiment concerned fairly complex algorithms for manipulating data structures.

The experiments mentioned above concern low-level flowcharts and small programs. Flowcharts at the macro level, for instance diagrams in which each node represents a module, might well be helpful in bringing across the structure-in-the-large of software systems. Flowcharts may also help in cases where the flow-of-control is complex, since they emphasize the mutual relation between components [Fitter79], or when the programming tasks involve tracing the control logic [Curtis89b].

From [Shneiderman82] it appears that information on the data structures being used often is more important than information on the control structure. We will come back to this topic in section 17.3.3.

17.3 PROGRAMMING LANGUAGE CONCEPTS

In the preceding section we discussed some notational matters independent of the programming language being used. We will now turn to specific programming language concepts.

The Whorfian hypothesis tells us that our thinking is constrained by the language in which we express our thoughts. The reverse seems to hold at least as strongly. Our way of thinking limits our language usage. There certainly is a strong interplay between the two. Since programs are probably read more often than they are executed, the notation of language concepts is of prime importance. Syntactic details play an important role in the visual perception and the building of a logical structure of the software in human memory [Green86].

Language constructs should also fit the tasks to be accomplished by a programmer. Early programming languages, for instance, offered one loop construct only. More recent languages offer a while- and repeat-variant besides the traditional for-loop. Still, we regularly feel the need to exit a loop construct from the middle, since that often corresponds most naturally to our way of thinking. Programming languages should be constructed such that they ease a natural way of expressing algorithms [Soloway83].

Syntactic details may differ considerably from one language to another. According to the cognitive model presented in section 17.1, knowledge of semantics and knowledge of syntax are not well integrated in human memory. As a consequence, we should be able to conduct experiments with non-realistic languages. One example hereof is the classic experiment done by Sime and his colleagues [Sime73], to be discussed below.

However, constructs in fully-fledged programming languages show up in combination and interaction with other language elements. There might well be a much closer interrelation between syntax and semantics than suggested by our simple model.

This is very similar to other forms of visual perception. If we draw a face where the nose is indicated as a V, and the eyes by Os, then these symbols are recognized as a nose and eyes, respectively. They are no longer recognized as letters. Symbols are being interpreted within the context in which they occur.

As with the notational matters discussed in the previous section, there are also fervent protagonists and antagonists of different language constructs.

For example, the loop construct in most languages exhibits all sorts of restrictions. In FORTRAN, the step size may take only on positive values. Pascal allows only stepsizes +1 and −1. While- and repeat-loops give us a little more leeway, although artificial wordings are often needed as well. Recursion provides an alternative to express loops. It is the natural method of expression in a language like LISP. What is striking is the persistency with which people defend their own viewpoints. Whence these trenches? Answers are lacking.

The experimental research into these notational questions mainly addresses the various control structures, such as nested if-statements versus non-nested if-statements versus gotos.

Much less is known about the influence of notations for data structures on the comprehension of software. Various experiments do seem to indicate that data structures may well be more important for program comprehension than its mere control structure.

17.3.1 If-statements

In a classic experiment done by Sime et al. a preference showed up for nested if-then-else constructs such as found in Pascal over if-goto's as found in FORTRAN [Sime73]. The results indicate that nested constructs are easier to handle. A similar experiment conducted later confirmed this [Sime77]. The 'programs' used in these tests contained a kind of cooking instructions; see figure 17.4. The NEST-INE version which combines nesting and repetition of conditions yielded the best results.

```
        JUMP                 NEST-BE                 NEST-INE
     IF hard GOTO L1     IF hard THEN          IF hard peel
     IF tall GOTO L2     BEGIN peel               IF green roast
     IF juicy GOTO L3      IF green THEN          NOT green grill
     roast stop           BEGIN roast            END green
L1   IF green GOTO L4     END                   NOT hard
     peel grill stop      ELSE                     IF tall chop fry
L2   chop fry stop        BEGIN grill            NOT tall
L3   boil stop            END                       IF juicy boil
L4   peel roast stop    END                        NOT juicy roast
                        ELSE                       END juicy
                        BEGIN                    END tall
                          IF tall THEN         END hard
                          BEGIN chop fry
                          END
                          ELSE
                          BEGIN
                            IF juicy THEN
                            BEGIN boil
                            END
                            ELSE
                            BEGIN roast
                            END
                          END
                        END
                      END
```

Figure 17.4:   Three formats for if-instructions (*Source: M.E. Sime et al., Scope marking in computer conditionals—a psychological evaluation*, International Journal of Man–Machine Studies **9** *(1977). Reproduced by permission of Academic Press Inc. (London) Ltd.*)

Note that the examples in figure 17.4 use a combination of language syntax and indentation patterns. Experiments reported in [Oman88] suggest that simple nested if-statements are best formatted in a tabular way such that the 1–1 relationship between logical condition and corresponding action is highlighted. Figure 17.5 gives two styles for formatting nested if-statements, one nested version with a traditional indentation style and one using a tabular format. Code comprehension proved to be significantly better for the tabular version. The transition from the nested version to the tabular version involves both structural changes (repetition of logical expressions) and a different spatial arrangement.

Shneiderman conducted an experiment aimed at the controversy between logical and arithmetic if-constructs as found in FORTRAN [Shneiderman76]. The question was whether

```
IF (HOURS .GT. 40) GOTO 150
```

is easier to comprehend than

```
IF (HOURS - 40.0) 100, 100, 150
```

```
IF A>B THEN
   S := 1
ELSE IF A=B THEN
   IF C>D THEN
      S := 2
   ELSE
      S := 3
ELSE IF C>D THEN
   S := 4
ELSE IF C=D THEN
   S := 5
ELSE
   S := 6;

IF         A>B       THEN S := 1;
IF (A=B) AND (C>D)   THEN S := 2;
IF (A=B) AND (C<=D)  THEN S := 3;
IF (A<B) AND (C>D)   THEN S := 4;
IF (A<B) AND (C=D)   THEN S := 5;
IF (A<B) AND (C<D)   THEN S := 6;
```

Figure 17.5:   Different styles of if-statements (*Source: P.W. Oman & C.R. Cook, A paradigm for programming style*, ACM SIGPLAN Notices **23**, *12 (1988) 69–78. Reproduced by permission of the authors.*)

The results did not show significant differences, though there turned out to be a clear interaction between the type of construct and the subject's experience. Novice programmers had greater difficulties with the logical form. Possibly, they still struggled with the syntactic structure, while expert programmers immediately translated this structure into the proper internal semantic structure.

From this type of research it shows that simple, well-structured if-constructs are to be preferred over constructs that involve complex conditional tests or arithmetic, or deep nesting.

17.3.2 Structured control structures

We may wonder whether—and, if so, why—if-then-else constructs are to be preferred over goto's. The argument often is that high-level constructs increase comprehensibility, since they are less complex.

In an experiment discussed in [Lucas76], students were asked to both write a program and change another program. One group was not allowed to use goto's, the other group was. Performance was measured by keeping track of programming time needed, compilation time, size of object code, and the like. Besides these objectively measurable factors, subjective factors were also taken into account, such as ease of debugging, the fun subjects had in carrying out their tasks.

The results suggest that subjects have difficulties circumventing goto's. However, by the time they had to carry out the second task, the changing of a program, they apparently had gained experience with structured programming. For the second task, performance was much higher.

Benander et al. studied over 300 student COBOL programs with respect to the use of goto's [Benander90]. They found that:

- programs with incorrect output had twice as many goto's as programs with correct output;

- programs with goto's had a significantly worse structure than programs without goto's;

- the mean time to debug programs with goto's was greater than the mean time to debug goto-less programs.

This type of experiment shows that the choice of control structures, structured versus unstructured, makes a clear difference. This experience supports the anecdote which says that the number of errors in a program is proportional to the number of goto's it contains. Though a program without goto's is not necessarily error-free.

In addition, the experiments show a distinct learning effect. For instance, in the experiment reported in [Sime77], each subject took part in three consecutive sessions. Performance was significantly higher in the later sessions. A similar kind of interaction shows up in other experiments. The more experience subjects have, the higher their performance.

Obviously we should not deduce possible merits of specific structured language constructs directly from the mere outcome of this type of experiment. Structured programming is a disciplined way of thinking, not just a bunch of language constructs. The various experiments do give very consistent, positive, results. A structured approach does help. A structured control structure eases the decomposition of a program into chunks. The demands on our memory processing capacity are thus decreased and we may direct our attention to other tasks [Curtis86a].

17.3.3 Data structures

An interesting result with respect to the effect of declarations is obtained by Gannon [Gannon77]. He studied the effect of declarations, i.e. the static binding of a variable to a given data type, on error statistics. In languages without these declarations a variable corresponds to a mere bit sequence. One subject group did a first exercise in a language with declarations and a second one in a language without declarations. The other group did the same exercises, but the order was reversed.

The results were significantly in favor of the language with declarations. The order in which the exercises were carried out also indicated that the data abstractions learned through the use of typed declarations are apparently transferred to the language without this binding.

A major advantage of data typing seems to be the ability to talk and think about objects in a program at a higher level of abstraction.

In an analogous way we may expect that the various forms of data abstraction increase program comprehensibility. Languages like Pascal offer the possibility to group logically related components, such as a name and the corresponding phone number, into one structure. This closely concurs with the corresponding semantic structure in human memory. The same type of structuring occurs in abstract data types, where a data structure and the corresponding set of operators is incorporated in one module. An experiment discussed in [Woodfield81b] indicates that such coupling increases comprehensibility.

[Dunsmore79] describes an experiment on the effect of the number of 'live' variables on programming effort needed. A variable is 'alive' from the first reference to the last reference to that variable (at execution time). Programs with a limited number of live variables turned out to be easier to adapt. The number of live variables is indicative of the memory capacity needed. We would thus expect that constructs which limit the number of live variables, such as Pascal's block structure and Modula-2's module concept, have a positive impact on the effort needed to manipulate program texts.

17.3.4 Modularization

During the design phase, a problem is decomposed into modules. In the chapter on design, we stressed the importance of notions like information hiding, notions that aim at a program structure where modules exhibit internal cohesion and loose mutual coupling. Modules should capture meaningful abstractions. At a lower level, procedures serve a similar purpose.

In the COCOMO cost estimation model, factors that relate to program structure have some, though not a very large, effect on program development cost [Boehm81]. When it comes down to software maintenance, though, such factors were found to have a much larger impact [Boehm83b].

For small programs, the effect of program modularization does not really show. [Tenny88] reports on an experiment to assess the impact of procedures and comments on program readability. The programs studied were fairly small (about 80 lines of code) and the use of procedures was found to have little effect on readability. Korson found that modular programs are faster to modify than their equivalent monolithic versions under the following conditions [Korson86]:

- the modifications are substantial enough;

- the program is long enough;

- the modifications concern a small set of modules which are called throughout the program (A), or they can make use of existing modules (B), or they require a significant understanding of the program (C).

By and large, cases A and B can be taken to refer to the proper use of information-hiding techniques. These experiments support our ideas that a proper program decomposition helps for larger programs.

In object-oriented programming and design, modules (classes) conceptualize real-world entities. Proponents of the OO-paradigm claim that this approach is more natural than the traditional, process-oriented design techniques. Program comprehension involves consideration of both the program and the application world. We speculate that programs (and designs) which explicitly link these worlds will lead to improved comprehension. Sound empirical evidence hereof though is still lacking [Rosson90].

17.4 USER INTERFACES

We can't worry about these user interface issues now. We haven't even gotten this thing to work yet!
[Mulligan91]

A system in which the interaction occurs at a level which is understandable to the user will be accepted faster than a system where it is not. A system which is available at irregular intervals, or gives incomprehensible error messages, is likely to meet resistance. In many systems, the user interface incorporates over 30% of the program code [Smith84]. Often, the user interface is one of the most critical factors as regards the success or failure of a computerized system. Yet, we know fairly little about this aspect of our trade.

There are many factors that impact human–computer communication. In this section we will just be scratching the surface. Important topics not discussed include the social-economic context of human–computer interaction (see [Kling80] and [Hirshheim86] for instance), input and output media and their ergonomics (see [Shneiderman86]), and workplace ergonomics.

In order to develop a better understanding of what is involved in designing user interfaces, it is necessary to take a closer look at the role of the user in operating a complex device such as a computer. [Norman83] distinguishes three types of models that bear upon the interplay between a human and the computer: the user's mental model, the system image and the conceptual model.

The user's **mental model** is a model of the machine that users create. Based on education, knowledge of the system and/or application domain, knowledge of other systems, general world knowledge, and the like, the user constructs a model, a knowledge structure, of that system. During interaction with the system, this model is used to plan actions and predict and interpret system reactions.

The mental model reflects the user's understanding of what the system contains, how it works, and why it works the way it does. The mental model is initially determined through metacommunication, such as training and documentation. It evolves over time as the user acquires a better understanding of the system. The user's mental model need not be, and often is not, accurate in technical terms. Instead, it may contain misconceptualizations and omissions.

The user's mental model is based on the **system image**, which includes all the elements of the system the user comes into contact with. The system image includes aspects ranging from the physical outlook of the computer and connected devices to the style of interaction and the form and content of the information exchange.

Finally, the **conceptual model** is the technically accurate model of the computer system created by designers and teachers for their purposes. It is a consistent and complete representation of the system as far as user-relevant characteristics are involved. The conceptual model reflects itself in the system's reactions to user actions.

The central question in human–computer interaction is to attune the user's mental model and the conceptual model as best as possible. When this is achieved to a higher degree, an interactive system becomes easier to learn and easier to use. Where both models conflict the user gets confused, makes errors, gets frustrated. A good design starts with a conceptual model derived from an analysis of the intended users and their tasks. The conceptual model should result in a system image and training materials which are consistent with the conceptual model. This, in turn, should be designed such that it induces adequate users' mental models.

The user of an interactive system has to accomplish certain tasks. Within the task domain, e.g. sending electronic mail or preparing documents, these tasks have a certain structure. Knowledge of these tasks and their structuring is present in human memory. The human–computer interaction then should have the same structure, as far as can be accomplished. If a certain action is seen as one conceptual unit within the task domain, it is confusing when we have to issue a whole sequence of commands to the system in order to achieve the effect intended. Actions that are close to one another within the task domain (i.e. they are semantically connected) should also be close to one another within the human–computer interaction, and vice versa.

Software engineers are inclined to model the user interface after the structure of the implementation mechanism, rather than the structure of the task domain. For instance, some structure-based text editor may force you to input ↑ 10 2 in order to obtain 10^2, simply because to the system the former is easier to recognize. This resembles the interface to early pocket calculators, where the stack mechanism used internally showed itself in the user interface [Gentner90]. Similarly, user documentation often follows implementation patterns, and error messages are phrased in terms that reflect the implementation rather than the user tasks.

Besides task-specific knowledge, general knowledge also plays a role in building a mental model. If hitting the 'u'-key in a text editor makes the cursor go one line up, the user will probably deduct that hitting the 'd'-key will move the cursor one line down. If, however, the effect of hitting the 'd'-key is that the file is deleted, such will lead to confusion and frustration on the part of the user.

This is not surprising in terms of the memory model discussed in section 17.1. New knowledge gets interwoven with knowledge already present. Obviously, limitations of short-term memory and attention also have their effect. Long command sequences, menus with a large number of entries, uncertainty about 'where we are' hamper interaction.

Such aspects together are referred to as the **cognitive load**. As the cognitive load increases, a system becomes more difficult to learn, we get tired sooner, we start to make more errors.

While learning to use an interactive system the user goes through a certain learning curve. The speed with which we manage to go through this learning curve depends on such factors as the complexity of the system and individual differences. Most people have learnt to ride a bicycle, though some of us will never master it. Few of us, however, know how to fly an aeroplane. The speed with which we go through a learning curve and become a skilled user is an important measure of the complexity of that system. This measure is a much better indicator of system usability than the rather inadequate notion of 'user-friendliness'.

Acquiring new skills or knowledge does not occur in a vacuum. We already possess certain skills and knowledge that we build upon. Skills and knowledge are transferred onto new task domains. A successful interactive system uses this fact. We use analogies (text editing looks like the use of a typewriter) and metaphors (such as a desktop). By keeping the repertoire of necessary skills small, they are used more often. It is paramount that the same skills are used in the same circumstances. Positive feedback, in which things look like what we have done earlier, strengthens the assimilation of these skills.

One way to help achieve these desirable properties is to make the interface consistent. Interface consistency, however, should not be carried to the extreme. Interface design is an engineering problem. As such, it involves trade-offs between many factors. [Grudin89] presents some convincing examples where consistency was sacrificed for schemes which better reflect user tasks and environments.

Consider for example the two function key layouts of figure 17.6. Interface experts are likely to prefer the star as the best design. It is a symmetric design, consistent with directional indicators on compasses. Yet studies have shown that the inverted T is the most usable configuration. With the index finger on the cursor left key and the ring finger on the cursor right key, the middle finger can efficiently cover both the cursor up and cursor down keys in this scheme. Designers of computer games seem to have known this fact for quite a while.

When going through a learning curve, the user sooner or later reaches a level that is acceptable to him at that moment, though chances are that he is by far no expert yet. This phenomenon is typical across a wide range of applications. Most UNIX users, for instance, know only a subset of the available UNIX commands well. Another subset they know about vaguely, but are not sure of their exact function. Yet a third subset contains commands the user has no idea about.

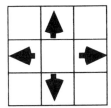 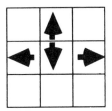

Figure 17.6: Two possible cursor key arrangements

Through training and/or documentation, the user builds up a first understanding of the facilities offered. Because of the task-orientedness of most users, they usually want to get to work with the system before having achieved a full understanding of it. If no further help is given, the chances are that users will never acquire this understanding. For the subset that is vaguely known, a passive help system may be of help. This help system may be available on-line, or off-line in the form of user documentation. As noted before, both the help system and the user documentation should follow the structure of the task domain, not the implementation structure of the system. For the commands that the user has no idea about, an active help system is required, one which guides and advises the user in his/her actions [Fischer86].

Since the full functionality of a system may also confuse inexperienced users and lead to errors, such functionality can be offered in layers. Novice users then are allowed to use only a subset of the commands, a subset with which simple yet meaningful tasks can be accomplished. As experience is being built up, successive layers of functionality can be peeled off.

How then do we go about designing an interactive system which is easy to learn, does not confuse the user, and fits the skills of the task domain? There exist extensive sets of guidelines that contain norms for response times, the use of color, form of commands, length of menus, styles of interaction, etc. An example of one such set is [Smith86]. [Shneiderman86] contains a well-supported discussion of many of these aspects. These guidelines are particularly useful in supporting the lower levels of the user dialogue.

The points raised in the above discussion on usability aspects are well reflected in a simple yet very useful set of usability principles formulated in [Molich90]. These design principles not only apply to traditional text-based dialogues, but to graphical user interfaces as well:*

1. **Simple and natural dialogue** Dialogues should not contain information that is irrelevant or rarely needed. Every extra unit of information competes with other relevant units for our attention. Information should appear in a logical and natural order.

---

* Source: R. Molich & J. Nielsen, Improving a human–computer dialogue, *Communications of the ACM* **33**, 3 (1990) 338–348. Reproduced by permission of the Association for Computing Machinery, Inc.

2. **Speak the user's language** Dialogues should use concepts and phrases that are familiar to the user. The dialogue should not be expressed in computer-oriented terms.

3. **Minimize memory load** The user should not have to remember information from one part of the dialogue to another. There must be easy ways to find out what to do next, how to retrace steps, and get general instructions for use.

4. **Consistency** Users should not have to wonder whether different words or actions mean the same thing (but recall the above remarks against consistency as the one and only driving force).

5. **Provide feedback** The system should keep users informed about what is going on. Though certain processes may take quite a while, the user should not be left in the dark as to what is going on. A percent-done indicator for example informs the user about the progress towards the goal.

6. **Provide clearly marked exits** Users make mistakes and may choose inappropriate functions. There must be ways to leave the unwanted state without having to enter an extensive dialogue with the system.

7. **Provide shortcuts** Novice users may not be hindered by an extensive question–answer dialogue. It gives them a safe feeling and helps them learn the system. This is not optimal for experienced users, and the system should provide clever shortcuts to accommodate the experts.

8. **Good error messages** Error messages should be expressed in plain language and not refer to the internals of the system. They should precisely state the problem and constructively suggest a solution.

9. **Prevent errors** As with any piece of software, it is better to prevent errors from occurring in the first place.

A second way to go about it is through **iterative design**. Assuming that the user interface cannot be designed right from the start, it is instead developed in a number of cycles. After each step the behavior of the user(s) is analyzed and evaluated. The future user plays a central role in this evaluation process. To make the iterative process economically viable, prototyping facilities are a necessary prerequisite. One example of a successful system developed along these lines, is the Speech Filing System of IBM [Gould83, 84]. The tools used in the development of this system were also used later in the development of the Olympic Message System [Gould87]. An iterative process has also been used in the development of the Star interface, well known from the Macintosh [Smith82, Bewley83].

Using iterative design, increasing use is being made of tools that help us build user interfaces. These tools are commonly classified as either **toolkits** or **User Interface Management Systems** (UIMS) [Hartson89]. A toolkit provides a set of routines to implement parts of the interface. Window management systems such as the X Window System [Scheifler86] fall into this category. A UIMS offers an integrated view of a user interface. Such systems support the specification of user interfaces at a high level of abstraction. Example UIMSs are SYNGRAPH [Olsen83] and RAPID/USE [Wasserman85].

Most UIMSs support the development of interfaces that are best categorized as being **conversational**. In conversational interfaces, human–computer interaction takes the form of a dialogue. Legal dialogues obey a certain grammar. Typical examples of conversational interfaces are the familiar command-language interfaces. Form-filling systems and menu-based systems can generally be modeled in linguistic terms as well.

A rather different class of user interfaces concerns the so-called **direct manipulation systems**. In a direct manipulation system, the interface can be viewed as a model world. In this model world, the user grabs objects, moves them around, changes their size, etc. It feels as if the user is in direct contact with the objects of the task domain. The direct manipulation style provides the user with a sense of direct engagement. In a traditional command-language mode of operation, the user does not perform a task directly, but is rather obliged to persuade the system to perform it [Laurel86].

Direct-manipulation systems have an object-oriented flavor. In command-driven interfaces, the operation is selected first and the objects are given as parameters, as in `print <myfile`. In a direct-manipulation interface, the object is selected first (for example by clicking on an icon) and the operation is selected next.

In direct-manipulation interfaces, the interaction does not follow a single thread of control, as in most conversational interfaces. Rather, the user may at some point select from among such different options as adding text, printing the contents of a file, or changing the size of a window. The communication is asynchronous, event-based.

One particular characteristic of direct-manipulation systems is the **semantic feedback** that is often offered, i.e. the application semantics is shown in the dialogue. For instance, when dragging a file object across a folder object, the folder icon is depicted differently to show that something meaningful will happen if the mouse button is released. Another example is when the cursor changes its shape when it is moved from one screen region to another. Semantic feedback is difficult to accomplish in most existing UIMSs.

Iterative design is a labor-intensive and costly affair. It would be nice if we could judge the quality of a user interface, not on the grounds of some empirical evaluation, but from an analysis of the system's description. In order to do so, we need a model of both the user and his tasks.

Seminal work in this area has been done by Card, Moran and Newell [Card83]. Two worked-out models are the GOMS-model (Goals, Operators, Methods, Selection rules) and the Keystroke-model.

The GOMS-model can be used to predict the time an expert needs to do routine-type tasks. The model has the following components: the goals stated (such as 'edit a manuscript' in text processing), operators (such as 'look at manuscript'), methods (such as 'change a line') and selection procedures (a certain line, for instance, can be searched by moving the cursor in case the distance is known, or by searching for a string contained in that line). Besides its use to predict the time needed for a given task, the model can also be used to predict which methods the user will apply. Application of the GOMS-model to text processing is described in [Card80b].

The Keystroke-model describes the interaction at the lowest level: keystrokes, mouse movements, and the like. In particular, the Keystroke-model gives performance predictions of these low-level user actions [Card80a].

The interaction with a system is often bound by certain rules. After a given action, only some continuations are allowed or meaningful. We may then describe the possible user dialogues using a context-free grammar. Based on the description of an interface as a context-free grammar, Reisner tried to predict properties of the user dialogue, such as how easy it is to remember certain command sequences, or what the probability is that errors are being made [Reisner81].

In the definition of the programming language ALGOL 68 a two-level (or van Wijngaarden) grammar has been used [Tanenbaum76]. At one level in such a grammar one describes how sets of similar things look like. This is next applied at the other level. For instance, we may once define a SEQUENCE, and next use both a P-SEQUENCE and a Q-SEQUENCE. Two-level grammars are applied to the description of human–computer interaction in [Payne83, 86]. They seem to offer perspectives to analyzing the consistency of user interfaces.

The research into analytical models to describe the user and the use of interactive systems is still in its infancy. Application of these models is mostly done after the fact, in an academic environment. In developing real interactive systems, you still have to rely on guidelines and a cyclic design process with the user at its center. The principle 'know your user' is more than a dummy cry. Knowledge of cognitive factors that play a role in human information processing is an essential prerequisite for obtaining successful systems.

17.5 SUMMARY AND FURTHER READING

Interest in psychological issues related to the use and construction of software has strongly increased since the publication of Weinberg's classic text in 1971 [Weinberg71]. Though published 20 years ago, it is still a valuable source of ideas and observations.

In the 1970s, a large number of experiments were carried out to measure various aspects of human–computer interaction. [Shneiderman80] discusses many of these. Other sources are [Surveys81] and [Coombs81]. In 1982 the first large international conference in this area was organised [Gaitersburg82].

Unfortunately, the results of many of the early experiments are not very convincing. Doing reliable experiments in human–computer interaction is a very complex affair. A large number of factors have to be taken into account. It is difficult to do realistic experiments, the experience of subjects is an important factor, personality traits cannot be neglected. It took some time before we became sufficiently aware of these problems [Moher81, 82], [Thomas89c].

Research in this area is gathering growing interest. Conferences are organized at regular intervals in both Europe and the US. [Curtis86a, b] gives an excellent overview of research in this area.

Many of the results obtained may be explained in terms of a cognitive model of the human as an information-processing system as discussed in section 17.1. As in other similar models, human memory has an active component of very limited capacity and a background memory which is (for all practical purposes) unlimited in size. Information is stored associatively and organized in a network.

These models offer good hooks for evaluating and designing interactive systems. A central issue in human–computer interaction is the mutual fit between the user's mental model of the system and the conceptual model embodied by the actual system. At the present state of our knowledge about the human as an information processing system, this is still largely a matter of trial and error. Successful systems are designed in a cyclic process where the user is at the center of the process. See for instance [Norman86].

The importance of theoretically oriented models such as those described in [Card83], [Payne86], or [Moran81], is that they allow us to judge the design of an interactive system before any code has been written. As we get to know more about the different factors that impact human–computer communication, better models can be developed. As a result, more effective interactive systems can be designed. An overview of formal modeling techniques in human–computer interaction is given in [deHaan91].

This chapter has touched upon only a few aspects of human–computer interaction. Text books devoted to human-computer interaction include [Rubinstein84], [Norman86] and [Brown89]. [Baecker87] is a collection of important articles on many aspects of human–computer interaction.

EXERCISES

1. Take a quick glance at the following algorithm and then describe what it does:

```
procedure sort(A: array [1 .. n] of integer);
var i, k, small: integer;
begin
   for i:= 1 to n do
       small:= A[i];
       for k:= i to n-1 do
          if small <= A[k] then swap(A[k], A[k+1]) end
       end
   end
end sort;
```

Next study the algorithm a bit more carefully and try to discern what it really does. Would less misleading mnemonics have increased its comprehensibility? To what extent might you have been misled by false beacons?

2. Write an essay on the impact of language constructs on problem solving ([Baecker87] contains a number of articles on this topic; [Rosson90] addresses consequences of object-orientation).

3. Study the desktop metaphor as it is commonly used in user interfaces for PCs and workstations. Can you spot places where the metaphor breaks down, or may even lead you astray?

4. Try to answer the following questions from the manual of your favorite word processor:
   — how do I swap two paragraphs?
   — how do I include the text of some other document at a given position?
   — how do I let the page numbering start at 0 rather than 1?
   — how do I align a picture at the top or bottom of the page?

   Assess whether the user documentation is organized after the functionality offered, or whether it addresses typical tasks faced by its users.

5. Discuss the requirements for on-line help facilities for a word processor.

6. Augment the waterfall model such that user interface issues are dealt with at appropriate phases.

7. Discuss pros and cons of the following approaches to user interface development:
   — discussion of manually constructed usage scenarios with prospective users;
   — prototyping screen displays and iteratively enhancing them;
   — developing the user interface after the functional parts of the system are completed and accepted by the users;
   — formally describing and analyzing the user interface prior to or concurrent with system design.

18

Software
Maintenance

Like living organisms and most natural phenomena, software projects follow a life cycle that starts from emptyness, is followed by rapid growth during infancy, enters a long period of maturity, and then begins a cycle of decay that almost resembles senility.
[Jones89]

Software, unlike a child, does not grow smarter and more capable; unfortunately, it does seem to grow old and cranky.
[Lyons81]

Consider the 'Gemeenschappelijk Administratiekantoor' GAK (Joint Administration Office), a typical large organization that is heavily dependent upon automation for its daily operation. Some one hundred Dutch organizations have commissioned the implementation of social security acts and schemes to the GAK. The GAK implements the Unemployment Benefits Act, Sickness Benefits Act, Disablement Insurance Act, and the like, on behalf of its affiliates. It also administers pensions and capital on behalf of pension funds and early retirement schemes. The annual cash flow runs into billions of Dutch guilders.

The GAK has 350 offices, spread all over the country. It has a number of mainframes at a central site, as well as over 7000 terminals and 3000 printers connected through a country-wide network. The workload is over 40 000 transactions per hour. The GAK has some 140 large application systems averaging 100 000 lines of code. Programs are written in a variety of languages, most notably COBOL, various 4GLs and JCL. The systems make use of huge data bases implemented under IDMS, INGRES, and the like. Some of the base registrations are used by many systems. Their structure has a large impact on the overall application portfolio.

GAK employees involved in software maintenance dread election time. Changes in the political climate forecast changes in the regulations implemented by GAK's information systems. The workload may become excessive if these changes have to be realized within a short period of time. Such is usually the case.

Within the DP department of the GAK, some 100 employees are engaged in software development, while over 160 employees do software maintenance.

There are many organizations like the GAK, organizations whose portfolio of information systems is vital for their day-to-day operation. At the same time, these information systems are ageing and it becomes increasingly difficult to keep them 'up and running'. An increasing percentage of the annual budget of these organizations is spent on keeping installed systems functioning properly.

It is estimated that there are more than 100 billion lines of code in production in the world [Lafue90]. As much as 80% hereof is unstructured, patched, and badly documented. It is a gargantuan task to keep these software systems operational: errors must be corrected, and systems must be adapted to changing environments and user needs.

This is what software maintenance is about. Software maintenance is defined as [IEEE83b]:

> The modification of a software product after delivery to correct faults, to improve performance or other attributes, or to adapt the product to a changed environment.

So software maintenance is in particular *not* limited to the correction of latent faults. Let us recall part of the discussion from chapter 1. Following [Lientz80], we distinguished four types of maintenance activities:

1. **Corrective maintenance** deals with the repair of faults found.

2. **Adaptive maintenance** deals with adapting software to changes in the environment, such as new hardware or the next release of an operating system. Adaptive maintenance does not lead to changes in the system's functionality.

3. **Perfective maintenance** mainly deals with accommodating new or changed user requirements. It concerns functional enhancements to the system. Perfective maintenance also includes activities to increase the system's performance or to enhance its user interface.

4. **Preventive maintenance** concerns activities aimed at increasing the system's maintainability, such as updating documentation, adding comments, improving the modular structure of the system.

Notice that 'real' maintenance activities—the correction of faults—accounts for about 25% of the total maintenance effort only. Half of the maintenance effort

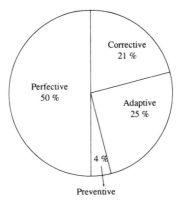

Figure 18.1: Distribution of maintenance activities

concerns changes to accommodate changing user needs, while the remaining 25% largely concerns adapting software to changes in the external environment (see figure 18.1).

Recall also that the total cost of system maintenance is estimated to comprise at least 50% of total life cycle costs.

The above data are based on [Lientz80] and reflect the state of the practice of the 1970s. More recent studies have shown that the situation has not changed for the better. [Nosek90] raised the major maintenance issues once again and came to the disturbing conclusion that maintenenance problems have remained pretty much the same, notwithstanding advances in structured development methodologies and techniques. The relative distribution of maintenance activities is about the same as it was ten years ago. Systems though have become larger, maintenance staff has grown, there are more systems, and there is a definite trend to an increase in maintenance effort relative to development effort.

Changes in both the system's environment and user requirements are inevitable. Software models part of reality, and reality changes, whether we like it or not. So the software has to change too. It *has* to evolve. A large percentage of what we are used to calling maintenance, is actually evolution.

When looking for ways to reduce the maintenance problem, it is worth bearing in mind the classification of maintenance activities given above. Possible solutions to be considered include:

— higher-quality code, better test procedures, better documentation and adherence to standards/conventions may help to save on corrective maintenance;

— finer tuning to user needs may lead to savings in perfective maintenance. Such may for example be achieved through prototyping techniques or a more intensive user participation during the analysis and design phase;

— by anticipating changes during requirements analysis and design and by taking them into account during realization, future perfective and adaptive maintenance can be realized more easily. Through its inheritance and virtual typing capabilities, the object-oriented development paradigm in particular offers perspectives to isolate parts that are susceptible to changes from those that are less so;

— less maintenance is needed when less code is being written. The sheer length of the source code is the main determinant of total cost, both during initial development and during maintenance. The reuse of existing software in particular has a very direct impact on maintenance costs.

These possible actions are all concerned with initial software development. This is not surprising, since the key to better maintainable software is to be found there. All these issues have been discussed at great length in previous chapters.

Yet, maintenance problems will remain. Some of these problems are inherent—systems degrade when they get changed over and over again—while others are caused by simple facts of life—real development and maintenance activities are carried out in less than perfect ways. The major causes of the resulting maintenance problems are addressed in section 18.1.

This discussion of maintenance problems suggests two approaches to improve the situation. The first one concerns various ways to rediscover lost facts ('what does this routine accomplish', 'which design underlies a given system', and the like) and restructure existing software systems in order to improve their maintainability. These are discussed in section 18.2.

The second approach entails a number of organizational and managerial actions to improve software maintenance. These are discussed in section 18.3.

18.1 MAJOR CAUSES OF MAINTENANCE PROBLEMS

The following story reveals many of the problems that befate a typical software maintenance organization. It is based on an anecdote once told by David Parnas and concerns the reengineering of software for fighter planes.

The plane in question has two altimeters. The onboard software tries to read either meter and displays the result. The software for doing so is depicted in figure 18.2. The code is unstructured and does not contain any comments. With a little effort though its functioning can be discerned. A structured version of the same code is given in figure 18.3. What puzzles us is the meaning of the default value 3000. Why on earth does the system display an, at first not very peculiar, value of 3000 when both altimeters cannot be read?

The rationale for the default value could not be discerned from the (scarce or nonexistent) documentation. Eventually, the programmer who had written this code was traced. He told that, when writing this piece of code, he did not know

```
IF not-read1 (V1) GOTO DEF1;
display (V1);
GOTO C;
DEF1: IF not-read2 (V2) GOTO DEF2;
display (V2);
GOTO C;
DEF2: display (3000);
C:
```

Figure 18.2:   Unstructured code to read altimeters

```
if read-meter1 (V1) then display (V1) else
if read-meter2 (V2) then display (V2) else
   display (3000)
endif;
```

Figure 18.3:   Structured code to read altimeters

what to display in case both altimeters were unreadable. So he asked one of the fighter pilots what their average flying altitude was. The pilot made a back-of-the-envelope calculation and came up with the above value: the average flying altitude is 3000 feet. Hence this fragment.

The reengineer rightfully thought that such was not the proper way to react to malfunctioning hardware. Fighter planes either fly at a very high altitude or very close to the ground. They don't fly in between. So he contacted the officials in charge and asked permission to display a clear warning message instead, like a flashing 'PULL UP'.

The permission to change the value displayed was denied. Generations of fighter pilots were by now trained to react appropriately to the current default message. Their training manual even stated a warning phrase like 'If the altimeter reader displays the value 3000 for more than a second, PULL UP'.

This story can't be true. Or can it? It does illustrate some of the major causes of maintenance problems:

- unstructured code,
- maintenance programmers having insufficient knowledge of the system and/or application domain, and
- documentation being absent, out of date, or at best insufficient.

We should add at least one other definite maintenance problem which is not illustrated by the anecdote:

- software maintenance has a bad image.

Unstructured code is used here as a generic term for systems that are badly designed and/or coded. It manifests itself in a variety of ways: the use of goto's, long procedures, poor and inconsistent naming, high module complexity, weak cohesion and strong coupling, unreachable code, deeply nested if-statements, and so on.

Even if systems were originally designed and built well, they may have become harder to maintain in the course of time. Much software that is to be maintained has been developed in the pre-structured programming era. Parts of it may still be written in assembly language. It was designed and written for machines with limited processing and memory capacities. It may have been moved to different hardware/software platforms more than once without its basic structure having changed.

This is not the whole story either. The bad structure of many present-day systems at both the design and code level is not solely caused by their age. As a result of their studies of the dynamics of software systems, Lehman and Belady formulated a series of Laws of Software Evolution (see also chapter 3). The ones that bear most on software maintenance are:

Law of continuing change A system that is being used undergoes continuing change, until it is judged more cost-effective to restructure the system or replace it by a completely new version.

Law of increasing complexity A program that is changed, becomes less and less structured (the entropy increases) and thus becomes more complex. One has to invest extra effort in order to avoid increasing complexity.

Large software systems tend to stay in production for a long time. After being put in production, enhancements are inevitable. As a consequence of the implementation of these enhancements, the entropy of software systems increases over time. The initial structure degrades and complexity increases. This in turn complicates future changes to the system. Such software systems show signs of arthritis. Preventive maintenance may delay the onset of entropy, but such is usually done to a limited extent only.

Eventually, systems cannot be properly maintained anymore. In practice, it is often impossible to completely replace old systems by new ones. Developing completely new systems from scratch is either too expensive, or they will contain too many residual errors to start with, or it is impossible to re-articulate the original requirements. Usually, a combination of these factors applies. Increasing attention is therefore given to ways to 'rejuvenate' or 'recycle' existing software systems, ways to create structured versions of existing operational systems in order that they become easier to maintain.

At a low level this process can be supported by tools such as code restructurers and reformatters. To get higher-level abstractions generally requires human guidance and a sufficient understanding of the system.

This leads us to the second maintenance problem: the scant knowledge maintenance programmers have of the system and/or application domain. Note that the lack of application domain knowledge pertains to software development in general [Curtis88]. The situation with respect to software maintenance is aggravated by the fact that there are usually scarce sources that can be used to build such an understanding. In many cases, the source code is the only reliable source. A major issue in software maintenance, then, is to gain a sufficient understanding of a system from its source code. The more spaghetti-like this code is, the less easy it becomes to disentangle it. An insufficient understanding results in changes that may have unforeseen ripple effects which in turn incurs further maintenance tasks.

Maintenance is also hampered if documentation is absent, insufficient, or out of date. Experienced programmers have learnt to distrust documentation; a disappointing observation in itself, albeit realistic. During initial development, documentation often gets the worst of it because of deadlines and other time constraints. Maintenance itself often occurs in a 'quick-fix' mode whereby the code is patched to accommodate changes. Technical documentation and other higher-level descriptions of the software then do not get updated. Maintenance programmers having to deal with these systems have become part historian, part detective, and part clairvoyant [Corbi89].

Careful working procedures and management attention could prevent such a situation occurring. But even then we are not sure that the right type of documentation will result. Two issues deserve our attention in this respect:

- A design rationale is often missing. Programmers and designers tend to document their final decisions, not the rationale for these decisions and alternatives rejected. Maintenance programmers then have to reconstruct this rationale, and may easily make wrong decisions.

- In trying to comprehend a piece of software, programmers often operate in an opportunistic mode. Based on their programming knowledge, in terms of programming plans and other stereotyped solutions to problems, they hypothesize a reasonable structure. Problems arise if the code does not meet these assumptions.

Finally, the noun, maintenance, in itself has a negative connotation. Maintaining software is considered a second-rate job. Maintenance work is viewed as unchallenging and unrewarding. Preferably, new and inexperienced programmers are assigned to the maintenance group, possibly under the guidance of an experienced person. The more experienced people are to be found working on initial software development. In the structure of the organization, maintenance personnel ranks lower, both financially and organizationally, than programmers working on the development of new systems.

This tends to affect morale. Maintenance programmers are often not happy with their circumstances and try to change jobs as fast as possible. The high turnover of maintenance programmers precludes them from becoming sufficiently familiar with the software to be maintained which in turn hampers future maintenance.

It would be far better to have a more positive attitude towards maintenance. Maintaining software is a very difficult job. The job content of a maintenance programmer is more demanding than the job content of a development programmer. The programs are usually written by other people, people who can often not be consulted because they have left the firm or are entangled in the development of new systems. When making changes in an existing system, one is bound by the very structure of that system. There is generally a strong time pressure on maintenance personnel. Maintenance work requires more skills and knowledge than development does. It is simply more difficult [Chapin87].

The maintenance group is of vital importance. It is them who keep things going. It is their job to ensure that the software keeps pace with the everchanging reality. Compared to software development, software maintenance has more impact on the well-being of an organization.

18.2 REVERSE ENGINEERING AND RESTRUCTURING

What we're doing now with reverse engineering is Archeology. We're trying to gain an understanding of existing systems by examining ancient artifacts and piecing together the software equivalent of broken clay pots. Then we look to restructuring and reengineering to save the clay.
[Chikofsky90b]

It is fashionable in our trade to coin new terms once in a while and offer these as panaceas to the software crisis. One of today's magical terms is **reverse engineering**. It comes under different guises and means altogether different things to different people. In the discussion below we will use the terminology from [Chikofsky90a]. The different terms are illustrated in figure 18.4.

Chikofsky defines reverse engineering as:

the process of analyzing a subject system to
- identify the system's components and their interrelationships and

- create representations of the system in another form or at a higher level of abstraction.

According to this definition, reverse engineering concerns only *inspection* of a system. Adaptations of a system as well as any form of restructuring such as changing goto's into structured control constructs, do not fall within the strict definition of reverse engineering. Reverse engineering is akin to the reconstruction of a lost blueprint. Retiling the bathroom or the addition of a new bedroom is an altogether different affair. If this distinction is not carefully made, the meaning of the term reverse engineering dilutes too much and it reduces to a fancy synonym for maintenance.

The above definition still leaves open the question whether or not the resulting description is at a higher level of abstraction. To emphasize the distinction, Chikofsky uses the notions of **design recovery** and **redocumentation**, respectively.

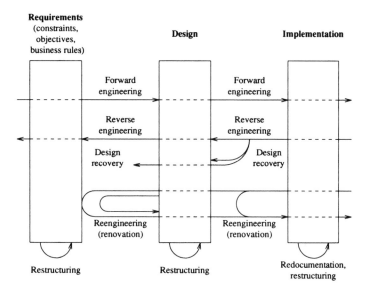

Figure 18.4:   Reverse engineering and related notions (*Source: E.J. Chikofsky & J.H. Cross III, Reverse engineering and design recovery,* IEEE Software **7**, *1 (1990) 13–18,* © *1990 IEEE.*)

Redocumentation, then, concerns the derivation of a semantically equivalent description at the same level of abstraction. Examples of redocumentation are the transformation of a badly indented program into one having a neat lay out, or the construction of a set of flowcharts for a given program.

Design recovery concerns the derivation of a semantically equivalent description at a higher level of abstraction. Some people limit the term reverse engineering to efforts that do result in higher level descriptions and thus equate the term to what we termed design recovery.

Obviously, reverse engineering is often done in circumstances where the target system is adapted as well. Two important subclasses hereof are **restructuring** and **reengineering**.

Restructuring concerns the transformation of a system from one representation to another, at the same level of abstraction. The functionality of the system does not change. The transformation of spaghetti-code to structured code is a form of restructuring. The redesign of a system (possibly after a design recovery step) is another example of restructuring.

Restructuring is sometimes done in conjunction with efforts to convert existing software into reusable building blocks. Such reclamation efforts may well have higher (indirect) payoffs than the mere savings in maintenance expenditure for the particular system being restructured [Garnett90].

With reengineering, also called **renovation**, real changes are made to the system. The reverse engineering step is then followed by a traditional forward engineering step in which the required changes are incorporated.

Each of the above transformations starts from a given description of the system to be transformed. In most cases this will be the program code, which may or may not be adequately documented. However, it is also possible to, say, restructure an existing design, or to reconstruct a requirements specification for a given design. For these transformations, too, the term reverse engineering applies.

Both reverse engineering and restructuring can be done manually, but such is a rather tiresome affair. Quite a number of tools have been developed to support these processes. These tools are discussed in section 18.2.2. There are, however, some inherent limitations as to how much can be achieved automatically. These limitations are discussed in the next section.

18.2.1 Reverse engineering and restructuring: inherent limitations

If you pass an unstructured, unmodular mess through one of these restructuring systems, you end up with at best, a structured, unmodular mess.
[Wendel86]

Reverse engineering will mostly not be limited to redocumentation in a narrow sense. We will often be inclined to ask why certain things are being done the way they are done, what the meaning is of a certain code fragment, and the like. We must therefore investigate how programmers go about when studying program text. These cognitive issues were discussed in chapter 17. In this section we address their implications with respect to maintenance. The relevance of these issues shows from results of a study into maintenance activities [Fjelstad79]:

- maintenance programmers study the original program code about one and a half as long as its documentation;

- maintenance programmers spend as much time on reading the code as they do on implementing a change.

Insight in the discovery process which takes place during maintenance activities will give us the necessary insights to put various developments regarding reverse engineering and restructuring into perspective.

Within forward engineering activities we usually proceed from high-level abstractions to low-level implementations. Information gets lost in the successive steps involved in this process. If we want to follow the reverse route, this information will have to be reconstructed. The object we start with, a piece of source code in general, usually offers insufficient angles for doing so.

The programmer uses varous sources of information in his discovery process. For example, if the design documentation is available, that documentation will reveal something about the structure of the system. A characteristic situation in practice is that the source code is the only reliable source of information.

So this source code has to be studied in order to discover the underlying abstractions. The question is how the programmer goes about when doing so.

Several theories to describe this comprehension process have been developed. Common to these theories is that expert programmers may draw on a vast number of knowledge chunks. Within the realm of programming, it is postulated that experts know of programming plans and/or beacons. Programming plans concern stereotypic instruction sequences, while beacons are kernel ideas embodied in some piece of software. These knowledge chunks are called in when software is developed.

The reverse process occurs when studying existing software. Meaningful units are isolated from the 'flat' source text. Knowledge from human memory is called in during this comprehension process. The more knowledge the reader has about programming and/or the application domain, the more successful this process will be. The better the source code maps onto knowledge already available with the reader, the more effective this process will be.

During the comprehension process, the reader forms hypotheses and checks these hypotheses with the actual text. Well-structured programs and proper documentation ease this process. If application domain concepts map onto well-delineated program units then the program text will be more easily understood. If the structure of a program shows no relation with the structure of the application domain, or the reader cannot discern this structure, then understanding of the program text is seriously hampered. Chapter 17 contains a more extensive discussion of these cognitive issues.

As a side remark we note that there are two extreme strategies for studying program text:

- the as-needed strategy, and

- the systematic strategy.

In the as-needed strategy, program text is read from beginning to end like a piece of prose and hypotheses are formulated on the basis of local information. Inexperienced programmers in particular tend to fall back onto this strategy. In the systematic strategy, an overall understanding of the system is formed by a systematic top-down study of the program text. The systematic approach gives a better insight into causal relations between program components [Littman86].

These causal relations play an important role when implementing changes. So-called delocalized plans, in which conceptually related pieces of code are located in program parts that are physically wide apart, may seriously hamper maintenance activities [Letovsky86], [Soloway88], [van Vliet89]. If our understanding is based on local clues only, modifications may easily result in so-called ripple-effects, i.e. changes are locally correct but lead to new problems at different, unforeseen places. Use of the as-needed strategy increases the probability of ripple effects [Nanja87].

During the comprehension process the programmer uses knowledge that has its origin outside the program text proper. To illustrate this phenomenon, consider the program text from figure 18.5.

```
for i:= 1 to n do
    for j:= 1 to n do
        if A[j, i] then
            for k:= 1 to n do
                if A[i, k] then A[j, k]:= true endif
            enddo
        endif
    enddo
enddo
```

Figure 18.5:   Warshall's algorithm to compute the transitive closure of a graph

The program fragment in figure 18.5 manipulates a boolean matrix A. Before this fragment is executed the matrix will have a certain value. The matrix is traversed in a rather complicated way (potentially, each element is visited n times) and once in a while an element of the array is set to true. But what does this fragment *mean*? What does it *do*?

An expert will 'recognize' Warshall's algorithm. Warshall's algorithm computes the transitive closure of a relation (graph). The notions 'transitive closure', 'relation' and 'graph' have a precise meaning within a certain knowledge domain. If you don't know the meaning of these notions, you haven't made any progress in understanding the algorithm either.

At yet another level of abstraction the meaning of this fragment could be described as follows. Suppose we start with a collection of cities. The relation A states, for each pair of cities i and j, whether there is a direct rail connection between cities i and j. The code fragment of figure 18.5 computes whether there is a connection at all (either direct or indirect) between each pair of cities.

Warshall's algorithm has many applications. If you know the algorithm, you will recognize the fragment reproduced in figure 18.5. If you don't know the algorithm, you will not discover the meaning of this fragment either.

As a second example, consider the code fragment of figure 18.6, adapted from [Biggerstaff89b]. The fragment will not mean much to you. Procedure and variable names are meaningless. A meaningful interpretation of this fragment is next to impossible.

The same code fragment is given in figure 18.7, though with meaningful names. From that version you may grasp that the routine has something to do with window management. The border of the current window is depicted in a

```
procedure A(var x: w);
    begin b(y, n1);
        b(x, n2);
        m(w[x]);
        y:= x;
        r(p[x])
    end;
```

Figure 18.6:   An incomprehensible code fragment

```
procedure change_window(var nw: window);
    begin border(current_window, no_highlight);
        border(nw, highlight);
        move_cursor(w[nw]);
        current_window:= nw;
        resume(process[nw])
    end;
```

Figure 18.7: Code fragment with meaningful names

lighter shade while the border of another window gets highlighted. The cursor is positioned in the now highlighted window and the process of that window is restarted. If we add a few comments to the routine, its text becomes fairly easy to interpret. Meaningful names and comments together provide for an informal semantics of this code which suffice for a proper understanding.

Common to these two examples as well as the altimeter anecdote from section 18.1 is that we need *outside* information for a proper interpretation of the code fragments. The outside information concerns concepts from a certain knowledge domain or a design rationale that was present only in the head of some programmer.

The window management example is illustrative for yet another reason. Tools manipulate sequences of symbols. In principle, tools do not have knowledge of the (external) meaning of the symbols being manipulated. In particular, a reverse engineering and restructuring tool has no knowledge of 'windows', 'cursor' and the like. These notions derive their meaning from the application domain, not from the program text itself. From the tool point of view, the texts of figures 18.6 and 18.7 are equally meaningful.

The above observations have repercussions for the degree to which tools can support the reverse engineering and restructuring process. Such tools cannot turn a badly designed system into a good one. They cannot infer knowledge from a source text which is not already contained in that text without calling in external knowledge as an aid. In particular, completely automatic design recovery must be deemed infeasible.

18.2.2 Reverse engineering and restructuring tools

During the reverse engineering process, the programmer builds an understanding of what the software is trying to accomplish, and why things are done the way they are done. Several classes of tools may support the task of program understanding [Wilde89]:

- Tools to ease perceptual processes involved in program understanding (reformatters). Tools may, for example, produce a neat lay out in which nested instructions are indented and blank lines are put between successive procedures. More advanced tools print procedure names in a larger font or generate page headers which contain the name of the component, its version number, creation date, and the like [Oman90b].

- Tools to gain insight in the static structure of programs. For example, tools to generate tables of contents and cross reference listings help to trace the use of program elements. Browsers provide powerful interactive capabilities to inspect the static structure of programs. Hypertext systems provide mechanisms to extend the traditional flat organization of text by their capabilities to link non-sequential chunks of information [Conklin87]. If system-related information is kept in a hypertext form, such opens up new possibilities for interactive, dynamic inspection of that information. Code analyzers may be used to identify potential trouble spots by computing software complexity metrics, highlighting 'dead code', or indicating questionable coding practices. Finally, tools may generate a graphical image of a program text in the form of flowcharts, control graphs or calling hierarchies.

- Tools to gain insight in the dynamic behavior of programs. Next to traditional text-oriented debugging systems there is a growing trend to provide graphical capabilities to monitor program execution, such as systems to animate data structures [Pazel89].

Note that these tools provide support for maintenance tasks in general (next to tools like test coverage monitors to keep track of program paths executed by a given set of test data, and source comparators which identify changes between program versions). With respect to reverse engineering, the above tools may be classified as redocumentation tools. By far the majority of present-day reverse engineering tools falls into this category. [Wilde89] contains a survey of commercial maintenance tools.

Tools which result in a description at a higher level of abstraction (design recovery tools) have some inherent limitations, as argued in the previous section. Similar arguments are given in [Biggerstaff89b].

Tools for design recovery need a model of the application domain in which the concepts from that domain are modeled in an explicit way, together with their mutual dependencies and interrelations. Completely automatic design recovery is not feasible for the foreseeable future. Concepts from an application domain usually carry an informal semantics. Tools for design recovery may, in a dialogue with the human user, search for patterns, make suggestions, indicate relations between components, etc. Such a tool may be termed a 'maintenance apprentice'. Various research efforts are aimed at developing interactive, programmer-guided tools to support maintenance tasks [Biggerstaff89b], [Devanbu91], [Hartman91], [Schwanke91].

A number of tools exist for restructuring program code. Such tools for example transform a program containing goto's into a semantically equivalent program containing only structured control instructions.

The history of restructuring tools goes all the way back to the late 1960s. In 1966, Böhm and Jacopini published a seminal paper in which it was shown that goto's are not necessary for creating arbitrary programs [Böhm66]. The roots of restructuring tools like Recoder [Bush85] can be traced to the constructive proof given in Böhm and Jacopini's paper. Recoder structures the control flow of Cobol programs. Other well-known tools in this category are the Cobol Structuring Facility (IBM), Superstructure (Group Operations) and Retrofit (The Catalyst Group).

Restructuring tools can be very valuable—a well-structured program is usually easier to read and understand. A study reported in [Gibson89] provides evidence that structural differences do impact maintenance performance. Specifically, it was found that eliminating goto's and redundancy appears to decrease the time required to perform maintenance, and to decrease the frequency of ripple effects.

Yet, the merit of restructuring tools is limited. They will not transform a flawed design into a good one. The improved versions of the system used in Gibson's experiment were constructed manually. The improvements incorporated may well go beyond what can be achieved automatically.

18.3 ORGANIZATIONAL AND MANAGERIAL ISSUES

The duties of maintenance management are not different from those of other organizational functions, and software development in particular. In chapter 2 we identified five entities that require continuous attention of management:

1. time, i.e. progress towards goals;

2. information, in particular the integrity of the complete set of documents, including change requests;

3. organization of the team, including coordination of activities;

4. quality of the product and process;

5. money, i.e. cost of the project.

In this section we address these issues from a maintenance perspective. We pay particular attention to issues that pose specific problems and challenges to maintenance. These issues are: the organization of maintenance activities, the control of maintenance tasks, and quality assessment.

18.3.1 Organization of maintenance activities

The primary question to be addressed here is whether or not software maintenance should be assigned to a separate organizational unit. The following discussion is largely based on an insightful study of different forms of systems staff departmentalization presented in [Swanson90]. The authors of this article explore the strengths and weaknesses of three alternative bases for staff

W-type	Departmentalization by work type (analysis versus programming) *Focal strength*: development and specialization of programming knowledge and skills *Focal weakness*: costs of coordination between systems analysts and programmers
A-type	Departmentalization by application domain (application group A versus application group B) *Focal strength*: development and specialization of application knowledge *Focal weakness*: costs of coordination and integration among application groups
L-type	Departmentalization by life-cycle phase (development versus maintenance) *Focal strength*: development and specialization of service orientation and maintenance skills *Focal weakness*: costs of coordination between development and maintenance units

Figure 18.8: Trade-offs between alternative organizational forms (*Source: E.B. Swanson & C.M. Beath, Departmentalization in software development and maintenance,* Communications of the ACM **33**, *6 (1990) 658–667. Reproduced by permission of the Association for Computing Machinery, Inc.)*

departmentalization. The three organizational forms with their focal strength and weakness are listed in figure 18.8. We will sketch the W- and A-type organizations and discuss the L-type organization with its pros and cons more elaborately.

Traditionally, departmentalization in software development tended to be according to work type. In such a scheme, people either analyze user needs, or design systems, or implement them, or test them, etc. Even though they cooperate in a team, each team member has quite separate responsibilities and roles.

In a W-type scheme, work assignments may originate from both development projects and maintenance. For example, a designer may be involved in the design of a (sub)system in the context of some development project, or in the design of a change to an existing system. Likewise, a programmer may be implementing an algorithm on behalf of a new system, or realize changes in an operational program.

Note that the development of new systems does not occur in a vacuum. Designers of new systems will reuse existing designs and must take into account constraints imposed by existing systems. Programmers involved in development projects have to deal with interfaces to existing software, existing data bases, etc. In the W-type scheme, the distinction between development and maintenance work is primarily a distinction between different *origins* of the work assignment: development versus maintenance.

A second form of departmentalization is one according to application areas, the A-type scheme. Nowadays, computerized applications have extended to almost all corners of the enterprise. Systems have become more diversified. Application domain expertise has become increasingly important for successful implementation of information systems. Deep knowledge of an application domain is a valuable but scarce resource [Curtis89a]. Nurturing of this expertise amongst staff is one way to increase quality and productivity in both development and maintenance. In larger organizations we may therefore find units with particular expertise in certain application domains, like financial systems, office automation, or real-time process control.

Finally, we may departmentalize according to life cycle phases, as is done in the L-type scheme. In particular, we may distinguish between development and maintenance. With an increasing portfolio of systems to be maintained and the increasing business need of keeping the growing base of information systems working satisfactorily, the division of development and maintenance in separate organizational units is found more often.

Separating development and maintenance has both advantages and disadvantages. The major advantages [Swanson90] are:

- Clear accountability: we may clearly separate the cost and effort involved in maintenance activities from investments in new developments. If personnel is involved in both types of work, they have some freedom in charging their time. It is then more difficult to measure and predict the 'real' cost of software maintenance.

- Intermittent demands of maintenance make it difficult to predict and control progress of new system development. If people do both maintenance work and development, some control can be exercised by specifically allocating certain periods of time as maintenance periods. For instance, the first week of each calendar month may be set aside for maintenance. But even then, maintenance problems are rather unpredictable and some need immediate attention. Many a schedule slippage is due to the maintenance drain.

- A separation of maintenance and development facilitates and motivates the installment of a meaningful acceptance test to be conducted by the maintenance organization before the system is taken into production. If such an acceptance test is not conducted explicitly, maintenance may be confronted with low-quality software and/or systems which still need a 'finishing touch' which the development team has left undone for lack of time.

- By specializing on maintenance tasks, a higher quality of user service can be realized. By their very nature, development groups are focused on system delivery, whereas maintenance people are service-oriented and find pride in satisfying user requests.

- By concentrating on the system(s) to be maintained, a higher productivity is achieved. Maintenance work requires specific skills of which a more optimal use can be made in a separate organization. If people are involved in both development and maintenance, more staff has to be allocated to maintenance, which partitions system familiarity.

On the other hand, the strict separation of development and maintenance has certain disadvantages as well [Swanson90]:

- Demotivation of personnel because of status differences, with consequential degradation of quality and productivity. Managerial attitudes and traditional career paths are the main causes for these motivational problems. Conversely, proper managerial attention to maintenance work goes a large way in alleviating the morale problem.

- Loss of knowledge about the system (with respect to both its design and the application domain knowledge incorporated) when the system is transferred from development to maintenance. Different forms of maintenance escort can be used to mitigate against this loss. For example, a future maintainer of a system may spend some time with the development team, or a developer stays with maintenance until the maintainers have become sufficiently acquainted with the system, or a designer instructs the maintainers about the design of a system.

- Coordination costs between development and maintenance, especially when the new system is going to replace an existing one.

- Increased cost of system acceptance by the maintenance organization. If the system is explicitly carried over from development, certain quality and documentation criteria must be met. Within an A-type organization these requirements can often be relaxed a bit, or their fulfillment is postponed. It is by no means clear though that this really incurs an increase in cost. In the long run it may well be cheaper to accept only systems which pass a proper maintenance acceptance test.

- Possible duplication of communication channels to the user organization.

Based on an analysis of existing departmentalizations and the resulting list of strengths and weaknesses, Swanson and Beath express a slight preference for having development and maintenance as separate organizational units. We concur with that. Careful procedures could be devised that overcome some or all of the disadvantages listed. We should stress that personnel demotivation is a real issue in many organizations. It deserves serious management attention.

Combinations of departmentalization types are also possible. In particular, combinations of A-type and L-type departmentalizations are quite common. So, within the maintenance organization, smaller groups can be identified that are specialized in some application domain, i.e. collections of information systems to be maintained. This may be termed the L–A-scheme. Conversely, in an A–L-scheme small maintenance units are found within groups that specialize in certain application areas. The L–A-scheme is more likely to exhibit the advantages of the L-scheme than the A–L-scheme does.

Too much specialization is a lurking danger, though. A system should never become someone's private property. A variation of the reverse Peter principle applies here: people rise within an organization to a level at which they become indispensable. Job rotation is one way to avoid people from becoming too much entrenched in the peculiarities of a system. There is a trade-off though, since such a step also means that in-depth knowledge of a system is sacrificed.

18.3.2 Control of maintenance tasks

Careful control of the product is necessary during software development. The vast amount of information has to be kept under control. Documentation must be kept consistent and up to date. An appropriate scheme for doing so is provided by the set of procedures that make up configuration control; see chapter 4. Configuration control pays particular attention to the handling of change requests. Since handling change requests is what maintenance is all about, configuration control is of vital importance during maintenance.

Effective maintenance depends on following a rigorous methodology, not only with respect to the implementation of changes agreed upon, but also with respect to the way change is controlled. After [Martin83] we suggest the following orderly, well-documented process for controlling changes during maintenance:

1. Require formal (written) requests for all changes.

2. Review all change requests and limit changes to those approved.

3. Analyze and evaluate the type and frequency of change requests.

4. Consider the degree to which a change is needed and its anticipated use.

5. Evaluate changes to ensure that they are not incompatible with the original system design and intent. No change should be implemented without careful consideration of its ramifications.

6. Emphasize the need to determine whether a proposed change will enhance or degrade the system.

7. Approve changes only if the benefits outweigh the costs.

8. Schedule all maintenance.

9. Enforce documentation and coding standards.

10. Require that all changes be implemented using modern programming practices.

11. Plan for preventive maintenance.

The above steps induce a maintenance model in which each change request is carefully analyzed and, once (and only if) the request is approved, its implementation is carried out in a disciplined, orderly way, including a proper update of the documentation. This control scheme fits in well with the **iterative–enhancement** model of software maintenance [Basili90]; see also figure 18.9.

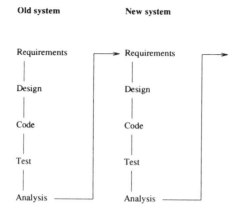

Figure 18.9:   Iterative–enhancement model of software maintenance (*Source: V.R. Basili, Viewing maintenance as reuse-oriented software development*, IEEE Software **7**, 1 (1990) 19–25, © 1990 IEEE.)

The essence of the iterative–enhancement model is that the set of documents is modified starting with the highest-level document affected by the changes, propagating the changes down through the full set of documents. For example, if a change necessitates a design change, then the design is changed first. Only as a consequence of the design change will the code be adapted.

Reality is often different. Figure 18.10 depicts the so-called **quick-fix model** of software maintenance [Basili90]. In the quick-fix model, you take the source code, make the necessary changes to the code and recompile the system to obtain a new version. The source-code documentation and other higher-level documents get updated after the code has been fixed, and usually only if time permits.

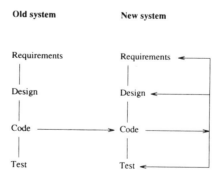

Figure 18.10:   Quick-fix model of software maintenance (*Source: V.R. Basili, Viewing maintenance as reuse-oriented software development*, IEEE Software **7**, 1 (1990) 19–25, © 1990 IEEE.)

In the latter scheme, patches are made upon patches and the structure of the system will degrade rather quickly. Because of the resulting increase in system complexity and inconsistency of documents, future maintenance becomes much more difficult. To be realistic, the quick-fix model cannot be completely circumvented. In an emergency situation there is but one thing that matters: getting the system up and running again as fast as possible. Where possible, though, the quick-fix model should be circumvented. If it is used at all, preventive maintenance activities should be scheduled as yet to repair the structural damage done.

18.3.3 Quality issues

Changing software impairs its structure. By a conscious application of software quality assurance procedures during maintenance we may limit the negative effects. If we know the software quality factors that affect maintenance effort and cost, we may measure those factors and take preventive actions accordingly. In particular, such metrics can be used to guide decisions as to when to start a major overhaul of components or complete systems.

Quality control issues get quite some attention during software development. Software quality assurance however should broaden its scope to maintenance as well. The implementation of changes during maintenance requires the same level of quality assurance as development work does. The ingredients of software quality assurance procedures as discussed in chapter 6 apply equally well to software maintenance.

Software quality assurance can be backed up by measurements that quantify quality aspects. With respect to maintenance we may focus on measures which specifically relate to maintenance effort, such as counting defects reported, change requests issued, effort spent on incorporating changes, complexity metrics, etc.

Relations can then be sought between such measures. Trends observed can be used to initiate actions, such as:

- If maintenance efforts correlate well with complexity metrics like Henri and Kafura's information flow or McCabe's cyclomatic complexity (see chapter 10), then these complexity metrics may be used to trigger preventive maintenance. Various studies have indeed found such correlations [Rombach85], [Gibson89], [Kafura87].

- If certain modules require frequent changes, or require much effort to realize changes, then a re-design of such modules should be given serious consideration.

A particular relevant issue during maintenance is to decide when to reengineer. At a certain point in time, maintaining an old system becomes next to impossible and a major reengineering effort is required. There are no real hard figures to decide on this, but certain system characteristics certainly indicate system degradation [Martin83]:

- Frequent system failures.
- Code over seven years old.
- Overly complex program structure and logic flow.
- Code written for previous generation hardware.
- Running in emulation mode.
- Very large modules or subroutines.
- Excessive resource requirements.
- Hard-coded parameters which are subject to change.
- Difficulty in keeping maintainers.
- Seriously deficient documentation.
- Missing or incomplete design specifications.

The greater the number of such characteristics present, the greater the potential for redesign.

Improvements in software maintenance requires insight in factors that determine maintenance cost and effort. Software metrics provide such insight. To measure is to know. By carefully collecting and interpreting maintenance data, we may discover the major cost drivers of software maintenance, and initiate actions to improve both quality and productivity [Grady87b], [Neil90].

18.4 SUMMARY AND FURTHER READING

Software maintenance encompasses all modifications to a software product after delivery. The following breakdown of maintenance activities is usually made:

Corrective maintenance concerns the correction of faults.

Adaptive maintenance deals with adapting software to changes in the environment.

Perfective maintenance mainly deals with accommodating new or changed user requirements.

Preventive maintenance concerns activities aimed at increasing a system's maintainability.

'Real' maintenance, the correction of faults, consumes approximately 25% of maintenance effort. By far the larger part of software maintenance concerns the *evolution* of software. This evolution is inescapable. Software models part of reality. Reality changes, and so has the software that models it.

Major causes of maintenance problems are discussed in section 18.1: the existence of a vast amount of unstructured code, insufficient knowledge about the system or application domain on the part of maintenance programmers, insufficient documentation, and the bad image of the software maintenance department.

Some of these problems are accidental and can be remedied by proper actions. Through a better organization and management of software maintenance, substantial quality and productivity improvements can be realized. These issues are discussed in section 18.3. Obviously, improved maintenance should start with improved development. Opportunities to improve the development process are a major topic in most chapters of this book.

A particularly relevant issue for software maintenance is that of reverse engineering, the process of reconstructing a lost blueprint. Before changes can be realized, the maintainer has to gain an understanding of the system. Since the majority of operational code is unstructured and/or undocumented, this is a major problem. Section 18.2 addresses reverse engineering, its limitations, and tools to support it.

The fundamental problem is that maintenance will remain a big issue. Because of the changes made to software, its structure degrades. Specific attention to preventive maintenance activities aimed at improving system structure will be needed from time to time to fight system entropy.

Like any other life cycle phase, software maintenance can be supported by tools. [Wilde89] presents a taxonomy of maintenance tools and contains a long list of commercial maintenance tools. MACS and REDO are major research efforts in this area, funded by ESPRIT [Bennett91].

Software maintenance used to be a rather neglected topic in the software engineering literature. Like programmers, researchers are more attracted to developing new, fancy methods and tools for software development. This situation is gradually changing. Major journals regularly feature articles on software maintenance (see for example [Software90a]), there is a bi-annual IEEE Conference on Software Maintenance (since 1985), and the journal *Software Maintenance: Research and Practice* (launched 1989) is wholly devoted to it.

EXERCISES

1. Discuss the major impediments to fully automated design recovery.

2. Assess opportunities of knowledge-based support for software maintenance (see [Devanbu91] for a very interesting application of such ideas).

3. Give a primary classification of your maintenance organization as W-, A-, or L-type (see figure 18.8). What are the major strengths and weaknesses of your particular organization?

4. Discuss advantages of software configuration control support during software maintenance.

5. Does your organization collect quantitative data on maintenance activities? If so, what type of data and how are these data used to guide and improve the maintenance process? If not, how is maintenance planned and controlled?

6. Discuss the possible structure and role of an acceptance test by the maintenance organization prior to the release of a system.

7. Study the technical documentation of a system whose development you have been involved in. Does the documentation capture the design rationale? In what ways does it support comprehension of the system? In hindsight, can you suggest ways to improve the documentation for the purpose of maintenance?

8. Discuss the impact of component reuse on maintainability.

9. Discuss the possible contribution of object-oriented software development to software maintenance.

APPENDIX A
The KWIC-index Programs

We discussed two possible modularizations of the KWIC-index problem in section 10.1. This appendix contains their realizations in Pascal.

To keep things simple, a number of assumptions have been made. We assume that the input is correct, that each input line contains one title, and that exactly one space is given between adjacent words. No spaces should appear at the start or end of a line. No effort has been made to make the output look typographically pleasing. Finally, we assume that the characters stored can be used directly in the sorting process. In particular, a distinction is made between upper- and lower-case letters.

In the implementation of modularization 1, the end of a line is indicated with a special character called `EndOfLine`. The particular choice made for this character is fairly arbitrary, but for two conditions. Firstly, the character should not occur in the input proper. Secondly, its ordinal value should be greater than that of any input character, because of the sorting process.

Figure A.1 contains an implementation derived from the first modularization, while figure A.2 relates to the second modularization. We argued in section 10.1 that changes are easier to accomplish with the second modularization. To illustrate this, figure A.3 contains an alternative version of the sorting module of the second modularization. Without any changes to the remainder of the program this module may replace the corresponding module in figure A.2.

Pascal does not offer the module as a language concept. Nevertheless, the various constituents of a module are placed together in the program texts given. This means that the texts given have to be reshuffled a bit in order to obtain correct Pascal programs. As for figure A.1, this means that the main program (lines 58–65) has to be moved to the end of the text.

```
 1  (* modularization 1 of the KWIC-index program *)

 3  (* Module 5: Control *)

 5  program kwic1(input, output);

 7  label 1000;

 9  const MaxWord = 10;
10          (* number of characters per word *)
11        MaxStore = 10000;
12          (* max. storage capacity, in words of *)
13          (* MaxWord characters *)
14        MaxLines = 1000;
15          (* max. number of input lines *)
16        EndOfLine = '%';
17          (* special character stored at the end of *)
18          (* each line; plays a role during sorting! *)
19        MaxShift = 10000;
20          (* max. number of shifts *)
21        MaxError = 25;
22          (* max. length of error messages *)

24  type TwordIndex = 1 .. MaxWord;
25        TwordIndex0 = 0 .. MaxWord;
26        TstoreIndex = 1 .. MaxStore;
27        TstoreIndex0 = 0 .. MaxStore;
28        Tstore = array [TstoreIndex] of alfa;
29        TlineIndex = 1 .. MaxLines;
30        TlineIndex0 = 0 .. MaxLines;
31        Tline = array [TlineIndex] of TstoreIndex;
32        Tword = array [TwordIndex] of char;
33        TshiftIndex = 1 .. MaxShift;
34        TshiftIndex0 = 0 .. MaxShift;
35        TshiftInfo =
36          record
37            LineIndex: TlineIndex;
38            StoreIndex: TstoreIndex;
39            WordIndex: TwordIndex
40          end;
41        Tshift = array [TshiftIndex] of TshiftInfo;
42        TerrorIndex = 1 .. MaxError;
43        TerrorString = array [TerrorIndex] of char;

45  var Store: Tstore;
46       StartOfLine: Tline;
47       NumberOfLines: TlineIndex0;
48       Shifts, Sort: Tshift;
49       ShiftIndex: TshiftIndex0;

51  procedure error(s: TerrorString);
52    begin
53      writeln;
54      writeln(s);
55      goto 1000  (* quit *)
56    end;

58  (* main program *)
59  begin
60    ReadInput;
61    MakeShifts;
62    SortShifts;
63    PrintOutput;
64  1000:
65  end.

67  (* Moduul 1: Input *)
68  (* Import from Control: Store, StartOfLine, *)
69  (*                      NumberOfLines. *)
70  (* Export: Store, StartOfLine, NumberOfLines. *)
```

Figure A.1: Realization of modularization 1 in Pascal

```
72  procedure ReadInput;
73    var WordIndex: TwordIndex0;
74        BeginStore: integer;
75        StoreIndex: TstoreIndex0;
76        word: Tword;
77        c: char;

79    procedure StoreWord;
80      begin
81        if StoreIndex = MaxStore then
82          error('too much input         ');
83        StoreIndex:= StoreIndex + 1;
84        pack(word, 1, Store[StoreIndex]);
85        WordIndex:= 0
86      end; (* store word *)

88    procedure StoreChar (c: char);
89      begin
90        if WordIndex = 10 then StoreWord;
91        WordIndex:= WordIndex + 1;
92        word[WordIndex]:= c
93      end; (* store character *)

95    procedure MarkEndOfLine;
96      (* The current word is closed, and the next *)
97      (* line starts with a new word. *)
98      begin
99        StoreChar(EndOfLine);
100       StoreWord;
101       if NumberOfLines = MaxLines then
102         error('too many lines         ');
103       NumberOfLines:= NumberOfLines + 1;
104       StartOfLine[NumberOfLines]:= BeginStore;
105       BeginStore:= StoreIndex + 1
106     end; (* mark end of line *)

108   begin
109     BeginStore:= 1;
110     NumberOfLines:= 0;
111     WordIndex:= 0;
112     StoreIndex:= 0;

114     while not eof do
115     begin
116       while not eoln do
117       begin
118         read(c);
119         StoreChar(c)
120       end;
121       read(c);   (* skip transition to the next line *)
122       MarkEndOfLine
123     end
124   end; (* read input *)

126 (* Module 2: Shift *)
127 (* Import from Control: Store, NumberOfLines. *)
128 (* Export: Shifts, ShiftIndex. *)

130 procedure MakeShifts;
131   var WordIndex: TwordIndex;
132       StoreIndex: TstoreIndex0;
133       line: TlineIndex;
134       word: Tword;

136   procedure NextCharacter;
137     begin
138       if WordIndex = 10 then
139       begin StoreIndex:= StoreIndex + 1;
140         unpack(Store[StoreIndex], word, 1);
141         WordIndex:= 1
```

Figure A.1: (cont'd)

```
142        end
143        else WordIndex:= WordIndex + 1
144      end; (* next character *)

146    procedure StoreShift;
147      begin ShiftIndex:= ShiftIndex + 1;
148        Shifts[ShiftIndex].LineIndex:= line;
149        Shifts[ShiftIndex].StoreIndex:= StoreIndex;
150        Shifts[ShiftIndex].WordIndex:= WordIndex
151      end; (* store shift *)

153    procedure FindStartOfNextWord;
154      begin
155        while not (word[WordIndex] in [' ', EndOfLine])
156          do NextCharacter
157      end; (* find start of next word *)

159    begin
160      StoreIndex:= 0;
161      ShiftIndex:= 0;

163      for line:= 1 to NumberOfLines do
164      begin
165        WordIndex:= 10;
166        NextCharacter;
167          (* we are now positioned at the start of the line *)
168        StoreShift;
169          (* the original line is the first shift *)
170        repeat
171          FindStartOfNextWord;
172          if not (word[WordIndex] = EndOfLine) then
173          begin
174            NextCharacter;
175            StoreShift
176          end
177        until word[WordIndex] = EndOfLine
178      end
179    end; (* make shifts *)

181  (* Module 3: Sorting *)
182  (* Implementation through a simple bubblesort *)
183  (* Import from Control: Store, StartOfLine, Shifts, *)
184  (*                        ShiftIndex. *)
185  (* Export: Sort. *)

187  procedure next(var charJ: char; j: TshiftIndex;
188                 var StoreIndexJ: TstoreIndex;
189                 var WordIndexJ: TwordIndex;
190                 var wordJ: Tword);
191      (* advance to the next position in the shift *)
192    begin
193      if charJ = EndOfLine then
194      begin
195        (* continue at the start of the line *)
196        StoreIndexJ:= StartOfLine[Sort[j].LineIndex];
197        unpack(Store[StoreIndexJ], wordJ, 1);
198        WordIndexJ:= 1
199      end else
200      if WordIndexJ = 10 then
201      begin
202        StoreIndexJ:= StoreIndexJ + 1;
203        unpack(Store[StoreIndexJ], wordJ, 1);
204        WordIndexJ:= 1
205      end else
206      WordIndexJ:= WordIndexJ + 1;
207      charJ:= wordJ[WordIndexJ]
208    end; (* next *)

210  procedure SortShifts;
211    var i, j: TshiftIndex;
```

Figure A.1:   (cont'd)

```
212        finished: boolean;

214    function GreaterThan(j, k: TshiftIndex): boolean;
215        (* yields true if and only if the shift in *)
216        (* Sort[j] lexically follows the shift *)
217        (* in Sort[k] *)
218      var wordJ, wordK: Tword;
219         WordIndexJ, WordIndexK, BeginWord: TwordIndex;
220         StoreIndexJ, StoreIndexK, BeginStore: TstoreIndex;
221         FirstTime: boolean;
222         cj, ck: char;

224      begin
225        StoreIndexJ:= Sort[j].StoreIndex;
226        BeginStore:= StoreIndexJ;
227        WordIndexJ:= Sort[j].WordIndex;
228        BeginWord:= WordIndexJ;
229        unpack(Store[StoreIndexJ], wordJ, 1);
230        cj:= wordJ[WordIndexJ];

232        StoreIndexK:= Sort[k].StoreIndex;
233        WordIndexK:= Sort[k].WordIndex;
234        unpack(Store[StoreIndexK], wordK, 1);
235        ck:= wordK[WordIndexK];

237        FirstTime:= true;

239        while (cj = ck) and
240          not ((StoreIndexJ = BeginStore) and
241               (WordIndexJ = BeginWord) and
242               not FirstTime) do
243        begin
244          FirstTime:= false;
245          next(cj, j, StoreIndexJ, WordIndexJ, wordJ);
246          next(ck, k, StoreIndexK, WordIndexK, wordK)
247        end;

249        GreaterThan:= cj > ck
250          (* in this routine, we assume that 'EndOfLine' has *)
251          (* a value which is greater than that of any other *)
252          (* character that may occur in the line *)
253      end; (* greater than *)

255    procedure swap (j, k: TshiftIndex);
256        (* swap Sort[j] and Sort[k] *)
257      var zi: TlineIndex;
258          si: TstoreIndex;
259          wi: TwordIndex;
260      begin
261        with Sort[j] do
262        begin
263          zi:= LineIndex;
264          LineIndex:= Sort[k].LineIndex;
265          si:= StoreIndex;
266          StoreIndex:= Sort[k].StoreIndex;
267          wi:= WordIndex;
268          WordIndex:= Sort[k].WordIndex
269        end;
270        with Sort[k] do
271        begin
272          LineIndex:= zi;
273          StoreIndex:= si;
274          WordIndex:= wi
275        end
276      end; (* swap *)

278    (* main bubblesort loop *)
279    begin
280      for i:= 1 to ShiftIndex do
281      begin
```

Figure A.1:   (cont'd)

```
282        Sort[i]:= Shifts[i];
283        j:= i;
284        finished:= false;
285        while not finished do
286          if j = 1 then finished:= true else
287          if GreaterThan(j - 1, j) then
288          begin
289            swap(j, j - 1);
290            j:= j - 1
291          end else finished:= true
292        end
293    end; (* sort shifts *)

295  (* Module 4: Output *)
296  (* Import from Control: Sort, ShiftIndex. *)
297  (* Export: --. *)

299  procedure PrintOutput;
300      (* simple output of the sorted shifts *)
301    var i: TshiftIndex;
302        StoreIndex, BeginStore: TstoreIndex;
303        WordIndex, BeginWord: TwordIndex;
304        word: Tword;
305        cj: char;

307    begin
308      for i:= 1 to ShiftIndex do
309      begin
310        StoreIndex:= Sort[i].StoreIndex;
311        BeginStore:= StoreIndex;
312        WordIndex:= Sort[i].WordIndex;
313        BeginWord:= WordIndex;
314        unpack(Store[StoreIndex], word, 1);
315        cj:= word[WordIndex];
316        repeat
317          if cj <> EndOfLine then write(cj);
318          next(cj, i, StoreIndex, WordIndex, word)
319        until (StoreIndex = BeginStore) and
320              (WordIndex = BeginWord);
321        writeln
322      end
323    end; (* output *)
```

Figure A.1:   (cont'd)

In figure A.1, the various type and variable declarations are contained in the control module. Such is necessary since different modules make use of these types and variables. They are therefore global. In figure A.2, these type and variable declarations are given in the modules that use them. Such is possible because of the application of the information hiding principle. In the second modularization, all information is passed through procedure calls.

```
 1  (* modularisation 2 of the KWIC-index program *)

 3  (* Module 6: Control *)

 5  program kwic2(input, output);

 7  label 1000;

 9  const MaxError = 50;
10          (* max. length of error messages *)

12  type TerrorIndex = 1 .. MaxError;
13       TerrorString = array [TerrorIndex] of char;

15  procedure error(s: TerrorString);
16    begin
17      writeln;
18      writeln(s);
19      goto 1000
20    end;


22  (* main program *)

24  begin
25    ReadInput;
26    PrintOutput;
27  1000:
28  end.

30  (* Module 1: Store *)
31  (* Import: -- *)
32  (* Export: InitStore, CloseStore, PutCharacter, *)
33  (*         Lines, Words, Characters, Character. *)

35  const MaxWord = 10;
36          (* number of characters per word *)
37        MaxStore = 10000;
38          (* max. storage capacity, in words of *)
39          (* MaxWord characters *)
40        MaxLines = 1000;
41          (* max. number of input lines *)
42        MaxWordsPerLine = 20;

44  type TstoreIndex = 1 .. MaxStore;
45       TstoreIndex0 = 0 .. MaxStore;
46       Tstore = array [TstoreIndex] of alfa;
47       TlineIndex = 1 .. MaxLines;
48       TlineIndex0 = 0 .. MaxLines;
49       TwordIndex = 1 .. MaxWord;
50       TwordIndex0 = 0 .. MaxWord;
51       Tword = array [TwordIndex] of char;
52       TwordInfo =
53         record
54           length: integer;
55           StoreIndex: TstoreIndex;
56           WordIndex: TwordIndex
57         end;
58       TnumberOfWordsIndex = 1 .. MaxWordsPerLine;
59       TnumberOfWordsIndex0 = 0 .. MaxWordsPerLine;
60       TlineInfo =
61         record
62           BeginLine: TstoreIndex;
63           NumberOfWords: TnumberOfWordsIndex0;
64           words: array [TnumberOfWordsIndex] of TwordInfo
65         end;
66       Tline = array [TlineIndex] of TlineInfo;

68  var Store: Tstore;
69      Line: Tline;
70      NumberOfLines: TlineIndex0;
```

Figure A.2:   Realization of modularization 2 in Pascal

```
71        LineIndex: integer;
72        WrdIndex: TwordIndex;
73        Word: Tword;

75    procedure StoreWord;
76      begin
77        if LineIndex > MaxStore then error('too much input    ');
78        pack(Word, 1, Store[LineIndex]);
79        LineIndex:= LineIndex + 1;
80        WrdIndex:= 1
81      end; (* store word *)

83    procedure StoreChar(c: char);
84      begin
85        Word[WrdIndex]:= c;
86        if WrdIndex = 10 then StoreWord else WrdIndex:= WrdIndex + 1
87      end; (* store char *)

89    procedure PutCharacter(r, w, c: integer; d: char);
90      begin
91        if (r > NumberOfLines + 1) or (r < NumberOfLines)
92          then error('PutCharacter: parameter r wrong');
93        if r = NumberOfLines + 1 then
94        begin
95          NumberOfLines:= NumberOfLines + 1;
96          with Line[r] do
97          begin
98            BeginLine:= LineIndex + 1;
99            NumberOfWords:= 0
100           end
101       end;

103       with Line[r] do
104       begin
105         if (w > NumberOfWords + 1) or (w < NumberOfWords)
106           then error('PutCharacter: parameter w wrong');
107         if w = NumberOfWords + 1 then
108         begin
109           if NumberOfWords = 20
110             then error('too many words on one line ');
111           NumberOfWords:= NumberOfWords + 1;
112           with words[w] do
113           begin
114             length:= 0;
115             StoreIndex:= LineIndex;
116             WordIndex:= WrdIndex
117           end
118         end
119       end;

121       with Line[r].words[w] do
122       begin
123         if c <> length + 1
124           then error('PutCharacter: parameter c wrong');
125         length:= length + 1;
126         StoreChar(d)
127       end
128     end; (* PutCharacter *)

130   procedure InitStore;
131     begin
132       WrdIndex:= 1;
133       LineIndex:= 1;
134       NumberOfLines:= 0
135     end; (* init store *)

137   procedure CloseStore;
138     begin
139       StoreWord
140     end; (* close store *)
```

Figure A.2:   (cont'd)

```
142  function Lines: integer;
143    begin
144      Lines:= NumberOfLines
145    end (* Lines *);

147  function Words(r: integer): integer;
148    begin
149      if r > NumberOfLines then error('Store: r > number of lines');
150      Words:= Line[r].NumberOfWords
151    end; (* words *)

153  procedure wrd(r, w: integer; var rw: TwordInfo);
154    begin
155      if w > Words(r) then error('Store: w > number of words   ');
156      rw:= Line[r].words[w]
157    end; (* wrd *)

159  function Characters(r, w: integer): integer;
160    var rw: TwordInfo;
161    begin
162      wrd(r, w, rw);
163      Characters:= rw.length
164    end; (* Characters *)

166  function Character(r, w, c: integer): char;
167    var rw: TwordInfo;
168        i, s: integer;
169        Word: Tword;
170    begin
171      wrd(r, w, rw);
172      with rw do
173      begin
174        if c > length then error('Store: c > number of karakters ');
175        i:= c + WordIndex - 1;
176        s:= StoreIndex
177      end;
178        (* now search for the right word *)
179      while i > 10 do
180      begin i:= i - 10; s:= s + 1 end;
181      unpack(Store[s], Word, 1);
182      Character:= Word[i]
183    end; (* Character *)

185  (* Module 2: Input *)
186  (* Import from Store: InitStore, PutCharacter, CloseStore. *)
187  (* Export: -- *)

189  procedure ReadInput;
190    var r, w, c: integer;
191        ch: char;
192    begin
193      InitStore;
194      r:= 1; w:= 1; c:= 1;
195      while not eof do
196      begin
197        while not eoln do
198        begin
199          read(ch);
200          if ch = ' ' then
201          begin w:= w + 1; c:= 1 end
202          else
203          begin PutCharacter(r, w, c, ch); c:= c + 1 end
204        end;
205        read(ch);
206        r:= r + 1; w:= 1; c:= 1
207      end;
208      CloseStore
209    end; (* ReadInput *)

211  (* Module 3: Shift *)
```

Figure A.2:   (cont'd)

```
212  (* Import from Store: Lines, Words, Characters, Character. *)
213  (* Export: InitShift, ShiftLines, ShiftWords, *)
214  (*           ShiftCharacters, ShiftCharacter. *)
215  (* Rather than constructing shifts explicitly, the routines *)
216  (* in this module call the corresponding routines from Store *)


218  var NumberOfShifts: integer;

220  procedure InitShift;
221    var i: integer;
222    begin
223      NumberOfShifts:= 0;
224      for i:= 1 to Lines do
225        NumberOfShifts:= NumberOfShifts + Words(i)
226    end; (* InitShift *)


228  function ShiftToLine(var l: integer): integer;
229    (* ShiftToLine returns the line number containing shift 'l' *)
230    (* and, in 'l', the number of that shift within the line *)
231    var i: integer;
232    begin
233      if l > NumberOfShifts then error('Shift: parameter l wrong');
234      i:= 1;
235      while l > Words(i) do
236      begin l:= l - Words(i); i:= i + 1 end;
237      ShiftToLine:= i
238    end; (* ShiftToLine *)


240  function ShiftCharacter(l, w, c: integer): char;
241    var lineno: integer;
242    begin
243      lineno:= ShiftToLine(l);
244      if w > Words(lineno) then error('Shift: parameter w wrong');
245      w:= l + w - 1;
246      if w > Words(lineno) then w:= w - Words(lineno);
247      ShiftCharacter:= Character(lineno, w, c)
248    end; (* ShiftCharacter *)


250  function ShiftLines: integer;
251    begin
252      ShiftLines:= NumberOfShifts
253    end; (* ShiftLines *)


255  function ShiftWords(l: integer): integer;
256    begin
257      ShiftWords:= Words(ShiftToLine(l))
258    end; (* ShiftWords *)


260  function ShiftCharacters(l, w: integer): integer;
261    var i: integer;
262    begin
263      i:= ShiftToLine(l);
264      if w > Words(i) then error('Shift: parameter w wrong');
265      w:= l + w - 1;
266      if w > Words(i) then w:= w - Words(i);
267      ShiftCharacters:= Characters(i, w)
268    end; (* ShiftCharacters *)


270  (* Module 4: Sorting *)
271  (* Implementation through a simple bubblesort *)
272  (* Import from Shift: ShiftLines, ShiftWords, ShiftCharacters, *)
273  (*                    ShiftCharacter. *)
274  (* Export: InitSort, Ith. *)


276  const MaxSort = 5000;
277          (* max. number of (sorted) shifts *)


279  type Tsort = array [1 .. MaxSort] of integer;


281  var Sort: Tsort;
```

Figure A.2:   (cont'd)

```
283  function GreaterThan(j, k: integer): boolean;
284      (* yields true if and only if the shift in Sort[j] *)
285      (* lexically follows the shift in Sort[k] *)
286  var wj, wk, w, upw, cj, ck, c, upc: integer;
287      charj, chark: char;

289      function min(i, j: integer): integer;
290      begin
291        if i < j then min:= i else min:= j
292      end;

294      begin
295        j:= Sort[j]; k:= Sort[k];
296        wj:= ShiftWords(j); wk:= ShiftWords(k);
297        w:= 1; upw:= min(wj, wk);
298        while w <= upw do
299        begin
300          cj:= ShiftCharacters(j, w); ck:= ShiftCharacters(k, w);
301          c:= 1; upc:= min(cj, ck);
302          while c <= upc do
303          begin
304            charj:= ShiftCharacter(j, w, c);
305            chark:= ShiftCharacter(k, w, c);
306            if charj <> chark then
307            begin
308              GreaterThan:= charj > chark;
309              c:= upc + 1; w:= upw + 2
310                (* to make sure that the final test works correctly *)
311            end
312            else c:= c + 1
313          end;
314          if (w <= upw) and (cj <> ck) then
315          begin
316            GreaterThan:= cj > ck;
317            w:= upw + 2
318          end
319          else w:= w + 1
320        end;
321        if w = upw + 1 then GreaterThan:= wj > wk
322      end; (* GreaterThan *)

324  procedure swap(j, k: integer);
325    var i: integer;
326    begin
327      i:= Sort[j];
328      Sort[j]:= Sort[k];
329      Sort[k]:= i
330    end; (* swap *)

332  procedure InitSort;
333    (* simple bubblesort *)
334    var i, j: integer;
335        finished: boolean;
336    begin
337      if ShiftLines > MaxSort then error('too many shifts  ');
338      for i:= 1 to ShiftLines do
339      begin
340        Sort[i]:= i;
341        j:= i;
342        finished:= false;
343        while not finished do
344          if j = 1 then finished:= true else
345          if GreaterThan(j-1, j) then
346          begin swap(j, j-1); j:= j - 1 end
347          else finished:= true
348      end
349    end; (* InitSort *)

351  function Ith(i: integer): integer;
352    begin
```

Figure A.2:   (cont'd)

```
353     Ith:= Sort[i]
354   end; (* ith *)

356  (* Module 5: Output *)
357  (* Import from Shift, ShiftLines, ShiftWords, *)
358  (*                  ShiftCharacters, ShiftCharacter, *)
359  (*        from Sorting: InitSort, Ith. *)
360  (* Export: -- *)

362  procedure PrintOutput;
363    var i, j, k: integer;
364    begin
365      InitShift;
366      InitSort;
367     .for i:= 1 to ShiftLines do
368      begin
369        for j:= 1 to ShiftWords(Ith(i)) do
370        begin
371          for k:= 1 to ShiftCharacters(Ith(i), j) do
372            write(ShiftCharacter(Ith(i), j, k));
373          write(' ')
374        end;
375        writeln
376      end
377    end; (* PrintOutput *)
```

Figure A.2:   (cont'd)

```
1   (* Module 4: Sorting *)
2   (* Import from Shift: ShiftLines, ShiftWords, *)
3   (*                    ShiftCharacters, ShiftCharacter. *)
4   (* Export: InitSort, Ith. *)

6   const MaxSort = 5000;
7          (* max. number of (sorted) shifts *)

9   type Tsort = array [1 .. MaxSort] of integer;

11  var Sort: Tsort;
12      last: integer;

14  function GreaterThan(j, k: integer): boolean;
15    (* see Figure A.2 *)

17  procedure swap(j, k: integer);
18    (* see Figure A.2 *)

20  procedure InitSort;
21  var i: integer;
22  begin
23    if ShiftLines > MaxSort
24      then error('too many shifts       ');
25    for i:= 1 to ShiftLines do Sort[i]:= i;
26    last:= 0
27  end; (* InitSort *)

29  function Ith(i: integer): integer;
30  (* invariant: Sort[1..last] is sorted and contains the *)
31  (* smallest elements; the rest has not been sorted yet. *)
32  (* last >= i after a call of Ith *)
33  var j, k, smallest: integer;
34  begin
35    if i <= last then Ith:= Sort[i] else
36    begin
37      for j:= last + 1 to i do
38        (* a step to search for the smallest remaining *)
39        (* value and place it at position 'j' *)
40      begin
41        smallest:= j;
42        for k:= j + 1 to ShiftLines do
43        if not GreaterThan(k, smallest) then smallest:= k;
44        swap(j, smallest)
45      end;
46      last:= i;
47      Ith:= Sort[i]
48    end
49  end; (* ith *)
```

Figure A.3:   Alternative sorting module for modularization 2

APPENDIX B
More on Formal Specifications

Formal specification techniques were introduced in chapter 11. We distinguished model-oriented and property-oriented specification techniques. This appendix elaborates on both these techniques.

Section B.1 deals with VDM, a well-known model-oriented specification formalism. Section B.2 contains some example algebraic specifications. Algebraic specifications are the major type of property-oriented specification methods. The algebraic specifications given are obtained by applying the guidelines given in section 11.4.3.

B.1 VDM

VDM stands for Vienna Development Method. It was developed in the early 1970s at the IBM Research Laboratory in Vienna—hence its name. In the early days, VDM was used to formally specify the syntax and semantics of programming languages. Subsequent evolution of the technique has led to two VDM 'schools', a Danish one and an English one. The differences between these schools are marginal. Current standardization efforts by the British Standards Institute try to amalgamate the two schools. We use the notation of [Jones90a, b], which follows this consolidation.

A VDM specification consists of two parts:

- a collection of abstract variables that constitute the internal state of the system;
- a collection of operations to manipulate the state.

The abstract variables are defined in terms of predefined objects. VDM has a number of built-in models, such as the natural numbers (N), positive natural numbers (N_1), booleans (B), real numbers (R), and characters (char). More complicated objects are built using **domain constructors**. VDM provides four such domain constructors:

1. **Sets** Sets are finite, unordered collections of objects. Sets can be enumerated in different ways:

   — explicitly, in {a, b, c},
   — implicitly, in {F(a) | a ∈ A • P(a)}, or
   — inductively, like in (**let** s = {a, b, c} ∪ {F(a) | a ∈ A • P(a)} **in** E(s)).

   A formula S = {F(a) | a ∈ A • P(a)} should be read as: S consists of the elements F(a) for which the condition a ∈ A • P(a) holds. The latter condition in turn stands for: the elements from the set A for which P(a) holds.
   The empty set is denoted by {}.
   The definition (declaration) of a state-variable T which is a set of objects of type X is denoted as T = X-**set**.
   Some of the built-in operations on sets are listed in figure B.1.

2. **Sequences** A sequence is a finite, ordered, collection of objects. The difference between sets and sequences is that sequences are ordered and may contain duplicate elements. Sequences can be enumerated in the same ways as sets, using square brackets ([]) rather than curly ones.
   VDM provides two ways to define sequences. X^* denotes a possibly empty sequence of elements of type X, and X^+ denotes a non-empty sequence of elements of type X.
   Some of the operations on sequences are given in figure B.2.

3. **Maps** Maps represent a mapping from *domain values* to *range values*. Maps look like partial functions. The relation between domain values and range values is explicit, however. We may view a map as a table of (domain, range) values, where a domain value is used as a key to obtain the corresponding range value. Maps may change dynamically, in the sense that both new entries can be added and existing entries can be changed. Maps can be enumerated explicitly, implicitly, or inductively. The denotation of a map contains (domain, value) pairs, and is written as in {a ↦ x, b → y}. Here, a and b are domain values, whereas x and y are range values.
   A map with domain T and range X is denoted as $T \xrightarrow{m} X$.
   Figure B.3 lists a number of operations on maps.

4. **Composite objects** A composite object describes a static aggregation of objects, like a record in Pascal. It describes elements from the Cartesian product of its constituents.

Symbol	Name/meaning
∈	membership
∉	nonmembership
⊂	proper subset
⊆	subset
∪	union
∩	intersection
=	equality
≠	non-equality
card	cardinality, the number of elements in a set

Figure B.1: Some operations on sets

Symbol	Name/meaning
⌢	concatenation of two sequences
hd	head element of a sequence
tl	tail
• (•)	application, i.e., s(i) yields the i-th element of the sequence s
len	length
ind	index set, i.e., for a sequence s, **ind** s yields the set $\{1, 2, \ldots,$ len s$\}$
elems	for a sequence s, **elems** s yields the set $\{s(1), s(2), \ldots,$ s(len s)$\}$
†	sequence override, to change the value of some sequence element. For example, s † $\{1 \mapsto a\}$ assigns a to the first element of s.

Figure B.2: Some operations on sequences

A composite object X with constituents A and B is written as X :: A B. (Note that the Cartesian product symbol × is not written in the type description).

If we have two domains X and Y that are both defined as the Cartesian product A × B, it is normally not possible to decide wether some element (a, b) belongs to X or Y. To make the distinction possible, VDM composite objects are *tagged*. In the context of X, Y :: A B, an element (a, b) of type X is different from an element (a, b) of type Y. We may conceive of these objects as (X, (a, b)) and (Y, (a, b)), respectively.

The fields of a composite object may be labeled, as in

```
date:: day: {1, ..., 31}
      month: {1, ..., 12}
      year:  N
```

Symbol	Name/meaning
dom	domain, i.e., **dom** m yields the set whose elements are the domain values from the map m.
rng	range, i.e., the set whose elements are the range values from the map.
$\cdot(\cdot)$	application, i.e., given a map M: D $\xrightarrow{m}$ R that contains an element (d, r), M(d) yields r.
†	map override. Given two maps M and N, the operation M † N yields a new map which contains all pairs from N plus those pairs from M whose domain value is not in **dom** N. For example, $\{a \mapsto x, b \mapsto y\}$ † $\{a \mapsto t, c \mapsto z\}$ yields the map $\{a \mapsto t, b \mapsto y, c \mapsto z\}$.
$\cup$	map union. The domains of both operands must be disjoint. So $\cup$ is the same as †, except that we know that $\cup$ is commutative, while † is not.
$\lhd$	map restriction. If s is a set and m is a map, s $\lhd$ m is the map of pairs from m whose domain value is in the set s. So s $\lhd$ m can be defined as: $\{d \mapsto m(d) \mid d \in (s \cap \textbf{dom } m)\}$.
$\lessdot$	map deletion. If s is a set and m is a map, s $\lessdot$ m is the map of pairs from m whose domain value is *not* in the set s.

Figure B.3:   Some operations on maps

Symbol	Name/meaning
mk-	make. In the context of T :: A B, an element (a, b) of type T is constructed by mk-T(a, b).
μ	modify. To modify one field of an object, as in μ(date, day $\mapsto$ 12).
field name	selection/projection. If the fields of a composite object are labelled, then those field names can be used to decompose the object. If X is of type date, then day(X) yields the day field of X.

Figure B.4:   Some operations on composite objects

These field names can be used as selector functions to obtain a projection from a composite object to one of its constituents. Some operations on composite objects are given in figure B.4.

We will illustrate the use of VDM in a non-trivial example. The example makes use of all four domain constructors and quite a few of the operations listed above. Since VDM has a rather rich notation, we will have to introduce quite some more as we go along.

The example concerns a library system. In this library, clients can borrow and return books. Since the library may include more than one copy of a given book, we make a careful distinction between a book and a copy of a book. If a client wants to borrow a book all copies of which are on loan, he can make a reservation.

Reservations are taken up on a first-come, first-serve basis. For simplicity's sake we assume that books have one author only. A client may ask for a list of all books by some given author. Finally, both clients and book copies can be added to and removed from the system. Some of the fine points are dealt with in the detailed discussion of the specification.

The full VDM specification for our library system is given in figure B.5. The line numbers are not part of the specification proper, but are used in the annotations to the specification.

The specification can be broken into three parts. Lines 1–15 contain definitions of constants and types that are used in the specification. Lines 16–33 give a definition of the state, its invariants, and the initial value of the state. Lines 34–122 contain the definitions of the various operations and functions.

The type definition part defines `Client`, `Book` and `Reservation` to be composite objects. By labelling the constituents of these objects, they can be selected. We will thus be able to select the address of a client, or the author of a book. `Client_Id` and `Book_Id` range over the set of positive natural numbers. They serve to uniquely identify clients and (copies of) books, respectively. The other types do not play a role at the level of detail we are dealing with and are simply defined to be character sequences.

The state definition part (lines 16–20) defines the information that is to be kept by the system. It includes the clients of the library, its stock of books, an administration of which books are borrowed by whom, and an administration of outstanding reservations. The clients are kept in a set. Since the library may possess multiple copies of the same book we cannot specify the stock of books as a set. It is rather kept in a map. The elements from the domain of this map are by definition disjoint and serve to uniquely identify book copies. The range values then contain the familiar information that is kept about books, such as its author and title. If the library has multiple copies of the same book, then different domain values will map onto the same range value. In a similar way, the information about which books are on loan is kept in a map from (unique) copy identifications to clients. Finally, the reservations are kept in a sequence of (book, client) pairs. The sequencing ensures that reservations can be handled on a first-come, first-serve basis.

Lines 21–27 contain the global invariants that the state has to satisfy. By stating these global invariants once we need not repeat them in the specification of the individual operations. The global invariants can be thought of as global pre- and postconditions, pre- and postconditions which are conjoined to the pre- and postcondition of every operation and function.

The following global invariants are specified:

line 22: Only copies of books that the library possesses can be borrowed.

line 23: Only clients of the library can borrow books.

line 24: Clients of the library are uniquely identifiable by their id.

```
1    values
2      maxBooks = 10 : N₁
3    types
4      Client:: name: Name
5             address: Address
6             id: Client_Id
7      Name = char*
8      Address = char*
9      Client_Id = N₁
10     Book_Id = N₁
11     Book:: author:   Author
12           title: Title
13     Author, Title = char*
14     Reservation:: book: Book
15                  client: Client
```

```
16   state Library of
17     clients: Client-set
18     books: Book_Id ─m→ Book
19     borrowed: Book_Id ─m→ Client
20     reserved: Reservation*
```

```
21   inv-Library (mk-Library(clients, books, borrowed, reserved)) △
22     dom borrowed ⊆ dom books ∧
23     rng borrowed ⊆ clients ∧
24     ¬ (∃ i, j ∈ clients) • (id(i) = id(j) ∧ i ≠ j) ∧
25     (∀ c ∈ clients) • BooksBorrowed(borrowed, c) ≤ maxBooks ∧
26     (∀ r ∈ elems reserved) •
27        (book(r) ∈ rng books ∧ client(r) ∈ clients)
```

```
28   init-Library(mk-Library(clients, books, borrowed, reserved)) △
29     clients = {} ∧
30     books = {} ∧
31     borrowed = {} ∧
32     reserved = []
33   end
```

```
34   operations
35     Borrow (c: Client, b: Book) bi: Book_Id
36        ext rd books: Book_Id ─m→ Book
37           rd clients: Client-set
38           wr borrowed: Book_Id ─m→ Client
39        pre (∃ copy ∈ dom books) •
40           (books(copy) = b ∧ copy ∉ dom borrowed) ∧
41           (c ∈ clients) ∧
42           BooksBorrowed(borrowed, c) < maxBooks
43        post let (copy ∈ dom books) •
44           (books(copy) = b ∧ copy ∉ dom ‾borrowed) in
45              borrowed = ‾borrowed ∪ copy ↦ c ∧ bi = copy
```

Figure B.5:   VDM specification of a library system (*Adapted from J. van Katwijk, Course Notes Software Engineering, University of Delft, 1991.*)

```
46    Return (copy: Book_Id)
47        ext wr borrowed: Book_Id ⟶ᵐ Client
48        pre copy ∈ dom borrowed
49        post borrowed = copy ⩤ ‾borrowed‾
50    AddCopy (b: Book)
51        ext wr books: Book_Id ⟶ᵐ Book
52        post let copy: Book_id • copy ∉ dom ‾books‾ in
53                books = ‾books‾ ∪ {copy ↦ b})
54    RemoveCopy (copy: Book_Id)
55        ext rd borrowed: Book_Id ⟶ᵐ Client
56            wr books: Book_Id ⟶ᵐ Book
57            wr reserved: Reservation*
58        pre (copy ∈ dom books) ∧ (copy ∉ dom borrowed)
59        post books = {copy} ⩤ ‾books‾ ∧
60            if ‾books‾(copy) ∈ rng books
61            then true
62            else reserved = RemoveBookRes(‾books‾(copy), ‾reserved‾)
63    AddClient (c: Client)
64        ext wr clients: Client-set
65        pre c ∉ clients
66        post clients = ‾clients‾ ∪ {c}
67    RemoveClient (c: Client)
68        ext rd borrowed: Book_Id ⟶ᵐ Client
69            wr clients: Client-set
70            rd reserved: Reservation*
71        pre c ∈ clients ∧ BooksBorrowed(borrowed, c) = 0
72        post (clients = ‾clients‾-{c}) ∧
73            (reserved = RemoveClientRes (c, ‾reserved‾))
74    HandleReservation (i: N₁)
75        ext rd clients: Client-set
76            rd books: Book_Id ⟶ᵐ Book
77            wr borrowed: Book_Id ⟶ᵐ Client
78            wr reserved: Reservation*
79        pre i ≤ len reserved ∧
80            ((∃ copy ∈ dom books) •
81                (books(copy) = book(reserved(i)) ∧
82                    copy ∉ dom borrowed)) ∧
83            BooksBorrowed(borrowed, client(reserved(i))) < maxBooks
84        post reserved = ‾reserved‾(1, ..., i-1) ⌢
85                ‾reserved‾(i+1, ..., len ‾reserved‾) ∧
86            let (copy ∈ dom books) •
87                (books(copy) = book(‾reserved‾(i)) ∧
88                    copy ∉ dom ‾borrowed‾) in
89                borrowed = ‾borrowed‾ ∪ {copy ↦ c}
90    AddReservation (b: Book, c: Client)
91        ext rd books: Book_Id ⟶ᵐ Book
92            rd clients: Client-set
93            wr reserved: Reservation*
94        pre b ∈ books ∧ c ∈ clients
95        post reserved = ‾reserved‾ ⌢ mk-Reservation(b, c)
```

Figure B.5: (cont'd)

```
96     ListBooks (a: Author) blist: Book-set
97        ext rd books: Book_Id ---m--> Book
98        post (blist ⊆ rng books) ∧
99           (∀ b ∈ blist) • (author(b) = a) ∧
100          ¬(∃ b ∈ rng books - blist) • (author(b) = a)

101    functions
102       BooksBorrowed: (Book_Id ---m--> Client) × Client -> N

103       BooksBorrowed (bor, c) △
104          card {b | b ∈ dom bor • bor(b) = c}

105       RemoveClientRes : Client × Reservation* -> Reservation*

106       RemoveClientRes (c, res) △
107          if card
108             {a | a ∈ elems res • a = mk-Reservation (-, c)} > 0
109          then let i ∈ ind res in
110             let res(i) = mk-Reservation (-, c) in
111                RemoveClientRes (c, res(1, ..., i-1)⌢
112                   res(i+1, ..., len res))
113          else res

114       RemoveBookRes : Book × Reservation* -> Reservation*

115       RemoveBookRes (b, res) △
116          if card
117             {a | a ∈ elems res • a = mk-Reservation ( b, -)} > 0
118          then let i ∈ ind res in
119             let res(i) = mk-Reservation (b, -) in
120                RemoveBookRes (c, res(1, ..., i-1)⌢
121                   res(i+1, ..., len res))
122          else res
```

Figure B.5: (cont'd)

line 25:   Clients can borrow up to maxBooks (arbitrarily set at 10) books only. The function BooksBorrowed (defined in lines 102-104) determines the number of books borrowed by a given client c.

line 26–27: Reservations can only be made for books that the library possesses. Only clients can reserve books.

The initialization part (lines 28-33) is straightforward. All elements from the state are initially empty.

The specification of the various functions and operations starts at line 34. VDM functions are like mathematical functions: they are expressions that map domain values onto range values. BooksBorrowed is a simple example of a function. VDM operations manipulate the state. We could define these operations as functions too, but then the state variables must be passed as parameters. Such will often necessitate copying large data structures, such as the set of all books from the library. This is not needed if we use operations, which may access these global data structures directly.

For functions, it is customary to first state the signature of the function (as in line 102), and next indicate the names of the parameters (as in line 103). For operations, the definition of the signature and the naming of parameters is usually combined in a procedure heading like notation, as in line 35. This difference in notation is historical and has no further significance.

The operations in our example are specified implicitly. *Implicit* specifications use pre- and postconditions to describe the effect of a function or operation. They require that the function or operation must satisfy the postcondition, given that the precondition is satisfied.

In contrast, *explicit* specifications contain algorithms that tell how the intended effect is obtained. As a simple example of the difference, consider the specification of a function to determine the larger one of two natural numbers. An implicit specification hereof might be the following:

```
max (i: N, j: N) r: N
   pre true
   post (r = i ∨ r = j) ∧ (i ≤ r ∧ j ≤ r)
```

An explicit specification of the same function could be:

```
max: N × N -> N
max(i, j) △
   if i ≤ j then i else j
```

Note that explicit specifications may have preconditions as well. For both implicit and explicit specifications, nothing is assumed if the precondition is not satisfied, i.e., the function or operation is *partial*. If the precondition is true the function or operation is *total*.

All operations in figure B.5 are specified implicitly. The (total) functions `RemoveClientRes` and `RemoveBookRes` (lines 105–122) are specified explicitly. Usually, operations and functions at the higher levels of abstraction are specified implicitly.

Each operation has a heading which includes the parameters of the operation and their types. If the operation returns some value, the name used for that return value is given also, together with its type (as in line 35). Next follows (after the keyword **ext**) a list of constituents of the state that are accessible from the operation. This can be viewed as a list of global variables used by the operation. Constituents that are read-only are prefixed with **rd**, constituents (part of which) can be overwritten by the operation are prefixed with **wr**.

The precondition of operation `Borrow` states that there must be a copy of the requested book which is not yet borrowed by someone (lines 39–40), that the person who requests the book must be a client of the library (line 41), and that the number of books already borrowed by that client has not yet reached the maximum number allowed (line 42). The postcondition selects a copy of the book requested (lines 43–44), updates the state by adding the pair (copy selected, client) to the map of books on loan, and returns the selected copy (line 45).

If an operation manipulates external variables from the state, we must be able to distinguish between the values of these variables before and after the operation is executed. In postconditions, the value of a variable prior to the execution of the operation is therefore marked with a backward-pointing hook (as in $\overleftarrow{\text{borrowed}}$). Line 45 should thus be read as: the new value of borrowed is the old value of borrowed plus the pair (copy, c). In the precondition we can only refer to the value of variables prior to the execution of the operation. In preconditions, these values are always written without the hook.

The specification of Borrow is an example of a non-deterministic, *loose specification*. The specification of an operation is loose if we can construct multiple, semantically different, implementations from it. In the postcondition of Borrow we select **a** copy of the book requested. The postcondition does not specify **which** copy to select if there is more than one. Once implemented, different invocations of this operation in the same state may lead to different results.

The precondition of AddCopy is true and has been left out. The postcondition states that the copy (with an id which does not yet exist) is added to the stock of books (lines 52–53).

The precondition of RemoveCopy states that the copy to be removed should be one from the stock of books, and not be on loan (line 58). Note that the copy to be removed may be the last copy of a given book. In that case, possible outstanding reservations for that book are cancelled by simply removing them from the sequence reserved (line 62).

The precondition of RemoveClient checks that the client about to be removed has returned all his books (line 71). The postcondition ensures that possible outstanding reservations are cancelled (line 73).

The actual removal of outstanding reservations of a given client is handled by the total function RemoveClientRes (lines 105–113). The specification of this function is explicit, and very much looks like an algorithm. It recursively removes reservations of client c until no such reservation remains. The specification of RemoveClientRes is *loose*, since the order in which reservations are removed is not specified. Loose specifications of functions are *underspecified*. Though the order of removals is not specified, the final result will be the same, no matter which implementation is chosen. The specification of RemoveBookRes is very similar to that of RemoveClientRes.

The specification of RemoveClientRes illustrates another VDM-feature, *pattern matching*. RemoveClientRes starts with a check for the number of outstanding reservations for client c. This check in lines 107–108 looks for reservations whose second element is c. It does so through a search for a pattern ("don't care", c), which is written as (-, c).

HandleReservation takes care of a single reservation. Its precondition states that a copy of the book requested must be available (lines 80–82), and that the client in question has not yet borrowed the maximum allowed number of books (line 83). The postcondition tells us that the corresponding reservation has been removed (lines 84–85), and that the map of books on loan has been updated (lines

86–89). (Note that the present specification of `HandleReservation` does not exploit the sequencing aspect of book reservations. It may deal with a reservation i in the presence of an earlier reservation j (i.e., i < j) for the same book.)

The final operation is `ListBooks` (lines 96–100). The postcondition states that the resulting set `blist` is a subset of the available books (line 98), that all books from `blist` have author a (line 99), and that we have not left out any book whose author is a (line 100).

An intriguing question with respect to this example specification is: is it 'correct'? Does it specify the library system we had in mind? Some of the formulas may look terrifying to the uninitiated. They may seem far less intelligible than plain English phrases expressing the very same idea.

A major advantage of formal methods over informal ones is that formal methods force you to reason methodically about each and every aspect of the design. VDM specifications for example give rise to so-called *proof obligations*. An important proof obligation concerns the satisfiability of functions and operations: for any function or operation, some result must exist for each valid input. Trying to prove *satisfiability* is a great help during the development of specifications.

In an earlier version of the library specification for example, line 42 was accidentally left out from the precondition of `Borrow`. As a result, clients could borrow 11 books. This conflicts with part of the state invariant. When trying to prove the satisfiability of `Borrow`, this error was quickly reveiled. Informal methods do not offer this type of support. In implementations derived from such informal specifications, this type of error may go undetected for quite a while.

Obviously, the use of formal methods does not guarantee correctness. Specification and design involve the modeling of a Universe of Discourse. Whether such is done properly can never be proved by formal means. This is why we need validation next to verification.

VDM has more features than can be discussed in this brief space. Two of these deserve at least to be mentioned. VDM does offer an, as yet not fully developed, mechanism to support the modularization of specifications. VDM specifications can be decomposed into modules that each consist of a state description and a collection of functions and operations. Such modules may import elements from other modules and export elements to other modules.

Next to a notation for specifications, VDM also offers a method to guide the development of software. Starting from a high-level specification, successive refinements result in a series of lower-level specifications. Each specification in this series must be proven correct with respect to the previous one. These proof obligations ensure that the final, executable, specification wil be correct as well. VDM distinguishes two types of refinement steps:

- **Data reification** In a data reification step, data types and domains are made more specific by adding implementation details. The term 'reify' is used to emphasize the transition from abstract to concrete data types.

- **Operation decomposition** In an operation decomposition step, implementation details are added to the operations and functions of the specification.

Normally, these refinement steps occur alternatingly. Some reification of a data type is chosen, after which operations and functions are made more specific, followed again by a data reification step, and so on.

For more details on VDM, see [Jones90a].

B.2 SOME EXAMPLE ALGEBRAIC SPECIFICATIONS

Let us recall some of the notions introduced in section 11.4.3. We categorized the operators of an algebraic specification of a data type X into four classes:

1. **Basic constructors** The set of basic constructors contains the operators with range X which are needed to generate each possible element of X.

2. **Extra constructors** This set contains the remaining operators whose range is X.

3. **Basic observers** Let S be the set of operators whose range is not X. The set of basic observers $S1$ is a subset of S such that each operator from S–$S1$ can be expressed in terms of elements from $S1$.

4. **Extra observers** The elements from S–$S1$.

In order to satisfy certain desirable properties, an algebraic specification should be *sufficiently complete*. This means that there is a set of operators F which suffices to generate all possible values of the data type that is being specified. For an algebraic specification of a data type X to be sufficiently complete, the following two facts must be proved:

1. Each closed term with range X which contains an operator not in F, can be rewritten such that we obtain a term which contains only operators from F. This rewriting is to be done using the axioms of the specification. This generating set F is exactly the set of basic constructors introduced before.

2. Each closed term with a range other than X can be rewritten to a term which does not contain an operator with range X. A term which has as its range a data type other than X, has an observer as its outermost operator.

A procedure that leads to an algebraic specification which is sufficiently complete involves the determination of a set of basic constructors and axioms for each observer and extra constructor such that the above proofs can be given (see section 11.4.3). This procedure is next applied to a few examples.

Let us consider the data type `Set` from section 11.4.1, with functions `Create`, `Isempty`, `Insert` and `Isin`. The basic constructors are `Create` and `Insert`. `Isin` and `Isempty` are basic observers. Suppose we want to extend the datatype with functions `Union` and `Intersect`. Both functions have their usual meaning from set theory. The signature of Set will be extended to include those two operations:

```
Union: Set x Set       ->     Set
Intersect: Set x Set ->     Set
```

In order to obtain a sufficiently complete specification we have to add axioms with the following left-hand sides:

```
Union(Create, s)
Union(Insert(s₁, x), s₂)
Intersect(Create, s)
Intersect(Insert(s₁, x), s₂)
```

(Note that we need not separately consider the various possibilities for the second argument of Union and Intersect. For, without considering the structure of the second argument, we may already remove these extra constructors from any term containing them. However, it is not erroneous to separately consider the various possible forms of the second argument. Doing so introduces some redundancy, since the rules will partly overlap. There also is a danger of introducing inconsistencies.)

The axioms could read as follows:

```
Union(Create, s) = s
Union(Insert(s₁, x), s₂) = Insert(Union(s₁, s₂), x)
Intersect(Create, s) = Create
Intersect(Insert(s₁, x), s₂) =
    if Isin(s₂, x) then Insert(Intersect(s₁, s₂), x)
                        else Intersect(s₁, s₂)
```

To clarify these axioms, we may observe the following. For the intersection of a set consisting of a first element x and tail s_1 with a set s_2, we distinguish two cases. If x is a member of s_2, it is also a member of the intersection. We may then proceed by taking the intersection of s_1 and s_2, and add x to the result. If x is not a member of s_2, it is not a member of the intersection either. The result is then simply the intersection of s_1 and s_2.

The second axiom for Insert is much simpler, since the existing axioms

```
Insert(Insert(s, i), j) = Insert(Insert(s, j), i)
```

and

```
Insert(Insert(s, i), i) = Insert(s, i)
```

will take care of the removal of possible duplicates in the union of the two sets.

The proof that a term of the form Union(s_1, s_2) or Intersect(s_1, s_2) can be rewritten to a term which only contains Create and Insert, follows easily by induction on the length of s_1.

Our second example concerns a sorted list `Slist`. Its signature is given in figure B.6.

```
type Slist;
operators
   Create:                    -> Slist
   Cons: Item x Slist         -> Slist
   Isin: Item x Slist         -> Boolean
   Isempty: Slist             -> Boolean
   Add: Item x Slist          -> Slist
   Delete: Item x Slist       -> Slist
   Merge: Slist x Slist       -> Slist
```

Figure B.6: Signature of `Slist`

Here, `Cons` is a function which cannot be directly called by the user. `Cons` and `Create` are the basic observers. Any non-empty sorted list can be written as $\text{Cons}(x_n, \text{Cons}(x_{n-1}, \ldots, \text{Cons}(x_1, \text{Create}) \ldots)$, where $x_n \geq x_{n-1} \geq \ldots \geq x_1$. If the user wants to add an `Item` to a sorted list, he calls `Add`. Internally, i.e. hidden to the user, `Add` will invoke `Cons`. The axioms for this specification may look as in figure B.7.

```
Isin(x, Create) = false
Isin(x, Cons(y, s)) = if x = y then true else Isin(x, s)
Isempty(Create) = true
Isempty(Cons(y, s)) = false
Add(x, Create) = Cons(x, Create)
Add(x, Cons(y, s)) = if x ≥ y then Cons(x, Cons(y, s))
       else Cons(y, Add(x, s))
Delete(x, Create) = Create
Delete(x, Cons(y, s)) =
   if x = y then s else Cons(y, Delete(x, s))
Merge(Create, s) = s
Merge(s, Create) = s
Merge(Cons(x, s₁), Cons(y, s₂)) =
   if x ≥ y then Cons(x, Merge(s₁, Cons(y, s₂)))
       else Cons(y, Merge(Cons(x, s₁), s₂))
```

Figure B.7: Axioms for `Slist`

An axiom `Merge(Create, Create) = Create` is not needed here, since it is induced by the other axioms for `Merge`. Also here, we must take care not to introduce inconsistencies. If the above scheme contains an axiom `Merge(Create, s) = s'`, with s ≠ s', then a term `Merge(Create, Create)` could be rewritten to different terms, using different axioms.

Again, rewriting terms so that the result contains only basic constructors or no operators with range `Slist` at all, can be easily shown by induction. For a term of the form `Merge(s₁, s₂)`, for instance, such can be done by induction on the sum of the number of occurrences of `Create` and `Cons` in s_1 and s_2.

Our final example concerns a binary search tree `Tree`, with the signature given in figure B.8.

```
type Tree;
operators
    Create:                          -> Tree
    Make: Tree × Item × Tree    -> Tree
    Left: Tree                       -> Tree
    Right: Tree                      -> Tree
    GetItem: Tree                    -> Item
    Isin: Item × Tree                -> Boolean
    Isempty: Tree                    -> Boolean
    Add: Item × Tree                 -> Tree
    Delete: Item × Tree              -> Tree
```

Figure B.8: Signature of `Tree`

```
Left(Create) = Create
Left(Make(t₁, x, t₂)) = t₁
Right(Create) = Create
Right(Make(t₁, x, t₂)) = t₂
GetItem(Create) = NullItem
GetItem(Make(t₁, x, t₂)) = x
Isin(x, Create) = false
Isin(Make(t₁, x, t₂)) =
    if x < y then Isin(x, t₁) else
    if x = y then true else Isin(x, t₂)
Isempty(Create) = true
Isempty(Make(t₁, x, t₂)) = false
Add(x, Create) = Make(Create, x, Create)
Add(x, Make(t₁, y, t₂)) =
    if x < y then Make(Add(x, t₁), y, t₂) else
    if x = y then Make(t₁, y, t₂)
    else Make(t₁, y, Add(x, t₂))
Delete(x, Create) = Create
Delete(x, Make(t₁, y, t₂)) =
    if x < y then Make(Delete(x, t₁), y, t₂) else
    if x > y then Make(t₁, y, Delete(x, t₂)) else
    if Isempty(t₁) then t₂ else
    if Isempty(t₂) then t₁ else
    Make(t₁, Leftmost(t₂), Minusleftmost(t₂))
Leftmost(Make(t₁, x, t₂)) =
    if Isempty(t₁) then x else Leftmost(t₁)
Minusleftmost(Make(t₁, x, t₂)) = if Isempty(t₁) then t₂
    else Make(Minusleftmost(t₁), x, t₂)
```

Figure B.9: Axioms for `Tree`

Again, Make(t$_1$, x, t$_2$) is a function not available to the user. The user will call Add to include an element in the search tree. Make is used internally. It is only used if both t$_1$ and t$_2$ are binary search trees, all elements from t$_1$ are less than x, and all elements from t$_2$ are greater than x. Create and Make are the basic constructors. A possible set of axioms is given in figure B.9.

Here, we see that the axioms for Delete make use of extra (hidden) functions Leftmost and Minusleftmost. If we remove a root of some subtree, that node has to be replaced by some other node. If either of its children is the empty tree, it is easy. Otherwise, the smallest element of its right subtree replaces the root. (Alternatively, we could have chosen the largest element from the left subtree.)

Note that the axioms for Delete are algorithmic in character. They closely mimic the well-known algorithm for node deletion in a binary search tree, as it is found in standard texts on data structures. This phenomenon occurs fairly often if we try to algebraically specify dynamic data structures.

APPENDIX C
ISO 9001: Quality Systems

ISO 9001 lists the following ingredients for a quality system[*]:

1. **Management responsibility** It is the management's responsibility to formulate the quality policy, to provide for an adequate organization of the quality system, and to conduct reviews of the quality system. Firstly, the supplier's management has to define and document its policy and objectives for, and commitment to, quality. The organization of the quality system includes a specification of the responsibility, authority and interrelation of all personnel involved, as well as the identification of verification requirements, the provision of resources and the assignment of trained personnel. Finally, the quality system adopted has to be reviewed on a regular basis to ensure its continuing suitability.

2. **Quality system** The product's conformity to requirements is to be ensured through a quality system. This is done through a set of procedures and instructions, to be prepared and implemented by the supplier.

3. **Contract review** Procedures have to be established for contract reviews. Contract reviews address the following issues:
   — requirements must be adequately defined and documented;
   — requirements differing from those in the tender must be resolved;
   — the supplier should be capable of meeting the contractual requirements.

4. **Design control** Procedures must be established to control and verify that the design meets its requirements. This includes procedures for planning design

---

[*] Reproduced by permission of ISO.

activities, identification and documentation of design input and output requirements, design verification and design changes.

5. **Document control** All documents and data that relate to this standard must be controlled. Changes to documents must be recorded and approved.

6. **Purchasing** The supplier must ensure that purchased products conform to the requirements. Amongst others, this includes an assessment of subcontractors.

7. **Purchaser supplied products** Products supplied by the purchaser must also be verified.

8. **Product identification and traceability** The supplier must have procedures to identify products. For traceability purposes, products must have a unique identification.

9. **Process control** The production and installation processes that affect product quality must be identified and carried out under controlled procedures.

10. **Inspection and testing** Incoming products must be inspected or verified before they are used. The product itself must be tested as required by the quality plan or other documented procedures.

11. **Inspection, measuring and test equipment** This equipment must be controlled and maintained. Test software must be checked to prove that it is capable of verifying the acceptability of the product.

12. **Inspection and test status** The inspection and test status of the product must be identified. Records should identify the inspection authority responsible for the release of the conforming product.

13. **Control of nonconforming product** Procedures must be established to ensure that a product which does not conform to the specifications is not inadvertently used or installed.

14. **Corrective action** The supplier should establish procedures for:
    — investigating the cause of nonconforming product and the corrective actions needed to prevent recurrence;
    — analyzing quality records, customer complaints and the like to detect and eliminate potential causes of nonconforming products;
    — initiating preventive actions to deal with problems to a level corresponding to the risks encountered;
    — applying controls to ensure that corrective actions are taken and that they are effective;
    — implementing and recording changes in procedures resulting from corrective actions.

15. **Handling, storage, packaging and delivery** Procedures for handling, storage, packaging and delivery of the product must be established and documented.

16. **Quality records** Procedures for identification, collection, indexing, filing, storage, maintenance and disposition of quality records must be established.

17. **Internal quality audits** A comprehensive system of planned and documented internal quality audits must be carried out to verify whether quality activities comply with planned arrangements and to determine the effectiveness of the quality system.

18. **Training** Procedures must be established for identifying the training needs and provide for the training of all personnel performing activities affecting quality.

19. **Servicing** Where servicing is specified in a contract, procedures must be established to ensure that it meets the requirements.

20. **Statistical techniques** Where appropriate, procedures must be established for identifying appropriate statistical techniques.

APPENDIX D
IEEE Standard 730: Software Quality Assurance Plans

IEEE Standard 730 specifies the following constituents for a software quality assurance plan:[*]

1. **Purpose** What is the purpose of this quality assurance plan? For which product(s) is it intended?

2. **References** Which other documents are referred to in this plan?

3. **Management** What are the tasks and responsibilities of the project's management and how is this management organized. The key parts of the project's organization and the responsibilities of the key roles are dealt with as well. One has carefully to delineate dependencies between people involved in development and those in charge of quality assurance. The tasks of the quality assurance team should be indicated, together with the order in which these tasks will be executed.

4. **Documentation** One has to indicate which documents will be produced in the course of the project, and in which way the quality of these documents will be assessed. This documentation encompasses at least the following: requirements specification, a description of the design, test plan, test report and user documentation. One has to specify the format and content of each of these documents.

---

[*] Reproduced by permission of IEEE.

5. **Standards** Which standards for coding, documentation, etc., will be used? One should also indicate how compliance with these items is assured.

6. **Reviews and audits** Under this heading is indicated how the technical and organizational assessment will take place. Technical assessment concerns the way in which verification and validation activities will be carried out in the various phases. Organizational assessment concerns the execution of the quality assurance plan.

7. **Software configuration management** How will the various documents be controlled and how will change requests be handled. Tools that are used to support this task are to be identified. If a separate software configuration plan is used (for instance the one discussed in chapter 4), a reference to that document suffices.

8. **Problem reporting and corrective action** Which procedures are being followed for reporting, tracking and resolving problems, and who is responsible for the implementation hereof.

9. **Tools, techniques and methodologies** Which tools, techniques and methodologies are used to determine whether or not the quality criteria are being met. Possible tools include debuggers, structure analyzers and test drivers. Possible techniques include formal verification, inspections and walkthroughs. Many of these have been elaborated upon in the chapter on testing.

10. **Code control** How are the different versions of the product stored and maintained. Once a baseline has been established, careful procedures for changing and protection of the associated documents is needed. If a configuration control plan is used, this is probably handled in that document.

11. **Media control** The physical protection against unauthorized access and damage is described here.

12. **Supplier control** Software written or delivered by others should also meet the quality criteria set for this project. How is the quality of this third-party software assessed?

13. **Records collection, maintenance, and retention** In which way is quality assurance documented, protected, maintained and preserved?

APPENDIX E
IEEE Standard 830: Software Requirements Specifications

The various components of IEEE Standard 830 should provide the following information:[*]

1. **Introduction** This section contains an overview of the complete document.

   1.1. **Purpose** What is the purpose of this document, and for whom is it written?

   1.2. **Scope** An identification of the product to be developed, what does it do (and what does it not do), why is the product being developed (including a precise description of its benefits, goals and objectives)?

   1.3. **Definitions, acronyms and abbreviations** This subsection contains definitions of all the terms, acronyms and abbreviations used in the document. Special attention should be paid to the clarification of terms and concepts from the domain of application.

   1.4. **References** References to all documents that are referred to in the remainder of the requirements specification.

   1.5. **Overview** This subsection contains an outline of the remainder of the document.

---

[*] Reproduced by permission of IEEE.

2. **General description** This section contains a description of matters that concern the overall product and its requirements. It provides a perspective for understanding the specific requirements from section 3 of this document.

2.1. **Product perspective** Does it concern an independent product or is it part of a larger product? In the latter case, the other components should be identified, and the interfaces with those components should be described. In this section, we also give an identification of the hardware to be used.

2.2. **Product functions** An overview of the functions of the system to be delivered. This should be confined to an overview. A detailed discussion of the functions is given in section 3 of the requirements specification.

2.3. **User characteristics** An indication of general user characteristics, in as far as these are relevant for the requirements specification. Experience, training and technical expertise of future users may influence specific requirements of the system to be developed.

2.4. **General constraints** An indication of any other constraints that apply. These may concern government regulations, hardware constraints, security regulations, and so on. Again, we are concerned with the rationale at this point. A further elaboration follows in section 3 of this document.

2.5. **Assumptions and dependencies** This does not concern constraints on the system to be developed, but things which may influence the requirements specification once they change. As an example, we may think of the availability of certain supporting software, such as some given operating system or a numeric library. If that operating system or library turns out not to be available, the requirements specification will have to be adapted accordingly.

3. **Specific requirements** This section contains all the details which are relevant for the design phase to follow. The ordering given here is just one way to present the specific requirements in a logical way. Specific requirements should be such that one may objectively determine whether they are fulfilled or not.

3.1. **Functional requirements** In this subsection, a description is given of how the transformation of inputs to outputs is achieved. The description is given for each class of functions, and sometimes for each individual function. To a certain extent, this description can be seen as a solution to the user. This component of the requirement specification is the main starting point for the design phase.

3.1.1. **Functional requirement 1**

3.1.1.1. **Introduction** A description of the purpose of this function and the approaches and techniques used. The introduction should include information to clarify the intent of the function.

3.1.1.2. **Inputs** A precise description of the function's inputs (source, quantities, range of acceptable values, and the like).

3.1.1.3. **Processing** A definition of the operations that must be performed, such as checking for acceptable values, reaction to abnormal situations, or a description of algorithms to be used. As an example of the latter, one may think of the use of some mathematical model for strength computations within a CAD-program.

3.1.1.4. **Outputs** A precise description of the outputs (destination, quantities, error messages, and the like).

3.2. **External interface requirements**

3.2.1. **User interfaces** A description of the characteristics of the user interfaces, such as screen layout, function keys, help functions. In order to support testing, verifiable requirements regarding learning time for the system functions should be included either here or in some subsection of 3.5 (Attributes).

3.2.2. **Hardware interfaces** A description of the logical characteristics of hardware interfaces, such as interface protocols, or screen-oriented versus line-oriented terminal control.

3.2.3. **Software interfaces** A description of software needed, such as a certain operating system or subroutine package. Interfaces to other application software is also discussed here.

3.2.4. **Communications interfaces** An example is a communication protocol for LANs.

3.3. **Performance requirements** Performance requirements encompass both static and dynamic requirements. Static requirements concern, amongst others, the number of terminals to be connected and the number of users that can be handled concurrently. Dynamic requirements concern the operational performance of the system: how frequently will certain functions be called for and how fast should the system's reaction be. It is important that these requirements be stated in measurable terms.

3.4. **Design constraints** Design constraints may result from such things as the prescribed use of certain standards or hardware.

3.4.1. **Standards compliance** Which existing standards or regulations must be followed, and what requirements result from these. For example, certain report formats or audit procedures may be prescribed.

3.4.2. **Hardware limitations** A description of the characteristics of the hardware environment, in as far as they lead to software requirements. An example of this might be the amount of memory available.

3.5. **Attributes** In this section, particular attention is paid to quality aspects. These requirements must be measurable and verifiable. They must be stated in objective terms (see also chapter 6). The subsections below by no means comprise a complete list of such attributes.

3.5.1. **Availability** Factors that guarantee a certain level of availability, such as restart procedures. In this subsection we may also enlist requirements regarding fault tolerancy (with respect to both hardware failures and software failures).

3.5.2. **Security** Requirements regarding unauthorized access and other forms of misuse. Certain cryptographic techniques may be prescribed, and we may put constraints on the communication between different parts of the system.

3.5.3. **Maintainability** Requirements to guarantee a certain level of maintainability of the system, such as a maximum allowable coupling between components.

3.6. **Other requirements** A description of requirements that are specific to certain software, and which have not been discussed yet.

APPENDIX F
IEEE Standard 1012: Software Verification and Validation Plans

The various constituents of IEEE 1012, the Software Verification and Validation (V&V) Plan, contain the following information:*

1. **Purpose** The purpose and scope of this plan. This includes the project for which the plan is written, the product items covered, and the goals of the V&V effort.

2. **Referenced documents** Documents referenced by this plan are identified, as well as documents that supplement or implement this plan. Examples of such related documents are the Quality Assurance Plan and Unit Test Plan.

3. **Definitions** The acronyms and notations used are explained. A definition of all terms is given, or a reference to a document which defines these terms.

4. **Verification and validation overview**

   4.1. **Organization** This section describes the organization of the test effort. It describes the relationships with other efforts, such as development, project management, and quality assurance. It defines the lines of communication within the V&V effort, the authority to resolve issues, and the authority to approve test products. For example, different test tasks, such as unit testing and integration testing, may be handled by

---
* Reproduced by permission of IEEE.

different groups. Results from one such task must be communicated to the relevant parties. A discrepancy between, say, some test results and the requirements specification may be due to a fault in either the software or the requirements specification. It must be clear where the authority lies which resolves such issues.

4.2. **Master schedule** This section describes the project's life cycle, its milestones and completion dates. This information can be copied from the project plan. It gives a summary of verification and validation tasks, and describes how the results of these tasks provide feedback to the development process. The description used here assumes a waterfall-like mode of operation. A different process model may necessitate adaptations in subsequent sections of this document. V&V efforts are highly iterative. Faults detected result in documents or products being updated, whereafter that V&V task is repeated. Enhancements or other changes to products under development result in iterations as well.

4.3. **Resources summary** This section summarizes the resources needed for verification and validation (personnel, tools, special requirements such as access rights, etc.). The planning of these resources should be done with care; projects tend to get under pressure, and V&V efforts tend to get the worst of it.

4.4. **Responsibilities** In this section, the organizational elements responsible for performing V&V tasks are identified. Since these responsibilities are also given for each of the development phases, a summary may suffice here.

4.5. **Tools, techniques and methodologies** The specific tools, techniques and methodologies for V&V tasks are identified. Each of these may require acquisition, training, or support, and the plan should include information on these aspects as well.

5. **Life-cycle verification and validation** This section contains the detailed verification and validation plan. In each of its subsections, the following topics must be addressed:

— *Verification and validation tasks* The identification of tasks for this phase. The contribution of these tasks to the overall goals of verification and validation should be stated. For each phase, Standard 1012 gives minimum tasks required for critical systems as well as a number of optional V&V tasks. Many of these tasks have been discussed in section 13.2. The required documentation for these tasks is indicated as well. Note that specific documents, for example those covering test designs, may be contributed to by tasks in different life-cycle phases.

— *Methods and criteria* The methods and procedures for performing each task are identified, together with the criteria used to evaluate the results. For example, the design evaluation task could be done using a review process, which involves certain rules for setting up meetings and procedures to follow up the results of such meetings.

— *Inputs/outputs* A specification of the input and output for each task. The input of a design evaluation for example is some design document. The output of this task includes documents like anomaly reports that provide feedback to both management and the development process.

— *Schedule* The schedule for V&V tasks, in particular the milestones for initiating and completing tasks, are listed under this entry.

— *Resources* The resources for performing tasks (personnel, training, tools, computer usage, etc.). A summary of resource requirements is given in section 4.3 of this plan.

— *Risks and assumptions* The risks and assumptions may relate to the schedule, resources, or approach. For example, we might have assumed that unit testing will start on a certain date and that certain qualified personnel will then be available. The V&V plan should specify a contingency plan for the case that such assumptions prove not to hold.

— *Roles and responsibilities* The organizational elements or individuals responsible for performing tasks must be identified. For each task, a specific responsibility should be assigned.

5.1. **Management of V&V** The management of V&V spans all phases of the development life cycle. Since software development tends to be iterative, and changes or enhancements necessitate iterations, V&V activities have to be reperformed as well.

5.2. **Requirements phase V&V** During the requirements phase, the requirements themselves are evaluated. Furthermore, plans for system and acceptance testing are generated at this stage.

5.3. **Design phase V&V** During the design phase, the design itself is tested. More detailed plans for unit and integration testing are developed.

5.4. **Implementation phase V&V** At this stage, the source code is evaluated. Test cases and test procedures for the various forms of testing are developed. In Standard 1012, this phase includes unit testing.

5.5. **Test phase V&V** The test phase encompasses integration, system and acceptance testing.

5.6. **Installation and checkout phase V&V** If the software is to be installed on a different configuration, that configuration package must be tested. This phase also includes making a summary of V&V activities and results.

5.7. **Operation and maintenance V&V** Modifications, enhancements and other changes must be treated as development activities and therefore require reperforming certain V&V tasks along the lines prescribed in this plan. Part of the activities that go under this heading (such as the handling of change requests) may also be covered by the Configuration Management Plan.

6. **Software verification and validation reporting** This section describes how the results of verification and validation activities are documented and reported. Examples of V&V reports include: task reports that document results and status of V&V tasks, phase summary reports to be delivered at the end of each phase, reports that describe anomalies detected, and a final report that gives a summary of the complete V&V effort.

7. **Verification and validation administrative procedures**

   7.1. **Anomaly reporting and resolution** Methods for reporting and resolving anomalies detected are given under this heading.

   7.2. **Task iteration policy** This section describes criteria used to determine the extent to which V&V tasks must be reperformed when their input changes. For example, depending on the type of change or the criticality of a system component, updating a design document may require certain V&V tasks to be reperformed.

   7.3. **Deviation policy** Specific procedures are needed for possible deviations of this plan. The possible effect of such deviations on system quality must be indicated. This section also identifies the authority for approving such deviations.

   7.4. **Control procedures** Like anything else, V&V efforts must be controlled as well. This section may refer back to plans for configuration control and quality assurance.

   7.5. **Standards, practices and conventions** Standards, practices and conventions that apply to the V&V effort are identified in this section.

References

[Abbott81] R.J. Abbott & D.K. Moorhead, Software requirements and specifications: a survey of needs and languages, *Journal of Systems and Software* **2** (1981) 297–316.

[Abbott90] R.J. Abbott, Resourceful systems for fault tolerance, reliability, and safety, *ACM Computing Surveys* **22**, 1 (1990) 35–68.

[Abdel-Ghaly86] A.A. Abdel-Ghaly, P.Y. Chan & B. Littlewood, Evaluation of competing software reliability predictions, *IEEE Transactions on Software Engineering* **12**, 9 (1986) 950–967.

[Abdel-Hamid86] T.K. Abdel-Hamid & S.E. Madnick, Impact of schedule estimation on software project behavior, *IEEE Software* **3**, 4 (1986) 70–75.

[Abdel-Hamid88] T.K. Abdel-Hamid, Understanding the '90% syndrome' in software project management: A simulation-based case study, *Journal of Systems and Software* **8**, 4 (1988) 319–330.

[Ackerman89] A.F. Ackerman, L.S. Buchwald & F.H. Lewski, Software inspections: an effective verification process, *IEEE Software* **6**, 3 (1989) 31–36.

[Ada83] *Reference Manual for the Ada Programming Language*, ANSI-MIL-STD 1815A, 1983.

[AdaMeth83] DoD, Ada Joint Program Office, Ada methodologies: concepts and requirements, *ACM SigSoft Software Engineering Notes* **8**, 1 (1983) 33–50.

[Adrion82] W.R. Adrion, M.A. Branstad & J.C. Cherniavski, Validation, verification, and testing of computer software, *ACM Computing Surveys* **14**, 2 (1982) 159–182.

[Agresti86] W.W. Agresti, The conventional software life-cycle model: its evolution and assumptions, in *New Paradigms for Software Development*, W.W. Agresti (Ed.), IEEE/North-Holland (1986) pp. 2–5.

[Akima89] N. Akima & F. Ooi, Industrializing software development: a Japanese approach, *IEEE Software* **6**, 2 (1989) 13–21.

[Alavi84] M. Alavi, An assessment of the prototyping approach to information systems development, *Communications of the ACM* **27**, 6 (1984) 556–563.

[Alavi91] M. Alavi & J.C. Whetherby, Mixing prototyping and data modeling for information system design, *IEEE Software* **8**, 3 (1991) 86–91.

[Albrecht79] A.J. Albrecht, Measuring applications development productivity, *Proceedings Application Development Symposium*, SHARE/GUIDE (1979) pp. 83–92.

[Albrecht83] A.J. Albrecht & J.E. Gaffney, Software function, source lines of code, and development effort prediction: a software science validation, *IEEE Transactions on Software Engineering* **9**, 6 (1983) 639–648.

[Alford77] M.W. Alford, A requirements engineering methodology for real-time processing requirements, *IEEE Transactions on Software Engineering* **3**, 1 (1977) 60–69.

[Alvey85] An Alvey survey: advanced information technology in the UK, *Future Generations Computer Systems* **1**, 1 (1985) 69–78.

[Ambler89] A. Ambler & M.M. Burnett, Influence of visual technology on the evolution of language environments, *IEEE Computer* **22**, 10 (1989) 9–24.

[van Amstel89] J.J. van Amstel & J.A.A.M. Poirters, *The Design of Data Structures and Algorithms*, Prentice-Hall, 1989.

[Anderson79] T. Anderson & B. Randell (Eds), *Computing Systems Reliability*, Cambridge University Press, 1979.

[Andrews83] C.L. Andrews & W.R. Dehaan, RXVP80: The verification and validation system for FORTRAN and COBOL, *Proceedings SOFTFAIR: A Conference on Software Development Tools, Techniques, and Alternatives*, IEEE Computer Society Press (1983) pp. 38–47.

[Appleby91] D. Appleby, *Programming Languages: Paradigm and Practice*, McGraw-Hill, 1991.

[Arango89] G. Arango, Domain analysis—from art to engineering discipline, Proceedings 5th International Workshop on Software Specification and Design, *ACM SigSoft Software Engineering Notes* **14**, 3 (1989) 152–159.

[Arthur85] L.J. Arthur, *Measuring Programmer Productivity and Software Quality*, Wiley, 1985.

[Baber82] R.L. Baber, *Software Reflected*, North-Holland Publishing Company, 1982.

[Babich86] W.A. Babich, *Software Configuration Management*, Addison-Wesley, 1986.

[Backus78] J.Backus, Can programming be liberated from the von Neumann style? A functional style and its algebra of programs, *Communications of the ACM* **21**, 8 (1978) 613–641.

[Baecker87] R.M. Baecker & W.A.S. Buxton (Eds), *Readings in Human–Computer Interaction*, Morgan Kaufmann, 1987.

[Baecker88] R. Baecker, Enhancing program readability and comprehensibility with tools for program visualization, *Proceedings 10th International Conference on Software Engineering* (1988) pp. 356–366.

[Bailey81] J.W. Bailey & V.R. Basili, A meta-model for software development resource expenditures, *Proceedings 5th International Conference on Software Engineering*, IEEE (1981) pp. 107–116.

[Baker72] F.T. Baker, Chief Programmer team management of production programming, *IBM System Journal* 11, 1 (1972) 56–73.

[Balda90] D.M. Balda & D.A. Gustafson, Cost estimation models for the reuse and prototype software development life cycles, *SigSoft Software Engineering Notes* **15**, 3 (1990) 42–50.

[Balzer83] R. Balzer, T.E. Cheatham, Jr. & C. Green, Software technology in the 1990s: using a new paradigm, *IEEE Computer* **16**, 11 (1983) 39–45.

[Banker89] R.D. Banker & C.F. Kemerer, Scale economies in new software development, *IEEE Transactions on Software Engineering* **15**, 10 (1989) 1199–1205.

[Baram89] G. Baram & G. Steinberg, Selection criteria for analysis and design CASE tools, *ACM SigSoft Software Engineering Notes* **14**, 6 (1989) 73–80.

[Barbacci85] M.R. Barbacci et al., The Software Engineering Institute: bridging practice and potential, *IEEE Software* **2**, 6 (November 1985) 4–21.

[Barfield86] W. Barfield, Expert-novice differences for software: implications for problem-solving and knowledge acquisition, *Behaviour and Information Technology* **5**, 1 (1986) 15–29.

[Barnard86] H.J. Barnard, R.F. Metz & A.L. Price, A recommended practice for describing software designs: IEEE Standards Project 1016, *IEEE Transactions on Software Engineering* **12**, 2 (1986) 258–263.

[Barnes91] B.H. Barnes & T.B. Bollinger, Making reuse cost-effective, *IEEE Software* **8**, 1 (1991) 13–24.

[Barstow84] D. Barstow, H. Shrobe & E. Sandewall (Eds), *Interactive Programming Environments*, McGraw-Hill, 1984.

[Basili80a] V.R. Basili, Product metrics, **in** V.R. Basili (Ed.), *Tutorial on Models and Metrics for Software Management and Engineering*, IEEE, 1980, pp. 214–217.

[Basili80b] V.R. Basili (Ed.), *Tutorial on Models and Metrics for Software Management and Engineering*, IEEE, 1980.

[Basili83] V.R. Basili, R.W. Selby, Jr. & T.-Y. Philips, Metric analysis and data validation across Fortran projects, *IEEE Transactions on Software Engineering* **9**, 6 (1983) 652–663.

[Basili87] V.R. Basili & R.W. Selby, Comparing the effectiveness of software testing strategies, *IEEE Transactions on Software Engineering* **13**, 12 (1987) 1278–1296.

[Basili90] V.R. Basili, Viewing maintenance as reuse-oriented software development, *IEEE Software* **7**, 1 (1990) 19–25.

[Bauer89] F.L. Bauer, B. Moeller, H. Partsch & P. Pepper, Formal program construction by transformations: computer-aided, intuition-guided programming, *IEEE Transactions on Software Engineering* **15**, 2 (1989) 165–180.

[Bazelmans85] R. Bazelmans, Evolution of configuration management, *ACM SigSoft Software Engineering Notes* **10**, 5 (1985) 37–46.

[Beizer90] B. Beizer, *Software Testing Techniques*, second edition, Van Nostrand Reinhold, 1990.

[Belady85] L.A. Belady, *New Software Engineering Programs—Worldwide*, Proceedings 8th International Conference on Software Engineering, IEEE (1985) pp. 128–130.

[Benander90] B.A. Benander, N. Gorla & A.C. Benander, An empirical study of the use of the GOTO statement, *Journal of Systems and Software* **11**, 3 (1990) 217–223.

[Benington56] H.D. Benington, *Production of Large Computer Programs*, Proceedings ONR Symposium (1956), reprinted in *Annals of the History of Computing* **5**, 4 (1983) 350–361.

[Bennett91] K.H. Bennett, Automated support for software maintenance, *Information and Software Technology* **33**, 1 (1991) 74–85.

[Bergland81] G.D. Bergland & R.D. Gordon, *Tutorial: Software Design Strategies*, IEEE Catalog nr. EZ389, 1981.

[Bergstra82] J.A. Bergstra & J.V. Tucker, The completeness of the algebraic specification methods for computable data types, *Information and Control* **54**, 3 (1982) 186–200.

[Bergstra83] J.A. Bergstra & J.V. Tucker, Initial and final algebra semantics for data type specifications: two characterisation theorems, *SIAM Journal of Computing* **12**, 2 (1983) 366–387.

[Bergstra89] J.A. Bergstra, J. Heering & P. Klint (Eds), *Algebraic Specification*, Addison-Wesley, 1989.

[Bersoff80] E.H. Bersoff, V.D. Henderson & S.G. Siegel, *Software Configuration Management*, Prentice-Hall, 1980.

[Berztiss83] A.T. Berztiss & S. Thatte, Specification and implementation of abstract data types, **in** *Advances in Computers*, Vol. 22, M.C. Yovits (Ed.) (1983) pp. 295–353.

[Bewley83] W.L. Bewley, T.L. Roberts, D. Schroit & W.L. Verplank, Human factors testing in the design of Xerox's 8010 "Star" office workstation, *Proceedings of CHI '83*, ACM (1983) pp. 72–77.

[Biggerstaff87] T. Biggerstaff & C. Richter, Reusability, framework, assessment and directions, *IEEE Software* **4**, 2 (1987) 41–49.

[Biggerstaff89a] T.J. Biggerstaff & A.J. Perlis (Eds) *Software Reusability, Volume I: Concepts and Models, Volume II: Applications and Experience*, Addison-Wesley, 1989.

[Biggerstaff89b] T.J. Biggerstaff, Design recovery for maintenance and reuse, *IEEE Computer* **22**, 7 (1989) 36–50.

[Birkhoff70] G. Birkhoff & J.D. Lipson, Heterogeneous algebras, *Journal of Combinatorial Theory*, Series A8 (1970) 115–133.

[Birtwistle73] G.M. Birtwistle, O.J. Dahl, B. Myhrhaug & K. Nygaard, *Simula BEGIN*, Auerbach Publishers, 1973.

[Björner82] D. Björner & C.B. Jones, *Formal Specification and Software Development*, Prentice-Hall, 1982.

[Blaschek89] G. Blaschek, G. Pomberger & A. Stritzinger, A comparison of object-oriented programming languages, *Structured Programming* **10**, 4 (1989) 187–197.

[Boehm74] B.W. Boehm, *Some Steps Towards Formal and Automated Design, Proceedings IFIP74*, North-Holland Publishing Company, 1974, pp. 192–197.

[Boehm75] B.W. Boehm, Some experience with automated aids to the design of large-scale reliable software, Proceedings International Conference on Reliable Software, *ACM SIGPLAN Notices* **10**, 6 (1975) 105–113.

[Boehm76] B.W. Boehm, Software engineering, *IEEE Transactions on Computers* **C-25**, 12 (1976) 1226–1241.

[Boehm78] B.W. Boehm, J.R. Brown, H. Kaspar, M. Lipow, G.J. MacLeod & M.J. Merrit, *Characteristics of Software Quality, TRW Series of Software Technology* **1**, North-Holland, 1978.

[Boehm81] B.W. Boehm, *Software Engineering Economics*, Prentice-Hall, 1981.

[Boehm83a] B.W. Boehm, Seven basic principles of software engineering, *Journal of Systems and Software* **3** (1983) 3–24.

[Boehm83b] B.W. Boehm, The economics of software maintenance, *Proceedings Software Maintenance Workshop*, IEEE Catalog nr. 83CH1982–8, 1983, pp. 9–37.

[Boehm84a] B.W. Boehm, T.E. Gray & T. Seewaldt, Prototyping versus specifying: a multiproject experiment, *IEEE Transactions on Software Engineering* **10**, 3 (1984) 290–302.

[Boehm84b] B.W. Boehm, Verifying and validating software requirements and design specifications, *IEEE Software* **1**, 1 (1984) 75–88.

[Boehm84c] B.W. Boehm, M.H. Penedo, E.D. Stuckle, R.D. Williams & A.B. Pyster, A software development environment for improving productivity, *IEEE Computer* **17**, 6 (1984) 30–45.

[Boehm84d] B.W. Boehm, Software life cycle factors, **in** C.R. Vick & C.V. Ramamoorthy (Eds), *Handbook of Software Engineering*, Van Nostrand Reinhold, 1984, pp. 494–518.

[Boehm86] B.W. Boehm, A spiral model of software development and enhancement, *ACM SigSoft Software Engineering Notes* **11**, 4 (1986), 22–42.

[Boehm87a] B.W. Boehm, Improving software productivity, *IEEE Computer* **20**, 9 (1987) 43–57.

[Boehm87b] B.W. Boehm, Industrial software metrics top 10 list, *IEEE Software* **4**, 5 (1987) 84–85.

[Boehm88a] B.W. Boehm, A spiral model of software development and enhancement, *IEEE Computer* **21**, 5 (1988) 61–72.

[Boehm88b] B.W. Boehm & P.N. Papaccio, Understanding and controlling software costs, *IEEE Transactions on Software Engineering* **14**, 10 (1988) 1462–1477.

[Boehm-Davis92] D.A. Boehm-Davis, R.W. Holt & A.C. Schultz, The role of program structure in software maintenance, *International Journal of Man–Machine Studies* **36**, 1 (1992) 21–63.

[Böhm66] C. Böhm & G. Jacopini, Flow diagrams, Turing machines, and languages with only two formation rules, *Communications of the ACM* **9**, 5 (1966) 366–371.

[Booch85] G. Booch, *Software Engineering with Ada*, Benjamin Cummings, 1985.

[Booch87] G. Booch, *Software Components with Ada: Structures, Tools, and Subsystems*, Benjamin/Cummings, 1987.

[Booch90] G. Booch & M. Vilot, The design of the C++ Booch components, OOPSLA '90 Proceedings, *ACM SIGPLAN Notices* **25**, 10 (1990) 1–11.

[Booch91] G. Booch, *Object Oriented Design with Applications*, Benjamin Cummings, 1991.

[Boudier88] G. Boudier, R. Minot & I. Thomas, An overview of PCTE, in [SIGSOFT88] pp. 248–257.

[Boyle84] J.M. Boyle & M.N. Muralidharan, Program reusability through program transformation, *IEEE Transactions on Software Engineering* **10**, 5 (1984) 574–588.

[Brilliant90] S.S. Brilliant, J.C. Knight & N.G. Leveson, Analysis of faults in an N-version software experiment, *IEEE Transactions on Software Engineering* **16**, 2 (1990) 238–247.

[Brooks75] F.P. Brooks, *The Mythical Man-month*, Addison-Wesley, 1975.

[Brooks83] R. Brooks, Towards a theory of the comprehension of computer programs, *International Journal of Man-Machine Studies* **18** (1983) 543–554.

[Brooks87] F.P. Brooks, Jr., No silver bullet: essence and accidents of software engineering, *IEEE Computer* **20**, 4 (1987) 10–20.

[Brown89] J.R. Brown & S. Cunningham, *Programming the User Interface*, John Wiley, 1989.

[Browne90] J.C. Browne, T. Lee & J. Werth, Experimental evaluation of a reusability-oriented parallel programming environment, *IEEE Transactions on Software Engineering* **16**, 2 (1990) 111–120.

[Budde84] R. Budde, K. Kuhlenkamp, L, Mathiassen & H. Züllighoven (Eds), *Approaches to Prototyping*, Springer Verlag, 1984.

[Burrell79] G. Burrell & G. Morgan, *Sociological Paradigms and Organizational Analysis*, Heinemann, 1979.

[Burton87] B.A. Burton, R. Wienk Aragon, S.A. Bailey, K.D. Koehler & L.A. Mayes, The reusable software library, *IEEE Software* **4**, 4 (1987) 25–33.

[Bush85] E. Bush, The automatic restructuring of COBOL, *Proceedings Conference on Software Maintenance*, IEEE, 1985, pp. 35–41.

[Buxton69] J.N. Buxton & B. Randell (Eds), *Software Engineering Techniques*, Report on a conference, Rome, NATO Scientific Affairs Division, 1969.

[CACM87] ACM forum, *Communications of the ACM* **30**, 11 (1987) 907–908.

[CACM90] Scaling up: a research agenda for software engineering, *Communications of the ACM* **33**, 3 (1990) 281–293.

[Caine75] S.H. Caine & E.K. Gordon, PDL, a tool for software design, *Proceedings National Computer Conference*, AFIPS, vol 44, 1975, pp. 271–276.

[Cameron89] J.R. Cameron, *JSP & JSD, The Jackson approach to software development*, IEEE Computer Society Press, 1989.

[Card80a] S.K. Card, T.P. Moran & A. Newell, The keystroke-level model for user performance time with interactive systems, *Communications of the ACM* **23**, 7 (1980) 396–410.

[Card80b] S.K. Card, T.P. Moran & A. Newell, Computer text-editing: an information processing analysis of a routine cognitive skill, *Cognitive Psychology* **12** (1980) 32–74.

[Card83] S.K. Card, T.P. Moran & A. Newell, *The Psychology of Human-Computer Interaction*, Erlbaum, 1983.

[Carroll80a] J.M. Carroll, J.C. Thomas & A. Malhotra, Presentation and representation in design problem solving, *British Journal of Psychology* **71** (1980) 143–153.

[Carroll80b] J.M. Carroll, J.C. Thomas, L.A. Miller & H.P. Friedman, Aspects of solution structure in design problem solving, *American Journal of Psychology* **93**, 2 (1980) 269–284.

[Celko83] J. Celko, J.S. Davis & J. Mitchell, A demonstration of three requirements language systems, *ACM Sigplan Notices* **18**, 1 (1983) 9–14.

[Cha88] S.S. Cha, N.G. Leveson & T.J. Shimeall, Safety verification in MURPHY using fault-tree analysis, *Proceedings 10th International Conference on Software Engineering*, IEEE, 1988, pp. 377–386.

[Chapin87] N. Chapin, The job of software maintenance, *Proceedings Conference on Software Maintenance*, IEEE (1987) 4–12.

[Charette86] R.N. Charette, *Software Engineering Environments*, McGraw-Hill, 1986.

[Chase73] W.C. Chase & H. Simon, Perception in chess, *Cognitive Psychology* **4** (1973) 55–81.

[Cheheyl81] M.H. Cheheyl, M. Gasser, G.A. Huff & J.K. Miller, Verifying security, *ACM Computing Surveys* **13**, 3 (1981) 279–339.

[Chen76] P.P. Chen, The Entity-relationship model—toward a unifying view of data, *ACM Transactions on Data Base Systems* **1**, 1 (1976) 9–36.

[Chikofsky90a] E.J. Chikofsky & J.H. Cross II, Reverse engineering and design recovery: a taxonomy, *IEEE Software* **7**, 1 (1990) 13–18.

[Chikofsky90b] E.J. Chikovsky, CASE & reengineering: from archeology to software perestroika, *Proceedings 12th International Conference on Software Engineering*, IEEE, 1990, p. 122.

[Chusho87] T. Chusho, Test data selection and quality estimation based on the concept of essential branches for path testing, *IEEE Transactions on Software Engineering* **13**, 5 (1987) 509–517.

[Clarke89] L.A. Clarke, A. Podgurski, D.J. Richardson & S.J. Zeil, A formal evaluation of data flow path selection criteria, *IEEE Transactions on Software Engineering* **15**, 11 (1989) 1318–1332.

[Claybrook80] B.G. Claybrook & M.P. Wyckoff, Module: an encapsulation mechanism for specifying and implementing abstract data types, *Proceedings of the ACM'80 Conference*, ACM, 1980, pp. 225–235.

[Coad90] P. Coad & E. Yourdon, *Object-oriented Analysis*, Prentice-Hall, 1990.

[Collofello89] J.S. Collofello & S.N. Woodfield, Evaluating the effectiveness of reliability-assurance techniques, *Journal of Systems and Software* **9**, 3 (1989) 191–195.

[Computer87] Special issue on integrated design and programming environments, *IEEE Computer* **20**, 11 (1987).

[Computer89] Special issue on prototyping, *IEEE Computer* **22**, 5 (1989).

[Conklin87] J. Conklin, Hypertext: an introduction and survey, *IEEE Computer* **20**, 9 (1987) 17–41.

[Conte86] S.D. Conte, H.E. Dunsmore & V.Y. Shen, *Software Engineering Metrics and Models*, Benjamin Cummings, 1986.

[Coombs81] M.J. Coombs & J.L. Alty (Eds), *Computing Skills and the User Interface*, Academic Press, 1981.

[Cooper84] J. Cooper, Software development management planning, *IEEE Transactions on Software Engineering* **10**, 1 (1984) 22–26.

[Corbi89] T.A. Corbi, Program understanding: challenge for the 1990s, *IBM Systems Journal* **28**, 2 (1989) 294–306.

[Coulter83] N.S. Coulter, Software science and cognitive psychology, *IEEE Transactions on Software Engineering* **9**, 2 (1983) 166–171.

[Cox84] B.J. Cox, Message/object programming, an evolutionary change in programming technology, *IEEE Software* **1**, 1 (1984) 50–61.

[Cox86] B.J. Cox, *Object-oriented Programming*, Addison-Wesley, 1986.

[Cox90] B.J. Cox, Planning the software industrial revolution, *IEEE Software* **7**, 6 (1990) 25–33.

[Cragon82] H.G. Cragon, The myth of the hardware/software cost ratio, *IEEE Computer* **15**, 12 (1982) 100–101.

[Crews82] P. Crews, D. Ward & J. Mungle, Ada requirements methodology (ARM), *Proceedings of the ACM '82 Conference*, ACM, 1982, pp. 149–155.

[Cristian82] F. Cristian, Exception handling and fault tolerance, *IEEE Transactions on Computers* **C-31**, 6 (1982) 531–540.

[Cristian84] F. Cristian, Correct and robust programs, *IEEE Transactions on Software Engineering* **10**, 2 (1984) 163–174.

[Cristian85] F. Cristian, A rigorous approach to fault-tolerant programming, *IEEE Transactions on Software Engineering* **11**, 1 (1985) 23–31.

[Crosby90] M.E. Crosby & J. Stelovsky, How do we read algorithms, *IEEE Computer* **23**, 1 (1990) 24–35.

[Currit86] P.A. Currit, M. Dyer & H.D. Mills, Certifying the reliability of software, *IEEE Transactions on Software Engineering* **12**, 1 (1986) 3–11.

[Curtis79] B. Curtis, S. Sheppard & P. Milliman, Third time charm: stronger prediction of programmer performance by software complexity metrics, *Proceedings 4th International Conference on Software Engineering*, IEEE, 1979, pp. 356–360.

[Curtis80] B. Curtis, Measurement and experimentation in software engineering, *Proceedings of the IEEE* **68**, 9 (1980) 1144–1157.

[Curtis81] B. Curtis, Substantiating programmer variability, *Proceedings of the IEEE* **69**, 7 (1981) 846.

[Curtis86a] B. Curtis, E.M. Soloway, R.E. Brooks, J.B. Black, K. Ehrlich & H.R. Ramsey, Software psychology: the need for an interdisciplinary program, *Proceedings of the IEEE* **74**, 8 (1986) 1092–1106.

[Curtis86b] B. Curtis (Ed.), *Tutorial: Human Factors in Software Development*, Catalog nr EZ577, IEEE, 1986.

[Curtis87] B. Curtis, H. Krasner, V. Shen & N. Iscoe, On building software process models under the lamppost, *Proceedings 9th International Conference on Software Engineering*, 1987, pp. 96–103.

[Curtis88] B. Curtis, H. Krasner & N. Iscoe, A field study of the software design process for large systems, *Communications of the ACM* **31**, 11 (1988) 1268–1287.

[Curtis89a] B. Curtis, Three problems overcome with behavioral models of the software development process, *Proceedings 11th International Conference on Software Engineering*, IEEE, 1989, pp. 398–399.

[Curtis89b] B. Curtis, S.B. Sheppard, E. Kruesi-Bailey, J. Bailey & D.A. Boehm-Davis, Experimental evaluation of software documentation formats, *Journal of Systems and Software* **9**, 2 (1989) 167–207.

[Cusumano89] M.A. Cusumano, The software factory: a historical interpretation, *IEEE Software* **6**, 2 (1989) 23–30.

[Daly80] E.B. Daly, Organisational philosophies used in software development, **in** *Infotech State of the Art Review*, 1980, pp. 45–66.

[Dart87] S.A. Dart, R.J. Ellison, P.H. Feiller & A.N. Habermann, Software development environments, *IEEE Computer* **20**, 11 (1987) 18–28.

[Date86] C.J. Date, *An Introduction to Database Systems*, Addison Wesley, 1986.

[Davis82] G.B. Davis, Strategies for information requirements determination, *IBM Systems Journal* **21**,1 (1982) 4–30.

[Davis88a] A. M. Davis, A taxonomy for the early stages of the software development life cycle, *Journal of Systems and Software* **8**, 4 (1988) 297–311.

[Davis88b] A.M. Davis, A comparison of techniques for the specification of external system behavior, *Communications of the ACM* **31**, 9 (1988) 1098–1115.

[DeGroot65] A.D. de Groot, *Thought and Choice in Chess*, Mouton, Paris, 1965.

[Delisle84] N.M. Delisle, D.E. Menicosy & M.D. Schwartz, Viewing a programming environment as a single tool, **in** [SIGPLAN84] pp. 49–56.

[DeMarco79] T. DeMarco, *Structured Analysis and System Specification*, Prentice-Hall, 1979.

[DeMarco82] T. DeMarco, *Controlling Software Projects*, Yourdon Press, 1982.

[DeMarco85] T. DeMarco & T. Lister, Programmer performance and the effect of the workplace, *Proceedings 8th International Conference on Software Engineering*, IEEE, 1985, pp. 268–272.

[DeMarco89] T. DeMarco & T. Lister, Software development: state of the art vs. state of the practice, *Proceedings 11th International Conference on Software Engineering*, IEEE, 1989, pp. 271–275.

[DeMillo79] R.A. DeMillo, R.J. Lipton & A.J. Perlis, Social processes and the proofs of theorems and programs, *Communications of the ACM* **22**, 5 (1979) 271–280.

[DeMillo91] R.A. DeMillo, Progress towards automated software testing, *Proceedings 13th International Conference on Software Engineering*, IEEE, 1991, pp. 180–183.

[Denning91] P.J. Denning, Technology of management, Editorial column, *Communications of the ACM* **34**, 3 (1991) 11–12.

[DeRemer76] F. DeRemer & H.H. Kron, Programming-in-the-large versus programming-in-the-small, *IEEE Transactions on Software Engineering* **2**, 2 (1976) 80–86.

[Dershem90] H.L. Dershem & M.J. Jipping, *Programming Languages: Structures and Models*, Wadsworth Publ. Co., 1990.

[Devanbu91] P. Devanbu, R.J. Brachman, P.G. Selfridge & B.W. Ballard, LaSSIE: a knowledge-based software information system, *Communications of the ACM* **34**, 5 (1991) 34–49.

[Dewhurst79] S.C. Dewhurst, A methodology for implementing structured flowcharting, *ACM Systems Documentation Newsletter* **6**, 1 (1979) 10–11.

[Dietz84] J.L.G. Dietz, PSL/PSA: a contribution to the development of better systems (in Dutch), *Informatie* **26**, 9 (1984) 722–733.

[Dijkstra76] E.W. Dijkstra, *A Discipline of Programming*, Prentice-Hall, 1976.

[Doe86] D.D. Doe & E.H. Bersoff, The Software Productivity Consortium (SPC): an industry initiative to improve the productivity and quality of mission-critical software, *Journal of Systems and Software* **6** (1986) 367–378.

[Dolotta78] T.A. Dolotta, R.C. Haight & J.R. Mashey, UNIX time-sharing system: the programmer's workbench, *The Bell System Technical Journal* **57**, 6 (1978) 2177–2200.

[Downs85] T. Downs, An approach to the modelling of software testing with some applications, *IEEE Transactions on Software Engineering* **11**, 4 (1985) 375–386.

[Downs88] E. Downs, P. Clare & I. Coe, *SSADM: Structured Systems Analysis and Design Method*, Prentice-Hall, 1988.

[Dowson87] M. Dowson, Integrated project support with Istar, *IEEE Software* **4**, 6 (1987) 6–15.

[Dunlop82] D.D. Dunlop & V.R. Basili, A comparitive analysis of functional correctness, *ACM Computing Surveys* **14**, 2 (1982) 229–244.

[Dunsmore79] H.E. Dunsmore & J.D. Gannon, Data referencing: an empirical investigation, *IEEE Computer* **12**, 12 (1979) 50–59.

[Duran84] J.W. Duran & S.C. Ntafos, An evaluation of random testing, *IEEE Transactions on Software Engineering* **10**, 4 (1984) 438–443.

[Ehrig85] H. Ehrig & B. Mahr, *Fundamentals of Algebraic Specifications, vol. 1, Equations and Initial Semantics*, Springer Verlag, 1985.

[Elshoff76] J.L. Elshoff, Measuring commercial PL—1 programs using Halstead's criteria, *ACM SIGPLAN Notices* **11**, 5 (1976) 38–76.

[Elswijk87] P.B.J. van Elswijk, *Performance Awareness Program*, DEC, 1987.

[Estrin86] G. Estrin, R.S. Fenchel, R.R. Razouk & M.K. Vernon, SARA (System Architect's Apprentice): modeling, analysis, and simulation support for design of concurrent systems, *IEEE Transactions on Software Engineering* **12**, 2 (1986) 293–311.

[Fagan76] M.E. Fagan, Design and code inspections to reduce errors in program development, *IBM Systems Journal* **15**, 3 (1976) 182–211.

[Fagan86] M.E. Fagan, Advances in inspections, *IEEE Transactions on Software Engineering* **12**, 7 (1986) 744–751.

[Feldman78] S.I. Feldman, *Make—A Program for Maintaining Computer Programs*, AT&T, 1978.

[Fenton91] N.E. Fenton, *Software Metrics*, Chapman & Hall, 1991.

[Fetzer88] J. H. Fetzer, Program verification: the very idea, *Communications of the ACM* **31**, 9 (1988) 1048–1063. See also reactions to this article in *Communications of the ACM* **32**, 3 (1989) 374–381 and **32**, 4 (1989) 506-512.

[Fischer86] G. Fischer, From interactive to intelligent systems, in *Software System Design Methods* J.K. Skwirzynski (Ed.), NATO ASI Series F: Computer and Systems Sciences, vol. 22, Springer, 1986, pp. 185–212.

[Fitter79] M. Fitter & T.R.G. Green, When do diagrams make good computer languages, *International Journal of Man–Machine Studies* **11** (1979) 235–261.

[Fitzsimmons78] A. Fitzsimmons & T. Love, A review and evaluation of software science, *ACM Computing Surveys* **10**, 1 (1978) 3–18.

[Fjelstad79] R.K. Fjelstad & W.T, Hamlen, Application program maintenance study: report to our respondents, *Proceedings of GUIDE 48*, 1979.

[Floyd67] R.W. Floyd, Assigning meaning to programs, in *Mathematical aspects of computer science*, J.T. Schwartz (Ed.), American Mathematical Society, 1967, pp. 19–31.

[Floyd84] C. Floyd, A systematic look at prototyping, in [Budde84] pp. 1–26.

[Floyd88] C. Floyd, Outline of a paradigm shift in software engineering, *ACM SigSoft Software Engineering Notes* **13**, 2 (1988) 25–38.

[Floyd89] C. Floyd, W.-M. Mehl, F.-M. Reisin, G. Schmidt & G. Wolf, Out of Scandinavia: Alternative approaches to software design and system development, *Human–Computer Interaction* **4** (1989) 253–350.

[Frakes90] W.B. Frakes & P.B. Gandel, Representing reusable software, *Information and Software Technology* **32**, 10 (1990) 653–664.

[Frakes91a] W.B. Frakes, T.J. Biggerstaff, R. Prieto-Diaz, K. Matsumoto & W. Schaefer, Software reuse: is it delivering, *Proceedings 13th International Conference on Software Engineering*, IEEE, 1991, pp. 52–61.

[Frakes91b] W. Frakes, C. Fox & B. Nejmeh, *Software Engineering in the UNIX/C Environment*, Prentice Hall, 1991.

[Frank83] W.L. Frank, The history of myth no. 1, *Datamation* (May 1983) 252–256.

[Frankl88] P.G. Frankl & E.J. Weyuker, An applicable family of data flow testing criteria, *IEEE Transactions on Software Engineering* **14**, 10 (1988) 1483–1498.

[Fraser91] M.D. Fraser, K. Kumar & V.K. Vaishnavi, Informal and formal requirements specification languages: bridging the gap, *IEEE Transactions on Software Engineering* **17**, 5 (1991) 454–466.

[Freeman83a] P. Freeman & A.I. Wasserman (Eds), *Tutorial: Software Design Techniques*, IEEE no EZ514, 1983.

[Freeman83b] P. Freeman, Reusable software engineering, concepts and research directions, in [ITT83] pp. 2–16.

[Freeman87a] P. Freeman, *Software Perspectives*, Addison-Wesley, 1987.

[Freeman87b] P. Freeman, A conceptual analysis of the Draco approach to constructing software systems, *IEEE Transacions on Software Engineering* **13**, 7 (1987) 830–844.

[Freeman87c] P. Freeman (Ed.), *Tutorial: Software Reusability*, IEEE Catalog nr EZ750, 1987.

[Frenkel85] K.A. Frenkel, Report on the Microelectronics and Computer Technology Corporation Conference, *Communications of the ACM* **28**, 8 (1985) 808–814.

[Friedman91] L.W. Friedman, *Comparative Programming Languages Generalizing the Programming Function*, Prentice-Hall, 1991.

[Gaitersburg82] *Proceedings Human Factors in Computer Systems*, Gaitersburg, ACM, 1982.

[Gallo87] F. Gallo, R. Minot & I. Thomas, The object management system of PCTE as a software engineering database management system, in [SIGPLAN87] pp. 12–15.

[Gane79] C. Gane & T. Sarson, *Structured Analysis and Systems Analysis: Tools and Techniques*, Prentice-Hall, 1979.

[Gannon75] J.D. Gannon & J.J. Horning, The impact of language design on the production of reliable software, Proceedings International Conference on Reliable Software, *ACM SIGPLAN Notices* **10**, 6 (1975) 10–22.

[Gannon77] J.D. Gannon, An experimental evaluation of data type conventions, *Communications of the ACM* **20**, 8 (1977) 584–595.

[Garey79] M.R. Garey & D.S. Johnson, *Computers and Intractability*, W.H. Freeman, 1979.

[Garland89] S.J. Garland & J.V. Guttag, An overview of LP, the Larch Prover, *Proceedings Third International Conference on Rewriting Techniques and Applications*, LNCS 355, Springer, 1989, pp. 137–151.

[Garland90] S.J. Garland, J.V. Guttag & J.J. Horning, Debugging Larch Shared Language specifications, *IEEE Transactions on Software Engineering* **16**, 9 (1990)1044–1057.

[Garnett90] E.S. Garnett & J.A. Mariani, Software reclamation, *Software Engineering Journal* **5**, 3 (1990) 185–191.

[Garvin84] D.A. Garvin, What does "product quality" really mean?, *Sloan Management Review*, Fall 1984.

[Gelperin88] D. Gelperin & B. Hetzel, The growth of software testing, *Communications of the ACM* **31**, 6 (1988) 687–695.

[Gentner90] D.R. Gentner, Why good engineers (sometimes) create bad interfaces, *CHI '90 Conference Proceedings*, ACM, 1990, pp. 277–282.

[van Genuchten91] M. van Genuchten, Towards a software factory, PhD Thesis, Technical University of Eindhoven, The Netherlands, 1991.

[Gerhart80] S.L. Gerhart, D.R. Musser, D.H. Thompson, D.A. Baker, R.L. Bates, R.W. Erickson, R.L. London, D.G. Taylor & D.S. Wile, An overview of AFFIRM: a specification and verification system, *Proceedings IFIP80*, North-Holland Publishing Company, 1980, pp. 343–347.

[Gibbs89] N.E. Gibbs, The SEI education program: the challenge of teaching future software engineers, *Communications of the ACM* **32**, 5 (1989) 594–605.

[Gibbs91] N.E. Gibbs, Software engineering and computer science: the impending split?, *Education & Computing* **7**, 1–2 (1991) 111–117.

[Gibson89] V.R. Gibson & J.A. Senn, System structure and software maintenance performance, *Communications of the ACM* **32**, 3 (1989) 347–358.

[Gilb86] T. Gilb, Estimating software attributes: some unconventional points of view, *ACM SigSoft Software Engineering Notes* **11**, 1 (1986) 49–59.

[Gilb88] T. Gilb, *Principles of Software Engineering Management*, Addison-Wesley (1988).

[Girgis86] M.R. Girgis & M.R. Woodward, An experimental comparison of the error exposing ability of program testing criteria, *Proceedings Software Testing Workshop*, ACM, 1986, pp. 64–73.

[Goguen75] J.A. Goguen, J.W. Thatcher, E.G. Wagner & J.B. Wright, Abstract data types as initial algebras and correctness of data representations, *Proceedings Conference on Computer Graphics, Pattern Recognition and Data Structures*, 1975, pp. 89–93.

[Goguen78a] J.A. Goguen, J.W. Thatcher & E.G. Wagner, An initial algebra approach to the specification, correctness, and implementation of abstract data types, in *Current Trends in Programming Methodology*, Vol 4, R.T. Yeh (Ed.), Prentice-Hall, 1978, pp. 80–149.

[Goguen78b] J.A. Goguen, Abstract errors for abstract data types, in *Formal Description of Programming Concepts*, E.J. Neuhold (Ed.), North-Holland Publishing Company, 1978, pp. 491–525.

[Goguen86a] J.A. Goguen, Reusing and interconnecting software components, *IEEE Computer* **19**, 2 (1986) 16–28.

[Goguen86b] J. Goguen, An introduction to OBJ: a language for writing and testing formal algebraic program specifications, in: N. Gehani & A.D. McGettrick, *Software specification Techniques*, Addison-Wesley, 1986, pp. 391–419.

[Goguen87] J. Goguen & M. Moriconi, Formalization in programming environments, *IEEE Computer* **20**, 11 (1987) 55–64.

[Goldberg83] A. Goldberg & D. Robson, *Smalltalk-80—The Language and its Implementation*, Addison-Wesley, 1983.

[Goldberg84] A. Goldberg, *Smalltalk-80—The Interactive Programming Environment*, Addison-Wesley, 1984.

[Good79] D.I. Good, R.M. Cohen & J. Keenan-Williams, Principles of proving concurrent programs in Gypsy, *Proceedings 6th ACM Symposium on the Principles of Programming Languages*, 1979, pp. 42–52.

[Goodenough75] J.B. Goodenough & S.L. Gerhart, Toward a theory of test data selection, *IEEE Transactions on Software Engineering* **1**, 2 (1975) 156–173.

[Goos83] G.Goos et al., DIANA - An intermediate language for Ada, *Lecture Notes in Computer Science* 161, Springer, 1983.

[Gould83] J.D. Gould & S.J. Boies, Human factors challenges in creating a principal support office system—the Speech Filing System approach, *ACM Transactions on Office Information Systems* **1**, 4 (1983) 273–298.

[Gould84] J.D. Gould & S.J. Boies, Speech filing—an office system for principals, *IBM Systems Journal* **23**, 1 (1984) 65–81.

[Gould87] J.D. Gould & S.J. Boies, The 1984 Olympic Message System: a test of behavioral principles of system design, *Communications of the ACM* **30**, 9 (1987) 758–769.

[Grady87a] R.B. Grady & D.L. Caswell, *Software Metrics: Establishing a Company-wide Program*, Prentice Hall, 1987.

[Grady87b] R.B. Grady, Measuring and managing software maintenance, *IEEE Software* **4**, 5 (1987) 35–45.

[Green86] T.R.G. Green, Design and use of programming languages, in *Software system design methods*, J.K. Skwirzynski (Ed.), NATO ASI Series F: Computer and Systems Sciences, Vol. 22, Springer, 1986, pp. 213–242.

[Green90] T.R.G. Green, The nature of programming, in *Psychology of Programming*, J.-M. Hoc, T.R.G. Green, D.J. Gilmore & R. Samurcay (Eds), Academic Press, 1990, pp. 21–44.

[Greeno80] J.G. Greeno, Trends in the theory of knowledge for problem solving, in D.T. Tuma & F. Reif (Eds), *Problem Solving and Education: Issues in Teaching and Research*, Erlbaum, 1980.

[Gries76] D. Gries, An illustration of current ideas on the derivation of correctness proofs and correct programs, *IEEE Transactions on Software Engineering* **2**, 4 (1976) 238–243.

[Gries81] D. Gries, *The Science of Programming*, Springer Verlag, 1981.

[Grudin89] J. Grudin, The case against user interface consistency, *Communications of the ACM* **32**, 10 (1989) 1164–1173.

[Grudin91] J. Grudin, Interactive systems: bridging the gaps between developers and users, *IEEE Computer* **24**, 4 (1991) 59–69.

[Guindon88] R. Guindon & B. Curtis, Control of cognitive processes during design: what tools would support software designers?, *Proceedings CHI '88*, ACM, 1988, pp. 263–268.

[Guindon90] R. Guindon, Designing the design process: exploiting opportunistic thoughts, *Human–Computer Interaction* **5** (1990) 305–344.

[Guttag75] J.V. Guttag, Specification and application to programming of abstract data types, PhD Thesis, University of Toronto, 1975.

[Guttag80] J.V. Guttag, Notes on type abstraction (version 2), *IEEE Transactions on Software Engineering* **6**, 1 (1980) 13–23.

[Guttag82] J.V. Guttag, J.J. Horning & J. Wing, Some notes on putting formal specifications to productive use, *Science of Computer Programming* **2** (1982) 53–68.

[Guttag85] J.V. Guttag, J.J. Horning & J.M. Wing, An overview of the Larch family of specification languages, *IEEE Software* **2**, 5 (1985) 24–36.

[Guttag86] J.V. Guttag & J.J. Horning, Report on the Larch Shared Language, *Science of Computer Programming* **6**, 2 (1986) 103–134.

[deHaan91] G. de Haan, G.C. van der Veer & J.C. van Vliet, Formal modelling techniques in human–computer interaction, *Acta Psychologica* **78** (1991) 27–67.

[Habermann86] A.N. Habermann & D. Notkin, Gandalf: software development environments, *IEEE Transactions on Software Engineering* **12**, 12 (1986) 1117–1127.

[Haies87] I. Haies (Ed.), *Specification Case Studies*, Prentice Hall, 1987.

[Hall90] A. Hall, Seven myths of formal methods, *IEEE Software* **7**, 5 (1990) 11–20.

[Halstead77] M.H. Halstead, *Elements of Software Science*, North-Holland Publishing Company, 1977.

[Hamer82] P.G. Hamer & G.D. Frewin, M.H. Halstead's software science—a critical examination, *Proceedings 6th International Conference on Software Engineering*, IEEE (1982) 197–206.

[Hamlet88] R. Hamlet, Special section on software testing, *Communications of the ACM* **31**, 6 (1988) 662–667.

[Hamlet89] R. Hamlet, Theoretical comparison of testing methods, Proceedings ACM Sigsoft '89, Third Symposium on Software Testing, Analysis, and Verification (TAV3), *ACM Sigsoft Software Engineering Notes* **14**, 8 (1989) 28–37.

[Hamlet90] D. Hamlet & R. Taylor, Partition testing does not inspire confidence, *IEEE Transactions on Software Engineering* **16**, 12 (1990) 1402–1411.

[Harel88] D. Harel, On visual formalisms, *Communications of the ACM* **31**, 5 (1988) 514–530.

[Harrison82] W. Harrison, K. Magel, R. Kluczny & A. DeKock, Applying software complexity metrics to program maintenance, *IEEE Computer* **15**, 9 (1982) 65–79.

[Hartman91] J. Hartman, Understanding natural programs using proper decomposition, *Proceedings 13th International Conference on Software Engineering*, IEEE, 1991, pp. 62–73.

[Hartson89] H.R. Hartson & D. Hix, Human–computer interface development: concepts and systems, *ACM Computing Surveys* **21**, 1 (1989) pp 5–92.

[Hecht72] M.S. Hecht & J.D. Ullman, Flow graph reducibility, *SIAM Journal on Computing* **1**, 2 (1972) 188–202.

[Hecht77] M.S. Hecht, *Flow Analysis of Computer Programs*, North-Holland, 1977.

[Hecht82] H. Hecht, *Final report: A Survey of Software Tools Usage*, National Bureau of Standards, NBS SP 500–82, Washington, 1982.

[Heemstra89] F.J. Heemstra, How much does software cost, PhD Thesis (in Dutch), Kluwer Bedrijfswetenschappen, 1989.

[Hekmatpour88] S. Hekmatpour & D. Ince, *Software Prototyping, Formal Methods and VDM*, Addison-Wesley, 1988.

[Henri81] S. Henri & D. Kafura, Software structure metrics based on information flow, *IEEE Transactions on Software Engineering* **7**, 5 (1981) 510–518.

[Hirschheim86] R.A. Hirschheim, The effect of a priori views on the social implications of computing: the case of office automation, *ACM Computing Surveys* **18**, 2 (1986) 165–195.

[Hirschheim89] R. Hirschheim & H.K. Klein, Four paradigms of information systems development, *Communications of the ACM* **32**, 10 (1989) 1199–1216.

[Hoare69] C.A.R. Hoare, The axiomatic basis of computer programming, *Communications of the ACM* **12**, 10 (1969) 576–583.

[Holbrook90] H. Holbrook III, A scenario-based methodology for conducting requirements elicitation, *ACM Software Engineering Notes* **15**, 1 (1990) 95–104.

[Hopcroft79] J.E. Hopcroft & J.D. Ullman, *Introduction to Automata Theory, Languages, and Computation*, Addison-Wesley, 1979.

[Horning82] J.J. Horning, Program specification: issues and observations, in Program Specification, .J. Straunstrup (Ed.), *Lecture Notes in Computer Science* **134**, Springer Verlag, 1982, pp. 5–24.

[Horowitz85] E. Horowitz, A. Kemper & B. Narasimhan, A survey of application generators, *IEEE Software* **2**, 1 (1985) 40–54.

[Hosier61] W.A. Hosier, Pitfalls and Safeguards in Real-time Digital Systems with Emphasis on Programming, *IRE Transactions on Engineering Management*, 1961, pp. 99–115.

[Houghton83] R.C. Houghton, *A Taxonomy of Tool Features for the Ada Programming Support Environment (APSE)*, National Bureau of Standards, NBSIR 82–2625, Washington, 1983.

[Houghton85] R.C. Houghton, Annotated bibliography of recent papers on software engineering environments, *ACM SigSoft Software Engineering Notes* **10**, 2 (1985) 62–76.

[Houghton87] R. C. Houghton & D. Wallace, Characteristics and functions of software engineering environments: an overview, *ACM SigSoft Software Engineering Notes* **12**, 1 (1987) 64–84.

[Howden76] W.E. Howden, Reliability of the path analysis testing strategy, *IEEE Transactions on Software Engineering* **2**, 3 (1976) 208–214.

[Howden82a] W.E. Howden, Validation of scientific programs, *ACM Computing Surveys* **14**, 2 (1982) 193–227.

[Howden82b] W.E. Howden, Contemporary software development environments, *Communications of the ACM* **25**, 5 (1982) 318–329.

[Howden85] W.E. Howden, The theory and practice of functional testing, *IEEE Software* **2**, 5 (1985) 6–17.

[Howden86] W.E. Howden, A functional approach to program testing and analysis, *IEEE Transactions on Software Engineering* **12**, 10 (1986) 997–1005.

[Huet80] G. Huet & D.C. Oppen, Equations and rewrite rules, a survey, in *Formal Languages: Perspectives and Open Problems*, R. Book (Ed.), Academic Press, 1980.

[Humphrey88] W.S. Humphrey, Characterizing the software process: A maturity framework, *IEEE Software* **5**, 2 (1988) 73–79.

[Humphrey89a] W.S. Humphrey, *Managing the Software Process*, SEI Series in Software Engineering, Addison-Wesley, 1989.

[Humphrey89b] W.S. Humphrey, D.H. Kitson & T.C. Kasse, The state of software engineering practice: A preliminary report, *Proceedings 11th International Conference on Software Engineering*, IEEE, 1989, pp. 277–288.

[Iannino84] A. Iannino, J.D. Musa, K. Okumoto & B. Littlewood, Criteria for software reliability model comparisons, *IEEE Transactions on Software Engineering* **10**, 6 (1984) 687–691.

[IEEE83a] *IEEE Standard for Software Configuration Management Plans*, IEEE Std 828, 1983.

[IEEE83b] *IEEE Standard Glossary of Software Engineering Terminology*, IEEE Std 729, 1983.

[IEEE83c] *IEEE Standard for Software Test Documentation*, IEEE Std 829, 1983.

[IEEE84a] *IEEE Standard for Software Quality Assurance Plans*, IEEE Std 730, 1984.

[IEEE84b] *IEEE Guide to Software Requirements Specifications*, IEEE Std 830, 1984.

[IEEE86a] *IEEE Standard on Software Quality Assurance Planning*, IEEE Std 983, 1986.

[IEEE86b] *IEEE Standard for Software Verification and Validation Plans*, IEEE Std 1012, 1986.

[IEEE87] *IEEE Recommended Practice for Software Design Descriptions*, IEEE Std 1016, 1987.

[ISO87] ISO Standards 9000–9004: ISO 9000: *Quality management and quality assurance standards—Guidelines for selection and use*, ISO, 1987. ISO 9001: *Quality systems—Model for quality assurance in design/development, production, installation and servicing*, ISO, 1987. ISO 9002: *Quality systems—Model for quality assurance in production and installation*, ISO, 1987. ISO 9003: *Quality systems—Model for quality assurance in final inspection and test*, ISO, 1987. ISO 9004: *Quality management and quality system elements—Guidelines*, ISO, 1987.

[ITT83] *Proceedings Workshop on Reusability in Programming*, ITT, 1983.

[Jackson75] M.A. Jackson, *Principles of Program Design*, Academic Press, 1975.

[Jackson83] M.A. Jackson, *System Development*, Prentice-Hall, 1983.

[Johnson88] R.E. Johnson & B. Foote, Designing reusable classes, *Journal of Object-Oriented Programming* **1**, 1 (1988) 22–35.

[Jones86] C. Jones, *Programming Productivity*, McGraw-Hill, 1986.

[Jones89] C. Jones, Software enhancement modelling, *Software Maintenance: Research and Practice* **1**, 2 (1989) 91–100.

[Jones90a] C.B. Jones, *Systematic Software Development Using VDM*, Prentice Hall, 1990.

[Jones90b] C.B. Jones & R.C. Shaw, *Case Studies in Systematic Software Development*, Prentice Hall, 1990.

[Joyce86] E.J. Joyce, SEI: The software battleground, *Datamation* (September 15, 1986) 109–116.

[Joyce87] E. Joyce, Software bugs: a matter of life and liability, *Datamation* (May 15, 1987) 89–92.

[JSS85] Special issue on the Gandalf Project, *Journal of Systems and Software* **5**, 2, 1985.

[JSS90a] Special issue on 'Oregon Workshop on Software Metrics', *Journal of Systems and Software* **12**, 3 (1990).

[JSS90b] Special issue on '*Using Software Metrics*', Journal of Systems and Software **13**, 2 (1990).

[Kaehler86] T. Kaehler & D. Patterson, *A Taste of Smalltalk*, W.W. Norton, 1986.

[Kafura87] D. Kafura & G.R. Reddy, Use of software complexity metrics in software maintenance, *IEEE Transactions on Software Engineering* **13**, 3 (1987) 335–343.

[Kamin80] S. Kamin, Final data type specifications: a new data type specification method, *Proceedings 7th ACM Symposium on the Principles of Programming Languages*, 1980, pp. 131–138.

[Kant84] E. Kant & A. Newell, Problem solving techniques for the design of algorithms, *Information Processing and Management* **28**, 1 (1984) 97–118.

[Kaposi87] A. Kaposi & B. Kitchenham, The architecture of system quality, *Software Engineering Journal* (1987) 2–8.

[Kelvin] W.T. Kelvin, *Popular Lectures and Addresses*, 1891–1894.

[Kemerer87] C.F. Kemerer, An empirical validation of software cost estimation models, *Communications of the ACM* **30**, 5 (1987) 416–429.

[Kernighan81] B.W. Kernighan & J.R. Mashey, The UNIX programming environment, *IEEE Computer* **14**, 4 (1981) 12–24.

[Kesler84] T.E. Kesler, R.B. Uram, F. Magareh-Abed, A. Fritzsche, C. Amport & H.E. Dunsmore, The effect of indentation on program comprehension, *International Journal of Man–Machine Studies* **21** (1984) 415–428.

[King88] D. King, *Creating Effective Software: Computer Program Design using the Jackson Methodology*, Yourdon Press, 1988.

[King89] R. King, My cat is object-oriented, *in Object-oriented Concepts, Databases and Applications*, W. Kim & F. Lochovsky (Eds), ACM Press/Addison-Wesley, 1989, pp.

23–30.

[Kitchenham84] B.A. Kitchenham & N.R. Taylor, Software cost models, *ICL Technical Journal* (1984) 73–102.

[Kitchenham85] B.A. Kitchenham & N.R. Taylor, Software project development cost estimation, *Journal of Systems and Software* **5** (1985) 267–278.

[Kitchenham87] B. Kitchenham, Towards a constructive quality model, Part I: software quality modelling, measurement and prediction, *Software Engineering Journal* (July 1987) 105–113.

[Kling80] R. Kling, Social analyses of computing: theoretical perspectives in empirical research, *ACM Computing Surveys* **12**, 1 (1980) 61–110.

[Klop80] J.W. Klop, *Combinatory Reduction Systems*, MC Tract 127, Centrum voor Wiskunde en Informatica, Amsterdam, 1980.

[Knight85] J.C. Knight & P.E. Ammann, An experimental evaluation of simple methods for seeding program errors, *Proceedings 8th International Conference on Software Engineering*, IEEE, 1985, pp. 337–342.

[Knuth81] D.E. Knuth & M.F. Plass, Breaking paragraphs into lines, *Software-Practice & Experience* **11** (1981) 1119–1184.

[Koontz72] H. Koontz & C. O'Donnell, *Principles of Management: An Analysis of Managerial Functions*, McGraw-Hill, 1972.

[Korson86] T.D. Korson & V.K. Vaishnavi, An empirical study of the effects of modularity on program modifiability, **in** [Soloway86b] pp. 168–186.

[Korson90] T. Korson & J.D. McGregor, Understanding object-oriented: a unifying paradigm, *Communications of the ACM* **33**, 9 (1990) 40–60.

[Kuntzmann-Combelles89] A. Kuntzmann-Combelles, ESPRIT: Key results of the first phase, **in** [Software89b] pp. 10–14.

[Lafue90] G.M.E. Lafue (moderator), Panel on software re-engineering, *Proceedings 12th International Conference on Software Engineering*, IEEE, 1990, pp. 118–124.

[Lampson77] B.W. Lampson, J.J. Horning, R.L. London, J.G. Mitchell & G.L. Popek, Report on the programming language EUCLID, *ACM SIGPLAN Notices* **12**, 2 (1977).

[Lanergan84] R.G. Lanergan & C.A. Grasso, Software engineering with reusable designs and code, *IEEE Transactions on Software Engineering* **10**, 5 (1984) 498–501.

[Laurel86] B.K. Laurel, Interface as mimesis, **in** [Norman86] pp. 67–86.

[Lawrence81] M.J. Lawrence, Programming methodology, organizational environment, and programming productivity, *Journal of Systems and Software* **2** (1981) 257–269.

[Leblang84] D.B. Leblang & R.P. Chase, Jr., Computer-aided software engineering: a distributed workstation environment, **in** [SIGPLAN84] pp. 104–112.

[Leblang87] D.B. Leblang & R.P. Chase, Jr., Parallel software configuration management in a network environment, *IEEE Software* **4**, 6 (1987) 28–35.

[Lehman74] M.M. Lehman, *Programs, Cities and Students—Limits to growth?*, Inaugural Lecture Series, vol. 9, Imperial College, London, 1974.

[Lehman78] M.M. Lehman, Laws of program evolution—rules and tools of programming management, *Proceedings Infotech State of the Art Conference 'Why software projects fail'*, 1978, pp. 11/1–11/25.

[Lehman80] M.M. Lehman, Programs, life cycles, and laws of software evolution, *Proceedings of the IEEE* **68**, 9 (1980) 1060–1076.

[Lehman85] M.M. Lehman & L.A. Belady (Eds), *Program evolution*, Academic Press, APIC Studies in Data Processing No. 27, 1985.

[Lehman87] M.M. Lehman, Process models, process programs, programming support, *Proceedings 9th International Conference on Software Engineering*, 1987, pp. 14–16.

[Letovsky86] S. Letovsky & E. Soloway, Delocalized plans and program comprehension,

IEEE Software **3**, 3 (1986) 41–49.

[Leveson86] N.G. Leveson, Software safety: what, why, and how, *ACM Computing Surveys* **18**, 2 (1986), 125–164.

[Leveson91] N.G. Leveson, Software safety issues in embedded computer systems, *Communications of the ACM* **34**, 2 (1991) 34–46.

[Lewis91] J.A. Lewis, S.M. Henri, D.G. Kafura & R.S. Schulman, An empirical study of the object-oriented paradigm and software reuse, Proceedings OOPSLA91, *ACM SIGPLAN Notices* **26**, 11 (1991) 184–196.

[Li87] H.F. Li & W.K. Cheung, An empirical study of software metrics, *IEEE Transactions on Software Engineering* **13**, 6 (1987) 697–708.

[Lieblein86] E. Lieblein, The Department of Defense Software Initiative—a status report, *Communications of the ACM* **29**, 8 (1986) 734–744.

[Lientz80] B.P. Lientz & E.B. Swanson, *Software Maintenance Management*, Addison-Wesley, 1980.

[Linger79] R.C. Linger, H.D. Mills & B.I. Witt, *Structured Programming, Theory and Practice*, Addison-Wesley, 1979.

[Liskov75] B.H. Liskov & S.N. Zilles, Specification techniques for data abstractions, *IEEE Transactions on Software Engineering* **1**, 1 (1975) 7–19.

[Liskov77] B. Liskov, A. Snyder, R. Atkinson & C. Schaffert, Abstraction mechanisms in CLU, *Communications of the ACM* **20**, 8 (1977) 564–575.

[Liskov86] B. Liskov & J. Guttag, *Abstraction and Specification in Program Development*, MIT Press, 1986.

[Littman86] D.C. Littman, J. Pinto, S. Letovsky & E. Soloway, Mental models and software maintenance, **in** [Soloway86b] pp. 80–98.

[Liu89] L.-C. Liu & E. Horowitz, A formal model for software project management, *Transactions on Software Engineering* **15**, 10 (1989) 1280–1293.

[Lucas76] H.C. Lucas & R.B. Kaplan, A structured programming experiment, *Computer Journal* **19**, 2 (1976) 136–138.

[Lyons81] M.J. Lyons, Salvaging your software asset (tools based maintenance, *AFIPS Conference Proceedings* **50**, National Computer Conference (1981) 337–341.

[Maarek91] Y.S. Maarek, D.M. Berry & G.E. Kaiser, An information retrieval approach for automatically constructing software libraries, *IEEE Transactions on Software Engineering* **17**, 8 (1991) 800–813.

[Macro87] A. Macro & J. Buxton, *The Craft of Software Engineering*, Addison Wesley, 1987.

[Maitland80] R. Maitland, NODAL,*in NBS Software Tools Database*, National Bureau of Standards, Washington, 1980.

[Marca88] D.A. Marca & B C.L. McGowan, $SADT^{TM}$, *Structured Analysis and Design Technique*, McGraw-Hill, 1988.

[Martin83] R.J. Martin & W.M. Osborne, *Guidance on Software Maintenance*, NBS Special Publication 500-106, National Bureau of Standards, Washington, 1983.

[Matsumoto84a] Y. Matsumoto, Some experience in promoting reusable software, presentation in higher abstract levels, *IEEE Transactions on Software Engineering* **10**, 5 (1984) 502–512.

[Matsumoto84b] Y. Matsumoto, Management of industrial software production, *IEEE Computer* **17**, 2 (1984) 59–72.

[Matsumoto87] Y. Matsumoto, A software factory: An overall approach to software production, **in** [Freeman87c] pp. 155–178.

[McCabe76] T.J. McCabe, A complexity measure, *IEEE Transactions on Software Engineering* **2**, 4 (1976) 308–320.

[McCall77] J.A. McCall, P.K. Richards & G.F. Walters, *Factors in Software Quality*, RADC-

TR-77-369, US Department of Commerce, 1977.

[McCarthy65] J. McCarthy, P.W. Abrahams, D.J. Edwards, T.P. Hart & M.I. Lewin, *LISP 1.5 Programmer's Manual*, MIT Press, Cambridge, USA, 1965.

[McClure68] R.M. McClure, Production-management aspects, **in** [Naur68] pp. 72.

[McCracken81] D.D. McCracken & M.A. Jackson, A minority dissenting position, **in** *Systems Analysis and Design—A Foundation for the 1980's*, W.W. Cotterman et al. (Eds), North Holland, 1981, pp. 551–553.

[McDermid84] J. McDermid & K. Ripken, *Life Cycle Support in the Ada Environment*, Cambridge University Press, 1984.

[McIlroy68] M.D. McIlroy, Mass-produced software components, **in** [Naur68] pp. 88–98.

[Medina-Mora82] R. Medina-Mora, Syntax-directed editing: towards integrated programming environments, PhD Thesis, Carnegie-Mellon University, 1982.

[Metzger87] P.W. Metzger, *Managing Programming People*, Prentice-Hall, 1987.

[Metzner77] J.R. Metzner & B.H. Barnes, *Decision Table Languages and Systems*, Academic Press, 1977.

[Meyer85] B. Meyer, On formalism in specifications, *IEEE Software* **2**, 1 (1985) 6–26.

[Meyer87] B. Meyer, Reusability, the case for object-oriented design, *IEEE Software* **4**, 2 (1987) 50–64.

[Meyer88] B. Meyer, *Object-oriented Software Construction*, Prentice-Hall, 1988.

[Meyer90] B. Meyer, Lessons from the design of the Eiffel libraries, *Communications of the ACM* **33**, 9 (1990) 68–88.

[Miller56] G.A. Miller, The magical number seven, plus or minus two: some limits on our capacity for processing information, *Psychological Review* **63** (1956) 81–97.

[Miller81] E. Miller & W.E. Howden (Eds), *Tutorial: Software Testing & Validation Techniques*, IEEE Catalog nr EZ365, 1981.

[Miller90] B.P. Miller, L. Fredrikson & B. So, An experimental study of the reliability of UNIX facilities, *Communications of the ACM* **33**, 12 (1990) 32–44.

[Mills87] H.D. Mills, M. Dyer & R. Linger, Cleanroom software engineering, *IEEE Software* **4**, 5 (1987) 19–25.

[Mintzberg83] H. Mintzberg, *Structures in Fives: Designing Effective Organizations*, Prentice-Hall, 1983.

[Mohanty81] S.N. Mohanty, Software cost estimation: present and future, *Software-Practice and Experience* **11**, 7 (1981) 103–121.

[Moher81] T. Moher & G.M. Schneider, Methods for improving controlled experimentation in software engineering, *Proceedings 5th International Conference on Software Engineering*, IEEE, 1981, pp. 224–234.

[Moher82] T. Moher & G.M. Schneider, Methodology and experimentation in software engineering, *International Journal of Man–Machine Studies* **16** (1982) 65–87.

[Molich90] R. Molich & J. Nielsen, Improving a human–computer dialogue, *Communications of the ACM* **33**, 3 (1990) 338–348.

[Moran81] T.P. Moran, The command language grammar: a representation of the user interface of interactive computer systems, *International Journal of Man–Machine Studies* **15**, 1 (1981) 3–50.

[Moranda78] P.B. Moranda, Is software science hard, *ACM Computing Surveys* **10**, 4 (1978) 503–505.

[Morell88] L.J. Morell, Theoretical insights into fault-based testing, *Proceedings Second Workshop on Software Testing, Verification, and Analysis*, ACM, 1988.

[Moriconi85] M. Moriconi & D.F. Hare, Visualising program design through PegaSys, *IEEE Computer* **18**, 8 (1985) 72–85.

[Mulligan91] R.M. Mulligan, M.W. Altom & D.K. Simkin, User interface design in the trenches: some tips on shooting from the hip, *Proceedings CHI '91*, ACM, 1991, pp.

232–236.

[Munck88] R. Munck, P. Obendorf, E. Ploedereder & R. Thall, An overview of DOD-STD-1838A (proposed), the Common APSE Interface Set, Revision A, **in** [SIGSOFT88] pp. 235–247.

[Musa85] J. D. Musa, Software engineering: the future of a profession, *IEEE Software* **2**, 1 (1985) 55–62.

[Musa87] J.D. Musa, A. Iannino & K. Okumoto, *Software Reliability: Measurement, Prediction, Application*, McGraw-Hill Book Company, 1987.

[Musser80] D.R. Musser, Abstract data type specification in the AFFIRM system, *IEEE Transactions on Software Engineering* **6**, 1 (1980) 24–32.

[Myers76] G.J. Myers, *Software Reliability*, Wiley 1976.

[Myers79] G.J. Myers, *The Art of Software Testing*, Wiley, 1979.

[Myers85] W. Myers, MCC: planning the revolution in software, *IEEE Software* **2**, 6 (1985) 68–73.

[Myers86] W. Myers, Can software for the SDI ever be error-free?, *IEEE Computer* **19**, 10 (1986) 61–67.

[Myers88] W. Myers, Shuttle code achieves very low error rate, *IEEE Software* **5**, 5 (1988) 93–95.

[Myers89] W. Myers, Allow plenty of time for large-scale software, *IEEE Software* **6**, 4 (1989) 92–99.

[Nanja87] M. Nanja & R.C. Cook, An analysis of the on-line debugging process, **in** *Empirical Studies of Programmers: Second Workshop*, G.M. Olson et al. (Ed.), Ablex, 1987, pp. 172–184.

[Nassi73] I. Nassi & B. Shneiderman, Flowchart techniques for structured programming, *ACM SIGPLAN Notices* **8**, 8 (1973) 12–26.

[Naur68] P. Naur & B. Randell (Eds), *Software Engineering*, Report on a conference, Garmisch, NATO Scientific Affairs Division, 1968.

[Neighbors84] J.M. Neighbors, The Draco approach to constructing software from reusable components, *IEEE Transactions on Software Engineering* **10**, 5 (1984) 564–574.

[Neil90] M. Neil, R.J. Cole & D. Slater, Measures for maintenance management: a case study, *Software Maintenance: Research and Practice* **2**, 4 (1990) 223–240.

[Nelson66] E.A. Nelson, *Management Handbook for the Estimation of Computer Programming Costs*, AD-A648750, Systems Development Corp., 1966.

[Newell72] A. Newell & H.A. Simon, *Human Problem Solving*, Prentice-Hall, 1972.

[Newsted73] P.R. Newsted, FORTRAN program comprehension as a function of documentation, University of Wisconsin, 1973.

[Nielsen90] J. Nielsen, Traditional dialogue design applied to modern user interfaces, *Communications of the ACM* **33**, 10 (1990) 109–118.

[Nierstrasz89] O. Nierstrasz, A survey of object-oriented concepts, **in** *Object-oriented Concepts, Databases and Applications*, W. Kim & F. Lochovsky (Eds.), ACM Press/Addison-Wesley, 1989, pp. 3–21.

[Norcio83] A.F. Norcio & S.M. Kerst, Human memory organization for computer programs, *Journal of the American Society for Information Science* **34**, 2 (1983) 109–114.

[Norden70] P.V. Norden, Useful tools for project management, **in** *Management of Production*, M.K. Starr (Ed.), Penguin Books, 1970, pp. 71–101.

[Norman83] D.A. Norman, Some observations on mental models, **in** *Mental models*, D. Gentner & A.L. Stevens (Eds), Erlbaum, 1983, pp. 7–14.

[Norman86] D.A. Norman & S.W. Draper (Eds), *User Centered System Design*, Lawrence Erlbaum, 1986.

[Norman89] R.J. Norman & J.F. Nunamaker, Jr., CASE productivity perceptions of software engineering professionals, *Communications of the ACM* **32**, 9 (1989)

1102–1108.

[Nosek90] J.T. Nosek & P. Palvia, Software maintenance management: changes in the last decade, *Software Maintenance: Research and Practice* **2**, 3 (1990) 157–174.

[Okimoto70] G.H. Okimoto, *The Effectiveness of Comments: A Pilot Study*, IBM SDD Technical Report TR 01.1347., 1970.

[Olsen83] D.R. Olsen Jr. & E.P. Dempsey, SYNGRAPH: a graphical user interface generator, *Computer Graphics* **17**, 3 (1983) pp 43–50.

[Oman88] P.W. Oman & C.R. Cook, A paradigm for programming style research, *ACM SIGPLAN Notices* **23**, 12 (1988) 69–78.

[Oman90a] P.W. Oman, CASE analysis and design tools, *IEEE Software* **7**, 3 (1990) 37–43.

[Oman90b] P.W. Oman & C.R. Cook, The book paradigm for improved maintenance, *IEEE Software* **7**, 1 (1990) 39–45.

[OOPSLA89] OOPSLA89 Conference Proceedings, *ACM SIGPLAN Notices* **24**, 10 (1989).

[OOPSLA90] OOPSLA90 Conference Proceedings, *ACM SIGPLAN Notices* **25**, 10 (1990).

[OOPSLA91] OOPSLA91 Conference Proceedings, *ACM SIGPLAN Notices* **26**, 11 (1991).

[Osterweil87] L. Osterweil, Software processes are software too, *Proceedings 9th International Conference on Software Engineering*, 1987, pp. 2–13.

[Palme76] J. Palme, A new feature for module protection in SIMULA, *ACM SIGPLAN Notices* **11**, 5 (1976) 59–62.

[Panzl78] D.J. Panzl, Automatic revision of formal test procedures, *Proceedings 3rd International Conference on Software Engineering*, IEEE, 1978, pp. 320–326.

[Parnas72a] D.L. Parnas, A technique for software module specification with examples, *Communications of the ACM* **15**, 5 (1972) 330–336.

[Parnas72b] D.L. Parnas, On the criteria to be used in decomposing systems into modules, *Communications of the ACM* **15**, 12 (1972) 1053–1058.

[Parnas77] D.L. Parnas, The use of precise specifications in the development of software, *Proceedings IFIP77*, North-Holland Publishing Company, 1977, pp. 861–867.

[Parnas78] D.L. Parnas, Designing software for ease of extension and contraction, *Proceedings 3rd International Conference on Software Engineering*, IEEE, 1978, pp. 264–277.

[Parnas85] D.L. Parnas, Software aspects of strategic defense systems, *ACM SigSoft Software Engineering Notes* **10**, 5 (1985) 15–23.

[Parnas86] D.L. Parnas & P.C. Clements, A rational design process: how and why to fake it, *IEEE Transactions on Software Engineering* **12**, 2 (1987) 251–257.

[Parnas87a] D.L. Parnas, SDI "red herrings" miss the boat, *IEEE Computer* **20**, 2 (1987) 6–7.

[Parnas87b] D.L. Parnas & D.M. Weiss, Active design reviews: principles and practices, *Journal of Systems and Software* **7**, 4 (1987) 259–265.

[Parr80] F.N. Parr, An alternative to the Rayleigh curve model for software development effort, *IEEE Transactions on Software Engineering* **6**, 3 (1980) 291–296.

[Payne83] S.J. Payne & T.R.G. Green, The user's perception of the interaction language: a two-level model, *Proceedings CHI '83*, ACM, 1983, pp. 202–206.

[Payne86] S.J. Payne & T.R.G. Green, Task-action grammars: a model of the mental representation of task languages, *Human–Computer Interaction* **2**, 2 (1986) 93–133.

[Pazel89] D.P. Pazel, DS-Viewer—an interactive graphical data structure presentation facility, *IBM Systems Journal* **28**, 2 (1989) 307–323.

[Penedo88a] M.H. Penedo & W.E. Riddle, Guest editor's introduction: software engineering environment architectures, *IEEE Transactions on Software Engineering* **14**, 6 (1988) 689–696.

[Penedo88b] M.H. Penedo, E. Ploedereder & I. Thomas, Object management issues for software engineering environments, **in** [SIGSOFT88] pp. 226–234.

[Perrone87] G. Perrone, Low-cost CASE: tomorrow's promise emerging today, *IEEE*

Computer **20**, 11 (1987) 104–110.

[Perry91] D.E. Perry & G.E. Kaiser, Models of software development environments, *IEEE Transactions on Software Engineering* **17**, 3 (1991) 283–295.

[Peters81] L.J. Peters, *Software Design, Methods and Techniques*, Yourdon Press, 1981.

[Peterson81] J.L. Peterson, *Petri Net Theory and the Modelling of Systems*, Prentice-Hall, 1981.

[Pintelas89] P.E. Pintelas & V. Kallistros, An overview of some software design languages, *Journal of Systems and Software* **10**, 2 (1989) 125–138.

[Pintelas91] P. Pintelas & S. Tragoudas, A comparative study of five language independent programming environments, *Journal of Systems and Software* **14**, 1 (1991) 3–15.

[Polya68] G. Polya, *Mathematical Discovery: on Understanding, Learning and Teaching Problem Solving*, Wiley, 1968.

[Porcella83] M. Porcella, P. Freeman & A.I. Wasserman, Ada methodology questionnaire summary, *ACM SigSoft Software Engineering Notes* **8**, 1 (1983) 51–98.

[Poston87a] R.M. Poston, Preventing most-probable errors in requirements, *IEEE Software* **4**, 5 (1987) 81–83.

[Poston87b] R.M. Poston, Preventing most-probable errors in design, *IEEE Software* **4**, 6 (1987) 87–88.

[Potts88] C. Potts & G. Bruns, Recording the reasons for design decisions, *Proceedings 10th International Conference on Software Engineering*, IEEE, 1988, pp. 418–427.

[Prentice81] D. Prentice, An analysis of software development environments, *ACM SigSoft Software Engineering Notes* **6**, 5 (1981) 19–27.

[Prieto-Diaz85] R. Prieto-Diaz, A software classification scheme, PhD Dissertation, University of California at Irvine, 1984.

[Prieto-Diaz86] R. Prieto-Diaz & J.M. Neighbors, Module interconnection languages, *Journal of Systems and Software* **6** (1986) 307–334.

[Prieto-Diaz87] R. Prieto-Diaz & P. Freeman, Classifying software for reusability, *IEEE Software* **4**, 1 (1987) pp 6–16.

[Prieto-Diaz90] R. Prieto-Diaz, Domain analysis: an introduction, *ACM SigSoft Software Engineering Notes* **15**, 2 (1990) 47–54.

[Prieto-Diaz91a] R. Prieto-Diaz, Implementing faceted classification for software reuse, *Communications of the ACM* **34**, 5 (1991) 88–97.

[Prieto-Diaz91b] R. Prieto-Diaz, Making software reuse work: an implementation model, *ACM SigSoft Software Engineering Notes* **16**, 3 (1991) 61–68.

[Process89] Proceedings of the 4th International Software Process Workshop, *SigSoft Software Engineering Notes* **14**, 4 (1989).

[Process90] *Proceedings of the 5th International Software Process Workshop*, IEEE, 1990.

[Putnam78] L.H. Putnam, A general empirical solution to the macro software sizing and estimating problem, *IEEE Transactions on Software Engineering* **4**, 4 (1978) 345–361.

[Putnam79] L.H. Putnam & A. Fitzsimmons, Estimating software costs, *Datamation* (Sept. 79) 189–198, (Oct. 79) 171-178 and (Nov. 79) 137–140.

[Putnam80] L.H. Putnam (Ed.), *Tutorial: Software Cost Estimating and Life-cycle Control: Getting the Software Numbers*, IEEE Catalog nr. EZ314, 1980.

[Raghavan89] S.A. Raghavan & D.R. Chand, Diffusing software-engineering methods, *IEEE Software* **6**, 4 (1989) 81–90.

[Ramamoorthy88] C.V. Ramamoorthy, V. Garg & A. Prakash, Support for reusability in Genesis, *IEEE Transactions on Software Engineering* **14**, 8 (1988) 1145–1154.

[Ramsey83] H.R. Ramsey, M.E. Atwood & J.R. van Doren, Flowcharts versus program design languages: an experimental comparison, *Communications of the ACM* **26**, 6 (1983) 445–449.

[Rapps82] S. Rapps & E.J. Weyuker, Data flow analysis techniques for test data selection, *in Proceedings 6th International Conference on Software Engineering*, IEEE, 1982, pp.

272–278.

[Rapps85] S. Rapps & E.J. Weyuker, Selecting software test data using data flow information, *IEEE Transactions on Software Engineering* **11**, 4 (1985) 367–375.

[Reddin70] W.J. Reddin, *Managerial Effectiveness*, McGraw-Hill, 1970.

[Redmond90] J.A. Redmond & R. Ah-Chuen, Software metrics—a user's perspective, *Journal of Systems and Software* **13**, 2 (1990) 97–110.

[Redwine85] S.T. Redwine & W.E. Riddle, Software technology maturation, *Proceedings 8th International Conference on Software Engineering*, IEEE, 1985, pp. 189–200.

[Reisner81] P. Reisner, Formal grammar and human factors design of an interactive graphics system, *IEEE Transactions on Software Engineering* **7**, 2 (1981) 229–240.

[Reps84] T. Reps, *Generating Language-based Environments*, MIT-Press, Cambridge, MA (1984).

[Reps87] T. Reps & T. Teitelbaum, Language processing in program editors, *IEEE Computer* **20**, 11 (1987) 29–40.

[Rettig91] M. Rettig, Nobody reads documentation, *Communications of the ACM* **34**, 7 (1991) 19–24.

[Reubenstein91] H.B. Reubenstein & R.C. Waters, The Requirements Apprentice: automated assistance for requirements acquisition, *IEEE Transactions on Software Engineering* **17**, 3 (1991) 226–240.

[Rich83] C. Rich & R.C. Waters, Formalizing reusable software components, **in** [ITT83] pp. 152–159.

[Rich88] C. Rich & R.C. Waters, The Programmer's Apprentice: A research overview, *IEEE Computer* **21**, 11 (1988) 10–25.

[Robinson77] L. Robinson & K.N. Levitt, Proof techniques for hierarchically structured programs, *Communications of the ACM* **20**, 4 (1977) 271–283.

[Robinson79] L. Robinson et al., *The HDM Handbook*, SRI International, Menlo Park, California, 1979.

[Rochkind75] M.J. Rochkind, The Source Code Control System, *IEEE Transactions on Software Engineering* **1**, 4 (1975) 364–370.

[Rombach85] H.D. Rombach, Impact of software structure on maintenance, *Proceedings Conference on Software Maintenance*, IEEE, 1985, pp. 152–160.

[Ross77a] D.T. Ross & K.E. Schoman Jr, Structured analysis for requirements definition, *IEEE Transactions on Software Engineering* **3**, 1 (1977) 6–15.

[Ross77b] D.T. Ross, Structured analysis (SA): a language for communicating ideas, *IEEE Transactions on Software Engineering* **3**, 1 (1977) 16–34.

[Rosson88] M.B. Rosson, S. Maass & W.A. Kellogg, The designer as user: building requirements for design tools from design practice, *Communications of the ACM* **31**, 11 (1988) 1288–1298.

[Rosson90] M.B. Rosson & S.R. Alpert, The cognitive consequences of object-oriented design, *Human–Computer Interaction* **5** (1990) 345–379.

[Royce70] W.W. Royce, Managing the development of large software systems: concepts and techniques, *Proceedings IEEE WESCON*, 1970, pp. 1–9.

[Rubin83] H.A. Rubin, Interactive macro-estimation of software life cycle parameters via personal computer: a technique for improving customer/developer communication, *Proceedingss of the Symposium on Application and Assessment of Automated Tools for Software Development*, IEEE Catalog nr. CH1936–4, 1983, pp. 44-49.

[Rubin85] H.A. Rubin, A comparison of cost estimation tools (panel discussion), *Proceedings 8th International Conference on Software Engineering*, IEEE, 1985, pp. 174–180.

[Rubinstein84] R. Rubinstein & H. Hersh, *The Human Factor*, Digital Press, 1984.

[Sammet69] J. Sammet, *Programming Languages: History and Fundamentals*, Prentice-Hall,

1969.

[Saunders88] J.H. Saunders, A survey of object-oriented languages, *Journal of Object-Oriented Programming* (March 1988) 5–11.

[Scanlan88] D.A. Scanlan, Learner preference for using structured flowcharts vs. pseudocode when comprehending short, relatively complex algorithms: a summary analysis, *Journal of Systems and Software* **8**, 2 (1988) 145–155.

[Scanlan89] D.A. Scanlan, Structured flowcharts outperform pseudocode: an experimental comparison, *IEEE Software* **6**, 5 (1989) 28–36.

[Scheifler86] R.W. Scheifler & J. Gettys, The X window system, *ACM Transactions on Graphics* **5**, 3 (1986) 79–109.

[Schwanke91] R.W. Schwanke, An intelligent tool for re-engineering software modularity, *Proceedings 13th International Conference on Software Engineering*, IEEE, 1991, pp. 83–92.

[Selby87] R.W. Selby, V.R. Basili & F.T. Baker, Cleanroom software development, *IEEE Transactions on Software Engineering* **13**, 9 (1987) 1027–1037.

[Selby91] R.W. Selby & V.R. Basili, Analyzing error-prone system structure, *IEEE Transactions on Software Engineering* **17**, 2 (1991) 141–152.

[Seppänen87] V. Seppänen, Reusability in software engineering, in [Freeman87c] pp. 286–297.

[Sethi89] R. Sethi, *Programming Languages: Concepts and Constructs*, Addison-Wesley, 1989.

[Shapiro81] E. Shapiro, PASES: a programming environment for Pascal, *ACM SIGPLAN Notices* **16**, 8 (1981) 50–57.

[Shatz89] S. Shatz & J.-P. Wang, *Distributed Software Engineering*, IEEE CS Press Tutorial, 1989.

[Shaw77] M. Shaw, W.A. Wulf & R.L. London, Abstraction and verification in Alphard: defining and specifying iteration and generators, *Communications of the ACM* **20**, 8 (1977) 553–564.

[Shaw84] M. Shaw, Abstraction techniques in modern programming languages, *IEEE Software* **1**, 4 (1984) pp 10–27.

[Sheil81] B.A. Sheil, The psychological study of programming, *ACM Computing Surveys* **13**, 1 (1981) 101–120.

[Shen83] V.Y. Shen, S.D. Conte & H.E. Dunsmore, Software science revisited: a critical analysis of the theory and its empirical support, *IEEE Transactions on Software Engineering* **9**, 2 (1983) 155–165.

[Sheppard79] S.B. Sheppard, B. Curtis, P. Milliman & T. Love, Modern coding practice and programming performance, *IEEE Computer* **12**, 12 (1979) 41–49.

[Shepperd88] M. Shepperd, An evaluation of software product metrics, *Information and Software Technology* **30**, 3 (1988) 177–188.

[Shepperd90] M. Shepperd, Design metrics: an empirical analysis, *Software Engineering Journal* **5**, 1 (1990) 3–10.

[Shneiderman75] B. Shneiderman, Experimental testing in programming languages, stylistic considerations and design techniques, *Proceedings National Computer Conference*, AFIPS, Vol. **44**, 1975, pp. 653–656.

[Shneiderman76] B. Shneiderman, Exploratory experiments in programmer behavior, *International Journal of Computer and Information Sciences* **5**, 2 (1976) 123–143.

[Shneiderman77] B. Shneiderman, R. Mayer, D. McKay & P. Heller, Experimental investigations of the utility of detailed flowcharts in programming, *Communications of the ACM* **20**, 6 (1977) 373–381.

[Shneiderman80] B. Shneiderman, *Software Psychology*, Winthrop, 1980.

[Shneiderman82] B. Shneiderman, Control flow and data structure documentation: two experiments, *Communications of the ACM* **25**, 1 (1982) 55–63.

[Shneiderman86] B. Shneiderman, *Designing the User Interface: Strategies for Human–*

Computer Interaction, Addison-Wesley, 1986.

[Shooman83] M. Shooman, *Software Engineering: Design, Reliability and Management*, McGraw-Hill, 1983.

[SIGPLAN79] Preliminary Ada reference manual, *ACM SIGPLAN Notices* **14**, 6, 1979.

[SIGPLAN84] Proceedings of the ACM SigSoft/SIGPLAN Software Engineering Symposium on Practical Software Development Environments, *ACM SIGPLAN Notices* **19**, 5 (1984).

[SIGPLAN87] Proceedings of the ACM SigSoft/SIGPLAN Software Engineering Symposium on Practical Software Development Environments, *ACM SIGPLAN Notices* **22**, 1 (1987).

[SIGSOFT88] Proceedings of the ACM SigSoft/SIGPLAN Software Engineering Symposium on Practical Software Development Environments, *ACM SigSoft Software Engineering Notes* **13**, 5 (1988).

[SIGSOFT90] Proceedings of the Fourth ACM SIGSOFT Symposium on Software Development Environments, *ACM SigSoft Software Engineering Notes* **15**, 6 (1990).

[Sikkel88] K. Sikkel & J.C. van Vliet, Growing pains of software reuse, *Proceedings Software Engineering in the Nineties*, SERC, Utrecht (1988).

[Sime73] M.E. Sime, T.R.G. Green & D.J. Guest, Psychological evaluation of two conditional constructions used in computer languages, *International Journal of Man–Machine Studies* **5** (1973) 123–143.

[Sime77] M.E. Sime, T.R.G. Green & D.J. Guest, Scope marking in computer conditionals—a psychological evaluation, *International Journal of Man–Machine Studies* **9** (1977) 107–118.

[Simon80] H.A. Simon, Problem solving and education, **in** D.T. Tuma & F. Reif (Eds), *Problem Solving and Education: Issues in Teaching and Research*, Erlbaum, 1980.

[Smit82] G. De V. Smit, A comparison of three string matching algorithms, *Software-Practice and Experience* **12**, 1 (1982) 57–66.

[Smith82] D.C. Smith, C. Irby, R. Kimball, W. Verplank & E. Harslem, Designing the Star user interface, *BYTE* **7**, 4 (1982) 242–282.

[Smith84] S.L. Smith & J.N. Mosier, The user interface to computer-based information systems: a survey of current software design practice, *Behaviour and Information Technology* **3**, 3 (1984) 195–203.

[Smith86] S.L. Smith & J.N. Mosier, *Design Guidelines for User-system Interface Software*, Technical Report, MITRE Corporation, 1986.

[Sneed78] H. Sneed & K. Kirchoff, PRUFSTAND—a testbed for systematic software components, **in** *Infotech State of the Art Report on Software Testing*, 1978.

[Software85] Special issue on Ada environments and tools, *IEEE Software* **2**, 2 (1985).

[Software87] Special issue on Integrated environments, *IEEE Software* **4**, 6 (1987).

[Software88] Special issue on the emergence of CASE, *IEEE Software* **5**, 2 (1988).

[Software89a] Special issue on Software verification and validation, *IEEE Software* **6**, 3 (1989).

[Software89b] Special issue on ESPRIT, *IEEE Software* **6**, 6 (1989).

[Software90a] Special issue: Maintenance, Reverse engineering & Design recovery, *IEEE Software* **7**, 1 (1990).

[Software90b] Special issue on software metrics, *IEEE Software* **7**, 2 (1990).

[Software90c] Special issue on Software Tools, *IEEE Software* **7**, 3 (1990).

[Software90d] Special issue: Applications of formal methods: developing virtuoso software, *IEEE Software* **7**, 5 (1990).

[Soloway83] E. Soloway, J. Bonar & K. Ehrlich, Cognitive strategies and looping constructs: an empirical study, *Communications of the ACM* **26**, 11 (1983) 853–860.

[Soloway84] E. Soloway & K. Ehrlich, Empirical studies of programming knowledge, *IEEE*

Transactions on Software Engineering **10**, 5 (1984) 595–609.

[Soloway86a] E. Soloway, Learning to program = learning to construct mechanisms and explanations, *Communications of the ACM* **29**, 9 (1986) 850–858.

[Soloway86b] E. Soloway & S. Iyengar (Eds) *Empirical Studies of Programmers*, Ablex Publishing Corp., 1986.

[Soloway88] E. Soloway, J. Pinto, S. Letovsky, D. Littman & R. Lampert, Designing documentation to compensate for delocalized plans, *Communications of the ACM* **31**, 11 (1988) 1259–1267.

[Spector86] A. Spector & D. Gifford, A computer science perspective of bridge design, *Communications of the ACM* **29**, 4 (1986) 267–283.

[Spivey88] J.M. Spivey, *Introducing Z: A Specification Language and its Formal Semantics*, Cambridge University Press, 1988.

[Standish84] T.A. Standish, An essay on software reuse, *IEEE Transactions on Software Engineering* **10**, 5 (1984) 494–497.

[STARS83] Special issue: The DoD STARS program, *IEEE Computer* **16**, 11, 1983.

[Stephens78] S.A. Stephens & L.L. Tripp, Requirements expression and verification aid, *Proceedings 3rd International Conference on Software Engineering*, IEEE, 1978, pp. 101–108.

[Stevens74] W.P. Stevens, G.J. Myers & L.L. Constantine, Structured design, *IBM Systems Journal* **13**, 2 (1974) 115–139.

[Stroud67] J.M. Stroud, The fine structure of psychological time, *Ann. NY Acad. Sci.*, vol 138 (1967) 623–631.

[Stroustrup86] B. Stroustrup, *The C++ Reference Manual*, Addison-Wesley, 1986.

[Stroustrup91] B. Stroustrup, *The C++ Programming Language*, second edition, Addison Wesley, 1991.

[Stuurman88] C. Stuurman, Product liability for software in Europe. A discussion of the EC-Directive of 25 July 1985, **in** G. Vandenberghe (Ed.), *Advanced Topics of Computer/Law*, Kluwer Law and Taxation Publishers, 1988.

[Sunshine82] C.A. Sunshine, D.H. Thompson, R.W. Erickson, S.L. Gerhart & D. Schwabe, Specification and verification of communication protocols in AFFIRM using state transition models, *IEEE Transactions on Software Engineering* **8**, 5 (1982) 460–489.

[Surveys81] Special issue: The psychology of human–computer interaction, *ACM Computing Surveys* **13**, 1 (1981).

[Sutcliffe88] A. Sutcliffe, *Jackson System Development*, Prentice-Hall, 1988.

[Swanson76] E.B. Swanson, The dimensions of maintenance, *Proceedings 2nd International Conference on Software Engineering*, IEEE, 1976, pp. 492–497.

[Swanson90] E.B. Swanson & C.M. Beath, Departmentalization in software development and maintenance, *Communications of the ACM* **33**, 6 (1990) 658–667.

[Symons88] C.R. Symons, Function point analysis: difficulties and improvements, *IEEE Transactions on Software Engineering* **14**, 1 (1988) 2–11.

[Tahvanainen90] V.-P. Tahvanainen & K. Smolander, An annotated CASE bibliography, *ACM SigSoft Software Engineering Notes* **15**, 1 (1990) 79–92.

[Tanenbaum76] A.S. Tanenbaum, Tutorial on ALGOL 68, *ACM Computing Surveys* **8**, 2 (1976) 155–190.

[Tanenbaum83] A.S. Tanenbaum, H. van Staveren, E.G. Keizer & J.W. Stevenson, A practical toolkit for making portable compilers, *Communications of the ACM* **26**, 9 (1983) 654–662.

[Tanenbaum87] A.S. Tanenbaum, *Operating Systems: Design and Implementation*, Prentice-Hall, 1987.

[Tarumi88] H. Tarumi, K. Agusa & Y. Ohno, A programming environment supporting reuse of object-oriented software, *Proceedings 10th International Conference on Software*

Engineering, IEEE, 1988, pp. 265–273.

[Teichroew77] D. Teichroew & E.A. Herschey III, PSL—PSA: a computer-aided technique for structured documentation and analysis of information processing systems, *IEEE Transactions on Software Engineering* **3**, 1 (1977) 41–48.

[Teitelbaum81] T. Teitelbaum & T. Reps, The Cornell Program Synthesizer, a syntax-directed programming environment, *Communications of the ACM* **24**, 9 (1981) 563–573.

[Teitelman81] W. Teitelman & L. Masinter, The Interlisp programming environment, *IEEE Computer* **14**, 4 (1981) 25–34.

[Tenny88] T. Tenny, Program readability: procedures versus comments, *IEEE Transactions on Software Engineering* **14**, 9 (1988) 1271–1279.

[Thayer81] R.H. Thayer, A.B. Pyster & R.C. Wood, Major issues in software engineering management, *IEEE Transactions on Software Engineering* **7**, 4 (1981) 333–342.

[Thibodeau81] R. Thibodeau, *An Evaluation of Software Cost Estimating Models*, RADC-TR-81-144, 1981.

[Thomas89a] I. Thomas, PCTE interfaces: supporting tools in software-engineering environments, *IEEE Software* **6**, 6 (1989) 15–23.

[Thomas89b] I. Thomas, Tool integration in the Pact environment, *Proceedings 11th International Conference on Software Engineering*, IEEE, 1989, pp. 13–22.

[Thomas89c] J.C. Thomas & W.A. Kellogg, Minimizing ecological gaps in interface design, *IEEE Software* **6**, 1 (1989) 78–86.

[Tichy79] W.F. Tichy, Software development control based on module interconnection, *Proceedings 4th International Conference on Software Engineering*, IEEE, 1979, pp. 29–41.

[Tracz88] W. Tracz, Software reuse myths, *ACM SigSoft Software Engineering Notes* **13**, 1 (1988) 17–21.

[Tracz90] W. Tracz, Where does reuse start, *ACM SigSoft Software Engineering Notes* **15**, 2 (1990) 42–46.

[Trenouth91] J. Trenouth, A survey of exploratory software development, *The Computer Journal* **34**, 2 (1991) 153–163.

[Tripp88] L.L. Tripp, A survey of graphical notations for program design—an update, *ACM SigSoft Software Engineering Notes* **13**, 4 (1988) 39–44.

[TrSE84] Special issue on reusability, *IEEE Transactions on Software Engineering* **10**, 5 (1984).

[TrSE85] Special issue on software reliability—Part I, *IEEE Transactions on Software Engineering* **11**, 12 (1985).

[TrSE86] Special issue on software reliability—Part II, *IEEE Transactions on Software Engineering* **12**, 1 (1986).

[TrSE90] Special issue: Formal methods in software engineering, *IEEE Transactions on Software Engineering* **16**, 9 (1990).

[Tse91] T.H. Tse & L. Pong, An examination of requirements specification languages, *The Computer Journal* **34**, 2 (1991) 143–152.

[Verner89] J.M. Verner, G. Tate, B. Jackson & R.G. Hayward, Technology dependence in function point analysis: a case study and critical review, *Proceedings 11th International Conference on Software Engineering*, IEEE, 1989, pp. 375–382.

[Vessey85] I. Vessey, Expertise in debugging computer programs: a process analysis, *International Journal of Man–Machine Studies* **23** (1985) 459–494.

[Vincent88] J. Vincent, A. Waters & J. Sinclair, *Software Quality Assurance, Vol I: Practice and Experience*, Prentice-Hall, 1988.

[van Vliet85] J.C. van Vliet, STARS and stripes, *Future Generations Computer Systems* **1**, 6 (1985) 411–416.

[van Vliet89] J.C. van Vliet, Teaching software maintenance, **in** *Software Engineering Education*, N.E. Gibbs (Ed.), Lecture Notes in Computer Science 376, Springer Verlag,

1989, pp. 80–89.

[Volpano85] D.M. Volpano & R.B. Kieburtz, Software templates, *Proceedings 8th International Conference on Software Engineering*, IEEE, 1985, pp. 55–60.

[Vonk87] R. Vonk, *Prototyping of Information Systems* (in Dutch), Academic Service, 1987.

[Wake88] S. Wake & S. Henry, A model based on software quality factors which predicts maintainability, *IEEE Conference on Software Maintenance*, 1988, pp. 382–387.

[Wall86] R.S. Wall et al., An evaluation of commercial expert system building tools, *AI Research Highlights*, January 1986, 54–74.

[Walston77] C.E. Walston & C.P. Felix, A method of programming measurement and estimation, *IBM Systems Journal* **16**, 1 (1977) 54–73.

[Wang84] A.S. Wang, The estimation of software size and effort: an approach based on the evolution of software metrics, PhD Thesis, Dept. of Computer Science, Purdue University, 1984.

[Ward85] P. Ward & S. Mellor, *Structured Analysis for Real-time Systems*, Prentice-Hall, 1985.

[Warnier74] J.-D. Warnier, *Logical Construction of Programs*, Stenfert Kroese, 1974.

[Wasserman85] A.I. Wasserman, Extending transition diagrams for the specification of human–computer interaction, *IEEE Transactions on Software Engineering* **11**, 8 (1985) 699–713.

[Wasserman87] A. Wasserman & P. Pircher, A graphical, extensible integrated environment for software development, **in** [SIGPLAN87] pp. 131–142.

[Waters82] R.C. Waters, The Programmer's Apprentice, knowledge based program editing, *IEEE Transactions on Software Engineering* **8**, 1 (1982) 1–12.

[Waters91] R.C. Waters & Y.M. Tan, Toward a Design Apprentice: supporting reuse and evolution in software design, *ACM SigSoft Software Engineering Notes* **16**, 2 (1991) 33–44.

[Watt90] D.A. Watt, *Programming Language Concepts and Paradigms*, Prentice-Hall, 1990.

[Webster88] D.E. Webster, Mapping the design information representation terrain, *IEEE Computer* **21**, 9 (1988) 8–24.

[Wegner79] P. Wegner, Introduction and overview, **in** P. Wegner (Ed.), *Research Directions in Software Technology*, MIT Press, 1979, pp. 1–36.

[Wegner83] P. Wegner, Varieties of reusability, **in** [ITT83] pp. 30–44.

[Wegner84] P. Wegner, Capital-intensive software technology, *IEEE Software* **1**, 3 (1984) 7–45.

[Wegner87] P. Wegner, Dimensions of object-based language design, OOPSLA '87 Proceedings, *ACM SIGPLAN Notices* **22**, 12 (1987) 168–182.

[Wegner89] P. Wegner, Learning the language, *BYTE* (March 1989) 245–253.

[Wegner90] P. Wegner, Concepts and paradigms of object-oriented programming, *ACM OOPS Messenger* **1**, 1 (1990) 7–87.

[Weinberg71] G.M. Weinberg, *The Psychology of Computer Programming*, Van Nostrand Reinhold, 1971.

[Weinberg74] G.M. Weinberg & E.L. Schulman, Goals and performance in computer programming, *Human Factors* **16**, 1 (1974) 70–77.

[Wendel86] I. Wendel, Software tools of the pleistocene, *Software Maintenance News* **4**, 10 (1986) 20.

[Wensley78] J.H. Wensley, L.L. Lamport, J. Goldberg, M.W. Green, K.N. Levitt, P.M. Melliar-Smith, R.E. Shostak & C.B. Weinstock, SIFT: design and analysis of a fault-tolerant computer for aircraft control, *Proceedings of the IEEE* **66**, 10 (1978) 1240–1255.

[Weyuker88] E.J. Weyuker, The evaluation of program-based software test data adequacy criteria, *Communications of the ACM* **31**, 6 (1988) 668–675.

[Weyuker90] E.J. Weyuker, The cost of data flow testing: an empirical study, *IEEE Transactions on Software Engineering* **16**, 2 (1990) 121–128.

[Wiedenbeck91] S. Wiedenbeck, The initial stage of program comprehension, *International*

Journal of Man–Machine Studies **35**, 4 (1991) 517–540.

[Wieringa91] R.J. Wieringa, *Conceptual Modelling*, Vrije Universiteit, Amsterdam, 1991.

[Wilde89] N. Wilde & S.M. Thebaut, The maintenance assistant: work in progress, *Journal of Systems and Software* **9**, 1 (1989) 3–17.

[Wing88] J.M. Wing, A study of 12 specifications of the library problem, *IEEE Software* **5**, 4 (1988) 66–76.

[Winters79] E.W. Winters, An analysis of the capabilities of problem statement language: a language for system requirements and specifications, *Proceedings of IEEE COMPSAC '79*, 1979, pp. 283–288.

[Wirfs-Brock90] R. Wirfs-Brock, B. Wilkerson & L. Wiener, *Designing Object-oriented Software*, Prentice Hall, 1990.

[Wirth71] N. Wirth, Program development by stepwise refinement, *Communications of the ACM* **14**, 4 (1971) 221–227.

[Wirth85] N. Wirth, *Programming in Modula-2*, Springer Verlag, 1985.

[Wolverton74] R.W. Wolverton, The cost of developing large-scale software, *IEEE Transactions on Computers* (1974) 615–636.

[Wood88] M. Wood & I. Sommerville, An information retrieval system for software components, *Software Engineering Journal* (September 1988) 198–207.

[Woodfield81a] S.N. Woodfield, V.Y. Shen & H.E. Dunsmore, A study of several metrics for programming effort, *Journal of Systems and Software* **2** (1981) 97–103.

[Woodfield81b] S.N. Woodfield, H.E. Dunsmore & V.Y. Shen, The effect of modularization and comments on program comprehension, *Proceedings 5th International Conference on Software Engineering*, IEEE, 1981, pp. 215–223.

[Yau86] S.S. Yau & J.J.-P. Tsai, A survey of software design techniques, *IEEE Transactions on Software Engineering* **12**, 6 (1986) 713–721.

[Yin78] B.H. Yin & J.W. Winchester, The establishment and use of measures to evaluate the quality of software designs, *ACM Proceedings of the Software Quality and Assurance Workshop*, 1978, pp. 45–52.

[Young89] W.D. Young, Verified compilation in Micro-Gypsy, Proceedings Third Symposium on Software Testing, Analysis, and Verification, *ACM SigSoft Software Engineering Notes* **14**, 8 (1989) 20–26.

[Yourdon75] E. Yourdon & L.L. Constantine, *Structured Design*, Yourdon Press, 1975.

[Yu88] T.-J. Yu, V.Y. Shen & H.E. Dunsmore, An analysis of several software defect models, *IEEE Transactions on Software Engineering* **14**, 9 (1988) 1261–1270.

[Zahn74] C.T. Zahn, A control statement for natural top-down structured programming, Proceedings Programming Symposium, Parijs, *Lecture Notes in Computer Science* **19**, Springer Verlag, 1974, pp. 170–180.

[Zelkowitz78] M.V. Zelkowitz, Perspectives on software engineering, *ACM Computing Surveys* **10**, 2 (1978) 197–216.

[Zelkowitz84] M.V. Zelkowitz, R.T. Yeh, R.G. Hamlet, J.D. Gannon & V.R. Basili, Software engineering practices in the US and Japan, *IEEE Computer* **17**, 6 (1984) 57–66.

[Zelkowitz88] M.V. Zelkowitz, Resource utilization during software development, *Journal of Systems and Software* **8**, 4 (1988) 331–336.

[Zilles74] S.N. Zilles, *Algebraic Specification of Data Types*, Project MAC Progress Report 11, MIT, Cambridge, MA, 1974.

[Zucconi89] L. Zucconi, Selecting a CASE tool, *ACM SigSoft Software Engineering Notes* **14**, 2 (1989) 42–44.

[Zuse90] H. Zuse, *Software Complexity: Measures and Methods*, De Gruyter, 1990.

Index

Abstract class, 308, 312
Abstract data type, 182, 245
Abstract object, 220
Abstraction, 173, 183–186, 230
Acceptance testing, 350
Access audit, 74
Access control, 74
Accuracy, 74
Active design review, 334
Activity-on-arrow network, 132
Activity-on-node network, 130, 132
Actual complexity, 342
Ada Program Support Environment (APSE), 297,
    377–378
Ada Requirements Methodology (ARM), 165
Ada, 162–165, 296–300
Adaptability, 180
Adaptive maintenance, 14, 456
Adhocracy, 60
AFFIRM, 334
Algebraic specification, 235, 238, 246, 251–261,
    504–508
  axioms, 252
  completeness, 255
  consistency, 255
  construction of, 258–260
  convergence of axioms, 262
  difficulties of, 255–257
  error treatment, 255–257
  final semantics, 253–255
  hidden function, 255
  initial semantics, 253
  readability, 257
  rewrite rules, 252, 261

  semantic part, 252
  signature, 252
  sufficiently complete, 258
  syntactic part, 252
Aliasing, 274
All-C-Uses/Some-P-Uses coverage, 340
All-Defs coverage, 340
All-DU-Paths coverage, 340
All-Edges coverage, 339, 346–348
All-Nodes coverage, 339, 346–348
All-P-Uses coverage, 341
All-P-Uses/Some-C-Uses coverage, 340
All-Paths coverage, 339
All-Uses coverage, 340
Alphard, 247–248, 288–290
Alvey, 17
Analyst workbench (AWB), 374, 384–385
Anatools, 385
Application generator, 406–408
ASF, 261
ASSET, 328
Axiomatic specification, 238

Babbage, Charles, 296
Base class, 311
Baseline, 50, 53–54
Basic execution time model, 360
Basis set, 342
Beacon, 433–434, 465
Behavior of objects, 216
Big Bang effect, 39
Black box testing, 318, 336–338
Bottom-up testing, 350
Boundary value analysis, 337